EARLY
CHRISTIANITY
IN CONTEXTS

EARLY CHRISTIANITY IN CONTEXTS

An Exploration across Cultures and Continents

EDITED BY

William Tabbernee

B

Baker Academic

a division of Baker Publishing Group
Grand Rapids, Michigan

Published by Baker Academic
a division of Baker Publishing Group
P.O. Box 6287, Grand Rapids, MI 49516-6287
www.bakeracademic.com

Printed in the United States of America

Library of Congress Cataloging-in-Publication Data
Early Christianity in contexts : an exploration across cultures and continents / edited by William Tabbernee.
       pages cm
   Includes bibliographical references and indexes.
   ISBN 978-0-8010-3126-7 (cloth)
   1. Church history—Primitive and early church, ca. 30–600. 2. Church history—Middle Ages, 600–1500. I. Tabbernee, William, 1944– editor.
   BR145.3.E23 2014
   270.1—dc23   2014020859

14   15   16   17   18   19   7   6   5   4   3   2   1

For Kay Lynn Northcutt

My Beloved Coexplorer
of Christianity, Cultures, and Continents

Contents

Illustrations

Preface

One of my most prized possessions is a full-size ink rubbing of the famous "Nestorian" Monument erected in China in 781 (see chap. 4). The rubbing is a constant reminder to me that early Christianity spread across a wide range of cultures and continents. For us to understand fully the nature of Christianity, we need to engage in an exploration of such diverse cultures and continents— hence the subtitle (and unique focus) of this volume.

I am profoundly grateful to the other seventeen authors of this book (see the list of contributors). Each is an expert on the way Christianity entered one or more of the cultures and continents covered in these pages. Working with such a diverse and talented group of scholars from around the world has been a delight. Thanks are due also to Richard Engle for preparing the numerous beautiful maps that help us all to gain greater insight into precisely where the diverse early Christian communities were located.

Julia Chastain typed and retyped numerous drafts of the text of this book. Additional technical assistance was provided by Dolores Ferguson, Cheryl McGuire, Joshua McGuire, Kay Northcutt, Myrna Ranney, and Jennifer Sweeten.

I wish also to acknowledge coauthors Christopher Haas, Robin Jensen, Ken Parry, Peter Richardson, Graydon Snyder, Julia Valeva, and Athanasios Vionis for contributing their personal photographs of relevant sites and artifacts. Similarly, the generosity of other photographers and copyright holders, noted alongside each illustration, has significantly enriched the educational value and beauty of this volume.

The volume itself was first envisioned by James Ernest, senior acquisitions editor at Baker Academic and Brazos Press. His passion for the project and his expert editorial advice have been a great encouragement to me from the book's inception to its fruition. Great appreciation is due also to Brian Bolger, managing editor at Baker Publishing Group, and to his staff for producing a spectacularly beautiful book.

William Tabbernee

Abbreviations

General

b.	born	fl.	flourished
bp.	bishop	*Fr.*	Fragment(s)
ca.	about	i.e.	that is
Can.	Canon(s)	km	kilometer
cathol.	catholicos	lit.	literally
cf.	compare	m	meter
chap(s).	chapter(s)	n(n)	note(s)
cm	centimeter	no(s).	numbers(s)
col(s).	column(s)	NS	New Series
d.	died	r.	ruled
e.g.	for example	ser.	series
Ep.	epistle(s)/letter(s)	s.n.	without a publisher
esp.	especially	SS.	saints
ET	English translation	St.	saint
fig(s).	figure(s)		

Modern Versions

KJV	King James Version
NRSV	New Revised Standard Version

Hebrew Bible

Gen.	Genesis	Lev.	Leviticus
Exod.	Exodus	Num.	Numbers

Deut.	Deuteronomy	Prov.	Proverbs
1 Kings	1 Kings	Song	Song of Songs
Job	Job	Dan.	Daniel
Ps./Pss.	Psalms		

Christian Scriptures

Matt.	Matthew	1 Tim.	1 Timothy
Mark	Mark	2 Tim.	2 Timothy
Luke	Luke	Titus	Titus
John	John	Phlm.	Philemon
Acts	Acts	Heb.	Hebrews
Rom.	Romans	James	James
1 Cor.	1 Corinthians	1 Pet.	1 Peter
2 Cor.	2 Corinthians	2 Pet.	2 Peter
Gal.	Galatians	2 John	2 John
Eph.	Ephesians	3 John	3 John
Phil.	Philippians	Jude	Jude
Col.	Colossians	Rev.	Revelation
1 Thess.	1 Thessalonians		

Old Testament Pseudepigrapha

Hel. Syn. Pr.	*Hellenistic Synagogal Prayers*
Mart. Ascen. Isa.	*Martyrdom and Ascension of Isaiah*

Apostolic Fathers

1 Clem.	*1 Clement*

New Testament Apocrypha and Pseudepigrapha

Acts Barn.	*Acts of Barnabas*
Acts Paul	*Acts of Paul*
Acts Pet. Paul	*Acts of Peter and Paul*
Acts Phil.	*Acts of Philip*
Acts Thom.	*Acts of Thomas*
Ps.-Clem.	*Pseudo-Clementines*

Other Premodern Authors and Works

English translations of the titles of premodern works are not necessarily literal
translations of the original, but they are the titles most commonly used in
English for those works.

Act. Cypr.   *Acta proconsularia Sancti Cypriani espiscopi et martyris
[The Martyrdom of Cyprian]*

Acts Mar Mari   *Acts of Mar Mari*

Agnellus
  Pont. Rav.   *Liber pontificalis ecclesiae Ravennatis [The Book of Pontiffs of the
    Church of Ravenna]*

Ammianus Marcellinus
  Res gestae   *Rerum gestarum libri xxxi [Roman History]*

Anonymus Continuatus Dion
  Fr.   *Fragmenta [Fragments]*

Aphrahat
  Demon.   *Demonstrationes [Demonstrations]*

Apollonius of Rhodes
  Argon.   *Argonautica [Voyage of the Argo]*

Appian
  Bell. civ.   *Bella civilia [Civil Wars]*

Arnobius the Elder
  Nat.   *Adversus nationes libri vii [Against the Nations]*

Athanasius
  Apol. Const.   *Apologia ad Constantium [Defense before Constantius]*
  Apol. sec.   *Apologia secunda (= Apologia contra Arianos) [Defense against the
    Arians]*
  Ep. Aeg. Lib.   *Epistula ad episcopos Aegypti et Libyae [Letter to the Bishops of
    Egypt and Libya]*
  H. Ar.   *Historia Arianorem [History of the Arians]*
  Vit. Ant.   *Vita Antonii [Life of Antony]*

Augustine of Hippo
  Bapt.   *De baptismo contra Donatistas [Baptism]*
  Brev. coll.   *Breviculus collationis cum Donatistis [A Summary of the Meeting
    with the Donatists]*

Civ.	De civitate Dei [The City of God]
Conf.	Confessionum libri xiii [Confessions]
Don.	Post collationem adversus Donatistas [Against the Donatists]
Ep.	Epistulae [Letters]
Ep.*	Epistulae [Letters], Divjak 1987
Enarrat. Ps.	Enarrationes in Psalmos [Enarrations on the Psalms]
Serm.	Sermones [Sermons]
Dolb.	Dolbeau 1996
Mai	Mai 1930
Mainz	See Dolbeau 1996
Morin	Morin 1930

Auxentius of Durostorum

Ep. de fide Ullfilae Epistula de fide, vita et obitu Ulfilae [Letter on the Faith, Life, and Death of Ulfila]

Basil of Caesarea

Ep. Epistulae [Letters]

Bede

Hist. eccl. Angl. Historia ecclesiastica gentis Anglorum [Ecclesiastical History of the English People]

Cassius Dio

Hist. rom. Historia romana [Roman History]

Cedrenus

Hist. comp. Historiarum compendium [Concise History of the World]

Chron. Edess. Chronicle of Edessa

Chron. pasch. Chronicon paschal [Paschal Chronicle]

Chron. Se'ert Chronicle of Se'ert

Cicero

Phil. Orationes philippicae [Orations: Philippics]

Clement of Alexandria

Strom. Stromata [Miscellanies]

Cod. theod. Codex theodosianus [Theodosian Code]

Const. ap. Constitutiones apostolicae [Apostolic Constitutions]

Cosmas Indicopleustes

Top. Topographia christiana [Christian Topography]

Cyprian

Ep.   *Epistulae* [*Letters*]

Sent.   *Sententiae episcoporum numero xxxvii de haereticis baptizandis*
                         [*The Judgment of Eighty-Seven Bishops on the Baptism of Heretics*]

Cyril of Jerusalem

Catech.   *Catecheses* [*Catechetical Lectures*]

Diodorus Siculus

Bibl. hist.   *Bibliotheca historica* [*Library of History*]

Dionysius of Halicarnassus

Ant. rom.   *Antiquitates romanae* [*Roman Antiquities*]

Epiphanius

Mens.   *De mensuris et ponderibus* [*On Weights and Measures*]

Pan.   *Panarion (Adversus haereses)* [*Medicine Chest (Against Heresies)*]

Eusebius

Dem. ev.   *Demonstratio evangelica* [*Demonstration of the Gospel*]

Hist. eccl.   *Historia ecclesiastica* [*Ecclesiastical History*]

Mart. Pal.   *De martyribus Palaestinae* [*The Martyrs of Palestine*]

Onom.   *Onomasticon* [*Onomasticon*]

Vit. Const.   *Vita Constantini* [*Life of Constantine*]

Gennadius

Vir. ill.   *De viris illustribus* [*On Illustrious Men*]

Gildas

Exc. Brit.   *De excidio et conquestu Britanniae* [*On the Ruin and Conquest
                         of Britain*]

Gregory of Nazianzus

Laud. Bas.   *In laudem Basilii magni* [*In Praise of Basil the Great*]

Or.   *Orationes* [*Orations*]

Gregory of Nyssa

Vit. Greg. Thaum.   *De vita Gregorii Thaumaturgi* [*On the Life of Gregory
                         Thaumaturgus*]

Vit. Macr.   *De vita Macrinae* [*On the Life of Macrina*]

Gregory of Tours

Glor. mart.   *Liber in gloria martyrum* [*Glory of the Martyrs*]

Hist.   *Historiarum libri x* [*Ten Books of Histories*, popularly known as
                         Historia Francorum (History of the Franks)]

Hermas
  Vis.   *Visiones pastoris* [*Book of Hermas/Shepherd of Hermas: Visions*]

Herodotus
  Hist.   *Historiae* [*Histories*]

Hilary of Poitiers
  Ad Const. 1   *Liber I ad Constantium* [*To Constantius (Book 1)*]

Hippolytus
  Comm. Dan.   *Commentarium in Danielem* [*Commentary on Daniel*]

Hippolytus (attrib.)
  Ref.   *Refutatio omnium haeresium (Philosophoumena)* [*Refutation of All Heresies*]

Homer
  Il.   *Ilias* [*Iliad*]

Ignatius of Antioch
  Phld.   *Epistula ad Philadelphios* [*Letter to the Philadelphians*]
  Pol.   *Epistula ad Polycarpum* [*Letter to Polycarp*]
  Rom.   *Epistula ad Romanos* [*Letter to the Romans*]
  Smyrn.   *Epistula ad Smyrnaeos* [*Letter to the Smyrnaeans*]

Irenaeus of Lyons
  Haer.   *Adversus haereses* [*Against Heresies*]

Itin. Eger.   ***Itinerarium Egeriae* [*The Travels of Egeria*]**

Jerome
  Comm. Gal.   *Commentariorum in epistulam ad Galatas libri iii* [*Commentary on the Epistle to the Galatians*]
  Ep.   *Epistulae* [*Letters*]
  Vir. ill.   *De viris illustribus* [*On Illustrious Men*]

Jerome (attrib.)
  Mart. hier.   *Martyrologium hieronymianum* [*Martyrology of Jerome*]

John Chrysostom
  Exp. Ps.   *Expositiones in Psalmos* [*Commentary on the Psalms*]
  Hom.   *Homiliae* [*Homilies*]
  Stat.   *Ad populum Antiochenum de statuis* [*Homilies on the Statues to the People of Antioch*]

John of Ephesus
  Hist. eccl.   *Historia ecclesiastica* [*Ecclesiastical History*]

Josephus
- *Ant.*   *Antiquitates judaicae* [*Jewish Antiquities*]
- *B.J.*   *Bellum judaicum* [*Jewish War*]

Julius Caesar
- *Bell. Gal.*   *De Bello Gallico* [*On the Gallic War*]

Justin
- *1 Apol.*   *Apologia i* [*First Apology*]
- *Dial.*   *Dialogus cum Tryphone* [*Dialogue with Trypho*]

Juvenal
- *Sat.*   *Satirae* [*Satires*]

Koriwn
- *Varkʿ Maštocʿi*   *Varkʿ Maštocʿi* [*The Life of Mashtots*]

Lactantius
- *Mort.*   *De morte persecutorum* [*On the Deaths of the Persecutors*]

Lazar Pʿarpecʿi   **The History of Lazar Pʿarpecʿi**

Leontius Scholasticus
- *Sect.*   *De sectis* [*On the Sects*]

Lian Song
- *Yuan shi*   *Yuan shi: Er bai shi juan; Mu lu: Er juan* [*History of the Yuan Dynasty*]

Libanius
- *Or.*   *Orationes* [*Orations*]

Lib. pont.   **Liber pontificalis [Book of Pontiffs]**

Lucian
- *Peregr.*   *De morte Peregrini* [*On the Death of Peregrinus*]

Marco Polo
- *Travels*   *The Travels of Marco Polo*

Mart. Carp.   **Martyrium Carpi, Papyri, et Agathonicae [Martyrdom of Carpus, Papylus, and Agathonicê]**
- *(A)*   *(Recensio A)* [*Recension A*]
- *(B)*   *(Recensio B)* [*Recension B*]

Mart. hier.   **See Jerome (attrib.)**

Mart. Lugd.   **Lugdunenses martyres [The Martyrs of Lyons]**

Mart. Pol.	*Martyrium Polycarpi [Martyrdom of Polycarp]*
Mart. Simeon.	*Martyrium Simeonis bar Sabba'e [Martyrdom of Simeon bar Shaba]*

Martial
Epigr.   *Epigrammata libri xii* [*Epigrams*]

Minucius Felix
Oct.   *Octavius*

Movses Khorenats῾i
Hist. Arm.   History of the Armenians

Narr. Simeon.   *Narratio de Simeone bar Sabba'e [The Story of Simeon bar Shaba]*

Nicephorus Callistus
Hist. eccl.   *Historia ecclesiastica* [*Ecclesiastical History*]

Nicetas of Paphlagonia
Or.   *Orationes laudatoriae aliaeque nonnullae festivae* [*Prayers of Praise and Some Other Festive Prayers*]

Olympiodorus
Fr.   *Fragmenta* [*Fragments*]

Optatus of Milevis
Donat.   *Adversus Donatistas* [*Against the Donatists*]

Origen
Cels.   *Contra Celsum* [*Against Celsus*]
Comm. ser. Matt.   *Commentariorum series in evangelium Matthaei* [*Series of Commentaries on the Gospel of Matthew*]

Orosius
Hist. pag.   *Historiae adversus paganos libri vii* [*Seven Books of History against the Pagans*]

Otto of Freising
Chron.   *Chronica sive historia de duabus civitatibus* [*A Chronicle or History of Two Cities*]

Palladius
Dial. v. Jo. Chrys.   *Dialogus de vita S. Johannis Chrysostomi* [*Dialogue on the Life of John Chrysostom*]
Hist. Laus.   *Historia Lausiaca* [*Lausiac History*]

Pass. Crisp.	*Passio Sanctae Crispinae* [*Martyrdom of St. Crispina*]
Pass. Eust.	*Martyrdom and Passion of St. Eustace of Mtskheta*
Pass. Flor.	*Passio Beatissimi Floriani martyris Christi* [*Martyrdom of Florianus*]
Pass. Fruct.	*Passio Sanctorum Martyrum Fructuosi Episcopi, Auguri et Eulogi Diaconorum* [*The Martyrdom of Bishop Fructuosus and His Deacons Augurius and Eulogius*]
Pass. Max.	*Passio Sancti Maximiliani* [*Martyrdom of St. Maximilian*]
Pass. Pion.	*Passio Pionii* [*Martyrdom of Pionius*]
Pass. Sals.	*Passio Salsae* [*Martyrdom of Salsa*]
Pass. Scill.	*Passio Sanctorum Scillitanorum* [*Acts of the Scillitan Martyrs*]
Pass. Theod.	*Passio Theodoti Ancyrani* [*Martyrdom of Theodotus of Ancyra*]

Patrick of Ireland
Conf.	*Confessio* [*Confession*]

Paul the Silentiary
Ambon.	*Descriptio Ambonis* [*Description of the Ambo (of the Hagia Sophia)*]
Soph.	*Descriptio Sanctae Sophiae* [*Description of the Hagia Sophia*]

Paulinus of Nola
Carm.	*Carmina* [*Poems*]
Carm. nat.	*Carmina natalicia* [*Anniversary Poems*]

P'awstos Buzand
	Buzandaran Patmut'iwnk' [*The Epic Histories of P'awstos Buzand*]

Peter Chrysologus
Serm.	*Sermones* [*Sermons*]

Philo
Legat.	*Legatio ad Gaium* [*Embassy to Gaius*]

Philostorgius
Hist. eccl.	*Historia ecclesiastica* [*Ecclesiastical History*]

Pliny the Elder
Nat.	*Naturalis historia* [*Natural History*]

Pliny the Younger
Ep.   *Epistulae* [*Letters*]

Polybius
Hist.   *Historiae* [*The Histories*]

Polycarp of Smyrna
Phil.   *Epistula ad Philippenses* [*Letter to the Philippians*]

Pontius
Vit. Cypr.   *Vita et passio Cypriani* [*The Life and Passion of Cyprian*]

Priscus
Fr.   *Fragmenta* [*Fragments*]

Procopius of Caesarea
Aed.   *De aedificiis* [*On Buildings*]
Pers.   *De bellis: De bello persico* [*The Wars (of Justinian): The Persian War*]

Prosper of Aquitaine
Chron.   *Epitoma chronicorum* [*Epitome of the Chronicles*]

Pseudo-Dionysius of Tell Maḥrē
Chron.   *Chronicon* [*Chronicle*]

Ptolemy
Geogr.   *Geographica* [*Geography*]

Rufinus
Hist.   *Eusebii Historia ecclesiastica a Rufino translata et continuata* [*Eusebius's Ecclesiastical History Translated and Continued by Rufinus*]

Seneca
Helv.   *Ad Helviam* [*To Helviam*]

Socrates Scholasticus
Hist. eccl.   *Historia ecclesiastica* [*Ecclesiastical History*]

Sophocles
Aj.   *Ajax*

Sozomen
Hist. eccl.   *Historia ecclesiastica* [*Ecclesiastical History*]

Strabo
Geogr.   *Geographica* [*Geography*]

Suetonius
    Aug.   *Divus Augustus [The Deified Augustus]*
    Claud.   *Divus Claudius [The Deified Claudius]*
    Jul.   *Divus Julius [The Deified Julius]*
    Nero   *Vita Neronis [Life of Nero]*

Sulpicius Severus
    Chron.   *Chronicorum libri ii [Chronicle]*

Tacitus
    Ann.   *Annales [Annals]*
    Hist.   *Historiae [Histories]*

Tertullian
    Adv. Jud.   *Adversus Judaeos [Against the Jews]*
    Apol.   *Apologeticus [Apology]*
    Bapt.   *De baptismo [Baptism]*
    Cult. fem.   *De cultu feminarum [The Apparel of Women]*
    Mart.   *Ad martyras [To the Martyrs]*
    Nat.   *Ad nationes [To the Heathen]*
    Praescr.   *De praescriptione haereticorum [Prescription against Heretics]*
    Scap.   *Ad Scapulam [To Scapula]*
    Val.   *Adversus Valentinianos [Against the Valentinians]*

Theodoret of Cyrrhus
    Hist. eccl.   *Historia ecclesiastica [Ecclesiastical History]*
    Phil. hist.   *Philotheos historia [History of the Monks]*
    Therap.   *Hellenikon therapeutikē pathēmatōn [A Cure of Greek Maladies]*

Theophanes
    Chron.   *Chronographia [Chronicle]*

Theophylact Simocatta
    Hist.   *Historiae libri viii [History]*

Thomas of Marga
    Hist. mon.   *Historia monastica [Monastic History]*

Victor of Vita
    Hist. pers.   *Historia persecutionis Africanae provinciae [History of the Vandal Persecution]*

    Vit. Dan.   ***Vita S. Daniel [Life of St. Daniel]***

Zosimus
    Hist. nov.   *Historia nova [New History]*

Modern Works

AA	Athenian Agora
AAASH	*Acta antiqua Academiae scientiarum hungaricae*
AAEA	Anejos de Archivo español de arqueología
AASOR	Annual of the American Schools of Oriental Research
AASS	*Acta sanctorum quotquot toto orbe coluntur*
AB	Anchor Bible
ABD	*Anchor Bible Dictionary*
ABulg	*Archaeologica bulgarica*
AC	Antioche chrétienne
ACW	Ancient Christian Writers
AD	*Archaiologikon Deltion*
ADAJ	*Annual of the Department of Antiquities of Jordan*
AE	*Archaiologike Ephemeris*
AI	*Annales Islamiques*
AJA	*American Journal of Archaeology*
AJEC	Ancient Judaism and Early Christianity
AJP	*American Journal of Philology*
AKM	Abhandlungen für die Kunde des Morgenlandes
AnBoll	Analecta Bollandiana
ANF	*Ante-Nicene Fathers*
ANRW	*Aufstieg und Niedergang der römischen Welt: Geschichte und Kultur Roms im Spiegel der neueren Forschung.* Edited by Hildegard Temporini and Wolfgang Haase
AnSt	*Anatolian Studies*
AOB	Acta orientalia belgica
AOC	Archives de l'orient chrétien
AoF	Altorientalische Forschungen
APF	*Archiv für Papyrusforschung*
APP	Ancient Peoples and Places
APVG	Archiv für Papyrusforschung und verwandte Gebiete
ArSP	*Archivio storico pugliese*
ArtBul	*Art Bulletin*
ASA	*Annali di storia dell'esegesi*
ASoc	*Ancient Society*
ASP	*American Studies in Papyrology*
AT	*Antiquité tardive*
AW	*Ancient World*
BA	*Biblical Archaeologist*
BAC	Biblioteca de autores cristianos
BAH	Bibliothèque archaeologique et historique
BAR	*Biblical Archaeology Review*
BARBS	British Archaeological Reports British Series
BARIS	British Archaeological Reports International Series

BASP	*Bulletin of the American Society of Papyrologists*
BAT	Bibliothèque de l'Antiquité tardive
BAug	Bibliothèque augustinienne
BBA	Berliner byzantinische Arbeiten
BBE	Bibliothèque byzantine: Études
BBI	*Bulletin of the Byzantine Institute*
BCH	*Bulletin de correspondance hellénique*
BCTHS	*Bulletin du Comité des travaux historiques et scientifiques*
BE	*Bulletin épigraphique*
BEFAR	Bibliothèque des Écoles françaises d'Athènes et de Rome
BHG	*Bibliotheca hagiographica Graece*
BHL	*Bibliotheca hagiographica latina antiquae et mediae aetatis*
BHT	Beiträge zur historischen Theologie
BI	Beiträge zur Iranistik
BIAL	Brill's Inner Asian Library
BibE	Bibliothèque d'étude
BIFAO	*Bulletin de l'Institute français d'archéologie orientale*
BJRL	*Bulletin of the John Rylands University Library of Manchester*
BK	Bibliothek der Kirchenväter
BL	British Library
Add.	Additional Manuscripts
Or.	Oriental Manuscripts
BMC	British Museum Collection
BMHB	*Bulletin du Musée hongrois des beaux-arts*
BP	Bibliothèque de la Pléiade
BRIIFS	*Bulletin of the Royal Institute for Inter-Faith Studies*
BSAC	*Bulletin de la Société d'archéologie copte*
BSGRT	Bibliotheca scriptorum graecorum et romanorum Teubneriana
BSIH	Brill Studies in Intellectual History
BSL	Brill Scholars' List
BSOAS	*Bulletin of the School of Oriental and African Studies*
BSS	Black Sea Studies
BTG	Biblioteca teológica granadina
ByzZ	*Byzantinische Zeitschrift*
BZNW	Beihefte zur Zeitschrift für die neutestamentliche Wissenschaft und die Kunde der älteren Kirche
CA	Christianismes anciens
CAAD	*China Archaeology and Art Digest*
CAH	Cambridge Ancient History. 3rd ed.
CAHA	Collection archéologie et histoire de l'antiquité
CahArch	*Cahiers archéologiques*
CAJ	*Central Asiatic Journal*
CAP	*Collectanea antiariana parisina (Fragmenta historica).* [= CSEL 65.43–205]
CAR	Cahiers d'archéologie romande

CB	*The Cities and Bishoprics of Phrygia* (when cited by inscription number). Edited by William M. Ramsay
CCCM	Corpus christianorum: Continuatio mediaevalis
CCSL	Corpus christianorum: Series latina
CEASA	Collection des Études augustiniennes: Série antiquité
CEFR	Collection de l'École française de Rome
CELAMA	Cultural Encounters in Late Antiquity and the Middle Ages
CFM	Corpus fontium Manichaeorum
CHJ	*Cambridge History of Judaism*
CHVF	Collection Histoire des villes de France
CIG	*Corpus inscriptionum graecarum*
CIJ	*Corpus inscriptionum judaicarum*
CIL	*Corpus inscriptionum latinarum*
CIMOS	Corpus of Illuminated Manuscripts: Oriental Series
CRAI	Comptes rendus de l'Académie des inscriptions et belles-lettres
CRINT	Compendia rerum iudaicarum ad Novum Testamentum
CRIPEL	*Cahier de recherches de l'Institut de papyrologie et égyptologie de Lille*
CS	Collectanea serica
CSCO	Corpus scriptorum christianorum orientalium
CSCP	Cornell Studies in Classical Philology
CSEL	Corpus scriptorium ecclesiasticorum latinorum
CSIC	Cambridge Studies in Islamic Civilization
CSMLT	Cambridge Studies in Medieval Life and Thought
CSS	Cistercian Studies Series
CUASEC	CUA Studies in Early Christianity
CW	*Classical World*
DACL	*Dictionnaire d'archéologie chrétiennes et de liturgie.* Edited by Fernand Cabrol and Henri Leclerq
DCAE	*Deltion Christianikis Archaiologikis Etaireias*
DECL	*Dictionary of Early Christian Literature.* Edited by Siegmar Döpp and Wilhelm Geerlings
DJS	Duke Judaic Studies
DOP	*Dumbarton Oaks Papers*
DubRev	*The Dublin Review*
EA	Études alexandrines
EAA	Études d'antiquités africaines
EastCS	Eastern Christian Studies
ECS	Early Christian Studies
EEBS	*Epeteris Etaireias Byzantinon Spoudon*
EEC²	*Encyclopedia of Early Christianity.* 2nd ed. Edited by Everett Ferguson, Michael P. McHugh, and Frederick W. Norris
EECh	*Encyclopedia of the Early Church.* Edited by Angelo di Berardino
EG	*Epigrafia greca*
EncIran	*Encyclopaedia Iranica.* Edited by Ehsan Yarshater

EOMIA	*Ecclesiae occidentalis monumenta iuris antiquissima*
EPROER	Études preliminaries aux religions orientales dans l'Empire romain
ES	Études syriaques
EUS	European University Studies
EW	*East and West*
FC	Fontes christiani
FCh	Fathers of the Church
FGH	*Die Fragmenta der griechischen Historiker.* Edited by Felix Jacoby
FilCr	Filologia e critica
GAF	Guides archéologique de la France
GCS	Die griechische christliche Schriftsteller der ersten [drei] Jahrhunderte
GEF	Guides archéologiques de la France
GO	Göttinger Orientforschungen
GOTR	*Greek Orthodox Theological Review*
GRBS	*Greek, Roman, and Byzantine Studies*
GRM	Graeco-Roman Memoirs
HA	Handbuch der Archäologie
HAM	*Hortus artium medievalium*
HATS	Harvard Armenian Texts and Studies
HE	Historia Einzelschriften
HeyJ	*Heythrop Journal*
HO	Handbuch der Orientalistik
HP	Hypurgeio Politismu
HTR	*Harvard Theological Review*
HTS	Harvard Theological Studies
HUPRL	Harvard University Press Reference Library
IAAR	Israel Antiquities Authority Reports
IAnkyraBosch	*Quellen zur Geschichte der Stadt Ankara im Altertum.* Edited by Emin Bosch
IAsMinChr	*Recueil des inscriptions grecques chrétiennes d'Asie Mineure.* Edited by Henri Grégoire
IE	Impact of Empire
IG	*Inscriptiones graecae.* Editio minor. Edited by Friedrich Hiller von Gaertringen et al.
IKlaudiop	*Die Inschriften von Klaudiu Polis.* Edited by Friedrich Becker-Bertau
IKourion	*The Inscriptions of Kourion.* Edited by Terence B. Mitford
ILCV	*Inscriptiones latinae christianae veteres*
ILS	*Inscriptiones latinae selectae*
IMont	*Montanist Inscriptions and Testimonia* (when cited by inscription number). Edited by William Tabbernee
IMS	*Inscriptions de la Mésie superieure.* Edited by Fanula Papazoglu
InnisR	*The Innis Review: The Journal of the Scottish Catholic Historical Society*
IPont	*Recueil des inscriptions grecques et latines du Pont et de l'Arménie.* Edited by John G. C. Anderson, Franz V. M. Cumont, and Henri Grégoire
IRT	*Inscriptions of Roman Tripolitania*

IstMitt	Istanbuler Mitteilungen
JIAAA	Journal of Inner Asian Art and Archaeology
JAC	Jahrbuch für Antike und Christentum
JACE	Jahrbuch für Antike und Christentum: Ergänzungsbände
JAS	Journal of Archaeological Science
JCoptS	Journal of Coptic Studies
JEA	Journal of Egyptian Archaeology
JECS	Journal of Early Christian Studies
JEH	Journal of Ecclesiastical History
JHS	Journal of Hellenic Studies
JJP	Journal of Juristic Papyrology
JLA	Journal of Late Antiquity
JÖB	Jahrbuch der Österreichischen Byzantinistik
JRA	Journal of Roman Archaeology
JRASup	Journal of Roman Archaeology Supplementary Series
JRS	Journal of Roman Studies
JSNTSup	Journal for the Study of the New Testament: Supplement Series
JSRC	Jerusalem Studies in Religion and Culture
JTS	Journal of Theological Studies
LAA	Late Antique Archaeology
LAGPW	Late Antiquity: A Guide to the Postclassical World. Edited by Glen W. Bowersock, Peter Brown, and Oleg Grabar
LAS	Lincoln Archaeological Studies
LASBF	Liber annuus Studii biblici franciscani
LBNEA	ASOR Library of Biblical and Near Eastern Archaeology
LBW	Inscriptions grecques et latines recueillies en Asie Mineur. Edited by Philippe Le Bas and William H. Waddington
LDAB	Leuven Database of Ancient Books (http://www.trismegistos.org/ldab)
MA	Miscellanea agostiniana
MAB	Monuments de l'art byzantine
MAGHL	Monuments of Ancient Georgian Hagiographical Literature
MAMA	Monumenta Asiae Minoris Antiqua. Edited by William M. Calder et al.
MAPS	Memoirs of the American Philosophical Society
MBM	Miscellanea byzantina monacensia
MCA	Mitteilungen zur christlichen Archäologie
MECS	Middle East Culture Series
MEFRA	Mélanges de l'École français de Rome: Antiquité
MEMIW	Medieval and Early Modern Iberian World
MF	Madrider Forschungen
MIS	Materiali az istoriiata na Sofiia
MO	Monumenta occidentis
MPIL	Monographs of the Peshitta Institute, Leiden
MRTS	Medieval and Renaissance Texts and Studies
M-S	Millennium-Studien

MSBC	Manuali e saggi per i beni culturali
MSMAS	Monographs of the Society of Messenian Archaeological Studies
MST	Michigan Slavic Translations
MTA	Münsteraner theologische Abhandlungen
NEA	*Near Eastern Archaeology*
NEAEHL	*The New Encyclopedia of Archaeological Excavations in the Holy Land.* Edited by E. Stern
NewDocs	*New Documents Illustrating Early Christianity.* Edited by G. H. R. Horsley and S. R. Llewelyn
NHMS	Nag Hammadi and Manichaean Studies
NovTSup	Supplements to Novum Testamentum
NPNF²	*Nicene and Post-Nicene Fathers.* Series 2
OBC	Orientalia biblica et christiana
OCA	Orientalia christiana analecta
OEANE	*The Oxford Encyclopedia of Archaeology in the Near East.* Edited by Eric M. Meyers
OECS	Oxford Early Christian Studies
OJA	*Oxford Journal of Archaeology*
OLA	Orientalia louvaniensia analecta
OM	Oxbow Monographs
OMT	Oxford Medieval Texts
Or	*Orientalia*
OrChr	*Oriens christianus*
OrChrAn	Orientalia christiana analecta
OrOc	Oriens et Occidens
OTM	Oxford Theological Monographs
OTP	*The Old Testament Pseudepigrapha.* Edited by James H. Charlesworth
OV	Orientalia venetiana
OWS	Oxford-Warburg Studies
PAA	*Praktika Akadimias Athinon*
PAE	*Praktika Archaiologikis Etaireias*
P.Alex.	*Papyrus grecs du Musée gréco-romain d'Alexandrie*
P.Amh.	*The Amherst Papyri*
PAPhS	*Proceedings of the American Philosophical Society*
ParOr	*Parole de l'orient*
PB	Poikila byzantina
P.Bas.	*Papyrusurkunden der Öffentlichen Bibliothek der Universität zu Basel*
PC	Papyrologica Coloniensia
P.Col.	*Columbia Papyri*
P.Dura	*The Parchments and Papyri* (at Dura-Europos). Edited by C. Bradford Welles et al.
P.Egerton	*Fragments of an Unknown Gospel and Other Early Christian Papyri.* Edited by H. Idris Bell and T. C. Skeat
PETSE	Papers of the Estonian Theological Society in Exile
PF	Papyrologica Florentina

PG	Patrologiae cursus completus: Series graeca. Edited by Jacques-Paul Migne
P.Grenf.	*New Classical Fragments and Other Greek and Latin Papyri*
PHA	Pelican History of Art
PHC	A People's History of Christianity
PHS	Persian Heritage Series
PIFEB	Publications de l'Institut français d'études Byzantines
PL	Patrologiae cursus completus: Series latina. Edited by Jacques-Paul Migne
PLB	Papyrologica Lugduno-Batava
PMAA	Princeton Monographs in Art and Architecture
PMFIA	Papers and Monographs of the Finnish Institute at Athens
PMMAEE	Publications of the Metropolitan Museum of Art Egyptian Expedition
PMS	North American Patristic[s] Society Patristic Monograph Series
P.Ness. 2	*Excavations at Nessana: Literary Papyri.* Vol. 2. Edited by Lionel Casson and Ernest L. Hettich
PO	Patrologia orientalis
POC	*Proche orient chrétien*
P.Oxy.	*The Oxyrhynchus Papyri.* Edited by Bernard P. Grenfell, Arthur S. Hunt, et al.
PPP	Past and Present Publications
PRSt	*Perspectives in Religious Studies*
P.Ryl.	*Catalogue of the Greek and Latin Papyri in the John Rylands Library*
PS	Patrologia syriaca
PSI	*Papiri greci e latini*
PTS	Patristische Texte und Studien
PV	Papyrologica vindobonensia
RAC	*Reallexikon für Antike und Christentum.* Edited by Theodore Klauser et al.
RAr	*Revue archéologique*
RAug	*Recherches augustiniennes*
RB	*Revue biblique*
RCSS	Records of Civilization: Sources and Studies
REA	*Revue des études anciennes*
REArm	*Revue des études arméniennes*
REAug	*Revue des études augustiniennes*
RelC	*Religion Compass*
RevNum	*Revue Numismatique*
RGG	*Religion in Geschichte und Gegenwart.* 4th rev. ed. Edited by Hans Dieter Betz et al.
RGRW	Religions in the Graeco-Roman World
RH	*Revue historique*
RHR	*Revue de l'histoire des religions*
RivAC	*Rivista di archeologia cristiana*
RMCS	Routledge Monographs in Classical Studies

RSO	Rivista degli studi orientali
RT	*Revue Tunisien*
SAAus	Studia antiqua australiensa
SAC	Studies in Antiquity and Christianity
SAKDQ	Sammlung ausgewählter kirchen- und dogmengeschichtlicher Quellenschriften
SAOC	Studies in Ancient Oriental Civilization
SB	*Sammelbuch griechischer Urkunden aus Ägypten*. Edited by F. Preisigke et al.
SBLRBS	Society of Biblical Literature Resources for Biblical Study
SBLTT	Society of Biblical Literature Texts and Translations
SBLWAW	Society of Biblical Literature Writings from the Ancient World
SBLWGRW	Society of Biblical Literature Writings from the Greco-Roman World
SC	Sources chrétiennes
SCH	Studies in Church History
SCI	*Scripta classica Israelica*
SCJ	Studies in Christianity and Judaism
SEAug	Studia ephemerides Augustinianum
SecCent	*Second Century*
SFSHJ	South Florida Studies in the History of Judaism
SGKAO	Schriften zur Geschichte und Kultur des alten Orients
SH	Studia historica
SHR	Studies in the History of Religions
SIAL	*Studies on the Inner Asian Languages*
SIISA	Studi pubblicati dall'Istituto italiano per la storia antica
SKCO	Sprachen und Kulturen des christlichen Orients
SL	Sinica Leidensia
SNTSMS	Society for New Testament Studies Monograph Series
SOK	Studien zur orientalischen Kirchengeschichte
SPAW	Sitzungsberichte der preussischen Akademie der Wissenschaften
SPL	Studia patristica et liturgica
SPM	Studia patristica mediolanensia
SPNT	Studies on Personalities of the New Testament
SPon	Studia pontica
SR	Scavi e ricerche
SRCR	Studi e ricerche di cultura religiosa
SRS	Silk Road Studies
SSK	Studien zur spätantike Kunstgeschichte
ST	*Studia theologica*
STAC	Studien und Texte zu Antike und Christentum
StACr	Studi di antichità cristiana
StPatr	Studia patristica
StPB	Studia post-biblica
STT	Semitic Texts with Translations
TAB	*Terra antiqua balcanica*

TAMS	*Transactions of the Ancient Monuments Society*
TAPA	*Transactions and Proceedings of the American Philological Association*
TAVO	Tübinger Atlas des Vorderen Orients
TCH	Transformation of the Classical Heritage
TCRPOGA	Travaux du Centre de recherche sur le Proche-Orient et la Grèce antiques
TH	Théologie historique
TIB	Tabula Imperii Byzantini. Edited by Herbert Hunger et al.
TMCRHCB	Travaux et mémoires du Centre de recherche d'histoire et civilization de Byzance
TPL	Textus patristici et liturgici
TRE	*Theologische Realenzyklopädie.* Edited by Gerhard Krause and Gerhard Müller
TSAJ	Texte und Studien zum antiken Judentum
TSCIA	Toronto Studies in Central and Inner Asia
TTH	Translated Texts for Historians
TTL	Theological Translation Library
TRW	Transformation of the Roman World
UCOP	University of Cambridge Oriental Publications
USL	Untersuchungen zur syrischen Literaturgeschichte
VC	*Vigiliae christianae*
VCSS	Variorum Collected Studies Series
VCSup	Supplements to Vigiliae christianae
VKB	Veröffentlichungen der Kommission für Byzantinistik
W.Chr.	*Grundzüge und Chrestomathie der Papyruskunde, 1.2: Chrestomathie.* Edited by Ludwig Mitteis and Ulrich Wilcken.
WUNT	Wissenschaftliche Untersuchungen zum Neuen Testament
ZPE	*Zeitschrift für Papyrologie und Epigraphik*

General Introduction

WILLIAM TABBERNEE

In December 2009 Professor Elizabeth Bolman, a specialist in Egyptian Christian art, was supervising the cleaning and restoration of some beautiful artwork painted on the walls of a fourth-century tomb chamber. The funerary chapel containing the tomb chamber, discovered in 2002, is part of the so-called White Monastery in Upper Egypt (see chap. 5). Its most famous abbot was Shenoute of Atripe (346/7–465 CE). This long-lived scholar-monk from the hinterlands of the Nile, who played a prominent role in one of the great ecumenical councils of the early church (Council of Ephesus in 431), was long neglected outside Egypt because his writings, regarded as the high-water mark in Coptic literature, were not translated into Greek and Latin. But inside Egypt many Christians, including three popes of the Coptic Church, have been named after him.

One of the barrel vaults of the chamber where Bolman and her team were working is decorated with a painting of three standing figures. The depiction of the central figure has almost completely survived the ravages of time, unlike those of his companions. Barefooted, bearded, the man wears a monk's garb and a stole with four crosses. His hands are raised in prayer, the left hand holding a victory wreath. Around his head is a (square) halo. Perhaps to their surprise, when they cleaned the wall above the saint's head, the team discovered an inscription. The initial words and a couple of later letters are missing, but the whole text may confidently be restored thus: "[The (holy) tomb/shrine] of A[bb]a Shenoute Archimand[r]ite" (Bolman, Davis, and Pike 2010, 457, 461). The final resting place of the great ancient abbot had been found!

Recent Archaeological Discoveries

Bolman's is merely one of the latest significant archaeological discoveries made in recent years related to the history of early Christianity (ca. 30–ca. 400) or Christianity in Late Antiquity (ca. 400–ca. 640). In August 1998 a young Turkish villager, Murat Altıner, sold to the Uşak Archaeological Museum a broken marble slab. His grandfather had uncovered the slab while plowing and used it as a step for the family home.

In July 2002 the Greek and Latin bilingual inscription on the slab provided a vital clue leading to the discovery of Tymion and Pepouza, the long-lost "New Jerusalem" of the Montanists, adherents of an early Christian prophetic movement (Tabbernee 2003; 2012; Tabbernee and Lampe 2008).

Fig. I.1. "Tymion Inscription"

In May 2006 a stone pillar was unearthed in Luoyang, China, and sold on the black market before being recovered by the authorities. It is the second stele known to have been erected by Christians of the Church of the East describing the establishment of Christianity in China (see chap. 4).

In January 2010 workers repairing Davis Street in Jerusalem's historic Old City accidentally uncovered the original pavement of the Decumanus, the main east-west street built by the Romans after the Second Jewish Revolt. The discovery confirms the accuracy of the mosaic Madaba Map (see chap. 1). That map shows the Decumanus slightly south (to the right on the map) of the Church of the Holy Sepulcher. The colonnaded street shown in the middle of the map is the Cardo Maximus, the main north-south Roman street.

Five years earlier, Ramil Razilo was one of fifty Israeli prisoners clearing an area of ground for the construction of a new ward at the Megiddo prison when his spade struck what turned out to be the mosaic floor of a (probably) third-century church (fig. 1.8). Claims about the mosaic being the

Fig. I.2. Pavement of Roman Cardo Maximus, Jerusalem

oldest extant remnants of a building specifically constructed as a Christian church may be exaggerated, as that honor may belong to the mosaic flooring of the Theodorian Complex in Aquileia. On the basis of an inscription, that church can be dated between 313 and 319 (see chap. 9).

A number of other exaggerated or highly speculative claims, based on ancient artifacts, inscriptions, or other material evidence, have been made in

Fig. I.3. Madaba Map, Showing Jerusalem

recent years. These include the alleged identification of some early ossuaries as containing the bones of "James, the brother of Jesus," of other members of Jesus's family, and even of Jesus himself (Tabor and Jacobovici 2012). These claims are very controversial (see chap. 1). It is, nevertheless, important to recognize that our understanding of the past is always open to challenge and correction by the discovery of new "hard evidence" and/or by the reinterpretation of already-known material seen in a new light (Tabbernee 2013a).

The "Abercius" Inscription

Until the late nineteenth century, scholars believed, on the basis of the extant fourth-century *Vita Abercii* (*Life of Abercius*), that a man named "Abercius" was a second-century bishop of Hierapolis (modern Pamukkale, Turkey). In June 1883, however, William Ramsay, a Scottish classicist and epigrapher, discovered two fragments of the tombstone of an "Avircius" (Ramsay 1883, 424–27 no. 36; *CB* 657). The discovery was made not at Pamukkale (ancient Hierapolis), but near Koçhisar (ancient Hieropolis) in the Phrygian Pentapolis, approximately 110 km northeast of Hierapolis (fig. 7.2). Two years earlier, at nearby Kılandıraz, Ramsay had come across another tombstone, that of a man named Alexander, which had partially borrowed the wording of Avircius's epitaph (Ramsay 1882b, 518 no. 5; cf. Ramsay 1882a, 339–53; *CB* 656).

The whole text of Avircius's epitaph (see sidebar I.1) can be reconstructed on the basis of the additional information provided by the *Vita Abercii* (Nissen 1912, 1–55) and the wording of Alexander's epitaph. In somewhat cryptic language, but language intended to be understood by "those in the know," Avircius tells all who pause to read his epitaph that he is the citizen of a "heavenly city" as well as of his native city, Hieropolis; a disciple of Christ, the Holy Shepherd; an avid reader of the Gospels and the letters of St. Paul; and that he had traveled widely (as far west as Rome and as far east as Nisibis), everywhere sharing the Eucharist with people bearing the seal of baptism.

Fig. I.4. Avircius's Tombstone (Reconstruction), Vatican Museum, Vatican City

William Tabbernee

I.1 "Having Paul in the Carriage"—Avircius's Cryptic Epitaph

I, the (citizen of a select city,) have prepared this while still living so that I might have a notable tomb here for my body. Named Avirkios, I am the disciple of a
4 holy shepherd | who feeds flocks of sheep on mountains and plains, who has powerful eyes keeping everything in view. For he it was who taught me . . .
8 faithful writings, he who sent me to Rome | to behold the capital and to see a gold-robed, gold-sandalled queen. Also a people I saw there having a re-
12 splendent seal | and I saw the plain of Syria and all the cities, (even) Nisibis,
16 having crossed the Euphrates; | everywhere I had kindred spirits. Having Paul
20 in the carriage, Faith led the way everywhere and set before me as nourish-ment | everywhere a fish from a spring, immense, spotless, which a holy virgin
24 caught. And this she gave into the hands of her | friends to eat always, (and) having a good wine, giving mixed wine with bread. That these things should
28 be written in this way I, | Avirkios, ordered, of a truth celebrating (my) 72nd year. May the one who understands and is in harmony with all these things pray
32 on behalf of Avirkios. | However, one shall not put anyone else in my tomb. Consequently, (any violator) shall pay 2,000 gold pieces to the treasury of the Romans and 1,000 gold pieces to my auspicious native city Hieropolis. (trans. Tabbernee forthcoming b)

Avircius is presumably the same person as the Avircius Marcellus to whom, in about 193, a now-anonymous bishop (perhaps from one of the other cities of the Phrygian Pentapolis) sent, at Avircius's request, a copy of an anti-Montanist treatise, utilized extensively by Eusebius of Caesarea in his *Historia ecclesiastica* (5.16.2–5.17.4). Since Alexander's tombstone was erected in 216, Avircius's own epitaph must have been composed before that date, perhaps in about 200 or even earlier.

The Earliest Material Evidence for Christianity

Avircius's epitaph, though one of the earliest extant Christian inscriptions, is not the earliest nonliterary evidence of Christianity. It is possible that a tombstone dated 157/8, from the territory of Cadi in Asia Minor, may be Christian, but it is certain that another one, dated 179/80, from Cadi itself definitely is (see chap. 7). The decade of the 180s seems to be the time when distinctively Christian terms, symbols, and art become recognizable in the extant archaeological material (Snyder 2003, 2–3). This is especially the case in Rome, where, at least from the very beginning of the third century, Christian cemeteries within the catacombs provided a certain amount of security

for expressing in word or symbol the Christian allegiance of the deceased—
something that non-Christian neighbors knew anyway. Such security, however,
was not to be taken for granted before Constantine (r. 306–337) adopted
Christianity as his own preferred religion in the second decade of the fourth
century.

Periodic outbreaks of actual persecution and the potential threat of being
accused of disloyalty to the Roman Empire by refusing to participate in cultic
activities made Christians reluctant to declare permanently on tombstones
or walls that they were the monotheistic followers of Jesus. Even if they had
wanted to do so, many early Christians belonged to the lower classes and
could not afford to have even a simple grave marker, let alone to decorate
their homes with Christian art. The "epigraphic habit" (MacMullen 1982;
Tabbernee 2008a) was not an activity of the poor, and "graven images" (of
whatever kind) were frowned on by the majority of early Christians. This
began to change in the course of the third century and with the rise of social
Christian elites in the middle of the fourth century, especially in the Western
provinces of the Roman Empire.

Similarly, it was only when Christians stopped meeting and worshiping in
homes (house-churches) and began adapting synagogues or constructing new
basilicas, baptisteries, monasteries, and other specifically Christian buildings
that they were able to leave to posterity monumental evidence of the details of
their spiritual, liturgical, ecclesial, and communal lives. The great "building
boom" of ecclesiastical edifices initiated by Constantine and his mother in
Jerusalem, Rome, Constantinople, and elsewhere was paralleled in the fifth
and sixth centuries, especially in the East, by emperors such as Justinian.

Early Christianity in Contexts   *Realia*

This book focuses on utilizing the earliest available "material evidence" (realia)
not only to give information about the origins of Christianity in a given location but also to provide a physical and cultural context for the particular
kind of Christianity that existed in that location. The book is divided into ten
geographic regions, and each chapter attempts to summarize what its region
was like before the introduction of Christianity in terms of geography, politics,
economics, agriculture, social patterns, and, especially, religious thought and
practice. Each chapter then draws on inscriptions, coins, mosaics, remnants
of church buildings, baptisteries, decorative artwork, icons, crosses, symbols,
ecclesiastical vessels, reliquaries, and a host of other artifacts to describe and
explain the region's specific form of Christianity.

Knowledge of the time and manner in which Christianity was first introduced (or, in areas such as Britain, reintroduced) to and developed in these regions is not always able to be deduced from the archaeological evidence, given that in many regions Christianity commenced well before 180—that is, before there are recognizably Christian artifacts. Consequently, early literary texts and later documents containing earlier oral traditions are also essential sources for the history of some of the earliest Christians. Written sources also provide a great deal of information about Christianity in a particular region, even when archaeological or epigraphic evidence does exist. Literary texts are not confined to the writings of church historians such as Eusebius, theologians such as Origen, or polemicists such as Tertullian; they also include the letters of bishops such as Barsauma of Nisibis and scraps of papyrus written on by ordinary Egyptian Christians. There are Chinese Christian *sūtras*, discovered among a hoard of Buddhist and Manichaean manuscripts, and Syriac Christian poems; acts of the martyrs and lives of the saints; as well as records of church councils, travel guides, ancient maps, and the journals of early pilgrims. There are also liturgical texts, church manuals, sermons, exegetical essays, biblical manuscripts, and different versions of Christian Scriptures, including those that did not make it into the official Christian canon.

The surviving works of groups such as the New Prophecy (Montanism), various kinds of so-called Gnostics, Marcionites, Arians, Donatists, Nestorians, Monophysites, and others deemed heretical (or at least schismatic) by the winners of christological, pneumatological, and trinitarian controversies attest the wide diversity of early Christianity, so much so that it is almost possible to speak of early Christiani*ties*.

This book does not argue that a primal and essential (orthodox) unity devolved into diverse (heterodox) expressions, nor does it lament the repression of an original (creative and expressive) diversity into a set of monolithic orthodoxies. Instead, the authors of the book, all experts on their assigned region or subregion, present the various Christian communities that they document on their own terms and, as much as possible, with their own voice. For example, this book refers to a major component of Christianity east of the Euphrates not as Nestorian Christianity (which to Western ears inevitably suggests doubtful orthodoxy) but by its own self-designation: the Church of the East. Care is taken, however, to point out, rather than minimize, significant differences in practice and belief. To the extent that there was mutual awareness and communication between differing groups, care is also taken to note their perceptions of each other, including judgments as to "orthodoxy" and "heresy."

The broad geographical and chronological sweep of this book—from Ireland in the west to India and China in the east, from Germany in the north to Ethiopia and Equatorial Africa in the south, and (mainly) from the first century BCE to the ninth century CE—reflects current trends in the study of early Christianity and Late Antiquity as well as the broader movement within the humanities to take account of diverse cultures. In this way, the distinctive expressions of particular Christian groups can be seen in context as well as highlighted.

From the Roman Near East (chap. 1)—the region that includes Judaea and Galilee, where Jewish "Jesus followers" started a reform movement that eventually led to a new religion—the history of Christianity narrated in this book quickly moves beyond Rome's borders to Mesopotamia and Persia (chap. 2), the Caucasus (chap. 3), and into Central Asia as far as China and on to India (chap. 4). The second half of the book returns to trace the development of Christianity within the borders of the Roman and (later) Byzantine Empires, covering the world of the Nile (chap. 5), Roman North Africa (chap. 6), Asia Minor and Cyprus (chap. 7), the Balkan Peninsula (chap. 8), Italy and its environs (chap. 9), and the Western provinces, including some areas beyond those provinces (chap. 10).

Special attention is given to particular cities especially important for the history of Christianity: Jerusalem (chap. 1), Nisibis and Edessa (chap. 2), Alexandria (chap. 5), Carthage (chap. 6), the "Seven Cities of Asia" (chap. 7), Athens and Constantinople (chap. 8), Rome and Ravenna (chap. 9), and Lyons, London, and Canterbury (chap. 10). The archaeological or literary evidence for the earliest existence of Christianity in dozens of other cities, towns, and villages is also presented in this book. Numerous maps provide a helpful geographic context. Where possible, both the ancient name (or names) and the modern name of a place are given in the text. Only the ancient name, however, normally is recorded on the maps. From the data presented, there are some surprises in store for those who think that early Christianity was primarily an urban phenomenon.

Another surprise for some may be the realization that although the Romans were dominant politically in most of the lands immediately surrounding the Mediterranean during the time when Christianity was developing as a religion, there were equally, if not more, powerful empires or kingdoms to the east and northeast of the Roman Empire. More than one Roman emperor spent much of his reign trying to defeat neighboring Parthians or Persians and was ultimately killed in battle or imprisoned in the process. There were also unconquered tribes north of the Danube and the Rhine as well as on the other side of the North Sea and what is now called the English Channel. Although in some non-Roman territories Christianity was not established for a number of centuries after the new "religion" first began in Judaea, careful examination of traditions, literary texts, and archaeological data reveals that in many regions beyond Roman borders Christian communities were founded as quickly, if not more quickly, than within the Roman Empire (see chaps. 2–4, 10).

By the time Constantine convened the Council of Nicaea in 325, there were literally hundreds of Christian communities within the borders of the Roman Empire and a significant number outside those borders. Christianity was most prevalent in the larger cities, but many smaller towns and even villages had a Christian "church"—either still a "house-church" or one of the few new basilicas. The spread of Christianity to the countryside, however, had been

Fig. I.5. Fifth-Century Church, Kharab al-Shams, Dead Cities Region, Syria

sporadic and continued to be so during the fourth and fifth centuries. In the so-called Dead Cities region of northwestern Syria alone there are scores of remarkably preserved churches built from the fourth century to the seventh. The "ruins" of these churches look as if they were still in use quite recently. In fact, they, and the seven hundred towns and villages in which they were situated, were abandoned soon after the eighth century, in the aftermath of Sasanian occupation of the area and a series of natural disasters.

Despite the unsuccessful attempt of the emperor Julian (the Apostate) to reassert the dominance of classical paganism during the 360s, Christianity prevailed. Under Theodosius I, the last emperor to rule the Roman Empire before the empire was divided permanently into (Byzantine) East and (Roman) West, "orthodox" Christianity became the "official" (albeit not the only) religion in 393. Outside the Roman Empire, however, the kingdoms of Axum, Iberia, and Armenia had made Christianity their state religion a half century or more earlier. The reception of Christianity by the numerous communities inhabiting the "known world" during the first eight centuries or so of the Common Era was neither chronologically predictable nor theologically consistent. Similarly, the kind of Christianity that resulted from the interaction between those who introduced the new faith to a particular area and the local population with its own religious beliefs, traditions, and practices was far more diverse than has often been presumed. Only an exploration across cultures and continents, such as provided by the chapters of this book, can provide a comprehensive and insightful understanding of the diverse nature of early Christianity in its multifaceted contexts.

1

The Roman Near East

LINCOLN BLUMELL, JENN CIANCA, PETER RICHARDSON,
AND WILLIAM TABBERNEE

Introduction

Rome first intruded into the Near East in 64–63 BCE during conquests by Pompey
the Great (106–49 BCE). Initially, only Syria (including Phoenicia) was governed
through Rome's provincial system. Twenty years later the senate chose Herod
the Great (r. 37–4 BCE) to rule Judaea, Samaria, and Galilee as a client kingdom
(Richardson 1996), while Nabataea and Arabia were left alone. The earliest
Christian communities developed in Jerusalem, Judaea, and Samaria (Acts 1:8)
in the first century CE, and believers were soon found in Caesarea, Tyre, and
Antioch. Christianity entered a difficult period with the Jewish Revolts of 66–74
and 132–135 CE. Though there was no formal parting of the ways (Richardson
2006)—Judaism and Christianity maintained a symbiotic relationship theologically, liturgically, architecturally, and ethically—the tensions led to Christianity
developing independently and, ultimately, separating (S. Wilson 1995).

This chapter was written by **Lincoln Blumell** (Sinai and the Negev, Arabia Felix), **Jenn Cianca**
(Antioch, the Tetrapolis, and Syria Coele), **Peter Richardson** (Introduction, Judaea, Samaria,
Galilee, Syria Phoenice, Phoenicia/Phoenica Libanensis, The Decapolis, Northern Arabia, Central
Arabia, Southern Arabia, Complexity of Christianity in the Roman Near East), and **William
Tabbernee** (Jerusalem).

The Near East within the Roman Empire

Pompey's organizational solution did not last, partly because the region was ethnically complex and historically convoluted. Syria in the north and Judaea in the south included various subregions, while semiautonomous cities survived from earlier Hellenistic foundations: along the Mediterranean coastline were cities such as Gaza, Dor, Tyre, Sidon, and, while inland, a Decapolis (ten cities) included centers such as Pella, Gadara, Hippos, and Gerasa.

Herod's death in 4 BCE brought change. Galilee and Peraea went to Herod Antipas (r. 4 BCE–39 CE), while Hulitis, Gaulanitis, Batanaea, Auranitis, and Trachonitis were ruled by Herod Philip II (r. 4 BCE–33 CE). Judaea (including Samaria and Idumaea) was given to Herod Archelaus (r. 4 BCE–6 CE), but it was made a minor Roman province in 6 CE after he was deposed. Judaea was reunited and nominally autonomous between 41 and 44 CE, under Herod Agrippa I (r. 39–44 CE). It was briefly under direct Roman control, but Herod Philip's territories passed to Agrippa's son Marcus Julius Agrippa II in 48, with an imperial procurator responsible for taxes and peace. Following the Jewish Revolt of 66–74, Judaea was expanded to include most of Herod's old territories; when Agrippa II died (ca. 90–100), Rome assumed direct control.

In 106 Trajan (r. 98–117) absorbed Nabataea and created the province of Arabia, whose capital was Bostra. Some Decapolis cities were transferred to the new province (Millar 1993, 95), some to Judaea, and some to Syria. Hadrian's plan to make Jerusalem the new Roman *colonia* Aelia Capitolina, among other factors, triggered the Bar Kokhba Revolt of 132–135; in the aftermath Hadrian (r. 117–138) changed the province's name to Syria Palaestina. Under Diocletian (r. 284–305) the region was divided into Palaestina Prima (Judaea, Samaria, Idumaea, Peraea, coastal plain) with Caesarea as administrative center, Palaestina Secunda (Galilee, Gaulanitis, the old Decapolis areas) with Scythopolis (Beth Shean) as capital, and Palaestina Tertia (the Negev, Nabataea) with Petra as center.

Syria's divisions were similarly complex. Pompey had united Phoenicia, historically a collection of independent cities with extensive maritime trading contacts, with Syria; soon the "official use of the Phoenician language" died out (Millar 1993, 286). Syria Coele (Hollow Syria), an ambiguous geographical designation, once referred to the Decapolis region (Millar 1993, 423) but came to be used of the areas around and between the Lebanon and Anti-Lebanon Mountains (Strabo, *Geogr.* 16.2.1–2, 16, 21). Confusing matters, Septimius Severus (r. 193–211), when he split Syria, named the southern portion Syria Phoenice, though it included more than ancient Phoenicia, and

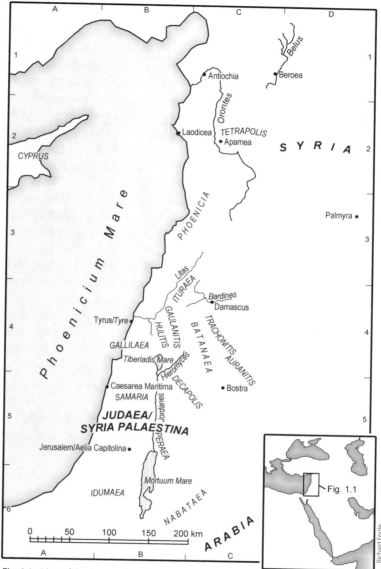

Fig. 1.1. Map of the Roman Near East

the northern portion Syria Coele, though that term once applied to areas in southern Syria. Theodosius I (r. 379–395) divided Syria in four: Syria Coele became Syria Salutaris and Syria Euphratensis; Syria Phoenice became Phoenice and Phoenica Libanensis.

Geography and Ecology

Three tectonic plates—Africa, the Arabian plateau, and Asia Minor—
collide within the Levant, generating earthquakes and volcanoes, rifts and
uplifted mountains. Because it is an important hinge, there have always been
substantial movements of humans, wildlife, and armies in the region. The
mountains and rifts of the Levant run mainly north and south, but there
are complicating transverse features, such as the hills of Upper Galilee and
the Carmel range. Four rivers arise between the Lebanon and Anti-Lebanon
ranges: the Orontes runs north and the Litani runs south from the Bekaa
Valley before they both turn west to the Mediterranean; the Barada runs
east from the Anti-Lebanons, evaporating in the desert; and the Jordan runs
south from Mount Hermon (2814 m), creating the Sea of Galilee (ca. 200 m
below sea level) and the Dead Sea (ca. 400 m below sea level). The paucity of
permanent rivers ensures that springs and oases acquire extra importance.
The climate is generally hotter and drier to the south and east, though there
are dramatic variations. Soil has formed from decomposed geological forma-
tions, mostly limestone; even where soil nurtures shrubs and trees, settlement
pressures and military actions (especially by Romans and Crusaders) have
denuded the hills of vegetation, resulting in serious erosion. The land's suit-
ability for settlement, herding, and agriculture is varied, though the valley
bottoms are usually fertile.

The Euphrates River, which marks the eastern limit of the Roman Near East,
forms, along with the Tigris River, a "fertile crescent" that includes northern
Syria and the coastal areas. This Fertile Crescent has indelibly stamped the
region as a cradle of human civilization. The crescent's interior is largely desert,
while the Sinai Peninsula is a wilderness appendage. Trachonitis, Auranitis,
and Gaulanitis include extensive volcanic areas.

Peoples and Religions

Settlements follow water, whether rivers and lakes (Apamea, Tiberias),
oases (Palmyra, Jericho), permanent springs (Jerusalem, Petra), or aqueducts
from mountain springs (Caesarea Maritima, Laodicea). Easily cultivated areas
were settled early, less hospitable areas had small farmsteads, while desert
areas supported nomadic or seminomadic groups who herded sheep and goats
(Strabo, *Geogr.* 16.2.11), though the contrast between "the desert and the
sown" (the title of Gertrude Bell's 1907 book) is less sharp than sometimes
thought. In the first century the Near East was a hodgepodge of local peoples
interspersed with Greeks and Romans. In his *Geographica* Strabo mentions
groups on the margins, such as Scenitae ("peaceful" [16.1.27]); Ituraeans and

Arabians ("all of whom are robbers" [16.2.18]); Idumaeans ("shared in the same customs" with Jews [16.2.34]); "tent-dwellers and camel-herds" (16.4.2); Sabaeans ("beautifully adorned with temples and royal palaces" [16.4.2–3]); Ichthyophagi ("fisheaters" [16.4.4]); Spermophagi ("seedeaters" [16.4.9]); and Creophagi ("flesheaters" [16.4.9]).

Phoenicians

A sense of ethnicity and religion continued for some time in Phoenician city-states, including Tyre, Sidon, and Byblos. Their influence depended on commerce (notably purple dye) and exploration, together with their coinage (especially the Tyrian shekel) that was widely used until the second century CE. Phoenician deities were assimilated to Greco-Roman gods: Melqart, for example, was equated with Rome's Heracles and Greece's Hercules. Phoenicia practiced a northwest Semitic religion, adopting customs such as sacrifice (whether this included human sacrifice is still debated), offerings, prayer, purity concerns, and festivals (Schmitz 1992, 359–62). Berytus (Beirut) was not a Phoenician city, having been founded as a Roman *colonia* in 15 BCE.

Ituraeans

Appearing desultorily in the historical record (Strabo, Josephus, New Testament, coins, inscriptions), Ituraea centered on Mount Hermon and extended into the Bekaa Valley, Trachonitis, Gaulanitis, Hulitis, and Upper Galilee. Widely dispersed inscriptions name Ituraeans as a Roman auxiliary unit noteworthy for archery; this auxiliary role continued after the ethnic group itself had virtually disappeared (E. Myers 2010). Nothing is known of their origins and very little about their religious activities, though they had cult centers on Mount Hermon (Dar 1993). Josephus (*Ant.* 13.11.3) claims that they were forcibly converted to Judaism by the Hasmonean Aristobulus I (r. 104–103 BCE), but he may exaggerate (Kasher 1988).

Palmyrenes

A distinctive culture emerged at Palmyra's desert oasis by the first century BCE, with worship focused on Semitic deities, such as Baal Shamim and Bel. Family or clan burials were often in tower tombs, incorporating distinctive grave sculptures. Its architecture blended Roman and indigenous traditions: the Temple of Bel, for example, had a Palmyrene *naos* (inner sanctuary) within a Roman *temenos* (sacred enclosure) that included an altar, banqueting hall, and a ritual pool (Richardson 2002, 25–51). Palmyra prospered from the late first century BCE through the third century CE, reaping tariff income through trading via the Euphrates, the Silk Road, and transdesert routes. After revolting against Rome under Queen Zenobia (r. 270–272), Palmyra only partially recovered.

NABATAEANS

By the second century BCE, Nabataeans had displaced Edomites (Idumaeans) from east of the Dead Sea to west of it. By the next century, Nabataeans formed a prosperous kingdom stretching from southern Syria to the Mediterranean and the Red Sea (Strabo, *Geogr.* 15.4.21–26), which often conflicted with Jews. They were famous for sophisticated management of limited water resources and a magisterial skill in contructing rock-cut buildings whose details were indebted to Hellenistic architecture (Markoe 2003). Nabataean religion focused on Semitic divinities such as Dushara, al-Illat, and Atargatis. As wealthy middlemen in international trade between the Mediterranean and the East, the Nabataeans joined Rome in a military expedition to Arabia Felix under Aelius Gallus in 25–24 BCE, but they lost their separate identity when Rome created the province of Arabia.

Peter Richardson

Fig. 1.2. Temple of Bel, Palmyra

1.1 Roman Roads

Rome's armies engaged in massive road building that spurred trade and communications. Some examples, though only a portion of the integrated network (Graf, Isaac, and Roll 1992), suggest their extent and importance:

- A road connected Seleucia Pieria and Antioch with Beroea (Aleppo) and eastward to the Euphrates, a large section of which still exists west of Aleppo.
- A paved road connecting Damascus with Tyre (es-Sur), through Panias/Caesarea Philippi (Banias), went over a mountainous height of land near modern Qiryat Shemonah, west of the Jordan River.
- Roads connected the Wadi Sirhan to Ptolemais (Tell Acco) and Caesarea Maritima (Qesaria) (built 69 CE [Graf, Isaac, and Roll 1992, 785]); parallel roads connected Philadelphia (Amman) with Caesarea Maritima and Joppe (Jaffa).
- Desert caravans arriving in Petra proceeded along roads through the Negev to Gaza.
- The Via Nova Traiana (built 111–114 CE) followed the much earlier King's Highway from Aila ('Aqaba) on the Red Sea to Damascus.
- A new road mirrored the Via Maris (Way of the Sea), paralleling the coastline; the part from Antioch to Ptolemais is the earliest datable road in the area (56 CE).

SAMARITANS

When the northern kingdom of Israel was destroyed in 722 BCE, the continuing peoples were known as Samaritans. Following its revolt against Alexander the Great (r. 336–323 BCE), Samaria was again destroyed, and the main city (also called Samaria) was moved nearer Mount Gerizim. Augustus (r. 31 BCE–14 CE) made Samaria part of Herod's kingdom. Herod built there extensively, including an imperial cult center at Samaria, which, in honor of Augustus, he renamed Sebaste (Sebastiya). Under Hadrian, a temple to Zeus Hypsistos (Highest) was built on the slopes of Mount Gerizim. Samaritanism, like Judaism, included animal sacrifice, ritual purity, and Torah (the five books of Moses). Samaritan synagogues were spread widely, in places such as Delos, Thessalonica, and Caesarea.

JEWS

During the Persian period, following the Babylonian exile of 587 BCE, Jews were loyal to Persia but restive under the Seleucids, until the Hasmonean Revolt (167–164 BCE) freed them from Syrian control. Dynastic conflicts led to Roman domination (63 BCE) and ultimately to an offer of the kingship to Herod. Though Herod was ethnically half Nabataean and half Idumaean, his grandfather had converted to Judaism (Richardson 1996). Herod rebuilt and extended the temple in Jerusalem, on which Jewish religion focused. Jews were found everywhere in the Roman Empire (possibly 10–15 percent of its population), worshiping in local synagogues (Richardson 2004, 111–85). Three revolts between 66 and 135 CE strained relations with Rome.

Trade, Commerce, and Roads

As Rome pursued extensive trade networks following Augustus's *Pax Romana* (Roman peace), the Levant became an important transportation hub. Trade followed traditional routes across the Syrian and Arabian deserts and up from the Red Sea, linking the Mediterranean with the Arabian Gulf, the Indian Ocean, and the Far East. Some infrastructure already existed in major commercial centers and entrepôts, such as Antioch, Palmyra, and Petra, and this made Rome's acquisition of Syria and Arabia inevitable. Herod's construction of the largest harbor in the Mediterranean at Caesarea Maritima provided a major boost, but smaller harbors, such as Gaza, Dor, and Seleucia Pieria, were also important. Roman roads sometimes mimicked caravan routes but primarily met military needs.

As goods traveled freely along the roads of the Levant, so did ideas. Dura-Europos shows, at the moment of its destruction in 256 CE, the competition

Peter Richardson

Fig. 1.3. Roman Road, between Antioch and Beroea

among various religious traditions, where new religions such as Christianity and Mithraism coexisted with established religions (Judaism, Atargatis, and the Palmyrene gods) and Greek cults (Adonis and Zeus). The Parthian style of the frescoed illustrations in several of these cult buildings emphasizes how they shared remarkably similar cultural features.

Contextual Influences

That Christianity benefited from the expanding road system is underscored by the fact that the three earliest archaeologically attested Christian buildings are deep within this road network. Aila on the Red Sea has the earliest purpose-built church (late third century); Dura-Europos, near Salihiya on the Euphrates, has the earliest surviving house-church (ca. 230–240); and Megiddo at an important road junction has another third-century church. Christianity benefited from religions jostling with one another on the same streets and being carried by the same camels or in the holds of the same ships (Vaage 2006; Donaldson 2000). The time and effort that emperors such as Hadrian devoted to the Levant show its importance to Rome, and soon emperors such as Elagabalus (r. 218–222) and Alexander Severus (r. 222–235) were chosen from the East. Eventually the first Arab emperor, Philip (r. 244–249), came from Shahba (renamed Philippopolis); his tolerance prompted Eusebius of Caesarea (ca. 264/5–ca. 339/40) to report that some considered Philip the first Christian emperor.

Christianity in the Levant

Almost from the beginning, visitors came to Judaea and Galilee for both scholarly and pious reasons. Melito of Sardis (fl. ca. 170), the earliest known "pilgrim," wanted to ascertain the biblical canon; Gregory Thaumaturgus (the Wonderworker), later bishop of Neocaesarea in Pontus (bp. ca. 238/9–ca. 270/5), came to study with Origen (ca. 185–ca. 253) sometime between 231 and 238; the mother of Constantine I (r. 306–337), Helena, wished to stimulate her piety. Helena traveled extensively in 326 and identified the burial place of Jesus, claiming to have found a relic of the true cross. The Pilgrim of Bordeaux in 333 was the earliest to produce a written record, but the most famous was Egeria, who left an important journal of her visit between 381 and 384 (Wilkinson 1999). About the same time, Paula and her daughter Eustochium visited the most famous places in the Holy Land in 385 (sometimes traveling with Jerome), before taking up monastic life and settling in Bethlehem. Remarkably, three of the more famous of these pious pilgrims—Helena, Egeria, and Paula—were women.

Christianity succeeded in wealth and power beyond all expectation, prompting some, like Paula and Jerome, to seek escape by establishing monasteries with an ascetic lifestyle in isolated wildernesses and deserts. The numbers were huge. Desolate areas were filled with ascetics, both males and females, seeking redemption with like-minded persons (Chitty 1966). Within three hundred years of Jesus's death, Christianity had transformed the Near East. From being the fount of Christian belief, the Near East had become a place of renewal, the ultimate destination of the pious, and a great intellectual center of the faith.

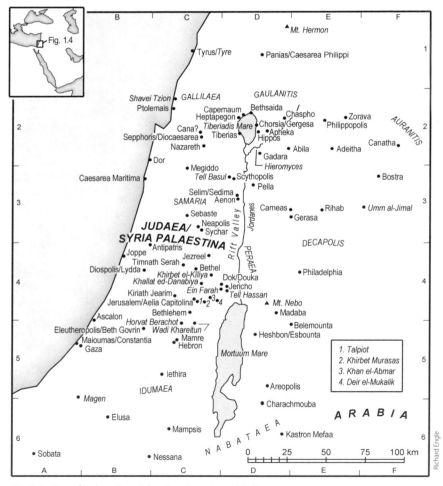

Fig. 1.4. Map of Judaea/Syria Palaestina, Samaria, and Galilee

Palaestina

Jerusalem

Christianity began in Jerusalem with a group of Jewish followers of Jesus in about 30 CE. At the time, of course, Christianity was not known as "Christianity," nor was Christianity's original beginning the only time when Christianity "began" at Jerusalem. There were periods in the tumultuous political history of Jerusalem when Christianity was virtually nonexistent in the city.

During the First Jewish Revolt many early Christians fled from Jerusalem, some settling for a time at Pella (Tabaqat Fahil), across the Jordan (Eusebius, *Hist. eccl.* 3.5.3; Epiphanius, *Mens.* 14–15). By the time of the Second Jewish Revolt (132–135), led by Simon Bar Kosiba (d. 135)—popularly known as Bar Kokhba, "Son of a Star" (cf. Num. 24:17)—a sizable Christian community again existed in Jerusalem. Justin Martyr (d. ca. 165) relates that Bar Kokhba persecuted Christians who acknowledged Jesus rather than him as messiah (*1 Apol.* 31.5–6). After the revolt Jerusalem was almost completely razed to the ground.

Colonia Aelia Capitolina

A new city, called Aelia Capitolina—a name chosen to emphasize its no-longer Jewish character—was built on the site of ancient Jerusalem. *Aelius* was the family name of Hadrian (P. Aelius Hadrianus), under whom the Bar Kokhba Revolt was quelled, and *Capitolina* referred to Jupiter Capitolinus, Rome's senior male god. Hadrian forbade Jews to live in the new city or even to visit it (Eusebius, *Hist. eccl.* 4.6.1–4). He erected pagan temples on sites sacred to Jews and Christians. On the site of the Jewish temple, demolished during the First Jewish Revolt by Titus (r. 79–81), he built a shrine to Jupiter, and on a newly leveled area that covered the rocky outcrop once known as Golgotha/Calvary and the nearby rock-cut tombs, one of which may have been Jesus's burial place,[1] he built a Temple of Venus (Aphrodite). Not until Constantine and Helena became interested in constructing Christian basilicas in Jerusalem were sites such as Golgotha and Jesus's tomb recovered for the Christian community.

---

1. A picturesque "Garden Tomb" outside the north wall of Jerusalem was taken by General Charles C. Gordon in 1884 to be the tomb of Jesus, and the hillside into which the tomb is cut to be Golgotha. The tomb in question, however, was constructed some six hundred to seven hundred years before the time of Christ and reused by Byzantine Christians four hundred to five hundred years after the time of Christ (see Finegan 1992, 282–84 nos. 236–38). Any alleged connection with Jesus himself is spurious.

JERUSALEM AS A CHRISTIAN CITY

Constantine demolished Hadrian's Temple of Venus and had rubble removed to uncover Golgotha and nearby long-buried tombs. Between 326 and 335 Constantine's chief architect, Zenobius, constructed the Church of the Holy Sepulcher. This magnificent basilica consisted of an outer court (entered from the Cardo Maximus, the main north-south street), the basilica itself, a second courtyard, and a rotunda (built over the rock-cut tomb identified as the tomb of Christ) named the Anastasis (Resurrection). Part of Golgotha was incorporated into the southeastern corner of the second courtyard, which led from the basilica to the rotunda.

An early fourth-century graffito of a sailing ship and the words *Domine ivimus*[2] (Lord, we shall go) can still be seen on one of the walls of a vault supporting the Church of the Holy Sepulcher. The inscription alludes to Psalm 122:1, "Let us go to the house of the Lord" (Vulgate: *in domum Domini ibimus*), as well as John 6:68, "Lord, to whom shall we go?" (Vulgate: *Domine, ad quem ibimus*). Psalm 122 was traditionally sung by pilgrims after they had arrived in Jerusalem,[3] and the graffito attests the safe completion of a journey by boat to Jerusalem by Christians who had come to the "house" that, at that very time, was being built to encompass the empty tomb of Jesus their *dominus* (Lord).

PILGRIMS AND HOLY PLACES

Pilgrims such as those who carved the ship on the foundations of the Church of the Holy Sepulcher made it a point to visit the Temple Mount. There they could visualize the Herodian temple in all its splendor and imagine Jesus being tempted by the devil (Matt. 4:5; cf. Luke 4:9), turning over the tables of the money changers (Mark 11:15), and prophesying that not one stone[4] would be "left here upon another" (Mark 13:2). Another historic landmark visited by Byzantine pilgrims was the Pool of Bethesda, where, according to John 5:2–9, Jesus healed a lame man. The pool actually consisted of two adjacent pools. One pool was an *oṣer*, a reservoir that collected rainwater and fed its "living water" into the smaller stepped pool, which was a *miqveh*, a Jewish bath for ritual self-immersion. Between the early second and early fourth centuries the Pool of Bethesda was part of an Asclepieum, a pagan healing center. By the fifth century a Christian church had been built at the site. Originally known as

---

2. That is, *Domine ibimus*; *b* and *v* were commonly substituted for each other in spoken Latin.

3. The whole text of Psalm 122:1–2 reads, "I was glad when they said to me, 'Let us go to the house of the LORD!' Our feet are standing within your gates, O Jerusalem."

4. That is, of the temple itself. Some of the temple enclosure's retaining walls, as already noted, were not destroyed and remain partially intact to this day, including the southeast corner, identified by some as "the pinnacle of the temple" (Matt. 4:5; Luke 4:9).

1.2 Ossuaries

A large number of ossuaries have been found around Jerusalem, all dating from before the Bar Kokhba Revolt (i.e., pre-135). Some were found in a cemetery at the traditional site where Jesus wept over Jerusalem (Luke 19:41) (Finegan 1992, 172 no. 63, 366–74 nos. 319–26), known as Dominus Flevit. Some scholars think that drawings and symbols on a few ossuaries there indicate Christian allegiance by some of those whose bones were inside (Finegan 1992, 372–74). This is unlikely.

Nor, despite views to the contrary (e.g., Shanks and Witherington 2003), is there incontrovertible evidence that the ossuary inscribed "James, son of Joseph, brother of Jesus" contained the bones of James the brother of Jesus of Nazareth. Given the extreme popularity of the names Jesus, Joseph, and James (Jacob) in first-century Jewish communities, and the early tradition that James was buried (in the ground) immediately following his martyrdom (Hegesippus, *Fr.*, in Eusebius, *Hist. eccl.* 2.23.18), it is difficult not to believe that the ossuary is that of some other James (Richardson 2004, 309–24).

Similarly, the ossuaries found at Talpiot, 5 km south of Jerusalem (Tabor and Jacobovici 2012), are unlikely to have any connection with Jesus of Nazareth, even though they include familiar names such as Jesus, Joseph, and Mariamne/Mary.[*] That some of the relatives of Jesus were deeply involved in the leadership of the early Christian community is, nonetheless, indisputable (Hegesippus, *Fr.*, in Eusebius, *Hist. eccl.* 3.20.8; 3.32.6).

[*] Attempts to identify other ossuaries found in or near Jerusalem with the families of Caiaphas (Matt. 26:57) or Simon of Cyrene (Mark 15:21) have also not been definitive.

the Church of the Lame Man, it was later called the Church of the Nativity of Mary, after the supposed birthplace of the mother of Jesus. A second church to St. Mary, the so-called Nea (New) Basilica, was dedicated by the Byzantine emperor Justinian I (r. 527–565) in 543. This huge church, the largest in Palaestina at the time, was built at the southern end of the Cardo Maximus, as indicated on a sixth-century mosaic map found at Madaba in Jordan. This map also depicts the Church of the Holy Sepulcher and, in addition to the Cardo, the Decumanus, the main east-west street (fig. I.2).

Fourth-century Christian pilgrims record that they were shown the house of the high priest Caiaphas, where Jesus was tried by the Jewish authorities (Matt. 26:57; Mark 14:53; Luke 22:54) and where St. Peter denied Christ (Matt. 26:69–75). In the sixth century the house taken to have been that of Caiaphas was made into a church named after Peter. By the twelfth century this church had been renamed as the Church of St. Savior, and the location was assumed to have been that of Pilate's *praetorium* (judgment hall), where

Fig. 1.5. Church of the Nativity of Mary, Jerusalem

Jesus was mockingly crowned with thorns (Matt. 27:27–31). The actual site of the *praetorium*, however, is more likely to have been the stone pavement (*lithostrōton*) next to what had once been Herod the Great's palace. Given the razing of Jerusalem before its reconstruction by Hadrian, it is not surprising that the precise location of many sites associated with Jesus and the earliest Christian community were lost to posterity. Two different churches, for example, commemorate the site of the house of another Mary the mother of John Mark.[5]

JAMES, FIRST BISHOP OF JERUSALEM

James "the Just," the brother of Jesus, was, along with the apostles Peter and John, acknowledged as one of the "pillars" of the church and deemed by Paul to have apostolic status (Gal. 2:9; cf. 1:18–19). The exact nature of James's role is difficult to ascertain. The earliest Christian community in Jerusalem was more a loosely knit movement within Judaism that believed Jesus to be the Messiah than a "church" with an episcopal hierarchical structure. In subsequent centuries, however, James was anachronistically deemed to have been the first bishop of Jerusalem and to have received his episcopate from the apostles or

5. Traditionally, Mary's house is considered to be the place where Jesus shared the Last Supper with his disciples (Mark 14:15; Luke 22:12) and at least one of the places in Jerusalem where the earliest Christian community gathered (Acts 2:1; 12:12).

even Jesus himself (Eusebius, *Hist. eccl.* 2.1.2–4; 2.23.1; 2.23.4; 7.19). James was martyred in about 61 by being thrown from the "pinnacle of the temple," stoned, clubbed to death, and buried in a simple tomb (Hegesippus, *Fr.*, in Eusebius, *Hist. eccl.* 2.23.18). Pilgrims to Jerusalem were shown, however, an elaborate tomb supposed to be that of James in the Kidron Valley, near the Temple Mount, and his (alleged) episcopal chair (Eusebius, *Hist. eccl.* 7.19) (Finegan 1992, 305–8 nos. 264–66).

CHRISTIAN JEWS IN JERUSALEM

If the information supplied by Eusebius (*Hist. eccl.* 4.5.1–4) is correct, counting James, there were fifteen bishops of Jerusalem before the time of Hadrian, all circumcised (i.e., Jewish). James was succeeded by Symeon, a cousin of Jesus and James (Hegesippus, *Fr.*, in Eusebius, *Hist. eccl.* 6.22.4; cf. Eusebius, *Hist. eccl.* 3.11.1–2; 3.32.1–4.5.3). Prior to Hadrian, it appears, the Christian community in Jerusalem comprised primarily Jews who continued to see themselves as Jews, even though they disagreed with their fellow Jews on the significance of Jesus of Nazareth. Using the term "Jewish Christianity" to describe Christianity in Jerusalem (or elsewhere) is, however, problematic, not only because the term is modern rather than ancient but also because it is unclear whether the underlying reference to Judaism is ethnic or religious. Especially pertinent is the extent to which Jewish practices such as circumcision and food laws were to be observed by early Christians who were not born as Jews or who had not formally converted to Judaism. It seems that in Jerusalem, at least during the earliest developments, there was a greater insistence on conformity to Torah than in areas of Pauline influence in Asia Minor (Gal. 2:1–21) and Greece.

Christian practice in Jerusalem may have differed little from Jewish practice, other than the church's regular communal meals (Acts 2:42, 46) and its distinctive form of baptism (Acts 2:38, 41). Although much of the Acts of the Apostles reflects later church tradition, its references to the daily breaking of bread in the homes of the earliest disciples and to the mandatory baptism of those joining the Jesus movement may well portray accurately these practices within the earliest church. Similarly, there is no need to doubt that members of the community renounced private ownership of property and, when necessary, sold what they owned for the common good (Acts 2:44; 4:32–5:11).

It is difficult to estimate the size of the earliest community of Jesus's followers in Jerusalem, a city of perhaps twenty thousand at the time. The figures in Acts—three thousand converts on the day of Pentecost (Acts 2:41), five thousand (male) believers in Jesus's resurrection (Acts 4:4), and the "many thousands of believers . . . among the Jews" in Jerusalem (Acts 21:20)—are rhetorical statements rather than reliable statistics (Stark 1996, 5). That the earliest "Christian" community in Jerusalem consisted of around 120 members (Acts 1:15), and that this group, like Christianity as a whole, experienced a growth rate of about 40 percent per decade as postulated by Stark (1996, 5–6; cf. R. Beck 2006, 233–52) seems reasonable. By the time Symeon became leader of the community in about 70 CE, there may have been hardly more than 450 Christian families in Jerusalem. How many returned with Symeon from Pella is debatable.[6]

Apart from their names, little is known about the other early "bishops" of Jerusalem. Many of the fifteen persons listed by Eusebius as bishops[7] may, in fact, have been leading elders who, alongside the apostles, appear to have had oversight of the Jerusalem Christian community (Acts 15:2, 4, 6, 22) (Horbury 2006, 58–59). Jerusalem also had a diaconate, which, according to Acts 6:5, included Stephen, the first martyr, and Philip the Evangelist.

Gentile Christianity

After Hadrian's founding of Aelia Capitolina as a Roman colony, Christianity in the city took on a distinctively Gentile character. Eusebius presents a list of fifteen non-Jewish bishops (*Hist. eccl.* 5.12.1b–2; cf. Epiphanius, *Pan.* 66.20) as a parallel to his earlier list of Jewish ones.[8] The second list concludes with Narcissus, bishop of Jerusalem (ca. 189–216), assisted in the latter part of his life by Alexander, formerly a bishop in Cappadocia (Eusebius, *Hist. eccl.* 6.11.1–2). It was Alexander who, along with Theoctistus of Caesarea Maritima (bp. 216–258), allowed Origen to preach to their congregations (ca. 230/1) while still a layman. Alexander later ordained Origen as presbyter (Eusebius, *Hist. eccl.* 6.8.4–5; 6.19.16–19). The bishops of Caesarea Maritima, the capital of Syria Palaestina, were much more important than those of Jerusalem. As ecclesiastical hierarchy developed, they became the metropolitans of the region, with the bishops of Aelia/Jerusalem being accountable to them. Jerusalem began to recover some of its earlier status as the historic mother church of Christianity only when the Council of Nicaea (325) mandated that, notwithstanding the status of the metropolitan of Caesarea, the bishop of Aelia be given due honor (*Can.* 7).

---

6. While the historicity of the temporary withdrawal of Christians to Pella seems assured, the details are sketchy, and the significance of the event has frequently been overestimated, both in ancient times and more recently (Horbury 2006, 69; see also Lüdemann 1980).

7. According to Eusebius (*Hist. eccl.* 4.5), they were Justus, Zacchaeus, Tobias, Benjamin, John, Matthias, Philip, Seneca, Justus, Levi, Ephres, Joses, and Judas.

8. The first group of Gentile bishops, according to Eusebius, consisted of Mark, Cassian, Publius, Maximus, Julian, Gaius, Symmachus, a second Gaius, a second Julian, Capito, a second Maximus, Antoninus, Valens, Dolichianus, and Narcissus.

Post-Constantinian Christianity

Macarius (bp. ca. 312–334) represented Jerusalem at Nicaea, following which he welcomed Helena to Jerusalem, starting the process by which Jerusalem became the preeminent site for Christian pilgrims. Jerusalem's reputation for orthodoxy was enhanced by the lectures to catechumens of Cyril of Jerusalem (bp. ca. 348/9–386/7). These annual lectures included an attack on the Montanists (*Catech.* 16.8) to counter their claims that the New Jerusalem (Rev. 21) would be established at Pepouza in Phrygia rather than at Jerusalem in Palaestina (see chap. 7). Perhaps earlier bishops had also felt the threat to the significance of Jerusalem from movements such as Montanists and Marcionites, as well as from the rising prestige of churches such as Rome (Irshai 2006, 105–12).

Juvenal (bp. ca. 420–458) had Jerusalem declared a patriarchate at the Council of Chalcedon in 451, in addition to the patriarchates of Rome, Constantinople, Alexandria, and Antioch. After the council, at which Juvenal had reversed his earlier "Monophysite" position, the Jerusalem church was for a time deeply divided between pro- and anti-Chalcedonian Christians. In 614 the Persians captured Jerusalem and retained control until 630/1. A number of Christians were killed, including some buried in a mass grave marked by a mosaic inscription: "Those whose names are known to the Lord" (Reich 1996). Some Christian churches, such as the Nea and St. Mary's at the Pool of Bethesda, were destroyed; others, such as the Church of the Holy Sepulcher, were seriously damaged.

Byzantine rule had scarcely been restored and the rebuilding of churches begun when, in 638, the city was conquered once again, this time by the Muslim caliph Umar (r. 634–644). Paradoxically, the Muslim occupants of the city were more tolerant than the Byzantines had been. Jews were allowed to live in Jerusalem, and various Christian groups, including "Nestorians," Manichaeans, and Maronites, were able to gain some ground, both literally and theologically. Ultimately, however, a group of Christians known as Melkites won the day, not only preserving Chalcedonian Christology but also developing a unique Arab Orthodox (as distinct from Greek Orthodox or Syrian Orthodox) Christian community. This community, though small, was still thriving in the Holy City when the first Crusaders arrived in 1099 (S. Griffith 2006).

Judaea

Caesarea

Although Eusebius emphasizes that "Hebrews" were consistently bishops of Jerusalem prior to the Second Jewish Revolt, we have little information about Christians in the rest of Judaea; the majority must have been Jewish, perhaps forming groups known as Ebionites and Nazoraeans. In the influential city of Caesarea, despite extensive archaeological excavation, little bears on Christian developments (Ascough 2000), though remnants of a (fifth-century?) chapel dedicated to St. Paul have been discovered in a warehouse area (Patrich 2000). The book of Acts hints at tensions between Jerusalem and Caesarea. In about 195 the bishops of Caesarea and Jerusalem jointly presided over the Council of Caesarea to mediate a dispute concerning the date of Easter, the troublesome Quartodeciman controversy between Alexandria and Antioch. Antioch argued for the older view that linked Easter with Nisan 14 (Passover), regardless of the day on which it fell, while Alexandria emphasized the day—the Lord's Day—rather than the date. With both Jerusalem and Caesarea siding with Alexandria, the Lord's Day won the struggle, and Judaea slid away from Christian-Jewish norms. From this point on, "Caesarea clearly became the most important church in Palestine" (Ascough 2000, 165), and not until 325 did Jerusalem regain its position.

When Origen came to Caesarea—first in 215 because of persecution in his native Alexandria and permanently in 231 because of a rift with Demetrius of Alexandria (bp. ca. 189–ca. 231/2)—it became a major Christian intellectual center, attracting not only orthodox Christians but also "innumerable heretics and a considerable number of the most eminent philosophers" (Eusebius, *Hist. eccl.* 6.18.2), suggesting a broad mix of beliefs. Origen's scholarship focused on the biblical text. Eusebius says that Origen gathered a library of over thirty thousand volumes. Among these were several Greek translations of the Hebrew Bible that he laid alongside the Septuagint in his *Hexapla*. Origen himself had found one of these "versions," by an unknown author, in a jar at Jericho. Another was by Symmachus, a late second-century Ebionite who kept Torah in a Jewish manner (Eusebius, *Hist. eccl.* 6.16–17). One of Origen's goals in producing polyglot editions of the Hebrew Scriptures, containing not only the Hebrew text and a Greek transliteration but also multiple Greek versions in parallel columns, was to carry on dialogues, or disputes, with Jews. Origen died around 253 from injuries sustained in the Decian persecution (250–251), twenty years after he had developed a theology of interior martyrdom in his *Exhortation to Martyrdom.*

Eusebius became bishop of Caesarea in about 313, about the time when Constantine officially became emperor of the western part of the Roman Empire. The eventual close cooperation between emperor and ecclesiastical leader gave Caesarea a new prominence, though Eusebius's shared interest with Arius (ca. 256/60–ca. 336) in a particular form of trinitarian theology first developed by Origen later required justification. Eusebius gives a firsthand view of conditions during the early fourth century in his irreplaceable works, especially his *Church History*, *Onomasticon*, *Martyrs of Palestine*, and *Life of Constantine*. Additional witnesses, such as Cyril of Jerusalem, Epiphanius of Salamis (bp. ca. 367–ca. 403/5) and Jerome (347–419), round out the picture.[9]

ARCHAEOLOGY AND LITERATURE

Among the numerous important archaeological finds in Caesarea (Richardson 2000, 11–34), none is more evocative than an inscription found in secondary usage that refers to Pontius Pilate (using his correct title), under whom Jesus was executed: [. . .]S TIBERIEUM/[. . . PON]TIUS PILATUS/ [PRA]EFECTUS IUDA(EA)E/[. . .] (Pontius Pilate, Prefect of Judaea, [built] the Tiberieum) (McLean 2000, 60–62; Richardson 2000, 23–24). This reference to Pontius Pilate, governor of Judaea (26–36 CE), in an archaeological context takes us back indirectly to the historical Jesus. Other archaeological sites are, of course, associated with events in Jesus's life. Since few shed any direct light, the main benefit of more than a century's excavations has been to clarify the contexts, whether Jewish, Roman, or Hellenistic, in which Jesus lived. One of the most important results has been the recovery of ordinary Jewish peasant life in Galilee, Peraea, Samaria, and Judaea (Charlesworth 2006).

Judaea in the early Christian period may be the provenance of several documents. The "Signs Gospel," a hypothetical source from the 50s–60s that underlies the Gospel attributed to John (Richardson 2004, 91–107) and reflects Jesus traditions before they were incorporated into the Fourth Gospel, probably is from Judaea. Two Egyptian papyri (P.Oxy. 5.840; P.Egerton 2), containing Jesus traditions, may also derive from Judaea, as may the Epistle of James. If James 1:1 should be understood as addressed to Judaeans in the Diaspora, then James's critical view of Paul's understanding of "faith" is an attempt to undermine Paul's influence where it was greatest. Jude and 2 Peter are more ambiguous; both may be early (Bauckham 1992) and could be set in Judaea, along with the early second-century *Acts of Pilate*. The *Martyrdom of Isaiah* and the *Ascension of Isaiah* are from the same period and locale, and both have later Christian interpolations, suggesting that Jesus's "disciples will abandon the teaching of the twelve apostles" (*Mart. Ascen. Isa.* 3.21). Some argue that *Sibylline Oracles* 6–8 are Judaean, and that Oracle 6 is from the Jordan Valley. Such possibilities imply substantial Christian Jewish literary activity that reflects a storyline different from the canonical Gospels, around but outside Jerusalem. The sources continue later in the second century with Hegesippus

---

9. Jerome's writings are particularly important for the history of this period, including his *Letters*, his *Lives*—for example, of Paulus (written ca. 374), Hilarion (ca. 390), and Malchus (ca. 391)—and his preface to the *Book on the Sites and Names of Hebrew Places* (ca. 388).

(110–170) and in the third century with Origen. The *Testament of Solomon* (third century) may also derive from Judaea.

PERSECUTIONS

Paul identified himself as formerly a persecutor of the church (Phil. 3:6). At first, persecution of Christians was by "vigilante" action, as in the cases of Stephen and James (brother of John) during the 30s and 40s. It became more official in the 60s with the death of James the brother of Jesus. Roman authorities soon became interested in Christians. For example, Peter and Paul appear to have been martyred during a brief but local persecution at Rome initiated by Nero (r. 54–

Fig. 1.6. Pilate Inscription, Caesarea Maritima

68), in about 64 (Eusebius, *Hist. eccl.* 2.25.5; cf. *1 Clem.* 5.1–7). Domitian (r. 81–96) interrogated, but released, two grandsons of Jude the brother of Jesus (Eusebius, *Hist. eccl.* 3.20.1–8). Atticus, the governor of Syria Palaestina in the reign of Trajan, executed the second "bishop" of Jerusalem, Symeon son of Clopas. Eusebius, on whom we are so dependent, cites Hegesippus to the effect that troubles were "sporadic" and "popular" (*Fr.*, in Eusebius, *Hist. eccl.* 3.32). Such occasional instances of persecution led to widespread martyrdoms, especially under Decius (r. 249–251). Locally in Caesarea under Valerian (r. 253–260), three men and one woman from the countryside went purposefully to Caesarea "to grasp the martyr's crown" (Eusebius, *Hist. eccl.* 7.12). There were renewed bouts of official persecution under Diocletian and Maximinus II Daia (r. 310–313): churches were leveled, sacred books burned, Christians removed from office, bishops imprisoned, and everyone was required to make sacrifices to the emperor. In the post-Constantinian era there was a brief renewal of persecution under Julian (r. 361–363).

WORSHIP AND CHURCH REMAINS

Large parts of Judaea became Christian during the third century, though there are few remains from that period, but soon increased pilgrim activity changed the landscape. By 330 four large imperial projects were under construction at Bethlehem (Pullan 2000), Mamre (Wilkinson 2002, 91; Freeman-Grenville, Chapman, and Taylor 2003, 13), and Jerusalem. Egeria describes Eleona (i.e., Olive Grove), a major basilica on the Mount of Olives covering a "cave in which the Lord was wont to teach" and "where hymns and antiphons suitable to the day and to the place are said" (Wilkinson 2002, 65, 67; cf. 71, 82, 85, 87). Bethlehem's Church of the Holy Nativity, before being rebuilt by Justinian, had an octagon over the cave marking the site of Jesus's birth. The octagon, which was attached to the basilica, emphasized the vertical relationship between God and God's action in history. At Mamre (Haram Ramet el-Khalil), near Hebron, a site associated with Abraham, Constantine constructed a basilica inside an enclosure that Herod the Great had built, counteracting the quasi-pagan nature of the site (Eshel, Richardson, and Jamitowski forthcoming).

Egeria's main interest was a site's liturgical and processional activities, shedding a bright light on Judaean Christians' late fourth-century worship. Among the churches she mentions are Timnath Serah, Kiriath Jearim, Bethel, and Shepherds' Fields in Bethlehem (Wilkinson 2002, 90–100). There are no certain Judaean remains of pre-Constantinian church construction. Fourth-century building activity, however, reflects a deep Christianizing of Judaea. Eusebius, for instance, notes in his *Onomasticon* that Iethira (Khirbet 'Attir, near Eleutheropolis/Beth Govrin [Bet Jibrin]) was a village comprised wholly of Christians. From the next century, the most important is a parish church at Lod (ancient Lydda/Diospolis), built over a Second Temple period building that may have been a synagogue, in which case it may be the earliest example of a church above a synagogue (Zelinger and Di Segni 2006). An inscription refers to "the most-reverend Bishop Dionysos," who attended the Council of Constantinople in 381 after having been persecuted under the Arian emperor Valens (r. 364–378). There were Christian cave shrines at Horvat Berachot (Tsafrir and Hirschfeld 1993, 207–18) and at Khallat ed-Danabiya, a church at Tell Hassan (near Jericho), and possibly an open-air church outside Caesarea's walls.

MONASTERIES

The Holy Land's first monastery, anticipating exponential growth during the next century, was Chariton's structure from around 330 at Ein Farah, 10 km east of Jerusalem along the Wadi Qilt (Hirschfeld 1990, 6–7). Chariton (d. ca. 350) also founded monasteries at Dok/Douka (Jebel Qarantal) near Jericho, in about 340, and, around 345, in the valley subsequently named Wadi Khareitun, after him. These three monasteries were lauras, with a mother house and scattered devotional cells for individual withdrawal. Communal activities took place on Sundays, when the monks gathered for a meal and corporate worship, while the remaining days were for private contemplation, worship, study, and work.

> Introspection much earlier than Augustine

As noted above, Paula and Eustochium in the mid-380s established a convent for women in Bethlehem, where Jerome had already founded a monastery for men. Only in 411 was the first monastery of a second type, the *coenobium*, built east of Jerusalem by Theoctistus. The *coenobium* (from *koinōnos*, "common") was a residential monastery where the monks lived a collective life of worship, work, and study, often in a walled complex of buildings. Early structures of this type are St. Euthymius's and St. Martyrius's monasteries, built around 480 at the sites of earlier lauras near the road between Jerusalem and Jericho. From then onward, churches and monasteries are attested at numerous locations.

Fig. 1.7. Monastery of St. Martyrius, near Jericho

Samaria

The book of Acts reports the risen Jesus speaking of witnesses in "Judea and Samaria" (1:8) and claims that "Samaria accepted the word of God" (8:14), but it gives no details. Acts also says that a scattering, because of persecution, brought Philip to work in Samaria in an unnamed city. One of Philip's converts was Simon Magus, who already had such a reputation for wonder working that he was known as "the power of God that is called Great" (8:10), though Peter and John rejected his request to share their power (8:4–24). A later Gnostic sect focused on Simon Magus, prompting Irenaeus of Lyons (in the late second century) and Eusebius of Caesarea (early in the fourth century) to consider him the "father of all heretics" (Irenaeus, *Haer.* 3 preface; cf. Eusebius, *Hist. eccl.* 2.13.5–6).

Fig. 1.8. Church Mosaic, Megiddo

Justin Martyr was born in about 100 in Flavia Neapolis (Nablus) of Roman parents and was converted to Christianity about the time of the Bar Kokhba Revolt, probably in Asia Minor. At about the same time Hadrian built a temple to Zeus Hypsistos near the Samaritan holy place, reached by 1,300 steps, according to the Pilgrim of Bordeaux (Wilkinson 2002, 27). Justin, regrettably, says little about Samaritanism or Christianity in Samaria. Samaritan theology and piety flowered during the third and fourth centuries, and Samaria as a whole reached its peak of settlement in the Byzantine period (Zertal, Dar, and Magen 1993), for the number of villages at that time was double the number during the Roman period. When the Samaritans were subsequently repressed, only a small group remained, near Nablus.

On the boundary between Samaria and Galilee a third-century Christian building has been discovered in a prison courtyard at Legio (Megiddo), with a floor inscription that reads, "The God-loving Akeptous has offered this table, as a memorial to the God Jesus Christ" (Tepper and Di Segni 2006, 36). Although mention of a table is noteworthy at this early period, the unique formulation "God Jesus Christ" is more surprising (fig. 1.8). The floor has not been stratigraphically dated and thus is still uncertain, but the building seems to reflect an early and vigorous Christian presence, like the buildings at Dura-Europos and Aila.

There were enough Samaritan Christians that Sebaste had a bishop, Marinus, who attended the Council of Nicaea in 325. Relics, notably John the Baptist's head, were located at Sebaste. Even after Julian the Apostate scattered the relics, Christians still venerated John's tomb. The area around nearby Nablus was equally important to Christians. Eusebius refers to Sychar, associated with the account of the woman at the well (John 4:4–30), and the Pilgrim of Bordeaux reports "a baptistery, which takes its water" from this well (Wilkinson 2002, 27), implying the baptistery was built sometime between 300 and 333. Egeria refers to two churches 50 m apart, one containing the well and the other Joseph's tomb (Wilkinson 2002, 93). The Pilgrim of Bordeaux also speaks of Mount Gerizim, above Neapolis/Nablus, which had a sophisticated octagonal church to St. Mary Theotokos (Godbearer) built in 484 as part of a Byzantine attempt to convert Samaritans, covering the ancient Samaritan place of sacrifice. Egeria also knew of nearby Aenon (Khirbet Khisas ed-Deir), where John baptized (Wilkinson 2002, 127). Remains of a third-century church adapted from a Roman fort have been found at Khirbet el-Kiliya (Magen 1990).

MONASTERIES

Samaria had fewer monasteries than Judaea, and none were as early, though between five and ten walled cenobitic monasteries, built of large ashlars with broad margins and decorated with crosses and other motifs, have been located within 2 or 3 km of each other between Antipatris and Jerusalem. Yizhar Hirschfeld (2002, 188–89) suggests that they were occasioned by the Samaritan revolt of 529/30 and were funded by tax exemptions to the Christian community as a result of damage to Christian estates in the region, a strategy that demonstrated the victory of Christianity. If we include Scythopolis here, a Decapolis city that the Pilgrim of Bordeaux visited in 333, which hints that it may have been an important Christian site, the number of monasteries is increased. There was a late fourth- or early fifth-century monastery at Tell Basul (just west of Scythopolis), with a courtyard paved with mosaics. Better known is the later Monastery of the Lady Mary (ca. 567), with a rich battery of mosaics, including a zodiac not unlike that found in some synagogues.

Galilee

Galilee stretched from Samaria to Tyre and over to the Sea of Galilee (Aviam and Richardson 2001) (for Peraea, see below), a region reestablished as Jewish by the Hasmoneans. Surprisingly, the earliest synagogue that has been archaeologically excavated is an early second-century synagogue at Khirbet Qana, the probable site of Cana (Richardson 2004, 55–71, 91–107; Runesson,

Binder, and Olsson 2008, 22–25). Hellenistic-Roman culture was also present, particularly in major cities such as Tiberias, Sepphoris, and Ptolemais, but in minor ways even in small villages. Gradually Galilee acquired a majority of Christians during the early Byzantine period; there were at least eighteen Christian communities in the third century, thirty-six in the fourth, and ninety-six in the fifth (Avi-Yonah 1984).

LITERARY MATERIAL

The earliest Gospel material, designated by scholars as "Q," was likely written in Galilee during the early years of Agrippa II. A source of the later Gospels attributed to Matthew and Luke, Q is a first-generation document from the 50s (Kloppenborg 2000; Arnal 2001, 159–64, locating Q in Capernaum) that presupposes agriculturally based communities that followed Jesus's precepts. Small groups no doubt met in houses (Richardson 2004, 73–90), though Virgilio Corbo's specific claims about the house of Peter in Capernaum (J. Taylor 1993, 57) and similar claims about a house in Nazareth are doubtful. Yet, there probably were early Christian worship groups in these places and others, such as Cana and Bethsaida.

Evidence of Galilean Christianity, however, is sparse for all sites. The book of Acts suggests that Christianity really began in Galilee (10:37; cf. 8:1; 9:31), but it notes nothing significant other than Judas the Galilean's uprising (5:37). Galilee appears neither in the rest of the New Testament nor in the Apostolic Fathers. Anthony Saldarini (1992, 23–38) suggests Matthew may have been written in Galilee, though Antioch and the Phoenician coastline are also possible provenances. Saldarini also maintains that the Matthean community formed a sectarian Jewish community operating within wider Jewish society. Albert Baumgarten (1992, 39–50) argues that the Pseudo-Clementine literature was Galilean, reflecting a group with such detailed knowledge of rabbinic Judaism that it implies "two groups in close proximity that maintained intellectual contact with each other" (47). Perhaps the early second-century *Gospel of the Hebrews* (often situated in Egypt) should be located in Galilee, as well as the *Protevangelium of James* in the mid-second century, if it does not belong to Phoenice. Eusebius is of little help, since he provides locations for neither of his two kinds of Ebionites (*Hist. eccl.* 3.27). He fails to note much of historical significance in Galilee, though he does refer to a statue of Jesus with a woman seeking healing in Caesarea Philippi (*Hist. eccl.* 7.18).

GROUPS

The literature hints at the development of Christian groups in Galilee through more than a century, implying that Galilean Christians operated largely within a Jewish context, though the history of Christianity there seems discontinuous. If Christians shared the fate of Jews in the revolt of 132–135, which included Galilee (Eshel 2006), that would help to account for the lack of continuity, with a fresh beginning coming just before the Constantinian period. When Epiphanius discusses the Ebionites, he implies a similar discontinuity. He focuses on Joseph of Tiberias (*Pan.* 30.4–12) (Manns 1990), who in the 330s built four churches at Constantine's request, in Tiberias, Diocaesarea (formerly known as Sepphoris), Nazareth, and Capernaum. He goes on to insist that the population in these places included no Hellenes, Samaritans, or Christians, implying that Joseph had no Christian foundation to build upon, even in Nazareth and Capernaum. The fact that the Council of Nicaea had no bishops from Galilee would support this supposition.

MATERIAL REMAINS

Only after Constantine does Galilee come into its own. The dating of the Christian house-church in Capernaum is controversial. Michael White (1997, 152–59) argues on archaeological grounds against a continuous Christian presence starting in the first century, suggesting the quadrilateral building is post-Constantinian, perhaps Joseph of Tiberias's building, while the octagonal church is fifth century. Egeria confirms that the "house of the Prince of the apostles" was a church in her day (Wilkinson 1999, 97). She also says that "the synagogue [of Nazareth] . . . is now a church," that there was a church (below the present church) at Heptapegon (Tabgha) along with one or two other churches, and that at Tiberias a church was built on top of the "house of the apostles James and John" (Wilkinson 1999, 96–98). Presumably, this was the church built by Joseph of Tiberias (J. Taylor 1993, 289). The Pilgrim of Bordeaux adds that Mount Tabor, Mount Carmel, and Jezreel also had churches.

By the Byzantine period Christianity was dominant in western Upper Galilee (forty-nine churches and monasteries, most relatively late), where synagogues were rare. Judaism remained strongest in eastern Upper Galilee (twenty-one synagogues), where churches were absent (Frankel et al. 2001, 114–15). The geographical separation between Judaism and Christianity followed exactly Josephus's western border of Upper Galilee. The same regional survey showed that while Jewish occupation of eastern Upper Galilee was continuous, when intense Christian occupation occurred in western Upper Galilee in the Byzantine period, it replaced a previously pagan occupation (Frankel et al. 2001, 131). Only around the Sea of Galilee were Judaism and Christianity found side by side. Some Christian Galilean church buildings, such as at Horvat Hesheq (Church of St. George), were unusual architecturally, with a nave at the second-floor level (Aviam 1990).

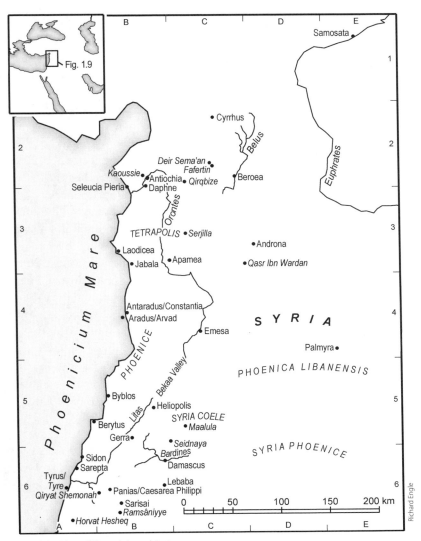

Fig. 1.9. Map of Phoenicia and Syria

Syria

As noted in the introduction, the Roman organization of Syria changed much during the period. For the sake of simplicity, we refer to the northern section of ancient Syria as the Tetrapolis and Syria Coele. Phoenicia was the coastal region similar to modern Lebanon, but reaching farther north and south. Syria Phoenice was similar to Diocletian's Augusta Libanensis, stretching inland.

Antioch, the Tetrapolis, and Syria Coele

The Syrian Tetrapolis, a group of four cities near the Orontes River, comprised Antioch, its port Seleucia Pieria, Apamea, and its port Laodicea. Combined with the villages of the Limestone (or Belus) Massif, they hold a special place as an early and intensively Christianized area. The cities were founded by Seleucus I Nicator (r. 311–281 BCE) in 300 BCE and soon were Hellenistic cities burgeoning with culture. When Pompey conquered Antioch in 64 BCE, he made it the administrative seat of the Roman province of Syria, just as it had been the capital of the Seleucid Empire. Situated perfectly between East and West, it was an important link with Rome and cities farther afield. Roman building programs outfitted Antioch with baths, a hippodrome, an amphitheater, a temple to Jupiter Capitolinus, and a colonnaded street—the first such street in the Roman Empire. It had all the trappings of a Roman imperial city (Ball 2003, 152–55). Since it enjoyed close connections with Rome, many emperors, including Trajan and Hadrian, spent considerable time in Antioch.

Antioch's position of political importance was checked, however, by earthquakes (in 115, 526, and 528) that changed the face of the city and left it crippled. Misplaced alliances under Septimius Severus (r. 193–211) relegated Antioch to a secondary role after Apamea (which hosted the second Parthian legion, 215–244); Apamea was the capital of Syria Secunda in the late fourth century. Antioch declined in the sixth century, while other parts of the region rose. At the same time, the villages of the neighboring Limestone Massif were thriving, sustained by their success in growing and harvesting olives (Foss 2000, 27).

RELIGION

Greco-Roman religion was alive and well at Antioch, where special affection was held for the gods Zeus/Jupiter and Apollo, especially at Daphne, the upscale western suburb of Antioch. As a cosmopolitan Hellenistic city, the religious affiliations of Antioch's people naturally included Egyptian, Roman, Greek, Phoenician, and other eastern cults. From the earliest days a community of Hellenistic Jews was present in Antioch, perhaps rewarded with land for their service as mercenaries under the Seleucids. They constituted a large portion of the Antiochene population (Zetterholm 2003, 43–62) and functioned as a *collegium*, with rights that may have exceeded those of other *collegia*. Numerous synagogues in three different areas of the city have been posited, although excavations have yielded no confirmation. This large Jewish community formed the beginnings of the fledgling Christian movement.

Acts 11:26 claims that Antioch was the first place where Jesus's followers were called Christians, so it is no surprise that it has been the locus of scholarly interest. The famous dispute in Antioch between Peter and Paul (Gal. 2) has been invoked in discussion of the "parting of the ways" between Judaism and Christianity (Zetterholm 2003, 202–24; N. Taylor 1992, 125–39). The Gospel attributed to Matthew may have been written in Antioch, reflecting Jewish and Gentile groups in the same community (Brown and Meier 1983, 13; Brent 2007, 25). Yet the angry homilies of John Chrysostom (ca. 347–407) "against Judaizing Christians" demonstrate that the boundaries between the groups remained blurred well into the fourth century (Brown and Meier 1983, 12; Brooten 2000, 35), so there was no simple transfer from one group to another. It was not just with Jews that Christians struggled in Antioch. Internal arguments flared over church authority, leadership, and theology; these involved movements such as Arians, Encratites, and Novatianists, as well as the teachings of Basilides (fl. ca. 125), Cerdo (fl. ca. 135), and Tatian (fl. ca. 165). Epiphanius, writing around 376 CE, refers explicitly to Encratites at Antioch in his own day (*Pan.* 47.1.2–3). Ignatius (d. ca. 115), the second bishop of Antioch (Eusebius, *Hist. eccl.* 3.22), claimed in his letter to the Romans that he was the "bishop of Syria" (*Rom.* 2.2) and elsewhere pushed for a common leadership (*Phld.* 4: "one eucharist . . . one altar . . . one bishop"), but rather than evidence of unity his struggle seems to indicate the opposite.[10] Eusebius (*Hist eccl.* 4.24.1) says that Theophilus, the sixth bishop of Antioch (bp. ca. 169–ca. 183), battled heretics "as though driving off wild beasts from Christ's sheep," and that he composed a treatise against Marcion, now lost.[11] Paul of Samosata, bishop of Antioch from 260, espoused views of a heterodox nature (Eusebius, *Hist. eccl.* 7.27–30) and was deposed by a synod of bishops in 268.

PERSECUTION

Martyrdom and persecution afflicted the Antiochene Christian community, beginning with Ignatius in the first quarter of the second century.[12] Although his letters provide crucial evidence for this early period, Ignatius says almost nothing about the reasons for his arrest and transport to Rome to face the beasts in the amphitheater. During the reign of Diocletian, a wealthy Antiochene

10. Literary sources for Christianity in Antioch are plentiful, including the writings of the fourth-century pagan rhetorician Libanius (ca. 314–ca. 393); the homilies, sermons, and treatises of John Chrysostom, who studied under Libanius in Antioch; the sixth-century chronicler John Malalas; and the other letters of Ignatius. An interesting letter found in Oxyrhynchus, Egypt, refers to "Sotas the Christian" and was sent from Antioch to Oxyrhynchus in the second or third century (*SB* 12.10772; P.Oxy. 36.2785); see also chap. 5 below.

11. The only extant work of Theophilus of Antioch is *Ad Autolycum* (*To Autolycus*).

12. Brooten (2000, 33) points out that 4 Maccabees, which may have been written in Antioch, also was interested in martyrdom.

woman, Domnina, and her two daughters threw themselves into a river to escape being raped by soldiers (John Chrysostom, *On Saints Bernike, Prosdoke, and Domnina*). The relics of Babylas (bp. 237–251), martyred in the Decian persecution, became part of a controversy between the Antiochene Christians and Julian the Apostate; they were placed at Daphne in about 350, removed by Julian in 362, and eventually moved back to a cruciform church built by Bishop Meletius (bp. ca. 360–381) especially to house them (Eusebius, *Hist. eccl.* 6.29.4; 6.39.4; John Chrysostom, *Babylas the Martyr*).

Fig. 1.10. Church of St. Simeon Stylites, the Elder (Qalaat Sema'an), Jebel Sema'an

CHURCHES AND WORSHIP

The limestone hills east of Antioch contain many church buildings, including some of the oldest known. In this area alone there are an estimated twelve hundred churches remaining (Ball 2003, 210).[13] A basilican church at Fafertin, southeast of Jebel Sema'an, is dated by inscription to 372; the church at Serjilla could be earlier, although the lack of an identifying inscription makes it impossible to be certain. Earlier still is the house-church at Qirqbize, the initial building phase of which is dated to 330 (White 1997, 27), though its identification as a church is certain only later, when "liturgical embellishments" make its function clear (White 1997, 136). In the fourth century it was given a triumphal arch, similar to many other churches in North Syria (Butler 1969; Tchalenko

---

13. This works out to one about every 4.5 km. At its peak, the population of the Limestone Massif was reported at about three hundred thousand (Ball 2003, 207), which indicates an extremely pious community at one church for every 250 people or so. As mentioned above, the area thrived through the olive trade, and economic growth presumably was strong enough to provide for such extensive church building. The ease of acquiring limestone in the area must also have played a role.

1980; White 1997). In the fifth century a *bema* (a raised speakers' platform or pulpit)[14] was added, and in the sixth century a martyrium. Antioch's material evidence is much later. The origins of the Cave Church of St. Peter, said to have been founded by Peter himself, are, of course, unsubstantiated, but the church became an important pilgrimage site. The cruciform church at the suburb of Antioch known as Kaoussie, dated by inscription to 387, is sometimes presumed to be the church honoring Babylas, built by Meletius; however, since Meletius died in 381, that church would probably have been completed before then.

Centrally planned churches are common in the Tetrapolis, the most spectacular being the tetraconch (four-apsed) church at Seleucia Pieria, built at the end of the fifth century, then rebuilt after the great earthquake of 526, when the baptistery was added (Kleinbauer 1973; 2000; Loosley 2001; Hickley 1966). It was constructed as a double-shelled tetraconch, its four sides squared by L-shaped piers. The nave has a grand U-shaped *bema* in its center, and its columns have "windblown" capitals, similar to those of Qalaat Sema'an (Kleinbauer 1973, 94). The church houses a beautiful mosaic, depicting a rich collection of animals parading around the ambulatory. Decorative wall panels (opus sectile revetments) depicting biblical scenes most likely belong to the later period of construction as earlier panels would probably have been destroyed in the 526 earthquake (Kondoleon 2000, 118).[15]

MONASTICISM

Both John Chrysostom and Theodoret of Cyrrhus (bp. 423–ca. 466) relate stories of monks entering the city from the mountains (Chrysostom, *Stat.* 17.1–2) or visiting the many ascetics who lived in the limestone hills nearby (Theodoret, *Phil. hist.* 9.14). Aphrahat (ca. 270–ca. 345), an ascetic from Edessa, settled near Antioch in 360, drawing visitors from all over the area (Harvey 2000, 41). "The region surrounding Antioch was noted for its unconventional and extreme expressions of Christian piety" (Kondoleon 2000, 10); these extremes are nowhere more evident than in the accounts of Simeon Stylites the Elder, the great pillar saint. St. Simeon (d. 459) was famous for living atop his pillar for over forty years, sustained by disciples who climbed a ladder to bring him provisions. After his death his body was brought to

---

14. *Bemas* are quite prevalent in the churches of Syria; Kleinbauer (1973, 94–95) notes that at least thirty-two other churches in northern Syria alone have U-shaped *bema*s. See also Loosley 2001; Butler 1969; Hickley 1966.

15. This church may have been a martyrium, possibly dedicated to Thecla (Harvey 2000, 41), but Kleinbauer (1973) sees it as an episcopal or diocesan seat, inspired in function by the now lost Great Church or Golden Octagon of Constantine, described by Eusebius (*Vit. Const.* 3).

Antioch, but the pillar upon which he had lived for so long became one of the greatest centers for pilgrimage in the Late Antique and Byzantine periods. The initial building phase of Qalaat Sema'an, on the slopes of Jebel Sema'an (Simeon's Mountain), took place in about 480–490, and the site gradually became larger and more complex, with multiple annexes, two monasteries, a convent, a baptistery, and a martyrium. What remained of the pillar itself was encircled by an octagon, four sides of which were squared off by four basilicas. This huge complex bears witness to the importance of the ascetic saint in the region, as do the hundreds of medallions found bearing his image that had been taken away by pilgrims seeking blessings. St. Simeon inspired another pillar saint, Simeon Stylites the Younger (521–597), whose sixth-century complex on the summit of a nearby mountain west of Antioch attracted pilgrims of its own.

In other cities of the Syrian Tetrapolis and Syria Coele, Christianity had a similarly rich and varied history. Christianity came to Emesa (Homs) early; the earliest surviving remains are catacombs of the third century. This city also had a connection with the appropriation of December 25 for the birthday of Christ. Emesa had a prominent cult of Bel, with a sacred black stone, served by high priests of the city, one of whose daughters, Julia Domna, married Septimius Severus in 187. Severus rebuilt the Temple of Bel at Emesa to rival those at Baalbek and Palmyra. Julia Domna was the mother of Geta (r. 211) and Caracalla (r. 211–217), and the great-aunt of Elagabalus (r. 218–222). The latter had the sacred stone taken to Rome, where the cult of the Sun took hold,

Fig. 1.11. Pillar of St. Simeon Stylites, the Younger, near Antioch

though after Elagabalus's assassination the stone was sent back to Emesa. Responding to the popularity of this Sun cult, Christians appropriated the birthday of the sun for Christ's birth.

Androna (Anderin), a nearby desert town, must have been an important Christian center, for it has ten churches from relatively early periods, though the dates are uncertain. Qasr Ibn Wardan has an important centrally planned church, built under Justinian, which, like Bostra, Resafa, and others, is a part of the experimental architecture of Christian Syria. St. Mary's Church (also known as Umm al-Zennar, "Church of the Virgin's Girdle") in Emesa is a Syriac Orthodox church built over an underground church, which legend dates to the first century, though this is unlikely. In Apamea another tetraconch church (similar in construction to the church at Seleucia Pieria) is dated to the late fourth/early fifth century and decorated with mosaics (Balty 1977).

Syria Phoenice

DAMASCUS

When St. Paul spoke of his stay in Damascus, stating that he spent three years in "Arabia" (Gal. 1:17), overlapping with the period when Damascus was briefly under Nabataean control, contemporaries presumably deduced that he intended the eastern part of Syria Phoenice. Under Rome, the area flourished from the end of the second century, though its Christian community must have been quite modest for 250 years, for we hear little about it (Eusebius's only reference is to some unfaithful women who renounced Christianity by defaming its morality [*Hist. eccl.* 9.5.2]). But there were massive conversions to Christianity in some parts of Syria Phoenice during the third century (Bounni 1997, 137), and the region's religious status changed dramatically when Theodosius I abolished pagan worship; Damascus's enormous Temple of Jupiter became the Church of St. John the Baptist and the city's bishop gained status second only to that of the bishop of Antioch.

Two Aramaic-speaking villages, Maalula and Seidnaya, just north of Damascus on the slopes of the Anti-Lebanon Mountains, have unexpectedly survived from Antiquity. Maalula has a church dedicated to St. Sergius, parts of which may be from the fourth century, and Seidnaya has a Convent of Our Lady, dating from 547, when Justinian was camped nearby. Their main importance, however, is that the villagers have preserved a form of Aramaic close to that spoken in the first century. Philippe Le Bas and William Waddington found an important Marcionite inscription, dated 318/9, at Lebaba (Deir Ali), about 5 km south of Damascus: "The meeting-house of the Marcionists, in the village of Lebaba, of the Lord and Savior Jesus Christ. It was erected under the management of Presbyter Paul in the year 630" (White 1997, 140).[16] Marcionite Christianity was influential and widespread, and such an inscription underscores the diversity of Syrian Christianity. In the fifth century Syria was at the heart of Monophysitism, which was deeply influential from Damascus northeastward into Armenia, while Nestorianism dominated both sides of the Tigris River from Nisibis southward.

DURA-EUROPOS

Early Christian archaeological remains in eastern Syria are rare, so discovery of a house-church at Dura-Europos, overlooking the Euphrates River, is of unrivaled importance. It is the earliest unambiguous and securely dated early church, showing more clearly than any other site the fact and the form of adaptive church structures—in this case, a house built in about 231/2, and shortly afterward adapted for worship, that was destroyed in 256 (Snyder 2003, 128–34; White 1997, 123–31). A wall was demolished between two rooms, and a small baptistery constructed in another, with frescoes of Adam and Eve, David and Goliath, the Good Shepherd, the woman at the well, the paralytic, Peter and Jesus walking on water, and women approaching a tomb. The building included inscriptions and graffiti. One crucial lesson is the strategic similarity among ambitious new cults: the church, a synagogue (now removed to Damascus's National Museum), and a building for the worship of Mithra (mithraeum) all were located abutting the town wall, all were similarly renovated houses, and all have comparable frescoes.

Fig. 1.12. Christ Walking on Water (House-Church Baptistery, Dura-Europos)

16. The inscription's date of 630 reflects the Seleucid reckoning, a period that began in 312/1 BCE.

EARLY CHRISTIAN LITERATURE

A number of early Christian literary works, such as the *Gospel of Thomas*, the *Infancy Gospel of Thomas*, and possibly the *Protevangelium of James* (Vorster 1992) appear to be from Syria Phoenice. All three testify to a form of Christianity with strong connections to Judaism, reflecting, however, a different understanding of their heroes. Tatian, a major figure in Syrian Christianity, was born to a pagan family in east Syria and traveled widely in the West, becoming a Christian perhaps in Rome. He compiled a harmony of the four Gospels, the *Diatessaron*, which was used extensively in Syriac-speaking churches, though it may have been created in Greek, since a Greek fragment has been found at Dura-Europos (Kraeling 1935; see chap. 2). From about the same time a late second- or early third-century collection of synagogue prayers, deriving from the *Apostolic Constitutions*, includes a number of additions that Christianize them for worship—for example, "He submitted to birth, that (birth) through a woman; (how) he appeared in (this) life, having demonstrated himself in (his) baptism; how he who appeared is God and man; . . . by him you brought the gentiles to yourself, for a treasured people, the true Israel" (*Hel. Syn. Pr.* 5.4–8) (Fiensy and Darnell 1985, 682–83). The *Gospel of Peter*, probably Syrian from before 190, is a slightly Docetic document, and the work of Bardesanes (d. 222/3) is rather Gnostic, though it may be from farther east. The third-century *Didascalia apostolorum* hints at the continuing attractiveness of Judaism among Christians, especially in chapter 26, with its implicit use of the *miqveh* and a concern for menstrual and sexual fluids (Young 2002).

PALMYRA

Palmyra (Tudmur) is a desert city northeast of Damascus on the shortest direct route between the East and the Mediterranean, beside springs that still feed its oasis (Richardson 2002, 25–51). Pliny the Elder (ca. 23–79) says, "Palmyra is a city famous . . . for the richness of its soil and for its agreeable springs. Its fields are surrounded on every side by a vast circuit of sand" (*Nat.* 5.88), and Appian (ca. 95–ca. 165) emphasizes, "Being merchants, they bring the products of India and Arabia from Persia and dispose of them in the Roman territory" (*Bell. civ.* 5.1.9). Its four main churches are not especially early (a fourth was announced in 2008), but it is possible that there are other relevant remains to be analyzed.

HELIOPOLIS

Ituraeans occupied areas west and south of Damascus in the late first century BCE; they were significant players politically, and they continued strongly as an auxiliary force in the Roman army for hundreds of years, though they virtually disappeared politically (E. Myers 2010). Some of their small villages around Mount Hermon may have ultimately become Christian, such as Gerra (Anjar), but the most important site associated with them was Heliopolis (Baalbek), where remains survive of the exceptional Antonine expansion of an ancient site dedicated to Baal, rededicated to the cult of Iuppiter Optimus Maximus Heliopolitanus, with temples to Venus, Mercury, and Bacchus. Constantine suppressed its cult of Venus, and Theodosius I demolished parts of the Temple of Jupiter and the courtyard to build a church dedicated to St. Peter. The smaller Temple of Venus became a chapel to St. Barbara, martyred in 237. Nineteenth-century archaeologists destroyed the remains of the church to disclose the pagan altar and observation tower.

Phoenicia/Phoenica Libanensis

EARLY CHRISTIANITY

The word *Phoenikē* (red-purple) was applied historically to coastal peoples from Arwad in the north to Strato's Tower (Caesarea Maritima) in the south, a region centered on the Lebanon Mountains but not embracing the Bekaa Valley and the Anti-Lebanons. The Phoenician trade network reached from Africa's Atlantic coastline to Persia and from Nubia to the Black Sea. Acts notes the early spread of Christianity to Phoenicia (Acts 11:19; 12:20; 15:3; 21:2, 7; 27:3). We lack solid literary or archaeological sources for Christian Phoenicia, but communities of Christians probably developed relatively early. Oracle 7 of the *Sibylline Oracles* may have been written in Phoenicia in the second or third century, as maritime and other allusions suggest. For example, it mentions Jesus's baptism in the Jordan (7.66) immediately after referring to Berytus (Beirut). It echoes Revelation 2:9 and 3:9 in referring to prophets who "will falsely claim to be Hebrews, which is not their race" (7.135 [cf. Oracle 8]). The presence of bishops in both Tyre and Ptolemais by the mid-second century is stronger evidence of the strength of Phoenician Christianity (Eusebius, *Hist. eccl.* 5.25), in contrast to Galilee, which had no bishops until much later. Both bishops sided with Alexandria in the Quartodeciman controversy, deciding to celebrate Easter on the Lord's Day. We also hear of Marinus and Alexander of Tyre in connection with the end of the Novatianist divisions and the "new spirit of harmony and brotherly love" (Eusebius, *Hist. eccl.* 7.5). Martyrdoms in Phoenician territory began in the late third century; executions under either Diocletian or Maximian (r. 285–305) included Tyrannion, bishop of Tyre;

Theodosia of Tyre (Eusebius, *Mart. Pal.* 8.7.1–2); Zenobius, presbyter of Sidon (Saida); and Silvanus, for forty years bishop of Emesa (Eusebius, *Hist. eccl.* 8.13.3–4; 9.6.1).

CHURCH BUILDINGS

When the Pilgrim of Bordeaux traveled from Antioch in 333—through Laodicea, Antaradus, Berytus, Sarepta, and Tyre to Ptolemais and then onward to Jerusalem—he mentions no Christian sites, even though Tyre had a cathedral before 300 that was destroyed and rebuilt to great acclaim some years prior to the Pilgrim's visit. In his *Historia ecclesiastica* Eusebius provides a long description (10.3.1–10.4.72), with the general introduction that "cathedrals were again rising far surpassing in magnificence those previously destroyed" (10.2.1), and that the one in Tyre was the most magnificent in all of Phoenicia (10.4.1). He also records for posterity his own speech, addressed to Paulinus of Tyre (bp. pre-315–327) and delivered at the dedication of the church (10.4.2–72). The church was surrounded by a wall with a colonnaded courtyard that held fountains for "sacred purification," with numerous gates into the building. Eusebius notes that it had cedar ceilings, marble floors, benches, and altars. Little remains at Tyre, Ptolemais, Sidon, Beirut, or Byblos, since all are heavily built up. At Antaradus (modern Tartus), which Constantius II (r. 337–361) renamed Constantia in 346, a third-century chapel to the Virgin Mary was destroyed by an earthquake two centuries later; a Crusader church now covers it. ✳

Remains have survived, however, of a church at Dor (modern Burj et Tantura), a bishopric from the fourth century onward, even despite Dor's decline by the mid-third century. An early fourth-century church rests atop a pagan temple; when it burned, it was rebuilt that same century (E. Stern 1994, 319–22). A marble column had "a carved recess surrounded by four crosses [and an] inscription . . . states that 'A Stone of the Golgotha' was inserted in the pillar, i.e., a stone from the Church of the Holy Sepulcher in Jerusalem" (E. Stern 1994, 320), adding extra sanctity to the Dor church. There may be a late fourth-century church at Shavei Tzion, north of Ptolemais.

Arabia

Included here are areas that Trajan rolled into the province of Arabia in 106, such as Peraea (commonly linked with Galilee), the Decapolis, Auranitis, Trachonitis, and Nabataea. We also include Idumaea, the Negev, the Sinai Peninsula, and Arabia Felix (as Rome called modern Yemen).

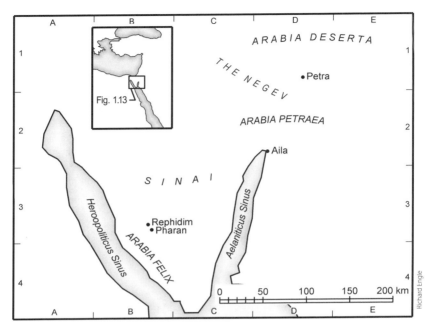

Fig. 1.13. Map of Arabia and Sinai Peninsula

The Decapolis

A dozen or so Hellenized cities that derived from Alexander the Great's conquests formed the Decapolis, a loose association that included Scythopolis, west of the Jordan River; Pella, Gadara, and Hippos, overlooking the Rift Valley; and cities farther inland, such as Gerasa, Philadelphia, and Abila (Richardson 2002, 77–102). Most were primarily cultural strongholds, new walled cities with Hellenistic *boulai* (councils) that promoted Greek religion, philosophy, education, architecture, and arts, within the prevailing rural Levantine cultures, whether Nabataean, Arabian, or Ituraean.

Jesus traveled through the Decapolis (Mark 7:31; cf. 5:20), but details about Christianity's growth in the region are lacking; Christian literature from and developments in the ten cities are speculative. The Gospel attributed to Mark possibly originated in a Decapolis city, perhaps especially one overlooking the Sea of Galilee, such as Hippos or Gadara or Pella. The *Epistle of Barnabas*'s provenance has never been satisfactorily settled, but it probably stems from the Decapolis in the 90s or from nearby areas in southern Syria (Richardson and Shukster 1983). Its Jewish-derived scriptural exegesis in the context of Hellenistic moral challenges would suit a city such as Gerasa. The hymnic *Odes of Solomon* (probably originally Aramaic or Syriac) might come from a location such as Pella, perhaps around 100 CE (Charlesworth 1985a, 725–71): "We can occasionally glimpse the earliest Christians at worship; especially their apparent stress on baptism, their rejoicing over and experiencing of a resurrected and living Messiah, Lord, and Savior" (Charlesworth 1985a, 728). ✳ A little later, Aristo of Pella (ca. 135–170) defended Christianity from Jewish critics in the mid-second-century *Dialogue of Jason and Papiscus* (Richardson 2006). These hints show a vital, though tantalizingly vague, early Christianity ✳ in the Decapolis.

Archaeological Evidence

Nevertheless, archaeological evidence suggests that the Christian community developed into a major cultural movement. For example, the Gerasa cathedral (ca. 350–375) was built over an earlier temple, perhaps to Dionysus and before that to the Nabataean Dushara, utilizing the existing entrance stair from the Cardo Maximus, a building only slightly later than the great constructions of Constantine. The remarkable number of churches at Gerasa (see sidebar 1.3) points in the same direction.

Fig. 1.14. Cathedral Church, Gerasa

Pella

An early text refers to Christians leaving Jerusalem during the First Jewish Revolt (see under the heading "Jerusalem" above), perhaps in 67/8, and going to Pella, returning later to Jerusalem. This has been seriously questioned (Lüdemann 1980), and some think that the story is modeled on accounts

1.3 Churches at Gerasa and Vicinity

East of the Rift Valley are several pockets with an unusual number of churches (Appelbaum and Segal 1993; Browning 1982). Gerasa has seventeen (twenty including chapels) within about two-thirds of the city's area (about one-third of the ancient city is covered by modern Jarash). (1) The building of the Cathedral Church (350–375) was followed by its Fountain Court (444–446) and then by (2) the Church of St. Theodore (464–466), which was integrated with it (and with two other chapels) in what must have been one of the great "triumphalist" church complexes of the Roman Near East. At the same time, (3) the Church of the Prophets, Apostles, and Martyrs was built near the North Gate (464–465). In the next century there followed in quick succession (4) Procopius's Church (526–527); the triple church, comprising (5) St. John the Baptist, (6) St. George, and (7) SS. Cosmos and Damian (all 529–533); then (8) the Synagogue Church (530–531); (9) Bishop Isaiah's Church (begun 540); (10) SS. Peter and Paul (540) with (11) an additional small chapel; (12) the Propylaea Church (565); (13) Bishop Marianos's Church (570); (14) the Mortuary Church (sixth century); (15) Bishop Genesius's church (611); and (16) undated churches on Artemis's altar terrace and in (17) Zeus's *temenos*. The Synagogue Church is a rare example of a church taking over a synagogue, though it is uncertain if the change was voluntary, forced, or gradual. The main structure was reused, though its orientation was shifted 180 degrees, and a new mosaic floor was laid, covering an earlier mosaic of animals heading toward Noah's ark. All these churches moved the center of the urban complex away from the Cardo westward to a street that accessed seven churches and southward to the Decumanus, which now replaced the Temple of Artemis's processional way as the main east-west route (Richardson 2002, 77–102).

An as yet unidentified smaller ancient city at modern Umm al-Jimal also had seventeen churches. In 1904/5 H. C. Butler dated Julianos's Church, the key building, to 344, based on an inscription on what he claimed to be a lintel. White (1997, 141–52) argues that the church is fourth/fifth century, that the Christian community previously met in a house, and that the lintel was in fact a memorial stone. Many of the other churches are late and adaptations of earlier buildings (Humbert 1990), yet this is still an unexpected situation for a modest rural town.

Other cities also had large numbers of churches. For example, Hippos (Horvat Susita) had eight churches, Adeitha (Khirbet es-Samra) had ten, and Kastron Mefaa (Umm ar-Rasas) had sixteen. Rihab's numerous churches have been overshadowed by unpersuasive claims of the alleged discovery there of Christianity's oldest extant church. These claims rest on a misreading of an inscription (Blumell and Cianca 2008). The conspicuous church building in nonbiblical cities without pilgrimage sites may be related sociologically to growing wealth or ecclesiastically to the liturgical calendar (see P.Oxy. 11.1357), where saints had churches dedicated to them so they could be celebrated on their feast day. Rural northern Arabia was densely Christianized, and Christianity must have played important social, religious, and political roles.

of Jewish leaders escaping Jerusalem. The early evidence for Christianity at Pella is not strong. The first-century civic complex was adapted as a church, beginning circa 400, while the East Church is from the last quarter of the fifth century. The earliest physical evidence may be a second-century sarcophagus (from about the time of Aristo of Pella), placed beneath the floor of the sixth-century West Church.

Northern Arabia

Beyond the Decapolis, the northern part of Rome's province of Arabia included most of Auranitis (the Hauran), Batanaea, and Trachonitis. There are reasons for thinking that there was an early Christian presence in the area. The *Didache*, an important late first-century noncanonical document, probably stemmed from the region (Van de Sandt and Flusser 2002, 52). It combines ethical instruction with requirements for worship and organization, including baptism, fasting, prayer, the Eucharist, apostles and prophets, bishops and deacons, and Sunday worship. Some parts reflect close contacts between Jewish and Christian practices, as in the case of baptism in "living water," keeping Wednesday and Friday fast days, and assemblies on the Lord's Day.

Peter Richardson

Fig. 1.15. Cathedral Church, Bostra

Bostra

Bostra, the capital of the province of Arabia, became an important bishopric in the third century. It had strong Monophysite tendencies—the belief that Christ had only one (divine) nature—a form of Christianity centered in this part of Syria. A third-century Roman basilica without aisles that still stands eave-high was converted to a church during the fourth century, underscoring how in some places there could be a shift from a civic to an ecclesiastical function. A few meters away the Cathedral Church of SS. Sergius, Bacchus, and Leontius was built in 512/3, experimentally utilizing a central dome over a square building. This was accomplished with a central colonnaded quatrefoil with corner exedra (perhaps copying the martyrium at Seleucia Pieria [see section on churches and worship under the heading "Antioch" above]). Bostra's cathedral was northern Arabia's greatest contribution to ecclesiastical architecture and a major inspiration for Constantinople's Hagia Sophia, the most creative and awe-inspiring Eastern church. Close by, at Ezraa (ancient Zorava), the lintel of the Church of St. George, which dates to 515, is inscribed: "What was once a lodging place of demons has become a house of God; where once idols were sacrificed, there are now choirs of angels; where God was provoked to wrath, now he is propitiated" (R. Burns 1994, 121). The church was built on the site of a pagan temple and is still in use, planned around an octagon within a square. Another nearby church, dedicated to St. Elias, dates to 542.

Canatha

At Canatha (Qanawat), a flourishing Christian city in the early Byzantine period, the Seraiah combines two basilicas at right angles to each other to form a church complex. The second-century west building and the third-century south building were converted to a church in the fourth/fifth century. The latter's transverse arches are a standard regional form of construction for roofing large areas, anticipating a technique used in Romanesque churches eight hundred years later.

Philippopolis

Farther north, Philippopolis (Shahba) was refounded by Philip the Arab and named after him, though building activities stopped at his death. Jerome, writing some 150 years after Philip's death, considered him the first Christian emperor (Jerome, *Vir. ill.* 54; cf. Eusebius, *Hist. eccl.* 6.34)—an exaggerated claim, but one that presupposes extensive regional Christianization at this period. For example, when Egeria visited Carneas (Sheik Sa'ad, north of Gerasa) to visit Job's tomb (Wilkinson 1999, 129), she mentions a bishop and a church, begun when a monk found a stone inscribed "Job" in a cave, over which an altar was built.

Christian Villages

The story of Christianity in northern Arabia is largely predicated on small villages, and thus minor pieces of evidence. Stephen Westphalen points out that a process of Christianization took place in the countryside in the early Byzantine period, seen clearly in the villages of Trachonitis. The steppe was urbanized by intensive clustering around churches, while clan and tribal structures influenced

Fig. 1.16. Seraiah Complex, Canatha

building patterns and local traditions (Westphalen 2006, 181–97). A major study confirms this picture for the adjacent Gaulanitis. Robert Gregg and Dan Urman's evidence is mostly late sixth century onward, but some is earlier. A martyrium dedicated to John the Baptist in Ramsâniyye is dated to 373 on the lintel, and a builder's inscription to 376, with undated inscriptions, such as *touto* (cross) *nika* (by this conquer), alluding to Constantine's famous "sign" (Gregg and Urman 1996, 186, cf. 191). Of the forty-four communities surveyed, nineteen preserve evidence of a religiously mixed population, while seventeen preserve evidence for only one group (Gregg and Urman 1996, 299). Christianized villages include Chaspho (Khisfin), Sarisai (Quneitra), and Apheka (Fiq) (Gregg and Urman 1996, 314–15). Other noteworthy inscriptions include "one God" (Gregg and Urman 1996, 120, cf. 158; Peterson and Markschies 2012, 90), "X M" ("Christ born of Mary" [Gregg and Urman 1996, 81]), and "the congregation itself of the catholic church" (Gregg and Urman 1996, 82). As in southern Syria and Jordan, that many villages had mixed populations, while others were dominantly Christian or Jewish or pagan (cf. Galilee, above).

Central Arabia

The literary sources and physical remains are meager for Peraea, the area east of the Jordan from the Hieromyces (Yarmuk) River to the territories of Philadelphia and Heshbon, where John the Baptist likely was active and through which Jesus probably traveled on his way to Jerusalem. But the area is virtually ignored in the sources, though Christians must have been there; we know nothing about them for several centuries.

PILGRIM SITES

On the eastern shore of the Sea of Galilee, also known as Lake Tiberias, the late fifth-century Kursi Monastery is important for its size (120 x 140 m; basilica of 25 x 45 m) and quality. Egeria notes a number of places, such as a church associated with John the Baptist at Selim/Sedima (modern Tell er Raghda) (Wilkinson 1999, 126–27), and farther south, opposite Jericho, 'Ain Musa's tiny church (Wilkinson 1999, 120). The Pilgrim of Bordeaux mentions the place of Elijah's ascension, but the main point of interest was Mount Nebo's church with the "burial place" of Moses beneath the altar (Wilkinson 1999, 121). Egeria says, "There is no doubt that it was the angels who buried him, since the actual tomb . . . cannot be seen today" (Wilkinson 1999, 121). Parts of the triapsidal church may date from the fourth century; although the splendid mosaics date from various periods, the earliest portion has a fourth-century inscription that reads, "Under the most reverend and pious priest and abbot, Alexios, the holy place was renovated," implying a yet earlier building.

Fig. 1.17. Mosaic, Mount Nebo Monastery

MADABA

Madaba's importance is underscored by its nine or ten churches, though it came to prominence relatively late. There is a cathedral (sixth century, with chapels of 562 and 575), a Church of the Apostles (578), a Church of the

1.4 Mosaic Floors at Madaba and Umm ar-Rasas

The skill of ancient Arabia's mosaic makers is legendary; nowhere is their work seen to better advantage than in the irreplaceable Madaba Map and in the beautiful vignettes in St. Stephen's at Umm ar-Rasas. The Madaba Map, from the mid-sixth century, is the oldest map of the Holy Land (the present building was built in 1896 over the remains of a Byzantine church), identifying Christian sites of interest to pilgrims and in many cases indicating major churches. It is no longer complete—originally it was ca. 15.60 by 6 m (94 m², of which only 25 m² are preserved)—but it once gave a full overview of the Levant from Lebanon to Egypt. Topographical features such as mountains and rivers, deserts, and palm groves figure prominently. Major cities such as Jerusalem (fig. I.3), Jericho, and Gaza are shown with recognizable details. Very little interest is shown in Jewish or pagan sites, but the interest shown in numerous Christian sites, both major and minor, is astounding.

The St. Stephen's mosaic (ca. 785) was constructed more than 200 years later than the Madaba Map—in fact, long after the Muslim conquest of the area. This mosaic's representations of settlements include, on the north row, Palestinian cities (the Holy City/Jerusalem, Neapolis, Sebaste, Caesarea Maritima, Diospolis/Lydda, Eleutheropolis, Ascalon, and Gaza); on the south row, Jordanian cities (Kastron Mefaa, Philadelphia, Madaba, Heshbon/Esbounta [Tell Hesban], Belemounta [Ma'in], Areopolis [Rabba], and Charachmouba [el-Kerak]); with two additional ancient, but not yet located, Jordanian cities, Limbon and Diblaton, in each aisle. Apparently, all these were still pilgrim destinations more than a century after the Muslim conquest.

Virgin Mary, and the Church of St. George, also known as the Church of the Map (both late sixth century). The latter contains the enormously important Madaba Map, which demonstrates graphically the growth in Christian sites between the fourth and sixth centuries, as well as their locations. Pilgrim sites dominated the mapmaker's consciousness. Since some sites are mentioned for the first time by the Piacenza Pilgrim (fl. ca. 570), a date around the same time is likely. Taken as a whole, even with its substantial gaps, the Madaba Map provides a remarkable overview of Christians' presence in the Holy Land before the Muslim conquest. Heshbon did not become a major Christian center, but farther into the desert, Kastron Mefaa (Umm ar-Rasas) had sixteen churches, including St. Stephen's, with its remarkable mosaic depictions of cities of the Holy Land. The Madaba Map and the St. Stephen's vignettes permitted Christians to savor the Holy Land even without visiting it.

The evidence cited above for northern and central Arabia stresses the importance of small villages and implies that they were crucial to the growth and spread of Christianity. It is often assumed, by contrast, that the Roman

Empire was Christianized from the cities (Stark 1996, 147). While this may have been true of Paul's missionary activity, as he went from provincial capital to provincial capital (R. Beck 2006), there were other models for Christian extension, such as in Palestine during the fourth and fifth centuries, a "movement from village out to Christian shrine on the peripheries of settlements" (Frankfurter 2005, 275).

[handwritten: Xianity moves to rural areas in 4th, 5th C.]

Southern Arabia

PETRA

Southern Arabia was the heartland of ancient Nabataea, with its capital at Petra, a bustling commercial, cultural, and religious center (Richardson 2002, 52–76). Petra became important to Christians because of its associations with Moses and Aaron, especially at 'Ain Mousa (Moses's Spring) at Wadi Musa, east of Petra, and Jebel Harun (Aaron's Mountain), west of the city. Petra declined when Bostra was made capital of Arabia, a trend that was reversed in the Byzantine period when Petra became the capital of Palaestina Tertia. Christian progress in Petra was "slow and uneven" (Fiema 2003, 239). Pagan worship continued at the same time as churches were being established during Eusebius's time (Hollerich 1999, 74). The earliest remains (mid- to late fifth century) are of the Ridge Church, possibly destroyed in the earthquake of 551, when a fire carbonized a church archive with more than 150 papyri scrolls. These have been carefully conserved by a Swedish team and can be dated between 528 and 582, detailing wills, contracts, loans, and property sales, with occasional references to church life. The monumental Urn Tomb was converted into Petra's cathedral (June 24, 446 [Fiema 2003, 239]), and the Blue Chapel complex possibly was the residence of the bishop (Bikai 2002).

AILA

During his extensive surveys in Jordan, Nelson Glueck discovered the remains of a chancel screen and two capitals from a Byzantine church at 'Aqaba (Glueck 1939, 13). A lintel with a Christian Greek inscription and symbols was found in excavations of the early Islamic quarter at 'Aqaba (Zayadine 1994, 489). This earlier evidence has been confirmed by the identification of a late third-century (ca. 290) purpose-built church, the oldest known church actually constructed for a Christian congregation. It approximates a basilica-style layout, is built of stone and mud brick, and hints at the sorts of structures that were, judging from the literary evidence, being built prior to Constantine's conversion and the beginnings of his massive building program that set a new style for church structures.

Sinai and the Negev

It is reported that during the Decian persecution many Egyptian Christians, including the bishop of Nilopolis (Dalas), fled to the wilderness of Sinai for refuge (Dionysius of Alexandria, *Ep.*, in Eusebius, *Hist. eccl.* 6.42.3–4). Nevertheless, direct evidence for Christianity in the Sinai is virtually nonexistent before the fourth century, despite this region's proximity to early Christian centers in Palaestina. At the turn of the Common Era much of the Sinai belonged to Nabataea, although different nomadic groups collectively identified as Saracens also occupied the area (Ptolemy, *Geogr.* 5.16.3; Ammianus Marcellinus, *Res gestae* 14.4; Eusebius, *Onom.* 166.12). Trajan incorporated the Sinai within the province of Arabia in about 106. At the close of the third century Diocletian reorganized the Eastern provinces, and the Sinai became part of Palaestina Tertia (Salutaris), although its upper northwest corner was administratively linked to Egypt (Dahari 2000, 13).

Christianization

In the fourth century, with the rise of Christian pilgrimage and monasticism, evidence for Christianity in the Sinai emerges around its highest peak, Jebel Musa, which Christians identified as the biblical Mount Sinai. Jebel Musa became a popular pilgrimage site, evidenced by nearly six thousand rock-cut graffiti inscriptions in the ravines leading to the mountain (Stone 1992–1994). The Christian provenance of many of these inscriptions is established by the presence of *nomina sacra*, symbols such as crosses (+, †) and monograms (X, ☧), and names that are characteristically Christian (e.g., Athanasius, Victor, Christopher, Stephen, Thekla). The earliest are written in Greek and date from the late fourth or early fifth through the seventh centuries (Negev 1977, 77), although later Christian inscriptions are also attested in Latin, Coptic, Armenian, and Georgian (Stone 1982).

Hardly any of the graffiti near Jebel Musa are Jewish, whether from the Christian or pre-Christian period; very few are written in Hebrew or Aramaic or contain distinctively Jewish symbols. The paucity of such inscriptions probably resulted from the widespread belief in postbiblical Jewish sources that Mount Sinai was located somewhere in northwestern Arabia (Kerkslager 1998, 151–69). Christian identification of Jebel Musa with the biblical Sinai therefore seems without precedent (Solzbacher 1989, 44–74). The earliest reference to a Christian center at Jebel Musa is the report by Theodoret (*Hist. eccl.* 6.14) that in the middle of the fourth century a Syrian monk, Julian Saba, founded a small monastic community on the mountain and built a church on its summit. Egeria, writing some twenty years later (ca. 384), reports there was a small church on the top of the mountain that contained cells for monks and a hostel for pilgrims (Wilkinson 1999, 109). The Piacenza Pilgrim likewise records the presence of a small church (Wilkinson 1977, 87).

St. Catherine's Monastery

Procopius of Caesarea (ca. 500–ca. 565) claims that Justinian patronized the building of a church to the "Mother of God" on Mount Sinai and a fortress at the base of the mountain to defend against nomadic raids (*Aed.* 5.8.4–9). Archaeological surveys near the summit have confirmed the remains of this church, since a number of stone fragments contain the contraction standing for *Theotokos*, "God Bearer" (Dahari 2000, 36). Since the ninth century, Justinian's fortress, or fortified monastery, has been known as St. Catherine's Monastery; it lies at the southern base of Jebel Musa (Sinai?) in the Wadi ed-Deir (Valley of the Monastery). While the largest building in this complex was the Church of the Transfiguration of Moses and Elijah, with its large apse mosaic that commemorates the transfiguration of these two figures, the *sanctum sanctorum* of this complex was reputed to be the site of the burning bush. Later tradition has it that Helena ordered the construction of a small church at the site of the burning bush; however, the church that presently marks this spot was built in the Middle Ages (Galey 1980, 63–64). Fifteen Greek inscriptions are presently known from the earliest period of the monastery's history, from about 500 to 700 (Ševčenko 1966, 262–64). One inscription that has gained notoriety, because of its length and its location at the monastery's entrance, commemorates the completion of the fortress (*CIG* 4.8634). It appears to date from the late eighteenth century and contains inaccuracies, but it may reflect the content of the original commemorative inscription (Chitty 1966, 177n16).

St. Catherine's manuscript collection has attracted considerable attention. Its most famous text is the Codex Sinaiticus, discovered by Constantine von Tischendorf in the mid-nineteenth century and now housed in the British Library (von Tischendorf 1862, 25–114). This beautifully written fourth-century vellum codex preserves parts of the Old Testament (Septuagint) and the entire New Testament, as well as the *Epistle of Barnabas* and the *Shepherd of Hermas*. The discovery of this Bible in the library at the monastery is convoluted; its removal to St. Petersburg by Tischendorf in 1859 is notorious, but almost nothing is known about how it originally made its way to St. Catherine's. However, owing to a distinct scribal error at Acts 8:5, where Sinaiticus mistakenly reads that Philip traveled down to "Caesarea" instead of "Samaria," Caesarean provenance for this manuscript seems likely (Milne and Skeat 1963, 20–23). Consequently, Sinaiticus may be one of the fifty vellum Bibles that the emperor Constantine commissioned Eusebius of Caesarea to prepare in 332 (Eusebius, *Vit. Const.* 4.36–37). Two other important works still in the monastery's possession are the Codex Syriacus, a fifth-century Gospel in Syriac written over an erased older Greek Gospel, and the Codex Arabicus, a trilingual palimpsest (Syriac, Greek, and Arabic) that contains a number of accounts of martyrdoms and the oldest Arabic version of the book of Job (Atiya 1952, 584–85).

OTHER CENTERS

One other Christian site in the Sinai with significant remains is Pharan (Tell Mahrad), located 40 km northwest of St. Catherine's on the western edge of the Wadi Feiran oasis. With rising interest in the southern Sinai in the fourth century, Pharan grew, obtained the status of a city, and flourished until the Muslim conquest in the seventh century (Grossman 1996, 28). Christians identified it as the place where Hagar and Ishmael settled after being driven off by Abraham (Gen. 21:21), as well as the site of the biblical Rephidim, where Moses caused water to flow from the rock and where the Israelites defeated the Amalekites (Exod. 17) (Eusebius, *Onom.* 142.22–25). When the Pilgrim of Piacenza visited, the city was garrisoned and had a bishop (Wilkinson 1977, 88).

NEGEV

There is little evidence for Christianity in the Negev prior to the fourth century (Figueras 1995). Nessana (Auja el-Hafir), a Christian center on the northern Sinai boundary, rose to prominence as Sinai's administrative capital in the Byzantine period. At one time it had been a Nabataean city, and in this region Nabataean names continued, even those of bishops. The earliest of Nessana's six churches was the fourth-century North Church, with others ranging through the sixth century (Figueras 1995, 425–30). When the city was excavated in 1935, a substantial cache of papyri was discovered, including two sixth-century codices of the Gospel of John (P.Ness. 2.3, 4) and a seventh-century Pauline codex containing Romans, 1 Corinthians, Colossians, Philippians, 1 Thessalonians, Titus, and Philemon (P.Ness. 2.5). Other cities in the Negev were extensively Christianized. Fourth-century churches include Haluza's East Church (perhaps 350), Shivta's North Church, Mamshit's East Church (Zelinger and Di Segni 2006) and West Church, and Magen's Buildings B and C, the latter with crosses in its floor (Tzaferis 1993, 283–85).

The most prominent city of the Negev region with the strongest Christian evidence is Gaza. The city, situated on the Via Maris approximately 20 km south of Ascalon, was an important trading center, mentioned in the New Testament: Philip was instructed to begin his missionary activities by taking the road to Gaza (Acts 8:26) (Glucker 1987, 26–30). Its location along a major road would suggest that Christianity reached Gaza early. However, not until Diocletian's persecution is anything known about its Christian community; its most notable martyr at this time was its bishop Silvanus (Eusebius, *Mart. Pal.* 7.3, 13.4–11; cf. Eusebius, *Hist. eccl.* 8.13.5). The Gaza church must have recovered by 325, as a bishop from Gaza was present at Nicaea. At about this time the citizens of Maioumas, a port town administratively linked to Gaza, converted en masse to Christianity. Constantine was so impressed by this show of faith that he made it an independent *polis* and renamed it Constantia (Eusebius, *Vit. Const.* 5.38; Sozomen, *Hist. eccl.* 2.5), though its municipal status was reversed by Julian. At the same time, Gaza's large pagan population persecuted the city's Christians (Sozomen, *Hist. eccl.* 5.9). Christianity generally flourished in Gaza in the fourth and fifth centuries, though it became embroiled in the debate between Arians and Athanasians (Socrates, *Hist. eccl.* 2.15; Sozomen, *Hist. eccl.* 3.8). Its most famous Christian at this time was Hilarion (ca. 291–371), who established a hermetic monastery northeast of Gaza in about 340. Jerome devoted an entire treatise, *Vita S. Hilarionis eremitae* (*Life of St. Hilary the Hermit*), to him (Hirschfeld 2004, 67–69). Largely due to Hilarion's influence, at least ten other monasteries opened in the vicinity of Gaza between the fourth and sixth centuries (Bitton-Ashkelony and Kofsky 2000). In 1997 a large Byzantine church complex was discovered in northern Gaza that consisted of a fifth- or sixth-century church, a baptistery, and an adjacent Christian cemetery. Seventeen Greek mosaic inscriptions were also discovered in the church and baptistery that consisted mostly of prayers dedicated to church patrons, prayers of thanksgiving, and lists naming bishops and priests (Shanks 1998).

Arabia Felix

Greeks and Romans identified the fertile region in southwestern and southern Arabia as Arabia Felix (Happy Arabia), an area distinct from Arabia Deserta (central and northern Arabia) and Arabia Petraea (Stoney Arabia). Renowned for its production of aromatic resins and spices, illustrated by the description given in 1 Kings 10:2 of the caravan of the Queen of Sheba, this region was an international center of trade and export. Augustus initiated a campaign in about 26 BCE under the direction of Aelius Gallus to secure its natural resources (Strabo, *Geogr.* 16.4.24; Pliny the Elder, *Nat.* 6.160), an expedition that was largely unsuccessful. Still, Rome secured a foothold in the region by establishing a number of forts and trading posts along the Red Sea. Toward the end of the third century CE Arabia Felix fell under the control of Axum (Aksum), the capital of northern Ethiopia; though it regained temporary independence in 525, the Axumites subsequently reconquered the region (Trimingham 1979, 287–88).

There is little evidence that any substantial effort was made to evangelize Arabia Felix in the pre-Nicaean period, although Eusebius (*Hist. eccl.* 5.10) seems to imply that Pantaenus (d. ca. 200), the first head of the famous cat-echetical school in Alexandria (see chap. 5), may have preached in the region before assuming his teaching post around 177. Rufinus (ca. 345–ca. 411/2) reports that during the time of Constantine the kingdom of Ethiopia received the gospel by Frumentius, who was later ordained the first bishop of Axum, which could have hastened the spread of Christianity into Arabia Felix (*Hist.* 1.9–10; Athanasius, *Apol. Const.* 31). Regardless, it is Philostorgius (ca. 368–ca. 439) who preserves the first account of an official mission to Arabia Felix (*Hist. eccl.* 2.6; 3.4; 4a), which was led by the priest Theophilus during the reign of Constantius II. Perhaps, then, it is more than coincidence that the first monotheistic inscriptions from Arabia Felix begin to emerge within a century of this mission (Sima 2002, 165). While the gains Christianity made in Arabia Felix—to some extent a consequence of Byzantium's alliance with Ethiopia (Hoyland 2001, 147)—were rather modest and short-lived owing to the rise of Islam in the seventh century, the Christian communities established in cities such as Najran were able to flourish and thrive for some time before they were finally ended by Muslims (Trimingham 1979, 294–307; Cragg 1991, 38–40).

Complexity of Christianity in the Roman Near East

Important as cities were in Christian growth and influence—especially the roles of Antioch, Caesarea Maritima, and Jerusalem—attention must be paid to the truly surprising distribution of Christian groups in rural areas and to the quiet increase in the strength of the church in regions such as the Limestone Massif, northern Arabia (now southern Syria and northern Jordan), the Madaba Plains, and the Negev. In these areas, as the numbers of churches in smaller locales implies, there must have been different means of diffusion of Christianity, not so much from the cities outward as by the conversion of villagers and townspeople, which ultimately resulted, it seems, in wholesale conversions. Even in Palaestina, the original homeland of Christianity, the situation was not simple; its presence seems more widespread than expected, in Samaria, for example, but less powerful in Galilee than one might antici-pate. Overly simple portrayals of the growth and spread of Christianity should be abandoned in favor of a complex and multilayered picture that is built up from the surviving tangible evidence.

Alongside the indigenous developments of Christianity in the Roman Near East, especially in Palaestina, two external influences must be considered. On the one hand, the pilgrim movement resulted in knowledge of the Holy Land with its strong incentive to ensure that the holy places associated with the first generations of Christians were preserved and marked for future pilgrims. On the other hand, some who were driven by notions of a purer and simpler life were determined to stay in the Holy Land with other like-minded souls, establishing monasteries where they could keep the world at bay by solitude, contemplation, and study.

2

Beyond the Eastern Frontier

CORNELIA HORN, SAMUEL N. C. LIEU,
AND ROBERT R. PHENIX JR.

Introduction

Although Christianity began within the geographic border of the Roman Empire, it soon crossed those (somewhat fluid) boundaries, especially in the East.
Material evidence offers little insight into the arrival and spread of Christianity in northern Mesopotamia. Most of the extant inscriptions and visible
edifices come from the fifth century and later, when Christianity was already
well established in these regions. If one were to be restricted to the nonliterary
evidence, then for the first three centuries the Abercius/Avircius inscription ✳
(fig. I.4)[1] would be the only subject in the present section of this chapter. The
coins of Abgar VIII (r. 177–212) cannot be taken as evidence that this king was
a Christian. The obverse of these coins (G. Hill 1922, 91–92 and plate 13; Segal
2001, plate 28.b.i.) contains a mark that appears to look like an "X," which
some have interpreted to reflect a cross. However, given that the cross is not a
significant symbol in Christian art and depiction until the fourth century (Snyder ✳
2003, 58–64), and that similar marks occur on coins from other times and

---

This chapter was written by **Cornelia Horn** and **Robert R. Phenix Jr.** (Introduction, Northern
Mesopotamia), and **Samuel N. C. Lieu** (Persia).

1. See the general introduction, under the heading "The 'Abercius' Inscription."

places, it is best to interpret this as a numismatic mark rather than as evidence of the early official adoption of Christianity. Steven Ross (2001, 134–35) has provided further discussion of this alleged numismatic evidence, as well as of the controversial passage in the *Book of the Laws of Countries* of Bardaisan of Edessa (154–222) that claims King Abgar "believed" and then banned the practice of emasculation. Ross's conclusion, based on Sebastian Brock's assessment that this expression is a later interpolation, removes the last pillars of evidence on which to stand the argument that Abgar VIII was a Christian.

Any account of the region has to rely primarily on written sources. These reflect the cultural and religious diversity of northern Mesopotamia that confronted the first Christians and continued to be vibrant well into the later period when these sources were composed. It must be emphasized, however, that many of these written sources, which purport to describe the origins of Christianity in Mesopotamia, are, like the nonliterary material, much later than the events described. Many date to at least the fifth century and some as late as the seventh, and so they are highly unreliable as historical sources. Those few Syriac sources that are earlier present complex problems of interpretation. Consequently, far less is known about the origins of Christianity in this region than the size of the extant literature would suggest.[2]

Until the mid-fourth century there is scant evidence for Christianity in this region. After this period, the written sources reveal that Christianity in Edessa (Şanlıurfa) and other urban areas in northern Mesopotamia emerged into a rich intellectual climate, as the teaching of Bardaisan and his school, as preserved in the *Book of the Laws of Countries* (Cureton 1965; H. Drijvers 1965), indicates.[3] Bardaisan's work was edited first by Cureton in 1855, as were the other texts whose dates and circumstances are more difficult to interpret. The *Letter of Mara bar Serapion*, for instance, is dated by some (e.g., Millar 1993) to 70 CE, but this dating is problematic, with Kathleen McVey (1990) suggesting that the text is a fourth-century school exercise (see also Chin 2006; Ramelli 2006; Rensberger 2010). The *Oration of Meliton the Philosopher*, an apology for Christianity, contains tantalizing information about the practice of religion in Mesopotamia, but it has received very little scholarly attention since it was first edited in 1855. Other works include the *Odes of Solomon*, the *Acts of Thomas the Contender*, and two hagiographies: the *Acts of Habib the*

2. Most of the earliest Syriac sources (to the fourth century CE), of which only the literary sources are undisputedly Christian, are presented in a very useful appendix in Millar 1993, 553–59, which includes a brief bibliography; both are no longer up to date.

3. For a summary discussion of the relevance of this work for the study of early Syriac Christianity, see Ross 2001, 119–23.

Deacon and the *Acts of Shmona and Guria*, all three of whom were martyred in Edessa in about 310 CE.[4]

More substantial evidence comes only from the fourth-century writers Aphrahat (ca. 270–ca. 345) and Ephraem (ca. 306–373). Another important work is the *Liber graduum* (*Book of Steps*). However, this is a work to be situated in the polemics arising from divisions within the Christian church in the Sasanian Empire to the east of Mesopotamia proper (Greatrex forthcoming). Both Aphrahat and Ephraem reveal in their polemical material a diverse Christianity, from Jewish Christians to those influenced by Hellenistic ideas, "Gnostic" Christianity, as well as the presence of Jews and Manichaeans. Edessa in particular may have been attractive for Christians of all types because of its liminal position between the Roman Empire and Persia. In the fourth century the Christianized Roman state was less effective in enforcing its view of orthodoxy in this region, in part because of Edessa's strong identity as an independent church, but also for fear of driving the population of the region into the arms of the Sasanid Empire. Arians, Docetists, Gnostic Christians, and eventually, in the fifth century, anti-Ephesians and then anti-Chalcedonians all found a home in Edessa. To be sure, orthodox writers railed against these groups and their beliefs, but it was only toward the end of the fifth century that Rome felt secure enough to persecute them in northern Mesopotamia. Despite a strong bias, the texts of these various groups remain valuable in determining the character of Christianity in the fourth century, including the age and origins of its diverse forms. In what follows, coverage of nontextual material is reasonably complete, but there is no such claim for the textual material; the works of Bardaisan, Aphrahat, and Ephraem, not to mention the biblical material, must be treated only in passing, and much is omitted altogether.

Most of the direct textual evidence is recorded in Syriac, an eastern dialect of Late Aramaic, which was the language of the local population in northern Mesopotamia and, along with Greek, a language of trade and wider communication from the Euphrates to the western edge of the Zagros Mountains. In the course of the second century CE, Syriac became synonymous with Christians broadly defined and their literature, and eventually it also developed into the language of worship for Christianity across Central Asia, China, and southern India. Syriac was also an important vehicle for transmitting the ideas of Bardaisan and his followers as well as those of Manichaeism. After Greek and Latin, Syriac texts form the third largest corpus in the first through the

---

4. For an overview of bibliographical information, see Millar 1993, 556–57; also more recent general bibliographies in Brock 1996b, updates in *Hugoye* and Ross 2001, 119–31; Edwell 2008; Mosig-Walburg 2009.

early seventh centuries in the Mediterranean and Near Eastern world. They also constitute the third-largest corpus of Christian textual and epigraphic materials before the rise of Arabic for Christian writers after the seventh century. The early third-century works relating to Bardaisan and his school, and the fourth-century writings of Ephraem and Aphrahat, still provide the best local information about early Christianity in this region. Despite the paucity of archaeological material, the reconstruction of early Christianity in this region is aided by the antiquity of some of its written sources.

The geographical scope of the first part of this chapter covers northern Mesopotamia, roughly from the Euphrates in the west to the Zagros Mountains in the east, and from southern Anatolia in the north to the southern limit of the Jazira (northern Iraq) in the south. Christianity in northern Mesopotamia emerged and evolved as part of an organic whole with southern Mesopotamia and regions to the east (modern Iraq, Kuwait, and Iran). The second part of the chapter deals with ancient Persia, the region east and southeast of Mesopotamia, encompassing much of the territory that now comprises (southeastern) Iraq and Iran. The early sections of this chapter focus narrowly on non-Christian materials and on some of the important Christian literary witnesses in Syriac.[5] A comprehensive history of Syriac Christianity in the region, taking full account of the military, political, religious, economic, and social dimensions of the scattered and difficult evidence to the mid-fourth century, remains a desideratum.

Northern Mesopotamia

The area defined here as northern Mesopotamia includes the pre-Roman kingdom of Osrhoene, which corresponds mostly to the metropolitan ecclesiastical province of Edessa; Mygdonia (later the Roman province of Mesopotamia) and its most important city, Nisibis (Nusaybin); and the kingdom of Adiabene on the upper Tigris River. That latter kingdom was briefly incorporated in the Roman Empire in the second century.[6]

---

5. Millar 1993 provides a framework for the historical setting, and Ross 2001 specifically for Edessa; see also more recently Sommer 2005; Edwell 2008; Mosig-Walburg 2009.

6. The existence and exact location of Roman Assyria has been called into question by Chris Lightfoot (1990, 121–26). This article rejects the traditional view that Assyria was essentially Adiabene, and that Roman Assyria, if it extended south to Ctesiphon (near modern Baghdad), did so only for a brief period of time (see Millar 1993, 101). What is known about Christianity in this region comes largely from later fifth-century apostolic legends, and this suggests that Roman control of the region was short and Christianity was not well established in Adiabene and southern Mesopotamia until the third century. Lightfoot has provided translations and discussions of the Roman historians on this question. More work needs to be done to assess

Fig. 2.1. Map of Northern Mesopotamia

Boundaries

The first problem in addressing Christianity in northern Mesopotamia is that this region was a border area among greater powers in the Near East since at least the beginning of urbanization in the Early Bronze Age (ca. 3400–2350 BCE). After Alexander the Great (d. June 11, 323 BCE), the boundaries continued to fluctuate between the great powers of the Seleucids, Parthians, Romans, and Sasanid Persians. According to a common pattern in the Near East, when the great powers were weakened, regional kingdoms emerged, such as the Armenian kingdom under Tigran II "the Great" (r. 95–55 BCE), or the local kingdoms of Adiabene, Osrhoene, and Commagene, which were at times under Parthian hegemony, and at other times under Roman control. The Roman-Parthian border (*limes*) moved frequently by war and by treaty (Poidebard 1934; Lauffray 1983–1991).[7] The Roman province of Assyria, if it ever existed, would have been located in northern Mesopotamia east of the Tigris and acquired by Trajan in

the dispositions of fourth-century Roman historiography of the activities of Trajan (r. 98–117) and Julian (r. 361–363) in this region and the later Syriac apostle legends.

7. On aspects of the archaeology, history, geography of, and cultural exchange at, the Roman *limes* in the relevant regions in the East, see also Parker 1979; 2006; Konrad, Baldus, and Ulbert 2001; Khouri 2003.

[handwritten marginal note: Dura Europos was under Roman control]

115 CE. Whatever the precise status of this region, Trajan abandoned it to the Parthians in 117 CE (Millar 1993, 101), before Christianity put down firm roots there. Later, much of Roman Mesopotamia, including Nisibis, was ceded to the Sasanians in 363 following the murder of Emperor Julian on June 20, 363 (Greatrex and Lieu 1994, 1–13). Only Osrhoene, the former kingdom centered on Edessa, passed from being a Roman vassal state to becoming a part of the Roman Empire in the third century. Thus from the earliest Roman control until about the mid-third century, Roman rule of the region extended along both sides of the Euphrates south of the confluence with the Chaboras River, including Dura-Europos and, farther north, the five *coloniae* of Edessa, Nisibis, Singara, Harran/Carrhae, and Resh'aina (Millar 1993, 485). After the death of Julian in 363 the Roman border moved westward, with the loss of territory to the east of the region of Edessa and Harran to the Sasanids.

In the attempt to define Christian origins in the region, a related problem is that the development of Christianity in northern Mesopotamia, at least after the mid-fourth century, is only artificially separated from the rest of Mesopotamia and western Persia. The permeability of the Persian frontier first to anti-Ephesian (inappropriately named "Nestorian") and then later to anti-Chalcedonian (later Syrian Orthodox, also inaptly called "Jacobite") Christian agents reflects the somewhat artificial character of the borders. Already in the third century there is considerable evidence that goods and persons moved and even migrated between Persian and Roman territories in this period with relative ease, despite the periodic military hostility between the two nations, especially in the second half of the fourth century (Millar 1993, 483–84). Where "border" seems to have been relevant was in the realm of church organization. The Christian church in Persia was virtually independent of Antioch (Antakya), the mother church of the Roman Diocese of the East. It was officially independent from the Synod of Seleucia-Ctesiphon (410 CE) onward. That synod recognized and to some extent reorganized the administration of the church, which eventually would stretch from the Sasanian-Roman frontier in the West (although the Church of the East would eventually establish dioceses west of this line) eastward to China and southern India (Baum and Winkler 2003). The anti-Chalcedonian church, which was to become the dominant ecclesial body of Christians in Edessa, the former region of Osrhoene, and much of Roman Mesopotamia, gradually established itself beginning in the course of the second half of the fifth century in areas of Mesopotamia under Persian control (Gero 1981). Both churches (and their parallel Catholic lines of succession, which were initiated not earlier than the thirteenth century) dominated the Christian culture of southeastern Turkey and northern Iraq until the present (Horn and Phenix 2005; Phenix and Horn 2005).

It is important to bear in mind that the cradle of Syriac Christianity, Edessa and Nisibis, was closely connected through trade with regions to the south, and that economic documents in Syriac dating to the third century have been found in the region of the Middle Euphrates (the region of Dura-Europos) and on the west bank of the Euphrates (Millar 1993), some of which mention Nisibis. These documents cannot be considered Christian documents, but they do provide key evidence for the social and commercial network in which Christianity was introduced and propagated in this region.

Ethnicity

The ethnicity of northern Mesopotamia was diverse. The presence of speakers of Aramaic is most clearly attested in a number of Syriac mosaics, inscriptions, incantation bowls, and charms. Some of the mosaic inscriptions predate the earliest manuscripts. Speakers of Arabic played a key role in the formation of Christianity in this region; the names of the kings of Edessa found in Old Syriac inscriptions and struck on coins are Arabic. Armenians were also present in northern Mesopotamia. This, again, may be inferred indirectly from onomastic evidence, but also from the fact that most of the region came under Armenian control between 80 and 65 BCE under Tigran II the Great. Armenian was not yet a written language during this period, making it all but impossible to track the presence of Armenians in northern Mesopotamia at that time.

A hoard found at Nisibis in 1955 contains coins in Greek minted at Natunia (al-Shirqat), which was the royal mint of Adiabene. From this evidence some derive that there were Greek colonies in Adiabene (Seyrig 1955, 104; Milik 1962, 51–52; Chaumont 1988, 39). The region was a Parthian dominion until the early third century CE, a detail arguing in favor of a Parthian presence. Parthian presence elsewhere in northern Mesopotamia is attested by an ostracon with a fragment of a business letter found at Dura-Europos (Boyce 1983, 1153–54). Moreover, the influence of Parthian culture is present in the dress of figures on portraits found on early mosaics and reliefs from Edessa (Segal 2001, plates 12, 14–17). It is probable that there were other ethnicities from the regions of modern Iran and the Caucasus that would have contributed to the urban population of this region.

Language and Culture

The evidence for language in northern Mesopotamia in the first three centuries CE is to be gleaned from Old Syriac inscriptions (Jadir 1983; Drijvers and Healey 1999; Briquel-Chatonnet, Debié, and Desreumaux 2004), most of which come from Edessa; a few Greek inscriptions, which cannot be reliably dated; and legends on coins from the hoard found in Nisibis. The pattern that emerges indicates that the rulers of Edessa spoke a dialect of Arabic but used Syriac as a written language. There is no evidence that Syriac was a written language before the advent of the kingdom of Osrhoene in the first century BCE. The Nisibis hoard reveals that even local rulers followed the example of the Parthian kings and struck all their coins with Greek legends. Despite the clear importance of Syriac, it existed alongside Greek in a state of diglossia into the seventh century CE. Greek remained the commercial language that linked this region with the wider Mediterranean world. It also was a language of cultural prestige under the influence of Hellenism. The importance of Syriac translators of Christian and classical Greek works (other than the translation of biblical texts) is well known from the fifth century, but is likely to have begun earlier. One may characterize Syriac culture as a partly Hellenized, Greek-speaking society mixed with contributions from Iran that took root in the course of the second century BCE, when large sections of the area were incorporated into the Parthian kingdom during the reign of Mithridates II (r. 123/2–88 BCE). Hellenism in this part of the world was not uniform and probably was restricted to the cities and larger towns, with Syriac, other Aramaic dialects, and other languages for which no written evidence from this period survives likely having been predominant in urban as well as nonurban areas.

Religion

The Parthians, who were the dominant political force in this region, were tolerant of religious diversity, and the kingdom of Osrhoene, being essentially a satellite of Parthian political culture, inherited this tolerance. This open attitude toward foreign ideas may be one reason why Christianity in Edessa and Nisibis maintained its broad spectrum of diversity long after the "Peace of Constantine" brought infringement of civil rights and outright persecution waged against "heterodox" Christians, Jews, and adherents of other religions elsewhere. Edessa and Nisibis did not experience such Christian-on-Christian persecution until well into the fifth century. In effect, the diversity of Parthian society lived on in the Syriac Christian regions long after the Parthian kingdom had been absorbed into the Roman and Sasanian Persian Empires. This diversity survived primarily because the kingdom of Osrhoene, which finally was incorporated into the Roman Empire in 213 under Caracalla (r. 211–217), remained independent long enough for its social institutions to become stabilized.[8]

8. The local monarchy of Edessa returned in 239/40, after which the city reverted to its status as a Roman *colonia* in 241.

Sources

As noted above, prior to the fourth century there is little or no direct evidence for the existence of Christians in the regions of northern Mesopotamia. The earliest mention of Christians in this area is found in the New Testament's Acts of the Apostles. Independent of whether one assumes that Acts 1–2 is historically reliable, the "tableau of nations" in Acts 2:9 lists "Parthians, Medes, Elamites, and residents of Mesopotamia" among those who were reportedly present in Jerusalem at Peter's speech on Pentecost. To what "Mesopotamia" precisely refers here is unclear, but the author may have had in mind the Roman province of Mesopotamia, the metropolis of which was Nisibis in the first century CE until 363. Nisibis was a center of Jewish learning at least from the early to mid-second century onward. Acts 2:41 states that after Peter's speech, "those who welcomed his message were baptized, and that day about three thousand persons were added." Addressed as it was to the Israelites (Acts 2:22, 29), this speech is consistent with what other sources, such as Josephus (*Ant.* 20.3.3), reveal: Jews lived in Mesopotamia in the first century in areas such as in Adiabene that were under direct Parthian hegemony. Nowhere does the New Testament describe the arrival of Christians in northern Mesopotamia or mention the existence of churches there.

The earliest mention of Christians in northern Mesopotamia outside of Acts is in the Abercius inscription.[9] Abercius (fl. 180/90 CE) was the bishop of Hieropolis in the Phrygian Pentapolis whose epitaph mentions the presence of Christians in Nisibis, without further comment. The dearth of data on the earliest Christians in the region, however, should be understood as a result of historical circumstances rather than as an indication of a relatively late establishment of a Christian presence in northern Mesopotamia. Dionysius of Alexandria (bp. ca. 247/8–264/5) was familiar with Christian communities in Mesopotamia (*Ep.*, in Eusebius, *Hist. eccl.* 7.5.2) but does not specify them. Presumably, they were some of the communities represented in 325 by their bishops at the First Council of Nicaea: Amida, Arbela, Edessa, Macedonopolis/Birtha, Nisibis, and Resh'aina (Mullen 2004, 56–57).[10] When later literary texts witness to the presence of Christianity in northern Mesopotamia, they strongly suggest that Christian roots in the area were already well established and of ancient provenance.

9. Evidence for Abercius is witnessed in the form of the inscription on his tombstone, and also in the form of a separately transmitted literary text (Wischmeyer 1980; Ross 2001, 117, 137).

10. For the location of other (including possible) early Christian communities in the region, see Mullen 2004, 57–65.

Archaeology and Art

The number of artifacts and edifices created by Christians in the first four centuries in northern Mesopotamia may have been considerable. What remains—or more accurately, what has been excavated from these remains—however, is limited. In part, this lacuna is the result of destruction or reuse of earlier buildings, but also it is due to the almost complete absence of any systematic archaeology of late-antique Christianity in this region. Nearly all information about Christians in northern Mesopotamia must be derived from the reports of travelers and from geographical surveys, as well as from ancient written sources.[11]

Most of what is known about the geographical landscape of Christianity in northern Mesopotamia comes from Iraq. Here the work Jean-Maurice Fiey conducted from the 1930s to the 1980s remains a monumental and exceptional contribution (Fiey 1965–1968). Fiey and others have plausibly identified many of the locations in northeastern Mesopotamia and in the region of Nisibis related to Christian history that are mentioned in Syriac chronographies, bishop lists, and other sources. However, there has been little or no systematic excavation of any of these sites. The situation for nearly all sites in western Mesopotamia (in modern Syria and Turkey) is not much further advanced. This is not to say that there is absolutely no archaeological work on specifically Christian sites in this region, but most of the data brought to light pertain to the Mediaeval period (Abbasid, Ottoman). Archaeology of Christian artifacts is largely limited to objects, specifically inscriptions or larger edifices partly or entirely visible above ground that are accessible with little or no excavation.

The bulk of artifacts from the early Christian period in northern Mesopotamia that have been found and published come from Edessa and its immediate vicinity, primarily inscriptions and some architectural remains visible above ground. None of the Christian inscriptions from Edessa, however, can be dated to a time before the fifth century. Even the famous inscription of the *Letter of Jesus to King Abgar* found at Philippi is a later copy of a Christian apocryphal text.[12] Furthermore, there has never been any attempt to undertake

11. If one were to venture a comparison with the evolution of the archaeology of ancient Israel, the archaeology of Christian Mesopotamia is not much more advanced than the stage reached by Edward Robinson and Eli Smith's geographical survey of Palestine, conducted in 1838 (E. Robinson 1970; Silberman 1991, 78). Finding a remedy for this problem will require the concerted will of the governments and archaeologists of the nations in whose lands these Christian sites are located, primarily Turkey and Iraq, as well as strong interest from Western archaeologists and historians of Christianity in this region.

12. For a modern depiction of the encounter between Addai and King Abgar, featuring an inscription of a good part of the correspondence as shown in the Church of St. George in Aleppo, see Balicka-Witakowski et al. 2001, 50.

Fig. 2.2. Rabbula Gospels: Illumination (Crucifixion)

a complete archaeological survey of the city or of any other site in the Tur Abdin, the region in southern Turkey where many churches and monasteries of ancient provenance are located (Hollerweger, Palmer, and Brock 1999). One important exception to the general lack of excavations of Christian sites in this region consists of work in Nisibis, where the excavation of the Church of St. Jacob, one of the oldest Syriac Christian churches whose date is verified on the basis of textual sources, is under way.

In addition to these, there is a body of numismatic and textual evidence of significance for the history of Roman Edessa and Nisibis, from the first to the mid-third century CE. The finding of commercial documents in spots along the Middle Euphrates that mention these two cities has shed new light on the problematic chronology of the period and on the problem of establishing the cultural contacts of the later centers of Syriac Christianity with the rest of Syria and Mesopotamia. However, these documents are of limited value in assessing the earliest stages of Christianity in these cities (Ross 2001).

Other important material sources of information from Late Antiquity consist of illuminations in manuscripts, such as the Rabbula Gospels manuscript completed in 586 (Cecchelli, Furlani, and Salmi 1959), and objects associated with magical practices (Naveh and Shaked 1993; Morony 2003), such as amulets (Naveh and Shaked 1985) and incantation bowls (Hunter and Segal 2000; Morony 2007). However, the dating of magical objects possibly used by Christians in Late Antiquity is problematic. The illuminations in manuscripts are more easily dated. Although these depictions do not necessarily provide direct evidence for the earliest instances of Christianity, through their use of distinctive styles they offer further evidence of a local incorporation of motifs that suggests a considerable prior history of Christian art in the region.

Early commentaries on the Bible, such as the commentary of Ephraem on Exodus and Genesis, as well as other exegetical material from the fourth and early fifth centuries (some of which is preserved not in Syriac but in Armenian), show connections with earlier depictions of art in northern Syria, such as found at the early third-century church in Dura-Europos (Haider 1996), and especially in the synagogue there (Langer 1996, 250–53, 258–60). The scholarly consensus is that Judaism played an important role in the formation and development of Syriac Christianity; in all periods of Syriac literature, writers transmitted Jewish traditions, particularly exegetical material. This makes such artifacts, and their connection to later Syriac exegetes, important for understanding the formative period of Christianity in northern Mesopotamia.

Supporting the almost complete absence of archaeological remains are the writings of Greek Christian historians, Syriac and Arabic chronicles, hagiography, and other literature, including Islamic geographies and historiographies. Even with these texts, for much of the region outside of Edessa the evidence for the earliest presence of Christians must be sifted out from the legends of Christianization that were composed long after their historiographical settings.

Adiabene

Adiabene is the Greek rendering of the Aramaic *Hadyab* or *Hedayab*, the name for the heartland of Assyria comprising the region between the Greater and Lesser Zab Rivers to the northeast of the Tigris, bounded on the northeast by the Zagros Mountains (Reade 2001). In ancient time, Ammianus Marcellinus (ca. 325/30–post-391) had provided a spurious etymology from the Greek *diabainein*, "to ford," with the meaning "a (river) which cannot be forded" (*Res gestae* 23.6.22). Eventually, the name encompassed the region to the north, which was one of the independent kingdoms between Rome and Parthia in the first century CE. Trajan annexed this kingdom in 115. In 118, under Hadrian (r. 117–138), the territory returned to Rome's eastern rival, Parthia, and then was inherited by the Sasanid Empire in 224. Ammianus Marcellinus mentioned that several cities belonged to Adiabene, including Nineveh, Gaugamela, and Arbela (*Res gestae* 23.6.22). He distinguished Assyria from Adiabene, assigning to the former the cities of Babylon and Ctesiphon (*Res gestae* 23.6.23). In light of other evidence, Assyria here is a region rather than a Roman province.

As for Babylon, since its establishment in the Early Bronze Age that city had never been considered a part of Assyria.

Ammianus seems to have assumed that the political and possibly ecclesiastical geography of the fourth century was unchanged since before the Roman period, but there is much confusion among historiographers concerning Roman Assyria and Trajan's campaigns in this region. Christian sources dating after the fifth century mention the regions of Marga and Beth Garmai to the south of Adiabene, and Ba Nuhadra or Beth Nuhadra to the west, which included the important Christian center of Nineveh. The geography of this region and the development of the ecclesiastical organization of the Church of the East for the period beginning in the early fifth century have been reconstructed by Fiey in his monumental *Assyrie chrétienne* (1965–1968). However, there is little or no information about the organization of Adiabene and its surrounding regions in the first three centuries CE.

ARBELA

The center of Adiabene was the city of Arbela (Irbil), first mentioned in a Christian context in the acts of the Council of Seleucia-Ctesiphon (410 CE) as the metropolitan see of Adiabene. The city was located in the region of Beth Huzaye, one of the important ecclesiastical provinces of the Church of the East in Persia, whose catholicos-patriarch had resided originally in Seleucia-Ctesiphon.

Ecclesiastical organization of Adiabene in the fifth century adopted ecclesiastical regions delimiting the bishoprics that were subordinate to the metropolitan of Arbela. The *Acts of Mar Mari* mentions these regions as being among those which, according to the legend, Mari the apostle from Edessa and disciple of Thaddaeus/Addai converted when he worked his way through the entire Mesopotamian region down to what is now Khuzistan in southeastern Iran (*Acts of Mar Mari* 26–27) (Harrak 2005, 58–61). Among the notables of Adiabene whom Mari allegedly converted were Aphrahat the king of Arbela, the head of the royal army and his son, and the chief priest of the king; the story has it that King Aphrahat gave the idols of the city's temple to Mar Mari, who, according to the account (an adaptation of Exod. 36), ground the idols into dust and scattered the dust into the Tigris (*Acts Mar Mari* 25) (Harrak 2005, 56–57). It is hardly possible that this account can accurately describe a period before 115, when Trajan incorporated Adiabene into the Roman Empire, as the ruling house was Jewish, beginning with Izates I (d. 55 CE). Moreover, the fact that the ruler of Arbela is called a king need not reflect an early date. Under the Parthians (specifically the Arsacid rulers of the Parthian kingdom), local dynasties continued to exercise authority on behalf of the Parthian king, and they could have used the title king in the small dependent territories that they governed.

As the foregoing anachronism suggests, the evidence of the *Acts of Mar Mari* should be used with caution to reconstruct early Christianity in Persia. The claim advanced by Christelle Jullien and Florence Jullien (2003, 6–9), that the geographical features of the acts point to an original story from before the third century CE, is based on thin evidence. As they and other scholars have maintained, this work in its final form is a consciously anti-Manichaean treatise, which could not have come into existence until the late third century but almost certainly dates to the early fifth century. Among the many facts that lead to this conclusion is that the *Acts of Mar Mari* is an expansion of the *Doctrine of Addai*, a work that dates perhaps to the end of the third century but likely was redacted in its final form after the start of the fifth century (see also Harrak 2005, xiv–xvii, xix–xxvii; S. Griffith 2003; Ramelli 2006). The most plausible explanation for the origin of the *Acts of Mar Mari* is that the story reflects an attempt to establish Edessa as the source of Persian Christianity in order to support the claim of an apostolic foundation for the church in Persia, later known as the Church of the East.

Thaddaeus/Addai

The tradition that Thaddaeus/Addai,[13] rather than Mari, was the apostle to all of Mesopotamia and southern Armenia became the "canonical" account of the Christianization of Persia in the Church of the East after the fifth century. The reason for this may rest with the activities of anti-Ephesian ("Nestorian") scholars who came to dominate the church in Persia and who brought this story with them as the "founding narrative" of the church in Edessa, which linked the city explicitly with Jesus and the apostles. Eventually, in later historiographical documents such as the *Doctrina apostolorum* and the *History of Karka de Beth Slok and Its Martyrs*, Addai became the apostle to all of Persia, including Adiabene. Additionally, in these later documents the apostle Thomas is identified as the apostle to the Parthians, Medes, Bactrians, and others, as well as to India. Adiabene would have fallen within the territory associated with the Parthians in this legend, which probably is also of Edessene origin. Yet this legend never seems to have had canonical status in the church in Persia.

Judaism

Before the arrival of Christianity the local ruling house of Adiabene adopted Judaism as its religion. Queen Helena (d. ca. 56 CE) and her sons Izates I and Monobaz II (d. ca. 70 CE) are perhaps best known in this regard, Helena and

---

13. According to Eusebius of Caesarea (ca. 264/5–ca. 339/40), Thaddaeus was a member of the larger circle of seventy "apostles" appointed by Jesus (*Hist. eccl.* 1.13.11 [cf. Luke 10:1–12]).

Izates having received mention by Josephus (*Ant.* 19.2.5) for their conversion to Judaism. The remains of Izates and Helena (Josephus, *Ant.* 20.4.3) were transferred to the vicinity of Jerusalem and are said to have been buried in what is commonly called the *Qurqur al-Muluk*, "Tomb of the Kings," located north of Jerusalem; her alleged sarcophagus is now in the Louvre (Vailhé 1912, 561; Finegan 1992, 314–18).

With the exception of this tomb and the scant mention of the kingdom by Josephus and in Roman historiography, practically nothing is known about the material history of Adiabene pertinent to establishing the conditions by which Christianity arrived there. What is clear is that Adiabene was connected to Mesopotamia and to the Mediterranean by routes used in long-distance trade. It is possible that in the aftermath of the two Jewish revolts in Roman Palaestina, in 66–73 and 132–135 (Monobaz II helped fund Jewish resistance to the Romans in the First Jewish Revolt), some Jews fled to Adiabene. One may imagine that Christians would have established a presence in Adiabene by the middle of the second century. One of the great early philosophers and theologians of Edessa, Bardaisan, likely traced his roots to a family who arrived in Edessa from Adiabene (Chaumont 1988, 6).

HISTORIOGRAPHY

Adiabene appears in later Christian historiography. Sozomen (fl. ca. 445) describes the persecution against Christians under the Sasanian emperor Shapur II (r. 309–379) and notes that Adiabene was almost entirely Christian (*Hist. eccl.* 1.2). The first of two local historiographies of Adiabene is the highly controversial work attributed to the alleged seventh-century monk Meshiha Zeka, the *Chronicle of Arbela* (Mingana 1907; Kawerau 1985).[14] The work, if authentic, was composed in the first third of the third century, and it mentions the existence of twenty bishoprics of the Persian church, seven of which are of regions in Adiabene (Chaumont 1988, 32).

A second source concerning the Christianization of this region is the *History of Karka de Beth Slok and Its Martyrs* (Bedjan 1968, 2:507–35; Hoffmann 1966, 43–60; Braun 1915, 179–87). This city, now Kirkuk, Iraq, whose ancient name means "Fortress of the Land of the Seleucids," was the see of the bishop of Beth Garmai, which is in the eastern part of Adiabene. As in the case of the *Chronicle of Arbela*, the historical value of this work has been debated. Jean-Maurice Fiey (1964, 219; 1970, 23) and, more recently,

---

14. On the authenticity of the *Chronicle of Arbela*, contrast, for example, the defense of the work's authenticity by Christelle Jullien and Florence Jullien (2001) with the negative judgment on the matter by Joel Walker (2006, 287–90).

Marie-Louise Chaumont (1988, 38–41) have argued that there is much in this account that is reliable to a reasonable degree of certainty. They assigned this work to Bar Sahdê, a hagiographer who is otherwise unknown but was writing between 581 and 637 (Chaumont 1988, 38n65); its historical reliability is therefore questionable. This text presents both Addai and Mari as evangelizers of Karka de Beth Slok and states that from the time of the conversion of the first Christian according to the *History of Karka de Beth Slok and Its Martyrs*, Christianity continued to grow for ninety years, until the twentieth year of the reign of Shapur I (r. 240/42/43–270/72). As Shapur was allegedly enthroned on 1 Nisan (April 12) in 240, 242, or 243, his twentieth year would have been between 260 and 263. If the *History of Karka de Beth Slok and Its Martyrs* were to be trusted, it would provide evidence of the very early arrival of Christianity in Mesopotamia. However, the text's late date makes it, on the whole, an unreliable source. Moreover, the combination of the facts that the actual date of the coronation of Shapur I is unknown, that for a time he probably reigned with his father as co-regent, and that 240 corresponds to the first public appearance of the prophet Mani (ca. 216–276) cast further doubt on any precise chronology based on Shapur's coronation (Bickerman 1983, 783).[15]

Another important source of information about Adiabene is the *Legend of Mar Qardagh* (J. Walker 2006, 17–69). Created sometime in the early seventh century, this story recounts the failed rebellion of the Christian population of Adiabene against Shapur II in the fourth century. After Qardagh's execution his hagiographer created a portrait of him that combines elements of hagiography with symbols drawn from the literature of royal inscriptions and art. Joel Walker (2006, 249–52) has concluded that the martyrdom account preserves many elements of the indigenous Christian culture of Adiabene, some of which may have been adapted from the Assyrians. Assyriologists might receive Walker's judgment with skepticism, yet some elements of the tale may indeed reflect the experiences and practices of Christians in this region prior to the seventh century. This incorporation of pre-Christian, potentially Assyrian imagery into Christian narratives reflects a broader Christianization of ancient Near Eastern culture in this region.

ARCHAEOLOGICAL REMAINS OF EARLY CHRISTIANITY
The excavation by Japanese researchers of a church in Hirta/al-Hira (modern Hira in southern Iraq) has revealed that the church sits on the footprint of an earlier building, and the stratigraphy suggests a continuous rebuilding

---

15. Chaumont (1988, 56) takes for granted the difficulty in establishing any firm dating based on this evidence.

of this structure since the Iron Age (Okada 1991; J. Walker 2006, 248). The precise nature of this building awaits analysis, but the hypothesis that Christians adapted earlier cult sites in Assyria (be they Assyrian or Parthian) can be tested. However, the archaeology of Christian sites in northern Iraq remains largely dormant.

One of the few Christian sites that have received significant attention is the Church of St. Sergius at Qasr Serij, about 60 km northwest of Mosul. Its floor plan is similar to that of basilica churches found in northern Syria at about the same period and therefore serves as the basis for the dating of this church to the fifth century, contemporaneous to many of the basilica churches farther to the west in Syria. The structure includes a martyrium that was added later. In the sixth century a monastery formed around the Church of St. Sergius, and the buildings of this monastery are still preserved (Oates 1968, 106–17).

Aphrahat

The Christian history of Adiabene belongs properly to the history of Christianity in Persia, as this territory passed from the Romans to the Parthians in 118 and was absorbed into the Sasanian Empire in 226. The two local chronicles, as well as the Qardagh legend and other information that can be gleaned from Manichaean, Persian, and Christian sources, offer a basis for reconstructing an outline of this history.[16] The earliest Christian author from this region whose work survived is Aphrahat, whose *Demonstrations* offers insight into the close and at times uneasy relationships between Christians and Jews in Adiabene. However, there is practically nothing known about Aphrahat himself. Among the earliest names offered for the author of this collection is "The Persian Sage," found in the earliest manuscripts, the oldest being BL Add. 17,182 (474 and 510 CE, written in two parts). This name is also found in several later Syriac writers until the tenth century. Other attributions are to Jacob of Nisibis (also found in BL Add. 17,182, in the colophon to the part dated to 510). The earliest mention of Aphrahat as the author is in the lexicon of Bar Bahlul (fl. tenth century). The popularity of Bar Bahlul's work inspired this attestation, which is taken up by later Syriac writers such as Michael the Syrian (d. 1199), but not to the exclusion of Jacob (as in BL Or. 1017, dated 1364 [see Pierre 1988–1989, 1:33–35, 42–45; Lehto 2003]). Aphrahat's corpus offers neither reference to the origins of Christianity in his domain nor specific information about his opponents due to the difficult circumstances in

16. Chaumont (1988, 29–53) discusses this evidence, offering arguments for the general historical reliability of the ancient Syriac chronicles based on correlations with the Cologne Mani Codex and other sources, and a detailed, if not uncontroversial, picture of the early history of Christianity in Persia.

the Sasanian Empire.[17] It is most likely that Aphrahat addresses his criticism to Jewish Christians who retained observance of Torah while rejecting Paul's presentation of the exclusionary relationship between Torah and belief in Jesus as the Messiah (Pierre 1988–1989, 1:86–93).

Mygdonia/Roman Mesopotamia

NISIBIS

The heart of Mygdonia was the city of Nisibis, which has a history beginning at least in the tenth century BCE. Seleucus I Nicator (r. 311–281 BCE) refounded the Assyrian city as a Hellenistic colony, Antioch-in-Mygdonia.[18] After falling under the rule of the Armenian king Tigran II between 80 and 68 BCE, Nisibis and the surrounding region at times were dependent on Rome after Lucullus (ca. 118–57 BCE) captured the city in the winter of 68. After the Parthians recaptured Nisibis, King Artabanus II (r. ca. 10–38 CE) granted Nisibis to Izates I of Adiabene (Josephus, *Ant.* 20.3.3). The region then was incorporated again in 115 CE into the Roman Empire by Trajan when he annexed to Rome the territory of the Tigris and Euphrates Rivers from the mountains of Armenia (modern southeastern Turkey) to the Persian Gulf (Cassius Dio, *Hist. rom.* 68.23). During the Quietus (or Kitos) War (115–117), which was an uprising of Jews that spread to Mesopotamia and engulfed Edessa and Nisibis, the city was briefly lost but then regained. In 118 Hadrian was forced to cede most of this territory to the Arsacid Persians, but Rome maintained control of the northern region, today referred to in Arabic as the Jazira (island), between the upper courses of the Tigris and the Euphrates. Mygdonia may have been independent or may have been a dependency of Osrhoene after 118, but then it lost its nominal independence in 164 under Lucius Verus (r. 161–169).

Nisibis became the capital of Roman Mesopotamia in 197 after the defeat of the Parthians by Septimius Severus (r. 193–211). This area was incorporated as a Roman province with Roman colonies at Carrhae (biblical Harran, now Altınbaşak), just 40 km southeast of Edessa, and at Singara (Balad Sinjar). The city was again conquered from the East, this time by the Sasanian emperor Shapur I in 243. For a short time in the late third century it was under Palmyrene control. Then in 298 Roman Caesar and future emperor Galerius

---

17. He is called Jacob in early sources, and he was confused with Jacob of Nisibis (bp. 290–338) in the Armenian translation of the *Demonstrations* and in Gennadius (*Vir. ill.* 1). The name Aphrahat is attested first in a ninth-century manuscript of Gennadius, *De viris illustribus* (PL 58.1060–62). See Bernoulli 1968, 60–61; see also, for the Armenian evidence, Bruns 1991, 1:35–36.

18. This section cannot provide a full account of the historical events. See Millar 1993, 159–73; Edwell 2008; Mosig-Walburg 2009.

(Caesar, 293–305; Augustus, 305–311) acquired the province for Rome through a treaty with the Sasanian emperor Narseh (r. 293–302) (Dodgeon and Lieu 1994, 125–31). In June 363, after the death of Julian at Seleucia-Ctesiphon, Julian's successor, Jovian (r. 363–364), ceded half of Roman Mesopotamia to Shapur II. From 363 until the Arab conquest exactly three centuries later, Roman Mesopotamia was organized with its metropolis at Amida (Diyarbakır). Its border extended as far as the area around Dara (Oğuz), a fortified town founded later in the sixth century, just a few kilometers west of Nisibis (Preusser 1911, 44–49, and plates 53–61; Dillemann 1962).

CHRISTIANITY

The legendary *Acts of Addai* (Palmer 2002; 2005) ascribes to Addai the evangelization of Edessa and Amida. Specifically, *Acts of Addai* 7.6 (Palmer 2005, 658) mentions that Addai preached for five years in Amida and converted many Jews to Christianity. This apocryphal work dates to sometime between the fifth and seventh centuries. Consequently, Eusebius (*Hist. eccl.* 1.13) could not have relied on it, at least not in its present form, for his account of the conversion of Amida (Palmer 2005, 645–49). The importance of conversions of Jews in the account may reflect the presence of robust Jewish communities in the cities of this region in Late Antiquity. Another apocryphal work that is a reflection of fifth- and possibly fourth-century writers on the origins of Christianity in northern Mesopotamia, the *Acts of Mar Mari*, describes the evangelization of Nisibis as coming from Edessa. In contrast, the *Chronicle of Arbela* maintains that Christianity came to Nisibis from Adiabene. Given that each of these works is tendentious, with an attempt to claim Nisibis and its surrounding territory as being dependent on one of two rival sees (Edessa and Arbela), it is nearly impossible to resolve the question of the actual origins of Christianity in Nisibis.

Nisibis was an entrepôt and a center of religious influences. The city is mentioned in *Talmud Bavli Sanhedrin* 22a as the location of a school around the *tanna* Rabbi Judah ben Bathyra (fl. ca. 60), who may have sought refuge there after the First Jewish Revolt (66–73). The disciples of Rabbi Aqibah (ca. 50–ca. 150) arrived in Nisibis after the martyrdom of their teacher following the Second Jewish Revolt (132–135). It is possible that the presence of this Jewish community provided refuge for Christians fleeing from Syria Palaestina and was the nucleus of the first Christian community of Nisibis.

Nisibis, like its sister city, Edessa in Roman Osrhoene, was a city of rich religious and cultural diversity. What is known about this diversity is reflected in the writings of the city's most famous poet, Ephraem, whose polemical works against Marcionites, Manichaeans, Bardaisanites, Jews, and Judaizing Christians reveal the religious plurality of his hometown, Nisibis, as well as of his later adopted hometown, Edessa. Along with many other Christians, Ephraem immigrated to Edessa in 363, when Jovian had to cede the city of Nisibis to Shapur II. In Edessa, struggles with Arian Christianity occupied much of Ephraem's energies.

After Jovian had ceded Nisibis to the Persians, under the catholicate of Seleucia-Ctesiphon the city became the center of Beth Arbaye, one of the metropolitan provinces of the Church of the East (Fiey 1977, 1). Nisibis is most famous for its school, which was established when Emperor Zeno (r. 474–491) closed the "School of the Persians" in Edessa in 489 for supporting a "Nestorian" theology. The Christians of Nisibis, who were under pressure from Sasanid religious policy, welcomed the learned scholars from Edessa, led by Narsai (d. 502/3), celebrated as the founder of the School of Nisibis. The canons of the school, composed in 496, still survive (Vööbus 1961; 1965; Becker 2006).

Of the material remains of Nisibis, the baptistery that Jacob of Nisibis had erected during the reign of Constantine I (r. 306–337) remains an important monument. It is also one of the few ancient buildings in the region that is currently under excavation. The church dedicated to the Diocletianic martyr Febronia (Bedjan 1968, 5:573–615; Brock and Harvey 1987, 152–76) is also known, having been incorporated into the Zain al-Abidin Mosque.

Jacob of Nisibis is the earliest bishop of the city attested in sources other than those that originate in or concern only his city. He was a pivotal figure in its early Christian history. Jacob participated in the First Council of Nicaea (325) and had as his pupil Ephraem the Syrian, who later was responsible for training students in biblical exegesis (Bruns 2000, 195).

The native sources for reconstructing the history of Nisibis are limited to the *Liber pontificalis* (*Book of Pontiffs*), which contains a list of the city's bishops beginning with Jacob (Fiey 1977, 17–18), and to a reference to Jacob offered by Ephraem in *Carmina Nisibena* (*Songs of Nisibis*) 21.10,[19] by which Ephraem compares Jacob, as the first priest of Christianity in the city of Nisibis, to Constantine, the city's first Christian ruler. Significantly, Ephraem does not mention a succession that could be traced back to Addai or Mari. After Jacob's death Shapur II began a series of sieges in an attempt to wrest the city from Roman control (in 338, 346, and 350). Jacob's successor, Babu (bp. 338–350), received Emperor Constantius II (r. 337–361) in 345 and died in the course of Shapur II's third siege. In 359 Bishop Vologeses (bp. 350–361/2) constructed the baptistery of the church, which still stands and whose dedicatory inscription is the oldest Christian epigraph in the city (Fiey, 1977, 29–33; Jarry 1972, 243; Brock 1990, 11; P. Russell 2005). In the crisis of 363 Abraham,

19. E. Beck 1961–1963, 1.1:58, 1.2:72; Féghali and Navarre 1989, 77; cf. Fiey 1977, 1–26.

who as successor to Vologeses had assumed the office of bishop in 361/2, had the remains of Jacob of Nisibis carried from the city when, along with the rest of the Christian population, he was forced to leave. Many of these Christians from Nisibis subsequently settled in Edessa or Amida.

The Roman province of Mesopotamia included a number of cities with sizable churches, some of which were centers of pilgrimage. This province also comprised the eastern part of the Tur Abdin, the heartland of Syriac Christianity (Palmer 1990). Here, as well as at other locations, one still finds the remains of churches dating at least to the seventh century, but some of which may be as early as the fourth. The architecture of these churches, many of which are basilicas, reflects Greek and Mesopotamian elements, among the latter of which is the use of a vaulted cupola that may have been incorporated into Christian buildings first in this region (Strzygowski 1973, 51–74; Koch 1982). Amida and Resafa (since the third century known as Sergioupolis, modern al-Risāfah) each presents many examples of this type of architecture (fig. 2.4) that are not older than the sixth century (van Berchem 1910, 135–224; Leclercq 1933, 512).

Osrhoene

The heartland of the Syriac language, Osrhoene and its metropolis, Edessa, remain the best documented of all the regions in Roman Mesopotamia. More is known about the earliest stages of Christianity at Edessa than anywhere else in Mesopotamia. Christianity reached the city by the middle of the second century, though whether from Syria or from Adiabene and Nisibis is debated (Ross 2001, 130–31). Christianity in Edessa represented a broad spectrum, a new faith interacting with existing ideas and symbols. This is clear from Bardaisan to the reports of Ephraem and later writers about the diversity of "heterodox" Christians. Yet despite Edessa's importance for the history of Christianity, up until today no single archaeological excavation of a Christian site in the city or its surrounding territory has occurred.

Like Mygdonia, Osrhoene and, in particular, Edessa were located on the long-distance trade routes that linked Central Asia and the Caucasus with Mesopotamia and the Mediterranean. Edessa was built on Hellenized Parthian culture and was subject to Arab rulers who were tolerant of the many religions that came into its purview.

EDESSA

Many of the sites in Osrhoene probably had been occupied already in the Assyrian, Babylonian, and Achaemenid periods. After the death of Alexander in 323 BCE this region was incorporated into the Seleucid kingdom, and many of the cities were refounded by Seleucus I Nicator and his successors. Seleucus I reestablished the city of Orhay as Edessa in about 303/2 BCE, thus giving it the name of an important city in Macedonia. Edessa is a Slavic word reflecting the good waters of the (Macedonian) city. Perhaps the River Daisan (Greek: Skirtos, modern Karakoyun Deresi), as well as the many springs in the city, reminded Seleucus of Alexander's home. Edessa's waters also inspired the many names that later Seleucid kings gave to it, including Antiochia ad Callirhoem (lit., pleasantly flowing), referring perhaps to the Daisan or to the famous fish pools, one of which still remains at the Mosque of Abraham (Segal 2001, 6). Edessa possessed an important citadel, which still overlooks the city and serves as a reminder of the city's strategic relevance, commanding the fertile plains of the western bank of the bend in the Euphrates that forms part of the Jazira. Despite the importance of this citadel, it has not been excavated.

The slow breakup of the Seleucid kingdom after the death of Antiochus IV Epiphanes (r. 174–163 BCE) created a vacuum that allowed for greater autonomy of the many small local dynasts between the Euphrates and the Zagros Mountains in northern Mesopotamia. Many of these "dynastic houses" comprised Nabataeans or Arabs, who had established a network of local city-states based on trade between Mesopotamia, the Mediterranean, and the Arabian Peninsula. The Arab "House of Edessa" likely became independent shortly before the crushing victory of the Parthians over the Seleucids in Media in 130–129 BCE (Segal 2001, 9). The Parthians did not maintain a centralized administration, and so the local dynasty of Osrhoene remained independent, with the brief interlude of Armenian control (89–78 BCE) and other short periods of either direct Parthian or Roman administration. Edessa became a Roman *colonia* under Emperor Elagabalus (r. 218–222), and it was definitively incorporated into the Roman Empire by 243 (Ross 2001, 59; Segal 2001, 15).

The borders of Osrhoene moved in the Roman period, the area being administered at times by the Parthians, at times by the Romans. Moreover, Edessa and its dependent territory were just one of several political entities in the region, attested in the first century by the emissaries who greeted Trajan on his march east of the Euphrates. Cassius Dio (ca. 150–235) mentions an embassy from one "Augaros" the "Osrhoenian," no doubt from the ruling house of Edessa, and another from "Mannos," who ruled "the neighboring part of Arabia" (the name that the Greeks gave to much of the region east of the Euphrates). These various territories probably did not have fixed boundaries, and so establishing the extent of the dependent territory of Edessa in the earliest period is difficult, if not impossible (Millar 1993, 457).

Mygdonia (and its metropolis Nisibis) was incorporated into the fluctuating territory in certain periods, as the local Abgarids periodically sought to test Rome's strength in this region, and military operations against Nisibis were undertaken. Although the kings of Edessa played the Romans off against the Parthians, Osrhoene was the only one of the three provinces of Roman northern Mesopotamia that remained in the Roman fold until the Arab conquest in the seventh century. After Osrhoene became a Roman province, the region enjoyed relative stability and prosperity, founded on its rich soil and its importance as a center of trade. The region had been a strategic part of the Roman-Persian frontier ever since Rome began its expansion into the former territories of the Seleucid kingdom during the course of the first century BCE. Edessa remained an important part of the Roman border regions (*limes*), and consequently Edessa's fortifications were expanded throughout the late fifth and sixth centuries CE.

Despite the important contribution of the Romans that ensured the stability of Edessa and Osrhoene in later years, Christianity arrived in Edessa under the Hellenized Parthian Abgarids. Although most of the fourth- and fifth-century literary material concerning the first Christian missions to Osrhoene falls under the designation of Christian apocrypha[20] and was designed to emphasize the independence of Edessa and its ecclesiastical territory, the references to the kings of Edessa in this material seem to reflect a fairly accurate historical framework.

The Legend of Abgar and Jesus

The earliest attested legend about the relationship of the Abgarids to Christianity centers on Abgar V Ukkāmā (meaning "The Black" [r. 4–7 and 13–50 CE]). The account of this Abgar's story exists in many witnesses, which have been presented in German translation with notes and discussion by Martin Illert (2007, 178–97), including several Greek inscriptions. The oldest datable version is told and retold by Eusebius in two extracts (*Hist. eccl.* 1.13.1–20; 2.1.6–8) (Brock 1992, 212–34). Eusebius claims that the church in Edessa preserved a correspondence between Abgar and Jesus. The Abgar legend spread far and wide in Oriental Christian literature and was modified extensively, having been combined with other accounts of the evangelization of Edessa. The core of the story is that Abgar, hearing of the miraculous healings of Jesus, asked Jesus to come to Edessa to cure him of an unspecified disease (Horn 2013, 79–85). Jesus supplied a written reply, carried by Ananias (or Hannan) the courier, in which Jesus promised to send one of his disciples in his place. Eusebius's first extract recounts that after Jesus's ascension Thomas

---

20. For an overview of Syriac Christian apocrypha and the evidence from Christian Arabic sources, see the contributions in Debié et al. 2005. See also Horn and Phenix 2010; Horn 2010.

sent Thaddaeus (as Eusebius and the Syriac translation of Eusebius name him, but he is known as Addai in the *Doctrine of Addai*) to Edessa, not specifically to heal Abgar but rather to bring Christianity to the city. Eusebius states that the written records documenting these events are found in the record office of Edessa. He then provides Abgar's letter to Jesus and the letter of Jesus's reply, which Eusebius extracted and translated from the Syriac "word for word."

Eusebius also includes the long postscript subjoined to Jesus's reply, which recounts the arrival of Thaddaeus/Addai to Edessa. Abgar heard of miraculous healings by the apostle, suspecting that Thaddaeus/Addai was the one whom Jesus had promised, and assembles the people to hear the preaching of Addai, which Eusebius claims took place in the year 340 of the Greeks, or 30 CE. The postscript, however, is not part of the letter itself, as Eusebius maintains. It is clear that this account of Abgar and Thaddaeus/Addai represents an independent tradition that was appended to the letter of Jesus in order to harmonize the two accounts (Segal 2001, 62–68). The account does not mention that Addai actually converted Edessa. The ending of the passage is perhaps the most interesting part. Abgar orders gold and silver to be given to Thaddaus/Addai, but the apostle refuses, saying, "If we have left our own property behind, how can we accept other people's?" This statement may suggest that the purpose of the narrative was an *apologia* for ascetic renunciation of the world and a polemic against the secular administration of the city, which would have greater meaning in the course of the late third and early fourth centuries,[21] when asceticism in Edessa had evolved from a charismatic phenomenon to one in which individuals could choose to enter and develop a personal vocation. In any case, it is difficult to speak in this period of a monastic institution in Edessa, given the lack of evidence.

Eusebius's second account, a brief synopsis not supported by documentation, states that Thaddaeus/Addai converted Edessa, primarily through his miracles, and since then "the whole city" was converted to Christianity. The many references to Jews and Marcionites (among others) in Ephraem the Syrian (in Edessa 363–373) and in the *Life of Rabbula* (ca. 436) do not support such a statement, unless Ephraem referred primarily to Jewish Christians and Eusebius's statement understands Christianity in a broad sense.

Later accounts of this story claim that Thomas, rather than Addai, brought Christianity to Edessa. The Abgar legend was modified in the *Doctrine of Addai*, which contains a story of Jesus's blessing over Edessa, a reference to the building of the first church in Edessa, and regulations for church organization and liturgy (Howard 1981, 9, 65–67, 83–95).

---

21. Eusebius wrote his *Historia ecclesiastica* to the year 324 and died in 339/40.

The *Letter of Jesus to Abgar* also circulated as an independent apocryphal text (*Epistle of Christ and Abgar*), with a reception history of its own (Desreumaux, Palmer, and Beylot 1993; Segal 2001, 73–76). It is mentioned neither in Ephraem's works nor in any of the early West Syrian chronicles, such as the *Chronicle of Edessa* (Guidi 1955), but is referred to (ca. 429) first by Augustine of Hippo (bp. ca. 395/6–430), then by Jacob of Serugh (bp. 519–521), and also in the *Chronicle of Joshua the Stylite* (ca. 503). The expanded form of this letter contains Jesus's alleged final promise that no enemy would be able to take the city. It is associated with Sasanian sieges of Edessa beginning in the third century with the unsuccessful defense of the emperor Valerian (r. 253–260) against Shapur I in 259, and continuing into the seventh century. The pilgrim Egeria devoted an entire episode in her journal to this letter, indicating that it was known in the West but not in its longer form as she saw it in Edessa in about 384 (*Itin. Eger.* 9.19) (Wilkinson 1999, 135; Franceschini and Weber 1965, 62).[22]

Another tradition that is related to the Abgar correspondence is the "Portrait of Jesus," also known in Byzantine tradition as the "Icon Not Made by Human Hands." The legend concerning the portrait/icon as preserved in the *Doctrine of Addai* begins with Abgar V sending Hannan, his secretary, to the Roman governor of Syria. Hannan and his two assistants then continue on to Jerusalem. They meet Jesus, write an account of his "acts," and then return. It is possible that the author of the legend wished to tacitly identify the name Hannan with the first-person narrative of the Gospel attributed to John. Abgar sends Hannan back to Jesus with a letter. Jesus replies with an oral message to Hannan, and Hannan paints a portrait of Jesus, which Abgar gives a place of honor in his palace (Howard 1981, 2–9). The legend developed so as to minimize and then ultimately eliminate Hannan as the painter of this portrait, with the result that, in later versions of the legend, Jesus himself is reported as having impressed his image onto a cloth. The narrative recounts that the impression was subsequently treated as a sacred object. Its miraculous character, like the *Letter of Jesus to Abgar* itself, is again associated with the deliverance of Edessa from Sasanian sieges in the course of the sixth century. Judah Segal (2001, 77) has postulated that the icon of Jesus was associated with the Chalcedonian Orthodox (Melkite) community in Edessa, while the *Letter of Jesus to Abgar* was in the possession of the anti-Chalcedonian (Jacobite) church. It is at least as likely that the portrait of Jesus was an attempt to imitate the central holy object of the Manichaeans—namely, the portrait of Mani that played a central role in their most important ritual, the Bema Festival.

22. See also Gingras 1970, 81; Segal 2001, 74.

In the *Doctrine of Addai* (Howard 1981, 20–35) Addai recounts to Abgar that Protonike, the (alleged) wife of Emperor Claudius (r. 41–54), found the true cross of Jesus (J. Drijvers 1992, 147–63; 1997). The name Protonike is here to be regarded as a corruption of the name of Berenice of Panaeus, an alternative name for the Veronica who, according to Western texts, obtained a portrait of Jesus from the handkerchief with which she wiped Jesus's face (Cameron 1981). Thus the Veronica legend has been grafted onto the trunk of the Abgar legend in the *Doctrine of Addai*. Both stories involve a punitive persecution of the Jews for the death of Jesus. In the *Doctrine of Addai* (Howard 1981, 12–13) Abgar states that he would have sent an army to destroy "the Jews" who crucified Jesus, but he refrained from doing so on account of his treaty with Tiberius (r. 14–37).

APOSTOLIC SUCCESSION

The *Doctrine of Addai* emphasizes that the Christianization of Edessa derives directly, rather than indirectly, from one of the twelve apostles of the New Testament Gospels. As noted already, Eusebius calls Thaddaeus/Addai "one of the Seventy," whereas the Syriac and the derivative Armenian legends identify him with the apostle Thaddaeus (Matt. 10:3; Mark 3:18). Addai's reported association with Judas Thomas may have been due to parallel passages in Luke 6:16 and Acts 1:13, where, instead of Thaddaeus, a certain Judas the son (or brother) of James is listed. The apostolic succession of the bishops of Edessa exists in two versions. In the Syriac *Doctrine of Addai* Addai appoints Aggai, who ministered in the church that Addai built, to succeed him. Aggai himself died as a martyr before he could ordain to the episcopate Palut, another of Addai's companions whom he had made a presbyter. Palut then goes to Antioch and receives episcopal ordination from Serapion (bp. ca. 199–ca. 211), who, the reader is told, had been ordained by Zephyrinus of Rome (bp. ca. 198/9–217), who, in turn, was a successor of the apostle Peter (Howard 1981, 104–5). This would place Palut's episcopacy sometime in the late second century.

The tradition concerning Palut as the first of the orthodox bishops of Edessa is featured in Ephraem the Syrian's *Hymns against Heresies* 22.6 (E. Beck 1957, 1:80; 2:78–79). Ephraem does not mention Aggai, and many lists of bishops of Edessa omit him, making Palut the direct successor of Addai. Given the diversity of Christianities in Edessa, but specifically in polemicizing against Arianism, which had established itself there, Ephraem desired to make clear that his own church was not founded by Palut; otherwise, Nicene Christians could be called Palutians.

Sidney Griffith (2003, 24–29) has explained the importance of Rome in the *Doctrine of Addai* as a feature of a work that was designed to show the allegiance of Edessa during the reign of Theodosius II (r. 408–450). More specifically, the version of the succession at Edessa presented in the *Doctrine of Addai* is likely the result of the conflicts surrounding two bishops of Edessa, Rabbula (bp. ca. 415–435) and Yehiba (Ibas) (bp. 435–457), in the first half of the fifth century. This connection to Rome through Antioch is also consistent with Yehiba's positive appraisal of the writings of the Greek "Antiochene" theologians Theodore of Mopsuestia (bp. 392–428) and Theodoret of Cyrrhus (bp. 423–ca. 466), the former of whom Rabbula seems to have vehemently opposed, and with their importance for the School of Edessa, which Yehiba directed. The *Doctrine of Addai* seems to be more concerned with preserving the distinct traditions of Edessa, such as attributing to Addai the practice of "reading from the Old Covenant and the New of the Diatessaron" in the churches (Howard 1981, 72–73). Additionally, this version contains a statement against forced conversion: "But neither King Abgar nor the Apostle Addai forced anyone by constraint to believe in the Messiah, because without human compulsion, the compulsion of signs compelled many to believe in him" (Howard 1981, 68–71). This statement may be a polemic against Rabbula, whom his hagiographer portrayed as "a second Joshua bar Nun" in his attempt to eradicate heterodox Christianity from his city (Doran 2006, 91; Phenix and Horn forthcoming). However, even if one can identify the different fifth-century tendencies of these two versions, it is impossible to determine which of them reflects the older tradition, leaving open the possibility that both are later elaborations (Phenix and Horn forthcoming).

The last tradition to be discussed concerning the evangelization of Edessa and its role in the spread of Christianity in Asia is associated with the apostle Thomas. The connection between Judas/Thaddaeus/Addai and Judas Thomas has already been noted. In apocryphal texts Thomas was recalled in a special way in connection with Addai. In apocryphal acts of apostles Thomas was associated with the evangelization of Iran and Addai with Adiabene (Segal 2001, 66). The *Acts of Thomas* (Wright 1968, 1:172–333 [Syriac]; 2:146–298 [English]), a work that may have been composed originally in Syriac at Edessa and Nisibis and that dates to the third century (S. Myers 2006), narrates the apostle's journey to and evangelization of India. One of the purposes of such a tale might be to demonstrate the dependence of Christianity in India on Thomas, who is associated with Edessa, thereby placing the church in India under Edessa's "apostolic" see. This tradition may well predate both of the Thaddaeus/Addai legends mentioned above. This being said, one is hesitant to claim that the Thomas traditions originated in Edessa; it is much more plausible that important early texts associated with Thomas, notably the *Gospel of Thomas*, radiated into Edessa from Antioch, at a date that would be difficult to determine but probably is no earlier than the late second century CE (Piovanelli 2009, 460–61).

MATERIAL EVIDENCE AND CHRONICLES

The number of extant early Christian inscriptions and other monuments in Osrhoene is quite small. There are pre-Christian mosaics and funerary inscriptions from the area around Edessa, but the dated Christian inscriptions found outside Edessa at Constantia (Viranşehir) are not older than the fifth century. There is no evidence that any of the undated inscriptions might be significantly older (Leclercq 1937). Indeed, the oldest attested Christian Syriac inscription is from Dar Qita (perhaps ancient Tyba/Deba), in the Limestone Massif west of the Euphrates in Syria, which is dated to 433/4 (Briquel-Chatonnet and Desreumaux 2004, 15). Two fourth-century Christian Greek inscriptions from this site refer to personal events in the mid-fourth century. These are unrelated to the later Syriac inscription. From these inscriptions of Flavius Eusebius, who had the earliest Greek inscriptions made in 350 and 355, it can be inferred that Christianity came to Dar Qita first from the Greek-speaking West; whether he was the village's first Christian inhabitant, as Frank Trombley (1993–1994, 2:268–69) claims, is not certain. There are other inscriptions in Greek in the vicinity of Edessa. One of these is at the tomb of Mar Elias, who died in either 493 or 528 (Briquel-Chatonnet and Desreumaux 2004, 19). None of the inscriptions that date to the second or third centuries, including the ones on the marvelous mosaics of Edessa, is Christian in origin. Some, however, are clearly Jewish, such as the Greek inscription at the cemetery of the nearby modern village of Kırkmağara (Forty Caves) (Segal 2001, plate 31). The presence of these letters in funerary contexts suggests some combination of their attested use as amulets to designate a location as Christian and as a statement of Edessa's independence from Roman and Persian hegemony, something like a sign of civic pride, perhaps.

The suggestion by Segal (2001, 186n3) that a copy of the letter of Jesus to Abgar inscribed at Kırkmağara may predate the one Egeria saw presumably on the West Gate of Edessa in the 380s remains uncertain. There are also Greek tomb inscriptions that use the "One God One Christ" formula found in the cemetery to the north of Edessa, near the tomb of St. Ephraem in the northwest, and other locations. Some of these can be dated to either the fifth or sixth century. There is a possibility that some of these Greek inscriptions with the "One God One Christ" formula may be from the fourth century, as the same formula is found on inscriptions from Syria. Yet even a fourth-century inscription is relatively late. Other than that they reveal the continued use of Greek in the region of Edessa, it is not clear whether these inscriptions were written for Greek speakers serving in official capacities in Edessa (but native use of Greek is also likely). A systematic study of the inscriptional evidence in light of more recent work on reconstructing the religious history of Edessa remains a necessity.

The oldest record of the existence of a Christian church in Edessa from a historiographical source comes from the seventh-century *Chronicle of Edessa* (Guidi 1955 [Syriac text]; Segal 2001). For the year 513 of the Greeks (201/2 CE), this text speaks of the damage caused by the flooding of the Daisan River and mentions that the waters destroyed the *hayklā* (either the nave or the sanctuary) of the church of the Christians (*Chron. Edess.* 8 [Guidi 1955, 1–2; Segal 2001, 24]). Even if the *Doctrine of Addai* preserves a historical kernel of the spread of Christianity in Edessa, it would still be impossible to determine whether the church mentioned in the *Chronicle of Edessa* was the one that, according to Addai's hagiographer, the apostle constructed (Howard 1981, 66–67).

The *Chronicle of Edessa* contains different traditions concerning the building of one or more early fourth-century churches in the city. Qūnē (bp. ca. 289–312/3) is reported to have laid the foundations for a church in Edessa, and his successor, Sha'ad (bp. post-312/3–pre-324), is said to have finished the church (*Chron. Edess.* 12 [Guidi 1955, 4]). In 324 Aitallaha (bp. ca. 324–ca. 330) completed the courtyard and built "the east side of the church" (*Chron. Edess.* 14 [Guidi 1955, 4]). It is impossible to determine the relationship between the building activities of Aitallaha and those of the earlier bishops without locating the remains of these Edessene churches and conducting archaeological excavations.

The dearth of archaeological evidence does not permit any firm conclusions concerning the degree of continuity in the Christian appropriation of pre-Christian buildings, including sites of worship erected by Jews or others. Based on archaeological evidence, it is clear that Christians in the city did continue to use older cemeteries. Each of the three ancient cemeteries in Edessa contained indigenous polytheists, Jews, and, later, Christians (Segal 2001, 27–28). At the northern cemetery outside the city walls of Edessa, beyond the dam that Justinian I (r. 527–565) ordered to be built, a church dedicated to martyrs and confessors was constructed that served as a martyrium for the deposition of the bones of those deemed to be holy men and women (Procopius, *Aed.* 2.2) (Palmer 2001).

The First Syriac Christians

What is known about religion in Osrhoene to the end of the fourth century is restricted almost entirely to Edessa. The data concerning Edessa come from two principal sources: the writings of the school of Bardaisan, and Ephraem the Syrian's polemics. In addition, the *Chronicle of Edessa* has been used, on the basis of Walter Bauer's controversial work, as evidence that the earliest

Syriac Christians were Marcionites. The sixth entry in the *Chronicle of Edessa*, dating to the equivalent of 137/8 CE, states that Marcion (d. ca. 160) left the universal church. This, along with the fact that Ephraem rejected the title Palutians for "orthodox" Christians, led Bauer (1934, 24–41) to conclude that the orthodox in Edessa were latecomers, presumably displacing the Marcionites in the course of the late fourth to early fifth centuries. There is little direct evidence to reject Bauer's thesis out of hand. However, the *Chronicle of Edessa* was written long after the second century. At the time when Ephraem was active in the city, between 363 and 373, Marcionites were present in Edessa, and Syriac sources from the fifth and sixth centuries imply that Marcionite Christianity may have been common, if not predominant, for Edessa and Mesopotamia more broadly. It is possible that the author of the *Chronicle of Edessa* inserted the notice of Marcion's exit from the universal church as a reminder to his contemporary readership that, from an orthodox perspective, Marcion was an apostate.

The opposition between two other hypotheses—namely, that the first Syriac Christians converted from Judaism (principally in places such as Nisibis and Adiabene), or that they were converts from the other religions of northern Mesopotamia—is somewhat artificial. The complexity of society in northern Mesopotamia precludes any such distinctions. It is likely that Christianity spread first in the cities of northern Mesopotamia and then radiated outward into the smaller towns; it is possible that many forms of Christianity arrived in multiple waves, and that Christianity was then to some extent syncretized with local religions, as well as with Hellenistic philosophy and later Manichaeism. An important exception to this is Harran, a city just south of Edessa, where worship of the Mesopotamian moon-god predominated well into Late Antiquity and remained vibrant even in the Islamic period (Green 1992).

Syriac Bible and Apocrypha

The Syriac Bible presents an important record of early Christianity in Edessa. The Peshitta (simple) translation of the Hebrew Bible was not executed at once, but rather in stages, by multiple authors over time, perhaps beginning in the second century CE. Generally, the Peshitta is a translation that is independent of the Aramaic Jewish Targumim, with the exception of Proverbs; it relies on translation techniques similar to those in the Aramaic Targumim but preserves in some instances distinct interpretative traditions. These and other similarities led some scholars to conclude that the text was a Jewish translation; this hypothesis is now debated, with no clear consensus as to a Christian or a Jewish origin (Weitzman 1998; van Peursen and ter Haar Romeny 2006). Many of the similarities in translation technique between the

Peshitta and Aramaic Jewish Targumim may be due to shared grammatical and lexical features of the languages of the Peshitta and Targumim. The existence of an independent Syriac translation of the Hebrew Bible (with minimal borrowing from Greek versions in the earliest stages) seems to reflect that Syriac Christianity adapted the Hebrew text that was used by Jews in Palestine and Syria in the first century CE, which in turn may point to the close connections between Judaism and the earliest Syriac Christians.

The New Testament is known in Syriac in a variety of recensions. In the case of the Gospels, there are three significant early recensions. The *Diatessaron*, a Gospel harmony attributed to Tatian (ca. 120–180), dates to the middle of the second century. Translated from Greek into Syriac, the *Diatessaron* was widely received in the Syriac-speaking churches, probably representing the exclusive Gospel text for Edessa and Nisibis. Scholars attribute a commentary on the *Diatessaron* either to Ephraem the Syrian or to his school (Lange 2008, 1:69–73), and it was only in the course of the fifth century that the text of the *Diatessaron* was replaced by the four canonical Gospels of the New Testament. In addition to the *Diatessaron*, the texts of the four canonical Gospels also existed in Syriac. Prior to the fifth century, these are known as the Old Syriac Gospels, which are only partially preserved (E. Wilson 2003). The Peshitta Gospels underwent two redactions: one by Philoxenus of Mabbugh (Hierapolis; modern Membidj, Syria) (bp. 485–512), which is now lost, and another by Thomas of Harkel,[23] bishop of Hierapolis/Mabbugh (bp. until 602). After Thomas's expulsion from Mabbugh he produced his recension of the Bible in 615/6 (Baumstark 1922, 18; Aland 1980, 189–96). These redactions tended to bring the Syriac text closer to a Greek type, with an increasingly literal translation, to the point of creating Syriac equivalents for Greek morphology and syntax. The New Testament canon of the early Syriac church lacked 2 Peter, 2–3 John, Jude, and Revelation.

DIVERSITY

Despite the many artifacts from the Parthian and Roman periods that illuminate the history and culture of northern Mesopotamia in these periods, very little has been recovered pertaining specifically to the origins of Christianity. In the absence of systematic surveys and excavation of Christian sites, the picture must be drawn from careful use of later sources, the earliest of which are not historiographical in any sense. It is clear that by the fourth century, when these

---

23. The location of Harkel (Syriac *ḥarqel*) has never been identified. It is highly unlikely that it corresponds to any of the Syrian localities known as Heraclea/Herakleia. It is possible that "Harkel" refers to Hierapolis/Bambyce/Mabbugh, or that the name refers to a lost town somewhere between Chalcis and Hierapolis (see Hatch 1937, 141–43).

sources do appear, Christianity in northern Mesopotamia is a diverse, vibrant, and well-established religion. Situated between two empires, it was home to a rich religious and cultural panoply. By the fourth century, Christianity among Syriac speakers had been present long enough for Aphrahat, but even more so Ephraem, to provide detailed responses to "heretical" Christian sects (including the followers of Bardaisan), Jews (and Jewish Christians), and Manichaeans. Should archaeology in this region continue, it is likely that important finds will fill in the many gaps in the material record and may even help to resolve some of the long-standing debates on the origins of Christianity and its development in the first three centuries in northern Mesopotamia.

The diversity of Christianity in this region is quite old; both Aphrahat and Ephraem imply that their opponents had long been established and argue for the even longer presence of their own "orthodox" Christianity. The growing consensus among New Testament scholars that the Synoptic Gospels, the *Gospel of Thomas*, the *Diatessaron*, and many of the earliest apocryphal texts were originally composed in Syria has implications for earliest Mesopotamian Christianity. It would seem to support, prima facie, that a major early wave of Christianization came from western Syria, and that much of the early diversity of the region was "imported" from the West. Many questions remain to be explored in this respect, and although no definitive answers can be given, the search for better hypotheses will yield insights. It is to be hoped that archaeology can one day play its proper role in Edessa, Nisibis, and northern Iraq, as it has in illuminating the formation of Christianity elsewhere in the Roman Empire and beyond.

Persia

Iran, the land of Zoroaster (fl. mid-sixth century BCE) and later a great center of Islamic (mainly Shia) civilization, is rarely associated with Christianity, except perhaps as the homeland of the legendary Magi who visited the infant Jesus. Yet the history of the Church of the East (often misnamed as "Nestorian") in the Sasanian Empire in Iraq and Iran is vital to our understanding of the premodern spread of Christianity into Central Asia, India, and China (see chap. 4). The extraordinary success of this mission in historic times has aroused considerable interest among modern scholars interested in religious dialogue and ecumenism who see the Syriac-speaking Persian church as an example of an early (and more pristine?) form of Christianity that had not been exported along with a heavy Western "cultural baggage" in train. The checkered history of the Christian church in pre-Islamic Persia, which is relatively

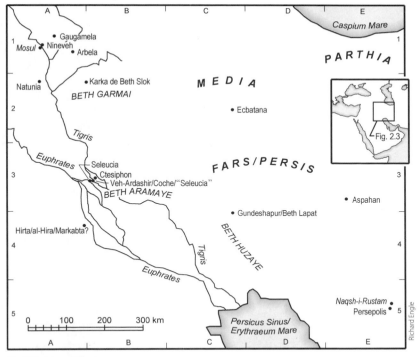

Fig. 2.3. Map of Persia

well documented by the Christians themselves, also provides an interesting paradigm for Christian communities in a number of modern Islamic states where they often constitute well educated, relatively affluent and influential minorities but are seen by the authorities and the religious majority as a foreign "race" with a large question mark hanging over their political allegiance.

Early Christianity in Palestine and adjacent Syria developed into a missionary religion at the time when the Parthian Empire held political sway over much of the Near East. It is widely assumed from the early church fathers that the Magi (the so-called wise men) who brought the three gifts in the Infant story (Matt. 2:1–12) came from lands under Parthian control, and the term "Magi" referred clearly to their possible links with Zoroastrianism. It was alleged that the Magi, from time immemorial, each year ascended a mountain at harvest time to await the appearance of the star that would show them where the Zoroastrian savior would be born (Herzfeld 1935, 61–62; J. Russell 1991, 524). The legend would take on an Iranian (and more particularly Zurvanite) tinge in that the three Magi were said to have visited the infant Jesus in a cave, and he appeared to them in the three ages "of man" (van Tongerloo 1992, 58–62). The Magi were almost always depicted in what the West thought was Persian costume, and, not surprisingly, they were recognized as compatriots on a Roman mosaic by the soldiers of the victorious Chosroes II Parvez (r. 590–628) in the seventh century (J. Russell 1991, 524).

Judaism had already established a strong presence in the Near East before the time of Jesus, thanks to the Babylonian exile and the growth of prosperous Jewish communities in the Hellenistic world in cities such as Antioch, Alexandria, and Cyrene. The presence of Jews in Parthian-held territories is alluded to in Acts 2:9. As Jacob Neusner has well remarked, "The movement of Christianity to the Iranian empire generally is parallel to that of rabbinical Judaism. In both instances, religious groups, formed within the heart of Palestinian Judaism, competed in the first place in winning over the Jews of the oriental diaspora" (1971, 2).

This strong link with Judaism would be sternly denied by the Church of the East in its own literature (Harrak 2005, 19). It did not, however, deny that early Christian missionaries such as Addai resided with Jews when they first set foot in Mesopotamian communities such as Edessa. According to a later legend (ca. 600–650), Mari, one of the disciples of Addai, was active in the conversion of client kings in the marches between Rome and Parthia, and he eventually established an episcopal see at the Twin Cities (al-Mada'in) of Seleucia-Ctesiphon on the Tigris. Seleucia had been founded originally by Seleucus I Nicator and rapidly grew in the Hellenistic period into the most important Greek city east of Antioch. Ctesiphon (al-Ma'aridh) was a neighboring city, directly across the Tigris, which originally served as the arsenal of Seleucia. It was developed by the Parthians into a major city to counterbalance Seleucia, which was annexed by treaty that guaranteed its Greek population a high degree of autonomy. Seleucia, the ruins of which are at Tell Omar near Salman Pak southeast of modern Baghdad, remained one of the chief cities of the Parthian Empire and later became the winter capital of the Sasanian Empire. The legendary *Acts of Mar Mari*, though written after that date as stated in the text (Harrak 2005, 38–39), contains interesting details on Seleucia as an autonomous city with its three-tiered city council (Harrak 2005, xxii–xxiii, 42–47). The level of the city's autonomy was remarked on by Tacitus (*Ann.* 6.42.1–2).

At some point in the second century the Tigris changed course, and a new Seleucia had to be built in order to remain a river port, and a new city, Veh-Ardashir, was built during the Sasanian period around a hillock called Coche, and it was here that the seat of the Christian bishopric came to be based. The old Seleucia became a deserted city, and Veh-Ardashir/Coche henceforth came to be known as Seleucia. This Seleucia, part of the new Twin Cities, became the seat of the metropolitan of the region of Fars (Greek: Persis), with undisputed primacy among the Christian communities east of the Tigris from the mid-fourth century onward.

Nisibis in northern Mesopotamia was, as noted already, an early center of Christianity, attested by the famous late second-century epitaph of Abercius. The evangelization of this key frontier city was vital to the history of Christianity in the Persian Empire as it frequently changed hands in the wars between Rome and both the Parthians and, after 224 CE, the Sasanians. Its population was active in cross-border trade, and many of its citizens, though native Aramaic speakers, would have had a good working knowledge of Greek. The presence of a Christian community at Dura-Europos, a frontier garrison town on the Euphrates, as attested by the remains of a house-church with its famous frescoes (fig. 1.12), provides further evidence of the eastward spread of Christianity along the Euphrates-route into Parthian-held Mesopotamia. The region of Adiabene that once embraced Judaism probably was home to Tatian; a fragment of his *Diatessaron* in Greek was among the papyri recovered from near Tower 18 at Dura-Europos (P.Dura 10, in Welles et al. 1959, 73–74). It would also have provided, through its Jewish colonies, stepping-stones for the evangelization of Mesopotamia and adjacent territories now composing Iran.

Deported Roman Christians

A major factor in the spread of Christianity across the frontier was the forced deportation of conquered cities by the early Sasanian kings. Many of the captives taken by Shapur I in his second and third campaigns (253 and 260) from cities in Syria, Cappadocia, and Cilicia would have been Christians, as the religion was already well established in both the cities and the countryside of these regions. Among those deported in 253 from Antioch was its bishop, Demetrius, along with a large number of the members of his congregation. Their arrival in the Eranshar (the Sasanian Persian Empire) contributed further to its religious diversity. The famous Cologne Mani Codex shows that at least one Judaeo-Christian sect, the Elchasaites, was well established in the marshy areas south of Seleucia-Ctesiphon under the Parthians (Lieu 1992, 33–50). The various strands of teaching that came together in the cosmogonic teaching of Mani also point to the presence of the followers of Marcion and Bardaisan and of some other Gnostic teachers in the area (Welles et al. 1959, 51–69).

Freed from persecution, the Christian captives prospered in their land of captivity. As colonists, they could acquire land in the more remote parts of the Persian Empire at little or no price, and they soon prospered economically (cf.

Chron. Se'ert 2, PO 4.223). Their superior skills gave them a clear edge over autochthonous competition. According to the later Arabic *Chronicle of Se'ert*, the Christian exiles flourished: "The Christians . . . multiplied in Persia, building churches and monasteries. Their number included priests who had been taken prisoner at Antioch. They colonized Gundeshapur and elected Azdoc of Antioch as their bishop, because Demetrius had fallen ill and died of sorrow" (*Chron. Se'ert* 2, PO 4.222) (cf. Peeters 1924, 294–98, 308–14). Being the most organized and cohesive of all the social groupings within the exile Roman community, the Christians undoubtedly were prominent, and as they rose in status, so did the church. For those pagan Roman captives who did not wish to become Persianized (i.e., become Zoroastrians), the Christian church, which at first preserved the use of Greek as a liturgical language, would have been an invaluable and cultural link with the Roman Empire (Lieu 1986, 481–82). Though Syriac would later become dominant within the Persian church, a separate Greek-speaking ecclesiastical hierarchy survived well into the fifth century to give rise to some concern at the Synod of Ctesiphon (*Can.* 21).

Syriac versus Persian

The variety of Christians within the Persian Empire seems to have been understood by Sasanian authorities, as we find them categorized in the Middle Persian inscription of Kirdir, the chief *mobed*,[24] on the ancient monument at Naqsh-i-Rustam near Persepolis (Parseh, near Istakhr) known as the Ka'ba (Cube) of Zoroaster. Line 10 of that inscription (conventionally abbreviated as KKZ) refers to four groups of Christians: (1) *n'cl'y* (= Syriac *nsry'*, i.e., Nazoreans, which most scholars interpret as native Syriac Christians); (2) *klstyd'n* (= Syriac *krystyn'*, i.e., deported Christians of Greek origin, including perhaps Marcionites); (3) *mktky* (= Syriac *mnqd'*, "purifiers," i.e., Judaeo-Christian baptists); and (4) *zndyky* "heretics" (= Arabic *zindik*, i.e., Manichaeans).

Significantly, in the entire corpus of Middle Persian literature this is the only attestation to the use of the term *n'cl'y* to designate Christians. In Syriac literature, which originated in the Christian community in Persia, the term "Nazorean" (*nsry'*) is used as a literary topos based on Acts 24:5, *Nazōraios*, the name by which the Christians were called or liked to be called by their enemies. Besides being known as *krystyn'*, the Christians in Persia and later in Central Asia were also popularly known by the Middle Persian name of *tarsag*, "(God)-fearer" (de Blois 2002, 9). The popularity of the latter is yet

---

24. Zoroastrian cleric.

another attestation to the gradual adoption of the Persian language as the religion established deeper roots in Persian society.

Thanks to the policy of deportation and resettlement, inside and outside Mesopotamia, a Christian community grew up in Fars, the center of early Sasanian power on the Iranian Plateau. The Christian deportees were said to be numerous enough to build two churches at Veh-Ardashir/Coche (*Chron. Se'ert* 2, PO 4.222), one for the "Romans" and the other for the "Karamanians,"[25] and the divine rites were celebrated both in Greek and Syriac (Kettenhofen 1994, 298–99). It is not surprising that this group, geographically distant from Mesopotamia, would, like the Jews in the region, gradually adopt the use of the predominant Middle Persian, the language of the Sasanian administration, as one of its ecclesiastical languages.

Unfortunately, very few examples of Christian texts in Middle Persian have survived. The best known of these are the thirteen fragmentary pages of a Psalter found in Bulayïq in Central Asia by the German expedition to Turfan in 1910 (see chap. 4). Research on these Psalter fragments in Pahlavi by Desmond Durkin-Meistererns (2006, 9–13) shows, importantly, that the text is translated not directly from Syriac versions of the Psalms, but rather from a mixture of Syriac and Greek (i.e., Septuagintal versions). This shows that as late as the seventh century knowledge of Greek was still maintained through its use as a liturgical language.

Unlike texts in Judaeo-Persian, which normally were written in Hebrew letters, the Christians did not employ a Syriac script for writing in Middle Persian, but employed the Pahlavi script instead. By contrast, the Manichaeans in Central Asia used their distinctive script derived from Palmyrene Aramaic, which is very similar to Estrangelo Syriac for writing their texts that had been translated into Middle Persian from Aramaic (P. Wood 2010, 78). This preference for Middle Persian in both language and script by Christians is also shown on some Christian inscriptions found in Kerala in South India. By the end of the century the use of Persian among Christians in Fars was so pervasive that John of Dailam (d. 738), an ascetic from the famous Monastery of Bet 'Abe, had to establish two monasteries, one for the Syriac-speaking monks and one for the Persian-speaking monks, in order to settle a running controversy over which language should be used for reciting the liturgy in the monastic church (§§39–41 [ed. and trans. Brock 1981–1982, 141, 150–51]). With the fall of the Sasanian dynasty in 651, the Church of the East reverted to the use of Syriac as its main ecclesiastical language until it was replaced by East Turkic (written in Syriac script) under the Mongols in the thirteenth century.

25. The inhabitants of Karamania, a Persian province extending as far as the Indian Ocean.

Toleration, Integration, and Persecution

The flow of Roman deportees into the Persian Empire probably slowed down in the reigns of Shapur I's immediate successors. Their military achievements were hardly spectacular. The last decades of the third century saw the consolidation and the social advancement of the exile communities in Persia as the policy of toleration was followed by Hormizd (r. 270–271) and probably Bahram I (r. 271–ca. 274). During the reign of the latter, however, under the guidance of the chief *mobed* Kirdir, Zoroastrianism steadily gained influence at court. The execution of Mani by Bahram II (r. ca. 274–293) in 276, at the instigation of Kirdir, occasioned a persecution that, though chiefly aimed at Mani's followers, adversely affected the Christians because many Manichaeans masqueraded as Christians, and the Sasanian authorities were not always able to distinguish between Manichaeans and the more orthodox Christians (*Chron. Se'ert* 9, PO 4.237–38) (cf. Decret 1979, 125–31).

Among the first Christian victims of this persecution was Candida, a favored concubine of Bahram II, who according to *Chronicle of Se'ert* 9 (PO 4.238) was of Roman origin. The Syriac account of her martyrdom says that she "belonged to those deported from Roman territory; she had been taken captive for (or by) the Persian king" (trans. Brock 1978, 173, 178). More probably her parents were captives, and they brought her up as a Christian in one of the new Sasanian foundations in which the captives had been settled. Her beauty was such that Bahram fell deeply in love with her and was willing to make her his chief concubine. At this, the other wives grew jealous and accused her before the *shahanshah* (king of kings) for her devotion to Christianity. Bahram summoned her and tried to entice her away from her faith by the promise of making her queen, but she stood her ground and suffered martyrdom in a most grotesque manner (Brock 1978, 178–81; Lieu 1986, 483–84).

With the exception of high-profile martyrs such as Candida, who was connected with the Sasanian court, the relationship between the Persian state authority and Christianity seems to have been relatively stable in spite of the grand designs of Kirdir. But things changed completely when Shapur II undertook to reestablish the Persian Empire in its old greatness. He considered the main means for achieving this end to be the raising in importance of the national religion and the war with Rome, winning back the provinces that had yielded to Galerius in 298. For both reasons, Shapur's policy necessitated a direction hostile to Christians. We have two accounts of martyrdom that, according to the dates included, precede the Great Persecution by Shapur, but these were very local affairs. If these dates are correct, and if it is not just a matter of spontaneous outbreaks, as is so often the case, then the famous letter of Constantine to Shapur in Eusebius's *Vita Constantini* (4.8.9) is to be interpreted as more than a gentle warning, and the summary of the letter by Sozomen (*Hist. eccl.* 2.15) may well be accurate.

Persecution under Shapur II

Constantine's meddling in the internal affairs of the Sasanian Empire, however, could not but cast doubt on the loyalty of all the Christians in Persia, be they of Roman or Iranian descent. Some halfhearted attempts at forced conversion were made by the Sasanian government with the encouragement of the Magian clergy and, according to Christian writers, also Jewish leaders. This merely revived the tradition of martyrdom that the Christians had brought with them from the Roman Empire. The news of Constantine's preparation for war against Persia in 337 must have held out hopes of deliverance to some Persian Christians who felt uncertain of their position within a pagan Sasanian Empire (Barnes 1985, 133–36). Aphrahat, the best known of the Christian writers in Syriac at that time and abbot of a monastery within the Eranshar, expressed his explicit hopes for Roman victory in some of his homilies (see sidebar 2.1).

2.1 Aphrahat's Homilies on the Persian/Roman Conflict

(1) Prosperity has come to the people of God, and success awaits the man through whom the prosperity came [i.e., Constantius II]. And disaster threatens the forces which have been marshaled by the efforts of an evil and arrogant man full of boasting [i.e., Shapur II] and misery is reserved for him through whom disaster is stored up. Nevertheless, my beloved, do not complain (in public) of the evil one who has stirred up evil upon many because the times were preordained and the time of their fulfillment has come.

(24) My beloved, as for what I have written to you about, namely that the kingdom of the children of Esau is being kept safe for its Giver, have no doubt about it, as that kingdom [i.e., the Roman Empire] will not be conquered. For a hero whose name is Jesus shall come with his power and his armor shall uphold all the forces of the kingdom. . . .

(25) For even if the forces [i.e., the Persian army] shall go up and triumph, realize that this is the chastisement of God, and if they win they shall be condemned in a righteous judgment. Yet, be assured of this, that the beast will be killed at its appointed time. But you, my brother, implore earnestly at this time for mercy that there may be peace upon the people of God. (Aphrahat, *Demon.* 5.1.24–25; text: PS 1.184–85, 234, and 238 [ET: *NPNF*[2] 13:352 and 361–62, altered])

The suspicion that widespread disloyal sympathies existed among the Christians seems confirmed when Simeon bar Shaba (bp. ca. 329–341), the son of royal silk dyers (*Mart. Simeon*. 7; PS 2.728, 14–17), refused to collect a special war tax from the Christian community after war had broken out between the two empires (see sidebar 2.2).

Simeon was, effectively, the ethnarch of the Christians within the Persian Empire. He declared, however, that he had no temporal power over his folk, and that although the Scriptures enjoin Christians to "render to all their dues: tribute to whom tribute is due," they do not speak of a double tax. His refusal to sign the royal decree was seen as an act of disobedience and treachery for which he and many of his followers suffered martyrdom.

One high-ranking Persian official who was a convert to Christianity in the fourth century was Guhaschtazad the chief eunuch of Shapur II. At the advice of some courtiers, he abandoned the faith and worshiped fire. For this, he earned the displeasure of Simeon bar Shaba, who, before his own execution, however, returned the chief eunuch to the faith. The latter also suffered martyrdom, probably at the site of the Hellenistic Seleucia (Tell Omar). While

---

2.2 Shapur II's "Double Tax" on the Christians

In the year 659 since the reign of Alexander, the year 296 since the Crucifixion, the year 117 of the rule of the Persian kings and the year 31 of the reign of Shapur, son of Hormizd [i.e., Shapur II], after the blessed Constantine had died, Shapur took the opportunity of attacking his sons on account of their virtue and of constantly making rapacious attacks into Roman territory. For this reason he felt particular hatred for the servants of God in his territory and set out to find a reason for the persecution of the believers. He thought of a ploy to oppress the Christians in Persia by double taxes. He wrote the following edict from Bet Huzaie [i.e., Huzistan/Khuzistan] to the officials of Bet Aramaie [i.e., Assuristan]: "As soon as you see this our divine command in this note sent by us, then seize Simeon, the head of the Nazarenes, and do not let him go until he seals a document, taking upon himself the responsibility of raising the paying a double poll tax and double taxes on all the people of the Nazarenes, who live in this, our land of the gods and who dwell in our kingdom. For we, the gods, are suffering the privations of war; they live in joy and contentment. They live in our land, but they are of the same turn of mind as the emperor, our enemy." Thus wrote the King Shapur from Bet Huzaie to the officials of Bet Aramaie. When they had received the king's edict they seized the blessed Simeon bar Shaba, read to him the royal communication and demanded that he should do what was written. (*Narr. Simeon*. 4; PS 2.789 [cf. Braun 1915, 8–9])

confessing his faith, Guhashtazad also declared his unflinching loyalty to the *shahanshah*. His final request was:

> May your mercy order that a herald climb on the wall, walking around with a drum and announcing: Guhaschtazad, who is being executed, is not being executed because he betrayed a state secret or was found out in any other offence, for which the laws would condemn him to death; but he is being executed because he is a Christian. The king ordered him to do his will and worship the sun, but he did not obey this command to deny his God. (*Narr. Simeon.* 58; PS 1.878–79 [cf. Braun 1915, 35; Wiessner 1967, 47–58])

The persecution under Shapur II first gave rise to the beginnings of an extensive martyr literature in Syriac, although some, such as the *acta* of the "bloodless" martyrdom of Mar Aba, might have been originally written in Middle Persian because of the large number of loanwords and *termini technici* in that language found in the Syriac version (Brock 1968, 300). These *acta* by and large followed closely the western models. These exulted in the ultimate triumph of Christianity over the pagan Zoroastrian state, and they also painted the Jews as accusers and denouncers rather than as fellow victims of Sasanian persecution. It is not impossible that the genre developed out of a need to counter the popular accounts of the death (or martyrdom) of Mani. In the Manichaean literature, descriptions of Mani's end are closely based on the pattern of that of Jesus in the Gospels, and many of the issues that led to the martyrdom of Simeon are echoed by those of Mani. As Sebastian Brock has put it succinctly: "The relationship between the deaths of Jesus and Simeon . . . is a quite different one, and it may well be that the rather surprising emphasis on this parallelism (rather than just *imitatio*) is in part, at least, due to conscious Christian rivalry of Mani's martyrdom" (1968, 303–4).

The Synods of 410 and 424

Shapur II died in 379, and the position of the church in the Persian Empire improved steadily under his successors, especially during the reign of Yazdgird I (r. 399–421), to whom the Zoroastrians would give the epithet "the Sinner" because he was alleged to have had a Jewish wife and was tolerant toward the Christians (Asmussen 1983, 940). The peace enabled the Church of the East to convene the first of a series of important synods at Seleucia-Ctesiphon in 410 at the instigation of the Roman envoy, Marutha of Maipherkat (bp. ca. 399–420). It accepted as orthodox the canons and decrees of the important Council of Nicaea. Isaac of Seleucia (bp. 399–410) was now addressed as "Grand Metropolitan and Head of Bishops," though not yet under his later and better-known title, Catholicos. Though the letter of the Western bishops in the acts of the so-called Synod of Isaac, presided over by Mar Isaac at Seleucia in 410, was signed by the bishop of Antioch and his suffragans, there was no claim of jurisdiction by Antioch on the Persian church. By 424, benefiting from another lull in Romano-Persian conflicts, another synod was convened, in which the "right of appeal" to the West was rejected. Though the canons and decrees of the ecumenical councils held in the Roman Empire were accepted, the gathered bishops were scornful of the lack of support and care shown to their coreligionists in times of persecution. The primacy of the see of Seleucia-Ctesiphon came to the fore, and to all intents and purposes the Persian church was autocephalous after the Synod of 424 held at Markabta (see chap. 4).

Barsauma and the School of Nisibis

In 363 the key frontier city of Nisibis was surrendered by the Roman emperor Jovian to the Persians by treaty, and among those who moved across the new frontier to Edessa via Amida was the Christian poet and theologian Ephraem. At Edessa he was said to have established a theological school that was nicknamed School of the Persians because among its students were a large number of refugees from Nisibis and other occupied territories. The school later acquired notoriety as a hotbed of "Nestorianism" and was persecuted by the "Monophysites" who had gained control of Edessa. By the time Zeno ordered its closure in 489, most of the school's staff and students had already fled across the border to Nisibis. There, as already noted, the school flourished. Soon Nisibis became the primary seat of theological and philosophical learning of the Church of the East in Persia.

The surviving statutes of the School of Nisibis reveal an austere regime for its students, and it is particularly interesting that they were not allowed to act as paid guides for cross-frontier travelers, to avoid the odium of espionage or smuggling (Vööbus 1961, 72–89). Under the leadership of Narsai, and of Abraham d'Bet Rabban (d. ca. 568/9), the school remained a major center of both classical and Christian learning for several centuries and provided training for many leaders of the Persian church, including Mar Aba. It was largely through the proficiency of its students in both Greek and Syriac that a substantial amount of Greek philosophical and scientific learning was passed on to the Islamic world (Vööbus 1965, 57–121).

At the "Synod of Isaac" in 410, the East Syrian metropolitan province of Nisibis was established as one of its five provinces and ranked second after the province of Elam. Its jurisdiction was initially confined to the five regions surrendered by Jovian in 363 (Arzun, Qardū, Bet Zabdaï, Bet Rahimaï, and

Bet Moksaye), and it remained an East Syrian metropolitan province without interruption between the fifth and the fourteenth centuries (Fiey 1977, 38–39; Wilmshurst 2000, 40–41). One of the first holders of the see of Nisibis was Barsauma (bp. 435–ca. 495), a refugee from the Byzantine Empire who came to prominence when he realized that he could exploit the precarious position of the Christian church in Persia to his personal advantage. Babowai (cathol. 457–484) entered into a secret correspondence with the bishops of the Roman Empire in the hope of getting help from the Roman government to put pressure on the *shahanshah* to lessen the persecution of Christians. Even more unwisely, Babowai made slighting remarks about the Persian government in his letter, which was sent hidden in a walking stick by a secret courier. However, Barsauma, who had gained so much of the *shahanshah*'s confidence as to be given the post of *marzban* of Bet Arabaye (i.e., the region of Nisibis), had the courier arrested and informed the *shahanshah* of the letter's contents. Although he was not made catholicos in Babowai's place after the latter's deposition at the Council of Bet Lapat in 484 and his subsequent execution by the order of the *shahanshah*, Barsauma played a major role in the Persianization of the church (Gero 1981, 33–41). The process was a deliberate one and is reflected in the introduction of a canon permitting clerical marriage, as celibacy was an ideal of Christian monasticism that was particularly offensive to the Zoroastrian clergy.[26]

Mar Aba and the Sasanian Church

The patriarchate of Mar Aba (cathol. 540–552) highlights many of the issues and problems concerning a Christian church that was now well established within the Persian Empire and was winning converts from Zoroastrianism. Aba himself once had excelled in his zeal for the Zoroastrian religion. The story of Mar Aba's conversion (see sidebar 2.3) from a haughty Persian grandee to a humble follower of Christ is a vignette of East Syrian hagiography made famous also through the influential work of Walter Bauer (1964, 27–29; ET 1971, 22–24) on orthodoxy and heresy in the early church.

After his conversion, Aba apprenticed himself to a Christian who, like him, had been holder of a governmental post, and he later went on to study theology at the School of Nisibis. More significantly, he traveled widely in the eastern Roman Empire as a pilgrim "to see the places of the Saints." He remained for a number of years at Constantinople. Later, at Alexandria, he

---

26. This canon of Barsauma was appealed to by a patriarch of the Church of the East in the early 1970s with fatal consequences. Mar Eshai Shimun was assassinated by an enraged member of his family in San Jose, California, on November 6, 1975 (Baum and Winkler 2003, 148–49).

2.3 Mar Aba's Conversion

Mar Aba was originally a pagan and exceeded most pagans in his (devotion to) paganism. He was also (educated?) in Persian literature. As he was very well schooled in literature, important people of his region saw that he was learned and quick-witted and persuaded him to become one of them, so that they could make him distinguished in the service of the state and in worldly status. As the blessed one listened to them, they made him Arzabed; he went in and out of their houses and was respected by many. He was a hard, confirmed pagan; he scorned the Christians and despised the sons of the Covenant. But when he was crossing the Tigris, Jesus threw His net over him and caught him in it. For the Lord usually acts thus, as He did to Saint Paul, who was on his way to Damascus to pursue His disciples, to chain them and to hand them over to death. He transformed him from a persecutor to one persecuted; he was chained, suffered and died for Him. The same happened to this saint, for when he was going to cross from the village of Chale to his home and was sitting with others in the ship in order to cross the Tigris, Jesus sent him a scholar [Syriac 'skwly'] as a teacher, a strict ascetic, a gentle, humble man, modest and humble in appearance, by the name of Joseph, with the second name Moses. On his fishing-hook he had placed the sweet and pleasing food of spiritual teaching, to return the saint from death to life.

When the blessed one was sitting on the ship to cross over (the Tigris), the scholar climbed aboard as well, to cross with them [i.e., Mar Aba and other passengers]. When the saint saw his dress and took him for a son of the Covenant [i.e., a Christian], he hit him, took the bag which he was carrying, threw it on to the shore and forced him to get out. The scholar said not a word, but got out and sat down on the bank of the Tigris. But after the saint and his companions had departed and were a little distant from the shore, by God's providence a strong wind blew towards them; like a zealous servant the Tigris became stormy and its waves rose against them as it roared at the saint, because he had struck and scorned Christ's disciples and prevented him crossing. Fear overcame him and he ordered the ship to be steered back to the shore. After he had landed and got out, the wind settled and there was a great calm. So he got in the ship again and the scholar got in as well and sat down with them in the ship, and once again the saint rose against him and forced him to disembark. And when they had gone a little way, once again the wind awoke against this pagan imprudence, which did not acknowledge the creator of the universe, and it became stronger than before. And again the saint and his companions returned and came back to the shore. That excellent scholar however was sitting on the bank of the Tigris.

When the saint looked at his dress which was chaste and (not) brightly-colored (?), he had doubts about whether he was a son of Christ's covenant, or rather a Marcionite or a Jew and he asked him: "Are you a Jew?" He said: "Yes." Again he said: "Are you a Christian?" He said: "Yes." Again he said: "Do you venerate the Messiah?" He said "Yes." The saint became very angry about the scholar's answer and he said: "How can you be Jew, Christian, and Messiah-worshipper?" For, according to local practice he called Marcionites Christians. The scholar said: "I am a Jew in secret. I worship the living God and believe in His Son, Jesus Christ, and in the Holy Spirit. I flee the service of idols and all impurity. I am a Christian in truth, not like the Marcionites who mislead and call themselves Christians. For Christ is a Greek word which means Messiah in Syrian. And if you ask me 'Do you venerate the Messiah?' indeed I venerate Him in truth and I flee all evil for the sake of true life."

When the saint heard that, he rejoiced in his spirit. He recognized the wisdom and humility of the scholar, Christ's disciple. Once more he got in the boat, sat down and the scholar got in too. And as the saint stopped despising the scholar, the wind stopped also, the waves of the Tigris grew calm; they crossed over and reached land. When both had got out, the scholar said: "What harm did it do to you to have me travel with you?" The saint was surprised at his calmness and was sorry that he abused him. He stepped up to him, fell down before him and said: "I beg you, by the living and true God, forgive me this sin I did to you." The scholar said: "The Lord commands us Christians to harbor anger for no-one, nor to repay evil with evil." Thereupon they stepped up to each other, greeted each other and separated. (*Vita de Mar Aba*, ed. Bedjan 1895, 210.5–214.9; cf. Braun 1915, 188–90, altered)

met Cosmas Indicopleustes (fl. ca. 550), the author of the famous Christian topography. Cosmas knew Aba as "Patrikios," the Greek version of Cosmas's name (Labourt 1904, 165–66). Aba/Patrikios returned to Nisibis, and, finding the church rent by internal division, he at first desired to escape to the desert but was prevented from doing so and soon found himself elected catholicos (*Vita de Mar Aba*, ed. Bedjan 1895, 216.18–226.8).

The Persian church under the rule of Mar Aba was an impressive organization. By 410, when the synod of Seleucia met under the auspices of Marutha of Maipherkat,[27] there were already six metropolitan sees and over thirty bishops. By the time the Sasanian dynasty was violently ended by the Arab armies in the seventh century, there were ten metropolitan sees (including the patriarchate) and ninety-six bishoprics (Brock 1982, 3; J. Walker 2006, 94–102). One of the more major problems confronting the new catholicos was that converts from Zoroastrianism carried over with them Zoroastrian marriage customs. The prominence of this topic in the sixth-century synods indicates how central a problem it was at that time; the earliest treatise of canon law, by

27. Maipherkat: Greek *Martyropolis* (because of the numerous relics deposited in the city by Marutha and others); modern Silvan.

Catholicos Aba, is also devoted to the subject (Brock 1982, 5n14). The increasing success of the Persian church in winning converts from Zoroastrianism earned Mar Aba the hatred of the Zoroastrian hierarchy, especially of the high priest, the *mobed* (*Vita de Mar Aba*, ed. Bedjan 1895, 236.9–237.11). Mar Aba was accused of being a friend of the Byzantine emperor, for winning converts, and, ironically, for persecuting Christians who had adopted certain Zoroastrian social customs. It is interesting that the reigning *shahanshah*, Chosroes Anushirvan (r. 531–579), who was on good terms with the catholicos, did his best to protect the victim from the zeal of the Zoroastrian clergy. Indeed, on more than one occasion the *shahanshah* issued specific orders that Christians were not to be molested by Magians. A consequence of this tension between the *shahanshah* and the Zoroastrian authorities was that martyrdoms were much more apt to occur when a shah had to rely on Magian support for his position (Brock 1982, 6). Chosroes refused to execute Mar Aba but had him exiled to Azerbaijan for fear of the political consequences his execution would have, such being the strength of the Christian community in the Eranshar (Persian Empire). When there was a rebellion against the *shahanshah*, he requested that Mar Aba write to pacify the Christians of the disaffected area, such being the prestige and authority of the catholicos. When peace was achieved, Mar Aba was released to die in peace, but not before he had won further converts from the Lakhmids of Hira (near Najaf) who were important Arab allies of the Eranshar (*Vita de Mar Aba*, ed. Bedjan 1895, 239.6–270.6; cf. Labourt 1904, 187–91; Hutter 2003, 167–73; P. Wood 2010, 245–55).

The Spread of Persian Christianity

The growing confidence of the Christian church in Persia is also reflected in its desire to conduct mission outside the confines of Sasanian power. Attempts to convert the Hephthalite Huns who threatened the eastern boundaries of the Eranshar made a tentative start under Mar Aba (*Vita de Mar Aba*, ed. Bedjan 1895, 266.15–267.12), and by the mid-seventh century there were "Nestorian" metropolitan sees at Samarkand (Samarkand, Uzbekistan) and Merv (Erk Kala, Turkmenistan) in Central Asia (see chap. 4). A handful of missionaries of the Church of the East even went west. A well-documented life of a late Persian saint who gave his name to St. Ives, a village just outside Cambridge in England, was Iba(s) (?) (Latin *Ivo*) of Asitania (*sic*) (Edgington 1985, 6–13).

By the late Sasanian period, both "Jacobites" (i.e., Monophysites) and Melkites had found the Persian Empire to be a fruitful field of mission. Shirin, the most beloved of the wives of Chosroes Anushirvan, was a "Jacobite," and she lavished gifts on the site of the shrine of Saint Sergius at Resafa in Roman

Venty Cridland/Wikimedia Commons

Fig. 2.4. Church of St. Sergius, Resafa

Syria (Fowden 1999, 136–41). However, missionary efforts by these two major Christian sects were too little too late, as the "Nestorian" Persian church was too well established by then in Iraq and Iran. The sudden collapse of the Sasanian Empire in the seventh century, however, marked the end of the growth of the Christian church beyond the Euphrates, especially in the heart of Iran, where Christian communities survived only in small pockets. In Iraq, however, Christian communities remained a major semiautonomously governed religious group (*millet*) under Ottoman rule, and their discovery by the major Western churches, which they nostalgically named the "Assyrian" Christians (because of their numerical strength in areas such as Kirkuk, Nineveh, and Mosul in northern Iraq, former Assuristan), has led to an important theological and liturgical reexamination of the roots of Christendom.

3

The Caucasus

CHRISTOPHER HAAS

Introduction

The Greek geographer Strabo (64 BCE–ca. 21 CE) describes Dioscurias, a bustling port on the eastern end of the Black Sea in Colchis, thus:

> [It is] the common emporium of the tribes who are situated (in the mountains) above it and in its vicinity; at any rate, seventy tribes come together in it, though others, who care nothing for the facts, actually say three hundred. All speak different languages because of the fact that, by reason of their obstinacy and ferocity, they live in scattered groups and without any dealings with one another. (*Geogr.* 11.2.16)

Strabo, who wrote his monumental *Geographica* during the reign of Augustus (r. 31 BCE–14 CE), was a native of nearby Pontus. Some fifty years later, Pliny the Elder (ca. 23–79 CE) informs us that in order to conduct business in this polyglot Colchian port, Roman merchants employed no fewer than 130 translators (*Nat.* 6.5).

Dioscurias (Sukhumi) stood in the shadow of the westernmost edge of the Caucasus Mountains. It is no wonder, therefore, that later Arab geographers

111

called the Caucasus *Jabal al-Alsuns*, the "Mountain of Tongues." The Caucasus, the highest mountain range in Europe, was home to numerous tribal/ethnic groups in Antiquity. The southern slopes of the Caucasus open onto a verdant region that extends to the south as far as the Lesser Caucasus and into the Armenian Highlands.

In Antiquity the region between the Greater and Lesser Caucasus was divided into three distinct kingdoms, whose nomenclature changed over the centuries. Beginning at the Euxine (Black Sea) in the west and proceeding east to what the Greeks called the Hyrcanian Ocean (Caspian Sea), there were the kingdoms of Colchis/Lazica, Kartli/Iberia, and Aran/Albania. The first two of these kingdoms today largely compose the Republic of Georgia. Aran/Albania corresponds most closely to modern Azerbaijan. Throughout the Classical Era Aran/Albania rarely achieved a status more independent than that of a vassal state, first to Armenia and then to Sasanian Persia. The two Georgian kingdoms, while often under the strong influence (if not outright control) of their larger imperial neighbors, were able to forge individual cultural identities that, in Late Antiquity, were shaped by their conversion to Christianity.

Armenia, by contrast, was situated in a far more strategically desirable position vis-à-vis both of its imperial neighbors. Armenia was located south of the Lesser Caucasus, and in classical times it constituted a lofty plateau, scored by valleys and numerous ridges, that occupied the high ground between Kurdistan and Iran to the south and east, and the Anatolian Plateau to the west. This placed Armenia between the wealthy cities of the Roman provinces of Anatolia and the rich heartland of the Parthian and, later, Sasanian empires. While Armenia was regarded by its inhabitants as an overall geographical unit, the rugged terrain of this upland region fragmented Armenia into many subregions that resisted attempts at political unification. Armenia possessed very few urban settlements and cult centers. With its continental climate, Armenia bakes in an intense summer heat and is prone to heavy snows in winter. Agriculture was limited to dispersed river valleys, and the uplands were given over to a pastoral economy, mostly cattle breeding.

Geography

To the north, Colchis/Lazica and Kartli/Iberia shared numerous cultural characteristics. However, their distinct political histories were, to a large degree, dictated by their very dissimilar geographies, which continue to have a profound effect on modern Georgia. The western region enjoys a warm, Mediterranean climate that is conducive to all manner of citrus fruits, tea, figs, and grapes.

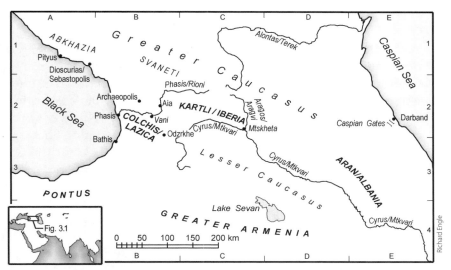

Fig. 3.1. Map of the Caucasus

In Antiquity the indigenous peoples generally shunned the coastline, which tended to be marshy. Apart from Greek colonies at Bathis (Batumi), Pityus (Bichvinta), Phasis (Poti), and Dioscurias, the major indigenous settlements in Colchis/Lazica were located on higher ground farther to the east at Vani (ancient name unknown), Aia (Kutaisi), and at Archaeopolis (Nokalakevi). This entire western region was separated from Kartli/Iberia to the east by the Likhis Kedi (see fig. 3.2), a heavily wooded steep ridge that averages just over 1000 m. There was only a handful of passes across this barrier.

After crossing the Likhis Kedi, one enters into eastern Georgia (Kartli/Iberia), which has a somewhat drier, more continental climate, as it is shielded from moist winds blowing from the west and the north. This has created a nearly perfect setting for viticulture and the growing of cereal grains. Topographically, Kartli/Iberia opens out to the southeast, toward modern Azerbaijan and Iran. As a consequence, this region has long tempted Persian monarchs, from the Sasanian *shahanshah* (king of kings) Shapur I (r. 240–270 CE) in the late third century to the Safavid king Shāh ʿAbbās I (r. 1587–1629), who reputedly slew over sixty thousand Georgians during campaigns in 1614–1615.

Cultural Identities

The rugged landscape of the south Caucasus divided the ancient Georgian kingdoms into numerous subregions, each with its own distinct cultural traditions, including cuisine, dialect, and architecture. There is, however, considerable evidence of the movement of people and goods between east and west even as early as the Bronze Age. Moreover, long before the medieval Bagratid dynasty unified the country politically in the eleventh century, Christianity provided an underlying cultural foundation for the emerging nation. The critically formative years of this common Georgian Christian identity were from the third through the seventh centuries, roughly the same period when Armenia underwent a similar crystallization of its own culture. At a time when the neighboring empires of Rome and Sasanian Persia were experiencing internal upheavals and invasions from external enemies (often from each other), the small kingdoms of Colchis/Lazica and Kartli/Iberia were experiencing a cultural efflorescence brought about by a common catalyst, Christianity. By the early seventh century, these kingdoms in the south Caucasus shared a recognizably Georgian style of Christianity that included hagiography, liturgy, hymnody, sacred architecture, decorative arts, monasticism, and ecclesiastical organization. These manifold expressions of Georgian Christianity provided the material out of which emerged a sense of common Georgian identity, enabling Georgians to endure a succession of invasions and imperial masters ranging from Sasanian Persians and Arabs to Mongols and Ottoman Turks.

A similar process took place to the south in Armenia. Like the dozens of kingdoms (*túatha*) of early medieval Ireland or the city-states of classical Greece, Armenia was characterized by a general sociocultural unity without an overarching political structure. This political fragmentation mirrored the fragmentation of the landscape. Throughout most of Antiquity Armenia was governed by a king whose weak central authority was resisted by powerful local independent warlords (*nakharars*). The Armenian monarchy, more often than not, was imposed and propped up by one of the two powerful external empires, creating considerable tensions with local princes. The feudal military structure that predominated in Armenia was far more similar to Persia, Macedonia, or medieval Europe than to the state-sponsored armies of the classical *polis* or larger Mediterranean empires—that is, heavily armed cavalry drawn largely from the noble class and their retainers, supported to a lesser degree by foot soldiers drawn from the peasantry. Consequently, Armenia's deeply rooted culture, which embraced Christianity by the fourth century, survived the kingdom's partition into extinction in 387 and the final abolition of the Armenian monarchy in Persarmenia in 428.

Strategic Importance

Besides the close connection with Armenia, the Georgian kingdoms themselves assumed a growing strategic importance in Late Antiquity. In the third and fourth centuries the normal patterns of nomadic life among Central Asian steppe peoples became disrupted, initiating a series of migrations that eventually led to the Gothic invasion of the Roman Empire in the 370s, and an even more serious incursion of Hunnic peoples in the fifth century. In the West, Attila (r. 433–453) led a large Hunnic confederation in a wide-ranging campaign of terror and plunder that came to an end only with the untimely death of the charismatic leader in 453. The Sasanian Persians faced an equally serious Hunnic threat, leading to a disastrous battle near modern Herat in 484 that claimed the life of the *shahanshah* Peroz I (r. 459–484) when he was defeated by the Hephthalite Huns.

The Caucasus, though a formidable barrier, was not impenetrable. Two passes from the north had been recognized for their strategic importance as far back as the Achaemenid Persians and Alexander the Great (r. 336–323 BCE). Almost in the center of the mountain chain, the Dariel Pass (2379 m) crosses near to the foot of Mount Kazbek (5033 m). The Dariel Pass connects the valley of the Terek River (ancient Alontas) in the north to that of the Aragvi River (ancient Aragos) to the south. Far to the east, the Caucasus almost reaches the Caspian Sea at modern Derbent in Dagestan. Under the Sasanian king Khusro I Anushirvan (r. 531–579 CE), the Persians erected fortifications nearly 40 km long between the mountains and the sea, effectively blocking a major invasion route from the northern steppes. These massive ramparts, with their thirty watchtowers, became known as the Caspian Gates (see fig. 3.1). The name "Derbent" itself derives from a Persian word signifying "closed gate." Although there were other passes through the Caucasus, the ability to hold the Dariel Pass and the Caspian Gates was considered crucial to the security of both the Byzantine and Sasanian Empires, thereby contributing to the ongoing interest of both in maintaining hegemony over the south Caucasian kingdoms.

In addition, once the center of gravity within the Roman Empire shifted decisively to the East with the inauguration by Constantine I (r. 306–337) of a new capital on the Bosphorus in 330, the east-west passage through the Georgian kingdoms assumed greater importance. Both Byzantium and Persia recognized that possession of ports on the Black Sea had the potential of endangering the security of Constantinople. At the very least, Persian armies in Lazica and Armenia could launch attacks on Trebizond and Roman provinces in the territory of Pontus. These new strategic considerations prompted a protracted war between the two empires over the control of Lazica, which engulfed the small kingdom throughout much of the 540s and 550s. Invasion could just as easily be launched from the Byzantine side. During the 620s the emperor Heraclius I (r. 610–641) used the region of the south Caucasus both for recruitment and as a staging point in his successful campaigns against

Khusro II Parwez (r. 590–628), a series of campaigns that so weakened the Sasanian Empire that, in 636, it easily succumbed to the Arab armies of Khālid ibn al-Walīd (592–642) and Sa'd ibn Abi Waqqas (595–664).

Georgia

Before Christianity

COLCHIS

The western Georgian kingdom of Colchis had long been in contact with the cultures of the eastern Mediterranean. Artisans in the south Caucasus were among the first in the Near East to alloy copper and tin to make bronze. Likewise, iron-smelting furnaces in Colchis dating from as early as the middle of the second millennium BCE support the common belief among classical authors that ironworking was discovered in this region. However, it was in the eighth and seventh centuries BCE that Colchis began to exploit its resources

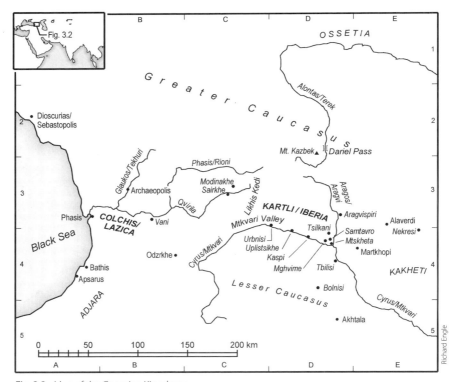

Fig. 3.2. Map of the Georgian Kingdoms

in gold with the concomitant development of the art of the goldsmith. Excavations at Vani, a major cultic and political center, have revealed scores of exquisitely fashioned golden grave goods, unmatched in the technical skill of their relief work and finely granulated gold decoration. It is no wonder that the Greeks were attracted by the wealth of Colchis, which became, in Greek legend, the fabled kingdom of Aeëtes and Medea, guardians of the golden fleece sought by Jason and the Argonauts "at the furthest limits of sea and earth" (Apollonius, *Argon.* 2.417). The possibilities for trade with the wealthy Colchian kingdom, as well as the ever-present desire for agricultural land, led adventurous Greeks to establish city-states scattered all along the Black Sea coast from Abkhazia in the north to Adjara in the south.

By the fourth and third centuries BCE Colchis had broken up into a handful of tiny kingdoms, each ruled by petty dynasts called *sceptukhs*. Only in the early portion of the first century BCE was the former Colchian kingdom in western Georgia drawn permanently into the wider Greco-Roman world. The ambitious king of Pontus, Mithridates VI (r. 120–63 BCE), seized western Georgia in 83 BCE as part of his much broader expansionist campaign to create a powerful counterweight to Rome's growing influence in the eastern Mediterranean. During the last of Mithridates's three wars against the Roman Republic, Georgia was invaded by Pompey the Great (106–48 BCE), who even campaigned across the Likhis Kedi and briefly conquered the eastern Georgian kingdom of Kartli/Iberia in 65 BCE. As part of the broader settlement of the East by Octavian (the future Augustus) after his decisive victory at Actium in 31, Colchis came under the supervision of the Roman provincial governor of Pontus. Outright annexation of the Colchian coastline occurred in 64 CE, and it is during this period that major Roman forts were established at Apsarus (modern Gonio, 14 km south of Batumi) and at the former Greek colony of Dioscurias, renamed "Sebastopolis." For the next three centuries this region saw a rich interplay of cultural, economic, and social influences, as Romans along the coastline traded and interacted with upland tribal groups.

KARTLI/IBERIA

While the Colchian kingdom disintegrated and eventually was absorbed into the Roman Empire, these same centuries saw the increasing consolidation of a stronger kingdom to the east in Kartli/Iberia. Strabo describes in glowing terms the prosperity of Iberia: "The plain of the Iberians is inhabited by people who are rather inclined to farming and to peace," and the kingdom "is so well built up in respect to cities and farmsteads that their roofs are tiled, and their houses as well as their marketplaces and other public buildings are constructed with architectural skill" (*Geogr.* 11.3.1–3). The central core of the kingdom

Yftach Herzog

Fig. 3.3. Mtskheta at Confluence of Mtkvari (left) and Aragvi (right) Rivers

grew up at the confluence of the Mtkvari and Aragvi Rivers. Over time, an urban center developed on the northern shore of the Mtkvari at Mtskheta, and by the first century CE Mtskheta had emerged as the Iberian capital. The development of a palace complex at Samtavro on the city's northwestern edge confirmed the growing influence both of the city and the Iberian monarchy.

The climate of the south Caucasus was conducive to many forms of agriculture, and the remains of numerous iron plows and irrigation systems suggest intensive cultivation of cereal grains and vegetables. Viticulture had long been one of the region's dominant forms of agriculture, perhaps as early as 4000 BCE. Throughout Georgia, archaeologists have discovered the remains of stone and wooden presses as well as huge double-walled clay jars known in Georgian as *kvevri*. Dating as early as the eighth and seventh centuries BCE, these *kvevri* were set into the ground to aid in fermentation and storage and on occasion were later reused as sarcophagi. In addition, the rearing of livestock was an integral part of the ancient Georgian economy, reflected not only by numerous skeletal remains but also by the figures of bulls in classical Georgian art.

While Strabo and other writers depict a land dotted with prosperous farmsteads, both Georgian kingdoms possessed nucleated settlements that certainly could be considered real towns, if not cities. Western Georgia appears to have experienced true urbanization first, not only at the Greek colonies along the Black Sea but also at the Colchian sites of the interior. Kartli/Iberia likewise boasted noteworthy towns by the first and second centuries CE. Besides the collection of settlements that aggregated into Mtskheta, the Mtkvari Valley also saw the growth of towns at Urbnisi, Uplistsikhe, Kaspi, and Odzrkhe. These towns flourished as market centers for their surrounding hinterland, and as production and trade emporia for local artisans and merchants.

During the general weakening of the Parthian Empire in the late first and second centuries CE, Roman contacts with the kings of Iberia reached their highpoint with the Romans seeking to employ the Iberian king as a tool against the Parthian client state of Armenia. High-level notices of friendship and alliance commemorated by royal inscriptions are echoed by more prosaic, but no less important, grave goods of the Iberian nobility, which frequently include silver dishes bearing imperial portraits and Roman gold coins bestowed as tokens of honor. Given patterns of Christianization elsewhere, one might expect that such a period of sustained contact between Rome and a distant kingdom would also be the most likely time for the introduction of a minor religion from Rome's Eastern provinces. As it turned out, Christianity took firm root in Iberia only when the eastern Georgian kingdom came under the political and cultural domination of Sasanian Persia.

From Strabo and from the medieval Georgian royal chronicle known as the *Kartlis Tskhovreba* (*History/Life of Kartli*), edited by the eleventh-century chronicler Leonti Mroveli, it is possible to discern the broad outline of Georgian society in the centuries just prior to the introduction of Christianity. Below the king stood a class of dynastic nobility, known in the sources as the *kartlosids*. Often related to the king, the *kartlosids* frequently chafed under royal authority. To counterbalance the threat posed by this aristocracy, the kings promoted the interests of the lesser nobility, known as the *aznaur*, who originated from the class of landowners, free warriors, and clan chiefs. It is from this class of *aznaur* that the kings selected *eristavis*, who functioned as dukes administering various provinces. Priests composed an additional high-ranking social group in Strabo's enumeration. Little is known of this priestly class, but priests seem to have exercised some judicial functions and occasionally were used as emissaries to foreign powers.

RELIGION

It is impossible to connect the Georgian priestly class with any one particular pre-Christian religious cult in Iberia. Nonetheless, the Georgian kingdoms served as a crucible for religious beliefs and practices of indigenous origin with those coming from both the Greco-Roman West and from the Persian East (Charachidzé 1968; Van Esbroeck 1990). In religion, as in virtually every other aspect of culture, Georgia displayed its dynamic role as a crossroads and as a cultural innovator. An early section of the *Kartlis Tskhovreba* credits Iberia's founding king, Parvanaz I (r. ca. 299–ca. 234 BCE), with the establishment in Mtskheta of a cult dedicated to the god Armazi, who thereafter became the head of the Georgian pantheon. Unfortunately, aside from these textual notices and the toponym of the fortress/acropolis of ancient Mtskheta, there is no archaeological evidence that would corroborate this cult. The same holds true for the cult of a fertility god, Zaden, established on a mountain northeast of Mtskheta by King Parnajom (r. ca. 109–ca. 90 BCE). In both cases, these gods have been identified by scholars with the remnants of earlier Hittite deities or with aspects of the Zoroastrian cult. Indeed, Armazi is frequently identified with the chief Zoroastrian deity, Ahura-Mazda. Even though definitive epigraphic or archaeological information about these gods is lacking, one noteworthy aspect of both cults is the assumption, or even the expectation, within the Georgian texts that the establishment of a new religious cult is the prerogative of the Iberian monarch. This, of course, creates a pattern followed in the fourth century by Mirian III's adoption of Christianity (see below).

Both Georgian kingdoms possessed sites that have been identified as cult centers by archaeologists. In Colchis the primary function of Vani evolved from its status as a royal and administrative center to one given over largely to cult activities. In its last phase of occupation, from the third to first centuries BCE, temple complexes, stone altars, and sacrificial pits predominate. Exquisitely fashioned images of Zeus, Pan, and Nike indicate that, at least in this last phase, Greek cults were the primary forms of religious expression at Vani. This predilection for Hellenized deities accords with excavated finds from other Colchian sites such as Phasis and Pityus. Phasis, at the mouth of the Rioni River, was the site of a temple to Apollo that attracted worshipers throughout the Classical Era. By the time that Colchis was absorbed into the Roman Empire, religion in western Georgia was overwhelmingly Hellenic (Tsetskhladze 1994; 1998; Lordkipanidze 2000).

Fig. 3.4. Uplistsikhe, Overlooking Mtkvari River

More indigenous forms of worship emerge from archaeological sites in Iberia, especially at the rock-hewn city of Uplistsikhe. From the time of the city's foundation in the early Iron Age (tenth/ninth centuries BCE), temples are the most significant structures on the site. In the four hundred years between 200 BCE and 200 CE dozens of temples were created or modified from previous buildings. Many of these cult structures are oriented toward the rising sun in the east, and some were designed to be open to the sky, leading scholars to conclude that the city's principal gods were solar and lunar deities. Many of the square temples also have fire-altars that suggest parallels with Zoroastrian cult places. However, there are enough discrepancies between these temples and the canonical fire-temple from Persia (e.g., one central column instead of the standard four columns) that the deity and its cult probably represented a local solar god. The sheer number and prominence of Uplistsikhe's sanctuaries suggest that the site had become a sacred center during the immediate pre-Christian period. The long history of worship at Uplistsikhe indicates that it may have functioned as a rival to the royal center at Mtskheta and, perhaps, helped to inspire the Iberian kings to develop their own cult centers in the capital (Khimshiashvili 1999; Sanikidze 2004; 2009).

In addition to a lively bestiary of animal imagery in early Georgian art (including stags, bulls, and horses), plant motifs are also quite common, especially grapevines and a local variant of the "tree of life" theme. The religious significance of viticulture in the south Caucasus can be seen as early as the second millennium BCE in the frequent depiction of drinking scenes and grape clusters on gold and silver goblets and even silver-encased grapevine cuttings. It also accounts for the widespread popularity of the cult of Dionysus in both Colchis and Iberia during the immediate pre-Christian period. This Georgian preoccupation with viticulture also blends easily into other plant motifs, notably that of the tree of life. Indeed, sacred trees are often depicted surrounded by grapevines. One of the most notable instances of this is a gilded silver bowl from the eastern Georgian region of Kakheti. The central image on the bowl is a tree with flowering branches extending in opposite directions. Birds and various small animals all find shelter among its branches. The edge of the bowl is decorated with grapevines, at one point harvested by two men holding a basket and a knife.

JUDAISM

One final element of the pre-Christian religious setting of the Georgian kingdoms is the presence of Jewish communities, and the deep respect accorded to Judaism, especially in the eastern kingdom of Iberia. While the existence of Jewish communities in the Greco-Colchian cities of the Black Sea littoral is not at all surprising, a Jewish presence in Iberia may at first seem unexpected. However, the trade corridor along the Mtkvari River may account for Jewish settlement in the Hellenistic and Roman periods. Georgian literary sources (notably the *Kartlis Tskhovreba*) claim that Jews began to settle the region in sizable numbers as early as the catastrophe of Nebuchadnezzar's siege of Jerusalem in the sixth century BCE. Another passage attributes Jewish immigration to the effects of the Roman destruction of Jerusalem in 70 CE. Archaeology confirms the presence of Jews in Iberia, notably at Urbnisi and at Mtskheta. The necropolis of Samtavro at Mtskheta has revealed two late-antique epitaphs of Jews. These epitaphs, as well as formulae possibly attributable to Jewish graves, suggest that the entire southern part of the Samtavro necropolis was given over to Jewish burials. This section of the necropolis is adjacent to the portion reserved for Iberian royal burials, suggesting that the Jewish community, a community of resident foreigners, had come under the patronage of the Iberian monarchy (Babalikashvili 1970; Ivashchenko 1980). Further testimony to the Jewish community of Mtskheta may be found in the *Martyrdom and Passion of St. Eustace of Mtskheta*, a medieval work that probably derives from a sixth-century source. In this text a Persian youth is depicted attending services in a local synagogue as part of his quest to find spiritual insight. The synagogue services are portrayed in such a way as to ascribe to them a status equal to those of Christian churches or Zoroastrian fire-temples (Mgaloblishvili and Gagoshidze 1998; C. Lerner 2003).

Jews figure prominently in Georgian traditions regarding the establishment of Christianity in Kartli/Iberia. Among the earliest is the story that the kingdom's most holy relic, the robe worn by Christ during his passion, was brought from Jerusalem by pious Jews who kept it within the Jewish community at Mtskheta. The later *vita* of St. Nino, the evangelizer of the Iberian kingdom, preserves the tradition that when Nino first came to Kartli, she stayed with the Jewish community at Mtskheta. Regardless of how one may wish to evaluate the historicity of such texts, it is clear that Georgian tradition places the Christianization of the Iberian kingdom firmly in the context of the local Jewish community.

Earliest Christianity

The period immediately prior to the establishment of Christianity in the Georgian kingdoms was a time of upheaval and dislocation throughout the Caucasus. This turmoil was just one facet of the so-called Crisis of the Third Century for the Roman Empire, during which the empire was wracked by political instability, military coups, the collapse of the imperial frontiers, and economic weakness. In the 250s several tribal groups from the Crimea, among them the Goths and Borani, attacked Roman settlements along the eastern and southern shores of the Black Sea (Zosimus, *Hist. nov.* 1.31–33). Both Pityus and Trapezus were sacked, and Phasis was besieged. Roman control in the region appears to have lapsed completely until the reign of Diocletian (r. 284–305) and the eastern campaigns of Galerius (r. 293–311) in 298. During the fourth century a Roman presence was reestablished in western Georgia, notably at the garrison forts of Apsarus, Sebastopolis, and Pityus. As the fourth century progressed, the Romans gave their support to the Lazi, who formed a successor kingdom that eventually incorporated the earlier Colchian kingdom as well as regions farther north in Svaneti and Abkhazia. This new kingdom of Lazica developed a fortified capital at Archaeopolis, on the left bank of the Tekhuri River some 50 km from the coast.

Fig. 3.5. Remains of Archaeopolis, Nokalakevi

The third century was, if anything, even more tumultuous for the eastern Georgian kingdom of Iberia, due principally to the overthrow of the Parthian Empire by Ardashir I in 224 and the establishment of the Sasanian dynasty in Persia. The repercussions of this dynastic revolution were felt in the Caucasus, especially during the reign of Shapur I, whose long reign was notable for his sack of Antioch in 256 and his victories over successive Roman emperors, including Valerian (r. 253–260), whom he captured in 260. In the immediate aftermath of his victory over Valerian, Shapur set up a trilingual inscription at Naqsh-i-Rustam in which the *shahanshah* enumerates the peoples in his empire and the rulers of these client states. Among them we find Amazasp, king of Iberia

(r. 260–265). He and his successor Aspagur (r. 265–284) sought to maintain close relations with the Sasanians, even though the Iberian kings were related to the last of the Parthian kings, the Arsacids. The Iberian branch of the Arsacid dynasty came to an end with Aspagur when the Sasanians installed the young Mirian (r. 284–361) on the throne. Mirian (*Mihran* in Armenian, *Meribanes* in Latin) was later believed to be a member of the Sasanian royal house, descended from a common distant ancestor, thereby inaugurating the Iberian dynasty of the Chosroids. It was this same Mirian who embraced Christianity as the state religion of Iberia in the 330s (Braund 1994; Rapp 2003).

Although Iberia came back under at least nominal Roman suzerainty after Galerius's campaigns in 298, the Sasanians remained the dominant cultural influence in the region. This influence extended to religious matters, and the late third and early fourth centuries witnessed the increasing presence of Zoroastrianism throughout the kingdom. This is reflected in a Middle Persian inscription set up in the 280s at Naqsh-i-Rustam by the *mobed* (high priest) Kirdir (see chap. 2). The Zoroastrian high priest boasts that he established fire-altars and colleges of priests throughout the newly conquered regions of "non-Iran" and includes Iberia in his list of territories (D. N. MacKenzie 1970). Although Zoroastrianism in Iberia may have adapted itself to the local cult of Armazi, it became associated with submission to Persian overlordship. As a result, it retained a place of influence in Iberia throughout Late Antiquity and served as the chief opponent to Christianity in later Georgian saints' lives and martyrdoms. After 363 Iberia was formally ceded to Shapur II (r. 309–379) by the Roman emperor Jovian (r. 363–364), and it remained a client state of the Sasanians well beyond the end of the Iberian monarchy in the 580s, indeed, until the Arab conquest of the south Caucasus in the mid-640s. It is under these new political and cultural conditions that Christianity makes its first appearance in the Georgian kingdoms.

We know relatively little about the introduction of Christianity into Colchis/Lazica. In Georgian tradition the apostles, after Pentecost, cast lots to determine where they should each preach the gospel. Georgia fell to the lot of the Virgin Mary (*Theotokos*), but Christ appeared to her and instructed her to send the apostle Andrew in her place. St. Andrew was accompanied by the apostle Simon the Zealot, and together they preached in the towns along the Colchian coastline. According to the late fifth-century Armenian historian Movses Khorenats'i, Simon the Zealot eventually was martyred in Colchis by being sawn in half. The fourteenth-century Byzantine historian Nicephorus Callistus (1256–1335) preserves an account not found in the late-antique church historians concerning St. Matthias, who was chosen as an apostle to replace Judas. After preaching in Judaea, he traveled to Sinope, on the Black Sea, and eventually came to Colchis, where he was martyred (Nicephorus Callistus, *Hist. eccl.* 2.40). Local tradition identifies the Roman fort at Apsarus/Gonio as the site of his martyrdom, and his burial place within the fort is still venerated (Licheli 1998; Machitadze 2006; Kakhidze 2008). By the time of Diocletian's persecution, in about 303–305, Colchis became one of the principal destinations for exiled Christians. Seven brothers who were also soldiers, most notably Orentius, were sent to the northern regions of the kingdom, where they died (*AASS* 4.809–11; 24 June). Even after the Christianization of the Roman state, Colchis/Lazica remained a prime destination for those punished by exile. The most famous of these, of course, was St. John Chrysostom (ca. 347–407), who died en route to his appointed exile in Pityus (Theodoret, *Hist. eccl.* 5.34; Palladius, *Dial. v. Jo. Chrys.* 11).

Perhaps a better indicator of the early presence of Christianity in Colchis/ Lazica is a group of burials at Modinakhe/Sairkhe, located at the extreme eastern edge of Lazica in the valley of the Qvirila River. Many of the more than eighty burials show the deceased arranged on their sides, but several burials from the early fourth century display the Christian practice of placing the deceased on their backs, with the arms crossed over the chest, and oriented with the feet toward the east. From about this same time we find the first clear textual evidence for a Christian bishop in Colchis/Lazica. Among the attendees of the Council of Nicaea in 325 there is mention of a bishop Stratophilus of Pityus. The presence of Christianity in this northwestern

Fig. 3.6. Roman Fort, Gonio

3.1 Summary of Rufinus's Account of the Conversion of Iberia

According to Rufinus, the agent for the royal conversion was "a certain captive woman who had fallen among [the Iberians], and who led a life of faith and complete sobriety and virtue, and throughout the days and nights unceasingly offered up prayers to God" (*Hist.* 1.10). Through her prayers and ascetic practices the unnamed captive woman developed a reputation locally as a healer. After her prayers had led to the healing of a sick child, the Iberian queen, who was suffering from a grave illness, went to the ascetic's hut and asked for prayers. The queen was healed immediately, and the young captive converted the queen to Christ. The king initially was resistant to his wife's new religion, until he too encountered a miracle one day while hunting. He had been riding through the woods, when suddenly he was enveloped by a threatening darkness. He called upon Christ, his wife's new God, and daylight returned, allowing him to return to safety. At the urging of the young Christian slave, the king laid the foundations of a church to commemorate his new faith. Upon the church's completion, the king requested that Constantine send clergy to help establish the faith in Iberia.

---

corner of Lazica was confirmed when, in 1952, excavators discovered a fourth-century, three-aisled basilica at Pityus. The floor of the apse area was adorned in the fifth century with a mosaic that is the earliest extant piece of large-scale Christian decorative art in either of the Georgian kingdoms. Unfortunately, textual information regarding the broader context of Christianity in Lazica is also lacking until the fifth century. It is only then that we begin to discern the contours of Christianity's impact on Lazican society and its relation to the Lazican monarchy.

We are in a much better position to trace the introduction of Christianity into Kartli/Iberia, not only because of the later Georgian historiographical tradition that focuses on the eastern kingdom, but also because of the interest taken by Greek and Latin church historians in the story of the conversion of the Iberian monarchy. However, there are archaeological indications that Christianity had already gained some adherents among the higher levels of Iberian society prior to the conversion of Mirian III in the early fourth century. Just as at Modinakhe/Sairkhe in the fourth century, Iberia witnesses a distinct shift in the manner of burial during the third century. Previously, Iberian interments arranged the corpse on its side, in a fetal position. Abundant deposits of grave goods commonly accompanied these burials. The new style of interment laid the corpse out on its back, with its feet to the east. By the end of the third century over half of the new interments at the Samtavro necropolis are oriented west to east. In addition, deposits of grave goods decline dramatically, although the paucity of material may owe more to economic conditions than to a reluctance to fortify the dead with possessions for the next life. Some of these third-century burials include Christian objects such as signet rings with a cross and fish or anchor and fish, clearly attesting their Christian affiliation. Third-century burials attesting to the progressive Christianization of Iberian society at sites are scattered across the kingdom, not only at Mtskheta and Aragvispiri but also along the Mtkvari River corridor as far west as Urbnisi (*Pass. Eust.* 7.43, 89; 9.73). As a consequence, the conversion of the Iberian royal house signifies less the advent of Christianity into the kingdom but more the monarchy's adoption of an increasingly popular religion as means to further the centralization of the kingdom and strengthen the hand of the king in the ongoing contest of authority with local lords.

The earliest narrative of the conversion of Iberia is related by Rufinus (ca. 345–ca. 411/2), who wrote a Latin continuation of Eusebius's *Ecclesiastical History* shortly after the year 400. This earliest and, admittedly, sketchy conversion narrative (see sidebar 3.1) is supplemented by a Georgian literary tradition that originates sometime in the seventh century. It is developed in several texts: *The Life of Nino*, embedded within the *Kartlis Tskhovreba* and the *Mokcevay Kartlisay* (*The Conversion of Kartli*), along with a second *Life of Nino*. The relationship among these texts is complicated and disputed, but they seem to have crystallized in their current form in the ninth and tenth centuries, though drawing on much older traditions (Toumanoff 1963; Alexidze 2002; Rapp 1998; 2003; C. Lerner 2003). It is only within this Georgian literary tradition that Rufinus's unnamed "captive woman" is identified as St. Nino, and she is endowed further with a more exalted pedigree: her father is a Roman general, and her maternal uncle is the patriarch of Jerusalem. She comes to Iberia on her own volition and takes up residence in Mtskheta's palace-suburb of Samtavro, where her *ascesis* attracts the notice of Queen Nana. She instructs the queen in the new faith partly through the use of a cross that Nino had fashioned from two vine branches tied together with strands of her own hair. The king is identified as Mirian III, and among Nino's most noted deeds is the heavenly destruction of the idol Armazi on a hill overlooking the capital and her subsequent setting up of a cross in its place, commemorated in the sixth century by a monastery and church on the site known as Djvari (the Cross). This composite account also fills out the narrative of the king's construction of the first church in the capital. The church was given the name "Svetiskhoveli," meaning "the life-giving pillar," from a miraculous central pier of the church that was set in place only through St. Nino's prayers. Its sanctity derived from two sources: the miraculous circumstances of its construction and that it was set up over the first-century tomb of a pious Jewish woman, Sidonia, who was buried clutching the sacred robe of Christ, brought back to Mtskheta from Jerusalem by her brother.

Elements in Rufinus's version and in the composite Georgian tradition show both how deeply rooted the story of the royal conversion is in earlier Iberian religious ideas and how this narrative influenced the later development of Georgian spirituality, literature, and art. One of the most distinctive conceptual elements in early Georgian Christianity is the multifaceted prominence accorded to the related notions of the cross, viticulture, and the tree of life. The Church of the Life-Giving Pillar is constructed on a holy relic associated with Christ's crucifixion, and it is accomplished through the prayers of a woman bearing a cross fashioned from grapevines. In this way, long-standing Georgian reverence for viticulture is Christianized, and wine drinking continues its sacral quality by its association with the eucharistic rite. This helps account for the presence of grapevines in relief sculptures on Georgian churches as well as the elegantly rendered fifth-century floor mosaic from Pityus. After the Arab conquest viticulture assumed an even greater prominence in Georgia's Christian identity, in view of Quranic prohibitions of wine drinking. The cross itself assumes a central place in early Georgian Christianity, to a degree unsurpassed in other early Christian cultures, with the possible exception of Ireland. By the early Middle Ages the most common decorative motif within the dome of Georgian churches is not the *Christos Pantokrator* of Byzantine churches, but a cross borne up by four angels. And as an echo of the planting of the cross at Djvari, ornately carved, freestanding crosses in either stone or metal, some of which are over eight feet tall, become standard decorative features within Georgian churches.

Mirian III's espousal of Christianity was a cultural choice with profound ramifications, both within the Iberian kingdom and on the wider stage of international politics. Despite his adoption of Christianity, there is no indication that he saw this conversion to the new religion of Constantine as a betrayal of Sasanian overlordship. Indeed, Mirian's conversion took place in a distinctly non-Roman context. It was presented at the time, and in later Georgian tradition, as occurring entirely independently of any Roman diplomatic initiative. Mirian and his successors proudly maintained that they were scions of the Persian royal house. It was only in the fifth and sixth centuries that Christianity served as a rallying point for Iberian resistance, and it is noteworthy that the earliest example of Georgian literature, the *Passion of Šušanik*, details the martyrdom of a noblewoman by her husband who was serving as a Persian governor along the Armenian-Georgian border.

Christianization

VAKHTANG GORGASALI

Mirian's successors are credited with the construction of churches throughout
Iberia, from Bolnisi in the west to Nekresi in the east, but it appears that Christianity did not make a substantial impact on Iberian society and culture until
at least a century later. This was accomplished, first of all, by the vigorous pro-
Christian stance of the long-lived warrior king Vakhtang Gorgasali (r. ca. 450–
502). In addition, the crucial task of Christianizing the Iberian countryside had
to wait a further half century until the arrival of a group of missionary monks,
venerated collectively as the Thirteen Syrian Fathers. Together, the combination
of Iberian royal initiative and missionary monasticism provided the foundation
on which a fully articulated Georgian Christian culture was established.

Unfortunately, as we enter the fifth and sixth centuries the Greek historical tradition all but ignores developments in the eastern Georgian kingdom.
The attention of Byzantine historians is fixed on Lazica, where the two great
empires fought fiercely to exert their dominance. With regard to the eastern
kingdom, Procopius (ca. 500–565) provides a laconic statement that is typical
of many Byzantine writers: "The Iberi are a Christian people and keep the
ordinances of the faith as zealously as any people we know. However, they
have long been subjects of the Persian king" (*Pers.* 1.12.2–3). Georgian sources
are much more promising, especially the lengthy *History of Vakhtang Gorgasali*, a component part of the much larger *Kartlis Tskhovreba*. From this
historical tradition, Vakhtang Gorgasali emerges as a Georgian King Arthur,
a semilegendary monarch who embodies all the virtues of a Christian king.
He acquired his sobriquet "Gorgasali" because of the distinctive helmet that
he wore bearing the face of a wolf. "Gorgasali" was thought to derive from
a Persian term for "wolf's head." Tales of Vakhtang's martial prowess, his
Christian piety, his sense of duty, and his justice as a ruler abounded during
the medieval period, so much so that the success of medieval Georgian rulers
was always measured against the high standard set by Vakhtang Gorgasali.

For much of his reign Vakhtang Gorgasali acted as a faithful vassal of the
Sasanian *shahanshah*. In 472 he assisted Peroz I in his campaign against Lazica
and Byzantine possessions in Pontus, thereby regaining territories in western
Iberia that previously had been annexed by Lazica. He expanded the Iberian
realm into Ossetia and Armenia, and he founded a new capital some 24 km
downriver from Mtskheta at Tbilisi. In the 480s, however, Vakhtang reversed his
stance toward Persia, joined Vahan Mamikonian (440–510/11) and a number of
Armenian warlords in a general uprising against Persian rule, and inaugurated
policies that led to a fatal military confrontation with the Sasanian Empire.

Throughout his long reign Vakhtang Gorgasali was also a fervent advocate of Christianity, his religious policies being part and parcel of his larger strategic aims. Indeed, his shift in alliance from Persia to Rome came as a result of this commitment to Christianity. Despite his long attempts to mediate between emperor and shah, the Persians eventually demanded religious conformity as a sign of political fidelity. In the words of the medieval chronicler, "The Persians took control of Kartli and destroyed the churches, while the Georgians hid their crosses. In all the churches of Kartli the Persians lit fires for the fire-worshippers" (Thomson 1996, 153).

The turning point came in 482, when Vakhtang executed Varsken, a Persian official of Georgian descent who governed a fiefdom that straddled the Armenian-Georgian border. Seven years earlier this same Varsken had killed his own wife, Šušanik, when she refused to give up Christianity and embrace the Zoroastrianism of Varsken's Persian overlord. The horrific domestic violence

Fig. 3.7. Davit Garedji Monastery

suffered by Šušanik at the hands of her apostate husband and her eventual martyrdom are described in the first product of Georgian literature, the *Passion of Šušanik*, composed shortly after the events. Although he looked to the Byzantine church to provide him with more clergy and a candidate for catholicos (patriarch) of Mtskheta, Vakhtang acted vigorously on behalf of Georgia's ecclesiastical independence. He achieved autocephaly for the Georgian church in 487/8, a self-governing status that it since has enjoyed with only two interregna. Despite his long-standing efforts to maintain a precarious peace with Persia, he did not hesitate to pull down Zoroastrian fire-altars and punish Iberian nobility who actively supported the Persian religion. In this way, Vakhtang Gorgasali can be seen as having completed the process of official Christianization begun by Mirian III, a policy that led to Vakhtang's death in battle in about 502.

MONASTICISM

Politically and militarily, Iberia began to decline after Vakhtang's death, until the monarchy was abolished just before 580 by Khusro I. Thereafter, authority in Iberia was largely in the hands of local lords, with one, singled out as *kouropalatēs* or "presiding prince," who was recognized as such by the Byzantine emperor but ruled at the whim of the *shahanshah*. In spite of this political weakness the sixth century was a dynamic period that witnessed a critically important phase in the Christianization of the former eastern kingdom. This resulted from the work of a group of foreign-born ascetics known in Georgian tradition as the Thirteen Syrian Fathers. According to the medieval *Life of St. Shio of Mghvime*, a mid-sixth-century catholicos of Mtskheta was instructed by an angel to welcome a band of monks who had traveled hundreds of kilometers and were, at that moment, nearing the city. On the basis of this heavenly introduction, the catholicos greeted the ascetics as honored guests. The band of thirteen monks had come to the Iberian kingdom under the leadership of a famed Syrian ascetic, John, later to be known as Ioane Zedazneli.

Once they received the blessing of the catholicos, John and his twelve ascetic followers did not remain long in the capital. Of the thirteen, John chose to settle the closest to Mtskheta, but it took a strenuous day's climb to reach

Fig. 3.8. Church Founded by St. Abibos, Nekresi

his dwelling at the top of Mount Zedazeni, reputed as the site of a prominent pagan sanctuary. He demolished the temple, and he became renowned
among the country people for his ability to cure illnesses, cast out demons,
and even tame the wild bears that roamed in great numbers on Mount Zedazeni (Abuladze 1971). John's disciples settled throughout the Mtkvari Valley,
from Urbnisi to Garedji and northward through Kakheti to Alaverdi, imitating
his example of asceticism, thaumaturgy, and evangelization. While there are
archaeological and literary hints of monastic foundations in Iberia prior to
the sixth century, notably at Tsilkani north of Mtskheta, it is principally with
the work of the Thirteen Syrian Fathers that monastic traditions took root,
with the attendant diffusion of Christianity into peripheral regions far from
the confluence of the Mtkvari and Aragvi Rivers.

The style of monastic life introduced into Iberia by John and his disciples
was of a distinctly Syrian variety, a quality that has endured to this day. Like
the Syrian monks described in Theodoret's *Religious History* and John of
Ephesus's *Lives of the Eastern Saints*, many of the Thirteen Syrian Fathers
chose mountains and hilltops as their monastic retreats, and at least one of
them, St. Anton, climbed a hilltop at Martkhopi overlooking western Kakheti,
and there he dwelt on a pillar for many years. John and his disciples came into
conflict with both Zoroastrianism and native cults throughout the Iberian
kingdom, and they engaged in a vigorous evangelistic campaign among the
inhabitants of the towns and villages. One of them, St. Abibos of Nekresi,
paid with his life for his opposition to Zoroastrianism. He was martyred
after he disrupted a local Zoroastrian ritual by pouring water on a fire-altar,
derisively asking, "What kind of god is this that I can extinguish him with a
jug of water?" St. Davit of Garedji first dwelt on a mountainside overlooking
Vakhtang Gorgasali's newly inaugurated political capital of Tbilisi, and he
functioned in the now-familiar role of the Syriac holy man, working miracles
and arbitrating in local disputes. He then retired to a semiarid desert in southeastern Kakheti, and he replicated in distant Iberia the austerities of the Syrian Desert. All together, the Thirteen Syrian Fathers established some sixteen
monasteries and other churches, many of whose sixth-century foundations
still can be observed today. As a consequence, monastic traditions took firm
root in the peripheral regions of the eastern kingdom and were linked closely
to the spread of a common Christian culture.

LAZICA

In comparison with Iberia, our understanding of the spread of Christianity
in Lazica is hampered by the lack of a detailed local historical tradition (with
its attendant critical challenges). Byzantine imperial policy demanded that the

kings of Lazica fall into line with the emperor's demands. At best, this led to a checkered relationship, since Persian armies frequently used Lazica as a staging ground for their conflict with the eastern Roman Empire. Consequently, Lazica appears much more frequently than Iberia in the Byzantine historical tradition, but even these notices have an anecdotal quality that makes it nearly impossible to trace the progress of Christianity in the Lazican kingdom. As but one example, the Lazican king Gubazes I (r. 455?–468?) traveled to Constantinople, where the emperor Leo I (r. 457–474) took him to see the celebrated stylite Daniel (ca. 409–493) on his pillar just outside the city's walls. In the words of Daniel's hagiographer, "When he saw this strange sight Gubazes threw himself on his face and said, 'I thank Thee, heavenly King, that by means of an earthly king Thou hast deemed me worthy to behold great mysteries; for never before in this world have I seen anything of this kind'" (*Vit. Dan.* 51). Later Lazican monarchs attempted to preserve the kingdom's independence; however, both of the great imperial powers intervened freely, employing tactics ranging from assassination to fortifying garrison citadels.

Georgian Christianity

Despite the military and political vicissitudes of the Georgian kingdoms, by the fifth and sixth centuries Christianity was firmly rooted and had become an integral part of their cultural identity. These kingdoms, in turn, contributed to the ongoing development of Christianity in the Mediterranean world. Georgian ascetics were drawn to the holy places, and some of them eventually settled in Palestine and in Egypt. Among these was the noted theologian and spiritual writer Peter the Iberian (d. 491), who sojourned first in Bethlehem and later became bishop of Maiuma near Gaza (Kofsky 1997; Lourié 2010; Horn 2006). In the following century several Georgian ascetical writers settled at the Monastery of St. Sabas (Mar Saba) near Jerusalem, maintaining a lively connection between the liturgical and ascetic traditions of Palestine and those of the Georgian kingdoms. Georgian monks (and their manuscripts) soon came to St. Catherine's Monastery on Mount Sinai. By the early Medieval period, Georgians had established important monastic communities at Gialia on Cyprus (tenth century), at the Djvari "Cross" Monastery in Jerusalem (eleventh century, though legends trace its Georgian origins to the fourth century), and at the Petritsioni Monastery in Bulgaria (eleventh century). By far the most famous of these monastic foundations was the Monastery of Iveron (of the Iberians), established on Mount Athos by SS. Tornike (d. 985) and Ioannes the Iberian (d. ca. 1002) shortly after 980. Through these monastic communities Byzantine and Georgian forms of Christianity continued to influence each other well into the Middle Ages.

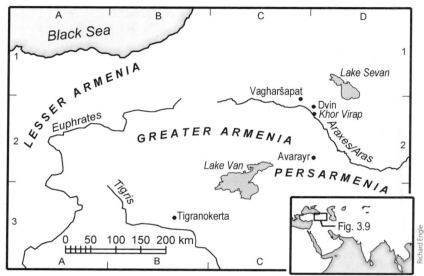

Fig. 3.9. Map of Armenia

Armenia

The spring of 451 was a time of great peril for Christianity. In April of that year Attila the Hun had crossed the Rhine and was ravaging with impunity the cities of Gaul. In the East, fresh controversies surrounding the nature of Christ had caused division among the major churches, resulting in the Council of Chalcedon. In the meantime, the Christian kingdom of Armenia had suffered a military catastrophe on the highland plains south of Mount Ararat.

The troubles in Armenia began the year before, when the *shahanshah* Yazdgerd I (r. 438–457) sought to impose Zoroastrianism on his provinces in the Caucasus. Armenia had been without a king since 428, when the monarchy was abolished by the Persians. The princes of the Armenian nobility (the *nakharars*) were led by the *sparapet* (chief military duke), an office that rested with the powerful Mamikonean clan. To crush the resistance of the Armenians, Yazdgerd sent an enormous army south through Azerbaijan. The *sparapet*, Vardan Mamikonean, had urgently requested assistance from the eastern Roman emperor, but with no result. Vardan and the rest of the Armenian nobility finally engaged the Sasanians near the small village of Avarayr on May 26, 451. The Armenians faced off against a seasoned Persian army nearly six times their size, fresh from campaigns against steppe nomads in the east and equipped with war elephants. In the ensuing slaughter, Vardan Mamikonean and the flower of Armenian nobility were crushed (Elishē', *History of Vardan and the Armenian War*; *Lazar P'arpec'i* [Thomson 1991]).

This military disaster became a defining moment in Armenian historical consciousness, akin to the defeat in 1389 of Prince Lazar and the Serbian nobility at the Battle of Kosovo near Priština. The Battle of Avarayr also highlights one of the principal problems of Armenian historiography: the tendency to view a long and variegated history in the light of a handful of historical moments. Of course, the other principal event that has shaped Armenian national consciousness in the modern era was the series of massacres perpetrated against Armenians between 1915 and 1923. However, the horrors of the twentieth century are beyond the purview of this chapter. At the same time, both may be interpreted as an indirect consequence of Armenian adherence to Christianity. By 451, Armenian Christianity had a history going back for a century and a half to the conversion, around 314, of Trdat (Tiridates) III (r. ca. 287–330). The Battle of Avarayr, moreover, fits into a broader historical narrative conditioned by the ongoing dynamics of Armenian historiography. Many of the historical sources for the battle were composed centuries after the events that they describe, their outlook shaped by literary patronage, ecclesiastical politics, and other contemporary concerns. Not surprisingly, they often project a historical framework on the past that distorts and sharpens divisions in what probably was a more complex and fluid historical reality. Nonetheless, the heroism of Vardan Mamikonean became identified with that of the Maccabees, who likewise defended their religion and independence on the battlefield against a much larger imperial power (Thomson 1994; Garsoïan 2004; Panossian 2006).

Before Christianity

As a historical entity, Armenia coalesced sometime after the collapse of the Urartian kingdom in the early sixth century BCE. However, Armenia took shape not as a single kingdom, but as a region dominated by powerful local clans sharing a common language. These disparate local clans evolved into the nearly seventy Armenian princely houses, which traditionally formed the core of the Armenian nobility.

By the time the Romans were expanding into the eastern Mediterranean in the first century BCE, they initially patronized the nascent Armenian kingdom of Tigranes II the Great (r. 95–55 BCE), who forged a vast kingdom that extended from the Mtkvari River in modern Georgia and Azerbaijan to Damascus in Syria. Tigranes's expansive kingdom, centered on his new capital at Tigranokerta, eventually alarmed both the Romans and the Parthians. His short-lived empire was broken up into a number of smaller client kingdoms, and control of Armenia itself became fiercely contested between the two empires.

In 63 CE the Romans and the Parthians came to a modus vivendi regarding Armenia that was to last for nearly two centuries. The king of a greatly reduced Armenian realm would be a scion of the Parthian Arsacid dynasty but would reign as a vassal of the Roman emperor. This arrangement endured reasonably well until the third century, when the Arsacid Parthians were overthrown by the Sasanians. However, Arsacid kings continued to rule in Armenia, thereby introducing a potentially threatening element into Armenia's relations with Persia. Even though there was nominal parity between the two empires in their relations with Armenia, Persia had always been the dominant power in culture and politics, a position that it had held since the Achaemenid dynasty (Hewsen 2000).

Knowledge of religion in Armenia prior to the fourth century is sketchy and is based largely on scant archaeological remains, notices in classical writers, and historical reconstructions posited by later Armenian historians and hagiographers. Not surprisingly, the main influences appear to have been preclassical Anatolian polytheism and various forms of Persian religion. Semitic deities, some in thinly Persian form, were widely worshiped, including Barshamin (Baal Shamash) and Astghik (Astarte). Zoroastrianism was the most significant Persian religion to take root in Armenia. The late third-century inscription of the high priest Kirdir at Naqsh-i-Rustam specifically lists Armenia among those regions of Anīrān (non-Iran) where fire-altars and their attendant priests were established. The diffusion of these fire-altars has been confirmed archaeologically, and the cult of Ahura-Mazda continued to have adherents, especially among the nobility, long after the Arsacid monarchy converted to Christianity (D. N. MacKenzie 1970; J. Russell 1987; Hewsen 2000). By contrast, the imprint of Greco-Roman civilization on pre-Christian Armenia was very slight. There were few cities, very little monumental architecture, and virtually no traces of Greco-Roman literature. Tigranes settled numerous Jewish captives throughout his kingdom. They dwelt mainly in Armenia's few cities and larger settlements and conducted a lively trade in luxury items with the Roman Empire. This Jewish presence became one facet of the cultural influences that began to filter into Armenia from Syria and Cappadocia.

Earliest Christianity

The principal Armenian chroniclers affirm that the monarchy was first converted through the efforts of Grigor Lusavorich, better known as St. Gregory the Illuminator (ca. 257–ca. 331), in the early fourth century. However, like every important center of early Christianity, the church in Armenia has its own traditions of apostolic foundation. *The Epic Histories*, attributed to Pʿawstos Buzand, links the famous story of the conversion of Abgar V of Edessa to the preaching of the apostle Thaddeus (Addai), who then continued his evangelization north into Armenia, where eventually he was martyred (*Pʿawstos Buzand* 3.1) (Garsoïan 2005–2007). It seems easy to pass off these tales as products of apostolic wishful thinking, but it is worth noting that the vast majority of early Armenian sources refer to the work of St. Gregory as "the *renewal* of the Armenian priesthood" and that his consecration established him "on the throne of the holy apostle Thaddeus" (Movses Khorenatsʿi, *Hist. Arm.* 2.34, 74; *Pʿawstos Buzand* 3.12; 4.3). Beyond the intriguing hints of these early apostolic associations, Eusebius informs us that Dionysius of Alexandria (bp. 247/8–264/5) wrote a treatise, *On Repentance*, that was addressed "to the brethren in Armenia, of whom Merozanes was bishop" (*Hist. eccl.* 6.46.2). This seems more substantive than Tertullian's rhetorical inclusion of the Armenians in a list of nations who had believed in Christ (*Adv. Jud.* 7).

Although Armenia's checkered relations with surrounding empires often led to tragedy, it is perhaps ironic that the tetrarchic emperor Galerius, a virulent persecutor of Christianity, provided the opportunity for the Arsacid monarchy to convert to Christianity. Galerius inflicted a humiliating defeat on the *shahanshah* Narsēs (r. 293–302), who was forced to acknowledge Roman suzerainty over the Upper Euphrates and the entire south Caucasus. This created a respite from Persian rule for Armenia that was to endure until 363. As

Fig. 3.10. Khor Virap Monastery, Mount Ararat in Background

a consequence, the Arsacid king Trdat was restored to his throne after he had been raised in Rome following the assassination of his father Khosrov II in 252.

Trdat's pro-Roman policy allowed for numerous cultural influences to enter unhindered into Armenia, principally from Cappadocia and from the Syriac regions to the south, especially from Edessa. According to most commonly repeated versions of the story, Trdat at first followed the religious policies of his Roman imperial patrons and persecuted Christianity, especially when he learned that one of Christianity's chief proponents in Armenia, Gregory, was related to his father's assassin. Gregory was imprisoned (traditionally at the site of the Monastery Church of Khor Virap ["deep pit"]), and Trdat executed several noted virgin martyrs. Trdat eventually became deathly ill. The king's sister was granted a vision in which she was told that only Gregory could heal the king. Gregory was brought forth from the pit of his imprisonment, with the desired result. Trdat was immediately healed, and he embraced the religion of his former enemy.

The date of Trdat's conversion is usually given as 314, the year Gregory received consecration as bishop in Caesarea of Cappadocia (Agathangelos 1976, 805–6). However, an unrelated text in Eusebius's *Historia ecclesiastica* may suggest an earlier date. In the context of discussing the persecutor Maximin Daia (r. 305–313), Eusebius says that "he had the further trouble of the war against the Armenians, men who from ancient times had been friends and allies of the Romans; but as they were Christians and exceedingly earnest in their piety towards the Deity, this hater of God, by attempting to compel them to sacrifice to idols and demons, made them foes instead of friends, and enemies instead of allies" (*Hist. eccl.* 9.8.2).

After Gregory's consecration, one of Christianity's principal centers in Armenia was located at the king's temporary court at Vagharšapat or Etchmiadzin (Descent of the Only-Begotten). A basilica was built there in the fourth century over an earlier fire-altar. The church was destroyed by Persians shortly after 363, and later it was rebuilt and modified into a quadriapsidal cross-in-square. In all, Vagharšapat became the site of four (fourth–fifth centuries) structures: a monastery church, churches dedicated to the virgin martyrs SS. Gayanē and Hřip'simē, and finally Zvartnots Cathedral, an ornately decorated seventh-century tetraconch church.

A Church between Rome and Persia

After an initial period of growth during the reigns of Trdat and his immediate successors, the geopolitical pendulum swung back once again in Sasanian Persia's favor. Julian (r. 361–363) attempted an ill-advised invasion of Persia in

363, which led to his death on the battlefield and an utter military defeat for the Romans. Jovian, the new emperor, ceded control of Armenia to Shapur II, who conducted widespread punitive campaigns. Armenian towns were destroyed (including the capital of Vagharšapat), King Arsaces II (r. 350–368) was taken off into captivity, and thousands more were either captured or slaughtered. Soon, even worse events unfolded. In 387 the great powers decided to settle the Armenian question by simply partitioning the kingdom. The smaller portion eventually became the Roman province of Armenia Minor, while the larger Persian allotment continued on as the closely controlled vassal state of Persarmenia. On the Persian side of the frontier a line of kings continued until 428, when the Sasanians abolished the monarchy. Henceforth, a Sasanian governor (*marzban*) was established in the administrative capital of Dvin. While the *marzban* was responsible for collecting taxes, each of the *nakharars* provided contingents of troops to the *shahanshah* in exchange for control over their ancestral lands (Blockley 1987; Garsoïan 1997).

After the partition in 387, the end of the monarchy in 428 in Persarmenia, and the defeat at Avarayr in 451, the church took on an increasingly central role in the definition of Armenian identity. It was the only institution that straddled the Byzantine/Sasanian border, and in the end it did not depend on either monarchy or nobles for its ongoing existence.

Gregory's work of evangelization and church organization focused on the northern regions of Armenia. He and his successors were supported by the pro-Byzantine Mamikonean clan that held sway in this area. Under these conditions it seemed natural for Gregory's successors to be consecrated at Caesarea in Cappadocia. Once monasticism became rooted in Armenia, it developed along the lines established by St. Basil (bp. 370–379) in Cappadocia. Moreover, the musical forms used liturgically were adapted from the eight modes used by the Greek churches in Anatolia. However, the influence of Syriac Christianity emanating from Edessa was of decisive importance in the shaping of Armenian Christianity. This was in large part due to the work of St. Mashtots (360?–440) and his disciples (Koriwn, *Vark῾ Maštoc῾i* [Koriwn 1941]). Mashtots is credited with the invention of an Armenian alphabet at the beginning of the fifth century. Previously, both royal court and church appear to have employed Greek and Syriac, though Aramaic sometimes was used for early Armenian inscriptions. Many of Mashtots's learned disciples were dispatched south and west in order to translate Syriac and Greek texts into Armenian. These included liturgical texts, theological treatises, exegetical works, and saints' lives. In less than a century an indigenous Armenian Christian literature developed that enshrined the faith and deeds of Armenians at a time when they faced political and military catastrophe (Crowe 2011; Thomson 1994).

By the mid- to late fifth century, Armenian writers were beginning to identify Christianity as an inalienable portion of their "ancestral, patrimonial and familiar tradition" (*Lazar P'arpec'i* 49; cf. *P'awstos Buzand* 3.11; 5.4, 44). Despite claims by Agathangelos that Gregory had baptized vast numbers of Armenians and consecrated hundreds of bishops, it appears that the actual process of Christianization was much slower and more piecemeal. In part, this may be attributed to the way the church's organization mirrored the decentralized nature of Armenian society. Since there were very few towns or cities, bishops were established within the major noble families. Of the twenty-seven bishops who attended the Second Council of Dvin in 555, twenty were attached to *nakharars*. Even the head of the Armenian church, the *katholikos*, was a hereditary office that remained within the clan of Gregory the Illuminator until the death of Sahek in 439. After the Sasanians abolished the monarchy in 428, the Armenian *katholikos* transferred his residence to Dvin, the principal urban center of Persarmenia and the seat of the *marzban*. On occasion, such close proximity to the Sasanian administration facilitated the deposition of the Armenian *katholikos* at the whim of the *shahanshah*. It also had the potential to foster better relations between *katholikos* and *marzban*. Indeed, three decades after the Battle of Avarayr another significant shift occurred in Armenian-Persian relations, precipitated by the death in battle of the *shahanshah* Peroz I. His successor, Balash (r. 484–488), needed the support of the Armenian *nakharars*, so he appointed Vahan Mamikonean, Vardan's nephew, as the new *marzban*. Persian representatives signed a treaty with Vahan in 484 at Nvarsak that granted the Armenians de facto religious toleration. During the course of this tumultuous fifth century, Armenian Christian culture continued to develop, especially within Persarmenia. It is this period that sees the first flowering of Armenian literature, the construction of numerous distinctive churches, and the beginnings of Armenia's rich liturgical traditions (Garsoïan 1997; 2004; Thomson 2008).

Estrangement, Conflict, and Endurance

During the late fifth and sixth centuries, Armenian Christianity gradually became estranged from the Byzantine church in Constantinople, the Georgian church in Mtskheta, and the East Syrian church in Seleucia-Ctesiphon. Throughout this period the principal concern of Armenian theologians was to guard against "Nestorian" influences coming from Armenians who returned to their homeland after having been forcibly settled in southern Iran. In 451 the Armenians were too preoccupied with preserving their national existence to become caught up in the Chalcedonian turmoil that embroiled the churches of the Byzantine East. Armenian bishops and theologians rallied to the *Henotikon* (*Act of Union*), issued in 482 by the emperor Zeno (r. 474–491), and continued to uphold it as a safeguard against "Nestorianism," even after the compromise formula was repudiated within the empire by Justin I (r. 518–527) and Justinian I (r. 527–565). Theologically, the Armenian bishops were ardent supporters of the Council of Ephesus (431), but they were suspicious of Chalcedon. After all, the *katholikos* was not represented at Chalcedon, but only bishops from western Roman Armenia. As time progressed, the majority of Armenian bishops considered themselves faithful adherents of traditional christological formulations, and they viewed radical Chalcedonians as "Nestorians" (Thomson 2000; 2008).

Meanwhile, Justinian was inexorably eroding the autonomy of the noble *nakharars* within the provinces of Byzantine Armenia. In 528 their private armies were disbanded, traditional Armenian laws of inheritance were made to adhere to Roman practice, and their patrimonial fiefdoms were transformed into four new Roman provinces. Although Justinian and later emperors deployed talented Armenian warriors throughout their empire, Armenian identity and culture were continually undermined on the Byzantine side of the border. Generally, the situation was more favorable in the larger region of Persarmenia.

For centuries, both emperor and shah had vied for indirect control in Armenia. By the sixth century, this policy shifted to one of forcible integration. This created a dilemma for both bishops and *nakharars* of competing allegiances from imperial overlords who tolerated no variation from the norm. However, it was not until the 570s and the sixty-year conflagration that came to engulf both empires that Armenians within the Sasanian Empire were caught between their loyalty to a Zoroastrian monarchy and their devotion to Christianity. In the end, neither the Byzantine emperor nor the Persian *shahanshah* could count on their fealty. An often-quoted, but probably apocryphal, letter from Maurice (r. 582–602) to Khusro II Parwez says of the Armenians that they are "a perverse and disobedient nation, who stand between us and disturb us. I shall gather mine and send them off to Thrace. You gather yours and order them to be sent to the east. If they die, it is our enemies who die. If they kill, they kill our enemies. Then we shall live in peace. For if they remain in their own land, there will be no repose for us" (Sebeos 1999, 15 <86>).

For the Armenians, the end of Antiquity was marked by deportations, desperate rebellions, and the ongoing attempt of both imperial powers to co-opt *nakharars* and clergy. Nonetheless, by the early seventh century the various elements of culture had coalesced into a unique Armenian Christian identity. After the rapid spread of Islam in the seventh and eighth centuries, Armenia and Georgia were the only distinct cultures within the larger Near East to remain predominantly Christian.

4

Deep into Asia

SAMUEL N. C. LIEU AND KEN PARRY

Introduction

Lack of access to primary sources in original languages and the common assumption among Western scholars that Islam had eradicated all traces of Christianity meant that, before the twentieth century, the study of early Christianity in Asia was largely neglected. This was to change, however, with discoveries made in Central Asia and China during the early twentieth century. Expeditions to ancient cities on the Silk Road, organized by European scholar-explorers such as Albert von Le Coq, Aurel Stein, and Paul Pelliot yielded large quantities of manuscripts and artifacts, many of which are still housed in archives and museums in London, Berlin, and Paris.

Christianity first reached Central Asia, China, and India largely as a result of the terrestrial and maritime trading networks. Thanks to Christian traders from the Middle East, communities were established in all three lands by the seventh century. As these communities grew, their pastoral needs were met by patriarchs who consecrated bishops for their far-flung dioceses. Remarkably, despite great distances from their spiritual homelands, these communities flourished. That they did so is a witness to their strength and sense of identity

This chapter was written by **Samuel N. C. Lieu** (Introduction, China) and **Ken Parry** (Introduction, Central Asia, India).

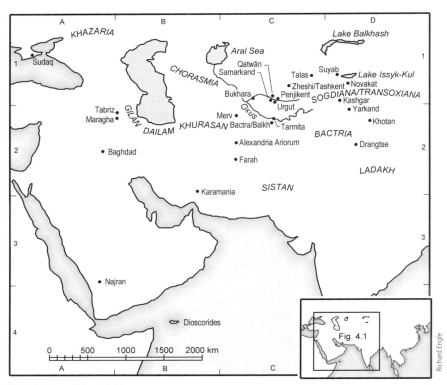

Fig. 4.1. Map of Central Asia

as minorities in foreign environments. Christianity always remained a minority religion in these areas, yet its message and influence certainly were recognized by different rulers over the centuries.

Central Asia

Knowledge of Central Asia in the ancient world increased after Alexander the Great (r. 336–323 BCE) conquered Bactria[1] and Samarkand in Sogdiana[2] and established satrapies in the region of the Oxus River (Amu Darya). By early Christian times, traders using the Silk Road were carrying merchandise from China through Central Asia and Iran to the eastern Mediterranean and Rome. Among the merchants operating on the Silk Road were Christians of Syrian, Iranian (including Sogdian), and Turkic origin. During the first

1. The country of Bactria consisted of parts of modern Uzbekistan, Tajikistan, and Afghanistan.
2. North of Bactria, the country of Sogdiana also comprised regions of what is now southern Uzbekistan and western Tajikistan.

millennium CE there is evidence for a variety of religious communities in Central Asia, including Jews, Christians, Manichaeans, Zoroastrians, and Buddhists. People from different ethnic and religious backgrounds lived side by side in the Silk Road oasis towns on both sides of the Pamirs, the high mountain range that divides Central Asia in two. Only later did Islam become the unifying religious force throughout this vast region.

The overland trade routes saw the establishment of various Eastern Christian communities, including Melkite (Byzantine rite), Syrian Orthodox ("Jacobite"), and Church of the East ("Nestorian"). Only in the late twentieth and early twenty-first centuries have scholars begun to form a clearer picture of these communities. We have no example of Christianity being made a "state" religion in Central Asia, unlike Manichaeism, which became the state religion of the Uighur Empire in the eighth century (Mackerras 1972), or Judaism, which became the state religion in Khazaria (northern Caucasus region) in the ninth century (Brook 2006). What we do see is Christianity being embraced by various settled communities, nomadic tribal leaders, and groups within khanate confederations.

The situation in Central Asia focuses to some extent on the relationship between nomadic and sedentary communities. None of the nomadic tribes founded a world religion based on their native traditions, nor did they demand conquered peoples to convert to their practices. Enforced conversions were not the order of the day, as respect for other traditions was enshrined in customary law (Khazanov 1994). It was only over time that the Mongols, for example, accepted Islam in the west and Buddhism in the east. Despite this, Christianity was practiced by members of leading Mongol families, so that it enjoyed patronage under a series of khans.

Unfortunately, none of the Chinese Buddhist pilgrims, such as Xuanzang (602–664) in the seventh century, make reference to groups that can be identified as Christian. They were more focused on recording the Buddhist communities that they encountered in Central Asia as they journeyed to India to collect Buddhist *sutras*. Xuanzang passed through Turfan (Turpan), Zheshi (Tashkent), and Bactra (Balkh) on his way to India, places where Christian communities undoubtedly existed by the seventh century. However, Syriac writers and early Muslim historians do mention Christian communities in Central Asia. In the thirteenth century, when Rabban Sauma (ca. 1225–1294) traveled from China through Central Asia on his way to the West, he reported on the Christian communities with which he stayed (Budge 1928). Also in the thirteenth century a meeting is recorded between a Christian (Tarsā) leader and the Daoist Changchun (1148–1227) during the latter's travels in Central Asia to meet Genghis Khan (r. ca. 1162–1227) (Waley 1931, 82).

China

While individual Syriac- or Iranian-speaking Christians might have reached China using both the terrestrial and the maritime Silk Road in the fifth and sixth centuries, the official recorded date of the entry of the Church of the East (often referred to erroneously as "Nestorian Christianity") into China is given as 635 on the famous Xi'an Monument, which was erected in 781. The discovery of this unique inscription in both Syriac and Chinese in the seventeenth century made European missionaries and scholars aware of the early diffusion of Christianity in China. Monastic communities were set up at the two capital cities of China, Chang'an (Xi'an) and Luoyang, in the seventh and eighth centuries. The monks probably were initially Iranian speaking, but there were attempts at converting local Chinese and recruiting such converts into the monastery, although Christianity never grew to become a significant religious force in premodern China because of Christianity's unwillingness to inculturate. Unlike the Manichaeans, the Church of the East did not receive substantial patronage from the rulers of the day, and in the ninth century it was expelled along with other "Western" religions as part of a large-scale persecution aimed primarily at Buddhism.

Our knowledge of the Church of the East in China would be very limited had a number of Christian texts in Chinese not been found at Dunhuang among a large hoard of Buddhist texts. These documents probably came from a Christian monastery at ancient Shazhou (modern Dunhuang). They include hymns and sermons. The latter clearly were composed for a Chinese audience using scriptural material in Syriac, but they are not close translations. Their main purpose was to show the Confucian authorities that Christian monotheism was philosophically sound and that Christians adhered to the highest moral and ethical principles.

Despite its expulsion from China proper, the Church of the East continued to flourish in Central Asia and won converts among Turkic-speaking tribes that later would become important allies of the Mongols. After the latter had conquered the whole of China in 1279, the Church of the East returned to China proper as a religion of foreigners, but a small number of Chinese probably were converted to what was now one of the several religions of the conquerors. Kublai Khan (r. 1260–1294), the son of a Christian Turkic princess, Sorghaghtani Beki (ca. 1198–1252), was particularly tolerant toward Christianity as he tried to govern a vast and ethnically diverse Eurasian empire. His successors were less tolerant, and later, when the Mongols were expelled around 1368, the Chinese virtually wiped out all traces of the religion among the ethnic Chinese.

India

Christianity reached India as a result of the trading system linking the Red Sea, the Arabian Gulf, and the Indian Ocean. Tradition associated St. Thomas with the evangelization of India from an early period, and the third-century *Acts of Thomas* details Thomas's alleged journey to India by ship. Roman trade with the Malabar Coast was well established at the time of Christ and continued throughout the early Christian period. The question of where exactly Greek and Latin sources located India has often been raised, but perhaps not enough credit has been given to the ancient writers with regard to this issue. Although there is some confusion between Ethiopia and Arabia, both the first-century *Periplus of the Erythraean Sea* and the sixth-century *Christian Topography* give clear indications that India corresponds to the country we know today. Pepper from South India was an especially prized commodity, and the use of the seasonal monsoon winds to sail to India and back made seafaring relatively straightforward.

The evidence indicates that it was Christians from Iran who first settled on the Malabar Coast in South India. Today, the "St. Thomas Christians" of Kerala claim the apostle Thomas as their founder, but there is no evidence for Christianity in South India before the sixth century. Material culture, in the form of stone crosses and inscribed copper plates dated to the eighth and ninth centuries, confirms the Syro-Persian connection. The Church of the East appears to be the earliest Christian community in Kerala, although we hear of Syrian Orthodox (*Yakoba*) as well. The presence of Christians in Cochin (Kochi) and other ports is attested by Western travelers such as Marco Polo (1254–1324), who also visited the shrine of St. Thomas at Mylapore in Tamil Nadu. With the arrival of the Portuguese in the sixteenth century, a period of Latinization followed, resulting in the burning of Syriac liturgical books and the imposition of foreign clergy. Still, India is the only region discussed in this chapter that can claim a continuous Christian tradition reaching back to the early period.

Christian Traditions in Asia

THE CHURCH OF THE EAST

The correct term for the East Syrian Christian tradition is "Church of the East" (Brock 1996a). So-called Nestorianism is an erroneous Byzantine construct resulting from the christological debates and ecclesiastical politics centered on Constantinople in the fifth century. It has little bearing on the Christian communities in Central Asia, China, and India. That being stated, the Antiochene theology of the Church of the East may be said to share characteristics with Dyophysite "Nestorianism," so long as we bear in mind that the Antiochene roots of this community predate the controversy over "Nestorianism." Nestorius, bishop of Constantinople (bp. 428–431), along with Diodore of Tarsus (d. 390) and Theodore of Mopsuestia (bp. ca. 392/3–428), was celebrated on the feast day of the three doctors in the Church of the East. All three were venerated as fathers of the Antiochene tradition.

The synod at Markabta in 424 is regarded as the occasion on which the Church of the East declared its autonomy, but it can be argued that it had been autocephalous since the Synod of Seleucia-Ctesiphon in 410 (Baum and Winkler 2003, 19). In any case, the church certainly was independent before the Council of Ephesus in 431; in other words, the condemnation of Nestorius at Ephesus was not the catalyst for establishing a "Nestorian" church. Nestorius himself never founded a church of his own and would have been dismayed by the suggestion that he had. He spent the last seventeen years of his life in exile at various monasteries in Upper Egypt, composing an apology, *The Bazaar of Heracleides*, which is extant in Syriac (Driver and Hodgson 2002). Although Nestorius's burial place is unknown (Parry 2013), Bar Hebraeus (1225–1286) mentions, in his *Chronography*, an episode concerning an attempt to return his remains from Egypt to Coche, near Seleucia-Ctesiphon, a center associated with the establishment of Christianity in Babylonia by Mar Mari (Budge 1976, 1:122). The Church of the East in Sasanian Iran declared its independence for political reasons, placing itself outside the jurisdiction of the Byzantine imperial and ecclesiastical authorities.

The condemnation of the Antiochene fathers Theodore of Mopsuestia, Theodoret of Cyrrhus (bp. 423–ca. 466), and Ibas of Edessa (bp. 435–457) at the Fifth Ecumenical Council at Constantinople in 553 under Justinian I (r. 527–565) reaffirmed the Christology of Cyril of Alexandria (bp. 412–444), at least as interpreted by Byzantine theologians in the post-Chalcedonian period. "Nestorian" became a term of opprobrium to be used against Christians of the Syrian Dyophysite tradition (Wessel 2004). Both the Melkites (Chalcedonian) and the Syrian Orthodox (non-Chalcedonian) applied the term to the Dyophysites, the name becoming a byword for heresy. It seems that Christians from the Church of the East were disparaged by their coreligionists regardless of their christological affiliations.

It cannot be stressed enough that the controversy between Nestorius and Cyril of Alexandria is irrelevant when it comes to looking for the origins of the Church of the East. The intellectual heritage of this community lies in the Syriac-speaking catechetical schools of Edessa and Nisibis. The so-called School of the Persians at Edessa, then on Byzantine territory, was closed under orders from Emperor Zeno (r. 474–491) in 489 for supposedly teaching

"Nestorianism," and it was obliged to move 200 km east to Nisibis in Sasanian Iran. The head of the school at Edessa at the time of its move was Narsai (d. 503), who, together with Barsauma the bishop of Nisibis (d. pre-496), created what was to become the Church of the East's principal teaching center (Becker 2008). This community in Iran lived first under Zoroastrianism and then later under Islam.

Merchants and priests from the Church of the East took Christianity to the oasis towns of Central Asia and eventually, by the seventh century, to China. These Iranian believers were the most evangelical of the Christians trading on the overland Silk Road, and their knowledge of international languages added to their ability to spread the Christian faith across a vast expanse of steppe and desert. The influence of their missionary activity in Central Asia, China, and India is reflected in the appointment of metropolitans for all three lands by Catholicos Timothy I (cathol. 780–823), and by the fact that Yaballaha III (cathol. 1281–1317) was still doing the same. At the nadir of its expansion, the Church of the East was more extensive geographically than both the Roman and Byzantine churches.

THE SYRIAN ORTHODOX CHURCH

The Syrian Orthodox Church came into being as a result of the christological controversies of the fifth century, especially after the "Definition of Faith" agreed on by the Council of Chalcedon of 451 became the standard by which the Greek and Latin churches measured orthodoxy. The Syrian Orthodox Church has been known historically as "Jacobite" and theologically as "Monophysite," but both terms are inappropriate. The name "Jacobite" derives from Jacob Baradaeus, bishop of Edessa from 543 to 578, who consecrated non-Chalcedonian bishops in the time of Justinian (Menze 2008). Today the name is repudiated, except in South India, where the term *Jacoba* is used by at least one Christian community. The term "Miaphysite" (referring to the single nature, *physis*, of Christ) rather than "Monophysite" is a more accurate rendering of the theological position of the Syrian Orthodox Church (Winkler 1997).

As far as Asia is concerned, the Syrian Orthodox were not as expansionist as members of the Church of the East. According to the *Chronography* of the historian and *maphrain* (head of the eastern Syrian Orthodox Church) Bar Hebraeus, there were bishops in Sistan and at Alexandria Ariorum (Herat) in today's Afghanistan in the seventh century (Budge 1976, 360). They were appointed to serve churches that had been established by members of the community at Edessa who had been deported there. Also in Afghanistan there was a bishop at Farah by the early ninth century. All three communities appear to have survived through to the eleventh or twelfth century. It is also possible that there were Syrian Orthodox communities at Yarkand on the southern Silk Road in Chinese Central Asia in the thirteenth century. There is some evidence for rivalry between the Syrian Orthodox and the Church of the East in Central Asia.

THE MELKITE CHURCH

The term "Melkite," meaning "loyalist" or "imperialist," from the Syriac *malka* (king), was applied from the sixth century to those Christians in the Middle East who remained loyal to the Council of Chalcedon and to the Byzantine Church in Alexandria, Antioch, and Jerusalem. Among these loyalists were Greek-, Syriac-, and later Arabic-speakers (Dick 1994). The term "Melkite" becomes more common after the Arab conquest of Byzantine territory in the eastern Mediterranean in the seventh century. It initially was used by non-Chalcedonians as a pejorative, but eventually it was applied by the Melkites to themselves. Members of this church saw themselves as belonging to a transnational community owing loyalty to the Oriental patriarchs, with a presence scattered throughout the Middle East. They regained some of their former status with the temporary reconquest by the Byzantines of territory in Syria in the tenth century. During the Crusades, however, the Melkite patriarchs of Antioch and Jerusalem were replaced by Latin patriarchs, resulting in the exile of the Melkite patriarchs to Constantinople, who were later subsumed into the Greek Orthodox Church under the Ottomans (Micheau 2006).

The presence of Melkites at Tashkent in Central Asia is attested from the eighth century (Parry 2012), and according to the *Chronology of Ancient Nations*, by the Muslim scholar al-Biruni (973–1048), there was a Melkite metropolitan at Merv in his lifetime (Sachau 1879, 289). There is little evidence for Melkites farther east, however, in spite of a bilingual psalm fragment in Greek and Sogdian found at Bulayïq, north of Turfan in Chinese Central Asia (Xinjiang). We have no clear evidence for Melkites in China and India, but this does not exclude the possibility of there having been individuals or families owing allegiance to this church whose presence is thus far unknown.

Central Asia

The Early Period

An early reference to Christians living southwest of the Caspian Sea and in Bactria under the Kushans is given by the Syrian Christian Bardaisan of

Edessa (154–222) around 196. In his *Book of the Laws of Countries* he tells us that the Christian women among the Gilanians and the Kushans did not have sexual relations with foreigners and that Christian men who lived in Iran did not marry their own daughters (H. Drijvers 1965, 61). This last reference is to the practice of consanguineous marriages among Zoroastrians in Iran. Who these Christians were, how they got there, and who evangelized them are not clear, but it would seem to confirm a Christian presence in Central Asia in the second century.

GILAN AND DAILAM

Writing in about 840, Thomas of Marga, the historian of the Church of the East, speaks of certain bishops who preached the message of Christ in the countries of the Dailamites and Gilanians. The metropolitan of Gilan and Dailam is named as Šubhāl-Išo, who is said to have known Syriac, Persian, and Arabic and to have died a martyr's death while returning to Iraq (*Hist. mon.* 4.20; 5.4.5). Today Dailam is part of the province of Gilan in Iran situated to the south of the Caspian Sea. The metropolitan is said to have been ordained by the catholicos at Baghdad, Timothy I, who also ordained a certain David as metropolitan of China (Bēt Zinayē). Thomas tells us that he knows something about this David from Timothy's letters. The Muslim historian Ibn al-Nadīm (d. 988), in his *Al-Fihrist* (*The Catalog*), reports meeting a Christian monk from China in 987 at the "House of the Greeks" (*Dār al-Rūm*) in Baghdad, the name of the Christian quarter near the main church of the catholicos (Dodge 1970, 2:836–37).

Thomas of Marga also mentions that the people among whom the bishops lived ate rice "bread," as they did not grow wheat (*Hist. mon.* 2.5.7). This statement is of interest in relation to eucharistic bread and wine, as wheat and grapes normally were absent from the diets of the nomadic peoples of Central Asia. Nomadic Christians, however, are reported to have carried wheat and grapes when they could get them, and this they may have done to fulfill the Pascha requirements (Mingana 1925, 309–11, 363). Turks, who were accustomed to eating only meat and milk, apparently substituted alcoholic mare's milk (*qumis*) for eucharistic wine. In Eastern Christianity it is customary to abstain from dairy products during Lent. In answer to a query from the metropolitan of Merv concerning Lenten food, John V (cathol. 1000–1011) nonetheless gave permission for Turks to drink milk.

TRANSOXIANA/SOGDIANA AND KHURASAN

Early evidence for Christians east of the Oxus River comes in 497, when the temporarily deposed Sasanian shah Kavad I (r. 488–496; 498/9–531) was forced to seek refuge among the White Huns (Hephthalites)—the old enemies of his father, Peroz I (r. 457–484). Among those who sought refuge with Kavad were two lay Christians, John of Resh'aina and Thomas the Tanner. They were later joined by Karadusat, bishop of Aran west of the Caspian Sea, together with four priests. Karadusat felt that he had been called by means of a vision to minister to Byzantine Christians held captive among the Huns. The bishop and priest stayed for seven years, and the two laymen remained for thirty. They preached and baptized, and they are said to have created the first written form of the Hunnic (Turkic or Iranian) language (Mingana 1925, 303–4).

Again we hear of Christians among the Hephthalites in 549, when the head of the Church of the East at Seleucia-Ctesiphon, Aba I (cathol. 540–552), dispatched a bishop to the region of the Oxus River in Bactria. This was in response to a request by the Hephthalites to ordain as bishop the priest who had been sent as an emissary to Chosroes I (r. 531–579) (Mingana 1925, 304–5). The Byzantine historian Theophylact Simocatta (d. post-647) records that in 591, among captives taken by Chosroes and sent to the Byzantine emperor Maurice (r. 582–602), were Turks who had crosses tattooed on their foreheads. They are reported to have adopted this facial decoration at the suggestion of the Christians among them as a prophylactic to ward off the plague (*Hist.* 5.10.13–15).

When a metropolitan of the Church of the East was first appointed to Samarkand is not entirely clear, but a mid-sixth-century date seems most likely (Colless 1986). Samarkand appears to have been the main center of the Church of the East in Central Asia at the time of the arrival of East Syrian Christians at the Chinese capital of Chang'an in 635. There may have been a metropolitan farther east at Kashgar (Kāshi) by the eighth or ninth century, but not until the twelfth century do we have confirmation of one (Hunter 1996). Although no early Christian buildings have been discovered at Samarkand, Marco Polo reports seeing a rotunda church dedicated to John the Baptist when he visited the city in 1272. The Armenian high constable Sempad (1208–1276) had also visited the city in 1248 and describes seeing a church in which he saw a painting of Jesus and the three Magi (Colless 1986).

At Urgut, 40 km south of Samarkand in Uzbekistan, a number of stone inscriptions written in Syriac and with carved crosses dating from the ninth century have been found (Klein 2000). Archaeological excavations in the vicinity have revealed a structure that has been identified as a Christian building. This could be the site of a monastery described by the Muslim chronicler Ibn Hawqal when he visited the area around 969. He writes, "Near Samarkand ones sees a monastery of the Christians, where they gather and have their cells. I encountered many Christians from Iraq, who moved here on account of the good and remote location and the healthy climate" (Baumer 2006,

169–70). Also south of Samarkand, from the Hephthalite city of Penjikent, in Tajikistan, is an eighth-century ostracon with lines from the Peshitta version of Psalms, written in the Estrangela script. And at Termiz in Uzbekistan, near the Oxus River, archaeologists have discovered two churches and a baptistery (Baumer 2006, 171).

Further archaeological evidence comes from Ak-Beshim (ancient Suyab) in Kyrgyzstan indicating two church structures from the eighth century. Also from Semireche, the Land of the Seven Rivers, located between Lake Balkhash in Kazakhstan and Lake Issyk-Kul in Kyrgyzstan, a large number of stone inscriptions (over five hundred) in Syriac and Turkish have been found, mostly dating from the thirteenth and fourteenth centuries (Klein 2000). The presence of Christians in this region is confirmed by the Franciscan William of Rubruck (traveled 1253–1255) and other Western travelers in the thirteenth century when the district was under the metropolitan of Kashgar and Novakat, near Lake Issyk-Kul, established by Elias III (cathol. 1176–1190) in the empire of the Qara Khitai (Pelliot 1973, 7; Biran 2005, 178).

The bringing of Christianity to Merv (Bairam Ali) in Khurasan is attributed to Bishop Bar Shaba (d. ca. 366) in the Syriac and Sogdian lives of the saint. He is said to have healed the consanguine wife of the Sasanian shah Shapur II (r. 309–379), which resulted in her becoming a Christian. She then was exiled to Merv, where she in turn converted her new husband, the *mobed* of the Zoroastrian community, and together with Bar Shaba built churches and helped with his missionary work (Brock 1995). The elevation of the bishop of the Church of the East at Merv to metropolitan status is not recorded before 544. Archaeology in the area has brought to light a range of ruins suggesting a Christian presence from the fifth and sixth centuries (Baumer 2006, 72).

In 644 Elijah, a metropolitan of Merv, is reported to have won converts among the Turks. According to one source, Elijah converted the khan of the tribe by making the sign of the cross to dispel a storm conjured up by the khan's shamans. The metropolitan baptized the khan and his army in a stream (Gillman and Klimkeit 1999, 216–17). A letter written by Timothy I in 781 indicates that another Turkish khan and his tribe had converted to Christianity and that a request for a metropolitan had been received (Dickens 2010). In a further letter addressed to the metropolitan of Elam (Khuzistan), Timothy speaks of having ordained a bishop for the Turks and says that he was going to ordain one for Tibet (Dauvillier 1948, 292). A ninth-century Sogdian inscription with three inscribed crosses at Drangtse (Tangtse) in Ladakh is thought to have been made by a Christian from Samarkand who had been sent as an emissary to the ruler of Tibet (Sims-Williams 1993). Other evidence for contact with Tibet by the Church of the East is less convincing (Uray 1983).

Fig. 4.2. Gilded Paten with   **Fig. 4.3.** Silk Fragment Depicting Women
Christian Scenes, Talas Region?   at the Tomb, Toyuk

The remote geographical areas of Central Asia made it impossible for bishops to attend the regular synods of the Church of the East in Iran. Dispensations for the metropolitans of Samarkand, India, and China allowed them to submit letters every six years, apprising the catholicos of the situation in their dioceses (Gillman and Klimkeit 1999, 219). The main cities of Transoxiana, Bukhara, and Samarkand fell to the Arabs in 712 and 713. The Battle of Talas in 751 saw the defeat of the Chinese army, the main church at Talas being converted into a mosque in 893 (Bartol'd 1977, 224). A gilded paten dated to the ninth or tenth century, with scenes of the crucifixion, the women at the tomb, and the ascension, may have originated in the Talas region (fig. 4.2). The changing political and demographic situation in Central Asia obliged Christian leaders to negotiate a modus vivendi with their new masters.

We learn of Melkites in Transoxiana in 762, when the Arab caliph al-Mansur (r. 754–775) transferred their community in Seleucia-Ctesiphon to Tashkent, together with their catholicos, who was known thereafter as the "Catholicos of Romagyris" (Parry 2012), but who by the end of the tenth century had changed his title to "Catholicos of Khurasan." In the fourteenth century, the title Romagyris appears to have been transferred to the catholicos of the Georgian Byzantine Church (Klein 1999). In 1253 William of Rubruck met Alans, whom he described as "Christians of the Greek rite who use the Greek alphabet and have Greek priests, and yet are not schismatic like the Greeks but honour every Christian without respect of persons" (Jackson 1990, 102). The king of the Alans in the Caucasus is said to have become Byzantine Orthodox in the early tenth century, but relations with Constantinople appear to have soured soon after (Alemany 2000, 187, 239). There is also evidence for Orthodox Christians among the Turks and Tatars at Sudaq in the Crimea (Sodak, Ukraine) in the thirteenth and fourteenth centuries (Vásáry 1988).

Chinese Central Asia

Interestingly, no Christian Sogdian texts have been found in Sogdiana itself, although most of those found at Turfan, in Chinese Central Asia (Xinjiang), probably originated there. At Toyuk in the Turfan oasis, a painted fragment found by a Japanese expedition in the early twentieth century has recently been identified as the women at the tomb (Parry forthcoming) (fig. 4.3), while a wall painting from the ruins of Gaochang (ancient Qočo, also in the Turfan oasis) is thought to be a Christian scene (fig. 4.4). The wall containing the eighth- or ninth-century fresco may have come from a church. The scene shows a (Sogdian?) deacon holding a thurible and chalice, and three worshipers/communicants (two [Uighur?] men and a Chinese woman) carrying branches. The presence of Christians so far east was a result of the Silk Road trade, with Sogdian being the lingua franca of the merchants, and with Sogdians the dominant entrepreneurs. The Armenian Het'um (ca. 1245–1276) wrote in 1307 that there were Christians called Sogdians in Chorasmia (the area south of the Aral Sea) who had their own language, celebrated the liturgy like the Greeks, and owed obedience to the patriarch of Antioch (Pelliot 1973, 117). This is confirmed by the Muslim scholar al-Biruni, a native of Chorasmia, who in his *Chronology of Ancient Nations* lists the feasts in the Melkite and

Fig. 4.4. Fresco Fragment Depicting Deacon and Communicants, Qočo

Saeki 1951, 408

Fig. 4.5. Silk Fragment Showing Christian Figure in Style of Bodhisattva (Fragment and Reconstruction), Dunhuang

Church of the East calendars and says he would have included the Syrian Orthodox as well had he known Christians of this community (Sachau 1879, 282–313). The existence of these Melkites may be evidence that Sogdian earlier had been used liturgically by them in Sogdiana (Sims-Williams 1992, 46). This suggestion gains support from the ninth-century *Life of Constantine the Philosopher*, in which Sogdian is included in a list of Christian liturgical languages. The Constantine of this *vita* is better known by his monastic name, Cyril (827–869), who, along with his brother Methodius (826–885), evangelized the Slavs (Kantor 1983, 71).

There were two churches by the ninth century at Khotan (Hotan), on the southern Silk Road in Chinese Central Asia, one situated inside the town and one outside. A Christian presence could still be found there in about 1214, when Christian monks took part in a religious debate initiated by Güchülüg (r. 1211–1218), a Naiman and former Christian who seized the Qara Khitai throne (Biran 2005, 179). Also by the ninth century, on the northern road, Christianity had put down roots in Turfan, where a large number of manuscript fragments have been found in a variety of languages. In 1265 the metropolitan of Hami (Qomul), located between Turfan and Dunhuang, left for the consecration of Dinkha I (cathol. 1265–1281) at Maragha (Baum and Winkler 2003, 75). At Dunhuang itself several Christian texts have been found, as well as a painted silk fragment depicting a Christian figure[3] in the style of a Bodhisattva, reflecting the inculturation of Christianity in Chinese Central Asia.

3. Three crosses are clearly depicted: a pectoral cross, a cross in the headdress, and a cross on the processional staff.

The Pax Mongolica

It is necessary to look at Central Asia during the *Pax Mongolica* (Mongol Peace) in order to understand that Christianity was not totally eclipsed by Islam in the period from the eighth to the twelfth centuries. At the start of the thirteenth century several Altaic tribes had Christians in their midst. Among these tribes were the Naiman, Merkit, Önggüt, Keörait, Tangut, and Qara Khitai. Any suggestion, however, that whole tribes had converted to Christianity should be treated with caution. Beginning in the middle of the thirteenth century we hear of Christians among the Mongols from the reports of papal envoys and merchants traveling through Central Asia to the court of the Great Khan.

The Latin occupation of Constantinople (1204–1261) as a result of the Fourth Crusade facilitated the passage of Western Europeans to the Levant. Latin Catholic emissaries and travelers journeying through Central Asia to China refer to many of the indigenous Christians they meet as "Nestorians" and brand their Christianity as "heretical." Nevertheless, the records of European visitors to the Far East during the *Pax Mongolica* provide invaluable evidence for the presence of Eastern Christians deep into Asia. Even after the devastations wrought by Tamerlane (r. 1376–1405) in the second half of the fourteenth century, we still hear of Syrian Orthodox, Armenian, and Melkite Christian communities in Samarkand (Markham 1859, 171).

Both William of Rubruck and Marco Polo report on the widespread presence of the Church of the East in Central Asia in the thirteenth century. They

---

4.1 The Legend of Prester John

When news filtered through to the crusaders in the Holy Land of the victory of the non-Muslim Qara Khitai over the Seljuk Muslim army at Qatwān near Samarkand in 1141, it was believed to be a Christian victory. The name of the founder of the Qara Khitai, and general of the victorious army, Yelü Dashi (r. 1124–1143), became associated with the legendary Prester John. The legend of a priest-king of this name who would come from the East to join forces with the West to drive out the Muslims from the Holy Land was first recorded by Otto of Freising (bp. ca. 1136–1158). In his *Chronicle* of 1146 he describes a meeting between Pope Eugenius III (bp. 1145–1153) and Hugh, bishop of Jabala in Syria (fl. ca. 1140), in which the latter speaks of Prester John as a Nestorian Christian and a descendant of the Magi (*Chron.* 7.33). The presence of East Syrian Christians within the empire and army of the Qara Khitai undoubtedly contributed to the legend of such a figure (Biran 2005, 176).

give tantalizing glimpses into the beliefs and practices of the Christians they encounter. For example, Rubruck found it difficult to comprehend the lack of the use of crucifixes by East Syrian priests, thinking that this implied a doctrinal divergence from his own Catholic faith (Jackson 1990, 117); images depicting the gory details of Christ's passion had become commonplace in Western Europe, largely as a result of Franciscan preaching.

The idea of an alliance between Mongols and Europeans (see sidebar 4.1) lay behind the diplomatic mission of Ilkhan Argun (r. 1284–1291), when he dispatched Rabban Sauma (ca. 1225–1294) to the Western powers in 1286. Rabban Sauma was an Önggüt from Khanbaliq (Beijing), who with his disciple Markus, another Önggüt from Koshang (in Inner Mongolia), had set out on a pilgrimage to the Holy Land in 1275. The presence of Christians in Inner Mongolia is attested by the remains of inscribed tombstones dating from the thirteenth and fourteenth centuries (Halbertsma 2008). The story of their journey (extant in Syriac) provides evidence for Christians among the Tangut and other Central Asian peoples, as they traveled on the southern Silk Road to Kashgar via Khotan. In 1281 Markus was elected catholicos of the Church of the East as Yaballaha III, while Rabban Sauma's diplomatic mission took him to Constantinople, Rome, and France, where he met the French and English kings (Budge 1928).

When the Syrian Orthodox historian and *maphrain* Bar Hebraeus died at Maragha in 1286, his funeral was attended by Yaballaha III, and in his *Chronography* Bar Hebraeus mentions Rabban Sauma's diplomatic mission to the West (Budge 1976, 492). After Tabriz replaced Maragha as the Ilkhanate capital, it was visited by many Western travelers, who report the presence of Armenians, Greeks, and Syrians. The Byzantine wife of Ilkhan Abaqa (r. 1265–1282), Maria Despina Khatun, the illegitimate daughter of Emperor Michael VIII (r. 1259–1282), had sent for iconographers from Constantinople to decorate a Greek church in Tabriz, and one of them was asked to decorate a church built by Bar Hebraeus (Budge 1976, xxvii). A Syriac illuminated manuscript from 1260 depicts the East Syrian wife of the Ilkhan Hülegü (r. 1256–1265), Doquz Khatun, with her husband as Constantine and Helena with the relic of the True Cross (Fiey 1975, 59–64).

It is not known how many Christians lived in Central Asia and China during the *Pax Mongolica*, but the fact that the Mongols set up the *Chongfusi* (Office for Christian Clergy) in 1289 indicates their importance. This office supervised the affairs of the Christian, Manichaean, Muslim, and other nontraditional religious communities in China, administering seventy-two regional offices (Lian Song, *Yuan shi*, chap. 89). The Chinese *Yuan shi* (*History of the Yuan Dynasty*) was compiled by Lian Song (1310–1381) and others from 1370 to about 1700. It contains a section on 'Isā Tarsā Kelemechi (Jesus the Christian and Interpreter), who is also mentioned by the Muslim historian Rashīd al-Dīn (1247–1318) in his *Successors of Genghis Khan* (J. A. Boyle 1971, 294). We are told that 'Isā was appointed head of astronomy and medicine in 1263, was sent on an embassy to Ilkhan Argun (r. 1284–1291) at Baghdad in 1285, and, on his return in 1291, was appointed head of the Office for Christian Clergy. He is said to have been a native of the Western Regions (*Fulin*), to have had a wife, Sarah, and to have had five sons, one of whom, Elias (*Yeliya*), succeeded him as head of the *Chongfusi* on his death in 1308 (Lian Song, *Yuan shi*, chap. 134).

Tolerance of world religions was enshrined in Mongol customary law (*Yasa*), and several leading Mongols were Christians, including, as already noted, Sorghaghtani Beki, the mother of Kublai Khan. Many of the Christian advisers to the Mongols came from the Central Asian tribes that made up the Mongol Confederation, and the unknown writer of *The Secret History of the Mongols* may have been a Christian (de Rachewiltz 2006, 1:xxvi). According to *The History of the World-Conqueror*, by the Muslim historian Juvaini (d. 1283), Ilkhan Güyük (r. 1248–1257) was brought up a Christian and respected Christians above adherents of other religions (J. A. Boyle 1958, 259). Güyük's supposed reputation as a Christian attracted Western emissaries (de Rachewiltz 2006, 1:259). Once Ilkhan Ghazan (r. 1295–1304) embraced Islam, however, the Christian influence at the Ilkhanate court waned, while Christians (*yelikewen*) in China under the Mongols found patronage through to the end of the Yuan dynasty in 1368.

China

Christian Monuments[4]

The history of the Church of the East in China was unknown to Western scholars until news reached Europe of the discovery of a large inscribed stele (ca. 270 cm high, 105 cm wide, and 30 cm thick). The stele (upright-standing stone slab) was found by workers in 1623 while digging a trench in the district of Zhouzhi about 75 km west of the historic city of Xi'an. The stele bears a long inscription in Chinese, but it also contains a number of lines in Syriac, which was then a closed book to scholars in China. However, Catholic missionaries

4. The author of this section is grateful to the Australian Research Council and the Chiang Ching Kuo Foundation for financial support for ongoing research on "Nestorian" monuments in China, both at Xi'an and Quanzhou/Zayton. The Humboldt Stiftung also provided extensions to his stipendium enabling him to consult scholars based at the Akadamienvorhaben Turfanforschung in Berlin.

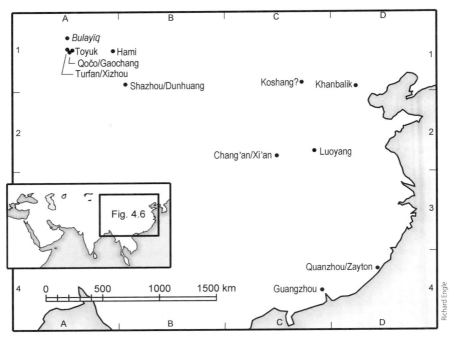

Fig. 4.6. Map of China

were by then active on the South China coast, especially in the Portuguese enclave of Macao, and the main text of the stele was soon recognized as pertaining to the establishment of the monasteries of a monotheistic (Christian) religion: "the Luminous Teaching [*Jingjiao*] of *Da Qin*."[5] The discovery of the so-called Nestorian (or Xi'anfu) Monument soon became public knowledge and is referred to in Edward Gibbon's famous *Decline and Fall of the Roman Empire* (see fig. 4.7; 1908, 149–50, 520–22).

Its authenticity and even its very existence, however, became the subject of a fiercely fought forensic debate, making strange bedfellows of *philosophes* such as Voltaire and countless Protestant scholars who commonly wrote it off as an ingenious "Jesuit forgery to deceive the Chinese and defraud them of their treasures" (Pelliot 1996, 151). Much of the debate was fueled by the

5. *Jingjiao*, the self-designated term for the Church of the East in Tang China, usually is translated as "Luminous Religion." Elsewhere (Lieu 2009, 241–45) I have tentatively argued for the character *jing* (luminosity, vista, etc.) being a homophonal mask meaning "reverence or fear," as the Christians in Iran and Central Asia had long been known by the Middle Persian name *tarsāg*, "God-fearer" (hence Sogdian *trs'q*). *Da Qin* is the traditional Chinese term for a great utopian nation situated in the Far West, which could only be the Roman Empire (see Saeki 1951, 320–33; Moule 1930, 35–52; Pelliot 1996, 173–80).

fact that very few scholars had actually seen the monument itself. We owe a huge debt to the Danish scholar Frits Holm (1924), who tracked down the monument in the early part of the last century and had full-size replicas made and distributed for exhibition in several of the most prestigious museums in the world. In 2006 came the news that a second but fragmentary "Nestorian" stele in Chinese only (i.e., no Syriac was used throughout) had been found in Luoyang, the eastern capital of Tang China. Although a transcription of the text is now available, major academic studies of this new text are not yet available. About two-thirds of the stele is preserved, but there is every hope that the missing portion may be discovered (Zhang Naizhu 2007).

The elder of the two stelae is a prime exhibit in the Xi'an Forest of Stone Tablets Museum (*Xi'an beilin bowuguan*), seen by hundreds of thousands of tourists each year (Xi'an beilin bowuguan 1993, 44). Earlier editions and translations of the long inscription normally included both the Chinese and the Syriac texts (Saeki 1951, 320–33; Moule 1930, 35–52). However, because the main body of the inscription on the monument is in Chinese, the text has been studied mainly by Sinologists and not by Syriac scholars. Consequently, some translations do not include the Syriac except for two lines, one placed at the beginning and the other at the end of the main Chinese text (e.g., Pelliot 1996, 173–80; Xu Longfei 2004, 95–101). The Syriac, though comprising no more than 300 words as compared to the 1,756 characters in 32 long lines of the Chinese, is an important and timely reminder of the Central Asian connections of the religion. Much of what it tells us about the Christian community's links with the Church of the East at large is not repeated in Chinese, as the Syriac and Chinese portions of the text are intended for different audiences. The very first line of the inscription, however, is bilingual, although the Chinese is clearly not a translation of the Syriac:

{Chinese} Recorded [i.e., authored] by Jing Jing, a monk of the *Da Qin* monastery.

{Syriac} Adam priest and *chorepiscopus* and *fapsh'* of Zinstan.[6]

6. Translations by the author. The transliterated term *fapsh'* in the Syriac, often misread as *fapshy*, is generally regarded as the Chinese religious term *fashi*, "monk, priest" (lit., man of law). "Priest of China," however, is simply too junior a title for a *chorepiscopus* who was also metropolitan. It is more likely that *fapsh'* is the Greek title *papos* (= Latin *papa*; i.e., pope) transcribed from its Syriac version into Chinese, and that it had become so commonly used that it was transcribed back into Syriac from the Chinese. The name for China in Syriac (from Middle Iranian) is "Zinistan." The variant "Zinstan" on the monument is usually emended by scholars to "Zin(i)stan" in translation. The form "Zynstan" is, however, attested in Sogdian, an important language of the Church of the East along the Silk Road (Henning 1948, 604, 606). The proper name for China in Syriac is "Bēt Zinayē" (Budge 1893, 2:238.15 [Syriac text]).

The Syriac resumes at the end (bottom) of the main part of the Chinese text and is preceded by a line in Chinese:

{Chinese} In the reign of Ningshu [i.e., Hananishu] as Patriarch [lit., King of the Law (= Buddhist Sanskrit: *Dharma*)] over the *Jing* congregations of the East.

{Syriac} In the days of the Father of Fathers Mar Hananishu Catholicus Patriarch.

In the year One Thousand and Ninety and Two of the Greeks [1092 Sel. = 781 CE] My Lord Izd-buzid priest and *chorepiscopus* of Khumdan [i.e., Chang'an] the metropolis, son of the late Milis priest, from Balkh a city of Tahuristan [i.e., Tocharistan], set up that tablet of stone. The things which are written on it (are) the law of him our Savior and the preaching of them our fathers to the kings of Zinaye.

{Chinese} Monk Lingbao Adam, minister, son of Izd-buzid *chorepiscopus*. (trans. Moule 1930, 48, altered)

Virtually none of the information contained in the Syriac lines is repeated in the Chinese. The Chinese monk-name of Adam son of Izd-buzid (i.e., Lingbao) is, interestingly, given in Chinese characters in the middle of the Syriac text, which would have been incomprehensible to a reader knowing only Syriac. Hananishu (cathol. ca. 774–780) had died toward the end of 780, but clearly news of his death had not yet reached distant China when the monument was erected in 781 (Moule 1930, 47n43). Izd-buzid hailed from Bactra (Balkh) in Tocharistan, which is significant because it was also the king of Tocharistan who requested (through what could only be described as diplomatic channels) that a Manichaean priest be presented at the Tang court (Lieu 1992, 229). The Church of the East had maintained the use of the Seleucid calendar, which is well attested in Syriac Christian texts and inscriptions from Iraq, Iran, and Central Asia. This, as we will see, would develop into an elaborate dating formula in Syro-Turkic Christian inscriptions found particularly in South China during the Mongol period. The names of some seventy monks and a handful of bishops

William Tabbernee

Fig. 4.7. Rubbing of the Top Panel of the Xi'an "Nestorian" Monument

are given on the side panels of the stele. These are given first in Syriac and then Chinese. The latter are rendered in some cases by phonetic translation but more often by the adoption of Chinese Buddhist-style monk-names (a name of religious significance adopted by a monk at the time of his ordination). There were four monks with the name Sargis (i.e., Sergius) in Syriac, but their monk-names in Chinese are completely different.

The Xi'an Monument has an apologetic preamble on the superiority of monotheism and a treatise on the mystical character of the symbol of the cross (*shi*, which happens to be the Chinese character for the number ten). A central part of the apologetic section is on the soteriological role of the Messiah (see sidebar 4.2).

The purpose of the main (i.e., Chinese) part of the inscription is to record the arrival of the religion in China, the official status accorded it by the Tang court, and the implicit permission to propagate the religion. In this respect, it is a historical document of the greatest importance, given the paucity of attestations in Chinese literary and administrative sources to the diffusion of Christianity in Tang China. Individual Christians might have visited China as part of the caravan trade, but the arrival of a priest named Aluoben (Syriac

---

4.2 Xi'an Monument (Soteriological Section)

Upon this [i.e., the rise of the different sects] the divided Person of our Three in One [i.e., the Trinity], the brilliant and reverend Mishihe [i.e., the Messiah], veiling and hiding his true majesty, came to earth in the likeness of man. An angel proclaimed the good news; a virgin gave birth to the sage in *Da Qin* [i.e., the Roman Empire]. A bright star told of good fortune; the Persians [*Bosi*] saw its glory and came to offer gifts. He [i.e., the Messiah] brought to completion the letter of the ancient law of the twenty-four sages, regulating the state on the great principle; he founded the new teaching unexpressed in words of the most holy Spirit of the Three in One, modeling the practice of virtue on right faith. He laid down the rule of the eight conditions, cleansing from the defilement of sense and perfecting truth. He opened the gates of the three which abide, he disclosed by storm the halls of darkness; the wiles of the devil were then all destroyed. He rowed the boat of mercy to go up to the palaces of light; those who have souls were then completely saved. His mighty works thus finished, he ascended at midday to the spiritual sphere.

There were left twenty-seven books of scriptures which explain the great reformation to unlock the barriers of understanding. The water and the Spirit of religious baptism wash away vain glory and cleanse one pure and white. The figure of ten [i.e., the symbol of the Cross] which is held as a seal lightens the four quarters to unite all without exception. (cf. Saeki 1951, 2 [text section]; trans. Moule 1930, 36–37, altered)

rabban, "teacher") in 635 was regarded by the sect as the official date of the entry of the religion into China, as he was received by ministers of state at the instigation of the Tang emperor, and some Christian Scriptures were translated into Chinese. This led to the promulgation of an edict in 638 that permitted the diffusion of the religion in China because the *Dao* (Way) could manifest itself in more than one manner (cf. Saeki 1951, 3–4 [text section]; trans. Moule 1930, 38–39). The same edict is preserved in a collection of administrative texts known as the *Tang huiyao* (*Notabilia of the Tang Dynasty*), which shows that the edict cited on the stele was genuine and not a Christian *pia fraus*.

Christian Texts from Dunhuang

The full title of the religion as given on the Xi'an Monument—*Da Qin Jingjiao* (the Luminous *Da Qin* [Roman] Religion)—enabled scholars to find a small number of written sources in Chinese on a foreign religion known as *Qinjiao* (short for *Da Qinjiao*), which flourished alongside Buddhism, Manichaeism, Zoroastrianism, and Islam in the Tang period, especially in the cosmopolitan capital cities of Chang'an and Luoyang (Saeki 1951, 1–4; Li Tang 2002, 145–208). However, these references are very meager, and the study of the Church of the East in China would have made very little progress had a number of Christian texts in Chinese not been identified among the large hoard of manuscripts (mainly Buddhist but some Manichaean) found by Aurel Stein in the Cave of the Thousand Buddhas in 1907 (Stein 1921). Most of the originals of the seven known Christian texts in Chinese from Dunhuang (see sidebars 4.3, 4.4, 4.5) are in the Stein Collection in the British Library. Others are in private collections, and the whereabouts of a few is still uncertain. The Japanese scholar Y. P. Saeki began collecting them into several collections both in English and in Japanese. The best-known of these was published in 1937. A less well-known and largely unavailable edition published in 1951 brought the collection up to date with texts found immediately before the outbreak of the Sino-Japanese War. His masterly study of the history of "Nestorianism" in Japanese (Saeki 1935), however, has never been translated into English.

Other Christian Texts

The discovery of "Nestorian" texts in Chinese from Dunhuang in Gansu province, an important stopping place on the Silk Road, was not an isolated phenomenon. Christian texts in a variety of Central Asian languages were also found among the many documents unearthed by German explorers at Bulayïq, about 10 km north of Turfan. In Gaochang, where Manichaean texts were found in abundance in 1905 by the second German Turfan expedition

4.3 Seventh-Century "Nestorian" Texts in Chinese from Dunhuang (with a Brief Summary of Their Contents)

Xuso Mishihuo jing (The Jesus-Messiah Sūtra): 170 lines, translated probably by Aluoben between 635 and 638/41. This is a theological treatise of some importance, as it summarizes a number of key issues: monotheism, the evils of idolworship, the Decalogue, Christian ethical principles as expounded in the Sermon on the Mount, the incarnation and early life of Jesus, and his passion. The final section (presumably on the resurrection) was said to be in such poor condition that it had been removed by the private Japanese collector (cf. Saeki 1951, 13–29 [Chinese text section], 125–60 [translation]; also Li Tang 2002, 145–46 [translation only]).

Yishen lun (Discourse on the One God): 410 lines in three sections, translated probably by Aluoben in about 641. It is a naturalistic and philosophical discourse arguing for the primacy of monotheism over polytheism. The arguments draw on few scriptural passages, not even from John 1, but utilize many standard early Christian arguments. Persia and Rome (*Fulin*) are mentioned as earthly empires whose boundaries were transcended by the limitless nature of the one God. The third section, titled the "Sermon of the Lord of the Universe on Almsgiving," however, draws extensively from the Sermon on the Mount and other ethical sayings from Matthew 5–7 (cf. Saeki 1951, 30–70 [Chinese text section], 161–247 [translation]; also Li Tang 2002, 157–81 [translation only]).

under Le Coq, the ruins of a Christian building on the eastern side of the city was also identified (Le Coq 1913, plate 7). The texts, mostly dated to the ninth and tenth centuries, are in Sogdian, Syriac, and Turkish (all three languages both in Syriac script and in cursive Sogdian or Uighur script) and include fragments of Psalters in Middle Iranian (in Pahlavi script) (Andreas and Barr 1933; Durkin-Meisterernst 2006) and New Persian (in Syriac script), and even the first line of a psalm in Greek (from Ps. 32:1 in the Septuagint). A Melkite origin of this particular text cannot be ruled out, as the knowledge of Greek among the priests of the Church of the East would have not been sufficiently high for it to remain even as a liturgical language.

The texts in Sogdian written in the Syriac script provided scholars of Middle Iranian dialects with their "Rosetta Stone," for Sogdian as the language was then still undeciphered. The "Nestorian" Syriac script is readily decipherable, and by using known proper names, one of the pioneers in the study of Turfan texts, Friedrich Müller (1907), was able to identify certain fragments as translations of the Peshitta into Sogdian. Incidentally, the system of vocalization used in "Nestorian" Syriac also gave many helpful clues to the pronunciation of Sogdian, as neither the Manichaean Estrangela nor the cursive Sogdian or Uighur scripts were vocalized. The ascetical tone of much of the texts recovered at Bulayïq suggests that the site is that of a Christian monastery (Sims-Williams 1990b). The employment of Middle Iranian beside Syriac probably indicates that the area was evangelized from Iran, perhaps specifically from Merv or Samarkand, the major centers of missionary activity of the Church of the East. The texts from Bulayïq include a Gospel lectionary in Sogdian (commonly cited as C5, i.e., [Sogdian] Christian Manuscript 5), containing substantial portions of the Gospels of Matthew, Luke, and John; several bilingual Gospel lectionaries in which the Syriac and Sogdian translations are given alternately; fragments of the Gospel of Matthew (C13); a bilingual lectionary of Pauline letters (e.g., C23, C77, C93) (Sundermann 1981, 171–95); and a Psalter including the East Syrian psalm headings, the first verse of each psalm being given in Syriac as well as in Sogdian (Sims-Williams 1990a). Besides these biblical texts, a large Sogdian manuscript (C2) contains a collection of ascetical writings and martyrologies that confirm the monastic nature of the community at Bulayïq (Sims-Williams 1985). Other ascetical literature includes the (spurious) *Acts of Sergius and Bacchus*, military martyrs who died in about 303 in Syria Coele; and the *Acts of Syriacus and Julitta*, a three-year-old child and his mother allegedly martyred in Tarsus around 304 (C22) (Müller and Lentz 1934, 520–22).

4.4 Eighth-Century "Nestorian" Texts in Chinese from Dunhuang (with a Brief Summary of Their Contents)

Da Qin Jingjiao Dasheng tongzhen guifa zan (Praise in Adoration of the Great Sage Penetrating the Truth and Returning to the Law of the Luminous Roman Religion [i.e., the transfiguration]): 14 lines, probably translated by Jing Jing (whose original name in Syriac was Adam) around 720. Jing Jing is known from Buddhist sources as an outstanding translator of scriptures into Chinese. He is credited with the translation of the *Satparamita Sūtra* from a *hu* (Iranian?) text. It is most likely that Jing Jing was a master of Sogdian, which would have enabled him to translate Buddhist and Christian texts into Chinese, as Sogdian was frequently used as an intermediary language for the translation of Buddhist texts and there was a large corpus of Christian literature translated from Syriac into Sogdian. This short hymn was copied by the monk Shuoyuan in the Christian/Roman (*Da Qin*) monastery at Shazhou. The latter is situated close to Dunhuang, and its existence helps to explain the presence of Christian texts in the hoard of predominantly Buddhist manuscripts in the Cave of Ten Thousand Buddhas at Dunhuang (cf. Saeki 1951, 100–101 [Chinese text section], 314A–314C [translation]; also Li Tang 2002, 203–4 [translation only]).

Zhixuan anle jing (Sūtra on Mysterious Peace and Joy): 188 lines, translated by Jing Jing (Adam) in about 780. This work is in the form of a discourse, commonly found in Buddhist texts, in which an enlightened disciple would ask the learned master a precise but also wide-ranging question on a theological or ethical topic, and the reply of the master would then form the main part of the text. Similar literary techniques are found in early Christian writings and, especially, among the Manichaeans. For example, the *Kephalaia*, which was translated from Syriac into Coptic in about the fourth century CE, already exhibits many such traits (Lieu 1992, 247–48). The text also displays a large number of Buddhist terms and concepts, but the use of Syriac words such as *ruha* (spirit) in phonetic translation (*luoji*) (line 43) shows that the author had no intention of completely camouflaging the Judaeo-Christian origin of the religion (cf. Saeki 1951, 77–95 [Chinese text section], 281–311 [translation]; also Li Tang 2002, 188–99 [translation only]).

Jingjiao Sanwei mengdu zan (A "Motwa" Hymn of the Luminous Religion in Adoration of the Three Powers [i.e., the Trinity]): 24 lines translated probably by Jing Jing (Adam) sometime in the eighth century. This is the famous Chinese version of the originally Latin hymn *Gloria in excelsis Deo* (Glory to God in the Highest). Its discovery caused a sensation among Chinese-speaking Christian congregations in the last century, and the text was quickly incorporated into hymnbooks as representative of an indigenous Christianity that could produce works of literature, albeit in the form of translation, long before many parts of Northern Europe were Christianized. A Sogdian version exists, but the Chinese version seems to be translated from both the Sogdian and the Syriac (cf. Saeki 1951, 71–73 [Chinese text section], 266–72 [translation]; also Li Tang 2002, 157–81 [translation only]).

Da Qin Jingjiao Xuanyuan zhi ben jing (The Sūtra of the Roman Luminous Religion Expounding the Origins and Reaching the Fundaments): a fragmentary work; the two fragments that came to light at different times yield about 41 lines in total, and the second fragment carries the colophon that the *sūtra* was the work of (copied by?) the monk Zhang Ju in 717. The authenticity of the second fragment has been called into question by scholars in China (Lin Wushu and Rong Xinjiang 1996). However, the newly discovered (2006) "Nestorian" inscription from Luoyang reproduces what it claims is the entire text of the *sūtra*, and comparative study of the epigraphical and manuscriptal versions of the text shows that the second fragment is completely genuine. The text is of a discourse given by a King of Law (*Dharma*) at the city of Nazareth (*Nasaluo*) in the Roman Empire (*Da Qin*). The discourse uses Daoist terms and depicts Christianity as the new and mysterious and superior *Dao* (the Way) (cf. Saeki 1951, 96–99 [Chinese text section], 312–313D [translation]; also Li Tang 2002, 199–201 [translation only]).

In comparison to the literary remains of the Church of the East in East Turkestan (Xinjiang), the extant Chinese corpus has a different outlook. This may be due to chance survival, but the seven texts described in sidebars 4.3–4.5

contain no ascetical or martyrological literature. Christian missionaries probably were aware that such material would make little impact on Chinese society, especially with the cultured elite, as it would only stress its alien origin. It was more important to concentrate on the production of apologetic literature intended for the Chinese audience. The Christian monks might have used Christian literature in Syriac or Sogdian for scriptural and other quotations, but apart from the *Gloria in excelsis Deo*, the Chinese texts have no known parallels in Syriac or Sogdian Christian literature. This is a striking contrast to Manichaean texts in Chinese, which are largely translated from Parthian, Sogdian, or even Old Turkish originals, with the exception of the so-called *Compendium*, a summary of the doctrines of the sect prepared for the Tang authorities.

Members of the Church of the East were deeply aware that they were missionizing in a much more sophisticated and intellectually competitive environment once they were established in the capital cities of Tang China, that they had to produce an apologetic literature that could meet the standards of Confucianist and Daoist philosophy and ethics, and that this could not be done purely by translation from the Syriac as in monastic centers in Samarkand, Balkh, or East Turkestan. Although a tenth-century Christian work called the *Zhunjing* (*Diptychs*) mentions a number of scriptural portions such as the *Sūtra of Moses the King of the Law* (*Mushi fawang jing*), the *Book of David the Sage King* (*Duohui shengwang jing*), the *Book of Paul the King* (*Baolu fawang jing*)—perhaps the Psalter and the Pauline Epistles—there is no evidence of a translation of the entire Bible into Chinese, not even of the whole New Testament. Such a task would have been beyond the efforts of a small body of monks who had to minister to the needs of the Christians among the foreign mercantile community in China (composed mainly of Sogdians), as well as try to impress the government of the day with the philosophical and ethical soundness of their doctrine in order to gain its official permission to missionize among the Chinese.

Cultural Adaptation

Unlike its passage through much of Central Asia, where Christianity was one of several major religious influences in lands that had no strong cultural barrier for its diffusion, in China Christianity was faced with a centuries-old culture with a Confucian official class and a form of emperor worship. Daoism had gained considerable prestige as a second school of philosophy in China, but Buddhism, a relative latecomer from India via Central Asia, opened Chinese society for the first time to foreign religious influence. Although some of the

---

4.5 A Late "Nestorian" Text in Chinese from Dunhuang (with a Brief Summary of Its Contents)

Zun jing (*The Book of Honor*): 20 lines, composed in about 800 or between 906 and 1036. This text consists mainly of lists of notables and scriptures. The list of notables includes the Trinity, the evangelists, and patriarchs. The list of scriptures includes catechisms, sermons, and similar material. Many of the latter are clearly Manichaean—for example, the *Sūtra of Three Moments* and the *Ning-wan Sūtra* (i.e., the *Letters* [*of Mani*]), which are also attested in lists of Manichaean works (cf. Saeki 1951, 74–76 [Chinese text section], 273–80 [translation]; also Li Tang 2002, 184–88 [translation only]). Most importantly, the monk who compiled these lists informs us of the two stages of the translation of Christian texts into Chinese:

> I respectfully note with regard to the list of all the books that the religious books of this religion of *Da Qin* are in all 530 works, and they are all on patra leaves in the Sanskrit [i.e., Syriac or, more likely, Sogdian] tongue. In the ninth Zhenguan period of the [Tang] emperor Taizong [i.e., 635 CE], a monk of great virtue from the West came to Zhongshia [i.e., China] and presented a petition to the emperor in his native tongue. Fang Xuanling and Wei Zheng made known the interpretation of the words of the petition.[*] Later by imperial order the monk of great virtue Jing Jing of this church obtained by translation the above thirty and more rolls of books. The great number are all on patra [leaves] or on leather in wrappers, still not translated. (trans. Moule 1930, 56–57, altered)

* Both were senior ministers of the Tang government. Neither was likely to have known Syriac, but both might have been able to summon help with Sogdian.

---

first Buddhist monks in China were Indians or Iranians, their zeal in translating Buddhist works into Chinese and the desire of local Chinese to travel to India to learn Sanskrit and Pali in order to translate more accurately from the original languages into more literary Chinese soon enabled Buddhism to pass into the mainstream of Chinese religious life.

Both the Church of the East and Manichaeism, being "religions of the Book," had to go through a similar process of translation and cultural adaptation. However, unlike Manichaean scribes who made liberal borrowings from Buddhism, especially names of Buddhist or Indian deities and religious concepts, the scribes of the Church of the East resorted to direct translation and restyling their basic teaching in a manner that was relatively easy for the educated classes to comprehend. With the exception of the *Gloria in excelsis Deo*, which was translated directly from both Syriac and Sogdian, the six other Christian texts from Dunhuang probably were composed solely for a Chinese audience, as there are no known examples of similar texts in Syriac or Sogdian (Deeg 2006, 122).

There are very few Buddhist terms of Sanskrit or Pali origin in the extant Christian texts in Chinese. While the Chinese term for "spirit" (*shen*) is used to denote God, the term *fo* (i.e., Buddha) was never used as an epithet for Jesus the Messiah, unlike Mani (ca. 216–276), who was transformed as the Buddha of Light soon after Manichaeism arrived in Tang China. The term *fo* was used in a generic manner in the *Xuso Mishihuo jing* (*The Jesus-Messiah Sūtra*) for "divine" or "deity" (Saeki 1951, 14–16 [Chinese text section]). Phonetically transliterated terms from Syriac abound in Christian texts—for example, *Yishihe* (or *Mishihe*) for "Messiah" (*meshihe* in Syriac), *Suodan* for "Satan," and *Aluohe* for "God" (from Syriac *aloha*). The latter was similar to the use of the transliterated name *Ala* by Chinese Muslims for "Allah." Although the Chinese characters used for transliterating *Aluohe* are the same as those sometimes used by Buddhists for *arhat* or *arhant* (Liščák 2006, 172), the context makes clear that it is the name of the supreme deity and not of a mortal who had attained Buddhahood. That Christianity has few names for deities and demons, save for the three persons of the Trinity and Satan, certainly makes adaptation of gods from Buddhist or Daoist pantheons unnecessary.

What strikes the modern reader about these extant texts is their surprising modernity. One of the oft-used terms for God is *tianzun* (lord of heaven), which is extremely close to that used by modern Chinese Catholics: *tianzhu* (master of heaven). The discourses on the Decalogue and the Sermon on the Mount are easily identifiable by readers of modern Chinese translations of the Bible. The name of Jesus was phonetically transliterated in a number of ways in the Christian texts. One that undoubtedly would have caused embarrassment had the text been read by an educated Chinese person was *Yishu*, which literally means "a migrant rat." However, the Tang Christians probably were less squeamish than we are, especially when it is obvious that a phonetic translation of a foreign name is involved. While eschewing Buddhist borrowings, the author(s) of the Chinese Christian texts cited Confucianist classics on numerous occasions to show that Christian teaching was on the same ethical and literary plane as that of the official cult of the state, and that loyalty to the emperor was essential to Christian social order (Li Tang 2002, 141–43; Liščák 2006, 172–73).

The Demise of Early Christianity

Like Manichaeism and Zoroastrianism, Christianity became established in China at a time of great openness to foreign luxury goods, technology, and ideas. The An Lushan Rebellion in the Late Tang period (755–762) led to a long period of unrest in which foreign influences and especially religions were seen as the root of the troubles. Unlike Manichaeism, which won the support of the Uighur Khan, whose Turkic troops were the main mercenaries of the tottering Tang government, the Church of the East had only fleeting patronage from the government of the day. When the Tang government turned against Manichaeism as a precursor to a more major onslaught on Buddhism, Christianity and Zoroastrianism fell under the same ban. With their monasteries situated in or close to the capital cities of Chang'an and Luoyang, the sect was extremely vulnerable, and few traces of the religion were left after their official expulsion in 843.

There is the well-known story told in *Al-Fihrist* by the tenth-century bibliophile al-Nadīm of Baghdad of his meeting with a Christian monk from Najran in Arabia who had made a special journey in 987 to inquire into the fate of the Christian church in China. To his dismay, he did not meet with one Christian in the whole of China (Dodge 1970, 2:836–37). Small pockets of Christians might have survived in cosmopolitan seaports such as Guangzhou (Canton) and Quanzhou (medieval Zayton), but a high degree of Sinicization would have been needed to camouflage the religion from the prying eyes of the authorities. The Church of the East, however, survived in border provinces such as Gansu and Xinjiang, especially at Dunhuang and Bulayïq near Turfan, which explains the survival of Christian documents among the hoard of predominantly Buddhist texts from Dunhuang. The religion found a strong following among the Turks of Central Asia, especially among the Turkic Keraits and Uighurs. When China came under Mongol rule in the thirteenth century, many Uighurs in particular served in the Mongol forces, and their presence as part of the Mongol occupying forces helped to reestablish the Church of the East in China, this time with the imperial patronage that it lacked under the Tang Dynasty. This second phase of the Church of the East is closely linked with the history of "Nestorianism" in Central Asia (Li Tang 2011; Lieu et al. 2012, 1–60, 83–122, 129–214, 243–62).

India

The Early Period

Two main traditions relate to the establishment of Christianity in India. The first concerns the mission of the apostle Thomas to India based on the third-century *Acts of Thomas*. This tradition maintains that Thomas landed at Cranganore (Kodungallur), on the coast of Kerala, in 52 CE, evangelized throughout the region, and eventually met a martyr's death at Calamina (Mylapore) on the Coromandel Coast, today a suburb of Chennai in Tamil

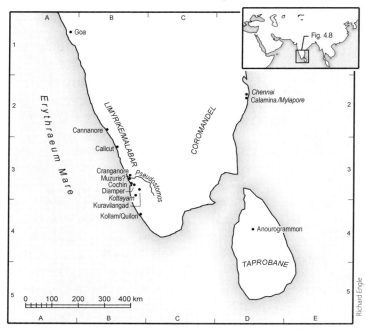

Fig. 4.8. Map of India and Sri Lanka

Nadu.[7] There are stories and songs from South India regarding St. Thomas, most of which stem from oral traditions providing testimony for the self-identity of various communities. The second tradition relates to a merchant, Thomas of Cana (Knayi Thoma), who reportedly landed at Cranganore in 345 with a group of seventy-two Christian families from Mesopotamia. The group was accompanied by a bishop and four priests, with Thomas helping to secure certain privileges for the Christians from the local raja. They appear to have migrated to South India as a result of persecution of Christians (Nazarenes) in the Sasanian Empire. If the date of 345 is correct, this occurred during the reign of Shapur II.

Associated with these traditions today are two ethnically distinct and endogamous communities in Kerala, the Northists and the Southists (*Vadakkumbhagar* and *Thekkumbhagar* in Malayalam). The Northists claim descent from those evangelized by Thomas and who lived on the north side of the raja's palace at Cranganore, while the Southists assert that they are descendants of the seventy-two families that migrated with Thomas of Cana and settled on the south side of the palace. The Northists claim apostolic

7. For discussion of the ancient names for Mylapore, see Medlycott 2005, 150–70.

4.6 Gregory of Tours on the Tomb(s) of St. Thomas

According to the history of his suffering the apostle Thomas is said to have been martyred in India. Much later his blessed body was transferred to the city that the Syrians call Edessa, and there buried. Thereafter, in that region of India where he had first been buried there is a monastery and a church that is spectacularly large and carefully decorated and constructed. (*Glor. mart.* 31; trans. Van Dam 1988, 51)

---

origins; the Southists claim the blessing of the catholicos at Seleucia-Ctesiphon (Kollaparampil 1992).

The Apostle Thomas

According to *Acts of Thomas* 170, after the apostle was martyred in India one of his followers took his bones away and conveyed them to the West. We first hear of a shrine to St. Thomas at Edessa in 371, when the emperor Valens (r. 364–378), an Arian, attempted to prevent the Nicene opponents of Arianism from worshiping at this shrine (Socrates, *Hist. eccl.* 4.18). At Edessa the relics of the saint were venerated until 1142, when, under threat from the Seljuk Turks, his bones were translated to the Greek island of Chios. In 1258 they were moved during the Latin occupation of Constantinople, this time to the Italian city of Ortona in the Abruzzi region. Today the Roman Catholic Church maintains that Thomas's relics reside at Ortona, while the Greek Orthodox Church claims to have his skull on Patmos in the Aegean. In India his tomb is venerated at Mylapore.

The tradition that Thomas went to India and died a martyr there is attested by many early Christian writers[8] (Gillman and Klimkeit 1999, 161–62). However, none of these authors records India as the location of Thomas's tomb, until Gregory of Tours (bp. 573–594), citing a traveler named Theodorus in his *Glory of the Martyrs* (see sidebar 4.6).

We have to wait until the ninth century for a further reference to the tomb. The *Anglo-Saxon Chronicle* informs us that the English king Alfred the Great (r. 871–899) sent an embassy to the tomb of St. Thomas in India (Medlycott 2005, 80–84). A more reliable account is given by a ninth-century Muslim merchant-traveler, Suleiman, who mentions Betuma in South India. This probably is "Beit-Touma" in Syriac, which means the "House or Church of Thomas" and refers to Mylapore. He informs us that from "Kaukam" (most probably

8. For example, Ephraem the Syrian (ca. 306–373), Gregory of Nazianzus (ca. 329–390), Rufinus (ca. 345–411/2), Jerome (ca. 347–419), and Paulinus of Nola (bp. pre-415–431).

Kollam), the tomb of St. Thomas could be reached in ten days' sailing (Renaudot 1995, 10a, 17b). Kollam was known to the Portuguese as "Quilon." In the thirteenth century Marco Polo visited Mylapore on his way home from China and tells us, in his *Travels*, that both Christians and Muslims prayed at the tomb of St. Thomas and that they took away soil to cure the sick (W. Marsden 1997, 232; cf. *Acts Thom.* 170). Several European travelers have left records of visits to Thomas's tomb in the thirteenth and fourteenth centuries (Medlycott 2005, 87–96).

MUZIRIS

Identifying the place names mentioned in early texts has long occupied scholars. The *Tabula Peutingeriana*, an early map of the *cursus publicus* (road network) of the late Roman Empire, shows the city of Muziris at the tip of India, together with a temple dedicated to the emperor Augustus (r. 31 BCE–14 CE), implying the presence of a Roman colony (Tomber 2008, 30). The identity of Muziris is still debated, but the most likely candidate is Pattanam, near Cranganore, about 38 km north of Cochin in the Thrissur district of Kerala.

Muziris is also mentioned in the anonymous first-century *Periplus of the Erythraean Sea*, where it is described as being approached by river and sea (54–56), which corresponds to the delta of the Pseudostomos (Periyar) River at Cranganore. It was also described by Pliny the Elder (ca. 23–79), who refers to Muziris as the primary emporium in India (*Nat.* 6.26). Archaeologists have found the remains of an ancient settlement at Pattanam, about 10 km south of Kodungallur, which, as noted, may well be the site of ancient Muziris. Pattanam has yielded Roman pottery, and gold and silver coins from the reigns of several first-century Roman emperors have been found in the vicinity (Tomber 2008, 140–43). A second-century papyrus records a transaction in a Red Sea port between a merchant who purchased a consignment from Muziris and an Egyptian shipping agent, the consignment consisting of nard, ivory, and textiles (Raschke 1975). In India Greeks and Westerners were known by the Sanskrit term *Yavanas*, and in a Tamil *Sangam* poem dating from the third century, the connection between *Yavanas* and Muziris is made clear when it speaks of the vessels of the *Yavanas* arriving with gold and departing with pepper (Casson 1989, 206).

ARIAN CHRISTIANITY

A reference to a mission by a certain Theophilus to India in 354 (see sidebar 4.7) is given by the fifth-century Arian church historian Philostorgius (368–ca. 439). Theophilus seems to have been a native of Diva (probably

4.7 Theophilus: Arian Missionary to India (ca. 354)

Theophilus . . . sailed off to the island of Diva, which, as has been said, was his homeland. From there he went on to the rest of the Indian country, where he corrected much that was not being done by them in a lawful way. They would, for instance, listen to the Gospel readings while seated, and they did other things not permitted by divine law. When, however, he had amended each of these matters with a view to their reverence and love of God, he confirmed the church's teachings. (Philostorgius, *Hist. eccl.* 44)

Socotra, Yemen) who was brought up at the court of the emperor Constantius II (r. 337–361) as a hostage and who later was ordained a bishop (Dihle 1998, 308–9). If this mission was sent in 354 under the emperor Constantius II, an Arian, then it seems to suggest that Theophilus confirmed Arian teaching on the church in India. The reference to the congregation being "seated" (see sidebar 4.7) indicates sitting on the floor in an Indian context, which is still the practice in most South Indian churches today.

The Church of the East

Although it certainly was possible to travel to India in the apostolic age, either overland or by sea, the first Christians to reach South India probably were Aramaic- or Syriac-speaking merchants from Iran and the Arabian Gulf, both of which had long-standing trading links with the seaports of Limyrike (the Malabar Coast). The involvement of the Greek patriarchate of Alexandria in international shipping is confirmed by the seventh-century *Life of St. John the Almsgiver*, patriarch of Alexandria (bp. 606–616) (Dawes and Baynes 1977, 217, 223, 239). Cosmas Indicopleustes (Cosmas the Indian Navigator), an otherwise unknown writer from Alexandria, composed, in the sixth century, a work in Greek titled *Christian Topography*, mentioning Christians in South India and on the islands of Socotra and Sri Lanka. Cosmas informs us that pepper grew on the Malabar Coast, where there was a church, and that at another place called Calliana[9] there was a bishop appointed from Iran (*Top.* 3.178). Cosmas probably belonged to the Church of the East, since he tells us that he received biblical instruction from Patricius, the later Catholicos Aba I (cathol. 540–552), referring to him as "a most divine man and great teacher" (*Top.* 2.124–25).

In addition to occasional references to the appointment of bishops to India in Syriac sources, there is local evidence from a series of copperplate inscriptions

9. Most probably also Kollam.

granting privileges to the Christians of South India. Two of the earliest of these, from 849, relate to privileges granted by the local ruler to the Terisa (Orthodox) Church in Kollam/Quilon, said to have been built by a certain Sabrišō, founder or refounder of Quilon in 825. Interestingly, 825 is the year in which the Malayalam era, or *Kolla Varsham*, named after Kollam, was inaugurated. Christians from the Church of the East in South India used the Seleucid calendar to date their manuscripts, but none of the known Syriac inscriptions in Kerala uses the Seleucid era. Among the privileges given to the Christians, besides permission to sit on carpets and to ride elephants (usually reserved for the highest caste), was the monopoly of the public weights and measures. While staying at Quilon in 1348, the Franciscan Giovanni de' Marignolli (ca. 1290–post-1357) reports that the local Christians were responsible for the public scales, a privilege that they appear to have relinquished by the time the Portuguese general Alfonso de Albuquerque (1453–1515) arrived in 1508 (L. Brown 1956, 75).

Socotra and Sri Lanka

According to Cosmas, Dioscorides (Socotra) in the Indian Ocean had Greek-speaking habitants settled there by the Ptolemies of Egypt, and the community of Christians had clergy ordained in Iran and sent to the island (*Top*. 3.178–79). It is not clear from his report, however, whether these Greek-speakers were Christians of the Byzantine rite and/or whether the Iranian clergy were members of the Church of the East. They could have been either, as there were both Melkite and Church of the East communities in Iran in the sixth century. The Muslim geographer al-Masudi (ca. 896–956) tells us that the people of Socotra were Arab Christians of Greek descent (Naumkin 1993, 31), while in the thirteenth century Marco Polo informs us, in his *Travels*, that the inhabitants were Christians whose archbishop was appointed by the patriarch in Baghdad (W. Marsden 1997, 247).

Cosmas Indicopleustes also provides the earliest reference to Christianity for Sri Lanka, or Taprobane, as it was known in ancient sources. He tells us, "The island has also a church of Persian Christians who have settled there, and a presbyter who is appointed from Persia, and a deacon and a complete ecclesiastical ritual. But the natives and their kings are heathens" (*Top*. 11.337). We can infer from this that the Christian community consisted of a colony of Iranians who had their own clergy to celebrate the liturgy. Given that Cosmas additionally informs us that there was a bishop at Quilon on the Malabar Coast who was also ordained in Iran (*Top*. 3.178), it appears that the Christian communities in South India and Sri Lanka had been formed as a result of Iranian trade in the region. The discovery of a stone cross in 1912 at Anourogrammon (Anuradhapura), the ancient capital of Sri Lanka, possibly dating from the ninth or tenth century, provides confirmation of a Christian presence there (Weerakkody 1997, 135).

The Arrival of the Portuguese

There were important commercial and diplomatic relations between South India and China during the thirteenth and fourteenth centuries. Chinese sources for the Yuan (Mongol) dynasty (1272–1368) provide details relating to trading links between the ports of Quilon and Quanzhou in South China, known as Zayton to Europeans (Lieu et al. 2012). This was the port from which Marco Polo embarked for India, and he remarks in particular on the large quantity of pepper arriving from Malabar (W. Marsden 1997, 201, 242). This trade was already taking place in the Song dynasty (960–1272), when the superintendent of shipping at Quanzhou, Zhao Rugua (1170–1231), wrote his *Description of Foreign Peoples* (*Zhufan zhi*). Zhao Rugua, also known as Chau Ju-Kua, reports that the chief priest of the Christians was appointed by the patriarch in Syria (*Da Qin*) and that he wore his hair in the manner of the local Indians (Hirth and Rockhill 1911, 112–13). Similar observations concerning the hairstyle and dress of the local Christians are found in early Portuguese reports (L. Brown 1956, 199). Lian Song (*Yuan shi*, chap. 10) relates that in 1282 a Chinese ambassador, Yang Tingbi, met representatives of the Christian (*yelikewen*) community at Quilon who subsequently sent tribute to Kublai Khan at Khanbalik.

A letter written from Kerala in 1504 to the catholicos of the East by Mar Jacob (bp. 1498–1552) gives some insight into the situation in South India at the time of the arrival of the Portuguese. Mar Jacob was one of several bishops consecrated for India by Shimun V (cathol. 1497–1501) and Elijah V (cathol. 1502–1504) in Mesopotamia (al-Jazira). The letter mentions that there were about thirty thousand Christian families in Kerala, and it goes on to say that new churches were being built and that the Church of St. Thomas at Mylapore was being restored. Just as important, the letter describes the arrival of the Portuguese and the impact that this had on the indigenous Christian population. The Portuguese are referred to as "our Frankish brothers," but their presence so infuriated the Muslims of Calicut (Kozhikode) that they persuaded the ruling raja to attack them. For safety, the Portuguese then moved down the coast to Cochin, where their cause was taken up by the local raja, resulting in civil war. After more ships arrived from Portugal, the Muslims and the raja of Calicut were defeated, and peace was restored (Mingana 1926, 468–74).

With the Portuguese in control of the Malabar Coast, Mar Jacob and the other bishops spent time with them at Cannanore (Kannur), where they were invited to celebrate the *Qurbana* (eucharistic liturgy) according to the East Syrian rite. It appears that Mar Jacob met Francis Xavier (1506–1552) in Cochin in 1548 and was eventually "converted" by the Franciscans. Unfortunately, Portuguese rule in South India turned out to be disastrous for the native Syrian Christian communities (Rogers 1962, 169–72). After the death of Mar Jacob in 1552, the situation was complicated by the establishment in Mesopotamia of a Chaldean (Catholic) patriarch, John VIII Sulaqa (bp. 1553–1555), in opposition to Shimun VIII Dinkha (cathol. 1551–1558) (Murre-Van Den Berg 1999). The brother of John VIII, Mar Joseph Sulaqa (bp. 1558–1569), was sent to Malabar as a Chaldean bishop, but he was not welcomed by the Portuguese, even with his Catholic allegiances. By this time the Portuguese were claiming the royal prerogative (known as the *Padroado*) over the Catholic jurisdiction of Malabar, and they were becoming increasingly intolerant of beliefs and practices construed as "Nestorian" (Neill 1984, 193–217).

By the second half of the sixteenth century East Syrian, Chaldean, and Latin hierarchies could be found in South India. The gradual Latinization of the Syrian Christians culminated in the Synod of Diamper (Udayamperur) in 1599, convened by the Portuguese archbishop of Goa, Alexis de Menezes (bp. 1595–1617). The synod imposed the Roman calendar and the decrees of the Council of Trent (1563) on the Syrian Christians, while condemning Nestorius and the adoption of Hindu customs (Baum and Winkler 2003, 114–15). Once the business of the synod was concluded, Archbishop Menezes ordered the destruction of books written in Syriac, although Syriac continued to be used liturgically.

Art Historical Evidence

When the Portuguese excavated St. Thomas Mount near Mylapore in 1547, they uncovered a stone tablet depicting a cross with a Pahlavi inscription (fig. 4.9). The Pahlavi inscription on the so-called

Fig. 4.9. "Persian" Cross, St. Thomas Mount

Fig. 4.10. "Persian" Cross, Valiyapally

Fig. 4.11. Freestanding Cross, Kuravilangad

Persian crosses (of which at least seven are known) has been variously translated. The most recent translation reads, "Our Lord Christ, have pity on Sabrišō, (son) of Čahārbōxt, (son) of Suray, who bore (brought?) this (cross)" (Cereti et al. 2002, 297). The style of the epigraphy appears to indicate a ninth-century date. That all known examples bear the same inscription seems to suggest that it served as a *eulogia* (blessing), so that having a replica would bring protection to the community that acquired it. St. Thomas Mount is the site traditionally associated with the martyrdom of Thomas, whereas his alleged tomb is in the crypt of St. Thomas Cathedral in Mylapore itself.

The iconography of the stone tablet shows a dove descending to a leaved cross that is mounted on a three-stepped pedestal, with the arms of the cross splayed to support pointed globes. A distinctive feature at the base is the downward-pointing leaf motif counterbalancing the upward-pointing leaves of the lotus flower. The cross is set in an arch resting on two pillars studded with pearl-like roundels in the Sasanian style, with the pillars emerging from the mouths of two animals crouching on capitals. The stepped pedestal and globular arms can be seen on Christian seals from the Sasanian period (J. Lerner 1977).

Interestingly, a cross on a lotus flower appears at the head of the eighth-century inscription from China written in Chinese and Syriac detailing the arrival of Christians at the capital Chang'an in 635 (fig. 4.7), a motif also found on Christian tombstones at Quanzhou in South China from the Mongol period (Parry 2006). If we accept that the earliest stone cross with the Pahlavi inscription is dated to about the ninth century, then it seems that Christians in both India and China started using the motif of the lotus cross at about the same time. Furthermore, it might imply that there was some contact between Christians in India and China as a result of international trade, although there is no direct evidence for such contact. That both communities used Syriac certainly points to their ecclesiastical origins in Mesopotamia and Iran and their affiliation with the Church of the East.

There are two "Persian" crosses in the Church of the Virgin Mary (Valiyapally) near Kottayam in Kerala. The larger of the two (fig. 4.10), on the south side of the sanctuary, bears the Pahlavi inscription together with a line in Syriac from the Peshitta version of Galatians 6:14: "May I never boast of anything except the cross of our Lord Jesus Christ, by which the world has been crucified to me, and I to the world." This cross has additional iconographic features above the Pahlavi inscription, but these are mostly hidden by a wooden frame. These features show two peacocks flanking a smaller version of the "Persian" cross with a floral banner arching over them (Parry 2005). Also, in the same church at the west end of the nave is a carved archway depicting on one side two elephants flanking a cross on a lotus pedestal, and on the other side two peacocks doing the same. Both the elephant and the peacock are ancient symbols in Indian art, and their depiction venerating the cross shows the assimilation of local cultural elements by the Christians of South India (Parry 2005).

In addition to the "Persian" crosses set up inside churches, tall freestanding granite crosses are located outside many churches in Kerala (fig. 4.11). These high crosses are objects of veneration, and local Christians light coconut oil around the plinths. Unfortunately, the heat generated by the burning oil has resulted in damage to many of the crosses and their plinths. The plinths have carved lotus petals and a variety of Indian iconographic motifs, such as elephants and serpents (Parry 2005). Appearing on some of the crosses are the *arma Christi*, or instruments of the passion, indicating their Latin Catholic origins from the Portuguese period. However, there is some evidence that the tradition of setting up freestanding crosses may be pre-Portuguese in origin. It is reported by the Franciscan Giovanni de' Marignolli, who stayed at Quilon in 1347 on his return to Europe from Quanzhou in South China, that he constructed a stone cross mounted on a marble pillar and consecrated it with oil. He tells us that he had the papal arms engraved on it, with inscriptions both in "Indian" and Latin letters (Parry 2005), but whether the tradition was begun by the Franciscans or was already established remains uncertain (Reitz 2001).

5

The World of the Nile

MALCOLM CHOAT, JITSE DIJKSTRA,
CHRISTOPHER HAAS, AND WILLIAM TABBERNEE

Introduction

The Nile River flows south-north for almost 7000 km from Equatorial Africa to the Mediterranean Sea. Headwaters flowing into and from Lake Victoria become what is known today as the White Nile. At Khartoum it merges with the so-called Blue Nile to form what from that point onward is simply called the Nile (Ancient Greek: *Neilos*; Latin: *Nilus*; Egyptian: *Iteru*).

As in Antiquity, the Nile winds its way toward the Mediterranean through a valley that it has cut through the (mainly) desert. At points this valley is up to 22 km wide. Since the construction of a number of dams, such as the ones at Aswan, the controlled release of water has negatively affected the fertility of the Nile River Valley—formerly inundated annually not only with water but also with soil-enriching silt now trapped behind the walls of the great dams. The course of the Nile itself has shifted slightly to the east since ancient times, and the two original northernmost branches, which once defined the Nile Delta, no longer exist. Similarly, some of the Delta's coastland has disappeared beneath the waves of the Mediterranean, including much of Alexandria's royal palaces and docks, and also the Martyrium of St. Mark.

This chapter was written by **Malcolm Choat** (Egypt), **Jitse Dijkstra** (Nubia), **Christopher Haas** (Alexandria), and **William Tabbernee** (Introduction, Axum).

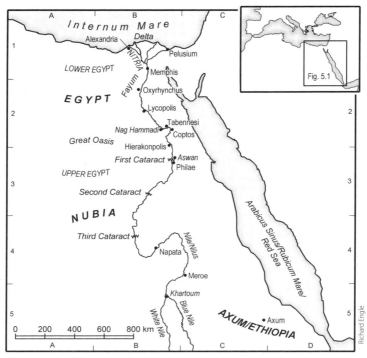

Fig. 5.1. Map of the World of the Nile

Ancient Kingdoms

As the White Nile makes its way north from Lake Victoria in Uganda and joins the Blue Nile to continue as the Nile into Egypt, it travels through the Republic of South Sudan and Sudan,[1] territory once belonging to the ancient kingdoms of Kush and Nubia. The Blue Nile originates in the Federal Democratic Republic of Ethiopia, the northern part of which, together with the State of Eritrea, once composed the kingdom of Axum. Fluctuating borders and overlapping spheres of influence with Egypt complicates the geography and history of the world of the Nile, especially in the pre-Roman period. Early Greek historians tended to call anything south of Egypt "Ethiopia," even including Arabia and India.

EGYPT

Following the unification of Upper Egypt and Lower Egypt in about 3150 BCE, Egypt was the dominant power in the region. This unification is evidenced by the Narmer Pallette, found at Kom el-Ahmar (ancient Hierakonpolis), the capital

---

1. South Sudan separated from Sudan in 2011.

of Upper Egypt and briefly the immediate first capital of unified Egypt. The Narmer Pallette depicts the same king (Narmer = Menes?) wearing both the Red Crown of Lower Egypt (fig. 5.2: obverse) and the White Crown of Upper Egypt (fig. 5.2: reverse).

Although Egyptologists disagree about some specific details such as the identity, dates, and achievements of particular pharaohs, Egypt was, on the whole, a strong, stable kingdom during the first millennium and a half after unification. There were, however, also a few not-so-stable periods caused by internal conflict or foreign invasion. For example, in the eighth century BCE Egypt's southern neighbor, the Nubian kingdom of Kush,[2] began to exert its influence and eventually conquered Egypt in about 743 BCE.

Fig. 5.2. Narmer Pallette

Egypt was ruled by a series of dynasties composed of kings, known from about 1550 BCE as pharaohs. The pharaoh was deemed to be the incarnation of the god Horus, symbolized by the pharaoh's "Horus name." Horus in Egyptian mythology was the son of Isis (queen of the goddesses and goddess of healing and magic) and Osiris (god of the dead). Horus is depicted most commonly as a man with a falcon's head wearing the double crown of Upper and Lower Egypt. As god of the sun as well as of hunting, war, and protection, in later times Horus merged with Ra, the sun-god, traditionally also depicted with the falcon's head but crowned with a disk representing the sun. The disk frequently was encircled by a golden cobra, which for later pharaohs became part of their distinctive headdress. "Son of Ra" became a

2. Not to be confused with the empire of Kush, on which see chap. 4.

common additional pharaonic title along with references to other gods, such
as the god of creation, Amun (e.g., Tutankhamun [r. ca. 1333–1323 BCE]).
Traditional Egyptian religion embodied a large pantheon of about eighty gods
and goddesses, each with relevant myths relating to their specific function.
With some local variations, neighboring kingdoms more or less adopted much
of Egyptian religion, and in Greek and Roman times the cults of the main
Egyptian deities (e.g., Isis) found fertile soil in the main cities of the world.

KUSH

At the time Kush took control of Egypt, it had its center at Napata (modern
Barkal). As pharaohs of the so-called Twenty-Fifth Dynasty, however, the kings
of Napatan Kush ruled their new extensive territory from Thebes (Luxor), the
capital of Egypt since about 1550 BCE. After less than a century the Kushitic
rule of Egypt came to an end as the result of defeat by the Assyrians. Taharqo
(r. ca. 690–664), probably the greatest of the Kushitic pharaohs, was forced to
retreat to Napata. His successor, Tanwetamani (r. 664–653), briefly recaptured
the throne of Egypt, but from 664 BCE Kush was essentially a Nubian rather
than Egyptian/Kushitic power. The kings of Kush, however, continued to rule
most of Nubia from Napata until about 250 BCE, when they moved the capital
farther south to Meroe (Bagrawiya). This instituted the Meroitic period of
Kushitic/Nubian history, which lasted until about 350 CE.

Meroe, like Thebes and Napata, was situated on the banks of the Nile.
Meroe was located at the intersection of ancient caravan routes, and the city
became an important center of trade. Skilled artisans of the region, which
was rich in gold and other metals, fashioned fine jewelry and bronze and iron
objects that were exported, along with locally produced ceramic and textiles,
to places as far away as China and India. Glassware, wine, and silks were
imported from Egypt, China, and the Greco-Roman world.

The kings of Napata and Meroe, greatly influenced by the religion, architecture, and burial practices of the Egyptian pharaohs, constructed pyramids for
themselves and their queens, albeit on a smaller scale. Over two hundred such
pyramids were built near Meroe, many still extant. Among the queens buried at
Meroe were some with the title *Candace*, designating not only consorts, queen
mothers, or regents but also queens, such as Shanakdakheto (r. ca. 170–150 BCE)
and Amanikhatashan (r. ca. 62–85 CE), who ruled in their own right. Meroe
eventually was conquered by the kingdom of Axum, its southern neighbor.

AXUM

While having an agricultural and pastoral economy sufficient to sustain its
own needs, Axum, like Meroitic Kush, was primarily a trading nation. It had

the advantage, however, of being situated right on the coast of the Red Sea, with easy access to the Arabian Gulf and the Indian Ocean. Its main, but not only, port was Adulis. Axum exported gold, ivory, obsidian, emeralds, animal skins, exotic monkeys, slaves, and salt.

By the first century BCE Axum rivaled Meroe in trade, and by the third century CE it had extended its territory to both sides of the Red Sea, including parts of what today are Yemen and Saudi Arabia but then was the territory of the Sabaeans. Unlike in Egypt or Meroe, the kings of Axum did not utilize pyramids for their burials. Instead, they erected huge stelae as grave markers, some as tall as 33 m. Some of these stelae are still extant in Aksum, the modern city on the site of ancient Axum. Axum was also the first nation in the region to mint its own gold coins as a means to facilitate trade. In about 350 CE King Ezana of Axum (r. ca. 333–360) defeated and incorporated the Meroitic kingdom of Kush, a detail listed among his other achievements on a trilingual stone (in Greek, Ge'ez, and Ge'ez written with Sabaean characters).

From the middle of the fourth century CE on, Axum began to utilize "Ethiopia" as a self-designation, laying the foundation for narrowing the name to apply to the area roughly corresponding today to the modern country of that name. The kingdom of Axum itself declined greatly in importance after the rise of Islam, as new Islamic states in the region gained control of the coast of the Red Sea and adjacent oceans (Grierson and Munro-Hay 2002). The last ruler of the Axumite dynasty was overthrown in about 950/60.

Between 1137 and 1270 a series of kings, the Zagwe dynasty, ruled the region now known as Ethiopia. In 1270 Yekuno Amlak (r. 1270–1285) became the first emperor of the so-called Solomonic dynasty. Subsequent claims deemed Yekuno Amlak to have been a direct male descendant not only of the last king of the old Axumite dynasty but also of the Hebrew king Solomon (r. ca. 970–931 BCE). Allegedly, the Queen of Sheba's visit to Solomon (1 Kings 10:1–13) had produced a son named Menelik, the legendary first emperor of Ethiopia. Solomonic descent remained a traditional aspect of the legitimation of the royal houses of Ethiopia, even as recently as the reign of Ethiopia's last emperor, Haile Selassie (r. 1916–1974).

Greeks and Romans

Like elsewhere in the Mediterranean world, the world of the Nile was impacted, especially in the north, by the conquests of Alexander the Great (r. 336–323 BCE). In October 332 Alexander and his armies occupied Egypt, entering the country at Pelusium, where he was met by Mazaces, the Persian satrap/governor. The Persians had first occupied Egypt from 525 to 404 and again

Fig. 5.3. Alexander the Great

from 343, only eleven years before Alexander ended the rule of Darius III (r. 336–330) in Egypt.[3] Although visiting Heliopolis, the cult center of the god Ra, protector of pharaohs, and Memphis, the capital of Lower Egypt, Alexander founded a new city, appropriately named Alexandria, as his Egyptian capital. As the new pharaoh, Alexander's royal name was *Meryamun Setepenre* (Beloved by Amun, Chosen by Ra) *Alexandros*. Alexander stayed in Egypt only for about six months. During this time he sent a delegation to the kingdom of Kush, headed by his official historian, Callisthenes of Olynthus (ca. 360–ca. 328). Callisthenes was the great-nephew of the Greek philosopher Aristotle (384–322), Alexander's own childhood tutor. No details are known about the delegation other than that they confirmed firsthand Aristotle's theories about the cause of the annual flooding of the Nile being due to rains in the south. In any case, Alexander decided to limit the extent of the southwest part of his new empire to the then-current southern borders of Lower Egypt.

Upon Alexander's death in 323, his body was intended to be returned to Macedon but instead was taken by Ptolemy, one of Alexander's generals and newly appointed satrap of Egypt, to Memphis. Following a power struggle, during which both Philip III Arrhidaeus (r. 323–317), Alexander's half-brother, and Alexander IV (r. 323–309 [Macedon]; 317–309 [Egypt]), Alexander's son, were murdered and Alexander's generals fought one another over the division of his empire, Ptolemy took the throne of Egypt as Ptolemy I Soter (r. 305–285). Either Ptolemy himself or his son and successor, Ptolemy II Philadelphos (r. 285–246), transported Alexander the Great's body from Memphis to Alexandria, where it was placed in a new tomb. In the time of Ptolemy Philopator (r. 222/1–205/4), the body was moved once again, this time to a mausoleum also housing the remains of members of the Ptolemaic dynasty. This dynasty continued to rule Egypt until August of 30 BCE. This was the month of the death of Cleopatra VII Philopater (r. 51–30) and her co-ruler son Ptolemy XV (r. 47–30). The latter is better known as Caesarion, his father being Julius Caesar (ca. 100–44).

3. The following year, Alexander conquered and destroyed Persepolis, bringing about the collapse of the Persian Empire, which was incorporated into his own after the death of Darius in 330.

Speculation by later writers that Cleopatra committed suicide by clasp-
ing an Egyptian cobra (asp) to her breast (e.g., Martial, *Epigr.* 4.59) may
simply be romanticized versions of the stark reality that she most likely
was poisoned (perhaps administering the poison herself) on the orders of
Octavian, the adopted son of Julius Caesar, later to become the emperor
Augustus (r. 31 BCE–14 CE). Octavian had defeated Cleopatra and Mark
Antony (83–30 BCE), his political rival, at the Battle of Actium in September
of 31 BCE. Within a year, Octavian invaded Egypt, where Mark Antony had
acquired power and influence through his relationship with and marriage
to Cleopatra. When Octavian arrived in Egypt, Mark Antony took his own
life on August 1, 30 BCE. Cleopatra's death occurred eleven days later, on
August 12. Coincidentally, Caesarion, the teenage (and now only) pharaoh,
lived only eleven days longer than his mother. He was murdered on August
23 by Octavian's soldiers. Having eliminated all opposition, Octavian made
Egypt a Roman province.

Egypt remained a Roman province until the Muslim conquest in 641 CE,
although its boundaries changed significantly during that period. Upper Egypt,
which had been partially abandoned by the Ptolemies, was restored to the
province by force under its first prefect, Gaius Cornelius Gallus, who governed from 30 to 26 BCE. Under the reorganization of the Roman Empire by
Diocletian (r. 284–305 CE), Egypt lost some of its western territory to Libya
Inferior and was divided into smaller provinces: Aegyptus Jovia, Aegyptus
Herculia, and Thebais. During the Byzantine period the new Diocese of Egypt
consisted of a number of smaller provinces: Aegyptus I and II, Augustamnica I
and II, Thebais Superior and Inferior, Libya Superior and Inferior, and Arcadia
(Bowman 2005, 316–22; Keenan 2000, 612–17; cf. Bagnall 1993).

Egypt

When Christian missionaries began to spread through the Mediterranean,
Egypt had been part of the Roman world for less than a century. While it
formed one province under a single prefect, the Romans encoded in the description of the capital, *Alexandria ad Aegyptum*, a belief that Alexander's
greatest foundation was not truly part of Egypt; rather, it was "on the way
to Egypt" (H. Bell 1946). Both administratively and culturally, the city stood
apart from Egypt. However, one should not overemphasize the divide between the capital and the countryside (*chōra*): native Egyptian iconography
is evident in the capital in the Roman period (McKenzie 2007, 192–99), and
Hellenic culture was strong in many of the capitals of the nomes (Egypt's

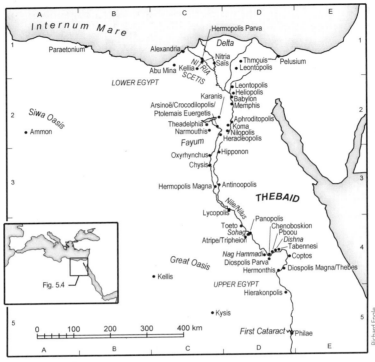

Fig. 5.4. Map of Egypt

ancient administrative divisions, still used in Roman times). Under the High Empire (70–192 CE), Egypt remained a single province. As noted, not until Diocletian reorganized the empire did Egypt split into additional provinces under their own *praeses*.

Religion

No less than the monumental buildings and tangible antiquity of the land, the myth of Egypt in the Greco-Roman mind still affected Roman engagement with Egypt. This is especially so in regard to religion (Dieleman 2005, 285–94; Frankfurter 1998, 198–237). Although Augustus and his successors steadily withdrew the financial privileges of the Egyptian priesthood and brought them progressively more tightly under the control of imperially appointed administrators (Kákosy 1995), the temple remained a social focus into the second century. In the third century, civic euergetism, which once had a strongly religious focus, began to be expressed more in secular civic terms (Bagnall 2008, 35). Combined with a continuing withdrawal of imperial support, the temples and their guardians were less and less able to fulfill their ancient roles, and some temples, such as that at Luxor (ancient Thebes, later Diospolis Magna), were reused for secular functions already in the third century (Bagnall and Rathbone 2004, 191–92; cf. Bagnall 2008, 33). At this time we witness the last regular use of Egypt's native scripts, although there are hieroglyphic texts in the catacombs housing the Buchis Bulls (the *Bucheum*) at Hermonthis (Armant) as late as 340 (Grenier 1983; 2002; 2003) and fifth-century Demotic texts from Philae (Dijkstra 2008, 175–92) (the same site preserves the last hieroglyphic text, from 394 CE).

The decline in the native scripts is mirrored in the rise of a new expression of the Egyptian language in foreign clothes—namely, Coptic. To be sure, the ancient traditions were not dead; into the fourth century some families in the capital cities of the nomes jealously guarded their inherited priesthoods (Willis and Maresch 1998; Maresch and Andorlini 2006). Both in their use of double Egyptian and Greek names and in their philosophical and priestly learning, these families show that the ancient priestly traditions of Egypt were being carried forward, albeit in a Hellenized, local, and less temple-centered form (Frankfurter 1998). It is into this world of partly Hellenized local traditions and classical culture overlaid with Roman administration that Christianity stepped.

The Spread of Christianity

If little is known about the introduction of Christianity to Alexandria (see below), even less can be securely deduced about how it first spread along the Nile. The later traditions that report first-century Christian activity in the province concern only the capital (Eusebius, *Hist. eccl.* 2.16.1–2; *Ps.-Clem.* 1.8–11, 13–14), and it is not commonly believed that the "Babylon" from which 1 Peter was written is the fortress town of that name near Memphis (Davis 2004, 4–5; Griggs 2000, 17–18). While Alexandrine Christianity comes into focus in the second century with Clement (ca. 140/50–ca. 220) and Origen (ca. 185–ca. 253), contemporary narrative sources state nothing about whether Christianity in general had spread to the towns and villages of the *chōra* (cf. Clement of Alexandria, *Strom.* 6.18). Information reported two centuries later about missionizing outside the capital by the famous Alexandrian "Gnostics" Basilides (fl. ca. 120–140) and Valentinus (fl. ca. 136–166) may not be reliable; even Epiphanius of Salamis (bp. ca. 367–ca. 403/5) was suspicious of some of the traditions that he transmits (*Pan.* 31.2.2–3; 7.1; 24.1.1) (Mullen 2004, 285; Pearson 2005, 3–4; Dunderberg 2005, 72–74). There is no archaeological or epigraphic attestation of Christianity before the fourth century (Pearson 2006, 331). Nor do the documentary papyri help (on the literary papyri, see below).

The supposed scriptural echoes and ambiguous monotheistic statements that appear in second-century letters on papyrus (e.g., Naldini 1998, nos. 1–3; Cugusi 1992, no. 169) are insufficient to assign them a Christian milieu. Nor can P.Oxy. 42.3057, from the turn of the first century, be easily accepted as Christian (Parsons 1980; Montevecchi 2000; Ramelli 2000; Blumell 2010). A Christian mummy label dated to the second or third century CE by its editors might just as easily belong to the latter century (Baratte and Boyaval 1979, 264 no. 1115; cf. *NewDocs* 4:260; Tabbernee 1997, 69).

In the absence of documentary or narrative literary evidence for the spread of Christianity through the Egyptian *chōra* in the second century, we have only Christian literature on papyrus to chart its diffusion (Choat 2012, 478–80). This has been used to excellent effect to demonstrate that second-century Christianity in Egypt did not have a "Gnostic" character, as Walter Bauer had supposed (Roberts 1979, 49–73; cf. Bauer 1964). The papyri provide geographical information irregularly, however, as many have come through the antiquities trade with little or no (and in some cases almost certainly false) indication of provenance. Their dating, of course, is entirely palaeographical and subject to challenge or adjustment (Bagnall 2009). For that reason, papyri normally dated to the second century CE and the late second or early third century CE are here treated together.[4]

Among papyri currently thus dated that were found *in situ* (confirming their provenance) are fragments of codices containing books of the Septuagint from Antinoopolis (Sheik Ibada) (*LDAB* 3087 [II]) and Hipponon (Qarara) (*LDAB* 3086 [II]). For reasons solely related to the scale of the papyrus finds at Oxyrhynchus (el-Bahnasa) (Bowman et al. 2007; cf. Parsons 2007), that site provides the largest number of Christian texts from this period, including four New Testament fragments (*LDAB* 2775, 2935, 2937 [II], 2938 [II/III]); a page from a codex of Genesis (*LDAB* 3094 [II/III] [Roberts 1979, 76–77]); three witnesses to the *Shepherd of Hermas* (*LDAB* 1095, 10575, 10576 [II/III]); two texts that may be from the *Gospel of Peter* (*LDAB* 4872 [II], 5111 [II/III]); and a part of the *Gospel of Thomas* (*LDAB* 4028 [II/III]). The interest in heterodox interpretations of Christianity is confirmed by a page from Irenaeus's *Adversus haereses* (*LDAB* 2459 [II/III]), being read in Oxyrhynchus within decades of its composition in Gaul.

Other texts from the period have come via the antiquities trade. New Testament fragments in the cover of a third-century codex of Philo (*LDAB* 2936 [II]

---

4. Indicated below as "II" and "II/III" respectively. On what follows, see Roberts 1979, 1–25; cf. Pearson 2006, 348–49. The papyri are cited by their number in the *Leuven Database of Ancient Books* (http://www.trismegistos.org/ldab/), where full details for each may be found.

[Skeat 2004]; the codex is *LDAB* 3541) may not be from Coptos (Qift), where the codex was reportedly found (if that is even true [Scheil 1893, iii; Merell 1938, 5; Worp 1998, 207]). The earliest witness to the *Shepherd of Hermas* (*LDAB* 1094 [II], though see Bagnall 2009, 42–45), purchased in Ashmunein (ancient Hermopolis Magna), probably was found in the vicinity. Two fragments of Psalms were purchased in the Fayum (*LDAB* 3092 [II], 3088 [II/III]). Of the provenance of other papyri, little can be said for certain; these include the earliest and most famous papyrus witness to the New Testament (*LDAB* 2774 = P.Ryl. 3.457 [II]), the "Unknown ('Egerton') Gospel" (*LDAB* 4736 [II/III]), the earliest stratum of the cache of biblical papyri now in the Chester Beatty Library (*LDAB* 3011, 3084, 3091 [II/III]), and sixteen other papyri featuring the New Testament, Septuagint, or treatises of unidentified authorship (cf. the lists in Hurtado 2006, 210–29).

It may reasonably be questioned whether the presence of these literary papyri confirms Christian activity at their findspot at the date they were copied; texts copied elsewhere may (perhaps sometime later) have been carried down the Nile and disposed of when they had outlived their usefulness. In some cases, the date at which a text was copied is demonstrably unrelated to the spread of Christianity in the area in which it was found. A large cache of classical and Christian texts in both Greek and Coptic, the core of which is now in the Bodmer Library, probably was found near Dishna in Upper Egypt (J. Robinson 1990). It includes a codex of the Gospel attributed to John that is commonly dated to the third century (*LDAB* 2777; on the dating see Nongbri forthcoming), a codex of Psalms that may be of similar date (*LDAB* 3098), and a copy of Proverbs in an archaic form of Coptic that suggests it too was copied in the third century (*LDAB* 107761). Yet the collection as we have it probably was formed in the first half of the fourth century, and some texts usually assigned to it certainly originated more than 100 km away in Panopolis (Bagnall 2002, 4–5). The assemblage tells us much about the preferences of its end-users (perhaps monks from the nearby Pachomian monastery at Pboou [Faw Qibli]) but little about those who copied its earliest texts. Similar remarks could be made about the Chester Beatty biblical papyri, perhaps from Aphroditopolis (modern Atfih, between Memphis and Heracleopolis) (C. Horton 2004, 153–59). Despite these caveats, it is unlikely that all the second- and early third-century Christian literary texts on papyrus are chronologically unrelated to the spread of Christianity in the areas in which they were found. Although they will not provide a totally accurate map of the expansion of Christianity through Egypt, they form our best evidence for the establishment of Christian communities in towns such as Oxyrhynchus, Antinoopolis, Hipponon, and Hermopolis, and the villages of the Fayum.

The Third Century

In the third century we encounter both narrative literary and documentary evidence for Christianity in the *chōra*. Eusebius of Caesarea (ca. 264/5–ca. 339/40) knew of "private letters" from the bishop of Jerusalem to the Christian community in Antinoopolis in the early third century (*Hist. eccl.* 6.11.3). A private letter on papyrus (P.Bas. 1.16 = Naldini 1998, no. 4), dated by its handwriting to the same period, is the first documentary text to use the Pauline formula "in the Lord" and the so-called *nomina sacra*, the characteristic Christian abbreviations of the sacred names.[5] Its correspondents' discussion of nomination to the gymnasiarchy and the council indicates that they are part of the municipal elite, though its provenance is, unfortunately, unknown; in light of other papyri from the same purchase, it might have been the Fayum.[6]

Certainly from the Fayum is *SB* 16.12497 (Sijpesteijn 1980), a list of nominees from among the class of minor landholders to undertake the liturgy of "supervision of the water-tower and fountains of the metropolis" (Arsinoë, modern Medinet el-Fayum). The text dates to the first half of the third century (perhaps later rather than earlier in that range) and includes among the nominees "Antonius Dioscorus son of Horigenes, Alexandrian"; a second hand that provides brief supplementary descriptions below each name notes that "he is the Dioscorus (who is a) Christian." Rather than being pejorative, the descriptions provide contextual information, perhaps to help locate the individual concerned (for another interpretation, see van Minnen 1994, 74–77). By the mid-third century the profile of the Christian community in the Arsinoïte capital was such that someone could be defined by membership of it.

Antonius Dioscorus brings us to the episcopate of Dionysius (bp. ca. 247/8–264/5) (Bienert 1978; Clarke 1998; Jakab 2001, 227–55). It is during his time that the church in Egypt steps decisively from the shadows in both the papyrological and narrative sources. Before this period we must rely on reports in later sources: Photius, patriarch of Constantinople (bp. 858–869, 877–886), mentions "Egyptian bishops" and gives the name of Ammonios, bishop of Thmouis (Tell Timai el-Ahmid) in the Delta (PG 103.387BC; PG 104.1229) (Martin 1996, 23–24). The "Antiochian" recension of the *Annals* of Eutychius (Sa'īd ibn Baṭrīq, Melkite patriarch of Alexandria, 932–940), asserts that Demetrius had ordained three bishops, and Heraclas twenty (PG 111.982, at 332).[7]

---

5. See the literature cited in Choat 2006, 119.

6. There seem no obvious grounds for Joseph van Haelst's (1970, 498) assignment of it to the Great Oasis (cf. Judge and Pickering 1977, 48, 51).

7. This information is missing from earlier, more reliable manuscripts of Eutychius (see Breydy 1985, 45n3; cf. Breydy 1983, 85).

In Dionysius's letters (Feltoe 1918; cf. Bienert 1978, 136–38; Legutko 2003) we find more secure contemporary information on the ecclesiastical hierarchy outside Alexandria. They indicate both how far Christianity had already spread (suggesting that Dionysius's predecessors did indeed consecrate bishops for the *chōra*) and how Christianity further expanded in the succeeding decades.

Dionysius addressed a festal letter (the kind by which the bishop of Alexandria announced the date of Easter) (Bienert 1978, 138–77) to Hierax, "bishop of those in Egypt," according to Eusebius (*Hist. eccl.* 7.21.2) (Bienert 1978, 157–62). The same title is given to Nepos (on whom, see below) (*Hist. eccl.* 7.24.1). Flavius, Domitius, and Didymus, other recipients of festal letters, are also likely to have been bishops (*Hist. eccl.* 7.20) (Martin 1996, 20), as probably was Hermammon, who, along with "the brethren in Egypt," receives a letter describing events under Decius (r. 249–251) (*Hist. eccl.* 7.22.12–7.23; cf. 7.1; 7.10) (Bienert 1978, 166–74, 143). Dionysius also writes to the bishops of Berenice in Cyrenaica (Mullen 2004, 295) and "of the parishes [*paroikia*] in the [Libyan] Pentapolis" (*Hist. eccl.* 7.26.1, 3) (Martin 1996, 19; Bienert 1978, 121–25). Within the province of Egypt, he mentions Chairemon, "bishop of the city called Nilos," who fled under Decius toward "the Arabian mountain." Nilopolis (Dalas), formerly part of the Heracleopolite nome, was by this time the metropolis of its own nome (Falivene 1998, 135–38, 225–26; Timm 1984, 498–502; Calderini and Daris 1935–, 3.4:327[1]) (it is attested as a bishopric between 325 and 347 [Worp 1994, 303]).[8] Konon (or Kolon), bishop of the *paroikia* of Hermopolis (Eusebius, *Hist. eccl.* 6.46.2; Jerome, *Vir. ill.* 69) (Bienert 1978, 54–55; cf. 180–85), who receives a "private letter on Repentance" from Dionysius, may have been bishop of Hermopolis Magna in the Thebaid or Hermopolis Parva in the Delta.

That the sees of Hierax and Nepos are never specified (the common assertion regarding Nepos's see notwithstanding [see below]) may be revealing. While there were bishops attached to cities in Egypt in Dionysius's time, the episcopal structure outside Alexandria might have initially developed (in Demetrius's time?) with a few bishops who had wide jurisdiction over the still-small Christian communities scattered through the *chōra*; the letters of Dionysius may witness the tail end of this system, overlapping with the growth of an episcopal structure more closely mapped to the administrative divisions of the province (Wipszycka 2006).

Throughout his tenure as bishop of Alexandria, Dionysius also wrote letters, festal and otherwise, to "the brethren in Egypt" (Eusebius, *Hist. eccl.* 6.46.1;

8. For what may be a second Nilopolis in the vicinity of Memphis, see Diodorus Siculus, *Bibl. hist.* 1.85.2, with Burton 1972, 246. It is not likely that a village in the Fayum named Nilopolis (Tell el-Rusas) had a bishop at this date.

7.22.11–12). The activity of one such group comes sharply into focus in Dionysius's report of an event that took place probably in the early 260s (Jakab 2001, 253). Dionysius traveled to the Fayum to engage in a three-day public conference to convince the local presbyters, teachers (or presbyter-teachers? [Martin 1996, 19n10]), and laity of the error of the millennialist beliefs that, according to Dionysius, had thoroughly taken hold among the Arsinoïte Christian communities ("for a long time" [*Ep.*, in Eusebius, *Hist. eccl.* 7.24.6]) (Bienert 1978, 193–96; Frankfurter 1993, 270–78; Davis 2005). The proof text of the millennialists was the *Refutation of Allegorists*, written by the now-dead "bishop of those in Egypt" Nepos, whose learning and psalmody Dionysius greatly admired (Eusebius, *Hist. eccl.* 7.24.2–4). Nepos is commonly considered to have been bishop of Arsinoë (Martin 1996, 20; Griggs 2000, 87; Feltoe 1918, 82) or (anachronistically) "of the Fayum" (i.e., Arsinoïte nome [Abbott 1937, 24]), but this is nowhere stated by ancient writers. That millennialist beliefs took such strong hold in the Fayum may have been because Nepos was bishop there, but it may equally have been due to the assiduous work of Coracion (d. ca. 280), "the author and originator of this teaching," who was present at the conference. At the conclusion of the conference Coracion acknowledged the superiority of Dionysius's arguments (Dionysius of Alexandria, *Ep.*, in Eusebius, *Hist. eccl.* 7.24.9), which the bishop later committed to writing in a work called *On the Promises* (Eusebius, *Hist. eccl.* 7.24.1).

Persecution

Some few years before these Christians in the Fayum gathered to debate theology with Dionysius, they, along with every other Roman citizen, had been required by Decius to reaffirm their allegiance to the gods of Rome by sacrificing and obtaining a signed certification of their act (Clarke 2005, 625–35; Scholl 2002). Of the forty-six extant "Decian *libelli*," forty-two come from the Fayum, thirty-four of these from the village of Theadelphia (Kharabet Ihrit). Yet this does not mean that this village, or the district, was a hotbed of Christianity. Something else may have linked these *libellicati*.[9] None of those who sacrificed to gain these particular certificates is indisputably Christian. The one distinctively Christian name among the *libellicati*, Thecla, is a doubtful reading, which more recent examinations of the relevant papyrus (P.Oxy. 12.1464) have rejected (Davis 1999). One declaration (W.Chr. 125) was filed by a priestess of the crocodile-god Petesouchus.

Two documents associated by some with the campaign of Valerian (r. 253–260) against Christians definitely record Christians, but they are not linked

9. For example, perhaps they all worked on the same estate (see Scholl 2002, 220–21).

with that emperor's actions (on these see Luijendijk 2008, 174–88). P.Oxy. 42.3035, issued on February 28, 256 (eighteen months before Valerian's campaign began in 257, and thus not associated with it), instructs officials in the village of Mermertha in the Oxyrhynchite nome to send "Petosorapis son of Horus, Christian" up to the city. His crime is not stated, but it cannot be his beliefs, not least because the "*komarchs* and superintendents of peace" are required to present themselves if he cannot be found. P.Oxy. 43.3119 is a fragmentary copy of an official letter, originating in the Saïte nome in the Delta (and thus perhaps concerns Christians in the neighborhood of Saïs), in which an assessment (perhaps of assets and buildings?) of Christians is mentioned (Whitehorne 1977). Yet nothing proves a persecution context, or even a date under Valerian.

The actions against Christians under Decius and Valerian find some of their best narrative evidence in the letters of Dionysius. Much of this concerns Alexandria, but Dionysius's reports also demonstrate the way in which these actions actually aided the further spread of Christianity through the *chōra* (Martin 1996, 22–23). Under Decius, Dionysius, with two companions, had hidden in a "desert and dry place in Libya, three days' journey from Paraetonium," but there he was "deprived of the other brethren" (Dionysius of Alexandria, *Ep.*, in Eusebius, *Hist. eccl.* 7.11.23; cf. 6.40.1–9). Such was not the case under Valerian. Dionysius was first sent to Cephro in the western edge of the Delta (7.11.5, 12, 15) (Calderini and Daris 1935–, 3.2:115–16; Mullen 2004, 277), then on to "more Libyan-like places," specifically the "district of Colluthion" (7.11.14–15), of which Dionysius had at least heard before his exile (7.11.16; cf. 11.15). Yet he lamented that it offered less opportunity for proselytization than had Cephro, despite being closer to Alexandria (7.11.17). Cephro had allowed the opportunity of increased contact with Christians "from Egypt," with the result that Dionysius "was able to extend the Church more widely" (7.11.17; cf. 7.11.12).

Dionysius's exile allowed him to interact with Christians from outside Alexandria; his ministers were able to spread the word even farther. During Decius's reign some of the clergy remained in Alexandria, but two of the better-known presbyters were sent "wandering in Egypt" (Dionysius of Alexandria, *Ep.*, in Eusebius, *Hist. eccl.* 7.11.24). This pattern of exiles was repeated under Valerian, but with more deliberation on the part of the prefect Amelianus. After being ordered to gather in the Mareotis, south of Alexandria, the Alexandrian clergy were "assigned to different villages throughout the country" (7.11.14), and although we hear no more of their activities, it is reasonable to conjecture that their enforced wandering provided the opportunity to reinforce the faith of local communities and perhaps to establish new ones.

Whether due to the actions of these exiled clergy or not, the expansion of Christianity through Egypt in the second half of the third century can be seen in the papyri. Christian literary texts on papyrus increase substantially in number, as do the range of genres represented. In addition to many more witnesses to the New Testament and the Septuagint we find Christian works of unidentified authorship (e.g., *LDAB* 3500–501, 5222, 5272, 5404–5, 5420–21), hymns and prayers (*LDAB* 5403, 5475), and further apocryphal Gospels (*Gospel of Thomas*: *LDAB* 4029–30; *Gospel of Mary*: *LDAB* 5406, 5329; the "Fayum Fragment": *LDAB* 5462). Alongside the provenances attested earlier, Christian literary papyri also come from the Fayum and Panopolis. Among the documentary papyri, *Papas* (pope) Maximus (bp. 264/5–282), Dionysius's successor, features in a letter sent from Rome detailing arrangements for the transfer of goods and money between the Fayum and Alexandria (P.Amh. 1.3a). Theonas[10] and an *anagnōstēs*[11] are also mentioned. That the letter concerns the economic dealings of a Christian community is reinforced by its subsequent use (by other scribes) for copying small sections of Hebrews (1:1 [P.Amh. 1.3b]) and Genesis (1:1–5, in both the Septuagint and Aquilan versions [P.Amh. 1.3c]).

Catechetical Instruction in the Chōra

The famous Alexandrian catechetical school, whatever its precise character (Pearson 2006, 340–44; van den Hoek 1997; Scholten 1995), had been long established when we find evidence for catechetical education in the *chōra* in the second half of the third century. This is primarily found in the "letters of recommendation,"[12] ten of which come from the last quarter of the third century or the first quarter of the fourth century. Most prominent are three letters (P.Alex. 29, PSI 3.208, PSI 9.1041 = Naldini 1998, nos. 19, 28, 29, the last two found in Oxyrhynchus) from a certain Sotas. The same man is addressed as *papas* in a letter (P.Oxy. 36.2785) to him from the *presbyteroi* of Heracleopolis (Ihnasya el-Medina). He is not, of course, the bishop of Alexandria, but it has been argued persuasively that he was the bishop of Oxyrhynchus, probably during the episcopate of Maximus or his successor, Theonas (bp. 282–300) (Luijendijk 2008, 81–144). In these letters Christian leaders recommend believers to other Christian communities both for assistance and edification (*oikodomē*); some are referred to explicitly as catechumens, and the stage of their spiritual education noted ("in the first stage of the gospel"; "in Genesis"). They show the ways in which the Christian community formed and maintained

10. A man bearing this name succeeded Maximus.
11. The title used for Christian readers.
12. Perhaps more accurately, "letters of peace" (see Teeter 1997; cf. Luijendijk 2008, 104–12).

its networks between the settlements on the Nile, seeking not only hospitality for those who traveled between them but often spiritual education as well.

Sotas is known also from two other letters. One (*SB* 12.10772) is sent from Antioch, where Sotas is currently, and explicitly calls him a "Christian" (which almost guarantees that its writer, an "Olympic victor," was not one). In the other, Sotas instructs his "holy son" Demetrianus on giving some land to the *topos* (the local church?) "according to the ancient custom" (P.Oxy. 12.1492). Several other letters from the same period (Naldini 1998, nos. 8, 13, 18) also bear witness to Christianity at Oxyrhynchus; the city is unusual only in the amount of papyri found there, and we may reasonably see its level of Christianization as roughly representative of other Egyptian cities.

ANTONY OF EGYPT

Alongside the growth of the institutional church, other currents were developing. In about 270, the son of well-off village landowners from Koma (Qiman el-Arus) in the Heracleopolite nome (Falivene 1998, 109–12; Calderini and Daris 1935–, 3.2:137) was inspired by the words of the gospel to forsake his inheritance for the spiritual guidance of men who practiced *ascesis* in solitude on the margins of their villages (Athanasius, *Vit. Ant.*; Sozomen, *Hist. eccl.* 1.13). When Antony (ca. 251–356) began this spiritual journey, the movement had no name; when he emerged from his seclusion across the Nile at Pispir (Deir Anba Antonius/Deir el-Memum [Mullen 2004, 285]) some thirty-five

Fig. 5.5. Coptic Monastery of St. Antony

years later, the phenomenon of monasticism had come to public attention, and the word *monachos* was soon to be used to denote such ascetics (Choat 2002). The flowering of the monastic movement lies in the fourth century, but the first developments of what became an alternate locus of religious authority on the margins of society yet still within it are to be found in the pre-Constantinian period (Goehring 1999c; Rubenson 2007).

Coptic Christianity

At the same time, an event of equal cultural significance was taking place. Knowledge of the Egyptian scripts had always been too restricted within Egyptian society to form a useful vehicle for translation; in the Roman period usage outside the temple context had diminished to nearly nothing (though it continued there into the third century [Ritner 1998, 8–9]). The development of Coptic, which used the Greek alphabet alongside a number of letters taken over from Demotic to write Egyptian, was thus a cultural imperative as much as a proselytizing tool. Unsystematized non-Christian transcriptions of Egyptian ritual texts predate Christian efforts by at least one hundred years (Satzinger 1991), but it is in the Christian texts of the second half of the third century that we see the beginnings of linguistic and orthographic standardization, and it is undoubtedly the decision to translate the Christian Scriptures into Egyptian that led to the development of Coptic into what it became in the fourth and later centuries. Although an imperfect guide, the dialects of Coptic provide some indication of where this was taking place in the third and the early fourth centuries. A bilingual school exercise, perhaps from the Great Oasis[13] (Crum 1934; Parsons 1970), which glosses on a Greek biblical text from the Fayum (Kenyon 1937), and a Greek-Coptic glossary from the neighborhood of Oxyrhynchus (Bell and Thompson 1925) both testify to an early stage of Coptic linguistic development. Bilingual codices (Diebner and Kasser 1989) and hymns (Brashear and Satzinger 1990) from the Fayum appear around the same time as the first full codices in Coptic among the "Dishna papers" (Kasser 1960; Goehring 1990), both in Upper Egyptian dialects. This new linguistic expression of Christianity in Egypt finds further voice through original Coptic compositions in the fourth century, such as in the letters of Pachomius (Quecke 1975) and perhaps in those of Antony (Rubenson 1995), the (lost) output of Hieracas, and, dwarfing all other Coptic authors, the voluminous works of Shenoute of Atripe (346/7–465), beginning during the last decades of the fourth century (Emmel 2004).

13. In Antiquity the neighboring oases now known as Dakhleh and Kharga were collectively known as the Great Oasis.

MANICHAEANS

Among the early adopters of the Coptic script were Manichaeans, who arrived in Egypt, probably both across the Red Sea and up the Nile from Alexandria, in the late third century (Lieu 1994, 61–105). Soon afterward a bishop of Alexandria (perhaps Theonas) was sufficiently alarmed by their progress to write an encyclical letter against them (P.Ryl. 3.469 [Gardner and Lieu 2004, 114–15]). Adopting the "Lycopolitan" dialect of Coptic (associated only by inference with the metropolis of Lycopolis), the Manichaeans produced Coptic versions of many of their sacred texts, which survive in fourth- and early fifth-century copies from Kellis (Ismant el-Kharab) in the Dakhleh Oasis and Narmouthis (Medinet Madi) in the Fayum (Gardner and Lieu 2004, 35–45). Private letters from Kellis show Manichaean missionaries traversing the length of the Nile in the fourth century and provide insight into that community's private life (Gardner, Alcock, and Funk 1999).

"GNOSTICS"

The "Gnostics" are, thanks to the heresiologists, better known than the Manichaeans, but they are less easy either to define or to locate anywhere outside their impressive literary inheritance. Not all of the twelve (plus leaves from a thirteenth) Nag Hammadi codices are "Gnostic"; notably, several Hermetic tractates feature, along with Sethian, Valentinian, and other dualist and demiurgical texts (M. Smith 1998, 730–33; Meyer 2007). Furthermore, the double (and on occasion triple) attestation of works among codices, differences in their dialect, manner of construction, and scribal practice, and the lack of any certainty on their *Sitz im Leben*, make the designation "library" hazardous (M. Williams 1996, 235–62; Khosroyev 1995). Nevertheless, they testify to an appetite among fourth-century readers of Coptic for this type of literature.

The Fourth Century

The turn of the third century brings a further rush of papyri documenting Christianity, particularly in private letters, where distinctive Christian scribal conventions and Pauline and other New Testament turns of phrase are increasingly noticeable (Naldini 1998, nos. 20–37; Choat 2006, 84–125). Again, where provenance is certain, most of the evidence comes from Oxyrhynchus, but one letter from the late third or early fourth century reveals a Christian *presbyteros* in Toeto (modern Tahta) in the Panopolite nome writing to another in Kysis (Douch) in the Kharga Oasis, part of what was known in Antiquity as the Great Oasis (P.Grenf. 2.73). The report therein of the body of a woman, "sent to the oasis by the government," may relate to the Great Persecution in the first decade of the fourth century (Llewelyn and Nobbs 1997; Łukaszewicz 1998), but regardless of that provides our earliest secure indication of Christianity in the Great Oasis[14] and the region of Panopolis (Akhmim).

With that, we are at the start of the fourth century and the organized government action against Christians that testifies in its scope to the scale of the movement that it was trying to suppress.

THE NUMBER OF CHRISTIANS

Although the report by Eusebius (*Hist. eccl.* 6.1) of martyrs brought from the Thebaid under Septimius Severus (r. 193–211) at the start of the third century may transmit exaggerated traditions, the numerical scope of suffering Christians in Upper Egypt a century later (*Hist. eccl.* 8.9) is much more believable.[15] By this time Christianity had reached well past the Nile *metropoleis* into villages such as Chysis in the Oxyrhynchite nome, where the local administration confronted the self-avowedly illiterate "reader" of the village church to confiscate its meager possessions (P.Oxy. 33.2673; 5.2.304). In the following decade a "deacon of the church" is registered on a taxation list in the village of Mermertha in the same district (P.Oxy. 55.3787; 313–320), and as Constantine I (r. 306–337) took sole control of the empire in 324, a farmer from Karanis (Kom Aushim) in the Fayum named a deacon and a monk as witnesses in a petition complaining of an assault (P.Col. 7.171; 6.6.324 [Judge 1977; Wipszycka 2001]).

In Dionysius's time we know of only a handful of bishops in Egypt apart from the Alexandrian *papas* (Martin 1996, 17–25); when Alexander of Alexandria (bp. 313–326/28) condemned his renegade presbyter Arius (ca. 256–336), he claimed the support of "nearly a hundred bishops of Egypt and Libya" (Socrates, *Hist. eccl.* 1.6.4). Fifty Egyptian and ten Libyan episcopal sees are known from Alexander's time or shortly thereafter (Martin 1996, 28–115; cf. Mullen 2004, 266–93), as Christianity becomes increasingly visible in public documents. During Alexander's tenure a bishop is listed in an account book from Diospolis Parva (Hiou) (Mitthof 2002, 59, line 262 [313/4 CE]); a list of properties in Panopolis includes a church (Borkowski 1975, III.27 [315–320 CE?]); and the "northern" and "southern" churches are noted matter-of-factly in a list of guardposts in Oxyrhynchus (P.Oxy. 1.43 verso [probably to be dated at least two decades after the text of 295 CE on the recto]). Shortly thereafter, onomastic analysis indicates that as much as 50 percent of Egypt's

14. See Wagner 1987, 355–65; for fourth-century churches in Kellis, see Bowen 2002; 2003.
15. For an assessment of the various *acta martyrum* and other data relating to the tradition of pre-Constantinian martyrs in specific locations in Egypt, see Mullen 2004, 266–93.

population was Christian (Bagnall 2003a; 2003b; but see Wipszycka 1986; Dijkstra 2008, 58–60; cf. Choat 2006, 51–56). Under Athanasius (bp. 328–373) and subsequent bishops of Alexandria, further bishoprics were created in Egypt and Libya, so that the total approached one hundred by the end of the fourth century (Martin 1996, 75–98). Churches and their clergy appear with increasing frequency in public documents, and Christian letters become numerically far superior to those that witness polytheistic or pagan beliefs (Choat 2006).

The Development of Monasticism

The ascetic impulse visible in the story of Antony's development from pious villager to monk and the theological speculation and scriptural exegesis that flourished in third-century Alexandria found another expression in the city of Leontopolis in the Nile Delta (Kom el-Muqdam or Tell el-Yahoudiyeh) (Goehring 1999a, 110n2). Under Diocletian, an Egyptian named Hieracas inspired people with his rigorous asceticism and learning (Epiphanius, *Pan.* 68) (Goehring 1999a; Elm 1994, 339–42; Brakke 1995, 45–48). This polymath, prolific writer (of lost works) in both Greek and Egyptian, and calligrapher led an ascetic group in Leontopolis and inspired ascetics farther afield (Epiphanius, *Pan.* 68.1.6). The influence of his ideas over ascetics in Alexandria was sufficient to necessitate a letter from Athanasius, arguing against his ideas (Lefort 1955, 1:73–99; cf. Brakke 1994, 19–25; 1995, 44–57, 274–91).

Anchorites. As the fourth century progressed, "cells arose even in the mountains, and the desert was colonized by monks" (Athanasius, *Vit. Ant.* 14). Forms of monasticism proliferated. Loose communities of like-minded anchorites formed around ascetics such as Amoun, who withdrew to Nitria (el-Barnuji) in the Western Delta shortly before 330 (Palladius, *Hist. Laus.* 8 [Harmless 2004, 279–80; on the location, see Evelyn-White 1932, 17–24]). Here and at Kellia, about 18 km south of el-Barnuji, to where Amoun departed in about 338 when he found Nitria insufficiently peaceful, monastic cells spread out across the landscape. Those at Nitria are known only from the reports of Palladius and others (*Hist. Laus.* 7 [Evelyn-White 1932, 43–59]); at Kellia surveys and excavations have revealed the remains of hundreds of cells and other buildings such as churches, spread over some 36 km^2 (Guillaumont et al. 1991; Grossman 2002, 262–66, 491–99). Macarius (d. ca. 390), later known as "the Great," went still farther into the desert in about 330 to found another community at Scetis (Wadi el-Natroun) (Evelyn-White 1932; 1933; Harmless 2004, 173–82; Innemee 2000; 2005).

At such settlements monks lived in well-appointed cells (each usually housing a senior monk and several disciples) and worked at a variety of trades (Palladius, *Hist. Laus.* 7), the exchange of which spanned the often merely

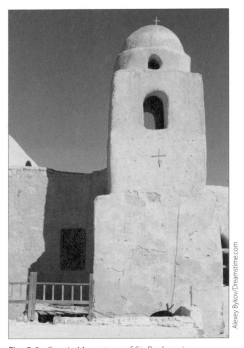

Fig. 5.6. Coptic Monastery of St. Pachomius

symbolic divide between "desert" and "world" (Goehring 1999e). In such communities a monk's ascetic program depended on no higher authority than his ascetic master (if he was a novice) or on no one if he was sufficiently experienced in the ascetic life. Priests who led communal worship, or councils of elders who watched over the settlements, provided little more than guidance and a forum for conflict resolution. The monks met for communal prayer in churches, and they shared resources such as bakeries, gardens, and guesthouses. However, there was no greater level of organization to their ascetic lives.

Pachomius. It was such a loose group of anchorites near the village of Šeneset (ancient Chenoboskion) in the Thebaid that Pachomius (ca. 292–ca. 346/7) left in the early 320s to form his own community in the village of Tabennesi (Rousseau 1999; Goehring 1999d). As ascetics gathered to him, he drew perhaps on his military experience of communal living, and certainly on his own early experiences with forming ascetic communities (which the *Lives* of Pachomius largely gloss over or downplay), to form his first *koinobion*, a community in which monks lived together according to a rule (Rousseau 1999, 57–76). Additional monks, and whole monastic communities, joined the *koinōnia*, so that by the founder's death in 346 the Pachomian federation encompassed eleven communities spread up and down the Nile. Within the walls of these monasteries the monks lived a far more regulated life than their semianchoretic brethren. The *Rules* as they were set down later in the fourth century governed the conditions of acceptance to the monastery (including a requirement for rudimentary literacy), contact with the outside world and one another, and the way they were to live, work, dress, and pray, along with many other regulations (Rousseau 1999, 87–104; Veilleux 1981, 141–223).

Other Monasteries. Pachomius is only the best-known early exponent of communal monasticism; a network of monasteries that owed their allegiance to the schismatic Melitian Church was well developed in the 330s, and it must have started around the same time as the first Pachomian community (Hauben 1998; Goehring 1999b; H. Bell 1924). Later in the fourth century there was a Manichaean monastery in the Dakhleh Oasis (Gardner 2000; cf. Koenen 1983; Lieu 1998, 76–97). In about 388, across the river from Panopolis (Achmim) just outside Atripe (ancient Tripheion [Waninna]), west of modern Sohag, Shenoute inherited the monastery founded by his uncle Pgol and turned it into one of the most influential monastic communities in Upper Egypt (Krawiec 2002; Schroeder 2007; Leipoldt 1903; Harmless 2004, 445–48). The Monastery of Apa Shenoute (Deir Anba Shenouda [the title White Monastery, Deir al-Abiad, is medieval]) did not follow the Pachomian system. Rather, Shenoute—a prolific writer (in Coptic), implacable opponent of paganism, and forceful leader—fashioned his own authoritarian rule, only now being pieced together from the thousands of pages of his writings (Emmel 2004; Layton 2007).

Other monks shunned both the influence of local ecclesiastical establishments and the rules of the communal monasteries. They lived, as Jerome disapprovingly noted, "in twos and threes . . . according to their own will and ruling" (*Ep.* 22.34) (Caner 2002, 19–49). Jerome's principal objection was that they would not submit to any authority, but his comments that they dwelt "in cities and fortresses" (*in urbibus et castellis*) echo the testimony of the documentary papyri: in these, monks wander through and dwell within the secular settlements of Egypt (Judge 1977; Choat 2007), owning property, and maintaining family relations (Bagnall 2001). Literary sources show these urban ascetics becoming increasingly visible in ecclesiastical politics (Brakke 1995; Wipszycka 1996).

Christianity and Other Religions

Even with the visibility of Christianity in the fourth century, however, it is clear that its dominance is not yet total. The traditional cultic infrastructure is still functioning in some form (Willis and Maresch 1998; Maresch and Andorlini 2006) during the reign of Constantine. In the early 320s highly educated Christians and worshipers of Hermes Trismegistus (the Greek version of the Egyptian god Thoth) cohabit the social circle of Theophanes of Hermopolis Magna (Matthews 2006), and a Hellenized Egyptian family in Panopolis argues over who will inherit the city's *propheteia* (Willis and Maresch 1998; Maresch and Andorlini 2006). Elsewhere, Greco-Egyptian gods and rituals live on in ritual (or "magical") texts (Betz 1986; Preisendanz 1973–1974). In the fourth and following centuries many such texts, written both in Greek and increasingly in Coptic (Meyer and Smith 1994; Kropp 1930–1931), come to incorporate Christian and Gnostic themes and terminology, and it is apparent that monks have replaced the temple priests as ritual experts (Frankfurter 1998, 198–237, 265–84). Yet into the sixth century some continue to feature references to Egyptian gods (Horus, Amun, Isis) and *historiolae* drawn from much earlier sources (Meyer and Smith 1994, nos. 43, 47–49, 72).

Beyond the first half of the fourth century, however, it becomes increasingly difficult to find documentary papyrological or archaeological evidence for the Greco-Egyptian cults. The temples and their priests appear more often in the fourth and fifth centuries in Christian accounts of how they were destroyed or converted, and the degree of rhetoric employed in these accounts (and consequently how they should be used historically) is debated (contrast Frankfurter 1998 with M. Smith 2002 and Bagnall 2008). Papyrological evidence for Christians, however, becomes increasingly evident, whether it be letters written by them, the appearance of their institutions in secular documents, or progressively more expertly produced (and more frequently encountered) copies of their sacred texts. The widespread distribution of the *Life of Antony* in the second half of the fourth century cements Egypt's reputation as the homeland of monasticism and both inspires Western imitators and attracts tourists and travel writers (e.g., Palladius, Egeria, and the authors of the *Historia monachorum in Aegypto*). These late fourth-century pilgrims found a society in which Christianity had spread to all regions of Egypt and beyond the borders of the Roman world south into Nubia.

The Arab Conquest

After the Arab conquest (640–642) Christians did not suffer immediately. Indeed, for the anti-Chalcedonian (traditionally labeled Monophysite but perhaps better called Miaphysite) establishment, the conquest brought both freedom from the agents of the emperor and the return of control over the churches of Alexandria and important shrines such as that at Abu Mina (Wilfong 1998; cf. Kennedy 1998). Christian chronicles such as the *History of the Patriarchs* record positive traditions about 'Āmir ibn-'As, who led the conquest, and have the Patriarch Benjamin (bp. 626–665) pray for him (Evetts 1904, 496–97). While conversion of Christians to Islam was slow in the early centuries of Islamic rule (motivated in many cases primarily by economic considerations [Wilfong 1998, 183]), the burden of taxation steadily increased on the non-Muslim population, including on the monasteries and individual monks (Simonsen 1988). Despite this—or perhaps because of it—as Christian intellectual life became concentrated in the monasteries, the early Islamic era in Egypt is witness to the golden age of Coptic manuscript production. The contents of great libraries, such as that at the Monastery of Apa Shenoute and the Monastery of St. Michael (Phantoou) near modern al-Hamuli in the Fayum, were transferred into the lavishly produced parchment codices that survived (though not always intact) into the modern period (Depuydt 1993, ciii–cxvi; Emmel 2005; Orlandi 2002). Yet outside the monasteries, as pressure steadily mounted on Christianity, Coptic was superseded as a spoken and written language by Arabic at the start of the second millennium.

Alexandria

During the early morning hours of November 25, 311, a consecrated virgin dwelling in Alexandria's eastern extramural region of Boukolou was finishing her prayers when she heard a heavenly voice pronounce, "Peter the first of the apostles, Peter the last of the martyrs." Shortly afterward in the same suburb, Peter I, bishop of Alexandria since 300, was beheaded by soldiers of the imperial prefect. There were later martyrdoms throughout the regions governed by the emperor Maximin II Daia (r. 310–313), but Peter of Alexandria was the most notable martyr during the last phase of a fierce persecution that had raged sporadically since February of 303. Within a year of Peter's death, Constantine won his landmark victory at the Milvian Bridge, and Christianity was on its way to becoming the empire's favored religion.

During the course of the next century, the church of Alexandria emerged as one of the preeminent centers of Christianity in the Mediterranean world. Its most notable bishops, Athanasius, Theophilus (bp. 385–412), and Cyril (bp. 412–444), profoundly influenced the forging of theological consensus around doctrines such as the Trinity and the nature of Christ. During this same century the reputation of Alexandrian scriptural exegesis became firmly established through the works of Didymus the Blind (ca. 310/13–ca. 398), who was one of a long line of gifted teachers and commentators. The fourth century also witnessed the flourishing of the monastic movement in Alexandria's hinterland regions of Mareotis and Nitria, following in the varied ascetic traditions developed in Upper Egypt by Antony and by Pachomius. In addition, elegant Alexandrian artistic styles influenced emergent forms of Christian art throughout the eastern Mediterranean in diverse media such as ivory carving, mosaic decoration, portraiture, and church architecture. Moreover, in 392 Alexandria was the site of a critical episode in the ongoing struggle between the empire's traditional pagan cults and Christianity, the destruction of the Temple of Serapis, described by the historian Ammianus Marcellinus (ca. 325/30–post-391) as one of the most magnificent temples in the world, second only to the Temple of Jupiter Capitolinus in Rome (Ammianus Marcellinus, *Res gestae* 22.16.12).

The city's most common designation, "Most-Glorious Alexandria," was well deserved. Ever since its founding by the Macedonian conqueror in 331 BCE, Alexandria flourished as the Mediterranean world's gateway to Egypt and as the principal transit point for trade through the Red Sea to the kingdoms of south Arabia and India. Alexander the Great established his port city on a narrow limestone ridge less than 3 km wide, located between the Mediterranean Sea and Lake Mareotis. Ships were guided past treacherous reefs to its twin ports by beacon and smoke from the Pharos, the great lighthouse that stood at the tip of the island of the same name, connected to the mainland by a causeway some 1260 m in length known as the *Heptastadion*. As the capital of the wealthiest of all the Hellenistic successor kingdoms, Alexandria was adorned by the Ptolemaic dynasty with magnificent palaces, temples, porticoes, and emporia. The celebrated *Mouseion*, with its vast library, served as a research institute under royal patronage and helped to establish Alexandria's reputation as the preeminent center in the Hellenistic world for physics, mathematics, astronomy, and literary criticism. Not surprisingly, Alexandria's population swelled to upward of half a million, creating a cosmopolitan society of Greeks, Egyptians, and other ethnicities. This included the largest settlement of Jews outside Palestine, who were accorded one of the city's five districts near the royal quarter of Bruchion. After the victory of Octavian over Mark Antony and Cleopatra at Actium, Alexandria was absorbed into the Roman Empire along with the rest of Egypt, and both were governed by an equestrian prefect headquartered in Alexandria (Capponi 2005). Besides its concern for the city's importance as a commercial, judicial, and administrative center, Roman strategic interest in Alexandria was guided above all by the city's role as embarkation point for the grain fleets that supplied Rome annually with nearly eighty-three thousand tons of grain.

While the later Egyptian church treasured traditions recounting the Holy Family's sojourn at sites in Middle and Upper Egypt, these same traditions ascribe the establishment of Christianity in Egypt to St. Mark the Evangelist. Mark is reputed to have converted a local cobbler, Annianus, who succeeded Mark as the city's bishop following Mark's martyrdom at the hands of an Alexandrian mob. The much-redacted *History of the Patriarchs of Alexandria*, following the information given by Eusebius of Caesarea, places Mark as the first of an unbroken succession of bishops who occupied what came to be known as "the throne of St. Mark." However, aside from sparse New Testament references to an Alexandrian Christian teacher named Apollos (e.g., Acts 18:24–28), and later lists of Alexandrian bishops, it is not until the early third century that historical material becomes plentiful enough to enable more than a cursory description of Alexandrian Christianity (Dorival 1999).

Earliest Alexandrian Christianity

Given the wealth of information available regarding Roman Alexandria (Haas 1997), it seems incongruous that next to nothing should be known of Christianity in the first two centuries. Modern scholars have long sought an explanation for this discrepancy. One of the most popular scholarly solutions of the twentieth century was set forth by Walter Bauer in his *Rechtgläubigkeit und Ketzerei im ältesten Christentum* (1934). Bauer argued that the earliest manifestation of Christianity in Alexandria was overwhelmingly Gnostic in character and that second-century teachers such as Basilides and Valentinus represented the majority viewpoint of the Alexandrian church. Later Christian leaders, horrified by the heretical quality of their church's infancy, pointedly avoided discussing these early centuries. It should be noted that Bauer argues almost entirely from silence. In addition, the vehemence with which he argues his thesis suggests an unwillingness to concede that early Alexandrian Christianity could share any commonalities with the faith taught and practiced by Athanasius and Cyril. As a result of Bauer's neatly drawn conspiracy theory, earliest Alexandrian Christianity has often been characterized as having doctrinal pluriformity and a relatively egalitarian structure of authority focused on the appeal of individual teachers and on the influence exercised by their circles of students.

More recent scholars, such as Colin Roberts (1979), Birger Pearson (1990; 2003; 2004; 2006), and Joseph Modrzejewski (1997), have argued that the proper context for understanding earliest Christianity in both Alexandria and in Egypt is within first-century Judaism. After all, later Alexandrian exegetes looked back on the brilliant Jewish philosopher and commentator Philo (ca. 20 BCE–50 CE) as a kindred spirit in his quest to find the inner, spiritual meaning of a biblical text (Dyck 2002). As the Alexandrian church developed, it relied on the Greek translation of the Hebrew Bible known as the Septuagint, which was produced within the Alexandrian Jewish community. Certain extrabiblical texts familiar to the Jerusalem church, with its strong Jewish flavor, were likewise used in Christian circles in Alexandria (Bagnall 2009). By situating the earliest Alexandrian Christian community within the larger Jewish community (van den Broek 1996), it becomes much easier to explain the silence of our sources surrounding Christianity in the first two centuries. This is because the Alexandrian Jewish community was all but obliterated during a widespread revolt among Diaspora Jews between 115 and 117 CE. If the Christians had constituted a small subset of the larger Jewish community, they too must have suffered near extinction during this period.

Both of the aforementioned interpretive models assume that the rarified intellectual climate of Alexandria surely produced an early Christian community in keeping with the city's size and reputation. It is imperative to resist the natural tendency to look in the first centuries for the seeds of later Alexandrian Christianity's fame and power. And in a city of about half a million, only a tiny fraction of the population was engaged in advanced intellectual and religious pursuits. There is no intrinsic reason why Christianity in Alexandria could not have developed later and more slowly than in other urban areas such as Antioch, Rome, or Carthage. In the episcopal lists provided by Eusebius, Mark's ten successors appear as not much more than mere names. This does not constitute a compelling argument for doubting their existence, but it is not until the election of Demetrius (bp. ca. 189–ca. 231/2) that the literary sources become plentiful enough to partially fill in the historical outline. The period on either side of 200 was an age when questions of apostolic succession, teaching authority, and the definition of orthodoxy came to dominate the work of churchmen such as Irenaeus in Lyons (bp. ca. 177–ca. 200), and Hippolytus (ca. 170–236/7) and Callistus (bp. ca. 217–222) in Rome. Likewise, it was during the long episcopate of Demetrius that the institutional structure of the Alexandrian church was regularized with the bishop asserting his authority over local congregations and over the Egyptian church as a whole.

The Catechetical School

Perhaps one reason for the assertion of the bishop's authority in matters of teaching was the emergence of a line of gifted theologians and teachers within the Alexandrian church. In later historical memory this group of teachers was seen as a succession of teachers at the head of an institution that usually is called the catechetical school (van den Hoek 1997). Eusebius speaks of the earliest of these teachers, Pantaenus (fl. ca. 175), in these terms: "About that time, Pantaenus, a man highly distinguished for his learning, had charge of the school of the faithful in Alexandria. A school of sacred learning, which continues to our day, was established there in ancient times, and as we have been informed, was managed by men of great ability and zeal for divine things" (*Hist. eccl.* 5.10.1). This included the brilliant theologian and philosopher Clement, whose erudition and fame were surpassed only by Origen, who was appointed by Demetrius to be head of the school in 202. Origen attracted a wide circle of converts and inquiring pagans, and during his thirty years as head of the school he penned a huge corpus of commentaries, theological reflections, apologetic works, and textual criticism. Eventually, Origen came into conflict with Demetrius, and he left for Caesaraea in Palaestina, to be succeeded as head of the catechetical school by Heraclas.

Institutional Development

With the appointment of Heraclas, the Alexandrian church moves into an important stage in its institutional development. Heraclas succeeded Demetrius as bishop in about 231/2, and for the rest of the third century all of Alexandria's bishops had previously served as head of the catechetical school. Heraclas's successor, Dionysius, sums up the enhanced doctrinal and institutional authority of his position when he states, "I inherited this rule and example from our blessed pope [*papas*] Heraclas" (Dionysius of Alexandria, *Ep.*, in Eusebius, *Hist. eccl.* 7.7.4). This is the first time that we encounter "pope" as a term of affection and reverence used of the Alexandrian bishop— a usage that predates its application to the bishop of Rome by nearly half a century (Wipszycka 2006). During the third century it also appears that the Christians of Alexandria became organized into a number of parishes, each with its own priest. By the time of Peter I's martyrdom in 311, Alexandria possessed several church buildings, including the Martyrium of St. Mark in the city's eastern suburbs and the newly built Church of Theonas, situated near the cemeteries on the western edge of the city (Tkaczow 1990; Gascou 1998; Venit 2004).

The second half of the third century appears to have been a pivotal period in the growth of Christianity within Alexandria (Goehring and Timbie 2007). The Christian community became visible enough that numerous individuals were targets for mob violence and official sanction during the persecutions under Decius and Valerian. Despite these sporadic pogroms, the number of Alexandrians who embraced Christianity grew apace, attracted in part by the care given by Christians to those who suffered during a horrific plague in 262, and by individual acts of mercy performed by Christians in the midst of civil wars in 262 and 273/4. It is also during this half century that some of Alexandria's earliest Christian tombs and *hypogea*[16] may be dated. Although this early attribution is by no means certain, the Karmuz Catacomb, with its painted scenes of the wedding at Cana and of the multiplication of the loaves and fishes, has sometimes been given a late third-century date. Likewise, Christian symbols decorate several of the third-century *hypogea* at Gabbari located just outside the ancient city's western walls. These tombs, sometimes situated side by side with tombs adorned with traditional deities, attest to Christianity's growing presence in this most cosmopolitan of the cities of the Roman Empire.

16. *Hypogea* are underground crypts with multiple burials, often in the form of *loculi*. Non-Christian *hypogea* frequently are accompanied by places for cultic ceremonies to honor the dead, and sometimes these carried over in the form of Christian meals to honor the departed.

Axum

In about 401 CE Rufinus of Aquileia (ca. 345–411/2) produced a Latin translation of Eusebius of Caesarea's *Historia ecclesiastica*, at the same time bringing
it more or less up to date by continuing the story of the church down to the
end of the reign of Theodosius I (r. 379–395).

Frumentius's Royal Connections

A fascinating part of the post-Eusebian narrative is Rufinus's account of
Aedesius and Frumentius, Christian youths from Tyre (*Hist.* 10.9–10). Ac-
companying their older relative Meropius on an exploratory excursion to
"Farther India," their ship entered a port (presumably Adulis) to take on water
and other supplies, only to be attacked. Everyone on board was killed except
these young men, on whom the barbarians took pity. They were brought to the
local king, who made Aedesius his cupbearer and made the older Frumentius
his secretary and treasurer.

Like Joseph and Daniel (cf. Theodoret, *Hist. eccl.* 1.22), Aedesius and Frumentius end up administering the country when the old king dies and the heir
to the throne is still too young to rule. Asked to do so by the king's widow,
they gain sufficient power to be able to seek out and protect Christian merchants who visit the country. Frumentius even provides building sites for the
construction of chapels or churches, doing all he can to foster the growth of
Christianity in the realm.

Later Byzantine church historians embellished Rufinus's narrative, adding
that Frumentius personally built churches for these Christian merchants and
for the indigenous people whom he converted (Socrates, *Hist. eccl.* 1.19; Sozomen, *Hist. eccl.* 2.24). Rufinus himself, however, merely recounts Frumentius's
support of the Christians and churches already there. According to Rufinus,
after the royal child had become of age, Frumentius, instead of returning home
to Tyre like his brother, traveled to Alexandria to tell Athanasius what had
occurred, beseeching him to send a worthy person to the kingdom as bishop.

Not surprisingly, Athanasius can think of a no more suitable person to send
than Frumentius himself. He ordains Frumentius and orders him to return with
God's grace. Frumentius does so, working miracles like those of the apostles,
converting (at that time, rather than earlier) countless barbarians, and appoint-
ing Christian clergy. Rufinus claims that the story he recounts of the beginnings
of the church in the kingdom is no idle tale based on popular rumors; he had
come to know of the events through the reports of Aedesius himself.

Independent corroboration that Athanasius ordained and commissioned Frumentius comes from none other than the emperor Constantius II (r. 337–361).

Constantius also reveals clearly that Rufinus's "Farther India" is Axum. In promoting the cause of Arianism, even beyond the official borders of the Roman Empire, Constantius, in 357, wrote a letter (in Athanasius, *Apol. Const.* 31) to the "princes of Axum," Aizana (Ezana) and Saizana (Sazana). The main point of the letter concerns Frumentius, bishop of Axum (Athanasius, *Apol. Const.* 29, 31). Constantius reminds the rulers that Frumentius was elevated to the episcopacy by Athanasius, the *deposed* bishop of Alexandria. He orders the rulers of Axum to send Frumentius immediately to Egypt to be interrogated by George, the new (Arian) bishop of Alexandria (bp. 356–361). Citing the need for the welfare of the churches of Axum to profess the same (Arian!) doctrine as churches in the rest of the world, Constantius warns that delay will be taken as a sign that Frumentius has been (and continues to be) influenced by Athanasius's wicked impiety. If Frumentius comes speedily to Alexandria, however, and answers satisfactorily the questions put to him he will be able to return home to Axum. Having received a great deal of important and relevant instruction in the (true) faith from George and other (Arian) clergy, Frumentius will be an even better bishop.

Rufinus assumes that Frumentius's consecration as bishop occurred soon after Athanasius's own in 328, but it is also possible that this happened as late as 346. If so, however, it is not necessary to assume, as does Françoise Thelamon (1981, 62), that Rufinus deliberately altered the facts in order to place the beginning of Christianity in "Farther India" during Constantine's reign rather than during that of (the Arian) Constantius. Regardless of exactly when Frumentius became bishop of Axum, there is little doubt that Ezana is the unnamed son of the king in Rufinus's account and that by the time of Constantius's letter, both he and his co-regent brother had personally embraced Christianity. According to Ethiopian ecclesiastical tradition preserved in the fourteenth-century *Senkessar* (*Synaxarion*), Frumentius converted the royal brothers, whose names are given as Abreha and Atsheba (Haas 2008, 102n3). The conflicting information is usually resolved by considering these names as alternate personal, "throne," or baptismal names.

A Christian Nation

Numismatic and epigraphic evidence support the literary and popular traditions that Axum/Ethiopia became a Christian nation in the mid-fourth century. Coins from Ezana's reign onward consistently contain the Christian cross, including ones bearing the legend "May this [the cross] please the country" (e.g., BMC Aksum 75; 90; see also Munro-Hay 1991, 109–10; Haas 2008,

101–3). An inscription found at the site of the ancient palace of Axum extolling Ezana's victories unambiguously declares his Christianity (see sidebar 5.1).[17]

Although Frumentius was the most important person for the establishment of Christianity in Axum/Ethiopia, he, as is clear from Rufinus's account, was not the only or first Christian there. Presumably, Christian merchants and other travelers had visited Axum even earlier. Origen (*Comm. ser. Matt.* 39; cf. 134) reports that at least some Ethiopians had heard the gospel preached (Mullen 2004, 331). Whether such preaching can be traced back all the way to the story of St. Philip and the Ethiopian (Acts 8:26–34) is theoretically possible, but debatable. The KJV translation of Acts 8:27 declares the man to whom Philip preached to have been "an eunuch of great authority under Candace queen of the Ethiopians." A more accurate translation of the Greek text, however, reveals that the Ethiopian was "a court official of the Candace, queen of the Ethiopians" (NRSV). As noted above, Candace was the title (not name) of the powerful female regents/rulers of Kushitic Meroe, which, at the time, was still independent of Axum although in the region popularly called Ethiopia. If the Ethiopian eunuch, on his return home, did anything to make public and spread his new baptismal faith, this would be evidence for "Christianity" in Meroe/Kush but not in Axum/Ethiopia.

Whether the Ethiopian queen of Acts 8 belonged to Meroe or Axum, the story illustrates that Christianity possibly first arrived in the region via contact with early Jewish Jesus followers in or from Judaea. The history of Judaism in Axum is complicated by the so-called Beta Israel (Black Jews, mostly now relocated to Israel) who trace their origins to the legendary Menelik I, alleged son of the Queen of Sheba and Solomon. Even the Ethiopian Orthodox Church, however, continues to perpetuate the tradition that Menelik traveled to Israel to visit his father. The central core of the tradition is that, unbeknownst to Menelik, his companions stole the ark of the covenant from Solomon's temple by substituting a fake. They brought the actual ark to Axum, where it is now housed in a chapel next to the Church of Mary of Zion. This church was first built in the time of Ezana and Frumentius, although few original remnants survive. There is no evidence, however, for knowledge of the Menelik/ark of the covenant tradition prior to the Middle Ages, suggesting that it was never part of Axumite Christianity but only developed with the claims of the later Ethiopian "Solomonic Dynasty."

Little is known about Christianity in Axum from the time of Ezana and Frumentius (d. ca. 383) to that of King Kaleb I Ella Atsheba (r. ca. 520–540). In

---

17. For the theory that this is the inscription of a later (fifth-century) Monophysite king also named Ezana, see Kobischchanov 1979; see also *NewDocs* 2:209–11. This theory has not been widely accepted (see Mullen 2004, 331–32).

5.1 Inscription of Ezana, King of Axum

In the faith of God, and the power of the Father and Son and Holy Spirit, who saved for me the kingdom by the faith of his son Jesus Christ, who helped and
5 always does help me, I, | Ezana, king of the Axumites and Himyarites and of Reeidan (?) and of the Sabaites and of Sileel (?) and of Hasa and of the Bougaites
10 and of Taimo; a man (of the tribe) of Alene (?), son of Elle-|Amida (?), servant of Christ, give thanks to the Lord my God and I cannot state fully his favors because my mouth and my mind cannot (embrace) all the favors which he has
15 given me, | because he has given me strength and power and favored me with a great name through his Son in whom I believed and he made me the guide
20 of all my kingdom because of (my) faith in Christ, by his will and | the power of Christ, because he has guided me and I believe in him and he has become my guide. I went out to make war on the Nubians, because there had cried out
25 against them the Mangurto, the Hasa, the Atiaditai (?), | the Bareotai, saying that, "The Nubians have ground us down; help us because they have troubled us by killing." And I rose up in the power of the God Christ, in whom I believed,
30 and he guided me. And I rose up | from Axum on the 8th day, a Saturday, of the Axumite month Magabithe (?), in the faith of God and I reached Mambaria (?) and there I fed my army. (*NewDocs* 1:143–45, altered)

525 Kaleb invaded Himyar (Yemen), territory first conquered by Ezana but lost to Axum in about 378. The king of Himyar, Yusuf As'ar Yat'an (r. ca. 517–525), belonged to a dynasty that had converted to Judaism. In about 523 Yusuf persecuted Christians in his kingdom, especially in Najran, which had a large number of resident Axumites. With the encouragement, and perhaps support, of the Byzantine emperor Justin I (r. 518–527), Kaleb defeated and deposed Yusuf (Procopius, *Pers.* 1.20), at the same time (at least temporarily) reasserting the dominance of Axum and Christianity in the region.

Kaleb abdicated in 540, becoming a monk. He sent his crown to the Church of the Holy Sepulcher (Jerusalem), on the roof of which, to this day, is an Ethiopian monastery. Local Axumite monasticism was influenced and stimulated by a group of ascetics traditionally referred to as the Nine Saints. These foreign monks from Syria and elsewhere came to Axum possibly in the aftermath of the Monophysite debates in the late fifth and early sixth centuries. They founded a number of Pachomian-like monasteries.

The library of the monastery founded by Abba Garima in about 494 in the far north of Axum, near Adwa, contains two illuminated Gospels written in Ge'ez. Carbon dating of small fragments of loose pieces of the goatskin vellum by Oxford University dates the Garima Gospels to between 330 and 650. While this theoretically could support the tradition that the manuscripts were written by Abba Garima, the Gospels, on the basis of the style of their Byzantine illuminations, are more likely to have been created in the last decades of the sixth century. This still makes them among the earliest extant illuminated Christian manuscripts, comparable to the Rabbula Gospels (see chap. 2).

Nubia

Nubia is the name used to denote Egypt's southern neighbor in Antiquity, an area that roughly corresponds with today's southernmost Egypt and northern Sudan.[18] The border between Egypt and Nubia lay at the first cataract (near modern Aswan), the first in a series of currents in the Nile when going upstream. However, on many occasions throughout history the real frontier was farther to the south. At the start of Roman rule in 30 BCE, for example, the southern Egyptian frontier was at the second cataract, thus comprising the land that is often called Lower Nubia (Locher 1999, 252–56; 2002, 73–75). From 25 BCE onward several conflicts arose between the new rulers of Egypt and the kingdom that dominated Nubia from the third century BCE to the third century CE, the kingdom of Meroe (Török 1988a; 1997, 409–531; Welsby 1996; D. Edwards 2004, 141–81). Because of these conflicts, Augustus decided to withdraw the southern frontier to Hiera Sykaminos (modern Maharraqa) in 21/20 BCE (Locher 2002). In 298 CE, finally, Diocletian withdrew the frontier even farther north, making it equivalent with the traditional border between Egypt and Nubia, the first cataract (Dijkstra 2008, 25–26).

In contrast to Egypt, Christianity seems to have arrived relatively late in Nubia, and there is no reliable evidence for it before the fifth century. To document the process of how Nubia became Christian, we also cannot rely on the same richness and diversity of sources that Egypt has to offer. Several archaeological campaigns conducted during the last century in Lower Nubia, related to the building of the Aswan dams, have brought to light a wealth of new information, but not all of this material has been (sufficiently) published. Except for Qasr Ibrim (ancient Primis), all these sites are now underwater, making archaeological (re)investigation impossible. As a result, much of the archaeological work since the 1970s has concentrated on the areas south of the second cataract, in Upper Nubia. Yet even if the archaeological and documentary evidence for the study of Nubian Christianity remains fragmentary and hard to interpret, this is at the same time its greatest challenge, as new material, from both north and south, gradually becomes available (D. Edwards 2004, 3–7).

18. I am grateful to Jacques van der Vliet, who also inspired in me an interest in Christian Nubia, and Geoffrey Greatrex for useful comments on an earlier draft of this section.

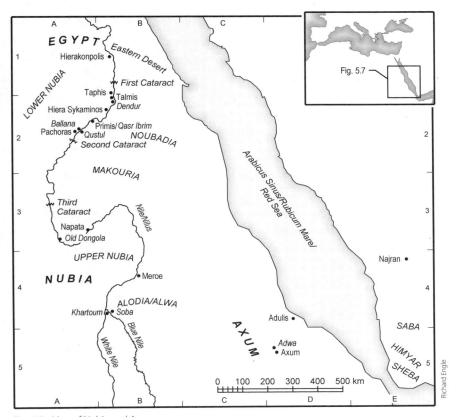

Fig. 5.7. Map of Nubia and Axum

It is perhaps because of the fragmentary documentary and archaeological evidence that most standard accounts of how Nubia became Christian use literary sources as the historical framework for this process. The most detailed of these literary works is the *Church History* of John of Ephesus (ca. 507–post-588). John mentions no fewer than three Byzantine missions to Nubia in the course of the sixth century. The first mission, which can be dated to between 536 and 548, resulted in the conversion of the king of Noubadia, a kingdom that had emerged in Lower Nubia at this time, after which a second mission was necessary in 569 to establish the church in Nubia. From Noubadia a third mission was sent in 579/80 to convert the king of Alodia (also known as Alwa), another kingdom that had come into being in the sixth century, the heartlands of which lay at the confluence of the Blue Nile and the White Nile. The other literary source that is often quoted is the *Chronicle* of John of Biclar (ca. 540–post-621), which refers to Makouria, a third sixth-century Nubian kingdom located between Noubadia and Alodia, as being Christian by 569. Although modern scholars are well aware that the first signs of Christianity predate the sixth century, they often downplay this evidence and reduce the "Christianization" of Nubia to the main events as described in the literary sources (Adams 1977, 440–45; Török 1988b, 69–73; Richter 2002, 139–48; Welsby 2002, 31–35). This approach seems, however, too narrow in focus. The literary sources mentioned above were written from an "outside" perspective, with a particular agenda, and may only provide part of the picture.

The Religious Transformation of Lower Nubia in the Fourth and Fifth Centuries

As is known from elsewhere, notably from Egypt, religious transformation was a complex and gradual process that was certainly not limited to a period of, say, forty years (Dijkstra 2008, 14–22). In the 1980s Sir Laurence Kirwan (1982; 1984), who excavated several important sites in Lower Nubia, already distinguished a first, formative phase well before the sixth century in which Nubia became influenced by Christianity through exchanges with Egypt, and a second phase in which Christianity became definitively organized through the Byzantine missions. This model allows us to see the establishment of Christianity in all three medieval Nubian kingdoms in the context of a dynamic process of religious transformation that was long under way (and also took longer to complete than the literary sources suggest). I therefore begin by tracing the roots of Nubian Christianity back into the post-Meroitic period, the fourth and fifth centuries, an important period of cultural change for Nubia (D. Edwards 2001, 89; 2004, 212; van der Vliet 2005, 221–23).

In 298 the southern Egyptian frontier was withdrawn from Maharraqa to the first cataract (Procopius, *Pers.* 1.19.27–37). Normally it would have been expected that the kingdom of Meroe would take possession of this region, called the Dodekaschoinos (Twelve Miles Land) in Greek. However, for reasons that are still vigorously debated, Meroe collapsed between the end of the third and the first half of the fourth century (Adams 1977, 383–90; Török 1988b, 33–46; 1997, 476–87; 1999; D. Edwards 2004, 182–85). The retreat of both Rome and Meroe from Lower Nubia brought an abrupt end to the commercial and other contacts between these two early states and, as seems reflected in the archaeological material (Adams 1977, 390–413; D. Edwards 2004, 198–207), probably caused a disintegration of the sociopolitical structure in the area. Several fourth- and especially fifth-century sources demonstrate that this sociopolitical void was filled by tribes originating in the Eastern Desert, the Blemmyes, and the original Nubian population, called the Noubades. These sources suggest that the situation south of the frontier was that of a complex tribal society, in which Blemmyan tribes were concentrated in places such as Taphis (Tafa) and Talmis (Kalabsha), whereas Noubadian tribes were located in Primis (Qasr Ibrim). The Romans tried to maintain the fragile stability on the southern frontier by granting these tribes concessions such as paying them money and giving them a federate status (Dijkstra 2008, 138–72; 2012).

Unlike in Egypt, where temples seem to have been increasingly abandoned in the course of the fourth century (Bagnall 1988; 1993; Dijkstra 2008, 125–27; 2011), there is a remarkable continuity of traditional cults and practices in northern Lower Nubia at this time. A late fourth-century inscription from Tafa (*SB* 1.5099) attests late cultic practice there, and several texts (Olympiodorus, *Fr.* 35.2; *SB* 1.1521–24; 5.8536; 5.8697; 14.11957) indicate that the Temple of Mandulis at Kalabsha was still open into the fifth century. The Romans even openly allowed the southern tribes to have access to the famous temple island of Philae, in the first cataract and thus on Roman territory, and to take a cult statue of Isis back south, only to return it to Philae after a while (F. Griffith 1935–1937, graffito no. 371; Priscus, *Fr.* 27; Procopius, *Pers.* 1.19.34–37). This practice is related by Priscus for as late as 452/3 (Dijkstra 2008, 138–46, 154, 159–60). From Qasr Ibrim there is archaeological evidence that some temples remained functioning into the post-Meroitic period (M. Horton 1991, 270–72). The forecourt of the Meroitic temple (temple 4), for example, was abandoned in the fifth century, after which the main sanctuary continued in use into the sixth century. Several blocks of the temple complex were then reused in the nearby cathedral church that was built in the later sixth or early seventh century (Rose 2007, 6).

It is in this "pagan" environment that the first signs of Christian influence begin to emerge. The expression "(the) god gave me the victory" in the Greek triumphal inscription of the Noubadian chieftain Silko from the Mandulis Temple at Kalabsha (*SB* 5.8536), in which he reports three victories over Blemmyan tribes, often has been cited in connection with the "conversion" of Nubia in the sixth century. However, this connection can be discarded because Silko is also mentioned in the fifth-century letter (*SB* 14.11957) of the Blemmyan chieftain Phonen to the Noubadian chieftain Abourni, Silko's successor, and therefore the inscription must date to that century. Moreover, the god mentioned in the Silko inscription more probably refers to the god of the temple, the Nubian god Mandulis, and there are no further signs of Christianity, such as crosses or Christian phrases, in the text. Such signs are present in the Phonen letter, for the son of Abourni has the Christian name Mouses (*SB* 14.11957.2), and the scribe used the Christian expression "I pray in God" (*SB* 14.11957.4). However, the contents clearly indicate that Phonen himself was not a Christian, since he was concerned only about the return of "the gods," probably cult statues, to Talmis (Kalabsha) (Dijkstra 2008, 160–67).

Illustrative for how Christianity would have reached Lower Nubia is the Coptic letter of the monk Mouses of Philae to the Noubadian tribal chief Tantani (Eide et al. 1998, no. 322). The letter on papyrus was found, with two other letters addressed to Tantani, wrapped together with the Phonen letter in Qasr Ibrim, which dates the Tantani letters to the fifth century too. In the letter, which is Christian in style, Mouses writes to Tantani about the exchange of luxury goods, purple dye, and pepper. Tantani may have been a Christian (Eide et al. 1998, 1175), but this is not certain (Dijkstra 2008, 60n54) and also is not the main point of interest of the text; more important, the text shows the existence of networks between Egypt and Nubia, which would have allowed Christianity to spread (van der Vliet 2005, 220).

The archaeological record bears witness to the dynamics of this process. A recent survey of the changing burial practices in Lower Nubia, even if the chronology remains a problem, points to a long-term and complex transitory phase, with, for example, Christian symbols appearing in traditional, post-Meroitic burials (D. Edwards 2001, 89–92; 2004, 217–18; cf. Adams 2005, 154). The most conspicuous example of the latter phenomenon is found in the tombs of Ballana and Qustul, situated 40 km to the south of Qasr Ibrim. It is commonly accepted that these were the burial mounds of Noubadian chiefs who were buried first (ca. 380–420) at Qustul and later (ca. 420–500) at Ballana, on the other side of the river. These tumuli were impressive, with diameters of up to 80 m and heights of up to 12 m. In the tombs of the kings numerous grave goods can be found, as well as traces of human and animal sacrifice, which show both continuity and change as compared with Meroitic practices (Török 1988b, 75–178; Welsby 2002, 20–22, 41–43; D. Edwards 2004, 206–7; Dann 2009). Among the finds are numerous diplomatic gifts from across the frontier, including, in the fifth-century tombs of Ballana, Christian objects such as baptismal spoons, a censer, and a reliquary, as well as objects with Christian inscriptions and symbols, thus showing that these kings were at least exposed to Christianity (D. Edwards 2001, 91; 2004, 218). There is therefore enough evidence to suggest that due to the frequent exchanges across the frontier, Christianity had reached Nubia already before the sixth century.

John of Ephesus's Account of the Missions to Nubia in Context

With this background of religious transformation in mind, it is time to return to the account by John of Ephesus. The Nubia passages are found in chapters 6–9 and 49–53 of the fourth book of the third part of his *Church*

History (Richter 2002, 42–98). Written in Syriac shortly after 588, John's work offers a history of the church as seen through Miaphysite eyes (van Ginkel 1995; Ashbrook Harvey and Brakmann 1998). Miaphysitism is the movement that came into existence out of disagreement with the christological formula adopted by the Council of Chalcedon in 451 and that subsequently found most of its adherents in Syria and Egypt.[19] In the sixth century, conflicts between Chalcedonians and Miaphysites became more severe, as emperors such as Justinian I (r. 527–565) and his successor, Justin II (r. 565–578), openly supported Chalcedon and persecuted the Miaphysites (Frend 1972). One should keep in mind John's Miaphysite agenda when reading through the Nubia passages.

John of Ephesus starts the first Nubia passage (*Hist. eccl.* 3.4.6–7) with the priest Julian in Constantinople. Julian takes up the idea to convert the Noubades and reveals his plans to Justinian's wife, Theodora, who often is portrayed as a champion of Miaphysitism. Theodora approves of the idea and informs her husband about it. But Justinian decides to send a rival, Chalcedonian mission to Nubia. Because of the wiles of Theodora, the Miaphysite mission arrives first at the Noubadian king's court. Julian converts the king and his entourage to Christianity and stays for two years in Noubadia. He then leaves the country to Theodore, bishop (ca. 525–post-577) of the southernmost Egyptian see of Philae, who had accompanied him south, and returns home. Because of circumstantial evidence, this first mission can be dated somewhere between 536 and 548.

John (*Hist. eccl.* 3.4.8–9) continues the story in 566, when Theodosius, Miaphysite bishop of Alexandria (bp. 535–566) living at the time in banishment in Constantinople, remembered the first Nubia mission of Julian on his deathbed. Theodosius appointed a protégé of his, Longinus, as bishop of the Noubades in order to finish the job and convert the whole country. The Chalcedonian emperor Justin II kept him in the capital for three more years, but in 569 Longinus escaped by wearing a wig on his bald head. Upon arrival in Noubadia, Longinus established an ecclesiastical hierarchy and built a church. He stayed until about 575, but then he was recalled to take part in the appointment of a new archbishop of Alexandria. Several chapters of disputes between the Miaphysite leaders concerning this appointment follow, after which a third mission to Nubia is reported, leading to the conversion of Alodia (*Hist. eccl.* 3.4.49–53). In 579/80, after Longinus had returned to Noubadia following repeated requests of the Alodian king, the bishop decided

---

19. The term "Miaphysitism" is a modern alternative for the still widely used, but more polemical and less correct, term "Monophysitism"; see the section "The Syrian Orthodox Church" in chap. 4.

to travel south. The journey was arduous because of the heat and the hostile lands of Makouria, but eventually they arrived in Alodia and converted the king, his entourage, and many more people.

These stories often have been interpreted as part of a struggle between the Miaphysite and Chalcedonian camps to convert the Nubian kingdoms to the preferred doctrine (e.g., Kraus 1930, 54–77; Monneret de Villard 1938, 61–70; Adams 1977, 438–47; Grillmeier 1990, 278–82; Welsby 2002, 32–33). But again it was Laurence Kirwan (1982, 142; 1984, 119) who argued that these missions would have primarily had political aims and would not have been so much about religious, let alone doctrinal, matters. The stories told by John of Ephesus are clearly aimed at making Miaphysite success appear as glorious as possible. For example, it is hardly credible that two rival missions were sent to Noubadia between 536 and 548 and this story appears to have been invented to enhance Miaphysite success. The missions to Nubia should rather be seen as a continuity of fifth-century imperial policy concerning the southern frontier, by which treaties often were concluded with tribes and concessions granted to them. It seems that Justinian, by sending the mission under Julian, wanted to continue or renew ties with the now-emerging Noubadian kingdom. As we have seen, Nubia itself was already familiar with Christianity for quite some time, and the king's conversion to Christianity would therefore not have been too large a step; what is more, the conversion would have won him an important ally (Dijkstra 2008, 282–92).

Despite the impression given by John of Ephesus, the building of churches and establishment of an ecclesiastical hierarchy had already taken place before Longinus arrived in 569, as is demonstrated by a Coptic inscription from Dendur, 70 km to the south of Philae (see sidebar 5.2; Richter 2002, 164–72; Dijkstra 2008, 300–302).

In the Dendur inscription King Eirpanome of Noubadia and a high official (the exarch) from Talmis (Kalabsha) order the construction of a church inside

5.2 Dendur Inscription

By the will of God and the command of King Eirpanome and the fervent advocate
5 of the word of God, Joseph, exarch of Talmis, and as we received the cross | from Theodore, bishop of Philae, I, Abraham, this most humble priest, have erected the cross on the day on which the foundations were laid of this church, on the
10 27th of Tobe, 27 [= January 22] | in the presence of Shai, the eunuch, Papnoute, the *stepharis* [?], Epephanios [*sic*], the *domesticus* and Sirma, the *veredarius*. Let everyone who will read these words be so good to say a prayer for me. Amen. (Dijkstra 2008, 300, altered)

the temple of Dendur, no doubt not long after the official conversion of the king in the period 536–548.[20] The project is sanctioned by Bishop Theodore of Philae (Maspero 1909; Richter 2002, 99–102; Dijkstra 2008, 299–333), to whom, as we have seen, Julian had left the country,[21] while the local priest Abraham performs the rituals of the dedication of the church in the company of a group of Nubian officials. The text not only attests the first steps in the organization, from the see of Philae, of the Nubian church before 569;[22] it also shows some of the remarkable transformations that Nubia had gone through by the sixth century. All the titles mentioned seem to be adopted from Byzantine administration, one of them being a Nubian equivalent (*samata*) of a Byzantine title (*domesticus*) (Richter 2002, 170). A similar mixture is present in the names of the Nubians mentioned: some bear Nubian names (King Eirpanome; Sirma), others Egyptian names (Papenoute; Shai), still others Christian names (Joseph; Abraham; Epiphanius) (van der Vliet 2005, 222–23). It is this mixture of Egyptian/Byzantine and Nubian elements that was to become characteristic of Nubian Christianity.

Nubian Christianity

In sum, we have seen that the "inside" sources provide a more complex picture of how Nubia became Christian than the Byzantine literary sources allow. Through the frequent exchanges on the frontier, Christianity started to spread already before the sixth century, which explains better why in the sixth century the rulers of the newly emerging kingdom of Noubadia adopted Christianity. At some point after the conversion of the Noubadian king in 536–548, a church was built in Dendur, where a clerical hierarchy was already

20. For a discussion of the date, preferring 544, see Dijkstra 2008, 300–302. However, it has been demonstrated (Ochała 2011) that the dating formula in line 9 contains not an indication of the year, as was previously thought, but only the month and day (first written out and then repeated in numbers), which makes it impossible to come to a closer dating than between the first mission to Nubia in 536–548 and the arrival of Longinus in 569. It still seems likely, though, that the church was constructed not long after the conversion of the Noubadian king, although it cannot now be said anymore exactly how long afterward.

21. It often has been assumed that there existed a direct causal relationship between the closure of the temples of Philae by Justinian in 535–537 (Procopius, *Pers.* 1.19.34–37) and the first mission to Nubia, and that both formed part of a deliberate, imperial anti-"pagan" policy. I have argued (Dijkstra 2008, 271–304), however, that the relationship between these two events probably was minimal and that the involvement of Bishop Theodore of Philae in the first mission to Nubia had more to do with the practical circumstance that Philae was the closest see to the kingdom of Noubadia.

22. Two complementary, undated inscriptions from Kalabsha (Richter 2002, 162–63), one of which uses the same formula of erecting the cross, mention the dedication of a church in the Temple of Mandulis by the priest Paulos and may be further evidence for the expansion of the Nubian church at about this time.

in existence. The organization of the Nubian church was further stimulated by the arrival of the first bishop of the Noubades, Longinus, in 569. By the end of the sixth century, Christianity probably had been firmly established in Nubian society, even though the transformation process was by no means complete at this time. The form that this Nubian Christianity had taken is embodied in the monumental church architecture built from the second half of the sixth century onward in Pachoras (Faras), the capital of Noubadia, with its magnificent wall paintings (Michałowski 1967; Richter 2002, 174–80; Seipel 2002).[23]

This discussion has focused mostly on Lower Nubia and on sources from the fifth and sixth centuries because the sources for the earliest stage of the religious transformation process are less abundant in Upper Nubia. However, there is no doubt that similar processes were under way more to the south, as Christianity would have reached these areas from the north and the southeast, where the kingdom of Axum, in modern Ethiopia, had already become Christian in the fourth century. The archaeological evidence from the south also still has much in store for us because systematic excavations are ongoing. For example, excavations at Soba, the site of the ancient capital of Alodia, have revealed the remains of at least five churches, even though their dating remains uncertain (Welsby 1998, 273–75; 2002, 120; Richter 2002, 188), and excavations at Old Dongola, the site of the capital of Makouria, have unearthed several churches dating from the second half of the sixth century onward and of a similar monumentality as those at Faras (Jakobielski and Scholz 2001; Richter 2002, 183–87). From all this material it becomes increasingly clear, as exemplified by the Dendur inscription, that Nubian Christianity was heavily influenced by the north but at the same time developed its own, distinctively Nubian features. In the end, Christianity had a larger impact on the medieval Nubian kingdoms than it had on Egypt itself, as it remained the official religion until as late as 1500, when Islam finally took over.

23. Not coincidentally, the sixth-century kings of Noubadia chose as their new capital a site that was close to the tombs of their ancestors at Ballana and Qustul.

6

Roman North Africa

JANE MERDINGER

Introduction

The origins of Christianity in North Africa are shrouded in obscurity. Although missionaries may have arrived on African shores sometime in the first century CE, no material or literary evidence attests to Christianity there until the late second century. Only in 180 CE can we start to pinpoint a Christian presence in North Africa with the condemnation of twelve converts by the Roman proconsul at Carthage (see below). Until recently, it was generally assumed that converts from Judaism initially brought the "good news" to Carthage from Rome or from Alexandria, both of which boasted sizable Jewish populations. With brisk trade between the imperial capital and Carthage, it would not have been difficult for Christians to make the three-day voyage to North Africa. From Alexandria, the new faith could have spread westward to coastal cities along the southern Mediterranean. Similarities in theology and liturgical practices with Syria and Asia Minor, however, suggest possible eastern roots for North African Christianity. Some historians contend that Christianity arrived in North Africa from many different locales (e.g., Telfer 1961; Dunn 2004, 13–15; Rebillard 2008, 303–4). Judaism remained the most potent element in the new faith, but indigenous Berber cults, harsh Punic rites,

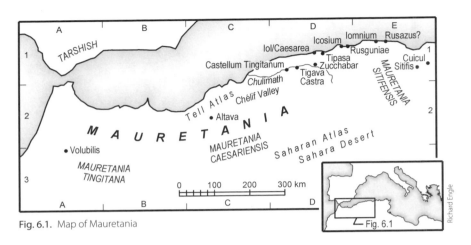

Fig. 6.1. Map of Mauretania

punctilious Greco-Roman ceremonies, and exuberant Eastern rituals would stamp North African Christianity with a rigorism peculiarly its own (Burns and Jensen 2014).

Geography

Strategically situated at the crossroads of the Mediterranean, North Africa has long attracted the attention of ambitious conquerors. Phoenicians, Romans, Vandals, Byzantines, and Arabs successively ruled North Africa. The modern countries of North Africa and their ancient counterparts roughly correspond to Morocco (Mauretania [fig. 6.1]), Algeria (Numidia [fig. 6.3]), Tunisia (Africa Proconsularis [fig. 6.3]), and Libya (Tripolitania [fig. 6.11]).[1] Poised at the northern end of the African continent, North Africa stretches about 2400 km from the Atlantic coast to the Gulf of Sidra (where the modern city of Benghazi is situated). In ancient times, to the east was Cyrenaica (fig. 6.11); farther east lay Egypt (fig. 5.4). Two major mountain ranges slice through North Africa diagonally in a northeasterly direction. For over 1500 km fronting the Mediterranean Sea, sheer cliffs and forbidding bluffs of the Coastal Range (the Tell Atlas) provide few inlets and bays. Only at Cap Bon do rolling hills and promontories supplant less inviting terrain. Fertile plains, dense forests, and pleasant valleys extend inland from the coast. Careful cultivation of the plains throughout antiquity produced abundant crops of wheat.

About 145 km inland, the landscape changes dramatically to high desert with dry, rough terrain, sandstone mesas, and protruding mountain spurs.

1. In Arabic, North Africa is known as the *Maghreb*, which means "the West."

Known as the High Plains, this region varies in altitude from 600 m to 1200 m. Its scattered, shallow salt lakes (Arabic: *chotts*) shrivel into salt flats during dry weather. Olives constituted one of the few crops capable of thriving in the harsh conditions. Consequently, the High Plains became famous for producing olive oil, a staple of the economy. At the southern edge of the High Plains the peaks of the second mountain range, the Saharan Atlas, effectively wall off North Africa from the rest of the continent. Immediately to the south, the Sahara Desert stretches for 9.4 million square kilometers. In summer the withering Saharan heat (the Sirocco) periodically smothers North Africa before engulfing southern Europe (Shaw 1995).

Berbers, Phoenicians, and Carthaginians

North Africa's indigenous people, the Berbers (also known as Libyans), began moving into the region twenty-five hundred to three thousand years ago. Their original homeland remains a matter of debate, though some certainly came from the Egyptian Sahara (Mattingly 1995, 19–21). Most Berbers were Caucasian, but some mixing occurred with black tribes that migrated from the sub-Sahara. Seeking pastureland for their goats and sheep, Berbers scattered throughout North Africa. Some of these Berbers settled down to farm, especially in the high plains of Numidia and mountainous areas of Mauretania. From Greek and Latin sources such as the writings of Herodotus (ca. 485–430/20 BCE), Pliny the Elder (ca. 23–79 CE), and Ptolemy of Alexandria (ca. 90–165 CE), scholars have identified dozens of ancient Berber tribes. Few Libyan inscriptions are extant, and they have proved to be challenging to linguistic experts. Nonetheless, over forty Berber dialects are still spoken in modern North Africa (Mattingly 1995, 17–21; Brett and Fentress 1996, 1–24; K. Stern 2008, 62–63). Little is known about ancient Berber cultic practices, though that is changing due to renewed scholarly interest. Springs and fountains were sacred sites because water is scarce in much of the Maghreb. The cult of the dead was especially important and, apparently, was associated with fertility. Berbers probably engaged in ancestor worship and communicated with spirits of the deceased (Mattingly 1995, 39; Brett and Fentress 1996, 35). For tombs, Berbers favored dolmens, especially westward from Byzacena; in Tripolitania, they favored tumuli. Corpses were arranged in the fetal position, with their faces painted red with cinnabar (Ben Khader and Soren 1987, 85–86; Lancel 1995, 53, 289–91; Raven 2002, 15).

In about 1000 BCE enterprising Phoenicians set sail from their homeland in search of metals for manufacturing weapons and agricultural implements. Fabled Tarshish (southern Spain) beckoned with silver and tin. Gradually, the

6.1 Carthaginian Cults

Initial Carthaginian cults were Semitic in character. The Phoenicians, who founded Carthage, hailed from the city of Tyre, which shared cultural ties with neighboring Israelites. At Tyre, Melqart and Astarte reigned as supreme god and goddess; at Carthage, the lesser-known Phoenician deities Baal-Hammon (Guardian of Eternal Values, Lord-Protector) and his consort, Tanit, soon replaced their Tyrian counterparts as the most popular divinities (Ben Khader and Soren 1987, 43). Possibly Baal-Hammon was associated with the Egyptian sun-god Ammon, but the origins of the cult remain a matter of debate. Tanit may originally have been a Libyan fertility goddess. Carthaginians worshiped her as "Mother of All" and "Queen of the Dead." As a Semitic people, the Carthaginians disapproved of physical representations of deities, preferring to symbolize them with emblems (a solar disc for Baal Hammon, a crescent moon for Tanit).

Like the God of Israel, Baal Hammon could sometimes be a vengeful, demanding deity. Rites in his honor called for meticulous attention to detail, reminiscent of injunctions in Leviticus. The high priest, the college of priests (always selected from aristocratic families), scribes, porters, musicians, butchers, groundskeepers—all had a role to play in appeasing the Lord-Protector of Carthage. In times of war or famine, Baal Hammon and Tanit demanded child sacrifice, a practice abhorrent to other peoples in the Mediterranean world. At Carthage's Tophet (fig. 6.2), the open-air Punic sanctuary where priests offered sacrifice, urns containing the immolated remains of infants and young children date from the seventh century BCE to the first century CE.* According to the historian Diodorus Siculus (ca. 90–21 BCE), five hundred children were sacrificed when Greeks from Syracuse invaded Carthaginian territory in 310 BCE (*Bibl. hist.* 20.14.4–7).†

Warfare, commerce, and the slave trade brought foreign gods to North Africa. By the fourth century BCE the Greek deities Kore and Demeter had become popular at Carthage, as well as Isis and Sarapis from Egypt, and the Great Mother, Cybele, from Syria. Much syncretism resulted, sometimes rendering it difficult for modern scholars to distinguish original characteristics from later Hellenistic accretions. Although Greek and Egyptian influences gradually persuaded Carthaginians to accept religious statuary, the humanism that suffused Greek culture with its drama, poetry, and athletics never appealed to North African tastes. In many respects, Carthaginian civilization remained fundamentally somber and austere.

* This is a practice expressly forbidden among the Israelite people (Lev. 18:21; 20:2–5; Deut. 12:30–31; 18:10).

† Some archaeologists are not convinced that such wholesale slaughter occurred there on any one occasion.

Phoenicians established ports one day's sail from each other along the southern Mediterranean for ship repairs and supplies. Around 800 BCE Phoenician mariners founded Kart-Hadasht,[2] later known as Carthago (Carthage), now a suburb of modern Tunis. Its excellent natural harbor and strategic location guaranteed that Carthage would become the capital of the Phoenician Empire.[3] For the next four centuries the Phoenicians' empire flourished, with colonies ringing the shores of southern Gaul, Spain, the North African coastline, and western Sicily. The Greeks figured as the Carthaginians' greatest rival, with settlements throughout southern Italy, southern Gaul, parts of Spain, and eastern Sicily. When Greece's fortunes declined in the third century BCE, Carthage faced a new enemy:

Fig. 6.2. Tombstone of Young Child in Carthage's Tophet

Rome had begun its relentless march to greatness. Three bitter Punic Wars ensued between the two rival powers during the next century, with Rome the victor each time.[4]

Carthaginian funerary practices incorporated elements from Berber, Punic, and Greek traditions. Both inhumation (burial) and cremation were common, the latter especially at Carthage as its population burgeoned in Hellenistic times. For the poor, the ancient Berber custom of burial sufficed: the corpse often was curled up and, as noted above, painted with cinnabar. Wealthier people chose burial in an underground chamber or a hillside tomb hewn out of rock. Excavations have revealed red ocher wall paintings depicting birds, plants, and the sign of Tanit, but most Carthaginian tombs are notable mainly for their austerity. Grave goods could be few or many, depending on the deceased's financial status and population constraints on the local necropolis. Practical items predominate near corpses: razors and lamps for men; perfume jars, mirrors, and hairpins for women; and decorated ostrich eggs (the symbol of life). Concerned that evil spirits might disturb the dead, Carthaginians also supplied graves with apotropaics such as grimacing masks, pop-eyed amulets,

2. Phoenician for "New City."
3. Carthage's legendary founder was a Phoenician princess named Elissa, whom Virgil (70–19 BCE) would recast as the tragic heroine Dido in the *Aeneid*.
4. "Punic" comes from the Latin *Poenus*, meaning "Carthaginian." During the final Punic War (149–146 BCE) the Romans slaughtered Carthage's citizens and reduced the city to ashes.

and small bells. However, since no Punic texts survive, scholars can only speculate about Carthaginian belief in an afterlife. The popularity of theophoric names remains a final testament to the religiosity of the Carthaginians (e.g., Hannibal signifies "Honored by Baal").

Roman North Africa

For six hundred years (146 BCE–439 CE) the Romans ruled North Africa, guaranteeing the region unparalleled productivity and peace for most of those centuries. Too valuable to lie dormant for long, Mauretania was prized by Rome for cedar wood, ivory, and wild animals. Numidia and Africa Vetus (Carthage and environs) promised wheat and olive oil. Enterprising Italian traders started plying the waters between Ostia and the Phoenician cities dotting the African coastline. An early attempt by the prominent politician Gaius Gracchus (b. ca. 159 BCE) to colonize Carthage failed upon his assassination in 121 BCE, but a decade later the Roman general Marius (157–86 BCE) granted land in North Africa to some of his veterans, a policy that would prove very effective for the Roman state. Land grants not only rewarded retired soldiers for their hard years of service, but also guaranteed loyalty, future recruits from family members, and payment of taxes in areas where Rome needed to build trust.

During the bloody civil wars that convulsed the Roman world throughout much of the first century BCE, Julius Caesar (ca. 100–44 BCE) won several battles on North African soil. To him and to his adopted great-nephew, Octavian (soon to be called Caesar Augustus), belong credit for the settlement of veterans in Mauretania, the old coastal cities, and Carthage itself. Sole victor of the wars by 31 BCE, and with the Roman republic in tatters, Octavian (d. 14 CE) reconstituted the Roman government as an empire. His ambitious plan for a new world order called for massive public works projects and the redevelopment of key cities, including Carthage. During the following decade, engineers reconfigured the old Punic capital into an orderly Roman city replete with a theater, odeon, baths, amphitheater, and an aqueduct stretching 120 km from mountain headwaters. Nero (r. 54–68 CE) designated North Africa as Rome's chief supplier of wheat.

Important also to the Roman state was the establishment of "client kingdoms"—native-ruled territories, friendly to Rome, bordering Roman-occupied lands. For helping defeat Hannibal (247–ca. 183/2 BCE) at the end of the Second Punic War in 202 BCE, the Berber chieftain Masinissa (r. 203–148 BCE) received eastern Numidia. In 46 BCE Julius Caesar granted western Numidia to the Berber king Bocchus of Mauretania (r. 50–33 BCE) for his assistance in vanquishing Pompey the Great (106–48 BCE). Caesar Augustus, in 25 BCE, bestowed all of Mauretania on Juba II of Numidia (r. 25 BCE–23 CE). Intrigue, factionalism, and revolts eventually convinced the Romans to disband all North African client kingdoms and annex them, a process completed by 42 CE, at which time the entire region became a senatorial province, ruled by a proconsul. From 42 CE until the late third century, Roman North Africa consisted of the provinces of Mauretania Tingitana; Mauretania Caesariensis; Africa Proconsularis, formed by combining Africa Vetus and Africa Nova; Tripolitania; and Numidia, which became a separate province around 200 CE.

The task of keeping this immense territory secure fell to the Third Augustan Legion. With 20,000 to 25,000 men (including auxiliaries), the legion quelled insurrections among Berber tribes, policed the city of Carthage, and patrolled several thousand kilometers of borders to protect against attacks by outlying tribes. Legio III Augusta also built bridges, dams, aqueducts, and almost 20,000 km of roads that knit together Roman North Africa.

Romanization

Romanization in North Africa occurred gradually and in patchwork fashion. Coastal Phoenician cities that had allied with Rome during the Punic Wars received full citizenship and favorable trading rights in the first century CE; some Punic towns were granted lesser status as *coloniae* or *municipia*; some cities retained their Punic governing bodies of suffetes and assemblies. In general, urban areas welcomed Roman customs and adopted Latin as their language, while many rural sites retained Punic traditions and the Punic language; in the highlands, Berbers continued to speak Libyan and remained relatively isolated.

By the second century CE, North Africa enjoyed remarkable prosperity. With a population of at least three hundred thousand, Carthage ranked as the second-largest city in the western half of the Roman Empire, surpassed only by Rome. In 193, for the first time ever, a North African became emperor: Septimius Severus (d. 211). His dynasty showered its homeland with magnificent temples, arches, and public buildings.

Warehouses outside Rome bristled with North African wheat, while a statesponsored shipping fleet ensured safe passage across the Tyrrhenian Sea for such cargo. In homes and taverns from southern Spain to Athens, people dined off African red-slip ware, a popular pottery mass-produced in Carthage and nearby cities. Manufacturers of garum, a popular fish sauce, packed it in *amphorae* made in North Africa for distribution throughout the empire. Efficient irrigation systems built by the Third Augustan Legion caused a boom in North African olive production for the rest of Antiquity.

Triggered by the murder of Emperor Alexander Severus in 235, political turmoil roiled the empire for the next fifty years. Crop failures, famine, plague, Gothic invasions, and war with Persia only added to the general misery. Stringent administrative and military reforms ordered by Emperor Diocletian (r. 284–305) saved the empire from collapse. Reorganization of provinces entailed division into smaller units. North Africa became segmented into eight provinces (which altogether now constituted the civil Diocese of Africa). Two new provinces were carved from Africa Proconsularis: Zeugitana in the north (a short-lived reform), and Byzacena in the south, with Proconsularis itself now much smaller. The new province of Mauretania Sitifensis was created out of eastern Mauretania Caesariensis. Tingitana, reduced in size by tribal incursions and too distant to protect, now came under Spain's control. Archaeologists have discovered, however, that North Africa (apart from Tripolitania) weathered the crisis of the late third century

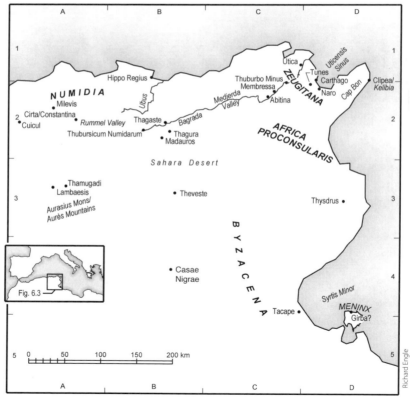

Fig. 6.3. Map of Numidia and Africa Proconsularis

relatively unscathed. Municipal projects continued to be funded, and civic life flourished, unlike in other Western provinces where permanent decline commenced.

Religion before Christianity

Roman North Africa boasted a rich array of cults. Over the centuries, merchants, slaves, and troops had imported to its shores their native beliefs. Typically, municipalities throughout Roman North Africa maintained temples to the Capitoline Triad (Jupiter, Juno, and Minerva); Saturn; Apollo; the Great Mother, Cybele; Ceres; and Asclepius. Berber and Punic elements became mixed with Greco-Roman practices, creating an assortment of hybrid cults unique to North Africa (Riggs forthcoming). For example, by the second century CE, Carthage's patron deity had metamorphosed from the Punic goddess Tanit into the Romano-African goddess Caelestis. Due to Phoenician influence, many North African sanctuaries contained not only a temple dedicated to a chief deity but also surrounding shrines to numerous other deities. The imperial cult figured prominently in North African cities as well. At Carthage fragments probably from an altar and an inscription dating to Augustus's reign confirm the early origins of emperor worship in the capital city. The first inscription attesting to a *flamen* (priest) of the imperial cult there is traceable to 54 CE (Rives 1995, 52–55, 58).

By 200 CE Jews constituted a small but thriving community at Carthage. No remnants of a synagogue have been discovered, but one must have existed by the early third century and another perhaps by the fourth century. In the suburb of Gammarth, just north of Carthage, a Jewish cemetery contains over one hundred *loculi* (tomb niches) with depictions of menorahs. A large synagogue with handsome mosaics nearby in the coastal town of Naro (modern Hammam-Lif) dates to the fourth century, testifying to a prosperous Jewish community there (Darmon 1994). Jewish inscriptions and artifacts from the third century have also been found at important North African cities such as Sitifis (Sétif), Volubilis (Ksar Pharaoun), Oea (Tripoli), and Cirta/Constantina (Constantine). With its monotheism, dietary laws, and strict moral code, Judaism offered a refreshing alternative to a polytheistic world awash in libidinous rites, abortion, infanticide, and blood sports. Some pagans converted completely to Judaism; others, shying away from circumcision and full observance of the law, participated in Jewish festivals and celebrations. New research indicates that many North African Jews interacted with pagans and Christians and adopted quotidian customs and burial practices from their neighbors (K. Stern 2008).

Contextual Challenges and Influences

The Romans believed that the gods had made the empire great; as long as traditional deities and the emperor received proper worship, the state would flourish. Centuries of conquest had taught the Romans to be tolerant of foreign religions as well, but subversive cultic activities necessitated exile and persecution or warranted death. With pagan rites and symbols permeating every aspect of civic life, the ancient world knew no distinction between religion and the state. Christianity upset that seamless balance by its absolute allegiance to a monotheistic God and by its newness. When persecution did strike North Africa periodically, it exacted a high toll, spawning serious divisions among Christians. The Donatist schism, born out of the Great Persecution of 303–305, cleaved the North African church in two for more than a century. No less challenging was the vast array of Christian sects that took root in Carthage. Monarchians, Marcionites, Valentinian Gnostics, Montanists, and Novatianists flourished in the teeming streets of the metropolis.

Also crucial to the spread of the gospel were the highways, bridges, and secondary roads that facilitated travel throughout the Roman Empire. The topography of Africa Proconsularis proved to be especially conducive for missionizing. From headwaters near the mountain town of Thubursicum Numidarum (Khamissa), the Medjerda (ancient Bagrada) River sprawls eastward for almost 250 km before reaching plains near Carthage. By 200, several hundred towns and villages, interspersed with wheat fields, dotted its flat, rich soil. With the average distance only a few kilometers between each community, Christianity spread rapidly throughout the Medjerda Valley in the early third century (Ben Khader and Soren 1987, 120–21). Rugged terrain in parts of Numidia and in the Mauretanias slowed the reception of the gospel there. Only in the latter half of the third century did significant portions of Numidia convert to Christianity. In Tripolitania and in Mauretania Caesariensis (Caillet 2008), coastal cities and municipalities on main roads embraced the new faith, but many settlements in the hinterlands remained faithful to traditional Romano-Berber deities.

Christianity by the Time of Constantine

Christianity in North Africa around 325 CE resembles a patchwork configuration. Although the new faith had taken hold in many areas (Mullen 2004, 294–329), polytheism remained widespread. Current archaeological research indicates no trend toward pagan monotheism in North Africa during Late Antiquity, and the view that the worship of Saturn as a Romanized Baal became dominant in the late third century (Leglay 1961–1966; Frend 1975) must be rejected. Moreover, Donatism had gained considerable momentum by 325, spurred by imperial repression, heroic martyrs, and a separatist ecclesiology. Peculiar to North Africa, Donatism never spread beyond its own provincial borders (apart from a token presence at Rome). Clashes with the Catholic church lasted until 420, quelled only by imperial intervention and eventually by Vandal occupation of the entire region (Frend 1971).

Carthage and Africa Proconsularis

Scillitan Martyrs

As already mentioned, the earliest evidence attesting to a Christian presence in North Africa dates only from 180 (Clarke 1984–1989, 4:249; Saxer 2000, 583). On July 17, 180, the governor of Africa Proconsularis, Vigellius Saturninus, sentenced twelve Christians to death for refusing to recant their faith. The title of the embellished record of their trial, the *Passio Sanctorum Scillitanorum* (*Acts of the Scillitan Martyrs*), indicates that the martyrs hailed from Scilli (or Scillium). This village probably was located near the capital city, since the proconsul arraigned them in his courtroom at Carthage (*Kartagine in secretario*) rather than out on circuit (*Pass. Scill.* 1; Musurillo 1972, 86, line 2; Rives 1995, 223; Shaw 2004, 298n45). Some scholars have mistakenly assumed that Scilli was located in Numidia (e.g., Mullen 2004, 317). Six of the martyrs' names appear only in the final lines of the *passio* (Barnes 1968, 519–20; Grig 2004, 24). Apparently, the proconsul had denounced those six at an earlier inquiry but they joined the others in martyrdom. Most scholars believe that all twelve came from Scilli, though possibly the previously condemned six were from Carthage (Tabbernee 2008b, 598). Tertullian (*Scap.* 3.4) notes that Vigellius Saturninus was the first Roman official in North Africa to persecute Christians.

The *Passio Sanctorum Scillitanorum* supplies valuable information about the spread of Christianity and its appeal in North Africa (Grig 2004, 24). By the late second century the new faith had taken root not only in cities but also in the countryside, attracting adherents such as those from Scilli. Nine of the latter bore Latin names, but three possessed Berber ones, an indication that Christianity was attracting indigenous people as well (Barnes 1971, 63; Saxer 2000, 584). Five of the martyrs were women and seven were men. It is difficult to ascertain the socioeconomic status of the twelve, but those from Scilli very likely were agricultural workers or tradespeople. The admission by Speratus, the martyrs' spokesman in the courtroom, that he possessed in his satchel "books and letters of a just man named Paul" (*Pass. Scill.* 12; Musurillo 1972, 89) supplies the first known evidence for a Latin translation of the Scriptures (or portions thereof) from the western half of the empire. The origins of the "Old Latin" Bible are controversial, but its provenance probably was second-century North Africa (Saxer 2000, 584–85; Yates forthcoming).

Namphano and Companions

On an unknown date, four Christians with Punic names were executed, presumably at Madauros, a community 24 km from St. Augustine's hometown, Thagaste. Correspondence between Augustine and Maximus, an old pagan grammarian who may have tutored the saint in his youth, reveals that by about 390 the cult of the Punic martyrs had become immensely popular at Madauros, the site of their tombs (Augustine, *Ep.* 16, 17). Deemed *archimartyris* (chief martyr) by local Christians, Namphano was especially venerated (Augustine, *Ep.* 16, written by Maximus). Misleading evidence in a fourth-century martyrology long convinced historians that Namphano and his companions suffered execution shortly before the Scillitans (Frend 1981, 313). The four Punic saints, however, are more likely to have been fourth-century Donatist martyrs (Barnes 1971, 261–62; di Berardino 1999, 550; but see Saxer 2000, 585).

Tertullian

Scant archaeological data for North African Christianity before the fourth century compels us to rely primarily on literary evidence for Christianity's origins. Tertullian (ca. 160/70–ca. 220) serves as our principal literary source for the early third century. His thirty-two extant treatises provide valuable evidence for theological, moral, sacramental, and liturgical issues affecting the church at Carthage. A skilled controversialist with an excellent philosophical and literary education, Tertullian was one of few members of the upper class at the time to embrace Christianity (Schöllgen 1984, 176–89). For over two decades he figured as a prominent lay leader and apologist for the North African church. His writings date from approximately 197 to 212 (Barnes 1971, 32, 55). In his *De praescriptione haereticorum* (*Praescription against Heretics*) Tertullian evinces great respect for the Roman church because of its apostolic origins (*Praescr.* 32, 36), but he does not conclude that Rome missionized North Africa. Very likely, he himself did not know who was responsible for bringing Christianity to his homeland.

Around 208 Montanism became increasingly attractive to Tertullian; many of his later treatises contain its distinctive features (Tabbernee 2012, 664–68; 2013b, 264–77). Montanism, a prophetic movement originating in Phrygia in the late second century, emphasized that the millennium was fast approaching. The New Jerusalem, Montanists believed, would descend on the Phrygian

6.2 The Size of the Christian Community in Carthage

How large the Christian community was at Carthage during the early third century remains debatable. Tertullian boasts that Christians crowd not only urban apartments, marketplaces, and the forum but also villages and the countryside (*Nat.* 1.14; *Scap.* 2; *Apol.*1.7; 37.34). His rhetoric mixes truth with much bravado to bolster fellow Christians in the face of persecution. Some scholars believe that Christians numbered only about five hundred to twelve hundred at Carthage circa 200 (Tabbernee 2001, 380–81n23); others suggest between five thousand and ten thousand (Hopkins 1998, 202). Few Carthaginian Christians were literate (Dunn 2004, 5).

settlements of Pepouza and Tymion (on their discovery, see Tabbernee 2003; Tabbernee and Lampe 2008). Caught up in the Spirit, adherents practiced strict asceticism, prophesied, experienced dreams, and insisted that revelation was ongoing (Tabbernee 1989). Historians long assumed that Tertullian left the catholic church to join the Montanist community at Carthage, but there is a growing consensus that the Montanists remained a subgroup within the Carthaginian church during the early 200s (Tabbernee 1997, 59; 2005; 2006; 2007, 268; traditional view in Saxer 2000, 785, 789). Cyprian, bishop of Carthage a half century later, esteemed Tertullian highly, an indication that the latter did not break from the Great Church (Jerome, *Vir. ill.* 53).

Carthage

Initially, Christians assembled in the homes of wealthier members (Barnes 1971, 89). As numbers increased, remodeling of such homes provided more space, though concerns for safety militated against any ostentatious additions. Tertullian indicates that the faithful gathered in a room, while the uninitiated penitents filled an adjoining vestibule (Saxer 2000, 593). Perhaps Christians rented a hall or space above a shop, as Justin Martyr did at Rome in the mid-second century (see chap. 9). Tertullian concedes that neighbors knew the whereabouts of Christian gathering spots and occasionally attacked or obstructed Christians as they departed their services (*Nat.* 1.7.19). Under the cover of night, pagans infiltrated burial grounds outside the city walls and mutilated Christian corpses, despite universal repugnance at such acts (*Apol.* 37.2). New research indicates that Christians at Carthage did not possess separate burial grounds; they buried their dead in cemeteries containing pagan graves as well (Rebillard 2009, 7–12; 1996; 1993; K. Stern 2008, 259n11, 294–96).

Fig. 6.4. Baptismal Font Commemorating Cyprian, Kelibia (Now in Bardo Museum, Tunis)

Centuries of invasions, vandalism, and rebuilding have left few traces of Christian structures at Carthage, especially in the city center. French annexation of North Africa in the nineteenth century spurred tremendous interest in the area's antiquities, but primitive excavation techniques caused archaeologists unintentionally to demolish valuable evidence (Frend 1996, 183–84).[5] Early Christian devotional habits also obscured artifacts. Third-century Christians frequently erected a shrine on the site of martyrs' graves. Large additions in the fourth and fifth centuries transformed such edifices into vast "cemetery" churches, attracting thousands of pilgrims each year, many of whom subsequently chose to be buried in close proximity to the saints—burial *ad sanctos* (Frend 1996, 87n22, 184; Sears 2007, 105–6). Such massive numbers often precluded any opportunity for archaeologists to exhume significant remains. No inscriptions at any Carthaginian Christian site can be dated with certainty prior to the fourth century. Similarly, though very important to the life of the church, early North African baptisteries are few. The late fourth and early fifth centuries, however, produced an efflorescence of them with elaborate and unusual designs peculiar to the region (Jensen 2005; 2012).

Martyrdom and Persecution

Until Constantine I (r. 306–337) declared Christianity legal in 312, martyrdom and persecution proved to be inescapable features of the new faith. Persecutions occurred sporadically and locally, ignited usually by a pagan mob or by merchants whose products Christians were boycotting. The psychological repercussions of living under such stressful conditions are beginning to be explored in depth (Grig 2004). Certainly, the heroism and faith that martyrs displayed as gladiators or wild animals slaughtered them is

---

5. The invention of stratigraphy in the 1940s finally curbed such destruction.

incontestable. Some onlookers were so moved that they decided to learn more about Christianity and eventually converted; that appears to have been Tertullian's experience. No ancient historian chronicled early persecution in North Africa, but it is possible to reconstruct some details from Tertullian's treatises. In about 190, a proconsul of Africa allowed Christians under arrest at Thysdrus (el-Djem) to go free after reciting a statement crafted by the proconsul himself (*Scap.* 4) (Frend 1981, 314). Tertullian records a further incident concerning that proconsul's successor, Vespronius Candidus. At the insistence of a mob, Candidus imprisoned a Christian for disturbing the peace but soon released him (*Scap.* 4) (Rebillard 2012, 35–38). Both examples demonstrate that some Roman officials harbored no ill will against Christians and were reluctant to convict them.

Around 197, persecution struck suddenly at Carthage, perhaps at the instigation of Septimius Severus. Those swept up in the dragnet may possibly have been the first Carthaginian Christians to face persecution, if all of the Scilli martyrs hailed from Scilli itself in 180 (Tabbernee forthcoming a). With Christians imprisoned under horrible conditions, Tertullian felt compelled to write an exhortation to martyrdom. A short, unpolished tract, *Ad martyras* (*To the Martyrs*), captures the essence of North African Christianity. If Christians are brought to trial, they need not fear what to say, for the Holy Spirit will guide them (Matt. 10:19–20). The Holy Spirit resides especially in the imprisoned (confessors) and in those about to be martyred. To confessors and martyrs belongs the power to absolve sins immediately without the mediation of the clergy (*Mart.* 1.6). Paradise imminently awaits those who die for the faith (*Mart.* 2.4). The end times are approaching; martyrdom simply expedites the process (Rev. 6:9–11). The true home of Christians is the heavenly Jerusalem and can never be any earthly state. Very likely, even at this early date North African Christians celebrated martyrs' feast days by reading aloud their *acta* on the anniversary of their death (Frend 1988, 155).

In 203 persecution again struck North Africa, possibly prompted by decrees issued by Septimius Severus prohibiting conversion to Judaism or Christianity (Shaw 2004, 292; on doubts about the decrees' authenticity, see Tabbernee 1997, 108–9). From Tertullian's *Ad Scapulam* we know that in 212 the proconsul of Africa, Scapula, launched a fierce persecution in Mauretania and Numidia. Christians suffered martyrdom by order of the provincial governors (*Scap.* 4.8). Although harm had not yet befallen Carthage, a sense of foreboding (and indignation) permeates the pages of Tertullian's text. "Spare Carthage," Tertullian pleads with Scapula (*Scap.* 5.3), who was beheading Christians in nearby Utica by late summer, but a bloodbath results (Barnes 1971, 260).

Perpetua and Felicitas

In March 203 a young noblewoman, Perpetua, and her servant, Felicitas, along with four others, were martyred at Carthage.[6] Perpetua's memoir of her trials in prison while awaiting martyrdom remains a priceless document in the annals of church history. Inspired by the Holy Spirit, Perpetua fearlessly forsook family and tradition to follow God. She experienced dreams and visions that fortified her faith and assured her of paradise. No one can read her "incandescent words" (Shaw 2004, 301) without being profoundly moved.

Fig. 6.5. Amphitheater, Carthage

Soon after Perpetua's death someone published her prison diary replete with additional details and commentary. The text of the *Passio Sanctarum Perpetuae et Felicitatis* (*Martyrdom of Saints Perpetua and Felicitas*) underwent further editing in the fourth century (Shaw 2004, 300–325). Debate still continues whether Tertullian was the first editor (Tabbernee 1997, 56–57; Shaw 2004, 309). Certainly, the *Passio Perpetuae* bears features that could be Montanist: Perpetua is filled with the Spirit immediately upon entering prison; her dreams and visions spur her toward martyrdom; paradise awaits her imminently, while quarreling clergy gain no admittance there. Yet rigorous catholics also demonstrated such traits. Consequently, it is "now impossible to determine definitely" whether Perpetua and her colleagues were Montanists (Tabbernee 1997, 57–59; 2007, 64).

The *Passio Perpetuae* does not specify Carthage as the site of the execution, but tradition strongly suggests that Perpetua and her associates suffered martyrdom in the amphitheater there (Amat 1996, 22–25; Shaw 2004, 286, 292–93). Possibly

6. The date remains disputed: Amat 1996, 19–22; Barnes 1971, 263–65.

6.3 Perpetua Inscription

Thirty-four fragments, discovered by A.-L. Delattre at the site of the Mcidfa basilica, form major portions of a sixth-century plaque commemorating Perpetua, her companions, and at least one other North African martyr.

Here are the martyrs Saturus, Saturninus, Revocatus, Secundulus, Felicitas

5 (and) Perpetua, who suffered on the 7th of March. | Maiulus. . . . (Tabbernee 1997, 106)

all six came from Thuburbo Minus (55 km from Carthage) (Amat 1996, 22; Shaw 2004, 292), but some scholars argue that Carthage was definitely their hometown (Tabbernee 2005, 424–27). Built by the Romans (first century CE), the amphitheater lies west of the Byrsa, accommodated thirty-six thousand spectators, and was Roman Africa's largest (156 m by 128 m [MacKendrick 1980, 62]). Today only the arena floor ringed by dilapidated columns and the inner wall remain.

A huge cemetery basilica in the northerly Mcidfa region of Carthage likely contained relics of Perpetua and her companions. Situated on a plateau with a commanding view of the city, the church measured 61 m by 45 m and boasted nine naves. It probably is the Basilica Majorum, mentioned by Victor of Vita in the late fifth century as "the burial place of Perpetua and Felicitas" (*ubi corpora sanctarum martyrum Perpetuae et Felicitatis sepulta sunt* [*Hist. pers.* 1.3.9]) (Frend 1996, 124).[7] Alfred-Louis Delattre, the French priest who discovered the dilapidated site and excavated it in 1906–1908, believed that he had found the saints' tomb in a subterranean crypt.[8] Moreover, several thousand graves covered the entire area of the basilica—testimony to the practice of burial *ad sanctos*. A badly damaged inscription commemorating Perpetua and her five companions (*CIL* 8,4.25038 [see sidebar 6.3]), and another inscription to "most beloved Perpetua" (*CIL* 8,4.25272), further convinced Delattre of the veracity of his discovery (Delattre 1907a; 1907b; 1908). The first inscription is Vandal or Byzantine, and the other is likely fourth-century (N. Duval 1972, 116–19; Y. Duval 1982, 2:682–83; Tabbernee 1997, 105–11). Carthaginian Christians often erected memorials to favorite saints long after their martyrdom.[9]

7. When he visited Carthage on ecclesiastical business, Augustine often preached about Perpetua and her fellow martyrs at the Basilica Majorum (Y. Duval 1982, 682; Sears 2007, 44).

8. A member of the Pères Blancs, Delattre deserves credit for the initial excavation of numerous Christian sites at Carthage, though his primitive excavation techniques caused significant destruction (K. Stern 2008, 13–14).

9. Many scholars think that the Mcidfa basilica probably is the Basilica Majorum and Perpetua's final resting place (N. Duval 1997, 318, 340; Tabbernee 1997, 115–16; Shaw 2004, 319; Sears 2007, 45), but some remain skeptical (e.g., Rebillard 2009, 11–12).

Fig. 6.6. Mosaic Medallions Honoring North African Martyrs, Carthage (Now in Bardo Museum, Tunis)

Several other artifacts scattered about Carthage memorialize Perpetua and her companions. In 1902 Paul Gauckler (1903, 416–18) discovered a pavement mosaic in St. Stephen's chapel in the Dermech district. The badly fragmented Byzantine mosaic (*CIL* 8,4.25037) depicts seven medallions, each measuring .65 m in diameter. On two medallions the names are clearly legible: Saturus and Saturninus, Perpetua's co-martyrs (N. Duval 1997, 324–25; cf. N. Duval 1972, 1097–98; Y. Duval 1982, 1:7–10). Two of the other medallions presumably honored Perpetua and Felicitas, testifying to the enduring popularity of the young saint and her associates (Tabbernee 1997, 112–14).

Cyprian

Literary evidence for North African Christianity sometime between 220 and 250 consists chiefly of eighty-one letters and a handful of treatises written by Cyprian during his tenure as bishop of Carthage (248/9–258). Cyprian mentions two African councils held prior to his episcopate. The first assembly, summoned by Agrippinus (bishop of Carthage ca. 220–ca. 235), dealt with the problem of heretical baptism. "Many bishops" attended, says Cyprian (*Ep.* 73.3), though he cites no exact figures (Y. Duval 2003, 239–43).

The other council specifically mentioned by Cyprian met between 236 and 248, probably at Carthage. Presided over by Cyprian's immediate predecessor, Donatus (bp. ca. 235–248), the conclave censured the bishop of Lambaesis for gross misconduct. Cyprian (*Ep.* 59.10) attests that ninety bishops attended from Africa Proconsularis and Numidia, an impressive figure that witnesses to the spread of Christianity in the region (Clarke 1984–1989, 3:77; Y. Duval 1984; 2003). It is difficult to ascertain the frequency and location of African conclaves prior to 250. Most likely, bishops met occasionally but not systematically, depending on political conditions and pressing ecclesiastical problems (Merdinger forthcoming; Y. Duval 2003; but see Clarke 1984–1989, 1:44).

In 250–251 fierce persecution by the emperor Decius (r. 249–251) caused stunning numbers of Christians to apostatize. In response to ensuing difficulties, Cyprian summoned seven councils during the course of his episcopate. He insisted that the guarantors of ecclesial purity were the clergy;

6.4 Rebaptism

Influenced by Tertullian's *De baptismo* (ca. 198), Agrippinus and his colleagues ruled that heretical baptism is lifeless because it is devoid of the Spirit; heretics seeking to join the catholic church must be baptized anew. We do not know whether some attendees dissented, but Eastern synods affirming rebaptism did experience opposition from some delegates (Firmilian of Caesarea in Cappadocia, cited by Cyprian, *Ep.* 75.7.4; 75.19.4 [Tabbernee 2007, 79–80]). Cyprian himself strongly endorsed rebaptism of heretics and schismatics. Old Testament regulations concerning purity and Tertullian's treatises caused Cyprian to regard heretics and schismatics as sources of pollution by the devil (J. Burns 2002). Whether North African Christianity always favored rebaptism remains a matter of debate (Cyprian, *Ep.* 71) (Frend 1984, 335; Clarke 1984–1989, 4:196). In the fifth century Augustine of Hippo (bp. 395/6–430) argued strenuously that the African church did not embrace rebaptism until Agrippinus's era (*Bapt.* 2.7.12). The topic is important because it lies at the heart of the Donatist controversy that ripped the African church apart in the fourth century.

any priests or bishops who had apostatized must be banned from the clerical ranks (*Ep.* 67). From his correspondence and from the proceedings of his final council in September 256 (which mustered eighty-seven bishops), more than one hundred bishoprics[10] are known. Because some bishops did not attend Cyprian's conclaves or correspond with him, North Africa probably numbered about 150 bishops altogether by the year 250 (Y. Duval 1984, 519; 2003, 250; Saxer 2000, 599–605). As bishop of Carthage, Cyprian exercised considerable authority over the North African church. It is difficult to know whether outlying areas accepted his leadership unquestioningly (Dunn 2002). Cyprian (*Ep.* 48.3.2) states that the African church comprised one single province governed by the bishop of Carthage, but Numidia and Mauretania appear to have exercised some autonomy (Y. Duval 1984, 516; 2005, 30–34; cf. Rives 1995, 290, 302–3).

Cyprian's writings afford glimpses of the well-developed organization and daily life of the Carthaginian church (Saxer 1984; 1995). Mirroring Rome, it maintained a hierarchy of seven grades: bishop, priests, deacons, subdeacons, acolytes, lectors, and exorcists (Saxer 2000, 800–802). Nascent ecclesiastical regions are apparent; by Augustine's era, the city would boast seven, also patterned after Rome (N. Duval 1997, 344; cf. N. Duval 1972, 1075, 1101). Parishes supervised by priests were beginning to develop within those regions (Frend

10. Mostly in Africa Proconsularis and Numidia, but at least two in Mauretania.

1977, 28–29). Priests celebrated the Eucharist and reconciled penitents in the absence of the bishop, but their main duties involved teaching and catechesis (Saxer 2000, 801–2). Deacons administered the finances and distributed food to widows, orphans, and the poor. The Carthaginian church was wealthy enough to pay higher clergy a monthly stipend (Cyprian, *Ep.* 39.5.2). In summer 252, when plague ravaged the capital city, Cyprian himself ministered to the dying (Pontius, *Vit. Cypr.* 8–9).

Cyprian's writings disclose little about ecclesiastical furnishings, buildings, or their locations (White 1990, 26). He does mention a pulpit (*Ep.* 39.4.1) and an altar (*Ep.* 59.18.1). House-churches remained the norm until Christianity became legal in the early fourth century (Ennabli 1997, 158), but full-fledged church buildings may have existed in Carthage by Cyprian's era (Clarke 1984–1989, 1:44). Shrines to Perpetua and other martyrs had already sprouted early in the third century on the periphery of the metropolis.

Care of the dead remained an important duty for Christians. When the plague struck, Christians even interred pagan victims whose family members spurned their corpses (Rebillard 2009, 93–95). New scholarship demonstrates that certainly as late as 250 CE, Christians continued to bury their dead next to pagans; no exclusively Christian burial grounds existed at Carthage at that time (Rebillard 2009, 11–12; but see Y. Duval 2000, 452–54).[11] Cyprian's letters also witness to the growing importance of the cult of martyrdom in North Africa. By the mid-third century, the Carthaginian church kept a list of the death dates of local martyrs. On the anniversary of their death (their *natalis*, or "birthday," into heaven) Cyprian celebrated the Eucharist in remembrance of them (*Ep.* 12.2.1 [Clarke 1984–1989, 1:249–50n12]; cf. *Ep.* 39.3.1 [Rebillard 2009, 98–100]). Episcopal control of the commemoration of saints supplanted spontaneous outpourings of reverence and affection characteristic of Tertullian's era. Now martyrs needed the intercession of the church to assure them a place in heaven (Frend 1982, 155).

In 257 persecution recommenced throughout the empire. Valerian (r. 253–260) cleverly targeted clergy, a strategy never employed previously by Roman authorities but designed to deprive the church of its leadership (Frend 2006, 515–16; cf. Rives 1995, 252–53). On September 14, 258, Cyprian suffered decapitation on the estate of Sextus (*Ager Sexti*) near the proconsul's palace. The reverent crowd placed cloths and handkerchiefs on the ground to catch drops of his blood (*Act. Cypr.* 5.4). That evening, the faithful carried

11. Rebillard's conclusions overturn a century of scholarly opinion about several sites considered to be solely Christian (e.g., *area Fausti*, *area Tertulli*, *Novae areae*) (Frend 1977, 24; N. Duval 1997, 318).

Fig. 6.7. Sainte Monique Basilica, Carthage

Cyprian's body to the cemetery of Macrobius Candidianus on the Mappalian Way and buried him by torchlight (*Act. Cypr.* 6) (Dunbabin 1978, 188–95). Cyprian's dedication to the unity of the church, tireless service to many, and heroic death catapulted him into the foremost ranks of North Africa's martyrs.

Soon after Cyprian's death, an altar table (*mensa Cypriani*) was erected on *Ager Sexti* at the site of his execution. There, the faithful could remember him in prayer and song (Lancel 2002, 195; Y. Duval 1982, 2:675–80). Archaeologists have not found the *mensa Cypriani*, but according to Victor of Vita (*Hist. pers.* 1.16), a vast basilica occupied the site by the fifth century. Augustine occasionally preached there to boisterous crowds on the anniversary of Cyprian's martyrdom (Perler and Maier 1969, 420–21). The exact locations of the Mappalian Way and Cyprian's tomb have also eluded archaeologists, but many believe that the ruined Sainte Monique Basilica, high on a bluff overlooking the Gulf of Tunis, is the place. Delattre excavated the site from 1915 to 1920, uncovering a vast church (35 m by 80 m) with seven naves and hundreds of epitaphs (Ennabli 1972). Augustine, in his *Confessions* (5.8.15), mentions a *memoria beati Cypriani* (shrine to the blessed Cyprian) overlooking the sea where Augustine's mother kept vigil the night that he sailed secretly for Rome (Frend 1977, 25, 27; Lancel 2002, 56). However, the *memoria Cypriani* may merely have been a funeral chapel that contained no remains of Cyprian. If so, the location of Cyprian's tomb remains unknown, leaving open the possibility of a third church at Carthage that actually contained his tomb (N. Duval 1972, 1103–7; 1993, 595; 1997, 315, 318, 340; Frend 1996, 183–94, 365–66; Ennabli 1997, 21–26).

The Donatist Schism

One final spasm of persecution wracked the empire in 303–305. Diocletian ordered that Scriptures be surrendered and church buildings demolished. In 304, Carthaginian authorities imprisoned Christians from the small town of Abitina in the Upper Medjerda River Valley, 4 km from Membressa (Y. Duval 1984, 509, 511; cf. Y. Duval 1982, 684–91). They had continued to gather together even after their bishop had apostatized. The Abitinians vigorously condemned anyone who handed over Scripture as a *traditor* (traitor). W. H. C. Frend (2006, 520–21) pinpoints their intransigence as the start of the Donatist schism. Perhaps in compliance with a recent imperial decree, the bishop of Carthage (Mensurius) and his archdeacon (Caecilian) physically prevented fellow Christians from bringing sustenance to the imprisoned Abitinians (Tilley 1996, 20, 25–26; Frend 2004, 261). The ill will engendered was not forgotten. Mensurius (bp. pre-304–307/8) had handed over heretical texts, but many clergy refused any compromise and, consequently, suffered martyrdom (Augustine, *Brev. coll.* 3.13.25). When Mensurius died in 307/8,[12] custom dictated that his successor be consecrated by Numidian colleagues (Optatus, *Donat.* 1.18). Instead, Caecilian's local supporters hastily consecrated him bishop of Carthage, even though one of the consecrators was rumored to be a *traditor*. Soon seventy Numidian bishops arrived at Carthage, declared Caecilian's election null, and elected their own candidate, Majorinus. Within a year Marjorinus died, and Donatus of Casae Nigrae (d. ca. 355)[13] became the new alternate bishop of Carthage. Under Donatus of Casae Nigrae (also known as Donatus the Great), the "Donatist Church" challenged the "Catholic Church" (Frend 1997; Y. Duval 2000), the opposition movement (eventually) bearing this Donatus's name.

Numidia

As already noted, evidence for Christianity in Numidia first appears circa 212 in Tertullian's tract *To Scapula*, reporting that Christians, as far away as in Mauretania but also in Numidia, suffered in the current persecution (*Scap.* 4.8) (Y. Duval 1984, 519). Also as noted, sometime between 220 and 235 Bishop Agrippinus of Carthage assembled a council to condemn heretical baptism. Bishops from Numidia as well as Africa Proconsularis attended, though we do not know which particular sees they represented (Cyprian, *Ep.* 59.10.1; 74.1).

12. Traditionally, scholars have listed Mensurius's death as 311/2, but Serge Lancel (2002, 165–66, 498n14), among others, argues convincingly for the earlier date.
13. Not to be confused with the earlier, pre-Cyprianic bishop of Carthage also named Donatus.

Fig. 6.8. Baptismal Font with Ciborium, Cuicul   **Fig. 6.9.** Ambulatory, Cuicul Baptistery

In the first century CE, as the Third Augustan Legion had gradually moved westward pacifying Numidia, a population boom had ensued. On the southern border of the High Plains a cluster of towns sprang up along the Roman road from Theveste to Lambaesis. On the High Plains' northern border the same phenomenon occurred along the Roman road from Madauros to Cirta and Cuicul. Bishoprics existed in many of these settlements by the early third century (Y. Duval 1984, 506, 509; Saxer 2000, 581–82, 603–4). With the Third Augustan Legion permanently headquartered at Lambaesis, that city became the military and political capital of Numidia. Its bishop enjoyed a regional prominence (tarnished, however, by the gross misconduct of Privatus, bishop of Lambaesis ca. 236–248 [Cyprian, *Ep.* 59.10]) (Clarke 1984–1989, 3:251–52; J. Burns 2002, 133). Cyprian's letters indicate that many Numidian bishops attended his councils and acted in concert to protect their interests (Y. Duval 1984, 515). For example, in 255 eighteen Numidian bishops wrote jointly to Cyprian for clarification about the rebaptism of heretics. *Epistula* 70 is Cyprian's reply (Clarke 1984–1989, 4:45–48, 191–205; Y. Duval 1984, 516). The list of signatories from Cyprian's Council of September 256 (*Sententiae episcoporum*) features almost two dozen Numidian bishops, and perhaps more, if the location of several obscure sees can be identified (Y. Duval 1984, 503–11; Saxer 2000, 601–4).[14]

14. In remote areas, as tribes ceased to move seasonally for pasturage, bishops established sees to serve them (Y. Duval 1995a, 806).

Lambaesis

Tazoult, the site of ancient Lambaesis, is rich in Roman ruins but offers few Christian artifacts. Cyprian (*Sent.* 6) indicates that Januarius, bishop of Lambaesis, attended the Council of September 256. Lambaesis's Asclepieum is famous for beautiful marble revetments and a series of chapels. The mithraeum possesses impressive frescoes (MacKendrick 1980, 221–26; Lepelley 1981, 416–24). A church excavated by Maurice Besnier in 1898 appears to be sixth-century; no earlier ecclesiastical buildings have been discovered (Gui, Caillet, and Duval 1992, 1.1:145–47).

Cirta/Constantina

Headquarters of Masinissa's ancient Massylian kingdom, Cirta is perched on a bluff 600 m high, with a precipitous drop of 100 m to the Rummel River below (Perler and Maier 1969, 232; Lepelley 1981, 383–98). Crescens, bishop of Cirta, was present at the Council of September 256 (Cyprian, *Sent.* 8). During Valerian's persecution (257–260) several Numidian bishops were deported to the mines near Cirta, where they suffered terribly (Cyprian, *Ep.* 76–79). The *Passio Sanctorum Mariani et Jacobi* (*Martyrdom of Saints Marianus and James*) records the last days of a lector and deacon traveling through Numidia in 259. Harassed by a mob, James and Marianus were tried and tortured at Cirta and then transported to Lambaesis, where they were beheaded with several others (Musurillo 1972, 194–213; Lancel and Mattei 2003, 16–20; Y. Duval 1982, 2:702–4). The *Kalendarium carthaginense* records their death date as May 6. Their *passio*, embroidered with eschatological imagery from Perpetua's *passio*, probably dates to the fourth century (Tilley 1997, 45–46). A Byzantine inscription honoring James and Marianus on a large rock in the Rummel Valley near Cirta was discovered by two French officers in the 1840s. It is difficult to ascertain whether the martyrs were venerated earlier than Byzantine times (Y. Duval 1982, 2:717; Frend 1996, 59).

The *Gesta apud Zenophilum* (*Proceedings before Zenophilus*), the record of a trial involving Christians that occurred in about 320 preserved by Optatus of Milevis (bp. pre-363–post-384), contains valuable information on Christianity at Cirta during (the earlier) Diocletianic persecution (Optatus, *Donat.* appendix 1 [M. Edwards 1997, 150–69]) (Lancel and Mattei 2003, 29–38). In 303 municipal authorities ordered clergy to surrender Scriptures. Bishop Paul and his subordinates initially prevaricated but then acquiesced. Christians at Cirta probably assembled at a house-church (*domum in qua Christiani conveniebant*), since stand-alone churches were still rare in Numidia, but one witness in 320 described their meeting place as a "basilica" (Lancel and

Mattei 2003, 75–76). Clergy at Cirta included the bishop, three priests, two deacons, four subdeacons, and several gravediggers. The church's resources were substantial: silver vessels, a sizable collection of clothing and shoes for the poor, and a library.

Sometime after 308 Constantine moved the capital of Numidia from Lambaesis to the more centrally located Cirta and renamed it Constantina. As a busy crossroads for merchants headed east to Carthage and south to the Sahara, Cirta flourished in the fourth century and remained a stronghold of Donatism. In 330 Donatists confiscated Cirta's Catholic basilica, which Constantine had donated earlier in his reign. When the Donatists steadfastly refused to surrender the edifice, Constantine appropriated funds for the Catholics to rebuild elsewhere in the city (Optatus, *Donat.* appendix 10 [M. Edwards 1997, 198–201]) (Frend 1984, 503). Few Christian artifacts have been found there due to continuous habitation over the centuries.

The *Gesta apud Zenophilum* also illuminates ecclesiastical organization in Numidia. By 305 the Numidian church had a primate—an office previously unattested for that province. Unlike Carthage, the Numidian primacy was not attached to any particular see; rather, the primacy devolved upon the Numidian bishop with the most longevity in episcopal office (Y. Duval 1984, 516; 1995b, 132; Sabw Kanyang 2000, 302–3; Lancel and Mattei 2003, 66).

Theveste

Theveste (Tébessa) lies on a broad plain along the main Roman road flanking the eastern Aurès Mountains about 200 km south of Hippo Regius. An ancient Massylian city, it came under Carthaginian rule when Hanno II (r. 280–240 BCE) subdued it in the mid-third century BCE (Polybius, *Hist.* 1.74.4). During Vespasian's reign (69–79 CE) Legio III Augusta made its headquarters there, transforming Theveste into a Roman garrison replete with gridded streets, stone barracks, and temples (*CIL* 8,1.215–30). When the legion began moving to Lambaesis late in the first century, Theveste prospered from olive cultivation. Remnants of olive presses are still abundant nearby (MacKendrick 1980, 272–73; Lepelley 1981, 185–88). Diocletian's reforms incorporated Theveste into the civil province of Africa Proconsularis, but ecclesiastically, Theveste remained in the Numidian province. Bishop Leucius of Theveste attended Cyprian's Council of September 256 (Cyprian, *Sent.* 31)—the first indication of Christianity there. It is highly likely that Leucius suffered martyrdom in 259, since his name appears in an early martyrology.

In 295 a young army recruit, Maximilian, refused to serve in the military despite his father's wishes. The *Passio Sancti Maximiliani* (*Martyrdom of*

St. Maximilian) records that he was beheaded at Theveste in 295 (Musurillo 1972, xxxvii, 244–49; Lancel and Mattei 2003, 22–25). According to the *passio*, Pompeiana, a wealthy woman, transported Maximilian's body by litter to Carthage, where she oversaw its burial below a hill not far from the governor's palace near the body of the martyr Cyprian (*sub monticulo juxta Cyprianum martyrem secus palatium condidit* [*Pass. Max.* 3.4; *BHL* 5813]). Thirteen days later Pompeiana died and was buried at the same site. Although her connections with Maximilian remain obscure, his interment near the great martyr-bishop represents the first known example in North Africa of burial *ad sanctos* (Saxer 1980, 108; Y. Duval 1988, 52–53).

Stunning Christian ruins at Theveste consist of a huge basilica complex, probably honoring the martyr Crispina (see the *Passio Sanctae Crispinae* [*Martyrdom of St. Crispina*]). A noblewoman from the small town of Thagura (Taoura), Crispina was martyred with five companions during the Diocletianic persecution on December 5, 304 (Musurillo 1972, xliv, 302–9; Frend 2006, 520). Taunted by the formidable proconsul Anullinus ("All of Africa has sacrificed. Why do you hesitate?"), Crispina remained steadfast and suffered beheading (*Pass. Crisp.* 1.7). Augustine preached about her on several occasions at Carthage, an indication of her enduring popularity (*Serm.* 286, 354.5; *Enarrat. Ps.* 120, 137). Some African red-slip lamps sported Crispina's image during Augustine's era, occasionally accompanied by the three youths in the fiery furnace from the book of Daniel (Herrmann and van den Hoek 2002, 40).

Situated just outside town on the great Roman road to Carthage, the basilica and adjoining buildings were visible for kilometers across the vast plain (Caillet 2005, 65). French excavation of the complex commenced in the 1850s, but only in the 1960s did Jürgen Christern's discoveries persuade most scholars that Theveste was a great pilgrimage center and not a monastery. In Christern's estimation, the original edifice was an early fourth-century martyrium constructed on the site where Crispina and her companions were martyred.[15] An inscription by the deacon Novellus and four (perhaps five) badly fragmented epitaphs indicate that clergy were buried there even before the mid-fourth century as privileged members of the community. A reliquary containing fragments of bone and teeth was deposited in the martyrium later in the fourth century as well as a pavement mosaic commemorating seven martyrs, presumably Crispina's companions (Christern 1976, 106, 293; *CIL* 8,1.215–16; *BHL* 1988ab, 1989; Y. Duval 1982, 1:127–28; Michel 2005, 91–94). An ambitious building program (ca. 388–420) added a huge three-naved basilica (on a high

---

15. Their graves have not been found.

podium), a trefoil chapel encompassing the martyrium, an elaborate double staircase down to the chapel, a baptistery, a garden, reflecting pools, a vast courtyard ringed by hostels for pilgrims, and feeding troughs for horses (Gui, Caillet, and Duval 1992, 1.1:311–17; Frend 1996, 127–29, 363–64; Y. Duval 1982, 1:123–28; Perrin 1995, 600; MacMullen 2009, 65–66, 131). Exquisite corbels and intricate stone tracery embellishing the walls attest to the fine craftsmanship for which Theveste was famous in Late Antiquity (Baratte 2005, 160–71). The complex remains the best-preserved ancient Christian site in Algeria (Lancel and Mattei 2003, 80–81).

Hippo Regius

Founded by Phoenicians prior to the late fourth century BCE, Hippo (Annaba) lies on one of the few sheltered bays along North Africa's coastline, 300 km west of Carthage. Diodorus Siculus mentions Hippo in his account of the Syracusan tyrant Agathocles's invasion of North Africa in 310–307 BCE (*Bibl. hist.* 57.6). The Ubus (Seybouse) River flows north through Numidia and reaches the coast at Hippo, where the river's mouth provides rich alluvial plains. The city's Phoenician heritage is most noticeable in its twisting streets and alleyways paved with large, irregular stones. As a favorite residence of Massylian kings in the second century BCE, Hippo earned the epithet "Regius" (Latin: *rex*, "king") (MacKendrick 1980, 188; Lepelley 1981, 113). Hippo figured as Roman Africa's third-largest port city and exported tons of grain and olive oil to Rome annually. With a population of forty thousand, Hippo boasted a theater, two bath complexes, sumptuous seashore villas, and the largest forum in North Africa (76 m by 43 m), replete with dozens of statues (MacKendrick 1980, 210–11; Lepelley 1981, 113–25; Lancel, Guédon, and Maurin 2005, 17). Hippo's fame derives chiefly from St. Augustine.

A Christian presence is first attested by Bishop Theogenes of Hippo, who attended Cyprian's Council of September 256 (Cyprian, *Sent.* 14). Possibly he suffered martyrdom during Valerian's persecution. The *Martyrologium hieronymianum* (attributed to Jerome) refers to a certain Theogenes, martyred January 26, 259, but gives no provenance (*Mart. hier.* 63–64) (Saxer 1980, 63–64; Lancel 2002, 240). On several occasions Augustine mentions a chapel dedicated to St. Theogenes outside the town walls, where his *natalis* probably was celebrated each year (*Serm.* 273.7 [PL 38.1251]; *Serm.* Mai 158.2; *Ep.* 26*.1 [BAug 46B, 390–93, 557–60]). Theogenes's cult waned, however, as new saints supplanted him (Marec 1958, 216–17; Saxer 1980, 174–75; Lancel 2002, 227, 240). When, around 420, Augustine listed popular North African shrines and saints (*Civ.* 22.8), he omitted Theogenes's name.

Augustine occasionally alluded to the "Twenty Martyrs" and the "Eight Martyrs," who apparently died during Diocletian's persecution (*Serm.* 148; 257; 325.1; 326.2; *Serm.* Morin 2.3). Although Augustine admitted that details about them were vague, his congregation celebrated their anniversaries with gusto (*Civ.* 22.8.10) (Saxer 1980, 175–76). A chapel to the Twenty Martyrs stood near the seashore, though its location remains unknown. Augustine preached there on many occasions (Perler 1956, 435–46; Marec 1958, 217–18; Lancel 2002, 240). A small chapel to the Eight Martyrs also existed somewhere on the periphery of town. Around 425 Augustine asked the priest Leporius to oversee construction of a new basilica to replace (or enlarge) the small *memoria* (*Serm.* 256.10) (Saxer 1980, 176; Lancel 2002, 237). Archaeologists have yet to discover its ruins.

Another church at Hippo mentioned by Augustine (*Serm.* 262 [PL 38.1208]) is the Basilica Leontiana, named for its founder, Bishop Leontius of Hippo. Possibly (but not certainly), Leontius was martyred during Diocletian's persecution (Lancel 2002, 238, 506n12). Both Donatists and Catholics venerated Leontius as a saint, an indication that he died before 308, when Donatism became a separate movement. Augustine preached at the Leontiana often; of the two Catholic basilicas at Hippo, it was the older and bigger edifice (*Ep.* 29 [CSEL 34.114–22]; *Serm.* 252.4 [PL 38.1174]; *Serm.* 260 [PL 38.1201]; *Serm.* 262 [PL 38.1208]) (Lancel 2002, 239). In 427 the Leontiana hosted the final plenary council of the African church during Augustine's lifetime (CCSL 149.248–53) (Merdinger 1997, 207–8). Most scholars believe that the Leontiana stood within the Christian quarter of Hippo, an area excavated by Erwan Marec in the late 1940s and 1950s. Ruins that Marec assumed to be the Leontiana (Marec 1958, 222–25; Saxer 1980, 178–79), however, probably are vestiges of a large private . house, so the search for the ancient basilica continues.

Hippo's Christian quarter itself is shaped like an irregular polygon and exemplifies efforts by Christians to sandwich their own edifices into a crowded urban area (Lancel 2002, 241). Marec also discovered a large three-naved basilica (49 m by 20 m) flanked by an oval baptistery (originally cruciform), a *secretarium* (meeting hall), and sundry annexes (Gui, Caillet, and Duval 1992, 1.1:349; Frend 1996, 333). Apparently, after 312 Christians partially demolished a house and its porticoed courtyard, constructing atop them the three-naved basilica. Very likely this church was the *Basilica Pacis* (Basilica of Peace, also known as the *Basilica Major*), Augustine's cathedral for thirty-five years (Marec 1958, 225–30; Lancel 2002, 241–42; Lancel, Guédon, and Maurin 2005, 17–18). Some archaeologists remain skeptical (Lassus 1958, 5–8; Marrou 1960, 146–48; Gui, Caillet, and Duval 1992, 1.1:349; Michel 2005, 72n22), but a recently discovered sermon by Augustine (*Serm.* 130A = Dolb.

19 [= Mainz 51]; 12 in Dolbeau 1996, 164, 171–75) mentions the axis of his church that corresponds exactly with the orientation of Marec's three-naved basilica (Lancel 2002, 239–40).

The Donatists maintained a basilica (not yet discovered) at Hippo, apparently not far from the Leontiana (Michel 2005, 103). While preaching at the Leontiana, Augustine (*Ep.* 29.11) once mentioned overhearing noisy Holy Day reveling from the Donatist basilica (Lancel 2002, 238, 497n32; Marec 1958, 219; but see Perler 1955, 305). Since we do not know exactly where the Leontiana was situated, Augustine's remark has not thus far been helpful. Theoretically, Marec's three-naved basilica may have been the *Donatist* cathedral (Saxer 1980, 181), but this suggestion has attracted scant support. The poor condition of the ruins yields no denominational clue. Donatists comprised a strong presence in Hippo, but no records survive indicating when they established their own separate ecclesiastical complex there.

In 431 Hippo fell to the Vandals (Victor of Vita, *Hist. pers.* 1.3) (Lancel and Mattei 2003, 99–100). With its thick walls and thriving port, it proved an attractive base for them. The Byzantine army recaptured Hippo in 533, but by then trade had declined, and the town sank into obscurity. Recent efforts to preserve ruins at Hippo have garnered some success, despite political instability in Algeria (de Vos 2003).

Mauretania

The earliest evidence for Christianity in Mauretania, as noted above, comes from Tertullian (*Scap.* 4.8). Some scholars doubt that Christianity had spread as far as Mauretania by 212 (Barnes 1971, 280–82; Rives 1995, 224; Février 1986, 780), but others believe Tertullian's claims that Christians were persecuted there then (Y. Duval 1984, 519; Lancel and Mattei 2003, 15). Unlike Numidia and Africa Proconsularis, Mauretania's coastline possessed numerous natural bays and inlets. Ancient Punic ports of call had developed into thriving cities (e.g., Icosium, Iol, and Iomnium), as had veterans' colonies (e.g., Rusguniae, Rusazus, and Zucchabar) founded by Augustus or his allies (Lancel 2002, 349; MacKendrick 1980, 184–86, 205). Trade with Spanish coastal communities had been common since Punic times. From Caesarea (the capital of Mauretania Caesariensis), Rome lay approximately eleven days away by sea, with prevailing winds dictating a stopover at Caralis (Cagliari) (Arnaud 2005, 154–55). Conceivably, Christian missionaries had sailed to Mauretania from Rome. Moreover, as the Roman army gradually moved westward, fortifying North Africa with roads and garrisons, towns sprang up in its wake, with

Christianity following soon thereafter (Saxer 2000, 581). Numidia and Mauretania Sitifensis share similar terrain, but travelers crossing the border westward
into Mauretania Caesariensis almost immediately encounter a more rugged
landscape of mountains, steep valleys, and desert. Isolated by its topography,
Mauretania Caesariensis remained more sparsely populated in Roman times
than did neighboring eastern provinces.

The earliest material evidence for Christianity in Mauretania is disputed.
An inscription dated 238 CE (*CIL* 8.9289, cf. 8.20856; *ILCV* 3319) from the
coastal city of Tipasa (70 km west of Algiers) commemorates a woman named
Rasinia Secunda. She appears to be Christian (Lancel and Mattei 2003, 10;
Saxer 1992c, 544; but contrast Février 1986, 771, 780–87; Barnes 1971, 281).
Cyprian's correspondence from around 250 CE sheds more light. He notes
how vast his province (Africa Proconsularis) and adjoining provinces (Numidia
and Mauretania) are, and how difficult communication can be with far-off colleagues (*Ep.* 48.3.2) (Clarke 1984–1989, 2:258–59; Février 1986, 794; Y. Duval
1984, 515–16). *Letter* 71 answers Quintus, a Mauretanian bishop seeking advice
on heretical baptism. Cyprian encourages Quintus to share the letter's contents with colleagues there (*illic*), a clear indication that Mauretania possessed
bishops by the mid-third century (*Ep.* 71.4.2). *Letter* 72.1.3 explicitly identifies
Quintus as Mauretanian, though his see remains unknown (Clarke 1984–1989,
4:205–7; Y. Duval 1984, 503, 518–19; Lancel and Mattei 2003, 15). In *Letter* 73
Cyprian replies to Bishop Jubaianus's queries concerning the validity of heretical baptism. Although the evidence is inconclusive, many scholars assume
that Jubaianus also hailed from Mauretania (Frend 1971, 137; Y. Duval 1984,
515n64, 518–19; Clarke 1984–1989, 4:221; Février 1986, 797; Saxer 2000, 604–5).

Even more problematic are the proceedings from Cyprian's celebrated Council of September 256. Although the preamble mentions that many bishops,
presbyters, and deacons assembled from Africa Proconsularis, Numidia, and
Mauretania, no vote is recorded from any Mauretanian bishops. Did their
close ties with Rome concerning the invalidity of heretical baptism cause
them to attend merely as witnesses or to boycott the council altogether? Did
distance prevent the Mauretanians from going, even though bishops from
southern Numidia (640 km from Carthage) managed to be present? After all,
some Mauretanian sees probably existed just west of the Numidian border.
Scholarly opinion varies widely on these questions (Y. Duval 1984, 519–20;
Février 1986, 796–97; Brett and Fentress 1996, 69; Saxer 2000, 599–605, 803).

After Cyprian's era no evidence is extant for Mauretanian Christianity for
forty years. Political and economic turmoil roiled much of the empire. From
289 to 297 the Quinquagentani ravaged large parts of Mauretania and western
Numidia, so much so that the co-emperor Maximian (r. 285–305) sailed to

Africa to quell their revolt (Raven 2002, 162). At the end of the third century, imperial demands for renewed allegiance to the gods served as a catalyst for several military martyrdoms. In about 299 Fabius, a Christian standard-bearer (*vexillifer*), refused to carry his staff in a ceremony at Caesarea.[16] Details are scant, but Fabius suffered martyrdom for his obstinacy (*BHL* 2818; Lancel and Mattei 2003, 22–23; Février 1986, 789). About the same time, Tipasius, a retired veteran recalled to duty at Tigava Castra (a military garrison southwest of Caesarea in the Chélif Valley), was decapitated after refusing to serve the gods (*BHL* 8354; Février 1986, 790; Lancel and Mattei 2003, 23). Inscriptions commemorating many other little-known Christians martyred in Mauretania sometime between 303 and 320 have prompted Yvette Duval (1982, 2:717–24) to conclude that Mauretania Caesariensis has yielded more martyrs' epitaphs than any other region in North Africa.

Mauretania is richly endowed with Christian archaeological sites dating back to the early fourth century. The oldest inscription mentioning a Christian basilica (*basilica dominica*) is from Altava (Ouled Mimoun), a Roman fort situated on a plain rimmed by jagged mountains in far western Mauretania Caesariensis (MacKendrick 1980, 251). The inscription (ca. 309–338), carved onto a large monumental stone, also mentions a *mensa* (altar table) dedicated to (a local?) martyr named Januarius and a *memoria* (shrine) to three unnamed martyrs (Y. Duval 1982, 1:412–17, 724; White 1997, 240–42; Lancel and Mattei 2003, 106; Sears 2007, 109n138). The *Martyrologium hieronymianum* records a Januarius martyred in Mauretania on December 2 (year unknown) along with numerous other Christians. The name, however, was common in Mauretania (Y. Duval 1982, 1:415) and thus the Januarius referred to in the *Martyrologium hieronymianum* may not be the martyr of Altava. Yvette Duval believes that the *mensa* is the oldest archaeological artifact at Altava; that the three unnamed martyrs were initially buried next to the *mensa*, with a martyrium covering the graves; and that a basilica was constructed on the site later. According to Duval, the inscription provides the earliest epigraphic example of burial *ad sanctos* (Y. Duval 1982, 1:417; cf. Perrin 1995, 599; but contrast Février 1986, 782–87).

Less controversy surrounds findings at Castellum Tingitanum (el-Asnam). An inscription dating from November 20, 324, on a stone block signifies that it was part of the foundation stone of a five-aisled Christian basilica—the oldest Christian church ever discovered in North Africa (Lancel and Mattei 2003, 12, 76–77; Gui, Caillet, and Duval 1992, 1.1:11–14; MacMullen 2009, 130). Its pavement mosaics still exist, but not the walls (Gui, Caillet, and Duval 1992, 1.1:75–76).

16. The army routinely decorated its standards with images of the gods and medallions of battle sites.

Caesarea Mauretania

The city of Caesarea Mauretania (Punic Iol, modern Cherchell) was founded by the Phoenicians on a bay surrounded by sheer hills, 95 km west of Icosium (Algiers). Juba II, king of Mauretania, renamed the city in honor of his patron, Augustus, and lavished it with temples, statues of the gods, baths, and a theater. Around 40 CE, when Rome annexed Juba's kingdom, Caesarea became the capital city of the new province. Equipped with both a naval harbor and commercial harbor, Caesarea figured as North Africa's second busiest port in Roman times (MacKendrick 1980, 205–8; Lepelley 1981, 513–14). Despite a sizable population of forty thousand, few Christian artifacts have survived (Gui, Caillet, and Duval 1992, 1.1:16). Caesarea probably had a bishop by the mid-third century, but none is attested until Fortunatus, who attended the Council of Arles in 314 (Optatus, *Donat.* appendices 4, 5; CCSL 148.15–17; Février 1986, 793–94). Few Christian burial inscriptions are extant at Caesarea; none bears precise dates (N. Duval 1990, 377n173).

Corpus inscriptionum latinarum 8.9585 is a famous fourth-century inscription on a marble plaque commissioned by the church at Caesarea. It honors Severianus, a wealthy patron who donated land for burials perhaps as early as the third century (Rebillard 2009, 31–32; Y. Duval 1982, 1:380–83; Février 1986, 793). The inscription's poetic language does not specify whether a chapel or tomb was constructed on the land.[17] Due to poor excavation techniques, *CIL* 8.9585's original location remains unknown (Y. Duval 1982, 1:381). Evelpius, who salutes readers at the end, may have been a priest or bishop at Caesarea and may have suffered martyrdom, but his status remains unclear (Y. Duval 1982, 1:381–82; Saxer 1992b, 138). A second inscription at Caesarea (*CIL* 8.9586; *ILCV* 1179), from a priest named Victor, has also proved problematic. Victor donated money to build a mausoleum for his mother and several others, describing it as a "gift to all the brethren." Clearly the inscription is Christian, but no date accompanies it, and the mausoleum remains unfound, making it difficult for archaeologists to utilize the inscription fully (Rebillard 2009, 32; Saxer 2000, 620).

Tipasa

About 30 km east of Caesarea lies the picturesque coastal city of Tipasa, which became one of the most popular Christian pilgrimage sites in Late Antiquity. Tipasa's early history is similar to Caesarea's: founded by Phoenicians perhaps as early as the sixth century BCE; granted *municipium* (self-governance)

---

17. No edifice has been discovered.

status in 46 CE; declared a *colonia* by Hadrian (r. 117–138) or Antoninus Pius (r. 138–161). Connected to Icosium and Caesarea along the coastal road, Tipasa was the terminus of an important commercial route into the interior of Mauretania (MacKendrick 1980, 186; Lepelley 1981, 543–46; Sears 2007, 66–67). Roman additions to Tipasa included a forum, capitol, baths, amphitheater, and an aqueduct. The population during the Roman era probably approached twenty thousand.

Christianity apparently came to Tipasa in the early third century. The 238 CE inscription of Rasinia Secunda is, as noted, most likely Christian. A basilica erected by Alexander, bishop of Tipasa in the late fourth or early fifth century, and named after him (*CIL* 8.20915), also provides evidence of earlier Christianity there. Situated in an ancient necropolis on the west side of town, the basilica was built over a crypt in which was found a mosaic inscription from Alexander commemorating nine (perhaps ten) "prior right ones" (*iusti priores*), presumably his episcopal predecessors (*CIL* 8.20903). Such a long line of antecedents could attest an episcopal presence at Tipasa at least by the mid-third century (Y. Duval 1995a, 808; Frend 1996, 116), but some scholars remain cautious about the dating (Gui, Caillet, and Duval 1992, 1.1:35; Sears 2007, 70). The church itself is not large, measuring 21.8 m by 13.5 m (Gui, Caillet, and Duval 1992, 1.1:33). Numerous *mensae* dedicated to local martyrs (e.g., Vitalis and Rogatus) are surrounded by scores of burials, marking Alexander's church as a significant cemetery basilica (Y. Duval 1982, 1:371–72; MacMullen 2009, 55, 60–61). The significance of the burial grounds and their contents remains debated (Rebillard 1996, 186–88, differing with Y. Duval 1982, 1:462). (On the difficulties with dating the *natalis* of martyrs at Tipasa, see Y. Duval 1982, 1:357–80.)

Fig. 6.10. Church of St. Salsa, Tipasa

The Church of St. Salsa, with its surrounding burial grounds, high on a promontory overlooking the Mediterranean, perhaps ranks as the "most moving seaside cemetery of all western antiquity" (Lancel and Mattei 2003, 80). According to the *Passio Salsae* (*Martyrdom of Salsa*), a colorful, late fourth-century narrative, Salsa was a young convert who enraged the local populace by casting the head of Tipasa's patron deity into the sea, probably in about 320 (*Pass. Sals.* 7–8 [*BHL* 7467]) (Lancel and Mattei 2003, 52; Sears 2007, 67–68). The citizens lynched her and threw her body into the sea; Gallic sailors recovered it and brought it ashore to the eastern promontory where it was interred in a small martyrium. A *mensa* was erected to celebrate *agapē* meals (love feasts), and many faithful sought burial near her tomb. Some scholars speculate that Donatism predominated at Tipasa, but by 373, when the city successfully repelled the usurper Firmus (d. 375) and his Donatist allies, Tipasa was strongly Catholic (Frend 1996, 334; 1988, 164) (Optatus, *Donat.* 2.18; Ammianus Marcellinus, *Res gestae* 29.5.15; *Pass. Sals.* 13). Crediting St. Salsa with their deliverance, the residents built a large church in her honor close by her martyrium on the promontory.[18]

Tripolitania

History of the Region

Tripolitania shares much history with the other North African provinces but differs significantly in geography, climate, and religiosity. Ancient Tripolitania comprised the curving stretch of Mediterranean coastline from the Syrtis Minor (Gulf of Gabes) eastward to the Syrtis Major (Gulf of Sidra) and extended southward 640 km to include the Fezzan (part of the Sahara Desert).[19] In the seventh century BCE Phoenicians began to establish trading posts (emporia) and ship repair facilities at three small natural harbors along the Tripolitanian coast, which grew into the thriving cities of Sabratha, Oea, and Lepcis Magna.[20] Carthage figured as their protector, though they maintained close ties with their homeland cities of Tyre and Sidon. In the second century BCE the Numidian king Masinissa seized control of the three emporia with Rome's blessing. In

18. Scholars disagree on the construction date, citing anywhere from 374 to 450. The archaeological history of the site is complex, not least because the remains of an older, pagan woman named Fabia Salsa were mistakenly buried next to the young martyr (Gui, Caillet, and Duval 1992, 43–44; MacMullen 2009, 56, 132). As Salsa's fame grew during the fifth century, pilgrims flocked to her grave from all parts of the Mediterranean.

19. Modern Tripolitania, much smaller than its ancient namesake, consists solely of northwest Libya.

20. The name Tripolitania derives from the Greek words for "three" and "city."

46 BCE Julius Caesar annexed the entire Numidian kingdom, including Sabratha, Oea, and Lepcis Magna. Around 27 CE Tiberius (r. 14–37) declared Tripolitania part of the new province of Africa Proconsularis. Only in 303 did Diocletian make Tripolitania a separate province with Lepcis Magna its capital. Detachments from the Third Augustan Legion patrolled the region to quell tribal unrest. Ruins of the legion's outposts are still visible, jutting up from the monotonously flat landscape.

People, Geography, and Climate

The indigenous people of Tripolitania were Berbers from the Egyptian Sahara who migrated to their new homeland circa 2000 BCE. Various tribal groups, subtribes, and clans coalesced over time; those on the coast intermarried with Phoenicians. Principal tribes (or confederations) during the Roman era included Libyphoenicians (in coastal cities and nearby oases); Gaetuli (numerous tribes in the predesert); Garamantes (in the Fezzan); and Austuriani (south of the Greater Syrtic Gulf), probably the tribe later called the Laguatan. Arid desert constituted over 90 percent of Tripolitania, but careful cultivation of coastal oases and predesert terrain yielded abundant crops of wheat, grapes, and barley. Mosaics also depict sheep herding, horse rearing, and harvesting murex shells for purple dye. Olive oil proved to be Tripolitania's premier export, with millions of gallons shipped annually to Rome. Many of Antiquity's most massive olive presses are situated in Tripolitania. Sumptuous villas ringing the seashore testified to the vast wealth of a coterie of families that monopolized the olive trade. Strong leeward winds rendered the

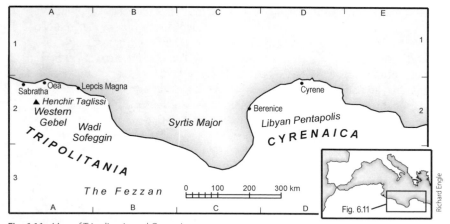

Fig. 6.11. Map of Tripolitania and Cyrenaica

Tripolitanian coastline notorious for shipwrecks, prompting Roman engineers
in the second century CE to expand the moles and harbors of the three cities.

Lepcis Magna

Founded by Phoenicians in the seventh century BCE, Lepcis ("Magna" was
added in the mid-first century CE) flourished as a port city. Despite annexation by Rome in 46 BCE, Lepcis (Lebda) retained much of its Libyphoenician
heritage. Its magistrates were called suffetes (as in Phoenicia) until Lepcis became a Roman *colonia* in 109 CE. Most of its wealthy citizens never became
proficient in Latin. Lepcis reached its apogee when its native son Septimius
Severus inaugurated an ambitious building program that endowed the city
with a magnificent new forum, civil basilica, and temples (Brett and Fentress
1996, 53–54; Laronde and Degeorge 2005; Gros 2008). Expenses incurred
(imported marble, foreign craftsmen) contributed to Lepcis's economic decline
shortly thereafter.

The origins of Christianity in Tripolitania remain obscure. Undoubtedly,
Christianity first took root in the port cities before penetrating the hinterland.
Bryan Ward-Perkins and Richard Goodchild (1953, 2) speculated that Cyrenaica, with its sizable Jewish contingent and close ties to Tripolitania, may
have supplied the first missionaries to Tripolitania, but scholars now believe
that Christianity probably arrived from several Mediterranean cities (K. Stern

6.5 Religion in Tripolitania

Great disparities existed between cultic practices in the coastal cities and the
hinterland (predesert and desert) of Tripolitania (Brouquier-Reddé 1992). Hinterland tribes worshiped ancient Libyan gods, most especially Ammon, whose cult
arose at the great oasis of Siwa in northwest Egypt, bordering Libya. Ram-headed
Ammon figured as protector of the dead and overseer of desert tracks, oases,
and travelers. Devotees flocked to the city of Ammon (modern Siwa) from all
parts of the eastern Mediterranean to hear the god's oracular pronouncements
that helped unify Libyan tribes in times of crisis. Shrines to Ammon proliferated
throughout rural settlements and desert oases. Gods associated with springs also
were popular with Libyans, given the paucity of rainfall in the region. Urban dwell-
ers preferred ancestral Phoenician gods, especially Milk'ashtart and Shadrapa from
Tyre. Shadrapa functioned as a healing god, while Milk'ashtart (Tyre's Melqart)
protected the populace. During the Roman era Shadrapa became assimilated with
Liber Pater, the god of fertility and wine (*IRT* 294); Milk'ashtart assumed Hercules's
name and attributes (*IRT* 289). More than forty different gods were worshiped at
Lepcis Magna (Mattingly 1995, 168).

2008, 89, 161). Tripolitania's first known bishop may have been Archaeus, who probably presided at Lepcis in the late second century. His Greek name suggests that he was not native to the area. A fragment exists (PG 5.1489–90) from a tract bearing Archaeus's name on the Easter controversy in support of Victor of Rome (bp. 189–198) (see Mai 1839–1844, 3:707; Saxer 1992a).[21] By the mid-third century, bishoprics existed at all three coastal cities. Shortly before the great Council of September 256, Cyprian wrote to Pompeius, bishop of Sabratha, to gain his support for rebaptism (*Ep.* 74). Bishop Natalis of Oea attended the council and cast votes for his two absent colleagues, Pompeius of Sabratha and Dioga of Lepcis Magna (Cyprian, *Sent.* 83–85) (Clarke 1984–1989, 4:236; Y. Duval 1984, 514n62). Also present was Monnulus, bishop of Girba (probably modern Houmt-Souk), capital of the island of Meninx (Gerba) off the coast of ancient western Tripolitania now in Tunisia (Cyprian, *Sent.* 10) (Maier 1973, 147, 365–66). Tacapa (Gabes), on Tripolitania's westernmost coast, acquired a bishopric sometime later (Ward-Perkins and Goodchild 1953, 3; Mattingly 1995, 127–28). In 397 the Council of Carthage referred to these five sees as the only bishoprics in the entire province of Tripolitania (*Can.* 38 [CCSL 149.45]) (Mattingly 1995, 210). Wadi Sofeggin (south of Lepcis Magna) became widely Christianized by the late fourth century (Ward-Perkins and Goodchild 1953, 3–5, 57; Mattingly 1995, 211).

Donatism existed in Tripolitania, though its extent remains obscure. Augustine (*Ep.* 93.8.24) attests that the Maximianist schism[22] originated in Byzacena and Tripoli in 393. Two Donatist bishops from Tripolitania attended the Colloquy of Carthage in 411: Marinianus of Oea and Salvianus of Lepcis Magna (Maier 1973, 183, 356; 161, 410). Only one Catholic bishop from Tripolitania participated: Nados of Sabratha (Maier 1973, 194, 367).

Archaeological evidence for Christianity in Tripolitania is abundant in the coastal cities but sparse in the hinterland. Italian experts made significant discoveries in the early twentieth century; since World War II, British archaeologists have also excavated numerous sites (Polidori et al. 1999; Reynolds 1976). Six churches have been found at Lepcis Magna, but only Church II is pre-Byzantine. Situated in the old forum atop vestiges of a late first- or early second-century temple, Church II dates to the early fifth century. It measures approximately 30 m by 20 m (Ward-Perkins and Goodchild 1953, 24–29; Kenrick 2009, 110–11; Mattingly 1995, 211). Churches IV and V remain undated due to poor site conditions, but they may yet prove to be early structures (Sears

21. Severus of Antioch (bp. 512–538), however, attributes the tract to Irenaeus of Lyons (bp. ca. 177–ca. 200), raising doubts about the existence of a bishop named Archaeus at Lepcis Magna (e.g., Höffner 2000, 46).
22. A movement within Donatism, led by a deacon named Maximian, which decried violence.

2007, 73; Mattingly 1995, 183). Most Byzantine churches in the coastal cities of Tripolitania share similar architectural features: three aisles, a raised apse at the west end, and a chancel extending to midnave with the altar placed there. Most altars were wooden. The only church (or private residence?) in Tripolitania bearing a Donatist inscription is at Henchir Taglissi, a fortified farm about 160 km south of Oea (*IRT* 863, bii; Mattingly 1995, 212; Ward-Perkins and Goodchild 1953, 37–43). No martyr cult or cemetery basilicas (Catholic or Donatist) have been discovered in Tripolitania, a puzzling fact because the rest of North Africa esteemed martyrs highly (Ward-Perkins and Goodchild 1953, 5; Sears 2007, 105). Few baptisteries and no decorative mosaics existed in Tripolitania until the Byzantine era, unlike neighboring provinces (Mattingly 1995, 211; Ward-Perkins and Goodchild 1953, 57–66).

In the 360s a massive earthquake and devastating raids by Austuriani precipitated a sharp economic decline in Lepcis Magna (Lepelley 1981, 341, 363–64; Mattingly 1995, 182–85; Kenrick 2009, 6, 11–12). Perhaps too Africa Proconsularis began to dominate African trade in olive oil, eclipsing Tripolitania in the process (Mattingly 1995, 209). Never considered essential to the empire, Tripolitania suffered further in the late fourth century with the evacuation of troops westward to territory deemed more strategic. African church councils at Carthage became accustomed to a single representative from Tripolitania (*Can.* 127 [CCSL 149.227–28] (Sears 2007, 82). In the seventh century Islamic invaders found willing converts among the pagan tribes of the Western Gebel and hinterland. The coastal cities submitted in 643–644. Pockets of Christianity survived into the eleventh century in the oases south of Oea (Mattingly 1995, 211).

7

Asia Minor and Cyprus

WILLIAM TABBERNEE

Introduction

Even a cursory glance at the books that, in the Christian Bible, follow the four
Gospels reveals that Asia Minor (Lesser Asia) was a crucially important region
for the spread of Christianity beyond the Levant and Syria. The canonical Acts
of the Apostles, for example, contains stories about the missionary activity
of Paul of Tarsus in Asia Minor (13:1–14:27; 15:36–18:21; 18:22–21:3). According to the account presented by the author of Acts, Paul (then still called
Saul), accompanied by Barnabas and a man named "John" but also known
as "Mark," first went to Cyprus (13:4–12), which had already been visited by
"Jesus followers" from Jerusalem (11:19) and was later to be evangelized more
extensively by Barnabas and John Mark (15:36–39).

As we will see, much of the information presented by the author of the Acts
of the Apostles was shaped by the issues and concerns of the author's own
time, which appears to have been the early part of the second century (D. Smith
2009, 47–49). Consequently, for those interested in tracing the precise historical development of Christianity in Asia Minor, the only valid starting place
is not Acts but the genuine letters of Paul (Koester 1982, 2:101–4). Similarly,
because of their highly theological format and concerns, the so-called letters

261

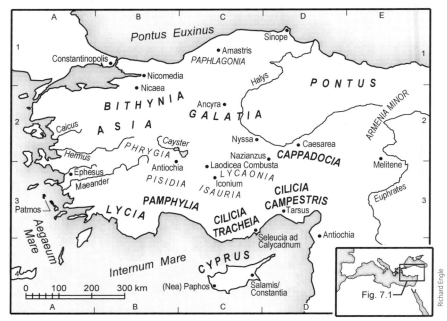

Fig. 7.1. Map of Asia Minor and Cyprus

to the seven churches in Asia (Rev. 2:1–3:15) require informed interpretation in order to yield any valuable historical information. Few, if any, reliable historical data can be gleaned from early second-century apocryphal acts such as that of *Paul and Thecla*. The later acts of the martyrs (*acta martyrum*) and lives of the saints (*vitae*) yield only snippets of useful information. Conversely, from the middle of the second century onward, inscriptions provide a wealth of evidence about individual Christians and Christian communities, but they do so unevenly for the various regions of Asia Minor and Cyprus.

Subjection to the Roman Empire

Roman occupation of Asia Minor commenced formally in 133 BCE when the Romans took control of the kingdom of Pergamum on the death of Attalus III (r. 138–133). Attalus "bequeathed" his kingdom to Rome—something that a number of subsequent "client kings" in Asia Minor also ended up doing. Forming a new province named Asia, the Romans rapidly annexed or extended political influence over a large number of formerly independent kingdoms, or "city-states," in the western half of what has been known since the tenth century CE as Anatolia (Turkish *Anadolu*) and what is now Turkey. Asia consisted of Mysia and the Troad in the northwest; Aeolis, Ionia, Caria, and Lycia in the south; and Lydia farther inland. Once the kingdom of Croesus (r. ca. 560–546 BCE), Lydia had become part of Pergamum in 188 BCE when the Seleucids of Syria lost control of the western part of the Hellenistic empire of Alexander the Great (r. 336–323 BCE). Phrygia, which under the semilegendary king Midas had also been an extensive kingdom in the eighth century BCE, still comprised a substantial area when it was incorporated into Asia between 129 and 116 BCE.

During the early years of Roman presence in Asia Minor, rampant piracy, conducted from bases in Cilicia Tracheia (Rugged Cilicia), troubled the eastern Mediterranean. "Rugged Cilicia," distinguished from "Smooth Cilicia" (Cilicia Campestris) farther east, had gained its name both from its rough mountainous terrain and its inhospitable inhabitants. The Romans took Cilicia Tracheia from the Seleucids in 101 BCE to form the second Roman province in Asia Minor. Cilicia Campestris, consisting primarily of the large fertile plain that included the city of Tarsus, the later birthplace of St. Paul, was annexed in 64. Cyprus, the island due south of Cilicia, was incorporated into the province in 58, becoming a separate Roman province in 30 BCE.

Provincial borders in Asia Minor frequently were redrawn as the result of new political alliances or opportunities. For example, in 56 BCE Cilicia was extended west to border Asia. Some of the same territory became part of Asia itself in 44 BCE. In 20 BCE Cilicia Tracheia was ceded to King Archelaus of Cappadocia (r. 36 BCE–17 CE). Cilicia Campestris was subsequently added to the province of Syria. Cappadocia became a Roman province in 17 CE, and in 70 CE the two regions named Cilicia were organized into a single province.

Galatia, an area in central Asia Minor occupied by Celts from Gaul in the third century BCE, was made a Roman province in 25 BCE on the death of its final king, Amyntas. At various times Galatia incorporated, in the south, parts of Phrygia, Pisidia, Lycaonia, and Isauria and, in the north, Paphlagonia (the kingdom situated between Bithynia and Pontus). One of southern Galatia's most important Roman colonies was Antioch-in-Pisidia.

In 43 CE another new Roman province, Lycia-Pamphylia, was created between Asia to the west, Galatia to the northeast, and Cilicia to the east. The new province comprised the former cities of the Hellenistic "Lycian League" and territory that had once been ruled by Pamphylian kings.

Whereas the western and southern coasts of Asia Minor respectively adjoined the Aegaeum Mare (Aegean Sea) and the Internum Mare (Mediterranean Sea), its northern shores ran along the Pontus Euxinus (Black Sea). Bithynia, in northwestern Asia Minor, had successfully resisted Alexander the Great and his successors and was still independent when Nicomedes IV Philopater (r. 94–74 BCE) bequeathed his kingdom to Rome. The (also independent) kingdom of Pontus was incorporated into the Roman province of Bithynia-Pontus in 63 BCE on the defeat of King Mithridates VI Eupator (r. 120–63 BCE). In 47, after easily quelling a revolt by Mithridates's son Pharnaces II (r. 63–47 BCE) near Zela, C. Julius Caesar (ca. 100–44 BCE) reputedly penned the much-quoted statement *Veni, vidi, vici* ("I came, I saw, I conquered" [Suetonius, *Jul.* 37]).

The extreme northeastern section of Asia Minor was originally part of the kingdom of Armenia. Armenia Minor (Lesser Armenia), west of the Euphrates River, long ruled by kings who were "subject allies" of the empire, was incorporated into the Roman province of Cappadocia by Vespasian (r. 69–79 CE) in 71–72 CE.

The Inception of Christianity

When Christianity first began to make inroads into the region, Asia Minor was, apart perhaps from the extreme northeast, solidly under Roman control, organized politically into six large provinces whose border fluctuated. Cyprus was no longer part of Asia Minor but made up a seventh Roman province. In succeeding centuries the original provinces of Asia Minor were subdivided to create smaller, additional provinces, especially during the reign of Diocletian (r. 284–305 CE) but also in the immediate post-Constantinian and Byzantine eras. The Romans exploited the rich resources of the various territories under their control, not only through heavy taxation but also through huge imperially owned agricultural estates worked by tenant farmers and supervised by imperial procurators. A number of such estates were in Phrygia. Phrygian marble, often streaked with purple, highly prized by the emperors and others given imperial permission to use it, was quarried on some of the estates. Gold mines in Lydia and copper mines in Cyprus also greatly enriched the empire.

Asia Minor's agricultural and mineral resources were as diverse as its peoples and topography. Whereas Cappadocia and the Phrygian Highlands were ideal for raising cattle and especially horses, the desert-like steppe lands of Galatia's central plateau were barely able to supply sufficient grass for sheep and goats. The Halys River, which wound its way through this same plateau to the Black Sea, however, watered the coastal lands of Bithynia and Pontus, which produced an abundance of fruit and nuts. Similarly, the Caicus, Hermus, Cayster, and the Maeander, flowing from the mountains of Phrygia to the Aegean coast, created fertile river valleys for cattle, grain, grapes, fruit, and figs. Forests, especially in Cilicia Tracheia but also in the hinterlands of Asia, supplied ample timber for shipbuilding. Numerous wrecked ships from Roman and Byzantine times recovered recently through marine archaeology off the coasts of Turkey attest considerable ancient fishing and maritime trading activities.

Asia Minor, the only land bridge between the East and the West, also provided major trade routes. Coastal cities such as Troas, Pergamum, Smyrna, Ephesus, Cyzicus, Sinope, Attalia, and Seleucia ad Calycadnum either were the starting points of trade routes or were linked to such routes. Cities such as Sardis, Ancyra, and Caesarea, located at the junctions of major inland roads, became prosperous trading centers. Other cities such as Tarsus, Laodicea, Philadelphia, and Thyatira were significant "staging posts." Getting from place to place in Asia Minor was relatively simple for early Christians and other travelers alike, as long as they followed well-established routes. Reaching out-of-the-way places in the hinterland, however, was extremely difficult.

Peoples and Religions

When Paul, Barnabas, and John Mark arrived in Cyprus, approximately four hundred thousand people inhabited the island. When they crossed the 70 km of the Internum Mare, which separated Cyprus from Asia Minor, they arrived in a part of the Roman Empire consisting of about fifteen million people. The population of Cyprus and the six provinces of Asia Minor was a mixture of the original inhabitants of the various regions and the descendants of those who settled there under a succession of external rulers: Hittites, Assyrians, Persians, Iranians, Greeks (including Hellenized Syrians or Egyptians such as the Seleucids, Attalids, and Ptolemies), and, finally, Romans. A significant number of Jews also existed in both Cyprus and Asia Minor. Although modified versions of local languages persisted in some rural areas, the lingua franca was Greek.

Each group of new settlers brought its own religions, gods, and goddesses. In an age when a multiplicity of deities was deemed advantageous, imported gods were either simply added to the religious culture or worshiped in a new local form. The native Phrygian mother goddess, Cybele, for example, frequently took on the characteristics of Artemis, the sister of Apollo.

In 29 BCE Augustus (r. 31 BCE–14 CE) established the cult of "Roma and [Julius] Caesar" for Roman settlers at Ephesus and Nicaea. Augustus also allowed the indigenous population to erect temples to (Roma and) himself at Pergamum and Nicomedia. In 23 CE Tiberius (r. 14–37) approved a second imperial temple (subsequently built at Smyrna) dedicated to himself, his mother (Livia), and the senate. A third imperial cult temple functioning on behalf of the whole province of Asia by the end of the first century was erected at Ephesus in 89/90 honoring Vespasian, Titus (r. 79–81), and Domitian (r. 81–96).

Numerous municipal imperial cults were also established by various cities throughout Asia and the other provinces in the region.

The large Jewish communities in Asia Minor, especially in Lydia, Phrygia, Lycaonia, and Lycia-Pamphylia, provided the religious milieu not only for the descendants of those who settled there during the time of the Seleucids onward but also for numerous "God-fearers." The latter were Gentiles attracted in particular by Judaism's monotheism and ethical precepts. Some God-fearers became proselytes and ultimately full members of Jewish communities; others remained functional polytheists or joined syncretistic sects, such as the Hypsistarians.

It is difficult to overestimate the effect of Hellenization on the culture, religion, and philosophic development of Asia Minor in the immediate pre-Christian period. Because of this Hellenization, Asia Minor differed significantly from most other regions of the Roman Empire, which in part explains the kind of Christianity that developed among the more educated and philosophically literate in the cities of Asia Minor.

Contextual Challenges and Influences

Because of their political, socioeconomic, demographic, and religious context, early Christians in Asia Minor and Cyprus faced serious challenges. The whole region was under the political control of the Romans, who had a vested interest in promoting the various expressions of the imperial cult. Any religion or religious group whose members could not or would not participate in acts of religious patriotism was seen as a potential threat to the empire. The challenge for early Christians was to prove to Roman officials that they were indeed loyal subjects who, in their own way, used their religion to support, rather than subvert, the empire. This loyalty, however, was sorely tested in times of local and empirewide persecution.

A similar contextual challenge to the earliest Christians in Asia Minor and Cyprus was the extensive religious pluralism in the region. The challenge for Christians was how to promote the One whom they believed to be the "one true God" while avoiding syncretism on the one hand and polytheism on the other. In Asia Minor, as elsewhere, the variety of different emphases on moral, ethical, and liturgical issues led to the development of a variety of forms of early Christianity. Phrygia, for example, was the birthplace of Montanism, an ethical renewal movement whose prophets and prophetesses made oracular pronouncements during ecstatic trances and who expected the New Jerusalem of Revelation 21 to be established in Phrygia rather than in Judaea (Tabbernee 2012).

A third challenge was how to relate the new "Jesus movement" to the Judaism of the Diaspora communities in Asia Minor and Cyprus. From Paul's letter to the Galatians it is clear that Paul took the view that Gentiles did not need to become Jews in order to be Christians (2:1–10; 3:28), but not all Christian leaders were of this opinion (2:11–14). From later sources it is apparent both that there continued to be conflict on this and other issues, and that in some areas of Asia Minor there were Jewish-Christian communities well into the third century.

Given the relative ease of travel along the main trade routes and the difficulties in getting into the hinterland, it is not surprising that Christianity in Asia Minor and Cyprus established itself first in the major cities and only gradually spread to more remote towns and villages. Similarly, the characteristics of Christianity in the large cities was inevitably, on the whole, more "mainstream" than those in isolated rural districts, where Montanists, Novatianists, Encratites, or members of other sects could practice their own kind of Christianity relatively undisturbed by imperial or ecclesiastical authorities, even in the post-Constantinian era.

Christianity by the Time of Constantine

This chapter concentrates on determining, especially from epigraphic and archaeological sources, the extent of Christianity in the region by the time Constantine I (r. 306–337) allowed Christianity to be a "tolerated" religion within the empire. In summary, it may be said that Christianity had established itself in most of the major cities of Asia Minor and Cyprus, especially in the province of Asia, including Phrygia. In some of the other provinces, and especially in the countryside, the spread of Christianity was extremely sporadic and idiosyncratic. In 325 there were still many areas of Asia Minor and Cyprus where either there were no Christians at all or "Christianized" villages or towns existed alongside totally pagan settlements.

In Asia Minor and Cyprus Christian communities, shaped by a variety of contextual factors, were very diverse. People calling themselves "Christians" belonged not only to "mainstream" groups but also to movements such as the "New Prophecy," castigated by their opponents as heretics. A number of others, also calling themselves "Christians," practiced forms of Christianity that, to a greater or lesser extent, were influenced and shaped syncretistically by various aspects of Greek philosophy, Judaism, or polytheistic religions. Consequently, Christianity also had an impact on Greek philosophy (especially Neo-Platonism), Judaism, and the native and imported religions of Asia Minor and Phrygia.

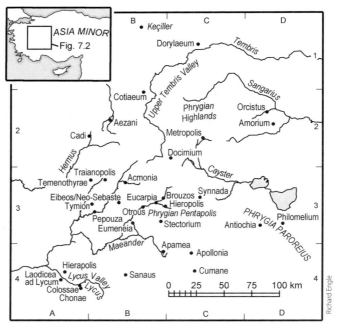

Fig. 7.2. Map of Phrygia

Asia Minor

Asia

PHRYGIA

As noted in the general introduction, William Ramsay discovered the now-famous tombstone of Abercius/Avircius (fig. I.4), which was known to have existed because its inscription had been copied more or less accurately by the author of the late fourth-century *Life of St. Abercius*.[1] This discovery, made in 1883, 5 km south of Koçhisar, "in the interior of the passage leading to the men's bath-room at the hot-springs" (Ramsay 1883, 424), showed that Avircius had been the Christian bishop of a city named Hieropolis[2] situated in the Phrygian Pentapolis, not the bishop of Hierapolis (modern Pamukkale) in the Lycus Valley, as assumed by earlier scholars.

1. The spelling "Aberkios," in the *Vita Abercii*, Latinized as "Abercius," is understandable given local pronunciation. For the text of the *vita*, see Nissen 1912, 1–55. The *Life of St. Abercius* itself is largely legendary, dealing with fourth-century rather than second-century issues (see Bundy 1989–1990).

2. "Hieropolis," rather than "Hierapolis," is an ancient, though erroneous, form of the name of the city in the Phrygian Pentapolis (TIB 7:272).

About 90 km northwest of Hieropolis, in an area of Phrygia bordering Mysia and Lydia, was a city called Cadi (Eski Gediz; i.e., "Old Gediz," 6 km south of modern Gediz). From the territory of ancient Cadi, at the village Çeltikçi, comes the earliest known dated inscription that, on the basis of its iconography, may definitely be considered Christian (Calder 1955, 33–35 no. 2). The epitaph was commissioned by P. Silicius Ulpianus for his foster brother Eutyches in 179/80. The tombstone itself portrays the deceased holding a bunch of grapes in his left hand and a round object stamped with a cross in his right hand. The round object, especially taken in conjunction with the grape symbol, is undoubtedly a *panis quadratus*—that is, a *panis eucharisticus* (eucharistic bread) divided into four quadrants by an incised cross. An even earlier tombstone from the territory of Cadi, dated 157/8, that commemorates a man named Beroneikianos and that shows the deceased in a pose similar to that of Eutyches holding a bunch of grapes in his left hand (Benoît 1959, 151 no. 32), may also be Christian (*MAMA* 10, xxxvi–xxxvii; Mitchell 1993, 2:38). Both tombstones were produced in the same workshop (Lochman 1991, 17–18). Beroneikianos, however, holds a pruning hook, rather than a *panis quadratus*, in his right hand. Consequently, since grape bunches were also common funerary reliefs depicting the agricultural environment in which the deceased had lived, the symbolism on Beroneikianos's gravestone is not as unambiguously Christian as that of Eutyches (Tabbernee 1997, 25).

No ambiguity exists regarding the Christian character of a series of tombstones from Temenothyrae (Uşak), a Phrygian city 40 km due south of Cadi and 75 km northwest of Hieropolis. The Temenothyrae tombstones (*IMont* 3–8) were produced in a local workshop sometime between 200 and 230. Five of the series contain the symbol of a *panis quadratus* on a communion paten (*IMont* 3, 5–8). Two of the tombstones (*IMont* 2, 5) commemorate bishops, and one (*IMont* 4) was commissioned by a bishop for a woman named Ammion, who is described as a *presbytera*. Given the other ecclesiastical titles

---

7.1 Cobbler's Tombstone with "Eumeneian Formula"

I, Aurelios Valens, son of Valens, cobbler, have prepared the tomb for myself
5 and for my wife Louliana | and for those who lie (here) with (us); but if anyone should wish to weigh down my bones [by placing other bones on top of mine] that person will be answerable to the One who has authority over every soul;
10 let no one open | (the tomb), the boundary (of which) is extensive. Whoever,
15 at any time, should throw a bone out of here | shall be answerable to God.
(*IMont* 33 [trans. Tabbernee 1997, 223])

and the eucharistic symbols on the tombstones in this series, the designation *presbytera* must mean "female presbyter," not merely "old woman." The geographical location of Temenothyrae, only about 20 km north of Tymion (near or at Şükraniye) and 34 km north of Pepouza (2 km southwest of Karayakuplu), both prominent Montanist sites (Tabbernee 2003, 87–93; Tabbernee and Lampe 2008), suggests that Ammion, and presumably at least some of the others commemorated by the Temenothyrae inscriptions, were Montanists (Tabbernee 1997, 62–86). Montanists, after all, were accused of having women as presbyters and even as bishops (Epiphanius, *Pan.* 49.2.5).[3] In the period before the emperor Constantine took up the cause of "Catholic" Christianity, the lines that later divided Christians into "orthodox" and "heterodox" groups were not yet drawn very strictly.

Unlike other parts of Asia Minor, such as North Galatia, Cappadocia, or even the western part of the Roman province of Asia itself, Phrygia has produced an abundance of second- and third-century Christian inscriptions (Blanchetière 1981, 473, 491–507). These inscriptions enable us to identify not just isolated individual Christians or Christian families but distinctive Christian communities (Mitchell 1993, 2:39), like the one at Temenothyrae (Tabbernee 1997, 61–86).[4]

A large number of inscriptions found at a variety of cities in the vicinity of Temenothyrae, such as Acmonia (Ahat), Eumeneia (Işıklı), and Apamea (Dinar), contain the so-called Eumeneian formula (Tabbernee 1983, 136–39). The earliest known dated example of this formula is on a tombstone found near Eumeneia (Calder 1955, 38). Its date is the equivalent of 246 CE. The Eumeneian formula warns potential grave violators that they "shall be answerable to God" (see sidebar 7.1). Since the identity of the god/God referred to by the Eumeneian formula is ambiguous, the formula, theoretically, could be utilized by pagans, Jews, and Christians alike. In the case of the Phrygian epitaphs, it appears that the Eumeneian formula was especially popular among Jews and Christians and that there was a great deal of interrelationship between Christians and members of the many Jewish communities of the region (Sheppard 1979; Trebilco 1991, 58–103; Mitchell 1993, 2:31–37). The addition of more and more specifically Christian terms or symbols to the Eumeneian formula helps to identify the Christian usage of the formula in specific instances

---

3. The possibility that the Temenothyrae Christians, including Ammion, belonged to "mainstream" Christianity, as argued by Ute Eisen (2000, 116–18) and Ronald Heine (1998, 825–27), should not be ruled out altogether (Madigan and Osiek 2005, 169–70).

4. Not every early Christian community in Asia Minor, or on the islands off the coast of Asia Minor, attested by epigraphic or literary data is referred to in this chapter. For additional locations, see chap. 8; Tabbernee 1997; Mullen 2004.

(e.g., *IMont* 20: *Christianoi*; *IMont* 32: ℟ *episkopos* [see also Tabbernee 1997, 144–47]). Distinguishing a Christian inscription from a Jewish one, however, remains a difficult task (Kraemer 1991, 141–62). Significantly, a number of the Christians commemorated by the third-century epitaphs displaying the Eumeneian formula were important citizens and often members of the city council (e.g., G. Johnson 1995, 82–87 nos. 3.2–4, 92–93 no. 3.6). Eumeneia had had a Christian bishop at least since Thraseas, who was martyred at Smyrna sometime prior to 190, perhaps in about 160 (Eusebius, *Hist. eccl.* 5.24.4). An especially touching third-century Christian inscription (in three parts) found near Acmonia (*CB* 455–57) records a gift of land to the Christian community by a man named Aristeas, on the condition that rose petals be strewn annually over the grave of his wife, Aurelia.[5]

Even when pre-Constantinian inscriptions are indisputably Christian, such as those originating from two workshops in the Upper Tembris Valley on the territory of Cotiaeum (Kütahya) displaying the formula "Christians for Christians" (e.g., *IMont* 24, 25, 27–29, 31, 38–52), issues of interpretation arise. Until recently, it was common to assume that the people who openly revealed that not only the deceased but also the surviving family members were Christians must have been Montanist Christians (Ramsay 1889, 398–400; Calder 1922–1923, 310, 317–19; Frend 1988, 32–34). There is, however, no independent evidence of the presence of Montanists in the specific area of Phrygia where the "Christians for Christians" inscriptions originated. Nor is there any indication that the "Christians for Christians" inscriptions were deliberately provocative. All they really revealed was something that undoubtedly was known by their neighbors anyway: the family that commissioned the epitaph was Christian (see sidebar 7.2). The "Christians for Christians" inscriptions, like other early Phrygian inscriptions containing the (single) word "Christian" or "Christians,"[6] merely seem to be indicative of a sense of security engendered by the tolerant attitude toward Christians and Christianity by the non-Christian inhabitants of West-Central Phrygia. Christianity, it appears, was not deemed to be an especially serious threat to the native Phrygian cults and the cults brought into Phrygia from elsewhere, at least not in the first three centuries of Christian presence in the area.[7]

5. Presumably on the anniversary of her death.
6. For example, *IMont* 9 (Traianopolis [Çarık]), *IMont* 12 (Kırkpınar, 15 km southwest of Orcistus [Ortaköy]), *IMont* 19 (Apamea), *IMont* 34 (Apollonia [Uluborlu, near Senirkent]).
7. A number of early Christian inscriptions in Phrygia have dates on them. For example, *IMont* 17 (Üçkuyu): 327 Sullan Era = 243 CE; Ramsay 1895–1897, 559–60 no. 447 (Karbasan): 338 = 253/4; *MAMA* 4.354, 355 (Sırıklı): 338 = 253/4, 340 = 255/6; *MAMA* 4.356, 357 (Dumanlı): 343 = 258/9, 358 = 273/4. The ancient sites corresponding to these Turkish villages, south of Pepouza, have not yet been identified.

7.2 Text of "Christians for Christians" Inscription Found at Keçiller

Eutyches for Ammia his daughter-in-law and for Tatia his granddaughter; and
5 Makedon for his son and for his wife Ammia; | and Eutyches their son, (who like his father and grandfather is still) living, constructed (this tomb for their relatives). Christians for Christians. (*IMont* 45 [trans. Tabbernee 1997, 285])

In Phrygia, as in other parts of Asia Minor, the cult of the mother goddess, known by various local names but most commonly as Cybele, was extremely prominent (Roller 1999). Shrines to Cybele, frequently cut into the sides of mountains, abounded throughout the countryside. The imported cult of Apollo and his mother, Leto, was also very popular in Phrygia and frequently became interrelated with the native cult of Cybele (Hirschmann 2005, 55–74) or that of Hosion and Dikaion (Holy and Just) (Mitchell 1993, 2:25). Zeus and Mēn, the moon-god, were also worshiped by many in Phrygia (Mitchell 1993, 2:23–25). There was, however, in Phrygia as well as elsewhere in Asia Minor during the time Christianity was establishing itself a gradual shift toward a kind of philosophic and syncretistic "monotheism" that, while still recognizing a plurality of gods, argued for the one ultimate God (Mitchell 1993, 2:43–50).

To open-minded pagans, the Christians' emphasis on "the One God" was not totally incomprehensible, but they did find it disconcerting that Christians were unwilling to participate in cultic activities, including (especially in the cities) activities associated with the imperial cult (Price 1998; Friesen 1993; 2001). Participating in the latter was a sign of loyalty to the Roman Empire and its rulers, and refusal to do so was considered not just an act of religious intolerance but also tantamount to treason. Before 250, however, Christians in Phrygia rarely had to prove their loyalty publicly, and even in the post-Decian period, at least until the so-called Great Persecution (303–313), there was little implementation of imperial anti-Christian legislation in the area. Consequently, Christianity in Phrygia was relatively free to make converts and to establish Christian communities. By the beginning of the fourth century, some of these communities had grown so significantly that, reportedly, the majority of the population in particular towns was Christian (Eusebius, *Hist. eccl.* 8.11.1 [Eumeneia?]; *MAMA* 7.305.i, lines 39–42 [Orcistus]).

Identifiable Christian pieces of decorative artwork, such as the exquisite marble sculptures now in the Cleveland Museum of Art, were being produced in West-Central Phrygia during the last quarter of the third century (Kitzinger

1978). Often, like the four Cleveland marbles portraying the "Jonah Cycle," the themes for such artwork were drawn from the Hebrew Scriptures. The Cleveland marbles probably were produced in a workshop associated with a marble quarry near Docimium (İscehisar).

Not all the numerous Christian communities known from inscriptions and other data to have existed in West-Central Phrygia during the second and third centuries (Ramsay 1895–1897; Harnack 1908, 2:218–20; Mitchell 1993, 2:38–41; Tabbernee 1997; 2009) were (what would later be called) "Catholic" or "Orthodox" communities. For example, around 165 Montanus, along with two prophetesses, Maximilla and Priscilla, started a prophecy-based ethical renewal movement, referred to by its supporters as the "New Prophecy" and by its detractors as the "sect named after the Phrygians." Based at Pepouza (Tabbernee and Lampe 2008), near where the Montanists expected the New Jerusalem to descend out of heaven (Rev. 3:12; 21:1–22:5) (Tabbernee 2003; 2012), Montanism (Heine 1989; Trevett 1996; Tabbernee 1997; 2009) spread rapidly to other parts of Phrygia, surrounding regions, and beyond. The epitaph of "Trophimus, apostle from Pepouza" discovered at Ankara (Mitchell 2005), shows that Montanists were still sending out missionaries from Pepouza as late as the sixth century. One of the other features of Montanism was its emphasis on the full participation of women in the ministerial leadership of its churches. Among the Montanists, women could be bishops, presbyters, or deacons, as well as prophetesses.

Fig. 7.3. Site of Pepouza, the Holy City of the Montanists

As already noted, early epigraphic evidence exists for what appears to have been a Montanist community at Temenothyrae. Similarly, the epitaph of a man named Paithos (*IMont* 23) may indicate the presence of Montanists at Eibeos/ Neo-Sebaste (Payamalanı) in the third century, something that is established for the fifth or early sixth century by the tombstone of a *koinōnos* called Paulinus (*IMont* 80). *Koinōnoi* were Montanist regional bishops, second in rank after the patriarch of Pepouza (Tabbernee 1993, 249–80). Other epigraphically attested Montanist communities in Phrygia were at Hierapolis (*IMont* 82); in the Phrygian Highlands (*IMont* 68); at Dorylaeum (Şarhüyük) (*IMont* 63); and, not surprisingly, in the general vicinity of Pepouza (*IMont* 21, 58, 77, 78).

A Novatianist Christian community existed in Cotiaeum by the fourth century (Tabbernee 1997, 347–48). The Novatianists were named after Novatian, a Roman presbyter and "antibishop" during the 250s. He took a strong stand against allowing Christians who had apostatized during the persecution of Decius (r. 249–251) back into the church too leniently. The Novatianists, like the Montanists, emphasized the purity of the church and advocated a highly rigoristic lifestyle for Christians. Perhaps at Cotiaeum, as elsewhere, Novatianism merged with Montanism in the post-Constantinian era (Socrates, *Hist. eccl.* 4.28; 5.22).

What we know about the Christian communities of Phrygia on the basis of extant inscriptions is, of course, by no means all that we know about the origins and development of Christianity in the region. Indeed, literary texts supply data relating to Christianity in parts of Phrygia that predate the epigraphic data by about a century. A complicating factor, however, is the questionable historic reliability of at least some of the literary data. For example, while the New Testament letter to the Colossians, attributed to St. Paul, attests the existence of Christian house-churches in Colossae (Col. 1:2; cf. Philem. 2, 23), Laodicea (Col. 4:15–16), and Hierapolis (Col. 4:13), it may not have been written by Paul but by a later author within the "Pauline circle." Consequently, the persons connected with the Christian communities of Colossae, Laodicea, and Hierapolis mentioned in Colossians may also belong to periods later than that of St. Paul. However, it may also be the case that the later writer accurately conveys reliable traditions about early Christianity in those locations. Whether Philemon (Philem. 1) was really the first bishop of Colossae (*Const. ap.* 7.46) is debatable and depends, in part, on the meaning of the term "bishop" during the first century. Perhaps Philemon was the owner of the house in which the house-church in Colossae met.

A large unoccupied mound 5 km north-northwest of Honaz (ancient Chonae) is the site of Colossae, which was abandoned during the ninth century CE in favor of Chonae. Parts of Colossae's defensive ring-wall and remnants of the theater are visible, along with a few architectural blocks. Remains of

Colossae's necropolis and of a large Byzantine church (probably dedicated to the archangel Michael [Ramsay 1895–1897, 1:213–16]) are on the north side of the Lycus River (Çürük Su), opposite the main city site.

Substantial remains of an octagonal fifth-century martyrium dedicated to St. Philip are a visible reminder of the tradition that the apostle Philip, already at an early time confused with Philip the Evangelist (Acts 21:8–9),[8] was buried at Hierapolis along with his daughters (Proclus, *Fr.*, in Eusebius, *Hist. eccl.* 3.31.4). Hagiography adds the legend that Philip instructed Bartholomew to appoint a man named Stachys (*Acts Phil.* 143, 148; cf. Rom. 16:9) or called Heros (Nicetas of Paphlagonia, *Or.* [PG 105.196]) as the first bishop of Hierapolis. The first reliably attested bishop of the city, however, is Papias (Eusebius, *Hist. eccl.* 3.36.1–2), sometime between 110 and 130. Under Apolinarius, bishop of Hierapolis during the 170s, a synod or local church gathering was held condemning Montanism (Tabbernee 2007, 15–20). Among the numerous early Christian inscriptions found in the extensive ancient cemetery with its above-ground sarcophagi at Hierapolis is a late second- or early third-century epitaph that reads, "For Ammia and Asklepios. The (coffin is that) of Christians" (*IMont* 10). A bishop named Flaccus represented Hierapolis at the First Council of Nicaea in 325, along with bishops from Laodicea,[9] and Sanaus (Sarıkavak), Aezani (Çavdarhisar), Dorylaeum, Eucarpia (Emirhisar), and Synnada (Şuhut).

Eucarpia was one of the five cities that composed the Phrygian Pentapolis, to which also belonged Hieropolis, Otrous (Yanıkören), Brouzos (Karasandıklı), and Stectorium (Kocahüyük, near Menteş). The Anonymous, in his correspondence with Avircius of Hieropolis, referred to one of their "fellow presbyters" (cf. 1 Pet. 5:1)[10] as "Zoticus of Otrous" (*Fr.*, in Eusebius, *Hist. eccl.* 5.16.5), not only indicating that there was a Christian community at Otrous but also suggesting that there may have been Christian churches in each of the five cities of the Pentapolis, and that the Anonymous may have been bishop of Brouzos, Eucarpia, or Stectorium in about 190. The Anonymous also reports that some years earlier another Zoticus, bishop of Cumane (Gönen), along with Julian of Apamea, went to Pepouza in order to exorcize the Montanist prophetess Maximilla (*Fr.*, in Eusebius, *Hist. eccl.* 5.16.17; cf. Apollonius, *Fr.*, in Eusebius, *Hist. eccl.* 5.18.3).

8. On the conflation of traditions concerning the tombs of the apostle Philip, Philip the Evangelist, and their respective daughters at Ephesus, Hierapolis, and Tralles, see Tabbernee 1997, 504–6; C. Hill 2006, 176–77.

9. On Laodicea, see below.

10. For a new assessment of the meaning of the terms bishop and presbyter in early Christianity, see Stewart 2014.

Fig. 7.4. Map of Asia

A late third-century ossuary with an inscription that reads, in part, "Here within are (the) bones of the martyr Trophimos" (*IMont* 35), may be the basis of the spurious *Acta Sancti Trophimi*, which relates that, during the reign of Probus (r. 276–282), Christians named Trophimus and Dorymedon were martyred at Synnada (1.1–3; [Tabbernee 1997, 236–40]). In the early part of the third century, Atticus, bishop of Synnada, allowed Theodorus, a layperson, to preach to the congregation (Eusebius, *Hist. eccl.* 6.19.18). The epitaph of a Christian soldier, Aurelius Gaius (Drew-Bear 1981; Tabbernee 2002, 123), martyred in about 303–305 during the persecution under Diocletian, has been found at Adaköy (23 km south of Cotiaeum). From Amorium (Hisarköy) comes the third-century epitaph (*MAMA* 7.297) of a man named "Paul" and his wife, "Kyriake" (popular early Christian names), decorated with a staff in the shape of a cross (or a T) and with a fish, which may represent the acrostic *I[ēsous] CH[ristos] TH[eou] Y[ios] S[ōtēr]* (i.e., Jesus Christ, God's Son, Savior), based on *ichthys*, the Greek word for fish.

The "Seven Churches in Asia"

Ephesus. Ephesus (Efes), founded as a Greek settlement in Ionia in about 1100 BCE, was the most important city of the Roman province of Asia, although Smyrna and Pergamum vied for that honor. From the time of Augustus, Ephesus was the official place of residence of the Roman governor, but the Romans purposely exploited the ambiguous status of Ephesus in relationship to Pergamum, the original capital of the province (Hemer 1986, 82–84). Paul's letter to the Galatians probably was written from Ephesus (ca. 52), as were the several letters that compose the canonical 2 Corinthians (ca. 54/5) and, assuming an Ephesian imprisonment, Philippians and Philemon (ca. 54/5). First Corinthians (ca. 54) certainly was written from Ephesus (1 Cor. 16:8).

Paul used Ephesus as his main missionary base but apparently did not found the church there. Sources (presumably) utilized by Luke indicate that Apollos had preceded Paul, and that it was he, along with Priscilla and Aquila, who first established a Christian community in Ephesus (Acts 18:24–26). During Paul's time in the city (ca. 52–55), a Christian house-church met in the home of Priscilla and Aquila (2 Cor. 16:19; cf. Rom. 16: 3–5).[11] Since Paul conveys greetings to the Corinthians on behalf of "the churches of Asia," we may assume that by the spring of 54, Christian communities had been founded in other cities of Asia, and possibly that there was more than one house-church in Ephesus. Multiple, diverse Christian communities are attested at Ephesus near the end of the first century, including an enigmatic group called the "Nicolaitans" (Rev. 2:6), which appears also to have existed at Pergamum (Rev. 2:15) and perhaps at Thyatira (Rev. 2:20–24). It is more likely that the major conflicts between Christianity and Judaism and between Christianity and the adherents of the cult of Artemis (the patron goddess of the city) occurred in Ephesus at the end of the first century rather than during the time of Paul (Koester 1995, 128–31).

Although there are no extant Christian inscriptions from Ephesus earlier than the fourth century (Mitchell 1993, 2:38), Dionysius of Alexandria (ca. 190–264/5) knew of two memorial tombs in Ephesus, each inscribed with the name "John" (*Ep.*, in Eusebius, *Hist. eccl.* 7.25.16). Both Dionysius and Eusebius (*Hist. eccl.* 3.39.6) use this epigraphic data to argue that the book of

11. Despite the views of scholars such as Helmut Koester (1995, 122–24), it seems more likely that Romans 16 is indeed what it purports to be, a list of greetings to Christians in Rome, rather than a cover letter for a copy of Paul's letter to the Romans sent to Christians in Ephesus (see also Lampe 2003a, 153–64). Consequently, the house-church referred to in Romans 16:5 is a house-church in Rome, not in Ephesus; but there is no reason why Priscilla and Aquila could not have hosted a Christian community (see chap. 9) in both locations at different times. The canonical letter to the Ephesians, like Colossians and the Pastoral Epistles, although in the Pauline tradition, was probably not written by Paul himself.

7.3 Ignatius of Antioch's Desire for Martyrdom

May I have joy of the beasts that are prepared for me (in Rome). I pray, too, that they may prove prompt with me. I will even entice them to devour me promptly, and not to refrain, as they have refrained from some, through fear. And, even though they are not willing without constraint, I will force them. Pardon me. I know what is expedient for me. Now I am beginning to be a disciple. May nothing of things visible or invisible seek to allure me, that I may attain unto Christ. Let there come on me fire and cross and conflicts with wild beasts, wrenching of bones, mangling of limbs, crushing of the whole body, grievous torments of the devil may I but attain to Jesus Christ. (Ignatius, *Rom.* 5.1–3 [trans. Stevenson 2013, 14, altered])

Revelation was written not by the apostle John but by another John, whom (as Eusebius points out [3.39.4–5]) Papias of Hierapolis calls "John the Presbyter." The tradition that the apostle John brought Mary the mother of Jesus to Ephesus and resided with her there may be nothing but pious fiction (Koester 1995, 138–39), despite the incorporation of the "tomb of John the Apostle" into the basilica built by Justinian I (r. 527–565) in honor of the apostle and the "discovery" of "Mary's house" in 1891. That a Christian prophet known as John the Presbyter lived in Ephesus toward the end of the first century, and that it was he who wrote the book of Revelation, need not be doubted. Revelation 2:1–7, addressed to the "church in Ephesus," is the first of the so-called letters to "the seven churches" in Asia (1:4, 11, 19–20), which, according to the author, were "dictated" to him, on the island of Patmos, by the risen Christ (1:1–20).

Ignatius (d. ca. 115), bishop of Antioch-in-Syria (Antakya), on his way under guard to trial in Rome and to ultimate martyrdom (see sidebar 7.3), was allowed to stop for extended periods in cities along the way. In Smyrna Ignatius met with Christian leaders from Smyrna, Ephesus, Magnesia ad Maeandrum (Tekke), and Tralles (Aydın), which Ignatius followed up with subsequent letters to those Christian communities. Ignatius, in his *Letter to the Ephesians*, refers to a man named Onesimus[12] as bishop of Ephesus (1.3; 2.1; 6.2), to Burrhus as a deacon (2.1), and to the presbytery (*presbyterion* [2.2; 4.1; 20.2]). Ignatius mentions three other members of the Ephesian delegation: Crosus, Euplus, and Fronto (1.3), who presumably were either presbyters or deacons. Whether a threefold ministerial structure reflects the actual situation at Ephesus at that time or was merely Ignatius's ideal model is debatable. Such a structure became the norm at Ephesus, as elsewhere, certainly toward the end of the second century. By the fourth century (Eusebius, *Hist. eccl.* 3.4.6), if not earlier (cf. 1 Tim. 1:3;

12. Not to be confused with the Onesimus of Phlm. 10.

4:14), there had also developed a tradition that Timothy (Paul's co-worker) had been ordained as the first bishop of Ephesus. Another unsupported tradition cites a man named John (John the Presbyter?), ordained by the apostle John, as the second bishop of Ephesus (*Const. ap.* 7.46.7).

Polycrates, who *was* bishop of Ephesus (fl. ca. 195), in addition to mentioning the tomb of John (whom he equates with the apostle John) at Ephesus (in Eusebius, *Hist. eccl.* 3.31.3; cf. 5.24.3), mentions, in a letter to Victor of Rome (bp. ca. 189–198), that the (no doubt suitably inscribed) tomb of one of the daughters of the apostle Philip was at Ephesus (3.31.3; cf. 5.24.2). The tradition conveyed by the *Acts of Timothy* that Timothy's tomb was on Mount Pion (Panayirdağı), the large hill into which the theater of Ephesus is built, may have led to the construction of one of the very few churches discovered thus far that precede the Council of Ephesus in 431 (Scherrer 1995, 23). Even the building identified earlier by archaeologists as the Church of Mary,[13] where both Councils of 431 and of 449 were held, appears now not to have been built until about 500 (Karwiese 1995).

Smyrna. The second church to which one of the seven letters in Revelation is addressed is Smyrna (2:8–11), indicating that by the end of the first century a Christian community was flourishing in the second most important harbor city of Asia. Smyrna (İzmir), like Ephesus, was part of the region of Ionia. The city had been refounded by Antigonus (r. 318–301 BCE) and Lysimachus (r. 301–281 BCE), the successors of Alexander the Great, and moved from its original site (Old Smyrna) to take advantage of the natural harbors. Nothing specific is known of the founding of the church at Smyrna. The reference to Aristo as the first bishop (*Const. ap.* 7.46.8), like the one to Strataeas, the son of Lois (cf. 2 Tim 1:5), as the second bishop of Smyrna, is unreliable. The vehement conflict between Jews and Christians alluded to in Revelation 2:9 may or may not indicate that some early Christians in Smyrna were originally Jews. That verse does, however, suggest with greater certainty that some members of the Christian community in Smyrna had suffered some form of persecution in the years immediately preceding the writing of the letter. More, although time-limited, persecution apparently was to be expected (Rev. 2:10–11). The author of the letter undoubtedly had in mind some impending persecution in the near future.

If there was active persecution of Christians at Smyrna in the time of Domitian (r. 81–96) or during the reign of Trajan (r. 98–117) no record of this has survived. The church at Smyrna appears to have flourished in the first half of the second century under its bishop, Polycarp. Ignatius of Antioch

---

13. Not to be confused with the "House of Mary."

visited Smyrna and, as noted, met with delegations from Ephesus, Magnesia ad Maeandrum, and Tralles. Ignatius's letter of appreciation to the Smyrnae-ans indicates that, in addition to a bishop (Polycarp), presbyters, and deacons (*Smyrn.* 12.2), there was an order of "virgins who are called widows" at Smyrna (13.1; cf. Ignatius, *Pol.* 4.1; also 1 Tim. 5:3–6). Polycarp calls such widows the "altar of God," referring to their role of praying constantly for members of the Christian community (*Phil.* 4.3). Ignatius also mentions two other women at Smyrna who appear to have been "real widows," women of means whose husbands had died but who continued to manage their own households and who did not join the "*order* of widows" (cf. 1 Tim. 5:14). Ignatius refers to the first of these widows by name, "Tavia" (*Smyrn.* 13.2), but simply calls the second "the wife of Epitropus" (*Pol.* 8.2). Other persons belonging to the church at Smyrna during the early second century named by Ignatius are Alce, Attalus, Daphnus, and Eutecnus (*Smyrn.* 13.2; *Pol.* 8.2). Polycarp mentions a certain Crescens (*Phil.* 14).

Interestingly, Ignatius thanks the Smyrnaeans for Burrhus, a deacon, whom they, "together with the church at Ephesus," had generously sent along with Ignatius to serve him as an amenuensis (*Smyrn.* 12.1; cf. *Phld.* 11.2). It is not clear whether Burrhus served in a double capacity as deacon of both Ephesus and Smyrna or whether the two communities simply graciously provided the financial means by which Burrhus (a deacon only of Ephesus) could accompany Ignatius.

As a youth, Irenaeus of Lyons (bp. ca. 177–200) was a member of Polycarp's congregation (Irenaeus, in Eusebius *Hist. eccl.* 5.20.5). At the same time, a man named Florinus, who appears to have been on the staff of the proconsul of Asia and who later became a presbyter in Rome (C. Hill 2006, 16–22, 130–31), was a prominent early second-century Christian at Smyrna (Irenaeus, in Eu-sebius, *Hist. eccl.* 5.20.4–5). Polycarp himself was martyred, around 155/6, in the stadium at Smyrna (*Mart. Pol.* 13–18). In the same stadium, during the Decian persecution, a "catholic" presbyter named Pionius was martyred, along with a number of others, including a woman named Makedonia from Carina (Yatağan), 90 km northeast of Smyrna, a presbyter "from the sect of the Marcionites" (see below), and a member of "the sect of the Phrygians" (i.e., Montanism) (*Pass. Pion.* 2.1; 9.2; 11.2; 21.5), indicating the presence of multiple Christian communities in and around Smyrna circa 250. Today, the stadium, which was located in the southwest part of the city, is, like most of ancient Smyrna, underneath the buildings of the city of İzmir. Only the agora and some sections of the Roman theater remain visible. Cybele, Hellenized as Nemesis (and portrayed uniquely as a pair of goddesses), was the patron god-dess of Smyrna, but remnants of an altar to Zeus and statues of Poseidon and Demeter have also been found in the agora. Tantalizingly, a recently discovered

---

7.4 Letter to the Church in Pergamum

And to the angel of the church in Pergamum write: These are the words of him who has the sharp two-edged sword: I know where you are living, where Satan's throne is. Yet you are holding fast to my name, and you did not deny your faith in me even in the days of Antipas my witness, my faithful one, who was killed among you, where Satan lives. But I have a few things against you: you have some there who hold to the teaching of Balaam, who taught Balak to put a stumbling block before the people of Israel, so that they would eat food sacrificed to idols and practice fornication. So you also have some who hold to the teaching of the Nicolaitans. Repent then. If not, I will come to you soon and make war against them with the sword of my mouth. Let anyone who has an ear listen to what the Spirit is saying to the churches. (Rev. 2:12–17 NRSV)

---

partial graffito (-karpos)[14] may be an incomplete reference to [Poly]karpos, perhaps made by an early pilgrim. Crosses on marble blocks in the agora attest the existence of a (sixth-century) church on the site, probably dedicated to St. Polycarp. A letter written to the church at Philomelium (Akşehir) in northeast Phrygia (*Mart. Pol.* preface), giving an account of Polycarp's martyrdom, attests the existence of an early Christian community in that city also.

Pergamum. Pergamum (Bergama), a city in Mysia, was ruled in the time after Alexander the Great by the Attalid dynasty (283–129 BCE). During the Roman Republic, Pergamum was the seat of Roman government in the province of Asia and even during the early empire seems to have considered itself the capital. The city is described, in the letter addressed to it in the book of Revelation (2:12–17), as the place "where Satan's throne is" (2:13). The description appears to be a double reference to Roman authority and to the Temple (and Altar) of Zeus, linked because of the association of the emperor Domitian with Zeus (Collins 1998, 166–76; 2006, 26–39).

Unlike in the letter to Smyrna, the identity of one Christian martyred earlier at Pergamum *is* recorded by the author. The author, however, provides no details other than the martyr's name: Antipas (Rev. 2:13). It is likely that Antipas was a member of the Christian community at Pergamum, but it is also possible that he was brought to Pergamum from elsewhere for trial and execution. Subsequent Christian martyrs at Pergamum certainly included nonresidents. Papylus, for example, who was martyred at Pergamum along with Carpus and Agathonicê, most likely during the Decian persecution (Barnes 1968, 514–15), came from

---

14. I owe this information to Professor Thomas Drew-Bear, who in 2004 discovered the graffito in the remains of the civic basilica adjoining the agora.

Fig. 7.5. Snake Symbol on Column Base at Entrance of Asclepieum, Pergamum

Thyatira (*Mart. Carp.* [A] 27; [B] 1). Carpus, according to the Latin recension, was bishop of Gordos (*Mart. Carp.* [B]), presumably Iulia Gordos in Lydia (Gördes). A late, speculative tradition makes Antipas the second bishop of Pergamum after Gaius (*Const. ap.* 7.46.9; cf. 3 John 1). Among the martyrs of Lugdunum, in about 177, was a Roman citizen, Attalus, whose family came from Pergamum (*Mart. Lugd.* 17, 37, 44).

From Revelation 2:14–15 it is clear that, during the last decade of the first century, there were factions within the church at Pergamum, disagreeing over the extent to which it was possible for Christians to participate in cultic activities, especially with respect to eating "food sacrificed to idols" (2:14). Numerous pagan cults existed in Pergamum, but apart from the Altar of Zeus, Pergamum was most famous for its Asclepieum. The healing center and sanctuary was dedicated to Asclepius, "the Savior." As elsewhere, the imperial cult linked itself where possible to local deities. The emperor Caracalla (r. 211–217) visited the sanctuary at Pergamum to "take the cure" and is shown on a Pergamese coin with his hand stretched out, in an ambiguous sign of blessing, adoration, or both, to the serpent, which was the symbol of healing. For Christians, however, a deity with the title "Savior," be it Asclepius, Augustus, or one of the other deified emperors, was a direct affront to the worship of Jesus as "Savior." No wonder that once Christianity became a tolerated religion within (and, subsequently, the preferred religion of) the Roman Empire, the Asclepieum was "Christianized" by the addition of a Christian chapel and baptistery (Rheidt 1998, 400–401). The whole appearance of Pergamum was radically changed during the fifth and sixth centuries by the transformation of formerly pagan temples into churches and monasteries, as well as the construction of new ecclesiastical buildings (Rheidt 1998, 395–423).

Thyatira. Whereas Ephesus, Smyrna, and Pergamum were very important, and each claimed to be preeminent in the province of Asia, Thyatira (Akhisar) was a relatively insignificant city on the border of Mysia and Lydia, functioning primarily as a garrison town on the imperial "post-road" (Ramsay 1904, 316). Thyatira's inclusion among "the seven churches in Asia" (Rev. 2:18–28), however, supports the validity of the theory that each of the "seven cities" was the center of a Christian "postal district" for other churches in their region (Ramsay 1904, 191–92, 196). Founded by Seleucus I (r. 311–281 BCE), Thyatira, like many other cities founded or refounded in Asia Minor by the successors of Alexander the Great, was populated by large numbers of Jews. Lydia, the "seller of purple" and Paul's first convert in Europe (Acts 14:14–15), was from Thyatira, where she had been a "God-fearer." The titular god of Thyatira was the sun-god Helios, syncretistically known locally as Helios Tyrimnaios Pythios Apollo.

As in Pergamum,[15] the Christian community at Thyatira was split over the issue of the legitimacy of participating in cultic activities. This issue was of particular concern to persons involved in professional guilds. Significantly, at Thyatira a lenient attitude toward cultic participation was being promoted forcefully by an unnamed, but obviously very influential, prophetess, referred to by the author of the book of Revelation (2:20–24) simply as Jezebel, the name of the treacherous wife of King Ahab (r. ca. 874–853 BCE) (1 Kings 16:31; 21:5–25).

Epiphanius of Salamis (bp. ca. 367–ca. 403/5) reports that the whole Christian community at Thyatira became Montanist and remained such for 112 years (*Pan.* 51.33.4). The most likely time when this happened was approximately between 223 and 335 CE (Tabbernee 1997, 138). If so, the aforementioned Papylus, the deacon of Thyatira martyred at Pergamum most probably in 250/1, may have been a Montanist (Tabbernee 1997, 140–41). At least by the middle of the fourth century, perhaps as a direct consequence of the anti-Montanist legislation of Constantine promulgated in 325/6 (Eusebius, *Vit. Const.* 3.66), the church at Thyatira was back in the "catholic" fold. Few archaeological remains of Christianity, however, have survived at Akhisar. An ancient large building with an apse, discovered in the center of the modern town, appears to have been primarily a civic basilica, not a church, although it may have been utilized as a church in the Byzantine period.

Sardis. Sardis (Sart) was the original capital of Lydia. A gold refinery made Sardis a populous and prosperous city. The fifth representative Christian congregation to which a letter was addressed by the author of Revelation (3:1–6) was the church at Sardis.

In contrast to the paucity of archaeological remains of Christianity at Thyatira, considerable remnants of four basilicas have been discovered thus far in Sardis. The largest and earliest of these was built in about 350, making it the oldest (partially) extant church in the region, if not in all of Asia Minor.

---

15. And probably in Ephesus, if the Nicolaitans (Rev. 2:6, 14–15) are to be equated with those who, analogically, held to the "teachings of Balaam" (cf. Num. 22:1–24:25; 31:16) by allowing the eating of food offered to idols.

Fig. 7.6. Fourth-Century Church and Temple of Artemis, Sardis

The most interesting surviving church in Sardis, able to be dated by coins also to the fourth century, was built at the southeast corner of the huge Temple of Artemis. The prominence of the cult of Artemis at Sardis was undoubtedly influenced by the political alliance between Sardis and Ephesus, frequently portrayed on Sardian coins by two statues of Artemis facing each other. The original partron goddess of Sardis, however, was Cybele, whose altar has been uncovered near the remains of the gold refinery. The cults of Artemis and Cybele seem to have been combined in the Hellenistic era. Zeus Lydios, Heracles, and Dionysus were the principal male gods. Sardis also had a large Jewish population, dating back to the fifth century BCE. A civic basilica next to the gymnasium was made into an extensive synagogue between 150 and 250 and further renovated between 320 and 340. Melito (fl. ca. 170) was Sardis's most famous early Christian bishop (Eusebius, *Hist. eccl.* 4.26.1–14). There is only one extant pre-Constantinian Christian inscription from Sardis (LBW 1654).

Philadelphia. Philadelphia (Alaşehir) in southeastern Lydia was named after Attalus II Philadelphus (r. 160–138 BCE), perhaps by himself but equally likely by his brother Eumenes II (r. 197–160 BCE), at a time when the Attalids of Pergamum ruled Lydia. During the early Roman period Philadelphia was an important commercial center strategically located on the imperial post road from Rome to the east. Zeus Helios was the patron god of Philadelphia, but, as elsewhere, other cults, including those of Asclepius and, after Augustus, of the imperial family, also existed.

Fig. 7.7. Ancient Synagogue, Sardis

The letter to Philadelphia (Rev. 3:7–13) indicates the presence of a Jewish (2:7–9) as well as a Christian community in about 95 CE. Nothing is known of the earlier history of Christianity at Philadelphia, since the tradition that a man named Demetrius was Philadelphia's first bishop (*Const. ap.* 7.46.9) is no more reliable than the information provided in *Constitutiones apostolicae* 7.46 about the first bishops of other cities in Asia Minor. Ignatius of Antioch, as noted, stopped at Philadelphia on his way to martyrdom in Rome and, from Alexandria Troas (near Odun İskelesi), wrote back a letter to the Christian community that had been hospitable to him and to his Christian travel companions, Philo and Rheus Agathopous, deacons respectively from Cilicia and Antioch-in-Syria (*Phld.* 11.2).

Although Ignatius did not observe open schism in the Christian community at Philadelphia, he did discern strained relationships (*Phld.* 3.1). Issues causing dissention included episcopal authority (2.1–2; 3.2–3; 7.1–2; 8.1; 9.1), Eucharists conducted by persons other than the bishop (4), the relationship of Christianity to Judaism (6.1), and the validity of "Scriptures" other than the "Hebrew Scriptures" (8.2; 9.2).

Ammia, a Christian prophetess claimed by both "mainstream" and Montanist Christians as belonging to the legitimate prophetic succession from Agabus (Acts 11:27–28) and the daughters of Philip (Acts 21:8–9) onward (Eusebius, *Hist. eccl.* 5.17.2–4), was based in Philadelphia sometime between 140 and 160 or a little earlier (Tabbernee 2007, 138–40).

The reference in the letter to the Philadelphians to the descent of the New Jerusalem out of heaven (Rev. 3:12; cf. 21:1–22:5) is the basis for the Montanist view that the New Jerusalem would appear in Phrygia near Pepouza and Tymion (Apollonius, *Fr.*, in Eusebius, *Hist. eccl.* 5.18.2), less than 100 km due east of Philadelphia. Attempts to identify Ardabau, the place where Montanus first began his ecstatic prophesying (Anonymous, *Fr.*, in Eusebius, *Hist. eccl.* 5.16.7), near Philadelphia, either at Kallataba (Ramsay 1895–1897, 1.2:573n3; Calder 1922–1923, 324) or at Adruta (Hemer 1986, 270–71n74), are unconvincing (Tabbernee 1997, 18). That there were Montanist congregations in the vicinity of Philadelphia at least is attested by the sixth-century epitaph of another *koinōnos* named Praÿlios, found at Mendechora (probably ancient Myloukome), 15 km northwest of Philadelphia (*IMont* 84).

Not long after Praÿlios was buried, a huge basilica in honor of St. John the Apostle was built at Philadelphia, as was the case in each of the cities to which, according to tradition, the risen Christ had written via the apostle. Little, however, can be said with certainty about the history of Christianity at Philadelphia between Ammia's lifetime and the building of the basilica during the reign of Justinian. A number of Christians from Philadelphia were martyred in Smyrna at the same time as, or a little earlier than, Polycarp (*Mart. Pol.* 19.1). Thus far, no pre-Constantinian Christian inscriptions have been discovered at Alaşehir itself.

Fig. 7.8. Basilica of St. John, Philadelphia (in the foreground, with a mosque visible between the columns)

Laodicea. The seventh letter in the book of Revelation is addressed to the Christian community at Laodicea (3:14–22). This Laodicea (Eskihisar), to be distinguished from other cities with the same name founded by the Syrian Seleucid dynasty, is Laodicea ad Lycum—that is, "Laodicea on the Lycus River," a tributary of the Maeander. The Lycus Valley, which was also the location of Colossae and Hierapolis, was a strategically located area providing access from the east to Lydia and Mysia and from the west to Phrygia, Caria, and Pamphylia. Antiochus II Theos (r. 261–246 BCE) appears to have been founder of the city, naming it after his wife, Laodice. Antiochus III the Great (r. 223–187 BCE) settled large numbers of Jews from the East at Laodicea and elsewhere in Asia Minor. The principal god of Laodicea was Zeus, but there was also a shrine dedicated to Mēn nearby with an associated medical school at Laodicea itself. Laodicea originally belonged to Caria before being assigned by the Romans to Phrygia.

Christianity may have been introduced to the Lycus Valley (Huttner 2014) in the time of St. Paul, perhaps by Epaphras, if the tradition contained in Colossians 4:12–13 is accurate. Similarly, from Colossians 4:14–15 it appears that a woman named Nympha was the patroness of an early house-church in Laodicea and that Paul had written a now-lost letter to that church.[16] Colossians 4:16–17 is presumably the basis of the unlikely view that Archippus was the first Christian bishop of Laodicea (*Const. ap.* 7.46.12).

Laodicea had running water, dispersed throughout the city by means of a water tower 4.8 m in height. The exact date of the construction of this tower and the aqueducts that brought water to the town from nearby hot and cold springs is uncertain and could have been during the early second rather than the late first century. The tantalizing references in Revelation 3:15–16 to hot and cold water, therefore, may (or may not) be an allusion to Laodicea's abundant, but often lukewarm, water supply. Among the ruins of several churches discovered at Laodicea is, not surprisingly, one dedicated to St. John the Apostle.

Sagaris, a second-century bishop of Laodicea, was martyred at Laodicea in the 160s (Melito, in Eusebius, *Hist. eccl.* 4.26.3; Polycrates, in Eusebius, *Hist. eccl.* 5.24.5). Presumably, Sagaris's tomb was still identifiable at Laodicea when Polycrates wrote in the 190s. A later Laodicaean bishop, Theophilus, was martyred along with several others at Laodicea during the Great Persecution. Altogether, more than fifty martyrs connected with Laodicea are

---

16. The extant letter to the Laodiceans attributed to St. Paul is apocryphal, and, despite early theories to the contrary, it is unlikely that the canonical letter to the Ephesians is actually St. Paul's "letter to the Laodiceans" (see Schneemelcher 1991–1992, 2:42–46).

Fig. 7.9. Water Tower, Laodicea   Fig. 7.10. Ancient Harbor, Alexandria Troas

known (TIB 7:323). A number of local ecclesiastical synods or councils were held at Laodicea. The most significant of these church gatherings took place between 343 and 381, dealing with, among other matters, the issue of "women presbyters" and/or "women presidents" (*Can.* 11) (see Tabbernee 1997, 70, 72; Madigan and Osiek 2005, 163–64).

Mysia, Lydia, and Caria

In addition to six of the seven "churches in Asia,"[17] numerous churches from the various regions that made up the province of Asia were represented at Nicaea. This council, held in 325, dealt, among other issues, with Arianism—the view that Christ's divinity was not essentially the same as that of God "the Father." The council produced the famous Nicene Creed, which emphasizes that Jesus Christ, the Son of God, is "of one substance with the Father" (see sidebar 7.5).

Among the bishoprics from Mysia represented at Nicaea were Aureliane (Havran), Ilium, the former Troy (Hisarlık), and Cyzicus (Erdek, near Bandırma). The vicinity of Bandırma has produced two pre-Constantinian Christian inscriptions (*IAsMinChr* 7–8) as well as numerous later ones, including the epitaph of an early fifth-century Montanist bishop (*IMont* 86). Alexandria Troas may have had a Christian community since the time of St. Paul (2 Cor. 2:12; cf. Acts 20:6) but certainly did so when Ignatius of Antioch visited this picturesque harbor town. Synaus (Simav) was a bishopric in pre-Constantinian times (TIB 7:396).

17. Pergamum is not listed.

7.5 Nicene Creed (as Formulated in 325)

We believe in one God: the Father Almighty, Maker of all things visible and invisible;
   And in one Lord: Jesus Christ, the Son of God, begotten of the Father, only begotten, that is from the substance of the Father; God from God, Light from Light, True God from True God; Begotten, not made; Of one substance with the Father, through Whom all things were made, Who for us and for our salvation came down, and became incarnate, and was made man, (and) suffered, And rose on the third day, And ascended into heaven, And is coming with glory to judge living and dead;
   And in the Holy Spirit. (trans. Stevenson 2013, 391–92, altered)

Lydian bishops at Nicaea included those from Ancyra Sidera (Boğaz Köy),[18] Bagis (Güre), Hierocaesareia (Arpalı), Hypaepa (Datbey), Silandus (Kara Selendi), and Tripolis ad Maeandrum (near Yenice). Selendi, the site of Choria, an ancient village within the territory of Hierocaesareia, has yielded the inscribed lid of a sarcophagus with a date corresponding to July 2 sometime between 212 and 248. The epitaph declares openly that "Aurelios Gaios son of Apphianus, a Christian, prepared (this sarcophagus) for himself and for Aurelia Stratoneikiane his wife, being herself a Christian" (*IMont* 13). An as-yet-unidentified ancient site at Karakuyu, 20 km northwest of Güre within the territory of Bagis, is the findspot of the epitaph of still another Montanist *koinōnos* (*IMont* 85).

   Carian bishops who attended Nicaea were from Antiochia ad Maeandrum (Aliağaçiftliği),[19] Aphrodisias (Geyre), Apollonia (Medet),[20] Cibyra (Horzum), Marcianopolis,[21] and Miletus (Balat). According to a tradition preserved by Acts 20:17–38, St. Paul stayed briefly at Miletus, meeting with Christian elders from Ephesus at the very end of his third missionary journey. Unlike in some other parts of Asia (especially Phrygia), no pre-Constantinian Christian inscriptions exist, due, perhaps, not to the lack of epigraphic discoveries thus far but to the unwillingness of Carian Christians to produce even "crypto-Christian" tombstones (Mitchell 1993, 2:38). That there were Christian communities throughout Caria, however, is demonstrated not only by the attendees at Nicaea but also by incidental references to the persecution of Christians, such as the one at Panamara (Bağyaka) during a visit by Maximin II Daia (r. 310–313) in 311 (Lane Fox 1989, 585).

18. Not to be confused with the Galatian capital.
19. To be distinguished from Antioch-in-Syria, Pisidian Antioch, and Antioch Minor in Isauria.
20. Not to be confused with Apollonia in Phrygia.
21. Ancient site not yet positively identified (see Mullen 2004, 100).

Galatia

SOUTH GALATIA

Even more problematic than the data contained in the Deutero-Pauline letters is that, while some scholars deem the historical information provided by the canonical Acts of the Apostles about St. Paul's "missionary journeys" to be absolutely reliable (e.g., Ramsay 1908; 1915; Hengel 1979; Frend 1984; Hemer 1990; Schnabel 2004), others consider the (albeit biblical) account of the journeys to be largely the construction of a creative early second-century author (Knox 1942; Pervo 2006; Tyson 2006) who wrote a "novelistic" or "poetic" history, modeling his work on Greek and Roman travel journals (e.g., Pervo 1987; Marguerat 2002). The author of Acts is traditionally assumed to have been Luke, one of Paul's co-workers (Philem. 24; cf. Col. 4:14; 2 Tim. 4:11), but more likely was an otherwise unknown Christian living in Ephesus sometime between 100 and 140. This author appears to have utilized a collection of Pauline letters and perhaps other written sources relating to Paul's journeys, which he amended to reflect the situation of his own times, such as the increasing conflict between Christianity and Judaism. Consequently, while there is no need to doubt the authenticity of the tradition that St. Paul traveled to Asia Minor, including Phrygia, much of the chronology and many of the specifics of Paul's missionary strategy, his invariable rejection by "the Jews," and the text of speeches made or sermons delivered do not stand up under the scrutiny of modern historiography (Lüdemann 2005, 169–86, 205–11, 240–83).

Regardless of the historicity of the specific details of Paul's journeys, the author of the Acts of the Apostles apparently knew the geography of Asia Minor very well. For example, despite the name Pisidian Antioch by which the city where, according to Acts, Paul made the first converts to Christianity in Asia Minor (13:14–52, 14:21–23) is now best known,[22] this particular Antioch was situated in a region called Phrygia Paroreius (Phrygia along the Mountain)[23] and belonged to the province of Galatia rather than to Asia (into which most of Phrygia was incorporated). The author of Acts refers to this region accurately in 16:6; 18:23.

That Paul appears to have made (Pisidian) Antioch (Yalvaç) the base for his missionary efforts in South Galatia is due, according to Acts, to the contact that he had made with the governor of Cyprus on the first leg of his journey to Asia Minor. The governor, referred to in Acts as Sergius Paulus (13:6–12), is identified by some scholars as L. Sergius Paullus (e.g., Mitchell 1993, 2:7).

22. Pisidia was not made a separate province until the time of Diocletian, with Antioch as its capital.
23. Namely, Mount Olympus (Sultan Dağ).

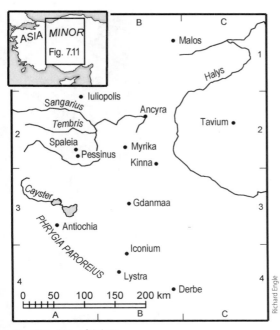

Fig. 7.11. Map of Galatia

Inscriptions show that Sergius Paullus was curator of the Tiber in Rome (*CIL* 6.31545) during the reign of Claudius (r. 41–54) and consul (*CIL* 6.253) during that of Vespasian. The Sergii Paulli owned estates in and around Antioch, having emigrated to the Roman colony there from Italia (Mitchell 1993, 1:151–52; 2:7–8).

The immediate post-Pauline history of Christianity at Antioch is undocumented. During the fourth century, however, two churches were built there. One of these is a martyrial church honoring three martyrs of the Great Persecution: Neon, Nikon, and Heliodorus (Mitchell and Waelkens 1998, 206–10). The other is a large basilica, which, judging from an inscription mentioning "the holy Paul"/"Saint Paul," was dedicated to the apostle Paul (Mitchell and Waelkens 1998, 210–17, esp. 215 and plate 143). This basilica can be dated rather precisely because of a reference to an inscription to Bishop Optimus in the church's extant mosaic pavement. Optimus, in about 377, corresponded with Basil of Caesarea (bp. 370–379) (Basil, *Ep.* 260) and attended the Council of Chalcedon in 381 (Mitchell and Waelkens 1998, 213). A third church, dating from the fifth century, has been discovered at the nearby Sanctuary of Mēn Askaenos (Mitchell and Waelkens 1998, 201–6). In his *Oration on the Martyrdom of St. Alpheus and Companions*, Eustathius of Thessalonica (bp. ca. 1175–1194) provides the information that Calytus, near Antioch, was the home of Alpheios, Zosimos, and Alexander, martyred during the Great Persecution (PG 136, 265d).

According to the Acts of the Apostles, Paul and Barnabas, after making some converts in Pisidian Antioch (13:48–49), went to Iconium (Konya) with mixed results (14:1–5). Iconium was, like Antioch, a Phrygian city in a region frequently controlled by Galatia. Similarly, Lystra (1.5 km northwest of Hatunsaray) and Derbe (Devri Şehri, 4 km south-southeast of Kertihüyük),

Fig. 7.12. Fourth-Century Church of St. Paul, Antioch-in-Pisidia

where reportedly the two Christian apostles went next (Acts 14:6–21), were in Lycaonia, a region also under the control of Galatia. Acts 20:4 contains the tradition that Gaius, a Christian from Derbe, was one of Paul's traveling companions on (at least the final part of) his third missionary journey. Exactly how the "South Galatian" churches fared during the ensuing decades is not clear.

No credible historical data other than geographic ones are contained in the legendary *Acts of Paul*,[24] which has Iconium as its primary setting. We do know that, sometime before 230, a bishop of Iconium named Celsus permitted a layperson named Paulinus to preach at Iconium (Eusebius, *Hist. eccl.* 6.19.18). By about 233–235 the church at Iconium, however, was sufficiently prominent to host a synod that was attended by the bishops of cities as far away as Caesarea (Kayseri) in Cappadocia. Among the issues discussed at the Synod of Iconium was whether to (re)baptize Montanists who wanted to become members of "mainstream" Christian communities (Firmilian, *Ep.*, in Cyprian, *Ep.* 75.7.4, 75.19.4). The "New Prophecy" apparently continued to concern the non-Montanist churches in the area, since, as late as the mid-370s, Amphilochius (ca. 340/45–398/404), the bishop of Iconium from 373, asked his mentor Basil of Caesarea about the same matter. Basil (*Ep.* 188.1) reaffirmed the decision made at Iconium 150 years earlier: Montanists and all other "heretics" needed (re)baptism (Tabbernee 2011, 920–23). In 268, the then-bishop of Iconium, Nicomas, attended a synod in Antioch-in-Syria (Eusebius, *Hist. eccl.* 7.28.1; 7.30.2).

Today the sites of Lystra and Derbe are unoccupied mounds. No early Christian inscriptions have been discovered at Lystra. Derbe has yielded the (fifth-century?) epitaph of "Michael, bishop of Derbe" (Ballance 1957). A

24. Including the *Acts of Paul and Thecla* (see Schneemelcher 1991–1992, 2:213–70).

Fig. 7.13. Site of Lystra   **Fig. 7.14.** Site of Derbe

large number of Christian inscriptions, many datable to before 260 (Mitchell 1993, 2:58–59), have been found in the nearby Çarşamba River Valley (*MAMA* 8.100, 116, 118–20, 131, 158–59, 161–65, 167, 199). An analysis of these and other inscriptions from the area has shown that approximately one-third of the population of this particular region was Christian before 260, increasing to 80 percent during the fourth century (Mitchell 1993, 2:58). This compares favorably with the statistics for the Upper Tembris Valley in Phrygia, where the "Christians for Christians" inscriptions were produced and where 80 percent of the tombstones datable to between 280 and 310 explicitly indicate Christianity (Mitchell 1993, 2:58).

Pisidia, Lycaonia, and Isauria

When Pisidia became a separate Roman province under Diocletian, it incorporated a number of originally Phrygian cities formally belonging to Asia. One of these was Apamea; the other was Metropolis (Tatarlı).[25] The bishops of Metropolis and Apamea represented Pisidia at Nicaea, along with the bishops of Baris (near Kılıç), Iconium, Limenae,[26] Neapolis (Şarkı Karaağac), and Seleucia Sidera (near Bayat). Late third- and early fourth-century inscriptions from Kindyria (Demiroluk) in northeastern Pisidia attest the presence of Encratite (e.g., *MAMA* 7.96, 106) as well as mainstream Christian communities in the area. Tatian (fl. ca. 160–200), a disciple of Justin Martyr (d. ca. 165), is credited with having founded the Encratites (Abstainers) in about 172 in Mesopotamia, from which they spread to Syria and Asia Minor. The Encratites, if all that is written about them by their opponents is to be believed, were even more rigoristic than the Montanists and the Novatianists. They abstained not

25. To be distinguished from another Metropolis (Ayazin) in the Phrygian Highlands. A large number of Byzantine rock-cut churches and monasteries are visible at and around Ayazin (Haspels 1971, 1:245–47).
26. Precise location unknown, probably east of Antioch-in-Pisidia (see Mullen 2004, 100 [Liminai]).

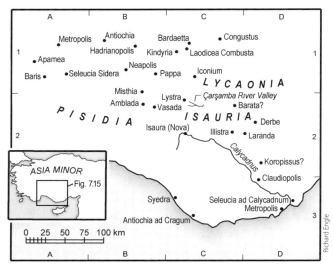

Fig. 7.15. Map of Pisidia, Lycaonia, and Isauria (Tres Eparchiae)

only from sex but also from marriage, meat, and wine, including substituting water for wine during their Eucharists.

In Lycaonia, Montanists and Novatianists appear to have merged a number of their communities during the immediate post-Constantinian period (Tabbernee 1997, 347–49). One inscription discovered near Laodicea Combusta (Lâdik/Halıcı) praises "Eugenios, the presbyter, who labored much for the sake of the holy Church of God of the Pure Ones" (G. Johnson 1995, 131–32 no. 4.10). Another inscription commemorates "Abras, most pious presbyter of the holy Church of God of the Novatianists" (G. Johnson 1995, 128–29 no. 4.8, altered).

The sarcophagus and epitaph of Marcus Julius Eugenius, the Montanist/Novatianist bishop of Laodicea Combusta (*IMont* 69), and a plaque honoring Eugenius's episcopal predecessor, Severus (*IMont* 70), have been discovered at Lâdik/Halıcı. Eugenius belonged to an influential family of the region and served as an officer at the headquarters of Valerius Diogenes, governor of Pisidia (ca. 311–313), at Antioch during a persecution of Christians by Maximin (see Tabbernee 1997, 434–35). Severus appears to have been martyred in about 312, as was another bishop from nearby Congustus (Altınekin), Gennadius (*IMont* 56).[27]

Eugenius's epitaph records that he was bishop of Laodicea Combusta for twenty-five years (ca. 315–ca. 340) and that during that time, at his own expense,

27. For further early Christian inscriptions from Laodicea Combusta and vicinity, see Mullen 2004, 99.

7.6 Text of Epitaph of Bishop Marcus Julius Eugenius of Laodicea Combusta

I, Markos Ioulios Eugenios son of Kyrillos Keleros a native of Kouessa a city-councilor, having been stationed as a soldier at the headquarters of the governor of Pisidia and having married Flaovia Ioulia Flaoviana, daughter of Gaios Nestoria-
5   nos, a senator, and having served as a soldier with distinction | and, meanwhile, when an order had been issued in the time of Maximinos that the Christians were to sacrifice and were not to be released from military service and having endured, repeatedly, very many tortures when Diogenes was governor, I hastened
10 to leave the service, keeping the faith of the Christians, | and having stayed a brief time in the city of the Laodikeians and having been appointed bishop by the will of almighty God, and having held the episcopal office for twenty-five
15 whole years with great distinction, and having rebuilt the entire church from its foundations, and having provided the | adornment of the whole including the surroundings, i.e., cloisters, antechambers, murals, mosaics, water-fountain, an entrance porch with all the attendant masonry work, and everything else, and when I was about to leave human life, I made for myself a supporting base and sarcophagus on which I commissioned the above to be engraved for the adornment of the church and of my family. (*IMont* 69 [trans. Tabbernee 1997, 428])

he completely renovated the church and its surroundings: its "cloisters, ante-chambers, murals, mosaics, water-fountain," and "entrance porch" (Tabbernee 1997, 428). Some of the building materials from Eugenius's church are still extant in Lâdik/Halıcı, including decorated stones embedded in the village's houses.

Eugenius did not attend Nicaea, but the bishops of other major Lycaonian cities did: Amblada (Hisartepe near Kızılca), Hadrianopolis (probably Koçaş), Pappa (Yunisler), Vasada (Bostandere), and, possibly, Misthia (Beyşehir).[28] Unfortunately, apart from the attestation of the pre-Constantinian existence of these Christian communities, nothing is known of their early history. Lycaonia has, however, produced numerous (mainly fourth-century) inscriptions belonging to other Christian ascetic groups such as the Encratites and Apotactites (e.g., Calder 1923, 84–91 nos. 8–11). Apotactites (Renouncers), like Encratites, abstained from sex, marriage, and certain kinds of food but also renounced the private use of property. Their origins are obscure, and they may simply have been a more extreme form of Encratism. The ministerial structure of both these groups, however, appears to have been similar to that of other Christian communities. An epitaph found near Sarayönü (ancient Bardaetta), for example, reads, "Here lies Anicetus, presbyter of the Apotactites. Eugraphius, presbyter,

28. See TIB 4:86, 206.

together with Brother Diophantus, presbyter, . . . erected this tombstone in remembrance" (Calder 1923, 86 no. 8, altered).

During the reorganization of Roman provinces under Diocletian, parts of western Cilicia, southern Lycaonia, and eastern Pamphylia were merged with Isauria. Isauria had formerly been part of Galatia and then of an administrative unit known as the Tres Eparchiae, consisting of Cilicia, Isauria, and Lycaonia. Beginning in the mid-third century Lycaonia was a separate province. Some of the pre-Constantinian inscriptions from the Çarşamba River Valley mentioned above come from the region by then part of the separate province of Isauria, as do others, especially from Isaura (Nova) (Zengibar Kalesi) and vicinity (Blanchetière 1981, nos. 513–14, 218–21, 225, 228, 234; Mullen 2004, 78). The expanded Diocletianic province of Isauria was represented at Nicaea by bishops from Antiochia ad Cragum (Güney Köy), Barata (probably Kızılkale), Claudiopolis (Mut), Ilistra (Yollarbaşi), Koropissus (probably Dağpazarı),

Fig. 7.16. Sarcophagus of Marcus Julius Eugenius, Laodicea Combusta

William Tabbernee

Fig. 7.17. Marcus Julius Eugenius's Epitaph

Drawing: Tabbernee 1997, 427, fig. 78b. Used with permission.

Fig. 7.18. Plaque Commemorating Severus of Laodicea Combusta

William Tabbernee

Laranda (Karaman), Metropolis (Tahta Limanı), Seleucia ad Calycadnum (Silifke), Syedra (Asartepe), and Umanada.[29] Claudiopolis is the city where Alpheios, Zosimus, and Alexander from Calytus were martyred, along with some other Christians. Orestes, a deacon martyred at Side—also during the Great Persecution—came from Umanada (Delehaye 1902, 814). Sometime dur-

29. Exact location unknown.

ing the early third century the first
known bishop of Laranda, Neon,
allowed a layperson named Euel-
pis to preach (Eusebius, *Hist. eccl.*
6.19.17). A different Neon and four
others were martyred in the same
city in the early fourth century
(Delehaye 1902, 43, 45, 178, 427).
On the outskirts of Seleucia, at a
location now known as Ayatekla, a
monastery and basilica were built
in the fifth century at the site where
Thecla is alleged to have spent her
final years (*Acts Paul* 43). During
the Byzantine period the cults of
the various martyrs spread rapidly
throughout Asia Minor, producing
a multitude of shrines, relics, and
(often completely legendary) *vitae*
(Mitchell 1993, 2:68–70).

Fig. 7.19. Basilica Dedicated to St. Thecla, Seleucia ad Calycadnum

North Galatia

In about 193 the now anonymous (Phrygian?) bishop who sent Avircius
Marcellus a copy of his anti-Montanist treatise had addressed the church at
Ancyra (modern Ankara) on the dangers of the New Prophecy movement
(*Fr.*, in Eusebius, *Hist. eccl.* 5.16.3). Consequently, we know that a Christian
community existed in Ancyra before the end of the second century. Presum-
ably, the Ancyran church had been founded much earlier.

Thus far, only one pre-Constantinian Ancyran inscription, an epitaph, commissioned by a woman named Aquilina for herself, her husband, and their children
Timothy and Paul (*IAnkyraBosch* 325), has been identified positively as Christian
(Mitchell 1993, 2:38n223, 2:62n56). That there were strong Christian communities
(including "sectarian" Christian communities) in and around Ancyra, however,
during the third and early fourth centuries is to be assumed on the basis of the
references to two martyrial churches in the *Passio Theodoti Ancyrani* (20, 26);
the Synod of Ancyra, held in 314, when Marcellus of Ancyra was bishop; and
Jerome's comment "Whoever has seen Ancyra, metropolis of Galatia, knows as

I do[30] by how many schisms it
is ripped apart even now. . . .
Vestiges of ancient foolishness
remain (there) to the present
day" (*Comm. Gal.* 2.2).

Dionysius, bishop of Al-
exandria in Egypt from 247/8
until his death (ca. 264/5),
refers to bishops of Galatia
in a letter, written in about
251/2, summarizing a no longer extant letter of Stephen I
of Rome (bp. 254–257). Unfortunately, Dionysius names

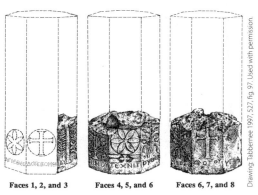

Faces 1, 2, and 3   Faces 4, 5, and 6   Faces 6, 7, and 8

Fig. 7.20. Column Base of Theodotus's Martyrium, Malos

Drawing: Tabbernee 1997, 527, fig. 97. Used with permission.

neither the bishops themselves nor the specific cities that they served (*Ep.*, in Eusebius, *Hist. eccl.* 7.5.4). One of the cities probably was Pessinus (Ballıhisar), as
a number of third-century Christian inscriptions (e.g., Blanchetière 1981, 508
nos. 164–65) have been found there and at nearby Spaleia (Sivrihisar) (Waelkens
1986, 294–95 nos. 772, 786). Another North Galatian city perhaps intended
by Dionysius may have been Iuliopolis (Sarılar), whose bishop, Philadelphus,
attended the Synod of Ancyra in 314 and, along with the bishops of Gdanmaa
(Çeşmelisebil), Kinna (Karahamzılı), and Tavium (Büyüknefes), was present at
Nicaea in 325. *Monumenta Asiae Minoris Antiqua* 7.417, found at Kerpişli,
may be evidence of ante-Nicene Christianity north of Gdanmaa. The cult of
St. Theodotus is attested epigraphically by Byzantine inscriptions (*IMont* 88,
89) at the martyrium built in his honor at Malos (Kalecik), approximately 50 km
northeast of Ancyra. The pre-Constantinian Christian community of Malos
(and Theodotus himself) probably was Montanist (Mitchell 1982; 1993, 2:93),
but this is not absolutely certain (Tabbernee 1997, 529–32). A reference to an
ancient village named Medicones[31] in the *Martyrdom of Theodotus of Ancyra*
(*Pass. Theod.* 10) perhaps indicates the existence of another pre-Constantinian Christian community in the vicinity of Ancyra (Harnack 1908, 2:217; but
see Mullen 2004, 131). Approximately 60 km southwest of Ancyra, Myrika
(Yeşilyurt) is the findspot of an inscription (Waelkens 1986, 298 no. 779) that
predates 212. It contains the names Peter and Paul, suggesting the existence of
a late second- or very early third-century Christian family (and community).
About 30 km farther southwest, a *tau* carved in the shape of a cross on the

30. Jerome had visited Ancyra in 373.
31. Exact location unknown.

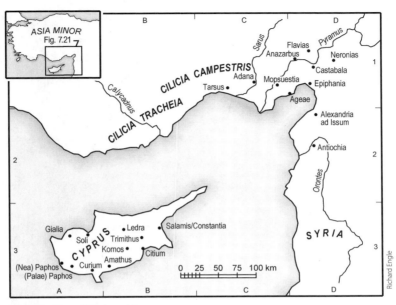

Fig. 7.21. Map of Cilicia and Cyprus

tombstone of a man named Irenaeus, found near Inlerkatrancı, probably points to a third-century Christian community at that as-yet-unidentified ancient settlement (Waelkens 1986, 302 no. 794).

CILICIA

From Acts 15:23, 41 it seems possible that there were Christian communities in Cilicia before Paul's so-called second missionary journey. Whether St. Paul had anything to do with the establishment of any of these churches, as perhaps suggested by Galatians 1:21 and Acts 15:36, is debatable. Frustratingly, Ignatius of Antioch does not tell us the exact Christian community in Cilicia from which the deacon Philo, one of his travel companions, came (*Phld.* 11.2).

Similarly, whether there was an early Christian community in Tarsus, where, according to Acts, St. Paul spent some time after his conversion to Christianity (9:30; 11:25–26a), is impossible to tell. The earliest reliably attested bishop of Tarsus[32] is Helenus (appointed ca. 250), who presided over a synod in Antioch-in-Syria that condemned Paul of Samosata, in 268 (Eusebius, *Hist. eccl.* 6.46.3; 7.5.1, 4; 7.28.1; 7.30.2). Subsequent bishops of Tarsus are recorded as having attended the Synod of Ancyra (314) and the Council of Nicaea (325). In the

---

32. The hagiographic reference to a man named Luke as the first bishop of Tarsus during the time of Nero (r. 54–68) may be dismissed as pious fiction (Delehaye 1902, 788).

Fig. 7.22. Roman Road, Tarsus

fourth century there was an Arian bishop of Tarsus, much to the annoyance of Basil the Great (*Ep.* 99, 102–3, 120–22, 128).

The earliest-known named Cilician bishop is Alexander, bishop of Flavias (Kadirli) (TIB 5:85–86, 378), during the reign of Septimius Severus (r. 193–211). Dionysius of Alexandria, around 251/2, refers to other, but unnamed, bishoprics in Cilicia (Eusebius, *Hist. eccl.* 7.5.1, 4). Presumably, these included Alexandria ad Issum (İskenderun), where another Alexander was bishop in about 188 (Pseudo-Dionysius of Tell Maḥrē, *Chron.* anno 2203).

In addition to the then-bishop of Tarsus, bishops from Adana, Ageae (Yamurtalık), Alexandria ad Issum, Castabala (Bodrum Kalesi), Epiphania (Gözene), Flavias, Mopsuestia (Yakapınar), and Neronias (Düziçi) attended Nicaea. Anazarbus (Anazarva Kalesi) was also a bishopric at that time (Theodoret, *Hist. eccl.* 1.4).

Lycia-Pamphylia

The capital and most important harbor city of Lycia-Pamphylia was Patara (Kelemiş Harabeleri). There, according to Acts 21:1–3, Paul embarked for Tyre (es-Sur) in Phoenicia on his way to Jerusalem at the end of his final missionary journey. When a Christian community was founded at Patara is not known, but, as with so many of the bishoprics of Asia Minor, it existed by 325. Eudemus, bishop of Patara, was present at Nicaea.

Olympus (Deliktaş) was the home of a prolific Christian author, Methodius. Like others of his time and Asiatic context, Methodius was strongly influenced by the Greek philosophers. He produced a number of "dialogues" against fictionalized opponents, including Origen (ca. 185–ca. 253) and Valentinus (fl. ca. 136–ca. 166). Methodius died around 311/2, perhaps as a martyr during the persecution under Maximin II (Jerome, *Vir. ill.* 83), but, contrary to Jerome, Methodius most likely was a layperson at, not the bishop of, Olympus

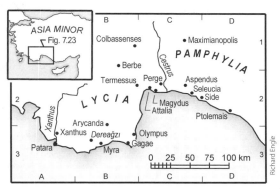

Fig. 7.23. Map of Lycia-Pamphylia

(Pauli and Schmidt 2000, 421). Perhaps, at the time of his death, he was bishop of Patara (Leontius Scholasticus, *Sect.* 3.1; TIB 8:781 [but see Mullen 2004, 103]).

In 312 Maximin published an edict in the Eastern provinces pressuring city officials to petition him to act officially against the Christian population in their midst. A number of cities responded positively to Maximin's edict, two of them being Arycanda (near Arif) and Colbassenses (Kuşbaba), as known from the text of extant inscriptions (*CIL* 3.12132; Mitchell 1988, 108).

According to tradition, St. Nicholas, patron saint of children and sailors, was born in Patara in about 300. Nicholas became bishop of Myra (near Demre). Acts 27:5–6 relates that St. Paul stayed briefly at Myra on his way to Rome for trial. Extensive remains of a basilica built in honor of St. Nicholas and restored by Justinian in the sixth century still exist, including a partially extant sarcophagus presumed to have been that of Nicholas.[33] Nothing, however, other than legend (e.g., *Acts Paul* 3.40–5.1) is known about the actual founding of Christianity at Myra. The story that a man named Nikandros was appointed Myra's first bishop by Titus, and that Nikandros was martyred along with a presbyter named Hermaios (see TIB 8:140, 344), is not credible.

Martyrologies report on a number of pre-Constantinian martyrdoms (and in some cases, martyr shrines) in cities of Lycia-Pamphylia other than Myra: Attalia (Antalya), Magydus (Lara), Perge (near Aksu), Ptolemais (Fığla Burnu), Side, Talmenia,[34] and Tritonion.[35] A third-century Christian community may have existed at Gagae (Yenice), the native town of a young man named Apphianus martyred at Caesarea Maritima (Qesaria) during the Great Persecution

33. In 1034 St. Nicholas's bones were taken by sailors to Bari, Italy, where they remain to this day in the crypt of the church dedicated to St. Nicholas in that city.

34. Location unknown.

35. Location unknown.

(Eusebius, *Mart. Pal.* 4.5). The ruins of four Christian basilicas in Xanthus (Kınık), one of which appears to be pre-Constantinian, attest the presence of Christianity in that city famous for its pillar tombs. Two amulets, one of which may be as early as the late third or early fourth century (Jordan and Kotansky 1996), reveal that at Xanthus, as elsewhere in Lycia-Pamphylia, the kind of Christianity practiced was very much influenced by Judaism.

From the originally Pamphylian sector of the Roman province of Lycia-Pamphylia, the bishops of Aspendus (Belkis Harabeleri), Berbe (Yelten), Magydus, Maximianopolis (near Kovanlık), Perge, Seleucia (near Kısalar),[36] and Termessus (Termesüs Harabesi) attended Nicaea. Perge, 16 km northeast of Attalia, in Roman and Byzantine times had an excellent harbor and is the site where, according to Acts, Paul, Barnabas, and John Mark disembarked on their journey from Cyprus (13:13), and where Paul preached prior to taking a ship back to Antioch-in-Syria from Attalia (14:24). Side, farther east along the Mediterranean coast, became Pamphylia's senior bishopric in the mid-fourth century.

Bithynia-Pontus

PONTUS

In about 112, probably at Amastris (Amasra) in Pontus during an assize tour (Sherwin-White 1966, 693–94), Pliny the Younger, the governor of the Roman province of Bithynia-Pontus (ca. 110/1–112/3), was presented with an unsigned document listing the names of a large number of people accused of being Christians (Pliny, *Ep.* 10.96.5). Pliny had never taken part in the trial of Christians and so, prudently, wrote to Trajan to give an account of the provisional action that he had taken, asking the emperor to instruct him further on the matter (10.96.1). Pliny reported that he had tested the loyalty of alleged Christians to the empire by getting them to curse Christ, recite a prayer to the gods, and offer a libation before statues of the gods and of Trajan himself (10.96.5). If they were not Roman citizens, Pliny had executed those who refused (10.96.3–4). Trajan confirmed that this was, indeed, the appropriate course of action (10.97.1). Trajan also stipulated that Christians were not to be sought out and that unsigned papers were not to be used as the basis for the trial of persons accused of Christianity (10.97.2).

The correspondence between Pliny and Trajan shows that, during the early part of the second century, Christianity was not an illegal religion (*religio illicita*) outlawed by universally binding laws. Instead, Christianity was a nuisance

---

36. Not to be confused with Seleucia ad Cadycadnus.

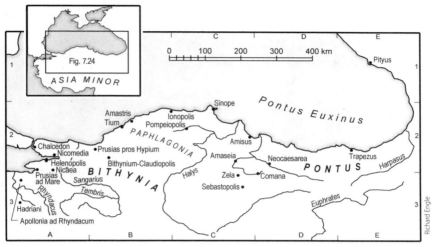

Fig. 7.24. Map of Bithynia-Pontus

cult whose members were considered potentially disloyal citizens because of their allegiance to Christ but who could easily prove their loyalty by renouncing Christ and participating in the customary religious rites associated with the imperial cult. The correspondence between Pliny and Trajan also shows that during the early decades of the second century, Christianity had spread to the villages as well as the cities of Bithynia-Pontus, and that there were Christians there of both sexes, of all ages, and of various ranks (10.96.9). According to Pliny, the temple-based economy of the region was suffering because of the high percentage of Christians in the population (10.96.10).

Among those named by the anonymous informer, some claimed that they had once been Christians but had given up being Christians long ago, some as long as twenty years previously (10.96.6). If accurate, this means that some former Christians had ceased being such in the early 90s and therefore must have become Christians in the 80s, if not earlier. Perhaps they had been members of the Christian communities in Pontus referred to in 1 Peter 1:1–2. First Peter was written sometime between 72 and 92 (Elliott 2000, 134–38), hence the Christian communities referred to by the author of 1 Peter must have been established no later than about 90 CE. Interestingly, Aquila, the husband of Priscilla, apparently was a Jewish native of Pontus (Acts 18:1) who settled in Rome at or before the time of Claudius. If accurate, this may mean that Priscilla too was from Pontus. The view that the apostle Andrew evangelized the area around Amastris (*Vita S. Andreae* [PG 120.221–24]) is, however, pure legend.

7.7 Pliny's Letter to Trajan Concerning Christians

1 It is my custom, lord emperor, to refer to you all questions whereof I am in doubt. Who can better guide me when I am at a stand, or enlighten me if I am in ignorance? In investigations of Christians I have never taken part; hence
2 I do not know what is the crime usually punished or investigated, or what allowances are made. So I have had no little uncertainty whether there is any distinction of age, or whether the very weakest offenders are treated exactly like the stronger; whether pardon is given to those who repent, or whether a man who has once been a Christian gains nothing by having ceased to be such; whether punishment attaches to the mere name apart from secret crimes, or to the secret crimes connected with the name. Meantime this is the course I
3 have taken with those who were accused before me as Christians. I asked them whether they were Christians, and if they confessed, I asked them a second and third time with threats of punishment. If they kept to it, I ordered them for execution; for I held no question that whatever it was that they admitted,
4 in any case obstinacy and unbending perversity deserve to be punished. There were others of the like insanity; but as these were Roman citizens, I noted them down to be sent to Rome.

Before long, as is often the case, the mere fact that the charge was taken
5 notice of made it commoner, and several distinct cases arose. An unsigned paper was presented, which gave the name of many. As for those who said that they neither were nor ever had been Christians, I thought it right to let them go, since they recited a prayer to the gods at my dictation, supplication with incense and wine to your statue, which I had ordered to be brought into court for the purpose together with the images of the gods, and moreover cursed Christ—
6 things which (so it is said) those who are really Christians cannot be made to do. Others who were named by the informer said that they were Christians and then denied it, explaining that they had been, but had ceased to be such, some three years ago, some a good many years, and a few even twenty. All these too both worshipped your statue and the images of the gods, and cursed Christ.
7 They maintained, however, that the amount of their fault or error had been this, that it was their habit on a fixed day to assemble before daylight and recite by turns a form of words to Christ as a god; and that they bound themselves with an oath, not for any crime, but not to commit theft or robbery or adultery, not to break their word, and not to deny a deposit when demanded. After this was done, their custom was to depart, and to meet again to take food, but ordinary and harmless food; and even this (they said) they had given up doing after the
8 issue of my edict, by which in accordance with your commands I had forbidden the existence of clubs. On this I considered it the more necessary to find out from two maid-servants who were called deaconesses, and that by torments, how far this was true: but I discovered nothing else than a perverse and extravagant

superstition. I therefore adjourned the case and hastened to consult you. The
9 matter seemed to me worth deliberation, especially on account of the number
of those in danger; for many of all ages and every rank, and also of both sexes
are brought into present or future danger. The contagion of that superstition has
penetrated not the cities only, but the villages and country; yet it seems possible
10 to stop it and set it right. At any rate it is certain enough that the almost deserted
temples begin to be resorted to, that long disused ceremonies of religion are
restored, and that fodder for victims finds a market, whereas buyers till now
were very few. From this it may easily be supposed, what a multitude can be
reclaimed, if there be a place of repentance. (*Ep.* 10.96.1–10 [trans. Stevenson
2013, 20–21, altered])

Exactly why the former Christians in or around Amastris had apostatized
some years before the governorship of Pliny is not clear, although, as Robin
Lane Fox (1989, 271) points out, it could not have been because of persecution.
Perhaps they, like other notable pagan apostates, such as Peregrinus (Lucian,
Peregr. 11–16), were attracted by more sophisticated forms of philosophy or,
like a man named Aquila (Epiphanius, *Mens.* 14–15), were Jews who returned
to Judaism. In any case, not all converts to Christianity remained such (see Lane
Fox 1989, 271). Many Christians, nevertheless, remained loyal to their faith. Dionysius of Corinth (fl. ca. 170) wrote a letter to Amastris and the other churches
in Pontus, mentioning by name Palmas, the bishop of Amastris (Eusebius, *Hist.
eccl.* 4.23.6). In the 190s this same Palmas, by then an old man, presided over a
synod of the bishops of Pontus dealing with the date of Easter (5.23.2).

Not long after the time when some of the Christians in the vicinity of
Amastris were abandoning their religion, a man named Marcion was born
in Sinope (Sinop), the predominant maritime city on the southern shores
of the Black Sea. According to a tradition known to Epiphanius, Marcion's
father was the "catholic" bishop (*Pan.* 42.1.3), attesting the existence of a
Christian community at Sinope prior to about 140, when Marcion moved to
Rome (perhaps following a scandal [42.1.3–6]). At Sinope, Marcion had been
a wealthy shipowner (Tertullian, *Praescr.* 30.1). At first, Marcion was well received by the Christian community at Rome, not least because of his generosity.
Marcion's financial gifts, however, were later returned to him when he was
excommunicated (30.2). Marcion subsequently established his own Christian
communities, which spread rapidly as far as Syria and Egypt (Justin, *1 Apol.*
26; Epiphanius, *Pan.* 42.1.1). The Marcionite communities utilized a unique
canon of Scripture consisting of truncated versions of the Gospel attributed
to Luke and ten Pauline epistles. Marcion and his followers, in "Gnostic-like"

fashion, distinguished between the (to Marcion inferior) God of the Hebrew Bible and the (good) God revealed by Jesus.

While there is no evidence of the New Prophecy in Pontus-Bithynia, Hippolytus (ca. 170–236/7) gives an account of a "Montanist-like" prophet in rural Pontus who, in about 200, predicted the imminent end of the world (Comm. Dan. 4.19).

The spread of Christianity along the south coast of the Black Sea must have been sporadic. According to a mainly legendary account of the life and ministry of Gregory the Wonderworker (ca. 210/3–ca. 270/5), when Gregory (a student of Origen's at Alexandria) became bishop of his native city Neo-caesarea (Niksar) around 238/9, there were only seventeen Christians; three decades later, at his death, there were only seventeen non-Christians (Gregory of Nyssa, Vit. Greg. Thaum. [PG 46.909b–c, 46.920a]; see Mitchell 1993, 2:53–57). Gregory had been consecrated bishop by Phaedimus, bishop of Amaseia (Amasya). Athenodorus, Gregory the Wonderworker's brother, also became a bishop in Pontus (Eusebius, Hist. eccl. 6.30; 7.14; 7.28.1). The paternal grand-parents of Gregory of Nyssa (bp. 372–ca. 395) and his more famous brother, Basil of Caesarea (see below), were third-century Christians in Pontus. During the Great Persecution they took refuge on their estates in Pontus before the grandfather was (most likely) martyred (Gregory of Nazianzus, Laud. Bas. [PG 36.501a]; Gregory of Nyssa, Vit. Macr. 2, 20.11; see Mitchell 1993, 2:65, 68). By the time of Licinius (r. 308–324), there were multiple church buildings in Amaseia, some of which Licinius leveled to the ground and some of which he closed, executing a number of bishops, including those of neighboring districts (Eusebius, Vit. Const. 2.1.2–2.2.1–2).

Pontus was well represented at Nicaea. The bishops of Amastris, Amaseia, Comana (Kılıçlı), Ionopolis (Inebolu), Pityus (Bichvinta, Georgia), Pompeiopo-lis (Taşköprü), Trapezus (Trabzon), and Zela (Zile) attended, indicating the existence of pre-Constantinian churches in those cities. Meletius, bishop of Sebastopolis (Sulusaray), was a supporter of Arius (ca. 256/60–ca. 336) at the time (Philostorgius, Hist. eccl. 1.8). Three late third-century inscriptions from Amisus (Samsun) and its vicinity also attest the existence of early Christian communities there (IPont 11, 15, 72).

BITHYNIA

The western part of the province ruled by Pliny consisted of the former king-dom of Bithynia, of which Nicomedia (İzmit) and Nicaea (İznik) were the most significant (and rival) cities. Pliny's official residence was at Nicaea. During his time in office, Pliny built a theater at Nicaea, parts of which are still visible today. As noted, in 325 Constantine hosted the first "ecumenical" council of Christian bishops at Nicaea. Small remnants of a sixth-century basilica built by Justinian that, in 787, was the site of the Second Council of Nicaea, are also extant.

Four pre-Constantinian Christian inscriptions have come to light from Nicaea and its immediate vicinity (Blanchetière 1981, 319, 515 nos. 241–44). One of these, an inscription recording that the construction of a tomb "for Aurelios Attikos, Aurelia Trophimia, and myself," was commissioned by "Aurelia Chreste, daughter of Polion" (G. Johnson 1995, 151), probably belongs to the late third century (Blanchetière 1981, 515), as does certainly the epitaph of an imperial bodyguard (see below).

Almost no traces of the Roman or Byzantine period have survived in İzmit, even though Nicomedia was the eastern capital during the tetrarchy established by Diocletian. According to Lactantius (ca. 250–ca. 325), it was at Nicomedia that Galerius (r. 293–311) persuaded Diocletian to commence the systematic action against Christianity, initiating the Great Persecution (*Mort.* 11.1–13.1). Significantly, one of the first anti-Christian activities undertaken was the physical destruction of the Christian basilica at Nicomedia, which, Lactantius tells us, was a very tall building, situated on high ground, and visible from the imperial palace (*Mort.* 12.2–5). Obviously, by the early fourth century the Christian community at Nicomedia was neither insignificant nor invisible (cf. Eusebius, *Hist. eccl.* 9.13b–22).

Earlier, Diocletian had agreed to make it illegal for court officials and military officers to be Christians (Lactantius, *Mort.* 11.3). As noted, a late third-century epitaph of a Christian member of the imperial *protectores* (bodyguards), a man named Flavius, has been discovered at Nicaea (G. Johnson 1995, 100–101 no. 3.10). Like some of the other pre-Constantinian inscriptions found at Nicaea, the Christian nature of Flavius's epitaph is guaranteed by its use of the word *koimētērion*.[37] Another late third-century Christian epitaph found at İzmit (G. Johnson 1995, 106–7 no. 3.14) commemorates a woodcarver named Papos, originally from Aradus (Arwad) in Phoenicia.

Pliny's comment to Trajan that there were Christians of every rank in his province (*Ep.* 10.96.9) is borne out by a third-century Christian epitaph (G. Johnson 1995, 80–81 no. 3.1) from Bithynium-Claudiopolis (Bolu) commemorating one Markos Demetrianos, who had served as senior magistrate, general administrator, and supervisor of games and public entertainment. Another pre-Constantinian Christian tombstone from Bithynium-Claudiopolis honors C. Offelius Iullus, a citizen of Ephesus (*IKlaudiop* 174; see Mitchell 1993, 2:38). At the outset of the Great Persecution in February 303, a citizen of Nicomedia described by Eusebius as "not obscure but very highly honored with distinguished temporal

---

37. That is, "sleeping-place" (see Tabbernee 1997, 423).

dignities" (*Hist. eccl.* 8.5.1 [*NPNF*[2] 1:326]) tore down Diocletian's edict, ripping it into pieces, while Diocletian and Galerius were still in the eastern capital (8.5.1). Not surprisingly, the unnamed but highly placed Nicomedian Christian was martyred, along with some others, including members of the imperial household and Anthimus, the bishop of Nicomedia (8.5.2–8.6.8a). At about the same time Autonomus, the first known bishop of Bithynium-Claudiopolis, was martyred in that city (Foss 1987, 187–98). Christianity, however, was present in Bithynium-Claudiopolis from at least the late second century, as attested by *IKlaudiop* 177: "Neither gold nor silver[38] but bones lie here but awaiting the trumpet call.[39] Do not disturb the work of God the begetter[40] [. . .]" (Prior 2002, 102).

A rescript by Maximin issued in 311 to explain his stringent anti-Christian measures attests that by the early fourth century there were still numerous Christians throughout Bithynia, especially in Nicomedia (Eusebius, *Hist. eccl.* 9.13b–22). Eusebius of Nicomedia (d. ca. 341/2), bishop of the Christian community in that city from 318 until 338/9, when he became bishop of Constantinople (İstanbul), was a supporter of Arius at Nicaea. Despite being out of favor with Constantine for a period of time over his pro-Arian views, this Eusebius, at Nicomedia, was the senior bishop among those who baptized Constantine on the latter's deathbed (Eusebius, *Vit. Const.* 4.61–64).

The early history of Christianity in Bithynia is not known. First Peter 1:1–2 suggests that, as in the case of Pontus, at least by about 90 there were Christian communities in Bithynia. A hundred years later Dionysius of Corinth wrote an anti-Marcionite letter to the church at Nicomedia (Eusebius, *Hist. eccl.* 4.23.4), perhaps indicating that the Christian community there was troubled by the teachings and especially the canon of Scripture promoted by the followers of Marcion. Dionysius of Alexandria, in letters written soon after the end of the Decian persecution (251/2), refers to unnamed bishops in Bithynia (*Ep.*, in Eusebius, *Hist. eccl.* 7.5.2). In addition to Eusebius of Nicomedia and Theognis of Nicaea, the bishops of Hadriani (Orhaneli), Apollonia ad Rhyndacum (Apolyont), Chalcedon (Kadıköy), Tium (Hisarönü), and two cities called Prusias (Prusias ad Mare [Gemlik] and Prusias pros Hypium [Konuralp]) attended Nicaea. There was a Church of the Martyrs at Helenopolis (Hersek), which Constantine visited just before his death in 337 (Eusebius, *Vit. Const.* 4.61). Novatianist churches existed in Bithynia during the fourth century (Socrates, *Hist. eccl.* 1.13; 4.28), if not earlier.

38. Cf. Acts 3:6.
39. Cf. 1 Thess. 4:16; 1 Cor. 15:52.
40. Cf. Rom. 14:20.

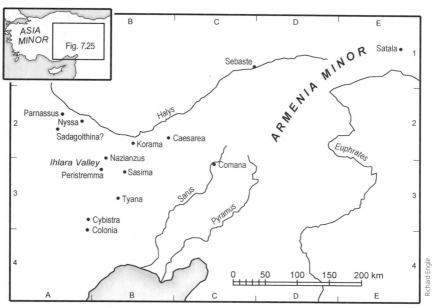

Fig. 7.25. Map of Cappadocia

Cappadocia

As in the case of Pontus and Bithynia, we know from 1 Peter 1:1–2 of the existence of Christian communities in Cappadocia by about 90 CE. Apart from this reference, however, the literary sources are silent about the development of Christianity in Roman Asia Minor's large eastern province until the middle of the second century.

The Martyrdom of Justin and His Companions relates that Euelpistus, one of those put to death along with Justin Martyr, came from Cappadocia, where he grew up in a Christian family (4.7), presupposing a Christian community in his hometown or village. According to Tertullian (ca. 160/70–ca. 220), the wife of Claudius Lucius Herminianus, the governor of Cappadocia sometime between 180 and 196, converted to Christianity. Furious, Herminianus took his revenge on the Christians, causing some through torture to apostatize until, so the story goes, his vital organs were eaten by worms and he saw the error of his ways (*Scap.* 3.4).

Early in the third century the Alexander who had been bishop of Flavias in Cilicia apparently became bishop of Caesarea in Cappadocia (Gregory of Nyssa, *Vit. Greg. Thaum.* [PG 46.905]; Harnack 1908, 2:194n1) before becoming bishop of Jerusalem, in about 212, where he established a library consisting mainly of the letters of contemporary bishops and other church leaders (Eusebius, *Hist. eccl.* 6.8.7; 6.20.1). As already indicated, one of Alexander's episcopal successors at Caesarea was Firmilian (bp. ca. 232–ca. 269). Firmilian's correspondence with Cyprian of Carthage (bp. 248/9–258) provides some information about the Christian community at Caesarea in the 250s, including the presence of a (Montanist?) prophetess (*Ep.*, in Cyprian, 75.10.1–11.1). Firmilian visited Origen in Caesarea Maritima (Eusebius, *Hist. eccl.* 6.27.1), but the view that Origen, in turn, visited Firmilian in Caesarea in Cappadocia and resided there for two years in the house of a Christian woman named Juliana is based on a mistaken reading of Palladius, *Historia Lausiaca* 64, and Eusebius, *Historia ecclesiastica* 6.17.1 (McGuckin 2004, 19–20). Only one definitely third-century Christian inscription from Caesarea has been discovered thus far: the epitaph of a wagonmaster originally from Phrygia (Grégoire 1909, 67 no. 46).

In 258 the forebears of Ulfila (ca. 306/11–383), the later "Bishop of the Goths," were among Cappadocian Christians kidnapped by Gothic invaders (Philostorgius, *Hist. eccl.* 2.5) from the ancient village of Sadagolthina (Karamollausaği?), near the city of Parnassus (Değirmenyolu). In 325 the then-bishop of Parnassus attended Nicaea, along with the bishops of six other Cappadocian cities—Caesarea, Tyana (Kemerhisar), Colonia (Aksaray), Cybistra (Ereğlı), Comana (Şar), and Spania[41]—attesting pre-Constantinian Christian communities in those cities. Five Cappadocian *chorepiscopi*[42] also attended Nicaea, indicating the presence of Christianity in the Cappadocian countryside.

By 325 part of northeastern Cappadocia had become the province of Armenia Minor, from which the bishops of Sebaste (Sivas) and Satala (Sadak) attended Nicaea. At Sebaste, during Licinius's persecution, a number of Christian soldiers had been martyred (Sozomen, *Hist. eccl.* 9.2.1). According to tradition, the "Forty Martyrs of Sebaste" belonged to the Legio XII Fulminata stationed at Melitene (Eskimalatya). Irrespective of the reliability of the tradition about the soldier-martyrs (Musurillo 1972, xlix), it appears that there was a considerable Christian population at Melitene (Eusebius, *Hist. eccl.* 8.6.8–10; 9.8.2) from which soldiers may well have been recruited (cf. 5.5.1–6). Melitene was a prosperous city on the Euphrates (Firat Nehri) located strategically on the main border crossing into the (non-Roman) kingdom of Armenia. Around 251/2, Dionysius of Alexandria wrote to the Christians

41. Location unknown.

42. That is, rural bishops without the full authority or function of city bishops. *Chorepiscopi* were numerous throughout Asia Minor during the third and fourth centuries, especially in Cappadocia (Mitchell 1993, 2:70–72).

in Armenia Minor, referring to Meruzanes as their bishop (Eusebius, *Hist. eccl.* 6.46.3). Whether this man was bishop of Melitene, Sebaste (Harnack 1908, 2:197), or some other city in any of the areas designated Armenia is now impossible to tell.

In 325 some bishops on their way to Nicaea halted their journey through Cappadocia at Nazianzus (near Bekarlar). There they converted the (future) father of Gregory of Nazianzus (ca. 329–390). Gregory the Elder and his family had belonged to the Hypsistarians, a sect that, in a syncretistic manner, worshiped the "Most High God" (*NewDocs* 1:25–29; Mitchell 1993, 2:49–51), kept the Jewish sabbath and dietary laws but not circumcision, and practiced Hellenistic tolerance (Gregory of Nazianzus, *Or.* 18.5). Presumably, the Christian community that gave hospitality to the bishops who converted Gregory had been established in the pre-Constantinian period (Harnack 1908, 2:193). Gregory's wife, Nonna, had been brought up in a Christian family.

By the time the son Gregory was born, the elder Gregory had become bishop of Nazianzus (ca. 326) and used some of his own considerable funds to construct Nazianzus's first church building. The younger Gregory was ordained in 361, for a time assisted his father at Nazianzus, and in 371 was, against his will, appointed bishop of Sasima (Hasanköy) by Basil of Caesarea as an anti-Arian political strategy. Although Gregory never took up the appointment, the appointment illustrates that there existed Christian communities even in insignificant rural villages throughout Cappadocia in the 370s. Gregory became bishop of an "orthodox" (i.e., non-Arian) congregation in Constantinople in 379 and patriarch of Constantinople in 381. He presided over the first part of the famous Council of Constantinople in the same year, before being forced out of office. In 382 he (again somewhat reluctantly) became bishop of Nazianzus, his hometown, retiring in 384 to the nearby family estate, where he died in about 389/90.

Gregory of Nazianzus (the Theologian), Basil of Caesarea (Basil the Great), and Basil's younger brother Gregory (Gregory of Nyssa) compose the so-called Cappadocian Fathers. These three men, along with Macrina (the sister of Basil and Gregory), significantly shaped both the theology and lifestyle of fourth-century Christianity not only in Cappadocia but also in the East as a whole, especially in terms of monasticism (Mitchell 1993, 2:109–21; Elm 1994). A large number of Byzantine rock-cut monasteries and churches are still extant in Cappadocia, especially in the Ihlara Valley near ancient Peristremma (Belisırma) and in the area around Korama (Göreme).

Cyprus

According to the author of the Acts of the Apostles, Paul and Barnabas were not the earliest "Jesus followers" in Cyprus. Acts 11:19 relates that the persecution that resulted from the confrontation of Stephen with the Jewish authorities and his ultimate execution by stoning (6:8–8:1) led to the scattering of some of the early disciples not only throughout Judaea and Samaria (8:2) but also to Phoenicia, Syria (Antioch), and Cyprus. As with much of the data presented in Acts, scholars disagree about whether the information about Cyprus is historically accurate or part of the theologically determined framework presented by the author about the spread of Christianity from Jerusalem "to the ends of the earth" (1:8).

Because of its closer proximity to Alexandria, the Ptolemies, in the second century BCE, moved the capital of Cyprus from Salamis (Ammokhostos) to Paphos—strictly speaking, Nea Paphos (New Paphos), now known as Kato Paphos (Lower Paphos). The refounded city was strategically located with a superb harbor. For most of the Roman occupation of the island, Paphos was also the capital; although, when Cyprus was first annexed by the Romans in 58 BCE, it was incorporated into the province of Cilicia in Asia Minor. During the Byzantine era Cyprus was allocated to the Diocese of Oriens and ruled directly from Constantinople. Salamis, renamed Constantia, once again became the (local) capital of the island. Salamis is the traditional birthplace of Joseph (or Josephus), nicknamed Barnabas (Son of Exhortation) by the apostles (Acts 4:36).

Pre-Constantinian Christianity

The fifth-century *Acts of Barnabas* compensates for the paucity of genuine historical data about the life and ministry of Barnabas in Cyprus. It contains legendary accounts such as the story that he and St. Paul baptized Heracleides, a man who allegedly had been their guide from Salamis to Paphos (cf. Acts 13:6), and the report that Barnabas subsequently consecrated Heracleides as the island's first bishop (*Acts Barn.* 16–17). The *Acts of Barnabas* also relates Barnabas's alleged martyrdom at Salamis (22–23). Anthemius, a late fifth-century bishop of Salamis,[43] fortuitously discovered the "tomb of St. Barnabas" with the body of Barnabas cradling his own handwritten copy of the Gospel of Mark in his arms. The discovery was made just in time to secure the independence of the Cypriot church from Antiochene control in

---

43. By then called Constantia, after the city's reconstruction in about 350 by Constantius II (r. 337–361).

William Tabbernee

Fig. 7.26. Tomb of St. Barnabas, Salamis

478. As already mentioned, the Acts of the Apostles relates that Paul and Barnabas, accompanied by John Mark, commenced their missionary activity in Cyprus at Salamis (13:4), that they made a favorable impression on the governor at Paphos (13:6–11), and that Barnabas and John Mark later returned to Cyprus (15:39). It is possible that John Mark also had familial ties with Cyprus (Col. 4:10).

Reliable data about the history of Christianity on Cyprus before the time of Constantine are scarce. Three bishops from Cyprus attended Nicaea. Two of these were the then-bishops of Salamis and Paphos, named Gelasius and Cyril respectively, suggesting (but not proving) the continuity of the Christian community from the time of Paul and Barnabas. The third Cypriot bishop present at Nicaea was Spyridon of Trimithus (Trimithousa). Some stories about Spyridon are preserved via Rufinus of Aquileia (ca. 345–ca. 411/2) by Socrates Scholasticus (ca. 380/1–ca. 450) and Sozomen (fl. ca. 445) in their ecclesiastical histories (Socrates, *Hist. eccl.*1.12.1–5; Sozomen, *Hist. eccl.* 1.11.8–9; cf. Rufinus, *Hist.* 10.5). The first bishop of Ledra (Lefkosia/Nicosia) known to us is Triphyllius (fl. ca. 340), famous for his erudition (Sozomen, *Hist. eccl.* 1.11.8–9) and for his commentary on Song of Songs, which Jerome claims to have read (*Vir. ill.* 92).

Archaeological Evidence

Judging from the numerous remains of basilicas, dating from the late fourth century onward at places such as Soli (Morphou), Christianity in Cyprus spread rapidly in the post-Constantinian era; however, it is almost certain that Christianity already existed in some of these places, as it did in Paphos and

Salamis. For example, tradition has it that in 327 Helena, the mother of Constantine, established a church and monastery near Citium (modern Larnaca) on the ruins of a temple to Aphrodite, allegedly putting a piece of the "True Cross" in the center of the church's own new wooden cross. At Kornos, not far from the "Monastery of the Mountain of the Cross," is the "Monastery of St. Thecla," built on the site of another fourth-century church allegedly built by St. Helena. That there were already Christian communities in the area even before 327 may be attested by an inscription from Citium utilizing the letter *chi*, tilted, perhaps to represent crosses (di Cesnola 1877, 434 no. 85).

Similar possibly "crypto-Christian" use of the letter *chi* occurs in extant third-century inscriptions from Curium (*IKourion* 150) and the territory of Amathus at Spitali, Gerasa, and Apesia (Mitford 1990, 2207–8). Philoneides of Curium (modern Kourion) was martyred during the time of Diocletian. At Amathus (Lemesos), as at Curium, the remnants of fifth- and sixth-century basilicas are being excavated. Perhaps one of these was that of Tychon of Amathus. His very existence, however, has been questioned (e.g., Usener 1907) as Tychon is also the name of a male fertility god associated with Priapos.

Sanctuaries or temples dedicated to Aphrodite existed in numerous Cypriot cities, the most splendid of which was at (Palae) Paphos (Old Paphos) near the village of Kouklia, 16 km southeast of (Nea) Paphos, closely rivaled by that of Amathus (Mitford 1990, 2186–87). Other popular cults in Cyprus were those of Apollo (often associated with Aphrodite) and of Zeus, especially Zeus Olympios at Salamis. During the third century CE, however, many of the cults imported to Cyprus, including the imperial cults, had lost some ground, particularly among more educated Cypriots, making them more open to embracing sects such as the Hypsistarians or adopting new religions such as Christianity (Mitford 1990, 2209).

Heterodoxy

Not all forms of Christianity in Cyprus were of the sort that were deemed to be "orthodox" in the post-Constantinian era. For example, Epiphanius, bishop of Salamis/Constantia and the early church's most renowned heresiologist, relates that it was in Cyprus that Valentinus separated from the true faith (*Pan.* 31.7.2). Valentinus, reportedly born in Egypt and educated at Alexandria (31.2.3), was one of the great Christian intellectuals of the second century. He lived, wrote, and taught in Rome during the episcopates of Hyginus, Pius I, and Anicetus (Irenaeus, *Haer.* 3.4.3)—that is, approximately 136–166. If Tertullian's information that Valentinus was upset at having been passed over for

Fig. 7.27. Remains of Epiphanius's Basilica, Salamis/Constantia

the position of bishop of Rome (*Val.* 4.1–2) is accurate, Valentinus may have left for Cyprus earlier rather than later during the time when Anicetus was bishop (ca. 155–ca. 166). It is also possible that an external event, such as the great plague that occurred around 166, provided the impetus for Valentinus's departure from Rome (Lampe 2003a, 294n8).

Shipwrecked on the way to Cyprus (Epiphanius, *Pan.* 31.7.2), Valentinus also, from an "orthodox" perspective, made a wreck of the Christian faith by perverting it through philosophical speculations. Such "Gnostic-like," but not necessarily "Gnostic," speculations (Markschies 1992, 402–7; cf. M. Williams 1996; King 2003), however, made "Valentinianism" extremely attractive to educated "pagans" tired of "paganism" in Cyprus as well as on the mainland in Asia Minor.

The Nature of Early Christianity in Asia Minor and Cyprus

Without overstating the case, there is little doubt that, at least for some forms of early Christianity in Asia Minor and Cyprus, certain aspects of paganism and Judaism influenced the type(s) of Christianity that developed. Regardless of whether Montanus had really been a priest of Apollo/Cybele, as claimed by some late opponents of Montanism, the role of prophetic oracles in the lives of ordinary people engaged in the cult of Apollo/Cybele cannot but have affected the nature of prophesying within the "New Prophecy." Similarly, the claim on legitimate prophetic succession via the daughters of Philip in Hierapolis and Ammia and Quadratus in Philadelphia by the opponents of Montanism (e.g., Anonymous, *Fr.*, in Eusebius, *Hist. eccl.* 5.17.2–3) shows that even "mainstream" Christianity in Lydia and Phrygia operated in a context in which prophesying and the utterance of prophetic oracles were considered the norm.

The legitimacy of the role of women as prophets, presbyters, and even bishops within Montanism and some other groups in Asia Minor may also owe something to the predominance of native Phrygian cults that venerated mother goddesses such as Cybele.

Judaism also continued to influence the life and thought of Christianity in Asia Minor and Cyprus, not merely because of common origins but because of close interaction between the two groups. This is seen especially by burial practices in cities such as Acmonia and Eumeneia and by the setting of the date of Easter by Christians in the region to accord with the Jewish Passover. Until Nicaea, all Christians in Asia Minor kept to the tradition that the fourteenth day of the Jewish month Nisan was the beginning of the Paschal festival (e.g., Polycrates, *Ep.*, in Eusebius, *Hist. eccl.* 5.24.2–7), regardless of the date of Easter set by Christian communities elsewhere. Even after the so-called Quartodeciman controversy (i.e., the controversy over the "fourteenth day") was allegedly settled in the immediate post-Nicene period, some Phrygian Novatianists and Montanists kept to the practice of correlating Easter with the Jewish Passover (Mitchell 1993, 2:98). The impact of Judaism (as well as certain aspects of Lydian and Phrygian paganism) may also be discerned in the prominence of angels, especially the archangel Michael, in Christian popular piety in Asia Minor and Cyprus.

The vastness of Asia Minor and the location of Cyprus as an island in the Mediterranean Sea meant that many communities within the region were geographically isolated, especially those in mountainous districts. Such isolation included isolation from the major centers of imperial power. Consequently, even in times of persecution elsewhere in the empire, Christians living in remote areas were unlikely to be threatened by civil authorities. For example, the pre-Constantinian "Christians for Christians" tombstones erected in the cities and villages of the Upper Tembris Valley testify to the peaceful cohabitation of pagans and Christians in that part of Phrygia. Presumably, imperial procurators were more interested in supervising the large agricultural estates in their jurisdiction than implementing anti-Christian edicts—if they even received copies of, or information about, such edicts. Similarly, the large proportion of the population that epigraphy attests as Christian in the Çarşamba Valley on the border of Isauria and Lycaonia during the third century demonstrates an unusually high degree of toleration for Christianity by local officials.

Elsewhere in Asia Minor and Cyprus, especially in the larger cities, Christians fell victim to local pograms in the period before Decius and to emperor-initiated persecutions after Decius. Numerous "acts of the martyrs" tell stories (some believable, others totally spurious) of a multitude of martyrs in the various provinces of Asia Minor and in Cyprus. From the second century, if not earlier, relics of martyrs were collected, and, especially in the post-Constantinian era, the cults of individual martyrs or of groups such as the Forty Martyrs of Sebaste were established throughout Asia Minor and Cyprus. Some, like the cult of St. Mamas, were established in both places. In Mamas's case there was a martyrial church with his relics at Caesarea in Cappadocia (where, according to one tradition, he was martyred) and another Church of St. Mamas with his relics at an ancient site near Güzelyurt in Cyprus (where, according to a different tradition, the coffin containing his martyred body washed ashore after having been set adrift on the coast of Asia Minor).

Major changes in political structures also affected the way in which Christian life and thought were shaped in Asia Minor and Cyprus. The most important political unit in the region during early Roman times was "the city" and "the territory" that the city controlled. Around 100 CE, if the estimates by Rodney Stark (1996, 131–32) are accurate, three cities in Asia Minor had populations of 100,000 or above (Ephesus: 200,000; Pergamum: 120,000; Sardis: 100,000). Smyrna had a population of about 75,000, and Salamis in Cyprus about 35,000. Most cities in Asia Minor and Cyprus, however, were much smaller. The population of Pepouza, for example, appears to have been around 5,000. The (often extensive) territory of each city encompassed a number of other settlements ranging from towns without city status to tiny rural villages. These settlements, at least during the first and second centuries CE, added significantly to the number of people under a particular city's control.

Judging from epigraphic evidence, by the middle of the third century a surprisingly large number of Christians in Asia Minor were local city councilors or senators. Their existence not only shows that, by that time, people of high social status had become Christians but also suggests that such Christians could, theoretically at least, have exerted considerable political influence on behalf of Christianity. As noted, by the beginning of the fourth century, some cities in Phrygia had declared themselves to be predominantly (if not totally) Christian.

The smaller settlements located on the territories of cities technically owed allegiance to the city on whose territory they were situated, but in reality they were more or less self-governing. Village elders and other local leaders determined much of what happened in these settlements, including the extent of toleration of Christianity in general or of Christian subsects in particular. This was the case in the post-Constantinian era as well as in pre-Constantinian times.

Whereas pre-Constantinian (pagan) emperors had sought to maintain the "peace of the gods" (the *pax deorum*) by occasionally persecuting all groups (especially Christians) deemed a threat to the well-being of the empire, after Nicaea (Christian) emperors sought to maintain the "peace of God" (the *pax Dei*) by persecuting all (Christian) groups suspected of heresy. "Orthodox" Christian bishops often worked hand in glove with imperial officials to root out Arians, Marcionites, Valentinians, Montanists, and members of other "deviant" groups. Frequently, the bishop himself became the imperial official, especially when ecclesiastical dioceses came to parallel imperial ones following the restructure of the provinces of Asia Minor in the fourth century.

Bishops such as Basil the Great, as metropolitan of Caesarea in Cappadocia, wielded a great deal of influence and authority both formally and informally. He appointed friends and colleagues (even, as in the case of Gregory of Nazianzus, against their will) to vacant sees in order to prevent these sees from being occupied by Arian bishops. In continuity with the politics of village life in Cappadocia (and elsewhere), Basil also appointed numerous *chorepiscopi*, illustrating that even the ecclesiastical hierarchy in rural Asia Minor was shaped by the sociopolitical context of the region.

Not only were Christian life and thought in Asia Minor and Cyprus shaped by the religious pluralism, geographical isolation, and the political structures of the region, but also each of these contextual factors was, in turn, affected and changed by Christianity. Syncretism ran in more than one direction. Christian monotheism could easily be incorporated into the worship of "the Highest God" by the Hypsistarians. Christian beliefs about angels affected the way Jews and pagans thought about angels. Christian Neoplatonist teachers influenced pagan Neoplatonists. Christian burial practices and epigraphic funerary formulae affected the way pagans and Jews buried and commemorated their dead. In time, the Christian "cult of the saints" subverted and replaced the pagan calendar of annual festivals with feasts celebrated on the anniversaries of the deaths of martyrs.

The strength of the rural Christian communities in Asia Minor and, to only a slightly lesser extent, in Cyprus overcame, at least partially, the isolation of communities separated because of geographical (or topographical) factors. By the end of the fifth century even the most remote or mountainous regions of Asia Minor and Cyprus had Christian churches, linked to one another through bishops or *chorepiscopi*. In Cappadocia, Phrygia, and Cyprus, canyons and mountaintops provided ideal locations for Christian rock-cut churches and monasteries, the inhabitants of which transformed the countryside.

The number of third-century Christians on the governing bodies of cities and the political power of bishops from the fourth century onward signaled the ultimate "defeat" of paganism in Asia Minor and Cyprus. During the fifth and early sixth centuries, pagan temples and shrines were systematically destroyed or converted into Christian sacred space by means of ritual purification, exorcism, and rebuilding.

One of the driving forces behind the late "Christianization" of much of Byzantine Asia Minor was John of Amida (ca. 507–post-588), known also as John of Ephesus and John of Asia. A favorite of Theodora, the wife of Justinian I, John was sent by Justinian in about 542 from the capital, Constantinople, to Asia Minor to convert Jews, pagans, and heretics. During the next thirty years, John, by his own account, converted seventy thousand people, built (and/or confiscated from "heretics") ninety-eight basilicas, turned seven synagogues into "churches," and established twelve monasteries (*Hist. eccl.* 3.36–37). Among the "heretical" basilicas that John of Ephesus confiscated and turned into Byzantine churches was the Montanist cathedral at Pepouza (*IMont* 1–2). John of Ephesus may also have been responsible for the establishment (or "Orthodox" use) of the monastery just outside Pepouza (on which, see Tabbernee 2003, 89–93; Tabbernee and Lampe 2008, 19–20, 209–30, 250–53).

Byzantine Christianity remained the dominant form of religion in Asia Minor from the sixth until the twelfth century, when the Seljuks invaded Asia Minor from the East. The Seljuks captured Nicaea in 1078 and made it the capital of an Islamic empire that stretched eastward beyond Asia Minor to India, encompassing Armenia, Syria, Mesopotamia, and Persia, and southward to the Gulf of Arabia. A relatively small part of western Asia Minor and Cyprus remained under Byzantine control until Constantinople fell in 1453 to Mehmet II (r. 1444–1446, 1451–1481), sultan of the Ottoman Empire, which had succeeded and expanded westward the Seljuk Empire. In 1571 the Ottomans conquered Cyprus.

8

The Balkan Peninsula

JULIA VALEVA AND ATHANASIOS K. VIONIS

Introduction

Land, Population, and Frontiers

The term "Balkan Peninsula" was coined in 1808 by Johann August Zeune, a German professor of geography, after the Balkan Mountains and by analogy with the designations Pyrenean Peninsula and Apennine Peninsula. Zeune was also influenced by ancient geographers who believed that the Balkan Mountains, called Haemus in Antiquity, stretched from the region of Istria in the west to the Black Sea in the east, thereby separating this territory from the rest of Europe. Actually, the mountain range extends across Bulgaria from the Black Sea to the northeast of Serbia. "Balkan" is Turkish (see Todorova 1997, 21–32) and means "steep wooded mountain ridge." The designation "Balkan provinces" is, therefore, a neologism, convenient for work and modern classification but not used in Antiquity. Nor was it used by Theodor Mommsen (1968, 206), who employed instead the term "Greek Peninsula," distinguishing the interior Haemus (Balkan) area from "the coast districts along the Adriatic

---

This chapter was written by **Julia Valeva** (Introduction, Thracia, Eastern Illyricum, Constantinople) and **Athanasios K. Vionis** (Achaea, The Greek Islands).

Fig. 8.1. Map of the Balkan Provinces

and the Black Sea." Indeed, the remarkable variety of natural resources, along with the region's mutability in history, implies a distinction that demarcates ancient Greece from the rest of the territory—a demarcation, which eventually was contingent not on geography but on civilization.

The Balkan Peninsula is the cradle of European civilization. Neolithic and Chalcolithic cultures (Nikolov 2006) were superseded by the Bronze Age, the last phase of which is familiar through the *Iliad* and the *Odyssey*. These epic poems illustrate the cultural equivalence of tribes on both sides of the Bosphorus (Hoddinott 1981, 58): Rhesos, king of Thrace, came to help the defenders of Troy along with other contingents from the Troad and the southeast part of the Balkan Peninsula, who were of the same ethnic origins as the Thracians (Homer, *Il.* 10.435–41, 474–97) (Kirk 1985, 257–60).[1]

The eighth century BCE saw the start of the split between Greeks, Thracians, and Illyrians. One of the main causes was the Greek city (*polis*) system of political and economic development, which was much more effective than the retrogressive monocratic system of the rest of the Balkan tribes. Another extremely important factor was Greek colonization. On the one hand, this gave great impetus to trade and economy in the region; on the other hand, it revealed to the Greeks the wisdom of the older civilizations of the eastern Mediterranean and Mesopotamia. The Classical Era marked the strongest cultural alienation of the Greeks from the rest of the Balkan population, which was only later overcome through intense Hellenization in the age of Alexander the Great (r. 336–323) and his successors (the *Diadochi*).

Macedonia and Greece became Roman provinces in 148 and 146 BCE respectively. After long and stubborn resistance, the interior Balkan territory was conquered by the Romans in the first decades of the empire. The lands between the Istros (Hister/Danuvius [i.e., the Lower Danube]) and the Haemus Mountains became the province of Moesia during the reign of Augustus (r. 31 BCE–14 CE). Domitian (r. 81–96 CE) divided the province into Moesia Superior and Moesia Inferior. When the province of Dacia to the northwest of the Danube was deserted in 270 under Aurelian (r. 270–275), part of Moesia Superior was restructured into Dacia Ripensis and Dacia Mediterranea. The latter was soon divided into Dardania and Dacia Mediterranea. The Balkans and the whole Pontus Euxinus (Black Sea) region were of great economic importance to the Romans for resources such as slaves, soldiers, grain, honey, wax, and fish (Polybius, *Hist.* 4.38.4–6).

After the administrative reforms of Diocletian (r. 284–305) and Constantine I (r. 306–337), the eastern part of the peninsula was organized into the Diocese of Thrace, part of the Eastern Prefecture (*Praefectura per orientem*). The *Dioecesis Thraciae* included the provinces of Thracia (with Philippopolis as its capital), Rhodope (capital: Enos), Haemimontus (capital: Hadrianopolis), Europa (capital: Selymbria/Eudoxiopolis), Moesia Secunda (capital: Marcianopolis), and Scythia Minor (capital: Tomis).

The western part of the Balkan Peninsula was organized by Diocletian into the Moesian diocese for military purposes. This turned out to be ineffective, and the territory was attached to the *Pars Orientalis* (eastern part)

---

1. The Rhesos myth reflects the political reality of the eighth to the seventh century BCE, and Song 10 itself is reminiscent of Thraco-Athenian contacts in the sixth century BCE.

8.1 Sources

Besides historiographical writings of traditional type, exemplified by Ammianus Marcellinus's *Res gestae*, sources of a new kind appeared during Late Antiquity (Demandt 1989, 1–33; Cameron 1993, 13–29, 199–207). Some, like the *Notitia dignitatum* (*Register of Offices*), produced in about 425–430 during the reign of Theodosius II (r. 408–450), were born by the need of bureaucratic systematization. The *Notitia dignitatum* is an official list of the titles of dignitaries, recording all the offices that existed in the Roman Empire at the beginning of the fifth century. For the *Notitia dignitatum*, the *Notitia urbis Constantinopolitanae* (*Register of the City of Constantinople*), and similar documents, see Seeck 1876; Fairley 1900; Speck 1973; Ireland 1997; the text is also in A. Jones 1964, 347–80. For illustrations from the *Notitia dignitatum*, see Cornell and Matthews 1982.

Knowledge of the administrative division and the towns in the eastern part of the empire is provided by Hierokles's *Synekdemos* (Honigmann 1939; A. Jones 1964, 712–13, 716–17), a travel guide produced in its final form shortly before 535. The law codes (*Codex theodosianus*, *Codex justinianus*) compiled in the time of Theodosius II (r. 408–450) and Justinian I (r. 527–565) contain not only legal principles but also details about all spheres of Byzantine life.

Numerous official documents from councils, official and private correspondence, and texts related to dogmatic controversies supplement the traditional histories of the church in the region (e.g., those of Eusebius, Lactantius, Socrates, Sozomen, Theodoret of Cyrrhus, and others). Lives of the saints and pilgrimage accounts were new genres, rich in details of fable-like material but nevertheless suggestive about many characteristics of the social life of that period.

of the empire in 395 and declared a praetorian prefecture, Eastern Illyricum.[2] The northern provinces of Eastern Illyricum were Moesia Prima (capital: Viminacium), Dacia Ripensis (capital: Ratiaria), Dacia Mediterranea (capital: Serdica), Praevalitana (capital: Scodra), Dardania (capital: Scupi), Epirus Nova (capital: Dyrrhachium), Macedonia Secunda (capital: Stobi), and, after 437, Pannonia (capital: Sirmium). Later the jurisdiction of Justiniana Prima encompassed this territory (Duval and Popović 1980, 369). The southern provinces of Eastern Illyricum were Macedonia Prima (capital: Thessalonica), Thessalia (capital: Larissa), Epirus Vetus (capital: Nicopolis), Achaea

---

2. The Diocese of Illyricum, part of the Italian Prefecture during the principate, was transformed by Diocletian into a separate prefecture (*Praefectura per Illyricum*) (see Rothaus 2000, 12). It was divided into two parts after the death of Theodosius I (r. 379–395) (see Duval and Popović 1980, 369; cf. Demougeot 1947; 1950; 1981; Bavant 2004). On the towns and cities of Illyricum during this period, see Dagron 1984b.

(capital: Corinth), the Cycladic Islands (capital: Rhodes), and Crete (capital: Gortyn[a]).[3] An important reality for Eastern Illyricum was the different cultural backgrounds within its two parts: Latin in the northern provinces, Greek in the southern ones.

Illyrian territory has been perceived differently through the ages. While for the Romans it was a border area between Italy and the East, for the Byzantines Illyricum formed the western part of their country as a counterpoint to Asia Minor (Dagron 1974, 68–76). The concept of "Illyricum" disappeared after the establishment of the medieval Byzantine administrative system in the seventh century, which utilized "themes" (territorial units under a military commander) rather than "provinces."

Two major imperial roads crossed the Balkan provinces: the Via Egnatia (from the Adriatic to Constantinople across Thrace) and the northern, sometimes called "diagonal," route from Singidunum (Belgrade) on the Danube to Constantinople. These roads are recorded on the *Tabula Peutingeriana* (*Peutinger Map*).

Polytheism, Oriental Cults, and Christianity

Even after Theodosius I reinforced the prohibition of all pagan cults and sacrifices with a series of edicts, the population of the Balkan Peninsula continued to venerate the gods of the Greco-Roman pantheon and numerous local deities. Most popular were the iatric deities Asclepius, Hygieia, Apollo, Dionysus, the Nymphs, and the Thracian Rider (Heros). Hundreds of votive plates have been found in sanctuaries dedicated to Zeus and Hera, Hekate, Artemis, Epona, and Silvanus. The imperial cult was practiced as well, and some cities, such as Perinthus and Philippopolis in Thrace, and Beroia and Thessalonica in Macedonia, were granted the status of *neokoroi* (cities that had a specific temple for the cult of the emperor) (Burrell 2004, 3–5, 10, 191–204, 236–45). Sacrifices to the emperor served to test affiliation to Christianity in the pre-Constantinian period. In general, the population remained faithful to such emblematic cultural events as the Olympic games, held as late as 393, and to classical philosophy and education. In 395/6, after the raids of Alaric I (r. 395–410), the Athenians restored the Library of Hadrian (Frantz, Thompson, and Travlos 1988, 63), and the Classical Era did not end in Athens until the closing of its Platonic school by Justinian in 529 (Frantz, Thompson, and Travlos 1988, 84–91).

---

3. The northern provinces of Eastern Illyricum correspond to modern Bulgaria, Serbia, the former Yugoslavian republic of Macedonia, Monte Negro, and Albania. Most of the territory of the southern provinces corresponds to modern Greece.

Fig. 8.2. Temple of Apollo, Corinth

During the third and fourth centuries the number of followers of oriental cults in the Balkan provinces as a whole continued to increase.[4] Most popular, although in single areas like the colonies along the coasts and only several cities in the interior, were the cults of Cybele and Attis, Isis and Serapis, Mithras, and Theos Hypsistos.[5] Statues of gods and emperors were considered sacred. After Christianity was promoted as the state religion by Theodosius I, the popularity of all other cults gradually declined (Momigliano 1963; Bowersock 1990; Fowden 1998; P. Brown 1998).

Christian inscriptions and archaeological data are instructive for giving specific details of the Christianization of the Balkan Peninsula. Most of the inscriptions are in Greek, the minority in Latin (Beševliev 1964; Feissel 1983; Barnea 1980). There are a few bilingual inscriptions and even some in Latin transliterated with Greek characters. Christian inscriptions from Corinth, Athens, Thessalonica, Odessos (Varna), Tomis (Constanţa), Philippi, Phthiotic Thebes (Nea Anchialos), and Serdica (Sofia) exist in substantial numbers. Many of the inscriptions are on stone, but there are others within mosaics or on ceramic, metal, and glass. There are only a few inscriptions, however, for which a pre-Constantinian date has been suggested. In most cases such an early date cannot be proved. One of the more secure is perhaps the small bronze lamp in the form of a ship, found in Smederevo, Serbia, ancient Vinceia in Moesia Superior. The lamp depicts Jonah vomited up by the marine monster. The inscription explains that Termogenes had made an offering to

4. For the oriental cults, see the EPROER series, edited by Maarten J. Vermaseren. For a modern discussion of monotheistic cults, see Mitchell and Van Nuffelen 2010.

5. For Thrace and Moesia, see Tacheva-Khitova1983; for Thessalonica, see Nigdelis 2010.

God: *Dei in domu Termogenes votum fecit* (*IMS* 1.83). The lamp was found with two hoards of coins from 247 to 250, suggesting a date of about the time of the Decian persecution (Barnea 1980, 465). Mass Christianization of the Balkan provinces started apparently after the middle of the fourth century. The transfer of the capital of the empire to the coast of the Bosphorus, on the edge of Europe and Asia, and that Constantinople was, from the beginning, a Christian city strongly stimulated this process. Among the first buildings in the new capital was the Church of the Holy Apostles, predestined to become an imperial mausoleum. Of particular importance is the fact that it was the first martyrium, to which sacred relics such as those of the apostles Andrew, Timothy, and Luke were transferred (Procopius, *Aed.* 1.4.18 and 21–22) (Mango 1990b). Otherwise, martyria appeared over the tombs of martyrs early in the fourth century and continued to be built in the fifth, presumably as a proof of the delayed Christianization of the Balkans (Ćurčić 2010, 58–65, 147–50).

In the Balkans Christianity established itself first of all primarily, but not exclusively, in the cities. Cities and towns within the Balkan Peninsula were far more numerous in Macedonia and Greece than in Illyricum and Thrace. Cities in the coastal areas of Thrace (most of them ancient Greek colonies) and those along the Danube (created by the Romans initially as military camps) were more densely situated as compared with cities in the interior. In general, early Byzantine cities inherited the town plan of their Roman predecessors. Town planning during the fourth to sixth centuries changed slowly. At first there were no principal differences in street systems, the location of necropolises, or the routes of aqueducts. The central square of the forum or agora type, however, became less important due to changes in the administrative system

Fig. 8.3. Ivory Depicting Transfer of Relics of St. Stephen from Jerusalem to Constantinople, around 421 (Now in Treasury of Trier Cathedral)

through which public buildings surrounding it largely lost their significance. *Gymnasia*, *bouleuteria*, and theaters gradually vanished, but public baths remained. The most important factor distinguishing the town planning of the Byzantine period was the appearance of Christian churches with related buildings concentrated around them: episcopal residences, monasteries, sheltered homes, and hospitals.

The precise origins of monastic life in the Balkan provinces eludes us, although clusters of rock-cut cells along the coast of the Black Sea and in the valleys of some rivers in the interior prove that adepts of eremitic or cenobitic life withdrew from secular life for the sake of moral perfection, probably as early as the fourth century. Later monastic life, organized in formal monasteries, is attested throughout the peninsula by archaeological evidence (S. Popović 1998; Ćurčić 2010, 142–46). Monks were especially active in Constantinople, the height of their social role being during the iconoclastic crisis from 711 to 843 (Hatlie 2007).

Challenges to Christianity

Christianity in the Balkans faced several specific challenges. One of them was the evangelization of barbaric tribes. Another was the intense conflict between the adherents of the Nicene Creed and followers of various heresies. Third, there was the issue of the status of the Constantinopolitan patriarchate. This was a political matter, on the whole solved in a relatively short time. There was, however, continuing rivalry between the bishop of Rome and the patriarch of Constantinople concerning supremacy over the churches in Eastern Illyricum. The bishoprics in Illyricum were under the control of the episcopate of Rome. At the same time, the provinces of Illyricum were under the secular administration of Constantinople, which presupposed that their episcopates were religiously bound to Constantinople's patriarchate as well. Pope Siricius (bp. 384–399) made the archbishop of Thessalonica his vicar, instructing him that "none be permitted to presume to consecrate bishops in Illyricum without our consent" (A. Jones 1964, 888). The Roman popes succeeded in controlling the vicariate of Thessalonica until the first half of the eighth century.

Church Planning and Liturgy

The intermediate location of the Balkan provinces between the eastern and western parts of the empire underlies the differences both in church planning and liturgy as observed in Constantinople, the Thracian diocese, and Eastern Illyricum (Mathews 1971; Pallas 1980; Taft 2004). The analysis of the ecclesiastical architecture in Eastern Illyricum shows that the liturgical tradition in this diocese was originally related to the liturgy of Roman type as described in the *Traditio apostolica*, attributed to Hippolytus (ca. 220). Gradually, an autonomous liturgical practice developed at the heart of this tradition, expressed in the *Testamentum Domini* (*Testament of the Lord*) and the *Apostolic Constitutions*, the prescriptions of which are clearly visible in the modification of Illyrian Christian church architecture and furnishing. A third phase becomes discernible at the end of the fifth century with further alterations in church architecture clearly under Constantinopolitan influence, which manifested itself to the fullest extent during the sixth century (Pallas 1980). In the Thracian diocese different liturgical traditions have been detected when studying ecclesiastical architecture in different parts of its territory: Constantinopolitan in the interior and along the coasts, Syriac in cities with Near Eastern diaspora, and Western in places close or related in some way to Eastern Illyricum. This observation has been explained as the result of the change in ecclesiastical jurisdiction over the Thracian diocese, which was initially Roman and after the Council of Chalcedon of 451, Constantinopolitan. Still, there was not an abrupt transition and both liturgies, Roman and Constantinopolitan coexisted until the end of the iconoclast crisis (Taft 2004, 181).

Achaea

Archaeological evidence from urban contexts in central and southern Greece (the Peloponnese, Attica, and Boeotia) and the Aegean Islands (the Cyclades, the Dodecanese, and Crete) makes clear that "public expressions of Christian identity" became manifested no earlier than the late fifth century (G. Sanders 2005, 420).[6] The Athenians, proud of their "city so full of idols" (Acts 17:16–17), were reluctant to convert to Christianity when, according to Acts 17:19–21, Paul preached on the Areopagus. The conversion of pagan temples into Christian churches and the complete Christianization of the city's monuments and inhabitants encountered even more resistance (Frantz 1965, 188). Similarly, at Corinth no identifiably Christian remains predate the fifth century (Rothaus 2000, 139). Natural disasters (e.g., the earthquake of 525) may finally have persuaded the Corinthian majority to accept Christianity in the sixth century (G. Sanders 2005, 442). The limited textual and extant epigraphic sources seem, nevertheless, to attest an early Christian community at Corinth in about 50–51.

Poverty and low social standing may have contributed to the admittedly small number of Christians in cities such as Athens and Corinth in the first two

6. See also Lalonde 2005; Saradi-Mendelovici 1990; Schowalter and Friesen 2005; Trombley 1989; 1993–1994, 1:283–332.

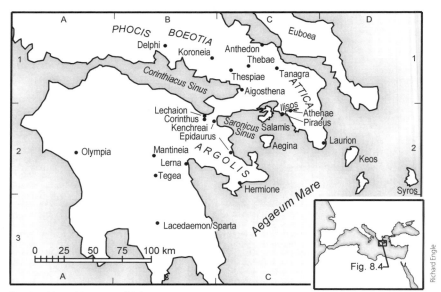

Fig. 8.4. Map of Province of Achaea

centuries, but certain studies picture some of the first converts to Christianity among the ranks of the social elite (J. Davies 1968, 1–3; Finley 1973, 52–53; White 1990, 141–42). Changes in the new civic plan and social structures of the cities (e.g., large basilicas at civic centers), the economic boom of Late Antiquity, and the growth of villas exploiting available agricultural land in close proximity to the city were "part of the continuum of classical antiquity," as were the religious practices related to the Greek and Roman pagan past (Rothaus 2000, 30).

From Paganism to Christianity

In much of central and southern Greece, pagan and Christian practices coexisted until the fifth and sixth centuries, much later than Constantine's law of 321 banning sacrifice (*Cod. theod.* 16.10.1), the most important practice of paganism. Christian communities existed in many Greek cities and towns by the time of the Council of Nicaea in 325 (Mullen 2004, 157–69). It is difficult, nevertheless, to draw a definitive line separating paganism from Christianity in the early centuries of our era or to determine exactly when Christianity became the dominant religion (Horsley 2005, 373). The main focus of pagan (polytheistic) religious activity was on rituals honoring the gods in order to receive protection and prosperity (Rothaus 2000, 1–7).

Both paganism and Christianity involved cultic activities of one form or another. However, the material testimonies for the presence of Christians during the first three centuries are limited to personal (noncultic) inscriptions.

During the second half of the fifth century, pagan activity still monopolized the ancient civic center of Athens, which Christians avoided, establishing neighborhoods elsewhere in the city. The physical separation of the two religious groups allowed for them to coexist and for paganism to survive until quite late. After damaging earthquakes during the third and fourth centuries, many pagan temples were never restored due to declining funds. This, though, does not mean that pagan cultic activity ceased at ruined temple sites (Rothaus 2000, 32–35; Saradi 2006, 356). The accession of Constantine in the early fourth century marked the beginning of a new era. Various later laws contained in the *Codex theodosianus* and *Codex justinianus* forbade pagan cults, closed temples, and forced conversion. These laws attest both the existence of paganism well into the sixth century and the transformation of the religious landscape to a predominantly Christian one.

Before and after Constantine

Following the administrative reforms of Diocletian most of central and southern Greece south of Thessaly and Epirus formed the province of Achaea. It incorporated Boeotia, parts of Phocis, Attica, the Peloponnese, the islands of Euboea, Aegina, Salamis, and some of the Cyclades (Keos and Syros). Systematic archaeological survey work in the Achaean countryside, such as within the rural territory of the city of Thespiae in Boeotia, confirms that the number of farm and hamlet sites decreased in early Roman times, while urban sites simultaneously contracted dramatically (Bintliff 2004, 200–201; Bintliff, Howard, and Snodgrass 2007). Villas replaced some of the many small classical Greek farm sites in the countryside, producing a landscape controlled by wealthy landowners with very few communities of

---

8.2 House-Churches

Like some other religious associations of the time, the Christian cult, in terms of its assembly and worship, was confined to the homes of its prominent and wealthier members (White 1990, 19). In Athens this was still the case as late as the fourth century (Frantz 1965, 188). The dining rooms of house-churches provided the physical setting that accommodated an *ekklēsia* in various locations throughout the Aegean region, possibly serving as stepping-stones for the establishment of house-church networks from Asia Minor to Rome (White 1990, 106).

free peasants. Towns became "dormitory centers" for estate workers. Towns and their *chōra*, however, slowly recovered during the mature Roman imperial era (ca. 200–400), paying taxes, contributing to the military, and honoring the Roman emperors. In Late Antiquity (ca. 400–640), especially throughout the Eastern empire, there was, once again, prosperity and economic vitality (Alcock 1993; Jameson, Runnels, and van Andel 1994). The development of Christianity in Achaea was, naturally, very much affected by the social and economic context of the times.

The Peloponnese

CORINTH

At Corinth there were possibly six church cells during the apostle Paul's time (White 1990, 105). Paul was offered hospitality at the house of Priscilla and Aquila (a Jewish couple expelled from Rome [see chap. 9]), who operated as co-workers with him when he arrived at Corinth around 50–51. The house of Titius Justus, adjacent to the synagogue, and the households of Stephanas, Crispus, Chloe, and Gaius (Acts 18:2–11; Rom. 16:23; 1 Cor. 16.15) also played a prime role in the Pauline Aegean strategy of establishing house-church networks.

A Christian community existed contemporaneously at nearby Kenchreai (Acts 18:18), Corinth's eastern seaport 7 km southeast on the Saronic Gulf. Phoebe, a friend and co-worker of Paul, was a "minister" or deacon of the local church community there (Rom. 16:1–2). In the mid-50s, as Paul's personal envoy, Phoebe was directed to the house-church of Priscilla and Aquila, now at Rome, before addressing several other house-churches in the capital (White 1990, 106).

House ownership and house-churches certainly place a portion of the early Christian community within the higher social strata (Theissen 1982; White 1990), although more recent studies on the social standing of Pauline congregations have argued that leadership within house-church assemblies seems to have come mostly from families living near subsistence level (Friesen 2005, 369–70).

Active assembly "leaders" such as Priscilla and Aquila were the heads of separate units based in larger towns, spreading to satellites such as Kenchreai (Horsley 2005, 395) and thus establishing Christian communities in the provinces of an impoverished agrarian Roman Empire. Paul's preaching also met the positive response of some local social elites such as Erastus of Corinth (Rom. 16:23), a treasurer responsible for public buildings and spectacles (Mavromataki 2003, 117). An inscription in Latin referring to Erastus's public works has been discovered to the north of the Roman Forum at Corinth.

Quoting Hegesippus (ca. 110–180), a chronicler of the early church, Eusebius refers to a man named Primus (*Hist. eccl.* 4.22) of Corinth (bp. ca. 150–155). Eusebius also mentions a Dionysius, bishop of Corinth during the reign of Marcus Aurelius (r. 161–180). Dionysius wrote a letter to the church of Lacedaemon (ancient Sparta) circa 170, "enjoying peace and unity" (Eusebius, *Hist. eccl.* 4.23.2), an important piece of information providing evidence that missionary work was being directed and carried out from Corinth throughout the Peloponnese. Bacchyllus, a late second-century bishop of Corinth, was among prominent leaders (*Hist. eccl.* 5.22) involved in the Quartodeciman controversy (Harnack 1908, 2:233). Bacchyllus supported Victor I of Rome (bp. ca. 189–198/9) in that controversy, and it is believed that he held a provincial synod with eighteen other bishops at Corinth around 195 (Peterson 1907, 189). Origen of Alexandria (ca. 185–ca. 253), who visited Corinth around 230, about the same time he visited Athens, refers to the church of God at both cities as "a peaceable and orderly body" (*Cels.* 3.30).

The textual attestations of the presence of Christian communities at Corinth, Kenchreai, and Lacedaemon during the first three centuries cannot be confirmed by archaeological evidence. There is plenty of evidence, however, both textual and archaeological, that Hellenic deities were still worshiped in Corinth as late as the fourth and early fifth centuries (Rothaus 2000, 13–17). Libanius (*Or.* 14.41) refers to prominent members of the Corinthian pagan ruling class in the fourth century actively engaged in public pagan cults until they were outlawed (Rothaus 2000, 13). A series of earthquakes at the end of the fourth century (Rothaus 2000, 16–18) and the sack of Corinth by Alaric in 396 (Gregory 1993, 141) account for the widespread catastrophe evident in the archaeological record of that period. Only after those years of destruction do recognizably public expressions of Christianity (in the form of architecture and burial customs) become manifest (G. Sanders 2005, 420).

The massive basilica at Lechaion, Corinth's western port along the Corinthian Gulf, exceeding 100 m in length, probably was built after the 525 earthquake (Rothaus 2000, 96; G. Sanders 2005, 440). It is one of the first Christian structures of a monumental nature in southern Greece, initially a pilgrimage center, associated with St. Leonidas and the seven martyrs who perished with him in about 250 at the site of the basilica (Pallas 1990). Its construction was an imperial donation (G. Sanders 2005, 439). Three more churches at the edge of Corinth—the Skoutelas, the Kodratos, and the Kraneion basilicas—were built in the early sixth century (Pallas 1979–1980, 105; 1990, 776–77, 779–85). The placement of basilicas at the periphery of Corinth has been puzzling. Perhaps they were built alongside roadways to impress anyone traveling into town (Rothaus 2000, 102).

Archaeological investigations at Kenchreai have revealed remains of a basilica and baptistery (on or close to the site of a Roman sanctuary of Isis), most likely also built in the early sixth century (Rothaus 2000, 77).[7] This church (very much like the other basilicas in the region), situated on the harbor, provided a landmark of Christianity to vessels entering port. The cruciform baptismal fonts (for the baptism of adult catechumens) preserved in the aforementioned churches (Lechaion, Skoutelas, Kraneion, and Kenchreai), and the large space provided by sixth-century Christian buildings, suggest a large number of unbaptized who postponed baptism until late in life (G. Sanders 2005, 441).

The first evidence of Christian burial practices in Corinth, similarly, is not until the last decades of the fifth century. The so-called Lerna court, between the Asclepieum and the Lerna springhouse, has revealed a large number of simple tile graves and a few infant Gaza-amphora burials of the late fifth and sixth centuries. A number of rock-cut tombs and Christian tombstones have been discovered near the Asclepieum. All the graves have an east-west orientation, with the feet of the deceased toward the east and their hands crossed over the abdomen (Rothaus 2000, 51; G. Sanders 2005, 428–34). Grave goods are confined to a few plain jugs (Rothaus 2000, 51, fig. 12). According to the tombstone inscriptions, the graves belonged to people of ordinary status, such as gardeners, goatherds, and bath attendants. Some similarly dated marble tombstones mentioning the humble occupation of the deceased (such as stockbreeders and goatherds) have also been found at Lerna, the summer resort of wealthy Corinthians in nearby Argolis (Papanikola-Bakirtzi 2002, 130–31 nos. 134–35).

A large number of early Christian basilicas have been excavated throughout the Peloponnese. The great majority of these date from the second half of the fifth century. It seems that the earliest was the five-aisled basilica at Epidaurus close to the Temple of Asclepius, dated to the late fourth, or first quarter of the fifth, century (Sotiriou 1929; Frantz 1965, 188).

Attica

ATHENS

Acts 17:16–34 appears to convey accurate information about the general Athenian skepticism toward Paul during his preaching at the synagogue and the Areopagus. There is very little information about conversion in Athens during Paul's visit, in about 49–50, apart from references to a woman named Damaris and to Dionysius, a member of the Council of the Areopagus (Acts

---

7. A late fourth-century date was initially proposed by the excavators (Scranton, Shaw, and Ibrahim 1978).

8.3 Christian Apologists

Eusebius (*Hist. eccl.* 4.23.2–3) mentions Quadratus as bishop of Athens in about 200. Aristides, a Christian apologist, possibly of Athenian descent (Harnack 1908, 2:232), may have attempted to lecture about Christianity in the presence of Hadrian (r. 117–138) during his visit to Athens around 124–125 (Mavromataki 2003, 103). The Christian philosopher Athenagoras of Athens addressed an apology for the Christian faith to Marcus Aurelius in about 177 (Trombley 1993–1994, 1:284n5).

17:34). Eusebius cites Dionysius of Corinth as referring to Dionysius the Areopagite as the first bishop of Athens (*Hist. eccl.* 3.4.11; 4.23.3). According to tradition, the Areopagite died as a martyr during the reign of Domitian.

Dionysius of Corinth wrote an epistle to the Athenian church cautioning against apostasy to Hellenic paganism after the execution of their bishop Publius (fl. ca. 155) (Eusebius, *Hist. eccl.* 4.23.2) (Trombley 1993–1994, 1:284n5). Origen visited Athens (as well as Corinth) in about 230 and again around 238–244 "for the conversion of heretics" (Eusebius, *Hist. eccl.* 23.32), and, as already noted, he describes the local church or "assembly of God" as "a peaceable and orderly body" (*Cels.* 3.30).

It is very difficult to be definitive about the extent of early Christianity in Athens. Literary texts tend to emphasize church leaders rather than the "ordinary members" of the Christian community, possibly composed largely of the financially weaker class of Athenian society. Since Pistus, bishop of Athens, is listed among the participants at Nicaea (Harnack 1908, 2:233), there must have been a sufficiently well recognized church by the first quarter of the fourth century (Frantz 1965, 188).

The earliest published Christian funerary epitaph from Athens belongs to a "faithful Christian" Maurus. The inscription is dated to the third or fourth century on the basis of the typically second- to fourth-century rounded *epsilon*, *sigma*, and *omega* (Bayet 1878a, no. 75; Trombley 1993–1994, 282–84). According to Frank Trombley, the expression "faithful Christian" on Maurus's tombstone suggests a time when adherence to Christianity was still unusual (before the accession of Constantine?), as does the absence of the *chi-rho* christogram, incised crosses, and use of the word *koimētērion* (resting place)—all typical of the period between the late fourth and sixth centuries.

A large number of Christian funerary inscriptions of the period 350 to 450 commemorate Athenians bearing names of deities with local popular shrines (e.g., Askleparion, Athenaos, Athenodora, Nike), suggesting the conversion of

Fig. 8.5. Erechtheion (Detail), Athens

many adults (Trombley 1993–1994, 1:289–91). The fourth/fifth-century funerary monument of a certain Dionysus, a silk worker from outside Athens and domestic servant of the proconsul Plutarch, implies that Christianity found converts in the rural estates of Attica, "where Christian churches and clergy hardly existed" (Trombley 1993–1994, 1:291). By the sixth century, Christianized Athenians came from all social strata, but mainly from the craftsman class. We are informed epigraphically about Erpidios the builder, Andrew the plumber, Epiphanes the potter, Euphrasios the glassmaker, Paul the shoemaker, and Isidoros (from the port town of Piraeus) the cutler and reader of the Holy Scriptures (Sironen 1997, nos. 66, 80, 250, 72, 68; Papanikola-Bakirtzi 2002, nos. 1, 244, 109, 113, 104, 98).

The Parthenon, Erechtheion, Hephaisteion, and the Asclepieum continued to dominate the Athenian skyline and public areas. The chronology of their "Christianization" has provoked controversy among scholars (Frantz 1965; Gregory 1986; Mango 1995; Trombley 1993–1994). Converting major Athenian pagan monuments into Christian buildings would have been a provocative act against the still-powerful pagan aristocracy of the fifth century (Frantz, Thompson, and Travlos 1988, 92), possibly explaining why the process took longer in Athens than in some other Greek cities. The conversion of the Parthenon and the Asclepieum occurred in the second half of the fifth century or early in the reign of Justinian, while the Erechtheion and the Hephaisteion had to wait another century (Saradi 2006, 360).

8.4 Neoplatonic Influences

Until closed by Justinian, Plato's Academy at Athens had a profound effect on the mentality and daily life of the Athenian pagan aristocracy, members of which converted to Christianity. Neoplatonic philosophy is discernible in a number of Christian funerary inscriptions. For example, the tombstone of Photius, son of Photius and Demostrate, talks about the soul ascending into the ether (Bayet 1878a, no. 38; Trombley 1993–1994, 1:286). In a city where philosophy was born, taught, and kept alive until the sixth century, Christian ethics blended with Neoplatonic theology and entered the Athenian aristocracy, potentially converting its members to Christianity without them having to totally abandon pagan traditions.

In the early fifth century, imperial initiative closed the temples and transferred temple property to the church (Sozomen, *Hist. eccl.* 3.17.3) (Saradi 2006, 356). Fear of demons inhabiting the ruins prevented Christian Athenians at first from utilizing temple sites or building material for the construction of churches (Theodoret of Cyrrhus, *Therap.* 8.68) (Saradi 2006, 358). Such fears were eventually overcome through practices of consecration and linking the qualities of pagan gods to those of Christian saints, as, for example, when the Asclepieum was turned into the church of the healing saint Andrew (Gregory 1986, 238–39; Karivieri 1995; Trombley 1993–1994, 1:343; Saradi 2006, 360).

The tetraconch basilica in the courtyard of the Library of Hadrian probably was constructed in the first half of the fifth century as the first episcopal cathedral (Snively 1984; Karivieri 1994; Saradi 2006, 360). The Ionic temple of Olympian Zeus, at the Ilissos River outside the city walls, was one of the earliest temples transformed into a large church cemetery, probably also already in the fifth century (Frantz 1965, 194; Frantz, Thompson, and Traulos 1988).

Rural Attica

A large number of basilicas have been identified in rural Attica, the majority of them dated between the second half of the fifth and the middle of the sixth centuries. Due to lack of systematically excavated and well-published data, a more precise chronology cannot be applied to most of them. There are also indications, however, of the construction of some Christian churches as early as the first half of the fifth century at or close to the municipal subdivisions of ancient Attica (*demes*), suggesting continuity of habitation and gradual conversion to Christianity, as in contemporary Athens. The five-aisled basilica in Laurion (Lavrion), for example, is dated to the second quarter of the fifth century by its mosaic style (Travlos 1988, 204–5). Baptisteries are preserved in a number of rural churches of relatively large dimensions, such as at Ai-gosthena (Porto Germeno) in southwest Attica (Koder and Hild 1976, 120). It seems that the average size of basilicas in central and southeast Attica ranged between 15 m and 20 m in length (Pallas 1986).

Boeotia

Thebae, Thespiae, Koroneia, and Tanagra probably were separate bish-oprics already in the fourth century (Harnack 1908, 2:230–31n4). Koroneia also appears in the participants' list of the Council of Ephesus in 431 (Koder and Hild 1976, 192–93). Thespiae is mentioned by Pope Leo I (bp. 440–461) in about 446 (Koder and Hild 1976, 275). Two inscribed statue bases from Thespiae, one of them belonging to the time of Constantine and the other to that of his sons Constantius II (r. 337–361) and Constans (r. 337–350), sug-gest that some Boeotian towns either favored Christianity earlier than others or favored their emperors more than others (Plassart 1926, 455 no. 99, 457 no. 101; Trombley 1989, 222–23).

THEBES

Although early traditions link St. Luke and even the Rufus mentioned by St. Paul (Rom. 16:13) with Thebes, epigraphic evidence and excavated ec-clesiastical remains compose the only reliable sources of information about early Christianization in Boeotia and its main city, Thebae (Thebes/Thivai). According to Trombley (1989, 221), "the latest token of the old religion" is a funerary inscription of the third/fourth century. A number of rock-cut chambers outside the city of Thebes were identified by the original excavator as "catacombs" or secret places of worship in use by a Christian community that survived the early persecutions (Keramopoullos 1917, 102–6, 111–22, 134; Trombley 1989, 221). Such underground burial chambers, however, probably were not secret and never used as places of worship but rather were, as in Rome, merely places where geology offered the option for the construction of underground cemeteries.

Pagan cult activity persisted in Thebes throughout the fourth century. The Temple of Ismenian Apollo, for example, was abandoned only after the edict of Theodosius I. It was around this time that the temple area on a hill out-side the Kadmeian walls started to function as a Christian cemetery filled with tile graves covered by slabs, some of them accompanied by oil lamps (Keramopoullos 1926, 127–29; Trombley 1989, 222). A marble sarcophagus was discovered at the temple site, bearing three Christian inscriptions dated to the fourth century (IG 7.2543–45; Trombley 1989, 222). The sarcophagus itself, now built into one of the walls of the modern Church of Luke the Evangelist, is dated to the second century (Bonanno-Aravantinou 1988, 318–19). The practice of establishing Christian necropolises in the precinct of pagan temples was common in central and southern Greece during Late Antiquity, appearing in about the late fifth and sixth centuries (such as the Lerna court cemetery in Corinth).

Hard archaeological evidence for Christian worship in Thebes is surprisingly rare. Evidence for the existence of a large basilica has only recently become available through the discovery of an apse, a few meters northeast of the present-day Church of Luke the Evangelist (Koilakou 2006, 1106). Another exceptional find is the so-called Mosaic of the Months, dated to the first half of the sixth century, with an inscription recording the conversion of its donor. The mosaic depicts the personified months and hunting scenes, and it is believed to have belonged to a basilica (Pallas 1977, 14–17), although the apse of the building in which the mosaic was found has not (yet) been located (Koilakou 2006, 1106). A certain Demetrios composed the mosaic with the help of his assistant Epiphanes (Pallas 1977, 15 no. 29; Trombley 1989, 224). Another (three-aisled) basilica has been excavated in Anthedon, the eastern port of Thebes, and dated to the second half of the fifth century on the basis of its mosaic floor remains (Koder and Hild 1976, 123).

TANAGRA

An abundance of fragments of the Late Roman 2 transport amphora-type (dated to the fourth through sixth centuries) indicates that the city was an important regional economic center of the period, especially for the production of olive oil frequently used for in-kind payment of taxes such as the *annona militaris*—the "military food ration" (Bintliff et al. 2004–2005, 568). Thus one would expect considerable investment in the appearance of the city after the firm establishment of Christianity by the fifth century. Indeed, excavations carried out in 1890 revealed the remains of a Christian basilica (40 m by 20 m) with mosaic floors of the fifth century on the highest point of the city, presumably on the site of an ancient temple (Konstas 1890, 34). Two (or possibly three) more basilicas have been identified within the city walls. The first of these, in the upper center of the town (the East Basilica), was a three-aisled church with an annex to its northwest (Bintliff 2005, 34). A Christian funerary inscription (probably of the first half of the sixth century) found in Tanagra commemorates a certain Lucian, an artisan of the building trades (*IG* 7.1648; Trombley 1989, 224).

Two early fifth-century Christian, but syncretistic, funerary inscriptions speak of the deceased in the old Ionic dialect (*IG* 7.582–84; Duchesne 1879;

Platon 1937; Trombley 1989, 225). This syncretism reflects the Hellenic *paideia* (rather than a purely religious syncretism) that prevailed even in agrarian regions such as Boeotia (Trombley 1989, 226).

The Greek Islands

Before and after Constantine

Under Diocletian most of the Aegean Islands were incorporated into the Provincia Insularum (Province of the Islands), forming, together with the provinces of Asia Minor, the Diocese of Asia. The *Synekdemos* lists Lesbos, Chios, and Samos in the eastern Aegean, most of the Dodecanese (including Rhodes, Kos, and Astypalaia), and most of the Cyclades (except Delos, Syros, Mykonos, Keos, Kythnos, and Kimolos). Rhodes was capital of the new province. The Cyclades experienced steady economic recovery and relative stability throughout the Roman imperial era from the second half of the

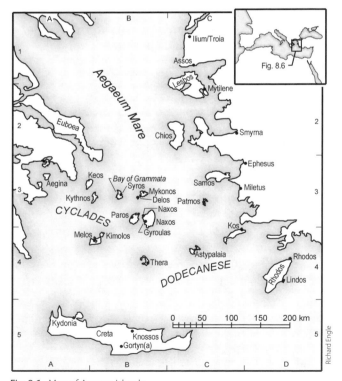

Fig. 8.6. Map of Aegean Islands

third to the early seventh century (Renfrew and Wagstaff 1982; Cherry, Davis, and Mantzourane 1991). Similarly, the period between 400 and 600 CE was one of prosperity for most of the Dodecanese, with evidence for an immense amount of Christian building activity.

The Cyclades

DELOS

The small island of Delos was home to one of the renowned ancient oracles, ranking among those of Delphi, Dodona, and Olympia. According to Theodoret (*Hist. eccl.* 3.21), the last known prophecy issued by the Delian oracle concerned the campaign of Julian the Apostate (r. 361–363) in the East. Timothy Gregory (1983, 290–91) has challenged the credibility of Theodoret's account, but it would not be surprising if indeed the oracle still functioned in the late fourth century, as did many other contemporary pagan sites. Significantly, the Temple of Apollo on Delos was never converted into a Christian church, as was, for example, the Temple of Apollo at Delphi (Laurent 1899).

The remaining pagan population on Delos lived side by side with Christians and Jews. Christian churches on Delos probably were built as early as the time of Theodoret (Orlandos 1936). One was near the Agora of the Delians. Others were constructed among the ruins of the ancient site, such as the Stoa of Philip, the Thesmophoreion, and the Sanctuary of Asclepius (Gregory 1983, 291). The Christian population on this small island was not large during the fifth and sixth centuries, but the churches erected in the Aegean center of the Apollonian cult can be seen as imperial attestation of the triumph of Christianity over Hellenic deities.

A large synagogue has been identified on the eastern shore of the island, adjacent to a residential quarter (White 1997, 335). The original structure dates to the first century BCE, but the building was renovated several times and seems to have been in use until the late first or second century CE (Bruneau 1963; 1982). An inscription recording the murder of two young Jewish women (*CIJ* 1.725; Frend 1996, 135) is further testimony to the existence of a Jewish community on Delos. The role of the Jewish population on Delos and other Aegean islands is of particular interest here, for it may be partly related to the beginnings and spread of Christianity in this part of the Roman Empire.

OTHER ISLANDS

On Aegina (off the west coast of Attica) another synagogue building and Jewish inscriptions have been identified and dated to the fourth century. A similar Jewish building inscription belonging to a synagogue has also been

Fig. 8.7. Catacombs, Melos

found in Mantineia in central Peloponnese (White 1997, 356, 359). A number of inscriptions from other Aegean islands also testify to the existence of established Jewish communities: on Thera, Naxos, Paros, Melos, Rhodes, Samos, Kos, and Crete (Kiourtzian 2000, 173–75). Most of these inscriptions date between the fourth and seventh centuries. The Bay of Grammata, a natural refuge harbor in northwest Syros, is of special importance because it preserves a number of Christian inscriptions engraved on the rocks, expressing thanksgiving and prayers, dated to the fifth, sixth, and seventh centuries (Kiourtzian 2000, 137–38). Two Jewish inscriptions have also been identified there (Kiourtzian 2000, 173–75 no. 108, 182–83 no. 118) and a few others as possibly Jewish on the basis of the sailors' names. In light of these inscriptions, it is highly likely that Christianity first found receptive soil within the Jewish communities of the Aegean region and that Jewish Christians became messengers of the new faith while sailing the Aegean from island to island engaged in maritime trade.

MELOS

Evidence for early Christian burial in the Provincia Insularum comes from the so-called catacombs on the island of Melos, probably the oldest and largest Christian funerary site in the Aegean. The underground chambers of Melos, however, did not necessarily function as family burial chambers until after Christianity was established as the official state religion (Bayet 1878b; Sotiriou 1928). Three main catacombs are linked by five galleries and a dead-end passage, making up a labyrinth 185 m long. Arched burial recesses (*arcosolia*) were cut into the side walls of the passageways. Individual graves were cut into the floors of the passages. In most cases, ceramic oil lamps accompanied the deceased; the decorative motifs on these lamps vary from pagan scenes (e.g., Eros playing panpipes) to Christian symbols (e.g., crosses), dated to the fifth, sixth, and early seventh centuries. Charles Bayet (1878b, 357) reports three hundred graves in the catacombs, burying fifteen hundred deceased. The graves are decorated with plant patterns and symbolic representations accompanied by inscriptions painted in red pigment (Sotiriou 1928, 40–45). The oldest inscriptions in the *arcosolia* are dated to the second half of the fourth century (Bayet 1878b, 356–59; Sotiriou 1928, 36; Kiourtzian 2000, 77–96).

Two of the catacomb inscriptions are of special importance for aspects related to the development of Christianity on Melos. The first belongs to the presbyter Melon, his wife, and children, and it is dated to the late fourth or early fifth century (Sotiriou 1928, 42; Kiourtzian 2000, 83 no. 22). It curses those who would attempt to place anyone other than Melon and his family in the tomb, conveying a sense of syncretism between Christian faith and past pagan traditions related to funerary inscriptions. The second, a fourth-century inscription, provides direct evidence for ecclesiastical offices (presbyter, deaconess, virgin) during this period on the island. It mentions the names of an ecclesiastical family consisting of Asklepis, Elpizon, Asklepiodotos, Agaliassis, Eutychia, and Klaudiani (Sotiriou 1928, 41; Kiourtzian 2000, 88). This inscription, likewise, curses any persons daring to put someone else in that grave in the name of the "guardian angel," echoing Jewish traditions (Pss. 34:7; 91:11) that blended with Christianity at an early stage (Matt. 18:10). Georgios Sotiriou (1928, 42) has argued that Melos provided a bridge for the spread of Christianity from Asia Minor via Jewish traders, as there was a prosperous Jewish community on the island exploiting and exporting Melian minerals.

Other than the catacombs, evidence for Christianity on Melos comes from the site of the "Three Churches." British excavations at the site in the late 1800s revealed the ancient agora of Melos, where a cruciform baptismal font and the foundations of a large building to its north were also located. A number of mutilated ancient statues were incorporated in various later structures at the site and around a Christian tomb. The manner in which these statues were packed around the tomb and below the foundation walls next to it "clearly reveals the intention to bury them out of sight, and suggests that those are the remains of a very early Christian church dating back to an age when those statues were still held in honour by part of the community" (D. MacKenzie 1897, 127).

PAROS

The final phase of the basilica of Katapoliani, dedicated to the Virgin Mary, in Paros has been dated to the sixth century. There are, however, indications that a church existed already in the early fourth century at the site. There, according to tradition, St. Helena prayed on her way to the Holy Land in 326 (Jewell and Hasluck 1920). Paros certainly had an organized church administration already at the beginning of the fourth century. Acedemius, bishop of Paros, is listed among the participants at Nicaea in 325, as is Athanasios at the Councils of Ephesus in 431 and Chalcedon in 451 (Konstantinidis 1998, 206–7). The cruciform baptismal font in the Katapoliani church complex is also dated to the fourth or fifth century, suggesting a rather large (adult) Christian community existing by that time. Despoliation of ancient temples and their consecration was not absent in the Cyclades. Some two thousand reused blocks were incorporated into the church complex of Katapoliani in the ancient city of Paros; eleven theater seats were reused for the *synthronon*—the amphitheatrically-placed benches for the clergy on the central apse of the sanctuary (Saradi 2006, 365).

NAXOS

On the large neighboring island of Naxos, seven basilicas have to date been identified, and there is evidence for the existence of an additional three. One of the earliest churches is the fifth-century Basilica of St. John at Gyroulas, built on top of the archaic Temple of Demeter and Kore (Lambrinoudakis, Gruben, and Korres 1976). A number of rooms around a courtyard have been excavated to the south of the basilica, identified as workshops operating from the sixth to the eighth centuries for the production of pottery, wine, and olive oil, suggesting that churches became the new centers of economic activity. Hélène Saradi (2006, 423) has argued that the connection of churches to the production and distribution through workshops and shops continued a pagan tradition.

The Dodecanese and the East Aegean Islands

According to Acts 20:13–15, Paul with Luke and their companions met at Assos during the course of Paul's third journey through Asia Minor (ca. 53–57), from where they sailed to Lesbos, Chios, and Samos. Nothing else is known about their visit to these large islands of the east Aegean, other than that their stay did not last more than three days. Following his visit, Paul disembarked at Miletus and sailed for Kos and Rhodes (Acts 21:1). According to tradition, Paul preached under the plane tree of Hippocrates the physician (ca. 460–360 BCE) on Kos. While on Rhodes, he also visited Lindos in the south of the island.

William Tabbernee

Fig. 8.8. "St. Paul's Harbor," Lindos

Presumably, the story of the association of the island of Patmos with the exiled St. John and the book of Revelation during the last decade of the first century would have spread to neighboring island communities.

The current Monastery of St. John the Theologian, above the main town of Patmos, was founded in 1088. It stands, however, on the foundations of an earlier "Grand Royal Basilica" built in honor of the saint sometime in the first half of the fourth century, according to inscriptions from the site of the basilica (destroyed possibly in the eighth century as a result of Arab raids). Nicaea provided a meeting place for members of the east Aegean ecclesiastical administration. Euphrosynus, bishop of Rhodes, and Meliphron, bishop of Kos, attended the council. A bishop existed on Lesbos at Mytilene in the days of Julian the Apostate (Socrates, *Hist. eccl.* 2.40) (Harnack 1908, 2:230). Nearly a hundred fifth- and sixth-century basilicas have been identified on Rhodes alone (Volanakis 1998; Kollias 2000). Neighboring Kos numbers some thirty basilicas (Kalopisi-Verti 1991).

Crete

Paul visited the island of Crete on his journey to Rome (Acts 27:8–15; Titus 1:5). The Epistle to Titus shows apostolic concern for the Cretans' fate, urging that "they may become sound in the faith" (Titus 1:12–13). Church tradition declares Titus the first bishop of Gortyn(a), the Roman capital of Crete. A significant part of Crete must certainly have been home to Christian communities in the second half of the second century. Dionysius of Corinth wrote, in about 170, to "the Church of Gortyn and the other Churches of

Crete" (*Ep.*, in Eusebius, *Hist. eccl.* 4.23.5) as well as a second epistle to the "Church of Knossos," whose bishop Pinytus wrote back a reply (Eusebius, *Hist. eccl.* 4.23.7–8). No representative bishop from Crete, however, is on the participants' list of the Council of Nicaea.

Crete also housed a large community of Jews during the first five centuries CE, as attested by Jewish sepulchral inscriptions found in Gortyn(a) and in the countryside west of Chania, ancient Kydonia (Spyridakis 1988). On one of the inscriptions, a certain Sophia is identified as a "leader of the synagogue" and the wife of the "head of the synagogue" (Bandy 1970, 142–43; Spyridakis 1988, 174–75).

Over one hundred Christian inscriptions from all over Crete have been published thus far. More than 60 percent of them are dated to the fifth and sixth centuries, while only a small number to the seventh and eighth centuries. Interestingly, there is also one third-century inscription (Bandy 1970, 128–29 no. 100). Jewish influences, mainly on the names of the deceased, are evident (e.g., Bandy 1970, 42–43 no. 10). Socrates mentions that a considerable number of Cretan Jews were converted to Christianity (*Hist. eccl.* 7.38).

Seventy early Christian basilicas have been identified on Crete (I. Sanders 1982, 89–131). The ecclesiastical administration of the island from the fourth century onward was at Gortyn(a). The remains of the large sixth-century cross-domed Basilica of St. Titus attest a thriving Christian community on Crete during Late Antiquity (Orlandos 1926). The basilica at Knossos was built on the site of an apparently third- or fourth-century Christian cemetery (Bandy 1970, 5).

Thracia

The urbanization of Thrace, which started in the time of Trajan (r. 98–117) and intensified its rhythm during the Antonine and Severan dynasties, transformed the social and spiritual landscape of these territories. The Thracian people experienced different cultures in the big, often cosmopolitan towns—like Philippopolis or the old Greek colonies along the coasts—where immigrants from the Eastern provinces settled in search of beneficial economic conditions. Troops were stationed for long periods along the Danube *limes* (the delimiting system of the boundaries of the Roman Empire), and veterans, recruited from Asia Minor, Syria, Palestine, Greece, and Macedonia, also settled in Thrace. As a result, religious life in Thrace acquired a complex and varied character (Danov 1979). The local deities retained their preponderance. Contamination of functions of local and Greek gods was widespread, such as Apollo-Kendrizos

Fig. 8.9. Map of Thrace

in Philippopolis. Self-evidently, the veneration of the Capitoline Triad was a manifestation of loyalty to the state and the emperor along with the cult offered to him. At the same time the Oriental cults progressively gained adepts, who were grouped in associations (Tacheva-Khitova 1982; 1983).

The Christianization of the Balkan provinces was emphatically uneven. While several cities of the Aegean such as Philippi, Thessalonica, and Athens heard the word of God from St. Paul himself in the first century, some of the highlanders, such as the Bessi in the Rhodopes, were converted to Christianity only in the fifth century by Nicetas of Remesiana (ca. 335–ca. 414). A well-known citation from Tertullian (ca. 160/70–ca. 220), in which he affirms that the barbarian peoples of the region were already Christianized in his time (*Adv. Jud.* 7.4; cf. Col. 3:11 [see Zeiller 1918, 29]), probably is not much more than a rhetorical device. Legendary names of followers of the apostles, like that of the martyr Amplias (cf. Rom. 16:8) from Odessos (Varna), suggest that small early Christian communities existed in the coastal areas and even in the interior. At the end of the second century, Aelius Publius Julius, bishop of Deultum (a Roman colony on the Black Sea coast), signed a letter by Serapion of Antioch (bp. ca. 198/9–211) against the Montanists (Eusebius,

8.5 Religious Diversity in Thracia

The towns along the coast of the Pontus Euxinus were Greek colonies. There the gods of the native Greek pantheon were venerated with piety. Temples and shrines dedicated to Apollo and Dionysus existed in all colonies on the coast (e.g., at Deultum, Apollonia Pontica, Mesambria, and Odessos). The supreme gods Zeus and Hera were venerated in all the towns as well. In Apollonia Pontica special honors were paid to the chthonic goddesses Gea and Hekate. Immigrants venerated their own native gods and goddesses, such as Cybele (especially at Troesmis, Histria, Tomis, Bizone, Marcianopolis, Dionysopolis, and Salmydessos), and those of the Egyptian cults (e.g., at Histria, Tomis, Callatis, Mesambria, and Anchialos).

The cults of Mithra, Jupiter Dolichenos, and Theos Hypsistos, to the contrary, were more popular in the interior of the diocese (Tacheva-Khitova 1983). The main Thracian cult of Heros often produced local epithets. The variety of religious practices in Odessos is expressive: temples and shrines were dedicated to Apollo, the Thracian Heros with the epithet Karabazmos, Zeus, the Great God Darzalas, Asclepius and Hygieia, Dionysus, Athena, and Poseidon, as well as to Roma and the emperor.

Hist. eccl. 5.19.3).[8] Bishop Philip of Heraclea, his deacon Hermes, and the presbyter Severus suffered martyrdom during the Diocletianic persecution in the first decade of the fourth century (*BHL* 6834).

These are, however, only sporadic signs of early Christianization in Thrace. In general, burial rites, religious practices, and epigraphic monuments definitely point to the pagan nature of the population's spiritual life in the Thracian diocese until at least the middle of the fourth century. From then on, Christian inscriptions appear en masse, with a tendency to increase in the fifth and sixth centuries. The majority of them are epitaphs. Inscriptions with the names of martyrs and famous saints have also been found. Ecclesiastical inscriptions record the names of bishops, presbyters, deacons, deaconesses, vicars, and vows of celibacy.

Thracian cities preserve the most Christian monuments, but there are also numerous remains of churches and funerary inscriptions that reveal how the new religion found its way into the countryside. The ideological context was heterogeneous. An ancient tomb from Osenovo, in the countryside 15 km north of Varna (ancient Odessos), is an eloquent example of the mixed character of the beliefs at that period. Side by side with the *chi-rho* monogram and the vine trellis, we see representations of the sun and the moon as guides of initiates, of

8. For the view that Aelius P. Julius actually signed a synodical letter by Apolinarius of Hierapolis (bp. ca. 170), later copied and circulated by Serapion, see Tabbernee 2007, 22–33.

Sol Invictus protector of the soldiers, and of pagan chthonic symbols: turtle and snake. Pre-Constantinian Christian monuments, however, are not securely dated. An anchor is depicted in a tomb in the village of Akchilar (17 km from Varna), although it is not clear whether the anchor provides evidence of a Christian context (Valeva 2001a, 196, 198).

In Thrace, as everywhere throughout the empire, Christian churches eventually replaced pagan temples and shrines. They were richly decorated with architectural sculpture, mosaics, and frescoes. Outside city walls, the churches were fortified, with good reason, since they contained many valuable objects. When archaeologists opened the crypt of the church on the hill Djanavar-tepe in the Odessos hinterland, miraculously untouched by treasure hunters, they found a marble reliquary in which a sheet of yellow silk was wrapped around a silver reliquary box, also in the form of a sarcophagus and decorated with Latin crosses. Inside the latter was a golden casket ornamented on the exterior by two bands with swastika-shaped beds of garnets and blue emeralds in the middle of each side. Its sliding lid was decorated with five precious stones and a band of cloisonné inlaid with garnets. The casket was created in the late fourth or early fifth century, most probably as a non-Christian object ending up as a Christian reliquary deposited in a sixth-century church (Weitzmann 1979, no. 569; Michev 2003, 15–18).

Marcianopolis

The metropolitan bishop's seat of the province of Moesia Secunda was at Marcianopolis (Hierokles, *Synekdemos* 636.2), a city 38 km west of Odessos (Angelov 2002). Several basilicas and mosaic pavements have been found in the city. One of these mosaics, decorated with a pattern of crosses, has a rare parallel at Kourion, Cyprus, suggesting intense cultural and economic exchanges within the Mediterranean region (Valeva 2001b). A basilica was erected at the end of the fifth or early sixth century at the eastern side of the amphitheater of the city. Another has been discovered outside of the walls in a northeastern direction and has been interpreted as belonging to a monastery. A third extramural basilica serviced the surrounding necropolis (Oppermann 2010, 109–10). Several tombs with painted decorations are known from Marcianopolis (Valeva 2001a, 196; Oppermann 2010, 234–35). Flowers, garlands, and birds decorated both pagan and Christian tombs in this syncretistic and spiritually dynamic period.

Tomis

Tomis was the metropolis of Scythia and the only bishopric of the province, at least until the fifth century (Sozomen, *Hist. eccl.* 6.21.3; 7.19.2; cf. Theodoret,

Hist. eccl. 4.35.1). The considerable number of martyrs from Tomis speaks of an important Christian community already in the early fourth century. Its bishop attended the Council of Nicaea (Eusebius, *Vit. Const.* 3.7.1). Several churches have been totally or partially excavated (Oppermann 2010, 57–64). A noteworthy feature is the presence of crypts under the presbyteria of the basilicas. Some of them are rather big, with separate spaces intended for burials. The crypt of a basilica, discovered near the Lyceum "Mihai Eminescu," is decorated with painted imitation of panels in opus sectile between pilasters (Barbet and Monier 2001; Oppermann 2010, 61). Two tombs from the fourth century with painted decorations, the Tomb of the Orants and the Tomb of the Banquet, are of distinct importance for the history of late antique painting (Barbet et al. 1996; Valeva 2001a, 201).

Philippopolis

Ever since its founding by Philip II of Macedon (r. 359–336 BCE) in 342 BCE, Philippopolis (Bospačieva 2005; Topalilov 2012; Bospačieva and Kolarova 2014) was one of the most prominent cities of Thrace. When Thrace became a Roman province in 45 CE, Philippopolis developed rapidly. The Hellenistic roots of the city's culture, however, remained strong: the administrative units (*phylai*) took their names from deities (e.g., Artemisias, Rhodopeis, Asklepias, Herakleis, Orpheis), and the citizens expressed their will in the Assembly (*Dēmos*), the Council of Citizens (*Boulē*), and the Council of Elders (*Gerousia*). Philippopolis was the metropolis of the Union (*Koinon*) of the Thracians, which existed from the first to the fourth centuries CE. The city also gained the right to have a temple dedicated to the emperor (Burrell 2004, 10, 243–44).

The agora of Roman Philippopolis (143 m by 136 m) is the largest excavated in Bulgaria (Dintchev 2009). It had four porticoes in Doric order with Ionic *propylaea* (monumental gateways) on the east, south, and west sides. During the final reconstruction of the agora in the third century following the Gothic raids, the porticoes were rebuilt in Corinthian order. The *bouleutērion* (where the Council of Citizens gathered) was situated at the northeast side of the agora, in close proximity to the library. On the south slope of the Three-Hills (Trimontium) area of the city is the theater, duly reerected in modern times. The ancient city had public baths, a stadium, temples, large colonnaded streets, and rich private residences (Valeva 2011b, 21–41; Bospačieva and Kolarova 2014).

Among the most interesting archaeological finds is the synagogue, discovered in the eastern part of Philippopolis (Kesyakova 1989a). Its floor is decorated with mosaics, depicting the menorah (seven-branched candlestick). A mosaic inscription gives the names of the donors: Joseph and Isaac. The continuous use of the synagogue from the third to the fifth centuries means that the Jewish community had a perpetual and important place in the history of the city.

We do not know in which circles the first Christians appeared, but legend speaks of a bishop named Hermes as early as the first century. Names of many other Philippopolitan bishops are known from the lists of the councils and other written sources (Mullen 2004, 149–50). What is believed to be the episcopal basilica of Philippopolis was lavishly decorated with floor mosaics, depicting dozens of species of birds (Kesyakova 1989b). A martyrium has also been discovered in the eastern necropolis of the city (Boyadjiev 2001; Bospačieva 2001). Philippopolis was the center of the Arian party during the time of the Council of Serdica in 343 (see chap. 9).

Church Architecture

The earliest Christian churches in Thrace were erected in the middle or second half of the fourth century. They exemplify the general type adopted in the area: a basilica with a nave and two aisles, covered by a ridge roof, a protruding apse on the east, and a narthex and atrium on the west. The congregation gathered in the atrium before the liturgy, then entered the church with the clergy through the narthex, in which the catechumens probably remained during the "Liturgy of the Faithful." The lack of an atrium in some early Balkan churches is the exception rather than the rule. The existence of a narthex (narrow, enclosed lobby) was essential (Oppermann 2010, 191–93). It was often tripartite to accommodate the stairs up to the galleries of large churches and to protective towers. Some basilicas had an exonarthex (outer entrance area) as well.

Inside the church, the nave was separated from the aisles by lines of piers or, more rarely, of columns and, in some cases, by means of barriers between them. That latter kind of partition was related to the liturgy and observed quite strictly in the Greek basilicas but not in Constantinople. The churches in Thrace tended to follow the Constantinopolitan tradition. The difference in the liturgical function between the nave and aisles was sometimes also emphasized by floor elevation. The nave, where the clergy moved about, was either elevated or lowered to allow better visual observance of the liturgy (e.g., Basilica 2 in Diocletianopolis-Hissar).

The inside shape of the apse was semicircular. The horseshoe-shaped apse, adopted from Asia Minor, was comparatively rare (Basilica 4a in Diocletianopolis-Hissar; basilicas in Karanovo and elsewhere; see Oppermann 2010, 187–88). The three-sided outer shape of the apse, the earliest example of which is believed to have been the basilica of the Studios Monastery in

Constantinople, was occasionally used in Thrace too (e.g., the so-called Old Metropolitan Church in Mesambria-Nesebar).[9]

The sanctuaries in the churches of the Thracian diocese conform to different liturgical traditions. The churches in which the Constantinopolitan liturgy was used did not have *pastophoria* (flanking chambers north and south of the apse) as was the tradition in the pre-iconoclastic churches of Constantinople. The erection of an ambo (raised podium) in the middle of the nave was also a mark of Constantinopolitan ritual influence, especially in the regions along the west coast of the Black Sea (Dosseva 2011). However, in many cases the organization and the decoration of the interior of the church was a combination of elements coming from different traditions: Constantinopolitan, Syrian, or from Asia Minor. The reason for this heterogeneity might have been the change in the ecclesiastical supremacy in respect to the Thracian diocese: from the end of the fourth to the middle of the fifth century it was under the supremacy of the bishop of Rome, until the Fourth Ecumenical Council in Chalcedon (451) postulated the transfer of the supremacy to the patriarch of Constantinople (Taft 1975, 180; Stanev 1999, 47; Dosseva 2011, 143).

The tripartite sanctuary was typical of Syrian early Christian architecture. In this type of sanctuary the central apse is flanked by two chambers related to the Preparation of the Gifts and the liturgy itself. A large number of Byzantine churches found in Bulgaria display this type of sanctuary. We see it in one of the most interesting basilicas, the so-called Eleussa in Nesebar. It has a U-shaped apse and two flanking small chambers in the east end, each provided with three *conchae* (semicircular apses, often domed). The plan resembles that of the church in Dereağzı in Lycia, 20 km northwest of Myra, suggesting cultural influences from the eastern parts of the early Byzantine Empire.

The altar could be situated in the apse (e.g., Basilica 8 in Diocletianopolis-Hissar; church in Chobandere), but often the apse contained the *synthronon* where the bishop and the clergy sat during the service. As in Constantinopolitan churches, *synthrona* in Thrace consisted of a semicircular tier of steps. Where a *synthronon* existed, the altar was moved a few meters into the nave. Under the altar table was a crypt with relics deposited in reliquaries (e.g., the churches of Djanavar-Tepe and Shkorpilovtsi near Varna, and Church 6 in Hissar).

The altar space normally was raised above the level of the nave (*Const. ap.* 8.11.10). The chancel barrier ran straight across the whole width of the nave (Church 1 in Krumovo Kale) or was *pi*-shaped (Isperikhovo, Novae—the episcopal basilica). The latter (on which, see Biernacki 1990) was to become

---

9. See Stanev and Zhdrakov 2009. For churches with this type of apse but dated earlier, see Oppermann 2010, 188.

Julia Valeva

Fig. 8.10. "Red Church," near Perushtitsa

standard in Constantinopolitan and Greek churches. In elevation, the barriers were either low chancel screens or high constructions with screens, colonnettes, and architrave (Dosseva 2002).

Another type of Christian cult building in Thrace was planned centrally. Scholars recognize its prototypes in Roman mausoleums or in palatial audience halls (Grabar 1972; Krautheimer 1981). A famous church with a central plan in Thrace is the so-called Red Church, near the town of Perushtitsa (Boyadjiev 1976; Ćurčić 2010, 241–42; Oppermann 2010, 198–99). The building has four *conchae* and a deambulatory (a passage around the central nave) built in the fourth century initially as a mausoleum or a martyrium. Later it was transformed into a church: the east *concha* was pulled down, and an apse with a foreapse space was constructed instead. An exonarthex was added with a baptistery on the north side, and a chapel for relics or a diaconicon (room containing liturgical books and vestments) on the south side. An annex was built on the west side (a portico?). The building was crowned with a dome.

A four-*conchae* building has been found in Augusta Traiana-Beroe, east of the city wall. The building could well be a martyrium with a monastery developed around it later. The church had an atrium, and graves with painted crosses and psalm citations have been found in the narthex (Ivanov 2002). The history of the monasteries in Thrace is, however, not yet well studied. The foundations of a monastery have been found in Karaach-Teke in the vicinity

8.6 Tomb Decoration

Both pagan and early Christian tombs from the provinces of the Thracian diocese illustrate the end of the antique decorative system, especially the idea that postulates that the decoration should give an illusion of the construction of the wall. Floral motifs—flowers and garlands—were widespread (e.g., tombs in Marcianopolis, Philippopolis, Diocletianopolis, and Durostorum). Crowning with flowers was considered to be a sign of divine protection, since people in remote Antiquity believed that gods reincarnated into plants. Vine trellises, which were chthonic symbols of Dionysus, acquired christological meaning.

In figural art, the most popular funerary iconography of the banquet gradually disappeared but contributed to the formation of the iconography of the procession (e.g., in a tomb from Philippopolis depicting a funerary banquet). In the well-known tomb in Durostorum, the standing frontal figures of the patron and his wife substitute for the classical variant of the *coena funebris* (funerary meal), with the reclining husband on the *klinē* (bed) and the wife sitting at his feet. The depicted servants are, however, already as big as the owners, and they bring objects that attest their master's prosperity. This is a ceremonial of private character (in the domain of the owner), exalted through the *concordia* between the patron and his wife expressed by means of the *volumen* (roll) in the hand of the man, the flower held by the *matron*, and the peacocks—birds of Juno, the protectress of matrimonial life.

The funerary banquet in late-antique Christian and pagan tombs was sometimes represented in a new version: a banquet around a *sigma*-shaped table. A tomb in Tomis displays the best-preserved variant of this iconography in the Eastern Roman Empire (see Valeva 2001a, 201). Another tomb in Tomis is decorated with orants (praying devotees [Barbet et al. 1996]), iconography familiar from the Roman catacombs. A recently excavated early Christian tomb in Philippopolis (Plovdiv) is decorated with depictions of two of the miracles of Christ: the healing of the paralytic and the resurrection of Lazarus. Most Thracian early Christian tombs were, however, decorated with crosses and monograms of Christ—secure protective signs. Very often the letters *alpha* and *omega* reinforced the eschatological meaning of the symbols. Crosses with vegetal motifs were semantically and graphically related to the idea of the "tree of life" (e.g., tombs in Augusta Traiana-Beroe). In a few tombs crosses are combined with psalm citations (Valeva 1998; 2001a, 192–94).

of Varna. A few rock-cut monasteries have also been discovered in the same area. Some of the more spacious rock-cut rooms presumably were used as churches, with natural *conchae* functioning as apses.

Building material in the Thracian provinces was traditional: stone, brick, and wood. The building technique was *opus mixtum*, with different layers of brick and the stones quite often only roughly chipped or crushed. The churches from the sixth century onward, having a far more complicated plan, were built entirely of brick, the stone being used only for the foundations (e.g., the church near Goliamo Belovo) (see Emerson 1946; Boyadjiev 1969; Grabar 1972).

Thrace suffered great losses during the incessant barbaric invasions from the third through the sixth centuries. Many tribes settled in Thrace as *foederati* (allies). Slavs inundated the peninsula in the sixth century, and Bulgarians, who came a little later, organized their state north of the Balkan Mountains in 681.

Eastern Illyricum

Early Christianity

The vast territory of Illyricum presupposes a great diversity in the spiritual and material development of its provinces (*Rapports* 1980; *Villes et peuplement* 1984). Illyricum appears for the first time in Christian literature in St. Paul's Epistle to the Romans. During his early missions Paul had traveled "as far around as Illyricum" (Rom. 15:19), which probably means up to the borders of Dalmatia and Pannonia (Zeiller 1918, 27). These provinces, which had recently been created out of the earlier Roman province of Illyricum, would hardly have offered a convenient spiritual setting for his missions. Therefore, we find Paul concentrating his activities among Jewish communities in cities such as Philippi and Thessalonica on the coast.

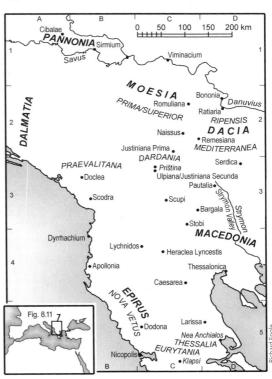

Fig. 8.11. Map of Eastern Illyricum

EARLY MARTYRS

By the early fourth century, many Christians had suffered martyrdom in the Illyrian provinces. In Pannonia Orientalis, for example, Pollio, a lector in Cibalae (modern Vinkovci, Croatia), perished on the stake during the Diocletianic persecution. His corpse was later transferred to Rome and buried in the Pontian cemetery (*BHL* 6869; Zeiller 1918, 73–75). A bishop of Cibalae named Eusebius appears to have been martyred even earlier, perhaps under Valerian (r. 253–260) (see Harnack 1908, 2:237). A famous martyr from Sirmium was Irenaeus, bishop of the local church,[10] who was questioned by the proconsul Probus (the same who accused Pollio) and then decapitated and thrown into the Sava River (*BHG* II 948; *BHL* 4466; Musurillo 1972, 294–301). This Irenaeus is not to be confused with Irenaeus of Lyons (bp. ca. 177–200), whose feast, nonetheless, impacted the feast of St. Irenaeus of Sirmium. Irenaeus of Sirmium's deacon, Demetrios, was also killed. He vanished from history, however, as his memory was replaced by that of St. Demetrios of Thessalonica (Zeiller 1918, 81–82). The latter is Eastern Illyricum's most famous martyr (d. ca. 306). St. Demetrios is patron saint of Thessalonica, and the huge basilica there today stands on the remains of a chapel dedicated in about 313, containing his relics.

A *mensa martyrum* (martyrs' table, for commemorative meals), found in Larissa, the capital of Thessaly, is inscribed with the names of John, Luke, Andreas, and Leonidas, commemorated on December 18. Leonidas was also venerated in Athens, Corinth (the Lechaion Basilica), and Klapsi in Eurytania (Barnea 1980, 453, 459). An invocation to the martyr Kodratos, who suffered martyrdom during the persecution of Valerian in 258, has been found at Corinth. Names of local martyrs also exist on reliquaries. One, made of silver and found in Praevalitana, additionally bears the names of SS. Peter, Paul, and John (Barnea 1980, 470). An engraved inscription on a terracotta reliquary from the district of Pautalia (Kyustendil, Bulgaria) reads, "Here are the relics of St. Thomas the apostle and St. Babylas the bishop and [those] of the three youths" (*Hic insunt reliquide sanct[i] Thomae apost[oli] et Babylae ep[iscopi] cum tribus parvulis* [Beševliev 1964, no. 42]). The names of the youths (Urban, Prelidianus, and Epolonus) are not inscribed on the reliquary.

OTHER INSCRIPTIONS

Apart from those mentioned above, pre-Constantinian inscriptions are very rare in Illyricum and usually are insecurely dated (Barnea 1980, 463). Mass

---

10. On Sirmium and its martyrs, see V. Popović 2003; on martyrs in Illyricum generally, see Bratož 2004a; 2004b.

8.7 Christian Epigrams and Classical Citations

Usually, inscriptions accompanied by representations of fishes or birds are considered to be possibly pre-Constantinian and Christian, but none such from Eastern Illyricum is securely dated. Other inscriptions convey biblical texts and citations from liturgical and other early Christian texts, but there are also fragments from classical pagan literature. An epigram from Apollonia in Epirus (*BE* 1969, no. 352) transmits a verse from Sophocles (*Aj.* 646). Another epigram, which is part of a mosaic in the sixth-century basilica of Bishop Dometios II (bp. post-516) in Nicopolis (Palaio-Preveza), also in Epirus (Barnea 1980, 471), cites verses from Homer's *Iliad* (17.447) and *Odyssey* (13.131).

Christianization began in the fourth century, hence the increase of Christian inscriptions during that century and even much more so in the fifth and sixth centuries. Philippi, according to Acts 16:12–15, was the first European town where the gospel was preached by St. Paul. Significantly, no Christian inscription earlier than the fourth century has been discovered there (Lemerle 1945, 7). Eusebius of Caesarea certainly was well informed when he wrote in 337 that the churches in Moesia and Pannonia were still young (*Vit. Const.* 4.43.2).

Many later inscriptions provide evidence concerning church organization in Eastern Illyricum. In these we see recorded the ecclesiastical offices of *archiepiskopos* (Thessalonica, Serdica, Crete) and *episkopos* (Philippi, Caesarea, Stobi, Bargala in Macedonia, Nea Anchialos in Thessalia, Delphi in Phocide, Athens, Corinth, Eurytania, Tegea and Hermione in Argolis, Naxos, Crete, and elsewhere). The names of some of these bishops exist in other written sources as well. They are often accompanied by epithets such as "most pious," "holy," "most holy," "most venerable." Inscriptions mentioning priests (*presbyteroi*) number about forty. Numerous inscriptions were made for deacons (both men and women), readers, virgins, *oikonomoi* (stewards/administrators), and other church officials. Neophytes (newly baptized Christians) also declared themselves. The usual name for adherents of the new religion was *Christianos*, although quite often we encounter "servant of God/Christ/the Lord" (Barnea 1980, 475).

Christian Topography

Even a short survey of the Christian topography of Eastern Illyricum shows the richness of monuments—witnesses of a long and turbulent history in which individual sacrifice for the sake of faith paralleled the unscrupulous bitter struggle for power and supremacy within the bosom of the church.

Thessalonica

One of the most important monuments not only for the history of art and religion in Thessalonica but also in the whole of the early Christian world is the so-called Rotunda of St. George (Torp 1963; Spieser 1984). There still are important questions about its building phases that remain unanswered, but the most widely accepted conclusion is that it was begun by Galerius (r. 293–311) to serve as his mausoleum (recently suggested as Constantine's mausoleum; Ćurčić 2010, 54). When the memorial complex at his residence in Romuliana (Gamzigrad) was conceived, the Thessalonica project was abandoned and was resumed only during the reign of Theodosius judging by the stamps on the bricks of the dome (Torp 1963, 1–12). Presumably, the dome was decorated with a full standing figure of Christ within a wreathed medallion carried by four angels, an iconography that reveals inspiration from imperial art. The preserved mosaic frieze with saints in the dome can be considered as the masterpiece of early Byzantine mosaic art (Ćurčić 2010, 71; best photos in Bakirtzis, Kourkoutidou-Nikolaidou, and Mavropoulou-Tsioumi 2012, 48–127).

By the middle of the fifth century Thessalonica became the seat of the prefecture of Illyricum at the expense of Sirmium, from where the relics of St. Demetrius were also transferred. Thessalonica was also the seat of a powerful bishop who, from the last quarter of the fourth century, was under the authority of the pope. The concentration of administrative and ecclesiastical power in the city contributed to its development, which made it second in size in the Balkans after Constantinople (Ćurčić 2010, 100–102). Despite the attempts of the patriarch of Constantinople to limit the prerogatives of the bishop of Thessalonica in his capacity as vicar of the pope, it was only in 535 that this power was shared with the head of the archbishopric of Justiniana Prima and was eventually and definitively transferred to the Constantinopolitan patriarchate in 732 by order of Emperor Leo the Isaurian (r. 717–741).

The most important church in Thessalonica, dedicated to St. Demetrius, patron of the city, was built in the second half of the fifth century and underwent some reparation after a fire in 620 (Bakirtzis 1988; Ćurčić 2010, 106). It is a five-aisled basilica with a large transept (the tranverse section of the building crossing the nave in a cruciform church), galleries over the side aisles, a narthex, and an atrium. Under the transept there is a crypt in which the body of St. Demetrius was at one time interred. An original opus sectile decoration is preserved on the nave arcade spandrels, as well as wall mosaics from the end of the fifth century to the eighth century (Bakirtzis, Kourkoutidou-Nikolaidou, and Mavropoulou-Tsioumi 2012, 128–79).

Another fifth-century basilica, well preserved in its original shape, is the Acheiropoietos (Not made by human hands). Its importance lies in its standard character: three aisles with galleries over the side ones, a semi-circular wide apse, and a narthex. It is believed that the church was built to honor the Virgin Mary after her proclamation as Mother of God (*Theotokos*) at the Third Ecumenical Council in Ephesus in 431. Reconstructions of the church occurred in the seventh century and, again, in the fourteenth and fifteenth centuries. The mosaic decoration dates from the middle of the fifth century (Bakirtzis, Kourkoutidou-Nikolaidou, and Mavropoulou-Tsioumi 2012, 196–237).

The Church of Hosios David, a small cruciform building with dome on pendentives and mosaic decoration of the apse, dates from ca. 500 (Bakirtzis, Kourkoutidou-Nikolaidou, and Mavropoulou-Tsioumi 2012, 180–95). It presumably belonged to a monastery (Ćurčić 2010, 110).

Philippi

Philippi, established by Philip II in 356 BCE, was an important station on the Via Egnatia (Ćurčić 2010, 114–19). In spite of the early acquaintance of its population with the word of God preached by the apostle Paul himself (Acts 16:9–10; Phil. 1.1), the Christianization of the city during the fourth century was slow. The building of an early church dedicated to a local martyr called Paul after 313 is known from a mosaic inscription. After a century a new, large cathedral with an octagonal floor plan was built in its place, incorporating a pagan *heroon* (shrine commemorating a hero) that stood on the site. This impressive octagon became the core of a large complex, which included the residence of the bishop, a baptistery, and a (public?) bath. Several more basilicas are known from Philippi, all of them remarkable for their plan and liturgical furnishing. Thus, in Basilica A the capitals of Prokonessian marble equaled in beauty the best similar architectural elements in Constantinople and Thessalonica. A particularly interesting material comes from Basilica C and the Extra-muros Basilica—namely, large quantities of colored glass, undoubtedly employed for more effective lighting of the interior.

Sirmium

Sirmium (Sremska Mitrovica, Serbia), the capital of Eastern Pannonia (P. Milošević 2001; V. Popović 2003), was the birthplace of several emperors: Aurelian (b. 214), Probus (b. 232), and Constantius II (b. 317). Decius (b. ca. 201) and Maximian (b. 250) were born in the environs as well. As a result of the administrative reforms of Diocletian, Sirmium became the residence of Galerius, one of the original Caesars of the tetrarchy, whose intolerance toward the Christians gave rise to severe persecutions; hence the high number of martyrs in the city. Later, Sirmium became the capital of Licinius (r. 308–324). Licinius built the public baths, attested by an inscription from the Island of

Brach referring to capitals made for the columns of these baths: *capitella columnarum ad thermas Licianas* (*CIL* 3.10107; V. Popović 2003, 201). He probably also started the construction of the hippodrome. Constantine resided in the city between 316 and 321, and again after his victory over Licinius in 324. Theodosius I was crowned in Sirmium in 379, but in the very next year barbaric invasions undermined the prosperity of Sirmium. The Avars destroyed the city irrevocably in 583 (John of Ephesus, *Hist. eccl.* 6.32–33).

The list of known fourth-century bishops of Sirmium (both Catholic and Arian) is almost complete. It begins with Domnus, who took part at Nicaea. Situated along the roads outside the city are graveyards in which the oldest Christian memorials have been discovered. One of them is the Martyrium of St. Synerotas (Sineros), an authentic victim of the Diocletianic persecutions, situated in the western necropolis (*CIL* 3.10232, 3.10233; Bratož 2004b, 223n105). In the eastern cemetery an inscription has helped the identification of another martyrium, dedicated to St. Irenaeus (Zeiller 1918, 79–80; Bratož 2004b, 216n54). An anonymous martyr was venerated in a *cella trichōra* (triconch funeral-banquet hall) in the eastern cemetery (Jěremić 2005; Duval and Popović 1980, 371).

VIMINACIUM

The painted tombs of Viminacium (Stari Kostolac, Serbia), the capital of Moesia Prima, have also yielded suggestive material for the Christianization of the society (Korać 2007). The well-to-do commissioned themselves to be painted with their opulent garments and jewels, attended by servants with large serving platters and drink vessels. In tomb 5517 the pagan iconography of the glorifying hunt was applied, but next to the rider we see the *chi-rho* monogram, accompanied by the apocalyptic letters *alpha* and *omega*.

RATIARIA

Evidence about the wealthy society of Ratiaria (Archar, Bulgaria), the capital of Dacia Ripensis, comes from archaeological excavations that reveal houses from the rich quarter of the town, an audience hall of a rich residence decorated with a mosaic of Orpheus charming the animals, and treasured jewelry and coins hidden in the walls of houses (Giorgetti 1983; 1987; Velkov 1966; 1977, 86; Kuzmanov and Valeva 2001). The pagan material, however, exceeds by far that relating to early Christianity. There must, nevertheless, have been a Christian community in Ratiaria by about 300. According to *Martyrologium hieronymianum* prid. kal. Jan. and kal. Jan., a Hermes of Ratiaria was martyred along with a man named Aggaeus and another named Caius, who came from Bononia. This occurred during the Great Persecution in about

304/5. Bononia (modern Vidin), 27 km north of Ratiaria, probably was the site of the martyrdoms. A prominent supporter of Arianism was Palladius, bishop of Ratiaria from 346 to 381 (Velkov 1966, 169).

Serdica

Serdica (also spelled "Sardica"; Sofia, Bulgaria) was one of the most important cities of the Balkan provinces (Kirin 2000; Boyadjiev 2002). Situated on a strategic crossroad, within a beautiful landscape and rich in mineral springs, the city almost became the capital of the empire under Constantine (Anonymus Continuatus Dion, *Fr.* 15 [*FGH* 4.199]; see Dagron 1974, 27). For a few years, between 303 and 309, Serdica was actually Galerius's capital, and the imperial mint was transferred from Thessalonica (Sutherland and Carson 1967, 54–55, 467–87). Probably at that time there was an imperial palace in the town, the precise location of which is still controversial (Kirin 2000; Valeva 2011a). In Serdica, Galerius, debilitated by illness, issued his Edict of Toleration on April 30, 311—his last hope to avoid death (Eusebius, *Hist. eccl.* 8.17.3–10). Serdica was Christianized in the fourth century. Some of the largest structures, such as those situated east of the forum, were turned into churches. One of them, built in the fourth century, has survived through the centuries and is now dedicated to St. George (Kirin 2000; Boyadjiev 2002, 152–61). The building

Fig. 8.12. Church of St. George and Remains of Late Fifth-, Early Sixth-Century Hagia Sophia, Serdica

probably was originally intended to be a bath (Grabar 1928, 87; Filov 1933; for the opinion that initially the building was a martyrium, see Venedikov and Petrov 1964). The dedication to St. George dates from the Middle Ages.

The Church of the Divine Wisdom (Hagia Sophia), which in the Middle Ages gave its name to the city, still stands in its reconstructed form most likely from the end of the fifth century (Filov 1913; Boyadjiev 2002, 162–75; 2009), although dating to the reign of Constantine V (r. 741–775) has recently been suggested on the grounds of similarities with Hagia Eirene in Constantinople (Fingarova 2011). Built originally probably as a memorial to a martyr or a saint in the middle of the large eastern necropolis of Serdica ca. 350–360 (Shalganov 2002), the Hagia Sophia was soon surrounded by burials *ad sanctos* (Shalganov 2005). During later building phases these tombs were preserved and can still be seen today under the present church. Several of these fifth- and sixth-century tombs are decorated with crosses and contain liturgical inscriptions (Valeva 2001a, 192–94).

Of noteworthy importance among the early Christian tombs in Serdica (Boyadjiev 1994) are ones decorated with representations of the Garden of Eden, and with the images of the four archangels, lords of the angelic host: Michael, Gabriel, Raphael, and Uriel (Valeva 1986).

The archaeological evidence about the solidity of the Christian community in Serdica is supplemented by data from written sources. We know the names of several bishops of Serdica, the first of whom, Protogenes, was addressed in a decree sent to him by Constantine in December 316 (Barnes 1982, 73). Protogenes attended the Council of Nicaea. In 343 an ecumenical council was held in Serdica, probably in virtue of the local church's dependence on the ecclesiastical jurisdiction of Rome (Hess 1958; Barnard 1983). The council became a battlefield between the Nicene "orthodox" party and the Arians, who withdrew to Philippopolis and organized their own sessions (see also chap. 9).

Pautalia

Several other cities and towns in Dacia Mediterranea continued not only to exist but even to thrive despite devastating barbaric intrusions. Pautalia (Kyustendil, Bulgaria) was one of them (Slokoska, Staykova-Aleksandrova, and Spassov 2002; Katsarova 2005). Situated in the fertile Strymon Valley, the town has a mild climate, mineral springs, and ore deposits. This originally Thracian settlement acquired its Roman urban aspect during the reigns of Trajan and Hadrian. Important roads connected Pautalia with Serdica, Stobi, and Thessalonica, a network recorded on the *Tabula Peutingeriana*. In Late Antiquity a second wall encircled the enlarged town. Seven early Christian basilicas have been excavated here (Katsarova 2005, 137–44), each with a nave, two aisles, and a semicircular apse. They date from the fourth to the sixth centuries. Basilica 2 is considered to have been the seat of the local bishop. The decoration of the apse in Basilica 7 shows Western influences in iconography, representations of lambs as symbols of Christ and the apostles (Spassov et al. 1999). A pious inscription in the south nave transmits the Thracian name of the donor: "Bitus and his kin (have made this). I beg you to pray for the sinner" (*Bitus cum suis. Peto orate pro peccatore*).

NAISSUS

Being a stop on the principal road from Central Europe to Constantinople was crucial for the prosperity of any town. Naissus (Niš, Serbia), where Constantine was born in 272/3, made the most of this circumstance. The city had an important Christian community as early as the fourth century (Rakocija and Todorović 2013). At Easter in 344, Athanasius of Alexandria (bp. 328–373), the champion of the orthodox party in the Arian controversy, visited Naissus after the Council of Serdica (Socrates, *Hist. eccl.* 1.36; 2.12). Of special interest is a sixth-century basilica with martyrium in the center of the eastern necropolis (G. Milošević 2004). A painted inscription, in a vaulted tomb, refers to Peter and Paul, the "Princes of the Apostles" (Rakocija 2008; Valeva 2001a, 201). The earliest known bishop of Naissus is Cyriacus, who preceded Gaudentius, the bishop who attended the Council of Serdica (Sozomen, *Hist. eccl.* 3.11.8) (see Zeiller 1918; Rakocija 2008).

SCODRA AND DOCLEA

The province of Praevalitana covered the territory of modern Montenegro and the north of Albania. The coastal area was much more developed and rich in towns, while the interior mountain region, with the metropolis Scodra (Shkodër) and the city of Doclea (Podgorica), contains little evidence about early Christianity. Martyrs are not known from this province, but many names of bishops have come down to us from different sources (Duval and Popović 1980, 378–80).

SCUPI AND ULPIANA/JUSTINIANA SECUNDA

Dardania, a Latin-speaking region, was culturally related to both Dacia Mediterranea and Macedonia (Duval and Popović 1980, 380–82). The seat of the archbishop probably was Scupi (Skopje, Macedonia), at least until the earthquake of 518. The main Christian city, however, was Ulpiana (near Gračanica, Kosovo), later (probably after 518) named Justiniana Secunda. The town produced two martyrs, the stonecutters Flaurus and Laurus. Churches and mausoleums have been explored (Snively 2005), although intense study of the early Christian antiquities of Dardania still awaits its peak.

DYRRHACHIUM AND LYCHNIDOS

From Dyrrhachium (Durrës, Albania), the capital of Epirus Nova, we have a unique image of Sophia—the Divine Wisdom—perfectly produced in mosaic in a chapel accommodated in the amphitheater. Another Epirotan town, Lychnidos (Ohrid, Macedonia), was situated on the Via Egnatia, which aided the town's prosperity in Late Antiquity. Lychnidos had been an important site in Hellenistic times, with numerous temples, rich houses, a theater, a gymnasium, and other buildings. The archaeological excavations on the Plaoshnik Plateau of the famous medieval Church of St. Clement and St. Panteleimon reveal that it was constructed on top of a three-aisled early Christian basilica. It has a spacious atrium with galleries on the four sides and a square baptistery with a round piscine (Bitrakova-Grozdanova 2006). Mosaics with rather naively depicted Christian symbolic compositions decorate both the basilica and the baptistery. Beyond the square across from the basilica is a polyconchal church from the second half of the fifth century. Archaeologists believe that the rather prompt construction of the basilica and the creation of the whole ensemble with square and basilica were due to the urgent need of support for the sake of the victory of orthodoxy over heresies.

STOBI

Stobi (near Gradsko, Macedonia), the capital of Macedonia Secunda since around 386 (Papazoglu 1988), was a rich town, as indicated by the solid construction of its vast churches and private residences. Its bishops were regular participants at ecumenical councils, beginning with Nicaea, which Bishop Boudius attended.

The center of the city consisted of numerous rich houses, the most prominent of which is the so-called Theodosian Palace, a fictitious name that hints at the visit of Theodosius I in the city in 388. The churches were incorporated into the plan of the town without significant alterations to the other buildings. Four of them were built within the town and three more were situated outside of the walls (*extra muros*). The Central Basilica was built in the fifth century on the grounds of a Jewish synagogue—a rare example of the continuity of the two religions (Duval and Popović 1980, 383–86, esp. 384). The episcopal basilica has in front of the façade a semicircular portico (a structure in vogue in Late Antiquity) that gives a monumental aspect to the ensemble. The altar is *pi*-shaped, with a crypt for the relics and an ambo in front of it in the south half of the nave, in accordance with the tradition of Greek churches. A privileged burial place in the church, which is unusual for the region, probably belonged to Bishop Philip, whose name is on a sixth-century lintel. A study of the atrium of the basilica revealed a preexisting church from the fourth century, the baptistery of which was covered by the later one, related to the cathedral (Ćurčić 2010, 111–14). The nearby theater was in use at least to the end of the fourth century.

HERACLEA LYNCESTIS

Heraclea Lyncestis (modern Bitola) was a city whose prosperity was a result of its location on the Via Egnatia. Heraclea became an important episcopal seat in the province of Macedonia. One of the bishops of the town, Evagrius, participated at the Council of Serdica (343); Bishop Quintilinus appeared at the Second Council of Ephesus (449). The episcopal palace and several churches have survived, of which the Great Basilica is most famous for its splendid mosaic pavement in the narthex, representing the Garden of Eden (Tomašević 1967).

JUSTINIANA PRIMA

One of the most interesting moments in the history of Byzantine Illyricum was the founding of the new archiepiscopal seat, Justiniana Prima (Caričin Grad, Serbia), by Justinian (Bavant, Ivanišević, and Trajković 2006). His aim was to oppose the aspirations of Rome and to reduce the power of the papal vicar in Thessalonica. The seat of the prefect of Eastern Illyricum (i.e., the civil administrative power), however, de facto remained in Thessalonica. At the same time, *Novella* 11, issued in 535 and titled *De privilegiis archiepiscopi primae Iustinianae*, honored the emperor's birthplace. Ten years later, in *Novella* 131 (*De ecclesiasticis titulis*), the administrative priority of Justiniana Prima was not reaffirmed, unlike the prerogatives of its archbishop, limited, however, solely to the diocese of Dacia (Markus 1979; Snively 2005, 216). Justiniana Prima was constructed virtually on virgin soil (Procopius, *Aed.* 4.1) and therefore can be taken as an example of early Byzantine urbanism. Situated on a promontory between two small rivers, the city was more than 500 m long and about 250 m wide. Archaeologists distinguish three parts of the city: acropolis, Upper Town, and Lower Town (Bavant, Kondić, and Spieser 1990). Each of these was protected with its own wall and towers. The residence of the archbishop and the cathedral (Basilica A) were situated on the acropolis (Caillet and Jěremić 2010). It has been observed with good reason that the fortified character of the episcopal residence is a mark of a new trend, which will culminate in the fortified palaces of the medieval period (Ćurčić 2010, 211). The Upper Town was organized around a circular space in the center of which was the statue of the emperor. The layout of Justiniana Prima conformed to some basic elements of classic town-planning, like the colonnaded streets and the infrastructure, and was at the same time inspired by the plan of Constantinople (Ćurčić 2010, 211). Several basilicas were erected on the plateau, implying that, from the beginning, Justiniana Prima was conceived of as an ecclesiastical center (Duval and Popović 1984). The types of the churches and their situation within the town suggest that they were halting places during liturgical processions (Duval and Popović 1980, 377). The cruciform church in the Upper Town is reminiscent of the urban martyria of Syria and points to Oriental prototypes along with the local Greek traditions.

Constantinople

There is no accurate information about apostolic missionary activity in Byzantium, the urban site on the Bosphorus that preceded Constantinople. Moreover, the total destruction of the ancient city by Septimius Severus in 196 would have dispersed any Christian community that, according to later legend, had been established there by the apostle Andrew on his way to Scythia. Therefore, the story of Christianity in Constantinople is the story not of known apostles and martyrs but of the church there as an institution that developed into the chief patriarchate of Byzantine Christianity. The ultimate prominence of the see of Constantinople was inevitable because the city was the capital of the Eastern provinces, soon to become, after the fall of Rome in 476, the only administrative center of the Late Roman Empire.

In Constantinople we are dealing with the political reality of the early church. The tumultuous history of the church of Constantinople, which at times resulted in bloody riots, disguised behind theological disputes the bitter

---

8.8 Ancient Sources about Constantinople

Details about the topography of Constantinople are fairly well preserved in the *Notitia urbis Constantinopolitanae*. Another important source is the *Patria sive origines urbis Constantinopolitanae*, based, in part, on a work written by Hesychius Illustrius (fl. ca. 550) and incorporated by other writers, including Pseudo-Codinus in his *Patria Constantinoupoleo* (*Patria of Constantinople*) in the fourteenth century (Preger 1901–1907; Dagron 1984a; Cameron and Herrin 1984; Berger 1988). Procopius's *De aedificiis* (*On Buildings*) and the *Chronicon paschale* (*Paschal Chronicle*) are important for knowledge about the city's monuments (see also Janin 1964; Mango 1990a; Barsanti 1992; Berger 1997; 2000; Bardill 1997; 1999; Basset 2004). The most detailed source for the Constantinopolitan court and imperial ceremonies, as well as for the topography of the city, is the *Book of Ceremonies*, by Constantine VII Porphyrogenitus (r. 913–959).

struggles for supremacy among the Eastern patriarchates. The development of
Christianity in Constantinople expressed itself in two related ways: through
the ecclesiastical canons of the early ecumenical councils, and through the
struggle against heresies "resolved" by these same councils.

A Christian City

From its very beginning, Constantinople was a Christian city (Sozomen,
Hist. eccl. 2.2.30–30.35; *FGH* 390). In a law (*novella*) dated December 1, 334,
Constantine refers to the divine providence that moved him to found the new
capital (*Cod. theod.* 13.5.7; cf. Eusebius, *Vit. Const.* 4.36). Significantly, St. Augustine (354–430) emphasized that Constantine had not built a single pagan
temple in the new capital, while he had laid several Christian foundations (*Civ.*
5.25). Constantine's establishment of Constantinople as a Christian capital is
the best indication of how the emperor viewed the future importance of the
empire as inextricably bound to Christianity (Bolotov 1994, vol. 3).

Several ecumenical councils were held in the new capital.[11] Through the
canons of these councils, the power of the bishop of Constantinople grew
quickly. Already at the Second Ecumenical Council, in 381, the see of Constantinople was acknowledged as second in rank after Rome. The enabling
canon (*Can.* 3), however, gave only honor rather than any real power to the
metropolitan bishop of Constantinople. He continued to be a suffragan of
the bishop of Heraclea. Real authority accrued in practice when, time and
time again, bishops from various sees in the region preferred to ask for justice
or intercession in Constantinople rather than from their own metropolitan
bishop. For example, Ambrose of Milan (bp. 374–397) interceded before the
Constantinopolitan patriarch Nectarius (bp. 381–397) for the deposition of
Gerontius of Nicomedia (bp. post-381–401) (see Bolotov 1994, 3:225). The
bishop of Constantinople also used to summon local synods or councils, attended by sympathetic local and foreign bishops who happened to be in town at
the time. This proved a successful tactic to expand influence and gain control.

During the late fourth century, the see of Constantinople had the good fortune of being led by strong personalities such as the former senator Nectarius
and John (bp. 398–404), named Chrysostom (Golden-Mouthed) because of
his eloquence. When John Chrysostom was in power, the ecclesiastical authority of the Constantinopolitan patriarch already encompassed the Diocese

11. The Second Ecumenical Council (Constantinople I [381]), the Fifth (Constantinople II
[553]), the Sixth (Constantinople III [680–681]), and the so-called Quinisext (Fifth-Sixth) Council
(also known as the Council "in Trullo" [692]). The last complemented the dogmatic resolutions
of the Fifth and the Sixth Councils but was not recognized by Pope Sergius (bp. 687–701).

of Thrace, with its six provinces, and the dioceses of Asia and Pontus, each with eleven provinces (Bolotov 1994, 3:227). The authority of the patriarch of Constantinople over the three dioceses was ratified at the Fourth Ecumenical Council in Chalcedon in 451. Canon 9 liberated the patriarch from the wardship of the Heracleian exarch, although the right of the latter to consecrate the patriarch of Constantinople was preserved out of respect to tradition. Canon 28 postulated equality between the sees of Constantinople and Rome (admittedly, this was not acknowledged by the pope).

The strengthening of the Constantinopolitan patriarchate evolved in an atmosphere of violent reaction on the part of the patriarchates of Alexandria and Antioch. Its victory, however, was predetermined by the very fact of its existence in the capital, in close proximity to and relationship with the secular power. Bishops often appealed to the emperor. Gradually, a specific bond between emperor and clerics developed in the East, the emperor tending to interfere in ecclesiastical affairs. Precedents occurred during Constantine's reign, and later, powerful rulers such as Constantius, Theodosius, and, especially, Justinian used to take ecclesiastical matters into their own hands (Dagron 1996). The emperor, nonetheless, was presumed to receive his rule from God, and he pretended to act according to divine law. Piety was ranked first among the virtues of a Christian emperor. Official imperial imagery was inconceivable without the victorious Christian symbol: the cross.

Arianism

The second important aspect of the history of the Constantinopolitan patriarchate was the patriarchate's struggle against heresies. As a result, the church of Constantinople gained ground and vastly contributed to the evolution of theology. Early heresies concerned the Holy Trinity. These were succeeded by debates about the nature of Christ. The definitive statement of orthodox faith was formulated at Nicaea in 325 (see chap. 7) and finalized at Constantinople in 381 (Gaddis 1999a; 1999d; see sidebar 8.9). Arianism (or better designated as Homoeianism) asserted that Christ is not of one substance with the Father, but rather is a creature raised by the Father to the dignity of Son of God.

Arianism, considered a product of the "School of Antioch" by scholars such as Vassilii Bolotov (1994, 4:1),[12] assumed dangerous proportions after Constantine's time, due to its protection by the imperial family (Barnard 1983, 38–39). The followers of Arius (ca. 256/60–ca. 336) dominated the capital

---

12. On the Arian controversy and the Council of Nicaea, see also Luibhéid 1982; Hanson 1988; Ayres 2004. On Arianism in Bulgarian historiography, see Snegarov 1944, 375–82.

8.9 Niceno-Constantinopolitan Creed (381)

We believe in one God: the Father Almighty, Maker of heaven and earth and of all things visible and invisible;

And in one Lord: Jesus Christ, The only-begotten Son of God, begotten from the Father before all ages, Light from Light, true God from true God, begotten, not made, of one substance with the Father, through Whom all things were made, Who for us and for our salvation came down from heaven, And became incarnate from the Holy Spirit and the Virgin Mary, and was made man, And was crucified for us under Pontius Pilate, and suffered, and was buried, And rose the third day according to the Scriptures, And ascended into heaven and sits on the right hand of the Father, And is coming again with glory to judge both living and dead, Whose kingdom shall have no end;

And in the Holy Ghost, The Lord and Giver of life, Who proceeds from the Father, Who with the Father and the Son is jointly worshipped and jointly glorified, Who spoke through the prophets;

In one holy Catholic and Apostolic Church; We acknowledge one baptism for the remission of sins, We look for the resurrection of the dead, And the life of the world to come. Amen. (trans. Stevenson 2012, 133–34, altered)

---

during the reign of Constantius II and were repulsed only after the death of Valens (r. 364–378), their ardent champion.

The recovery from Arianism/Homoeianism started in Asia Minor through the efforts of the three Cappadocian Fathers: Basil of Caesarea (330–379), his brother Gregory of Nyssa (331–ca. 394), and Gregory of Nazianzus (ca. 329–ca. 390). The last of these, known as "the Theologian," moved to Constantinople in 379 to fight for the orthodox cause in his capacity as patriarch and with his most effective weapons: his apologetic, eulogistic, and poetic talents. Gregory of Nazianzus began his preaching in Constantinople at the house of a relative, since all the churches were in the hands of the Arians. Later this house was transformed into a church called Anastasia (Resurrection) in honor of the victory of orthodoxy.[13]

"Nestorianism"

The decisive support of orthodoxy by Theodosius I put an end to the Arian controversy, which had so dangerously agitated the Eastern Church. Yet, soon a new conflict was to spread like wildfire: its firebrand was Nestorius (d. ca. 451),

---

13. Its remains are beneath the Mehmed Pasha Mosque at the southwestern part of the hippodrome in Istanbul.

appointed to the Constantinopolitan see by Theodosius II in 428. Nestorius insisted on the conceptual distinction between the divine and human elements in Christ and advocated calling Mary "Mother of Christ" rather than "Mother of God" (*Theotokos*). His position ran counter both to the growing popular piety for the Virgin Mary and to orthodox christological dogmas. Most crucial for his future destiny, however, was the powerful attack of his enemies, among whom were Cyril of Alexandria (bp. 412–444), Pope Celestine (bp. 422–432), and—a key person—Pulcheria (399–453), Theodosius II's sister and the empress from 450. Once Nestorius forbade her to take communion in the sanctuary of the church and sent her to the women's gallery—an offense that the Augusta, who considered herself the bride of Christ and compared herself to the Virgin Mary (Holum 1982, 141–45; Taft 1998, 70), could not forgive. The Virgin Mary was proclaimed to be *Theotokos* at the Council of Ephesus in 431 (Gaddis 1999c), and Nestorius was condemned by some of the participants as a heretic. He resigned his see not long afterward and was banished from Constantinople by Theodosius in 435.

"Monophysitism"

Monophysitism was a heresy that also emerged from christological arguments. It postulated the one and single nature of Christ (Winkler 1999). The controversial personality of Cyril, patriarch of Alexandria, is at the base of the Monophysite belief in the divine principle of the union of the two natures of Christ—the human one being absorbed by the divine (Gaddis 1999b). Monophysitism gained thousands of followers and survives today in the five so-called Oriental Orthodox Churches (Armenian; Coptic; Ethiopian; Syrian; Malankara [Indian]). Justinian's theological ambitions drove him to interfere constantly and in an authoritarian way in religious matters. He was a strong defender of the orthodox statements of faith produced at Nicaea (325) and Chalcedon (451) and tried to win over the Monophysites, although he had to show consideration for the Monophysite sympathies of his empress, Theodora (r. 527–548).

Churches

The churches of the new capital were numerous, and several of them gained fame throughout the Mediterranean.

CHURCH OF THE HOLY APOSTLES

The Church of the Holy Apostles was founded by Constantine as the main Christian place of worship of the new capital. The emperor planned to move the relics of all the apostles there, designating himself the thirteenth of them. The church was consecrated by his son, Constantius II, who buried Constantine there (Procopius, *Aed.* 1.4.19), establishing the tradition of imperial burials in Christian churches. The church had marble walls, a gilded dome, and galleries all around (Eusebius, *Vit. Const.* 4.58–59). It was later completely altered by Isidore of Miletus, the architect of the Hagia Sophia, by order of Justinian (Procopius, *Aed.* 1.4.9–18; 5.1.6) (Epstein 1982). The *naos* was covered by five cupolas, a type that was to be extensively adopted in later Russian church architecture. We can imagine Justinian's Church of the Holy Apostles as being similar to St. Mark's in Venice.[14] The church housed the holy skulls of SS. Andrew, Luke, and Timothy, the relics of Patriarch John Chrysostom, and a piece of the stake to which Christ was bound during his flagellation. The church was ransacked by the Crusaders, and the tombs of the emperors were desecrated.

CONSTANTINE'S "GREAT CHURCH"

Constantine probably also started the Hagia Sophia in 326 (*Chron. pasch.* 1.543–45, and discussion in Bardill 2004, 54–56, 107). This church was the cathedral of the new capital, consecrated on February 15, 360, by Eudoxius (bp. 360–370) in the reign of Constantius II. Originally it was simply called The Great Church (*Megalē ekklēsia*), and only later was it dedicated to "Divine Wisdom" (*Hagia Sophia*) (Socrates, *Hist. eccl.* 2.16; see also Hennessy 2009, 208). The foundations of this important structure are covered today by Justinian's church of the same name. Only part of the atrium and the small house for keeping the sacred vessels (*skeuophylakion*) remain of the original Constantinian building. John Chrysostom used to preach from the throne in the middle of the church. The church had an ambo and *solea* (passageway), made of stone (Cedrenus, *Hist. comp.* 1.531; Nicephorus Callistus, *Hist. eccl.* 17.10; John Chrysostom, *Exp. Ps.* 48.17; *Hom.* 5 [PG 55.507]) (Mathews 1971, 12–13). Golden drapes screened the entrances, and the altar was also made of gold, encrusted with precious stones (*Chron. pasch.* 1.544–45). The Constantinian Great Church and the nearby Senate House were ravaged by fire in the turbulences following the final deposition of John Chrysostom on June 9, 404.

CHURCH OF ST. JOHN THE BAPTIST

Constantinople's most famous early monastery was founded on the coast of the Propontis near the Golden Gate by the patrician Studios, consul of

---

14. There are descriptions of the Church of the Holy Apostles by Nikolaos Messarites and Constantinos Rhodios (tenth century) (see Downey 1957). Today, the Fatih Camii (mosque) stands on the site.

the East in 454 (*PLRE* II, 1037, s.v. Studius 2) perhaps in 463 as stated by Theophanes (*Chron.* 1.175). Modern studies, however, revise the founding date to shortly before 454 (Mango 1978; Peschlow 1982; Bardill 2004, 60–61, 109). Three of the monastery's monks became patriarchs of Constantinople, and several of its abbots (*hēgoumenoi*) contributed significantly to the development of monastic principles. The Rule (*Typikon*) of the Studios Monastery was developed during the iconoclastic period, and later it was followed by monastic communities at Mount Athos and elsewhere. The monks of the Studios Monastery suffered hardships as defenders of the images during the iconoclastic crisis. One of the most versed in christological matters was St. Theodore of Studios (759–826). The high spiritual and intellectual levels of the Studios monastic community were demonstrated in the fame of the monastery's calligraphic school and the books produced by its scriptorium. In the ninth century, for example, it created the well-known Chludov Psalter. The emperors Isaac I Komnenos (r. 1057–1059) and Michael VII (r. 1071–1078), after their reigns were over, became monks in the Studios Monastery. We owe descriptions of the monastery to the writings of the Russian pilgrims Anthony (ca. 1200) and Stefan (ca. 1348/49), both of Novgorod. The monastery was devastated twice: first during the Latin sack of Constantinople in 1204, and then during the Turkish invasion in 1453.

The monastery's church, dedicated to St. John the Baptist, still stands in substantial portions. It has a spacious nave and two aisles, preceded by a narthex. It is possible to reconstruct the setting in which the liturgy was performed. The apse had a high *synthronon* of six or seven gradines, on which the clergy sat on both sides of the throne of the *hēgoumenos*. A chancel barrier, built on a stylobate of *verde antico* and crowned by an architrave on elegant columns, separated the sacred altar from the nave. The altar table stood above a small cruciform crypt that could be entered by going down a few steps (Mathews 1971, 25–27).

CHURCH OF THE MOTHER OF GOD AT CHALKOPRATEIA

A similar crypt and configuration of the altar site, with a *synthronon* in the apse and chancel barrier encompassing a rectangular space in front of it, existed in the Church of the Mother of God at Chalkoprateia (Copper Market). Situated in close proximity to the Great Church, the Hagia Sophia, it was served by the same clergy as the cathedral. The holy relic of the Virgin Mary's cincture was venerated there, and, at least since the ninth century, all processions during the religious feasts dedicated to the Mother of God started or finished before its doors (Mathews 1971, 28n49). Medieval authors attribute the building of the church to Theodosius II and his pious sister Pulcheria, although the Justinian *Novels* name Verina, the wife of Leo I (r. 457–474), as its founder (Mathews 1971, 28–33). In either case, a mid-fifth-century date is in perfect agreement with the close resemblance between the Chalkoprateia Church and the Church of the Studios Monastery. The people of Constantinople chose the Mother of God to be their protectress.

THE CHURCH OF SAINTS SERGIUS AND BACCHUS

Under Justinian, the religious architecture in Constantinople became much more varied compared to the previous two centuries. Several churches from that period are fairly well preserved. One of them is the Church of SS. Sergius and Bacchus, martyrs and healers (Van Millingen 1912, 62–83; Ebersolt and Thiers 1913, 21–51). According to Procopius (*Aed.* 1.41.1–8), and confirmed by an inscription placed inside the church, it was built by Justinian. The site, known as the "Hormisdas Residence," belonged to Justinian as well. It is curious that the building of SS. Sergius and Bacchus was preceded by the construction of another church, dedicated to the apostles Peter and Paul, which later completely disappeared. This church was also connected with Justinian, whose full name was Flavius Petrus Sabbatius Justinianus.

Whereas the Church of SS. Peter and Paul was a basilica (Mathews 1971, 45–47), the Church of SS. Sergius and Bacchus is one of the "central type." Its core is a two-storied octagon enveloped by ambulatories on three sides and set within an irregularly quadrilateral exterior wall. The sanctuary on the east side was separated from the nave by a straight chancel screen. Procopius

Fig. 8.13. Hagia Sophia, Constantinople

wrote that the Church of SS. Sergius and Bacchus was part of the palace and its ornamentation (*Aed*. 1.41.7–8). Indeed, the superb architectural sculpture in the church betrays imperial sponsorship. The column shafts are of green and gray marble, and the bases, capitals, and entablature are of gray-white Prokonessian marble. The capitals belong to the so-called folded type, which developed from the classical Corinthian capital. The workmanship is of the highest quality. The overall impression is of an exuberance of forms, combined with the sharp graphic design of the open-work order elements (Frazier 1999, 268; Kautzsch 1936, 187–89). Some scholars consider the Church of SS. Sergius and Bacchus to be the model for Justinian's great foundation, the Hagia Sophia (Mathews 1971, 42–43).

Justinian's Hagia Sophia

From Procopius (*Aed*. 1.1.20–26) we know the story of the destruction of the Constantinian Great Church during the Nika uprising of 532 and the erection of the new church by Justinian. The architects were Anthemius of Tralles and Isidore of Miletus.

The new Hagia Sophia had an atrium "with a fountain in the middle" still extant in the sixteenth century, when the French traveler Pierre Gilles described the antiquities of Constantinople (Gilles 1988). The atrium had galleries along three sides, while the fourth side was the outer narthex of the church itself. Paul the Silentiary (d. post-575) wrote that the atrium was as richly faced with marble as the interior of the cathedral. He also adds, "In addition, here and there around the sides and further extremities you would see many open-air courts . . . outside the divine building. This has been contrived with beautiful design around the sacred temple to make it appear flooded with bright-eyed daylight, the early born" (*Soph*. lines 607–16 [trans. Mathews 1971, 90]). The faithful gathered in the atrium and entered the church first through an outer open entrance hall (exonarthex), covered by nine groin-vaults. Richly ornamented doors, screened by curtains, led to the inner narthex and then to the church itself (Sas-Zaloziecky 1936; Mathews 1971, 91). Apart from the entrances from the narthexes, there are numerous openings in the northern and southern walls of the church that enable us to imagine the immense crowdedness during religious feasts.

The fame of the Hagia Sophia is due largely to the special sight of its interior: the vastness of space flooded with light; the play of forms of the dome, half-domes, and apse; and the lavish marble revetment, combined with the perfect forms and execution of the architectural decoration. A special interest has been shown in the statics of the great dome, daringly high (55.6 m) and large (diameter ca. 32 m). To this we must add the beauty of the mosaic decor and the splendor of the liturgical vessels, fans, and chandeliers. Before the first collapse of the dome in 558, the sanctuary furnishings were embellished with forty thousand pounds of silver, according to Procopius's testimony (*Aed.* 1.1.65). Although later replaced by Justinian, they did not survive pillage by the Crusaders in 1204.

Four massive piers support the dome and the two half-domes of the church. The north and south aisles and galleries are divided into six bays on each floor, three on either side. The architectural partition of the interior was further emphasized by marble barriers. Such barriers screened the emperor's box and the *metatorion*, the section on the ground floor in the south aisle, set apart for the occasions when the emperor was participating in the liturgy.

The sanctuary of the Hagia Sophia had a *pi*-shaped plan, projecting from the two piers that flank the apse as far as the eastern arch of the dome (Xydis 1947; Mathews 1971, 96–97). The chancel barrier consisted of slabs with the monograms of Justinian and Theodora and twelve columns that carried an architrave adorned with images of Christ, the Virgin Mary, angels, and the apostles (Paul the Silentiary, *Soph.* lines 686–719). The church, like its predecessor, had an ambo and *solea*, the walled path that linked it to the entrance of the sanctuary, made of stone similar to onyx (Cedrenus, *Hist. comp.* 1.531). The ambo was located almost in the middle of the nave (Paul the Silentiary, *Ambon.* lines 50–51, 229, 232); it was encircled with a barrier of eight columns with chancel slabs between them and an architrave above (*Ambon.* lines 163–70). The apse had a *synthronon* with silver seats for the priests at the seventh top step. The altar table was of gold, ornamented with precious stones and set under a *ciborium* (canopy) of silver (*Soph.* lines 720–54); golden hangings screened the entrances (*Chron. pasch.* 1.544–45). The famous Turin shroud was in the church until the Crusaders' sack of Constantinople.

HAGIA EIRENE

Another important Constantinian church restored by Justinian was the Hagia Eirene, dedicated to "Divine Peace." It was built on the ruins of a temple of Aphrodite (Mathews 1971, 77–87) and has survived until present times. The Hagia Eirene is now situated in the first inner courtyard of the Topkapı Palace in Istanbul. The Second Ecumenical Council was held there in 381. As with the Hagia Sophia and several other churches, it burned down during the Nika uprising in 532. Justinian rebuilt the church in the form of a domed cruciform basilica. A violent earthquake in 740 destroyed all of the upper part of Hagia Eirene. It was rebuilt after 753, during the reign of Constantine V, virtually from its foundations but with the addition of a cross-domed plan on the gallery level with transverse barrel vaults

Fig. 8.14. Hagia Eirene, Constantinople

to eliminate the constructural failings of the preceding building (Peschlow 1977; Freely and Çakmak 2004, 136–44). The enormous mosaic cross that decorates the apse dates from the same period; there is an inscription on the inner face of the apse arch, citing verses 4 and 5 of the sixty-fourth psalm, and a citation from Amos 9:6 runs along the outer face of the arch (Freely and Çakmak 2004, 141).

Church of St. Polyeuktos

One of the most lavishly decorated churches in Constantinople was dedicated to St. Polyeuktos (d. ca. 259) by Anicia Juliana, the daughter of Emperor Olybrius (r. 472) and wealthy heiress of a number of members of the imperial family (Mango and Ševčenko 1961). The church was erected between 512 and 527/8 on property belonging to Anicia and probably linked to her nearby residence.[15] Today, not a single wall of this structure remains. The extremely solid foundations, however, still stand, consisting of mortared rubble walls and brick vaults. The church was of the basilica type, with a nave and two aisles, probably covered by vaults (Mathews 1971, 53). Gregory of Tours (bp. 573–594) mentions a golden ceiling (*Glor. mart.* 102). Many beautiful fragments of the sumptuous sculptural decor have been found on the site; besides, some pieces (e.g., the *pilastri acritani*) can be seen today at St. Mark's in Venice, having been transported there by the Crusaders.

15. Identified by an inscription in the church itself (Harrison and Fıratlı, 1967). The hint about the proximity of the church to the residence: *erat enim proximum domui ejus* (PL 71.794; Mathews 1971, 52).

ICONS AND OTHER BYZANTINE CHRISTIAN ART

The centralization of the secular and spiritual power in Constantinople gave the city the status of art legislator. Immense wealth flowed to the capital, wealth not only in gold but also in talented people—gifted artists and skillful craftsmen. The enormous intellectual and spiritual capacity of the city produced consummate Christian art designed both for secular and religious use. Such art was usually also of exquisite design and remarkable craftsmanship.

Unfortunately, most of the monuments and the movable property of Byzantine Constantinople perished in the sacking of the city by the Crusaders and the Ottoman Turks. Much that survived this plundering disappeared gradually in the subsequent alien cultural setting. Irrevocable was the loss of the books created in the scriptoria (copying rooms for scribes) of Constantinople. Only a few illuminated manuscripts from the early Byzantine period have survived. Among them are some leaves containing canon tables (concordance charts) that once belonged to a lavishly decorated Gospel book (Nordenfalk 1938, 127–46, plates 1–4; Weitzmann 1979, no. 441).[16]

Some of the earliest extant icons come from Constantinople. One of them depicts the Virgin Mary, sitting on a throne and holding the child Jesus—the Word Incarnate—on her lap, flanked by two military saints: St. Theodore (left) and St. George (right). The saints hold martyr crosses. They are dressed in the ceremonial garb of the imperial guard. The style of the icon is eclectic, nevertheless exquisite: the fully three-dimensional angels are painted in the purest Hellenistic tradition, while the frontal figures of the military saints are in developed early Byzantine style (Weitzmann 1979, 533–34, no. 478).

Iconic images were produced on ivory diptychs as well. On a famous piece from the sixth century, Christ and the Virgin Mary are carved in symmetrical centered compositions (Weitzmann 1979, 528–30, no. 474).[17] Behind the somewhat severe image of Christ are the princes of the apostles: SS. Peter and Paul. Respectively, on each side behind the Virgin Mary, who holds the child Jesus on her knees, we see archangels, most probably Michael and Gabriel. In the background are elaborate identical architectural settings, ornamented with order elements. These are not the only classicizing motifs in the diptych. The style of the figures is still dependent on the Hellenistic tradition despite the explicit Christian iconography.

A set of nine silver plates embossed with scenes from the life of David, from his anointment by Samuel to his covenant with Jonathan (Weitzmann

---

16. Eusebius of Caesarea, Constantine's confidential adviser in religious matters and court historian, created the canon tables to enable a reader to locate parallel passages in the Gospel.

17. On luxurious ivory objects, see Volbach 1976.

1979, 475–83, nos. 425–32), are among the most famous examples of early Byzantine silverware art. Though discovered in Cyprus, they are considered to have been produced by the imperial workshop in Constantinople, since imperial stamps on the back of each plate show a range of dates (613–630) from the reign of Emperor Heraclius (r. 610–641). The style of the plates is a brilliant example of the respect for the principles of Hellenistic art among the enlightened upper class in Constantinople. Although illustrating a biblical tale, the modeling, the illusion of space, the detail of the costumes, and some of the principles of composition strongly recall Hellenistic prototypes. By Heraclius's time, secular art was entirely Christianized. Images of Christ, the Virgin Mary, angels, saints, and the cross were represented on vessels, jewelry, and garments. The protective power of those Christian signs increased the worth of such objects of art beyond their material and aesthetic value.

9

Italy and Environs

ROBIN M. JENSEN, PETER LAMPE, WILLIAM TABBERNEE,
AND D. H. WILLIAMS

Introduction

Italy acquired its name from the kingdom of the third-century BCE Oenotrian
ruler Italus, whose kingdom comprised the Bruttian Peninsula, the southernmost part of the mainland. Between 900 and 800 BCE the greater part of the
Italian Peninsula was settled by the Etruscans. Etruria occupied what is now
Tuscany in central Italy, between the Apennine mountain range and the Tyrrhenian Sea. Etruscan civilization stretched from the Arno River in the north
to the Tiber River where, in the center of the peninsula, so the legend goes,
a small settlement founded by Romulus on April 21, 753, would eventually
become the great city of Rome.

Apart from archaeological evidence, much of what we know of Etruscan
culture comes mainly from Greek and Roman authors. Livy (59 BCE–17 CE)
and Virgil (70–19 BCE) believed that the migration of the Etruscans to central Italy was due to the fall of Troy. The Etruscans appear to have spoken a

---

This chapter was written by **Robin M. Jensen** (Ravenna), **Peter Lampe** (Rome), **William Tabbernee** (Environs), and **D. H. Williams** (Introduction, Central Italy, North Italy, South Italy
and the Islands).

non–Indo-European language, and Herodotus (fl. ca. 400 BCE) records the legend that they (also called Tyrrhenians) came from Lydia in modern western Turkey (*Hist.* 1.94.6). Contrarily, Dionysius of Halicarnassus (fl. ca. 100 BCE) declared that the Etruscans were indigenous to Italy, called themselves "the Rasennae," and were part of an ancient nation "which does not resemble any other people in their language or in their way of life, or customs" (*Ant. rom.* 1.30). There is little question, however, that early Roman accomplishments in engineering, art, religion, and politics were indebted to Etruscan culture. According to tradition, the overthrow of Tarquinius Superbus, allegedly the seventh and last Etruscan king of Rome, ushered in the Roman Republic.[1]

Hellanicus of Lesbos (ca. 480–ca. 395 BCE) linked "Italia" with the term *vitulus* (calf) because of the legend of how the calf of Geryoneus had run away from Hercules (Dionysius of Halicarnassus, *Ant. rom.* 1.35). The *Timaeus* of Plato (ca. 429–ca. 347 BCE) associates the name with this region's wealth in cattle. Timaeus himself was said to be from Locris in Italy. For that reason, some Italic communities minted coins bearing the image of a calf. By the second half of the fifth century BCE, the name "Italia" referred to the part of the peninsula extending in the west up to the river Laus and in the east to the river Bradanus.

Rome, at first, was just one of many cities within Italy. Italy was populated by numerous politically independent tribes and cities, all with different dialects, languages, and political structures. In the course of the fourth century BCE, Italia encompassed, with the Italiote League, also Tarentum and Poseidonia (Dionysius of Halicarnassus, *Ant. rom.* 1.73.4). Rome's treaty with Carthage in 306 BCE guaranteed its predominant influence in Italy. By the early third century BCE central Italy had become the heartlands, and "Rome" extended from the Tyrrhenian Sea to the Adriatic Sea. The lands stretching from southern Italy[2] to the Arnus (Arno) and the Rubico (Rubicon) in the north either belonged to Rome itself, or to its colonies, or was allied to Rome by treaties. This created a Roman confederation.

As a political entity, however, Italy as yet comprised only the peninsula (up to the river Aesis [Esino]), whose inhabitants were granted Roman citizenship in 89 BCE. In 81 BCE the Roman general Sulla (138–78 BCE) moved the border northward to the Arnus and the Rubico. In 49 BCE citizenship was extended to the Transpadani (Cassius Dio, *Hist. rom.* 41.36)—that is, those residing

1. The tradition explains how, after the end of the rule of kings, the senate handed power to two consuls, each of whom ruled Rome for one year along with the senate. Despite the name Republic, however, Rome, was never a democracy as understood today, nor as the Greeks understood it. In the early days of the Roman Republic all power remained in the hands of the Roman aristocracy, the so-called patricians (*patricii*).

2. Excluding the islands.

on the other side of the river Padus (Po)—but the province Gallia Cisalpina continued in existence until 43 BCE (Cicero, *Phil*. 3.15, 37). From 42 BCE on, Italy extended from the river Varus (Var) to the river Formio (Risano) and then, in the late Augustan period as far as the Arsia (Raša), the river dividing Venetia et Histria from Illyricum. This meant that Italy enjoyed a political unity that was otherwise enclosed by the sea and the Alps. Larger ethnic units were the Itali as opposed to the Italiotai (i.e., the Greek colonists), and the Italici as opposed to the Romans. Under early Roman rule, "Italia" was applied to everything south of the Alps.

Romanization and Unification

Rome's dominant position in Italia was neither inevitable nor the result of continuous expansion. Although Romanization was accomplished in the first instance through military conquests and alliances, the process of unification was dependent more on the ways in which Rome's relationships with its affiliated states was shaped and on the establishment of colonies. These *coloniae*, comprised primarily of army veterans, who shared in the spoils of war through land grants, were used consistently as a tool both to control and to Romanize their environment. Augustus (r. 31 BCE–14 CE) himself established twenty-eight colonies (Suetonius, *Aug*. 46). Placed as they were in potentially hostile territory, these communities developed a strong loyalty to Rome for their own protection.

Similarly, self-interest on the part of the Italian elites, with whom the Roman *nobiles* (aristocrats) had drawn up favorable treaties and maintained close personal relations, ensured both loyalty and Romanization. The elites relied on Rome's support should conflicts or foreign threats arise in their home communities. They consequently became de facto representatives of Roman interests and thereby the creators and protectors of "Roman" society. Additionally, the Romans brought to the conquered or affiliated territories an effective infrastructure, including an efficient network of roads, aqueducts, urban planning, and, as already noted, Roman citizenship in particular circumstances. All this enhanced the appearance, and to a certain extent the reality, of a unified Italia.

Romanization and unification was also aided by Roman literature. An example of this is the *Aeneid*, an epic heroic poem about the founding of Roman civilization by Aeneas, a Trojan hero fleeing the destruction of Troy. The real subject of the *Aeneid*, however, is the greatness of the Rome of the Augustan age and Roman values. Chief among these values were *pietas*, "piety, respect for authority"; *virtus*, "manliness, fortitude in the face of adversity"; and *officium*, "duty." While Latin as a language would eventually become famous for literary expression in Italy, one must not link Latin too closely with the rise of Italy or, later, with the emergence of Christianity. Not until the very end of the second century CE, as witnessed by the *Octavius* of Minucius Felix (fl. ca. 200) and the *Apologeticum* of Tertullian (ca. 160/70–ca. 220), is Latin first used by Christian intellectuals. Greek remained the church's primary liturgical language until the mid-fourth century.

Augustan Division

"Italia" was not actually applied to its current boundaries until the Augustan period. Under Octavian, the later emperor Augustus, Italia was separated into eleven regions, according to the *Descriptio totius Italiae* (see sidebar 9.1).

The new regions, however, did not erase previous identities; old names and boundaries remained largely the same. Ancient ethnic groups lived on in the names of Latium, Etruria, Samnium, Umbria, Picenum, Lucania, Apulia, and Calabria. Under the Augustan rearrangement, all the territory as far as the Alps was considered Italy.

After the death of Augustus, Rome underwent a series of profound changes. The empire itself grew dramatically. By the time of Trajan (r. 98–117 CE), Rome had acquired much of northern Africa, Germany, Great Britain, and Europe around the Black Sea, as well as Mesopotamia and the northern part of the Arabian Peninsula. At home, Rome struggled with its new institution of quasi-monarchical rule. Augustus had clouded the issue by declaring himself "first among equals" (*princeps*). His imperial successors stopped pretending such, simply calling themselves either "Caesar," to indicate descent from the royal house, or *imperator*, since they derived their power from the *imperium* over Rome and the military.

9.1 The Augustan Regions of Italia

Regio I:	Latium et Campania
Regio II:	Apulia et Calabria
Regio III:	Lucania et Bruttii
Regio IV:	Samnium
Regio V:	Picenum
Regio VI:	Umbria et Ager Gallicus
Regio VII:	Etruria
Regio VIII:	Aemilia
Regio IX:	Liguria
Regio X:	Venetia et Histria
Regio XI:	Transpadana

Diocletian's Dioceses

A second major political restructuring of Italy occurred three centuries later under Diocletian (r. 284–305). The whole of Italy became one of twelve dioceses that composed the empire. Now Italy was split into two major *partes*: *annonaria* (North Italy) and *suburbicaria* (lands to the south), which were divided into twelve provinces

Fig. 9.1. Map of Italia

(by the fourth century there were seventeen). As Augustus had done by expanding the borders beyond the old commonwealths, Diocletian's reorganization pushed Italia's borders up to the Alps and spread eastward toward Raetia. Thus the old Gallic names for parts of northern Italy gave way to smaller territories such as the Alpes Cottiae. Aemilia became a much smaller region, bordering Venetia et Histria to the north and Flaminia et Picenum in the south. In the southwest, the ancient name of Etruria was changed to Tuscia, while the other regional names remained the same. Campania was expanded farther into Latium. Sicily, Sardinia, and Corsica were regarded as separate provinces.

With the advent of Constantine I (r. 306–337) and his dynasty, Rome was further demoted as a political administrative center. As the emperor traveled with the armies chiefly along the northern frontiers, there was little need to visit Rome (see under North Italy below). This situation had an impact on the

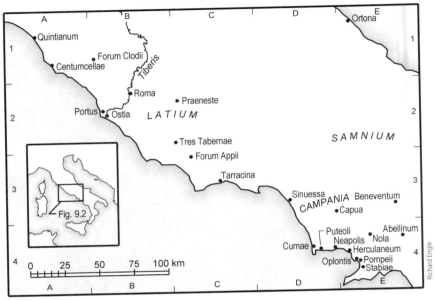

Fig. 9.2. Map of Latium and Environs

Western church's organization, at least for a time. It is no mere coincidence that once the imperial palace and court were established in Mediolanum (Milan), the city's bishop dominated ecclesiastical politics within Italy, as seen with the careers of Auxentius (bp. 355–374) and Ambrose (bp. 374–397). Certainly Milan had become the intellectual center of the West during the years of Ambrose (and so had Aquileia to a lesser extent). It was in Milan that Augustine (354–430) came into close contact with a fervent Christian Platonism. One of these Milanese Christian Platonists was Simplicianus (d. 400), a learned priest who had come from Rome and, while there, had befriended Marius Victorinus (b. ca. 300) during the 350s. Simplicianus had also baptized Ambrose and, in 397, succeeded him as bishop. The flowering of Milanese intellectual culture began drawing to a close once Ravenna became the capital of Italy in 402.

Early Christianity

We do not know precisely how or when Christianity first entered Italy, though it is certain that the development of Christian communities had begun well before the mid-50s, when Paul's letter to the Romans was written (cf. Rom. 15:25). Presumably, it was in the Jewish communities of Rome, Ostia, Puteoli, and elsewhere that the earliest followers of "the Way" arrived and grew in numbers (cf. Matt. 10:6; 15:24; Luke 4:14–15; Acts 3:1–10; 17:1–3). Jews were especially numerous in the city of Rome. Cassius Dio (*Hist. rom.* 60.6.6) states that in 41 CE the Jews posed a threat because of their large population and were denied the right of assembly. According to the Roman historian Suetonius (ca. 70–post-130), the emperor Claudius (r. 41–54) "expelled the Jews from Rome because they rioted constantly at the instigation of Chrestus" (*Claud.* 25.4). Perhaps Suetonius was speaking about an otherwise unknown person named "Chrestus."[3] Alternatively, it may be a misspelled reference to "Christ." Whatever Suetonius meant, Jewish Christians were affected by the ban of Jews in the city. It seems likely that this would have impacted Gentile Christians, since little or no distinction was made between Jews and Christians by the authorities at this time (contra Pizzuto-Pomaco 2001, 90).

Claudius's edict was issued in about 49 (Orosius, *Hist. pag.* 7.35), which was about the time when Paul encountered in Corinth "a Jew named Aquila, a native of Pontus, who had recently come from Italy with his wife Priscilla, because Claudius had ordered all Jews to leave Rome" (Acts 18:2 [cf. Eusebius, *Hist. eccl.* 2.18.9]). Paul's immediate cooperation with the husband-and-wife team suggests that they already shared the Christian faith (see Acts 18:3). Paul does not mention Aquila or Priscilla among those whom he baptized in Corinth (1 Cor. 1:14–16). It is therefore highly likely that Priscilla (also known as Prisca) and Aquila were Jewish Christians, forced to evacuate Rome along with the other Jews.

Patristic *testimonia* insinuate that Peter had come to Rome sometime before Paul arrived for trial. By the later second century, Irenaeus of Lyons (bp. 177–ca. 200) ascribed a founding role for Peter alongside Paul: "Peter and Paul were preaching at Rome, laying the foundations of the Church" (*Haer.* 3.1.1; cf. 3.3.2). There is no reason, however, to read into Irenaeus's sweeping remark that Peter or Paul started the church at Rome. Eusebius of Caesarea (bp. ca. 314/5–339) records the tradition that Peter went to Rome during the reign of Claudius, though with the specific purpose of foiling the plans of Simon the Magician, who earlier had tried to purchase the miraculous powers that Peter and John displayed in Samaria (*Hist. eccl.* 2.15.6; cf. Acts 8:18–23). Simon is said to have traveled to Rome to propagate his message, which appears to have been a variant of Gnostic Christianity (Irenaeus, *Haer.* 1.23.2). To thwart Simon's designs to likewise pollute the churches in the West, Peter "proclaimed the kingdom of heaven" there, though not in order to establish a

3. There are, e.g., two known Italian bishops named "Chrestus": Chrestus of Syracuse (*EOMIA* 1.379, 398.1) and another Chrestus who subscribed to the proceedings at the Council of Valence (ancient Valentia) in 374 (*EOMIA* 1.418.11, 422.8, 423.11).

church but rather to refute Simon's message and edify the believers.[4] Eusebius (*Hist. eccl.* 2.15.1) reports that John Mark was also at Rome[5] as Peter's disciple, and that Mark provided a "memoir" of what Peter received from Jesus probably at the request of the Roman churches.

As noted, by the time the apostle Paul wrote his one and only letter to the Romans during the mid- to late 50s, he was addressing an already active and sizable community. Paul was made familiar enough with the church there to call by name certain leaders of the *domus ecclesiae* (house-churches) as well as comment on their circumstances.[6] Priscilla and Aquila, for example, are now householders in whose residence a church meets (Rom. 16:3-5). There are also several believers whom Paul acknowledges are his seniors in the faith, such as Epaenetus, who was the first to convert to Christianity in the province of Asia, and Andronicus and Junia(s), perhaps husband and wife, who are called apostles (Rom. 16:5b, 7). Given their designations,[7] these individuals may have played a significant part in the founding of Roman churches.

The last four chapters of Acts provide an account of Paul's arrest and arraignment, and his journey to Rome triggered by his appeal to the emperor. Paul arrived by ship first at the port of Rhegium (Reggio), and then, in about 62, he sailed farther north to Puteoli (Pozzuoli). It was there that Paul was cared for by local Christians (Acts 28:13–14). Seven days later he came to Rome, and the report of his arrival was already circulating in the city and in the nearby communities of Christians in Forum Appii (Forum of Appius)[8] and Tres Tabernae.[9] While he waited for his trial under house arrest, Paul could receive visitors, among whom were leaders of the synagogues. Some expressed interest in Paul's message, but they were especially eager to learn about "this sect" that was spoken against everywhere (Acts 28:22). From these meager descriptions it follows that centers of Christian activity had quickly emerged beyond Rome and the port cities. Unfortunately, there is little specific

4. There is some confusion over the connection between the Simon who accosted Peter in Acts 8 and the Simon whose activities prompted the local populace in Rome to erect in his honor a statue declaring him as "a holy god."

5. Eusebius quotes from 1 Peter 5:13: "She that is in Babylon . . . sends you greetings, as does also my son Mark." Cf. Eusebius, *Historia ecclesiastica* 3.39.15, citing Papias of Hierapolis (bp. ca. 110–ca. 130).

6. I concur with the more generally accepted view that Romans 16 was originally attached to the epistle and addressed to the Christians in Rome (not Ephesus).

7. The term *apostolos* still carried a general, besides the specific, meaning. Given this flexibility, there is no reason why this designation could not refer to a woman.

8. Modern Faiti.

9. A small village on the Via Appia, southeast of Rome, at or near modern Cisterna, named after the "three shops" that composed the "halting station" on the journey to Rome (cf. Acts 28:15).

information in the two subsequent centuries regarding the Christian presence in Italian locations other than Rome.

Rome

Jewish Beginnings

Immigrants from the East were prolific in the biggest metropolis of the Roman Empire. Juvenal (fl. ca. 100) joked (*Sat.* 3.60–65) that the waters of the Syrian river Orontes flowed into the Tiber, carrying eastern rhythms, music, and customs with them. The city of Rome is Greek, he complained. The majority of the city's inhabitants were not born in Rome, as Seneca (ca. 4 BCE–65 CE) observed (*Helv.* 6; cf. Pliny the Elder, *Nat.* 3.6.). And what was true for the city population as a whole applied even more to the early Roman Jews and Christians. In Rome "all detestable and appalling things from all over the world come together," Tacitus (ca. 55/6–post-113 CE) regretted, with particularly the Christians in mind (*Ann.* 15.44.3).

Pompey (106–48 BCE), who had conquered Judaea in 63 BCE, had deported crowds of Jews to Rome as slaves. Soon, at the latest under Augustus, they were freed. At their manumission, most of them gained Roman citizenship and bequeathed it to their offspring (cf. Philo, *Legat.* 155, 157). In addition, imported Jewish slaves and freed slaves continued to stream into Rome through the imperial household and other large households such as that of Marcus Agrippa (64/3–12 BCE) and the Roman legate Volumnius (Lampe 2004b).

Volumnius had resided in Syria in 8 BCE as Augustus's personal emissary; King Herod (r. 37–4 BCE) enjoyed his friendship (Josephus, *B.J.* 1.535–538, 542; *Ant.* 16.277–283, 332, 351, 354). It is likely that this Volumnius brought Jews from the East to Rome and was the patron of those freed slaves and slaves who (or whose children) founded the Roman synagogue of the Volumnenses in the first century CE (*CIL* 6.29756; *CIJ* 1.343, 402, 417, 523). Marcus Agrippa had been active as Augustus's emissary in the East in 23–21 BCE and later, in 17–13 BCE, as general governor of the Eastern provinces. He had also maintained a close friendship with Herod the Great and had even sacrificed at the Jerusalem temple. Josephus describes him as friendly toward the Jews (*Ant.* 15.350–351; 16.12–16, 21–26). In all likelihood, the Jews who in the first century CE founded the Roman synagogue of the Agrippesioi (*CIG* 9907; *CIJ* 1.503, 425, 365) were his freed persons and slaves (and their offspring). In the same way, the emperor's household, which had branches all over the empire, transferred Jewish domestics to Rome. In the first century CE freed and enslaved Jewish members of the imperial household founded the Roman synagogue of the Augustesioi (*CIL* 6.29757; *CIG* 9902–9903; *CIJ* 1.284, 301, 338, 368, 416, 496). Many of the founders of these three synagogues, as freed slaves and children of freed slaves, were Roman citizens.

Three areas can still be identified where Roman Jews resided in the first century CE (Lampe 1989, 26–35; 2003a, 38–47). Many lived in Trans Tiberim (Trastevere), the crowded quarter west of the Tiber River across from Tiber Island. Others of poor economic means settled in the climatically unhealthy valley of the Appian Way outside the Capena Gate. Other Jewish groups lived in the northeast, where in the first century CE they founded a synagogue in the vicinity of the Viminal Gate, close to a fruit merchant's store. They probably also started the first Jewish catacomb (Villa Torlonia), on the Via Nomentana, northeast of the city as early as the first or second century CE, as radiocarbon dating suggests (Rutgers et al. 2005). It is unclear whether the Viminal Gate synagogue was identical with one of the synagogues already mentioned.

All three residential locations lay outside the Republican Wall, and the synagogue at the Viminal Gate was outside the sacred city limits, the *pomerium*.[10] The Egyptian cults, with which the Romans often associated Judaism, were banned from the *pomerium* as well.

For the first century CE, we know of at least two other synagogues existing in Rome besides the ones discussed: the synagogues of the Vernaculi (*CIJ* 1.318, 383, 398, 494) and of the Hebrews (*CIG* 9909; *CIJ* 1.510, 291, 317, 535). Another inscription mentions a synagogue of the (He)rodioi (*CIJ* 1.173). Although its existence cannot be documented for the first century CE, its name at least allows for the possibility that, already in the first century CE, Jewish slaves and freed persons of the Herodian royal household founded a synagogue for themselves in Rome. A branch of the Herodian household was located in Rome. Herod Antipas and Herod Agrippa I, for example, son and grandson of Herod the Great (r. 37–4 BCE), were raised and educated in Rome. In Romans 16 a possible Christian link to the Herodian household in Rome may be discerned (see below).

Altogether, inscriptions mention about fourteen Roman synagogues in imperial times. All these Jewish congregations in Rome were independent units and only loosely connected with one another. This fractionation was different from the situation in Alexandria, where the various synagogues constituted one political body.[11] Later, Roman Christianity would be organized with a similar fractionation (see below).

10. For a similar situation in Philippi, see Acts 16:13.
11. For Rome and Alexandria, see Lampe 1989, 367–68; 2003a, 431–32.

A fifth household with Jewish freed slaves worth mentioning was a Valerian one. A Roman inscription (*CIL* 6.27948) names a freed slave, Valeria Maria, of the first century CE, who was Jewish or Jewish-Christian. According to *1 Clement* (63.3; 65.1), Valerius Biton, a Valerian freedman or son of a freedman, was a prominent Christian in Rome, born in the 30s or 40s and still alive in the 90s. It is tempting to assume that the Christian Valerius Biton came into contact with the Christian gospel through Valerian Jewish-Christian freed persons such as Valeria Maria. Was she a close relative? New epigraphical material is needed to answer this question.

Despite the uncertainties in the patchy Valerian source material, at least it can generally be surmised that Jewish Christianity found one of its paths from the Syrian-Palestinian East into the city of Rome through some of the aforementioned Roman households, through their Jewish slaves, freedpersons, and their descendants.

Authors such as Suetonius cast more light on the scene. Jewish-Christian immigrants from the eastern part of the empire infiltrated one or several of the Jewish synagogues in Rome sometime in the 40s CE, most likely at the end of that decade. At that time, the apostle Paul still lived in Antioch, and the radius of his Christian mission had not reached farther than 500 km (Gal. 1:17, 21; 2 Cor. 11:32–33; Acts 9:22–25, 27, 30; 11:25–26; 13–14). It was not before 49–50 CE that Paul founded his famous congregations in Galatia, Macedonia (Philippi; Thessalonica), and Greece (Corinth). Preaching about Christ, the Jewish-Christian immigrants in Rome stirred up turmoil within the synagogues and attracted the attention of the Roman officials. The key

---

9.2 The Valerii and Possible Jewish Connections

When we look for a pagan Valerian aristocrat who had a connection to the Syrian East and to the Jewish people, the Roman rhetorician Marcus Valerius Messalla Corvinus (ca. 64 BCE–13 CE) comes to mind. In 29–28 BCE he served as governor of Syria. Earlier he had demonstrated a friendly attitude toward Herod the Great (Josephus, *Ant.* 14.384; *B.J.* 1.284; cf. 1.243). Unfortunately, we do not know whether or how this Valerian-Syrian connection may have preconditioned the existence of Jews and Christians in later first-century Valerian households in Rome. Marcus Valerius Messalla Corvinus was not a direct patron of Valeria Maria or Valerius Biton.

The same is true of Valerius Gratus, the predecessor of Pontius Pilate as prefect of Judaea in 15–26 CE (Josephus, *Ant.* 17), and even more of the republican senator Lucius Valerius, who had shown a friendly attitude toward the Jews (Josephus, *Ant.* 14.145).

persons in this inner-Jewish argument were expelled by Claudius's administration in 49 CE (Suetonius, *Claud.* 25.4; Orosius, *Hist. pag.* 7.6.15–16; cf.
Cassius Dio, *Hist. rom.* 60.6.6–7). As noted already in the introduction to
this chapter, among those forced to leave were the Jewish Christians Aquila,
an immigrant from Pontus, and his wife, Prisca (Acts 18:2) (Lampe 1998c).
Aquila and Prisca, free tentmakers who ran a workshop in Rome, were among
the first Christian activists in the city. It is unknown where or how they had
made contact with the Christian message; they could have done so even in
the synagogues of Rome itself.

Following the disruptive events of 49 CE, and no later than the mid-50s at
the time of Paul's letter to the Romans, the Christians began meeting separately
from the Jewish synagogues. The majority of Roman Christians by then were
of non-Jewish descent, although many of these Gentiles may, before their
baptisms, have been loosely connected with Jewish synagogues as (uncircum-
cised) sympathizers with Jewish monotheism. In 64 even Nero (r. 54–68) could
distinguish the Christians from the Jews in the city.

Despite separation from the worship of the synagogues, the Roman Christians maintained many Jewish traditions and influences in their thinking and
teaching. The *First Epistle of Clement* and the *Book of Hermas* exemplify
this well. Social contacts between Christians and Jews in the city continued,
as the Christian slave Callistus demonstrated in the 180s when he operated a
bank with Christian and Jewish customers decades before he became bishop
(Hippolytus [attrib.], *Ref.* 9.12) (Lampe 1989, 282–83; 2003a, 335). In the
second century a group of Jewish Christians still observed the Torah (Justin,
Dial. 47), withdrawing fellowship from other Christians who did not, but
probably maintaining contact with non-Christian Jewish synagogues. Cultural exchanges between Jews and Christians (in the fields of theology, art,
or catacomb architecture) existed throughout the second and third centuries.

"Bad Press"

In 64 CE a great fire severely damaged ten of Rome's fourteen regions. Nero
unjustly accused the Christians of arson, crucifying and burning many of them
as torches in the Vatican gardens (Tacitus, *Ann.* 15.38–44), thus imposing the
traditional punishment for arsonists of being burned alive. Many contemporaries suspected Nero himself of setting the city on fire because he needed
space for his construction plans. He designed his new palace, the vast "Golden
House," to stretch all the way from the Palatine to the slopes of the Esquiline.

Although the Christians were innocent, the fact that they could so easily
be scapegoated shows what a bad reputation they had. They were disliked in

William Tabbernee

Fig. 9.3. Dedicatory Inscription Marking St. Paul's Tomb in St. Paul's-Outside-the-Walls on the Via Ostiense

the pagan environment because they were as different as the Jews (see, e.g., Tacitus, *Ann.* 15.44; cf. Tacitus, *Hist.* 5.5.1; Suetonius, *Nero* 16; Pliny the Younger, *Ep.* 10.96.8; Justin, *1 Apol.* 1.1; also Mark 13:13, as a presumably Roman document written only six years later). Paul drastically illustrates this bad reputation under which particularly the early Christian missionaries suffered: "We have become like the rubbish of the world, the dregs of all things" (1 Cor. 4:13). Bad press, immigrant status, being an unimportant ingredient in a melting-pot city of people from all over the empire—this was early Christianity in the city of Rome.

It is probable that the apostle Peter was among Nero's crucified victims in 64 (*1 Clem.* 5.4; cf. John 21:18–19; Ignatius, *Rom.* 4) (Lampe 2003b). In the mid-second century at the latest—that is, no more than three generations after Peter's death—Christians appear to have identified a simple grave in the Vatican necropolis as Peter's burial place. This, however, is all that can be said in a scientifically responsible way about the history of this tomb prior to 160. Around that year, Roman Christians decorated the simple grave with a modest monument, an *aedicula*, before it gradually became the center of more and more architectural activity. Today the dome of St. Peter's Basilica soars high above it.

According to *1 Clement* 5.4–7 Paul also suffered martyrdom in Rome. At the end of the second century, if not earlier, Roman Christians held that his tomb was located on the Ostian Way (Eusebius, *Hist. eccl.* 2.25.7). This has been confirmed by recent excavations at St. Paul's-Outside-the-Walls. Acts, however, stops abruptly before Paul's martyrdom. Acts rather emphasizes that Paul, after his capture in Jerusalem, appealed to the emperor's court in

Rome, able to do so because of his Roman citizenship (16:37–38; 22:25–29; 23:27). Consequently, Paul was brought to Rome, where, guarded by a soldier, he could receive visitors relatively freely and teach in tenement lodging during his dragged-out trial (28:16, 30). Where possible, the author of Acts tried to keep negative sides of Roman rule, such as Paul's martyrdom, from his readers.

Contextual Influences

TOPOGRAPHY

Approximately one million people with various languages, customs, and religions from all over the empire crowded Rome in imperial times (Lampe 2005a). Persons who were more well-to-do lived in villas (*domus*), with floor heating, running water, and sewer pipes, or in luxurious apartments. The majority of the population, however, crowded tenements (*insulae*) built of brick and wood. The tenements, five or six floors high, often became deadly fire traps. Most of them had no water or latrines. The ground floors were used as stores, workshops, or storage rooms. The higher one climbed in the tenement houses, the smaller and darker the dwelling units became. Loud noises, foul odors, and crowded conditions were normal. At night, sleep was disturbed by carts clattering under the windows, since Caesar had banned daytime cart traffic from the jammed streets of the city. In the fourth century more than 44,000 entrances to *insulae* were counted in Rome, in addition to 1,791 entrances to *domus*.

The early Christians lived at the periphery of Rome outside the sacred city limits, the *pomerium*: in Trastevere and in the valley of the Appian Way outside the Capena Gate (Lampe 1989, 10–52; 2003a, 19–66; 2004a). Both areas, also settled by Jews, were permeated with immigrants from the provinces who swept into the city via the Appian Way and the Tiber River. People of the lower social strata populated these quarters. Martial (ca. 38/41–101/4 CE) caricatures the typical Trastevere inhabitant as a buffoon trading bits of glass for sulfur matches (*Epigr.* 1.41). Other Christians dwelt on the Aventine Hill, a much-preferred residential area, and still others on the Campus Martius.

On a map, areas infiltrated by Christians in Rome are shaped like a sickle curving around the city center. This was typical for an immigrant Eastern religious group in the capital. In the immediate neighborhood of the Christian "cells," other Eastern cults blossomed, venerating gods such as Sol of Palmyra, the Syrian Hadad, Atargatis, Simios, and Iuppiter Dolichenus, or Isis, Sarapis, Mithras, and Cybele.

The sickle shape helps to explain why Nero could so easily accuse the Christians of arson. Not only did they have the bad reputation of being misanthropes, but also they primarily lived outside the quarters that were affected by the disastrous fire in 64. Those in Trastevere, who could safely watch the fire from the other side of the Tiber, were ideal scapegoats.

SOCIAL ASPECTS

Topography reveals that the lower social strata predominated in pre-Constantinian Roman Christianity, although higher social strata were represented as well. This picture is confirmed by the literary sources. Most early Roman Christians were of very modest means (Minucius Felix, *Oct.* 36.3). This is to be expected, because lower-class people predominated in the city population as a whole (e.g., Seneca, *Helv.* 12.1). Roman Christianity, nonetheless, gradually infiltrated all social levels, even the senatorial. In 96, for example, a relative of the emperor Domitian (r. 81–96), Flavia Domitilla, was banished to an island because her Christian faith did not allow her to acknowledge Domitian as a god (Eusebius, *Hist. eccl.* 3.18.4; Cassius Dio, *Hist. rom.* 67.14.1–2).

Christianity entered the Roman upper classes primarily through women. Such gender imbalance, of course, made it difficult for aristocratic Christian women to find Christian spouses of equal rank (Hippolytus [attrib.], *Ref.* 9.12.24; *ILCV* 157–58 and 224 [third century]; Barbieri 1952, no. 2183). Callistus (bp. ca. 217–ca. 222) tried to find a solution by allowing Christian aristocratic women to live together with Christian men of lower social status without legal marriage. As bishop, he sanctified these relationships and the offspring resulting from them. Because they were not legally married, these women did not lose their high social rank (which was advantageous for the church). Callistus's decision also motivated them to avoid mixed marriages with pagan men of equal rank (which again was advantageous for the church).

With time, the average social position of the Roman Christians rose. In the first century socially elevated Christians were still few. Some Roman Christians even sold themselves into temporary slavery in order to raise money for the poor in the church (*1 Clem.* 55.2). It was not until the 90s that we hear about "wealthy people" among the Roman Christians, without, however, learning what "wealthy" or "rich" specifically means. Nevertheless, from the second century onward, well-off Christians were able to raise respectable sums for charity. At the turn of the second to the third centuries, not only the needy but also the church's office holders could be paid from these donations. In the last twenty years of the second century, under Commodus (r. 180–192) and Septimius Severus (r. 193–211), a fair number of generous imperial freed slaves and several Christian senators and women of senatorial rank belonged to Roman house-churches. A significant number of Christian senators are documented again in about 258. We are able to name almost forty pre-Constantinian Christian members of the senatorial class, most of them in the third century, with two-thirds of them being female. Forty is about 0.3 percent of the fifteen thousand senatorial individuals in the first three centuries. But the actual number presumably was higher than forty, with our prosopographical evidence being more accidental than representative (Lampe 1989, 94–103; 2003a, 117–26).

Parallel to this development within the church, the Roman senate itself, from the 190s onward, was composed of many more members from the Eastern provinces than before; the percentage of senators from those provinces jumped to almost one-third under Septimius Severus alone. It is tempting to suppose that this increase in the number of senators from the Eastern provinces also helped to push up the number of senators in the Roman churches. Prosopographically, we know of a Christian senator Astyrius from Syria-Palaestina in the 260s and of members of the senatorial class from Phrygia and Lycaonia. Senators from the provinces had to invest at least a quarter of their capital in Italian real estate, and one of their residences had to be in Rome. Thus Christian senators from the Eastern provinces both sat in Roman church services and played roles in their provincial churches, which made them influential links between Roman Christianity and the churches of the East.

The gradual rise of the average social status of Roman Christians mirrors the development in the society of the Roman Empire as a whole. In the second century the number of members of the higher social strata generally grew steadily, while the number of slaves decreased.

What, then, is different from society in general? Does the social history of early Roman Christianity exhibit anything special that is not reflected in the pagan environment? At least one point is worth mentioning. Those first-century Christians who sold themselves into slavery in order to support the needy of their church demonstrated an extreme solidarity among members of lower social strata that is rare in Roman society. Only the upper classes of the pagan empire presented themselves as fairly consolidated groups, above all the senatorial class, while the lower strata lacked a collective consciousness and supraregional cohesion. The early Christian representatives of the lower social levels, however, exhibited exactly this: a supraregional solidarity and a sense of belonging together in spite of ethnic and geographical distances. Christianity here contributed to the social integration of the whole Roman society.

Christianity's contribution to the social integration of Roman society as a whole is also true in another respect. Within the realm of the church (although not exclusively there), members of different social strata became extremely close to one another, supporting one another. The *Book of Hermas*, written in Rome in the first half of the second century, paints the lovely image of a vine climbing up an elm tree, the vine being the poor and the elm the rich in the church. The vine can bear grapes—spiritual fruit—only as long as the elm supports the vine; the unfruitful elm can bring forth fruit only as long as the vine grows grapes among its branches. The different social levels need one another. The donations and alms of the richer Christians raised the social position of those who, without Christian support, scarcely scratched out a living. The church offered subsistence to the needy and in this way, again, contributed to the social integration of Roman society.

Already in the early third century the church also assisted in acquiring burial space in the San Callisto Catacomb (Lampe 1989, 15–17; 2003a, 25–28). Even in the fourth century lower-class Christians predominated there, as is indicated by recent stable-isotope analyses of collagen from twenty-two randomly selected skeletons from different locations in the Liberian region of the catacomb. These simple people ate cheap freshwater fish from the unhealthy Tiber as their major protein supply and were buried in unassuming tombs (Rutgers et al. 2009).

It would be helpful to have more than just fragmentary demographic statistics for pre-Constantinian times. How many Christians lived in the city? In the middle of the third century, Cornelius (bp. 251–253) counted fifteen hundred Christians receiving assistance from the church (Eusebius, *Hist. eccl.* 6.43.11–12). However, this does not tell us how many Christians of meager means (*pauperes*), who formed the majority in Roman Christianity, lived in Rome. A *pauper*, often translated as "poor," usually did make a very modest living and did not receive subsidies from the church. Thus, the fifteen hundred should not necessarily be equated with the majority in Roman Christianity, and we are left in the dark when it comes to estimating the total number of Roman Christians.

Cornelius also enumerated forty-six presbyters in the city. During the first three decades of the third century about eight hundred Christians were buried in San Callisto (Lampe 1989, 15–17; 2003a, 25–28). However, we do not know by which factors these figures need to be multiplied. Already in the time of Nero, the Roman Christians formed a "large crowd," which constantly grew in the decades to come (cf. Minucius Felix, *Oct.* 31.7). In the last quarter of the second century, Irenaeus identified Roman Christianity as the largest Christian unit in the world (*Haer.* 3.3.2); no other city housed as many followers of the new faith. Modern guesses vary between ten thousand and thirty thousand Roman Christians in the mid-third century, while the total number of Roman Jews in early imperial times is estimated between fifteen thousand and sixty thousand. The murky waters of ancient population statistics reflect the limits of our knowledge.

Organizational Aspects

Fractionation. Jewish freedpersons and slaves of pagan households formed their own synagogues, as shown above. Pagan servants of an estate could form an independent religious unit within their household, administering the cult of the Lares or the cult of the master's *genius*. In the same way, Christian freedpersons and slaves of non-Christian masters organized Christian congregations of their own in Rome (cf. Rom. 16:10–11) within the houses and estates in which they lived and worked.

In all these cases the locale of work and living and the place of religious activity were concentric circles. Masters often practiced a religion different from that of their servants (Tacitus, *Ann.* 14.44.3; Philemon; 1 Tim. 6:1; Titus 2:9–10; Origen, *Cels.* 3.55; Council of Elvira, *Can.* 41), tolerating the religious plurality within their households, even if the servants were Christian.

In about 56 the apostle Paul, in Romans 16, sends greetings to various congregations in Rome (Lampe 1991), among them:

(i)   "those in the lord who are part of Narcissus's domestic staff" and
(ii) "those who are part of Aristobulus's domestic staff" (16:10–11);[12]
(iii) the house-church of Prisca and Aquila;
(iv) the Christians who were together with Asyncritus, Phlegon, Hermes, Patrobas, and Hermas; and
(v)   the saints who were with Philologus, Julia, Nereus and his sister, and Olympas.

If we assume that the fourteen other persons greeted in the chapter did not belong to any of the five Christian groups mentioned above and that the additional people could not have belonged to only one further group, then, in about 56 CE, at least seven different Christian "islands" existed in Rome. Another Christian circle was established when Paul himself, only half a decade later, gathered a group around himself in his Roman rental apartment (Acts 28:16, 30).

The individual groups celebrated their own worship services somewhere in private houses, in apartments, or in workshops. Thus early Christians in Rome formed various house-churches scattered throughout the city. There was no local center or central meeting place for Roman Christianity.

12. Translations by the author. Paul's formulations show that the two masters and part of their domestic staff were non-Christian. Furthermore, Aristobulus's name was very rare in Rome, which probably means that he had immigrated to Rome from the East or even lived in the East, with only part of his household being in Rome. The name Aristobulus was favored by the Herodian family (both the father and brother of Herod Agrippa I, for example, were named Aristobulus). A connection to the Herodian royal household is possible but cannot be proven.

This fractionation, similar to that of the Jews in the city, facilitated a theological pluralism (Lampe 1989, 320–34; 2003a, 381–96). Second-century Rome, for example, saw Christian groups moving in numerous theological directions: Marcionite, Valentinian, Carpocratian, Theodotian, Modalistic, Montanist, and Quartodecimanian teachings. There were Cerdo's followers and house-churches of (what was only later called) the "orthodox" faith. A Jewish-Christian circle existed that still observed the Torah. Some groups exhibited a *logos* theology that was too complicated for lesser-educated Christians. Some circles believed in a thousand-year-long eschatological reign of Christ (millennialism); others did not. Roman Christianity was extremely varied, with the groups often reflecting the original geographical or educational provenances of their members. The house-churches, scattered over the city, were only loosely connected. Some sent portions of their Eucharist to other Christian groups in the city to express fellowship and unity with them. Written material also was shared among the Christian groups in Rome.

On the whole, because of these loose connections the various circles in the city tolerated one another during the first two centuries. With few exceptions, no Christian group labeled another as heretical before the last decade of the second century. Consequently, communication with persons or congregations outside Rome was often coordinated among the groups. As a result, outsiders could perceive the various Roman house-churches as "*the* Roman church."

Late Development of Monepiscopacy. A monarchical bishop who oversaw at least the "orthodox" house-churches in the city, did not come into existence before the second half of the second century.[13] Earlier, the various house-churches were led solely by their own presbyters. The role of monarchical bishop emerged in connection with the needs for a centralized coordination of the foreign contacts of the Roman Christians. The first pioneers and proponents of a monarchical episcopacy were those presbyters who acted as "foreign ministers" of Roman Christianity. Also, the support of the poor called for more centralized structures in order to be effective.

One of the effects of the emerging monarchical episcopate was that the tool of excommunication began to be used more often. It was under Victor (bp. ca. 189–198/9), one of the first monarchical bishops in Rome, that Roman house-churches, regarding themselves as "orthodox," began to excommunicate other groups on a large scale. Victor, supported by Irenaeus, cut the ties to four Christian groups in the city.

13. See Lampe 1989, 334–45; 1998a; 1998b; 2003a, 397–408; 2003c; 2004c; 2005b.

CULTURAL ASPECTS

Languages. In the immigrant culture of early Roman Christianity, Greek was used as the main language. It was not until the 240s that the shift to Latin predominated, indicating that the majority of Roman Christians now came from a Latin background. In the second century, while Greek was still the dominant language of the educated Christians in Rome, a rather uncultivated Latin was being used by some lower-class Christian circles. In the first half of the third century, however, Latin and Greek were already equally represented in the Christian catacomb inscriptions.

At the beginning of the third century the Roman Christian lawyer Minucius Felix, a highly educated rhetorician probably of North African origin, composed a Latin dialogue of perfectly elegant style and Ciceronian form. The next important Latin author of the Christian faith in Rome was the presbyter Novatian (ca. 200–258/9). He was a man of profound rhetorical, philosophical, and literary education who skillfully used classical Latin writings; his knowledge of Stoic philosophy seems to have been molded by Seneca. In the 250s the Roman bishop's correspondence was composed exclusively in Latin, but the more educated circles remained bilingual. Both Latin and Greek could still be used as liturgical languages until the fourth century. The funerary inscriptions of the Roman bishops of the third century were also still formulated in Greek. Bilingualism, however, slowly disappeared from the second half of the third century onward. One did not need to be a prophet to predict that this shift toward Latin would open a gap between western and eastern ecclesiastical provinces.

Philosophy. First Clement, written at the end of the first century, exhibits Stoic elements, which probably had reached Roman Christianity via Hellenistic synagogues. Within the Greek-speaking Christian circles of Rome the

Fig. 9.4. Latin Inscription from Catacomb of St. Sebastian

ambitious assimilation of pagan education—that is, of Greek literature and philosophy—occurred in the second century. The apologist-philosopher Justin (d. ca. 165), for example, bridged Middle Platonism and Christian thought. The Theodotians (followers of Theodotus, an immigrant from Byzantium who taught at Rome in the 190s) explained the Christian faith by means of post-Aristotelian logic. Others, such as Valentinus (fl. ca. 140), were rooted in Platonism. These second-century intellectuals were the first Christians who extensively used and enjoyed the treasure chest of Greek culture and *paideia* (education). They rethought Christian doctrine on the basis of pagan philosophical presuppositions.

Greco-Roman Culture in General. Apologists such as Justin looked for as many points of congruence as possible between Greco-Roman and Christian cultures. They tried to bring the Greek and Christian traditions into a harmonious relationship in order to find a respectable place for Christianity in the Roman political and societal systems. Christians offered their loyal service to the pagan empire. Having insights into the allegedly definitive truth—a truth that Moses and many Greek philosophers had only partially discovered—Christians such as Justin reasoned that they alone could properly assess the actions of governments and the legitimacy of institutions and laws.

The question is whether the pagan environment was delighted with this offer of service. Not even all Christians thought it wise. Tatian, a student of Justin, sneered at the harmonization of thought. In about 165, although highly educated in Greek culture, Tatian wrote a harsh polemic, *Against the Hellenes*, declaring the incompatibility of Christian faith with Greek philosophy, rhetoric, science, art, and religion.

Pagan Reaction to Christianity. For pagan Romans, a multitude of deities and cults undergirded the order of their multipeopled empire. They therefore tolerated and even welcomed religious and cultic diversity. Philosophically minded pagans, adhering to a nonexclusive philosophical henotheism, speculatively pondered the unity of the divine essence. At the same time, however, these same persons in everyday religious praxis participated in more than one of the many cults. Thus, for pagan Romans the exclusive monotheism of the Christians, which ruled out any other veneration of the divine besides their own, was impious and ungodly. The Christians, consequently, were met with suspicion. They were regarded as potentially dangerous for the Roman order. Every governor, upon their denunciation, could examine Christians and punish, or even sentence to death, those who confessed their belief in Christ and refused to express cultic reverence for another deity or the *genius* of the emperor.

The apologists' writings did not change this legal position, but they probably altered the climate, at least a little. Tacitus, Suetonius, and Pliny the Younger (61/2–ca. 113) had labeled Christianity a "superstition" (Tacitus, *Ann.* 15.44; Suetonius, *Claud.* 25.3; *Nero* 16.2; Pliny the Younger, *Ep.* 10.96.8). From the second third of the second century on, however, Christian philosophers such as Justin worked to improve the Christians' image and claimed that Christianity was a respectable and loyal "philosophy," worthy of being received into the Greco-Roman world of *paideia*. The apologists' words usually went unheard, but not always. The pagan authors Lucian of Samosata (ca. 120–post-180) and Galen of Pergamum (129–199) indeed began to call Christianity a *sophia* (wisdom) and a "philosophy," although they were not impressed by it. In their eyes, this "school" lacked solid proof and was dogmatically encrusted. However, more and more cultivated and distinguished pagans found their way to the baptismal font during the second half of the second century. Christianity was, albeit gradually and slowly, recognized as a *paideia*.

Educational Processes. The Christian tradition, its doctrines and moral teachings, sometimes fused with pagan cultural elements, was transmitted within the church as a culture of its own. This "*paideia* in Christ," as *1 Clement* (21.8) called it, was taught on three levels:

(i)   Independent teachers and philosophers such as Justin or Valentinus gathered circles of students and held lectures. Justin gathered his audience in his rental apartment above the private thermal "Baths of Myrtinus," where he also worshiped with them.

(ii) Presbyters taught their house-church congregations. They also instructed the catechumens before their baptisms. The *Traditio apostolica*, a Roman work from the first half of the third century, ruled which pagan candidates could be admitted to this education and which could not.

(iii) In private homes children were taught by their parents. In the second century husbands often also taught their wives. Only for orphans and widows did the Roman house-churches appoint special woman teachers (Hermas, *Vis.* 2.4.3).

However, Christian instruction of children did not replace secular schools where children learned to read, write, do math, and analyze texts. Christians, consequently, continued to send their offspring to pagan elementary, grammar, and rhetorical schools (cf. Tertullian, *De idolatria*).

Pagan/Christian Assimilation. How much did Christian and pagan cultures amalgamate on the level of ordinary Roman Christians who did not have philosophical or rhetorical backgrounds of higher learning? The life of ordinary people often is revealed only by combining various source genres. In the case of Roman Christianity, archaeological, epigraphic, and literary sources reveal that many ordinary Roman Christians lived peacefully side by side with their pagan neighbors without any scruples or fear of contact. They often maintained pagan customs, particularly in funerary practices. Even in the post-Constantinian era Christians occasionally felt free to build tombs with openings for libations. According to several graffiti, Christians of the second half of the fourth century practiced libation in the Catacombs of San Sebastiano and of Priscilla. A Christian fresco and a drawing in the Catacombs of Domitilla and of St. Ermete/Bassilla depict the libation ritual as well. This coincides with other third- and fourth-century epigraphic and literary evidence according to which Christians often celebrated meals for the dead (*refrigeria*) at their tombs. Augustine of Hippo (bp. ca. 395/6–430) wrote that Christian meals for the dead did not differ all that much from superstitious pagan ones (*Conf.* 6.2). Christians brought wine with them, and those who honored several tombs in one day ended up coming home tipsy from the cemetery. Paulinus of Nola (bp. pre-415–431), a contemporary of Augustine, complained about the simplemindedness of those Christians who poured wine over graves (*Carm.* 27 [= *Carm. nat.* 9]).

In about 200 a cross and a Christian *acrostichon* (Jesus Christ God's Son Savior) were drawn into the wet plaster of an otherwise clearly pagan mausoleum under San Sebastiano. In other words, Christians buried one or more of their family members close to pagan graves. The same is true for San Callisto: in the surface area above the two original nuclei of this catacomb, pagan and Christian graves still lay side by side in the fourth century. In the third century, in the mausoleums of the Vatican necropolis, several Christians were buried in direct proximity to many pagan graves; the Christians decorated one little mausoleum with a Christ-Helios mosaic, not far from pagan frescoes and mosaics. In and above the two nuclei of the Pretestato Catacomb on the Appian Way, Christian and pagan tombs lay side by side in the third century. Nor did Jews have scruples about burying their dead beside pagans, as the Jewish funerary inscriptions of Ostia show. On the whole, the different groups coexisted peaceably.

In 217 freedpersons of the Christian imperial freedman Marcus Aurelius Prosenes were responsible for an interesting mixture of pagan and Christian elements. Their patron died, and they ordered for him a sarcophagus with a double inscription (*CIL* 6.8498). They juxtaposed a hint at Prosenes's Christianity (almost shyly hidden at the narrow side of the sarcophagus) with little cupids, winged *genii*, and a reference to a deified pagan emperor: *divus Commodus*. Another, clearly Christian, sarcophagus from the mid-third century similarly shows winged *genii*. On Christian frescoes and reliefs of third-century Rome, biblical figures such as Daniel and Jonah are often placed in traditional idyllic landscapes taken from pagan art. These pagan idyllic motifs frequently dominate the biblical ones, almost camouflaging the latter.

Church officials such as Cyprian of Carthage (bp. ca. 248/9–258) were upset about the intense assimilation of Christianity and paganism in the cemeteries (*Ep.* 67.6). However, ordinary early Christians had reasons to retain or adopt pagan elements. Tertullian points out an aspect that helps to interpret these sarcophagi, frescoes, and reliefs of the third century. According to him, Christian women defended their elegant attire and their jewelry by arguing that this was a sort of camouflage (*Cult. fem.* 2.11). If they did not wear such attire and ornaments, everybody would know right away that they were Christians. Interestingly enough, until the mid-third century the Christians' personal names usually were pagan. Specifically Christian or biblical names usually were avoided. This was also true for Jews both in Rome and in the Diaspora in general. Christians did not want to invite denunciations or molestations by constantly publicizing their faith in daily life.

Ordinary people speak also through our literary sources. The *Book of Hermas* was composed in Rome by a Christian freedman in the first half of the second century. The author betrays only a mediocre education and naively mixes pagan elements into his Christian writing. His Mother Church, an allegorical figure, exhibits features of the Sibyl of Cumae. Materials from pagan erotic novels and light reading are woven into the book. The pagan motif of the "divine beloved" is used without a qualm. Pagan bucolic literature inspires a great many pastoral motifs in the book. Popular Cynic-Stoic elements are picked up; the author, however, erroneously thinks that they are Pythagorean. His book "christens" manifold popular pagan conceptions and motifs. And had it not been for more-sophisticated theologians in the church, this book would have been included in the canon of Scripture by the masses of ordinary Christians who loved it and gladly read it, generation after generation.

The symbiosis of paganism and Christianity can also be shown to have existed within the same family. The following examples from the socially elevated strata are based on archaeological and literary evidence, respectively. The first is an anonymous, private catacomb on the Via Latina that dates from the fourth century. It exhibits gorgeous frescoes of both Christian and pagan contents side by side. In Room 11, soldiers gamble for Jesus's *tunica*, and Jonah is cast into the ocean, while in Room 12 Hercules steals apples from the Hesperides. He kills a hydra and offers Athena his hand.

The second example is the noble family of the *Ceionii* during the end of the fourth century and the first decades of the fifth. Two brothers of this family married two Christian women of high rank, but they themselves remained pagan. The daughters and granddaughters of these two marriages grew up Christian and also married Christian spouses. But the sons of these two marriages cultivated the old pagan roots of their family, although paganism had been officially suppressed by then. It was the women who gave the family the necessary Christian façade. The example again illustrates Christianity being introduced into aristocratic circles primarily through the women. However, it also shows how difficult it was to infuse these circles with the Christian spirit. Even after Constantine, aristocratic families remained bastions of paganism. Almost all Roman nobles were still pagan at the beginning of the fifth century, at the time of Augustine (*Conf.* 8.2.3). No Roman bishop before the mid-fifth century came from the leading circles of the empire. Even in the sixth century the pagan spirit and secular traditions of the city of Rome tenaciously survived in the Italian aristocracy under a thin Christian veneer.

Central Italy

Material and Literary Data

Both the material and literary evidence are too scarce for the historian to draw firm conclusions about how deeply or quickly Christian communities spread throughout Italy. There exists, for example, no equivalent sourcebook of second- and third-century events for Italy (or the West) as Eusebius's *Historia ecclesiastica* provides for the East. Although Eusebius shows interest in apostolic succession at Rome, he says nothing about bishops or churches elsewhere in Italy. The same limitations apply when it comes to the epigraphic evidence throughout Italy (sans Rome). There are no Christian funerary inscriptions that can be securely dated until the later fourth century (Galvão-Sobrinho 1995, 466), nor do the few dozen mosaics and church foundations (with the exception of Aquileia and, perhaps, Capua) offer information about Christian communities before the end of the fourth or early fifth century.[14]

Given that missionaries probably went out from Rome to nearby towns, we may assume that areas adjacent to Latium and Campania were the earliest to have Christian congregations,[15] despite Tertullian's hyperbolic remark to

14. For the dating of two crypt wall inscriptions in Venice (100), mosaics in Brescia (66), and the mosaics in the first stage of reconstruction of a sanctuary in Verona (83), see Caillet 1993. For the evidence relating to Aquileia, see below.

15. Among the writings of Cyprian of Carthage is a brief letter from the Roman clergy who admitted to Cyprian that the recent persecution led to the flight of a "large number" of Roman clergy and other bishops, "who are nearby and close to us, and some who are situated far off" (*Ep.* 30.8).

the contrary (*Apol.* 40.8). Adolf Harnack's estimate that one hundred episcopal seats could be found in middle and lower Italy by 250 (Harnack 1908,
2:252–54) probably is not far from the mark, although his count of 250 to 300
bishops by 300 lacks concrete justification. Scholars today are less enthusiastic
about attributing such rapid growth to Christianity before Constantine.[16] Yet
we may speculate that if 130 African bishops were convened at a council in
Carthage in 251, it is reasonable to argue that no less a number could be gathered in central Italy, with the likelihood of a larger number, given the greater
antiquity of Christianity in Italy.[17] Prior to the Councils of Rome (313) and
Arles (314), at which Italian clergy were in attendance, we have very little data
about which towns had Christian communities or could claim a bishopric.
While data on the social strata of Italian Christianity is important for seeing
its depth of impact,[18] it has little to do with its general spread geographically.
Another body of sources consists of medieval hagiographies, martyrologies,
lists of saints' festivals,[19] and episcopal registries (*fasti*) that claim a detailed
knowledge of Christian development in Italian cities since its earliest beginnings
(Humphries 1999, 53–71). The problematic nature of these sources, however,
limits their historical usefulness to the confirmation of other sources when
they coincide. Writings produced by Italian bishops before the mid-fourth
century are almost negligible.

Conciliar Data

THE COUNCIL OF ROME (251)

The most dependable data for determining the presence of Christianity in
Italian towns come chiefly from the canons and names of bishops indicated at
early synods. Before the fourth century there is only meager evidence for and
about the meetings of Italian bishops in Rome or elsewhere. For example, there
was a synod of Italian bishops under the headship of Cornelius of Rome that
convened in 251 just after Decius's death (Eusebius, *Hist. eccl.* 6.43.2; Cyprian,
Ep. 55.6.2). Its purpose was to give an official response to the North Africans'
decision that allowed those who lapsed during the recent persecution, now

16. Winrich Löhr (2007, 23) points out, "Growth in numbers can be assumed for the fifth
century; at the close of the sixth century the number of 250 episcopal sees seems to be realistic."
    17. The first attestation of Christianity in North Africa comes from the account of the Scil-
litan martyrs, 180 CE (see chap. 6).
    18. A tradition from the time of Damasus of Rome (bp. 366–384) identified M. Vibius Liberis,
consul suffectus in 166, as a Christian martyr. A wife of Posthumus Quietus (*consul* in 272) was
said to be a Christian (*CIL* 6.31749a). See Trombley and Rist 1999, cols. 1160–61.
    19. Most prominent are the *Martyrologium hieronymianum* and the *Aurea legenda* (*Golden
Legend*) by Jacobus de Voragine (ca. 1230–1298).

penitent, readmission to communion. This council also included a condemnation of Novatian for creating discord by his encouragement of the churches to reject flatly all those who had lapsed.[20] Apparently, Novatian convinced three other Italian bishops to side with his position, thus giving momentum to his claims. Based on a letter that Cornelius wrote to the Antiochenes about the conciliar judgments (in Eusebius, *Hist. eccl.* 6.42.3–22), we are told that there were sixty bishops present, subscribing according to name and see. However, none of these names or places, except for the church at Rome, is actually identified, though there is no need to doubt the report. That sixty bishops could convene so immediately after the severities of the Decian persecution suggests that a much larger number of episcopal sees existed in Italy by 250. Cyprian (*Ep.* 44.1) names two of these sixty bishops, Pompeius and Stephanus, who were sent to Carthage with the decisions of the council (Dunn 2007, 62), though nothing further is disclosed about them either in Cyprian's correspondence or elsewhere.

THE SYNOD OF ROME (313)

The next Italian council for which we have reliable data[21] is one prompted by Constantine in 313. Two years earlier, the election of Caecilian (d. ca. 345) as bishop of Carthage was challenged by his rivals[22] because one of his consecrators was allegedly a *traditor*.[23] Despite new conditions of freedom for Italy's Christians, only sixteen Italian bishops met in Rome in 313 under Miltiades (bp. ca. 310/1–314), though we should not read too much into this small number of attendees, seeing that the issue was not a provincial one. Optatus's *Against the Donatists* contains the only historical record of names (*Donat.* 1–23; PL 9.931A–932A).[24] Besides three Gallic bishops and Miltiades of Rome, fifteen names are listed: Merocles of Mediolanum (Milan), Florianus of Sinna [i.e., Saena] (Siena), Zoticus of Quintianum (Quintiano), Stennius of Ariminum, Felix of Florentia (Florence), Gaudentius of Pisae, Constantius of Faventia (Faenza), Proterius of Capua,[25] Theophilus of Beneventum (Benevento), Sabinus of Ter-

---

20. Giovanni Mansi (1960, 1:865–68) divides these events into three separate Italian councils.

21. Marcellus (*Lib. pont.* 30.2) tells how the bishop of Rome confessed to sacrificing to pagan gods before a synod of 180 bishops gathered at Sinuessa in about 300 in Campania. Such an assembly in the location described is likely enough, though it lacks substantiation.

22. That is, the supporters of Majorinus (d. ca. 312/3) who elected him as an uncorrupted candidate.

23. The legal process by which the case was handled by imperial authorities is recounted by Augustine (*Ep.* 162A.8).

24. The anachronistic location of the council (House of Fausta on the Lateran) and its erroneous dating to 314, however, cast a shadow of uncertainty on the accuracy of the list of names. See Humphries 1999, 47.

25. Modern Capua is near, but not on the exact site of, ancient Capua (modern Santa Maria Capua Vetera).

9.3 Italian Clergy at the Council of Arles

Epictetus of Centumcellae (Civitavecchia) (*EOMIA* 1.381)

Pardus of *Civitas Arpiensium* in Apulia; and Crescens, deacon (1.400.3);*

Quintasius of Caralis (Cagliari); and Ammonius (or Admonius), presbyter (1.412)

Chrestus of Syracusae (Syracuse) (Eusebius, *Hist.* eccl. 10.5.21); and Florus, deacon (1.398)

Theodorus of Aquileia; and Agathon, deacon (1.400)

Merocles of Mediolanum (Milan); Severus, deacon; and another cleric, Romanus (1.404.13)

Gregory of Portus (Porto) (Gregorius episcopus de loco qui est in Portu Romae) (1.381[b]; 414.42)

Proterius of Capua; and Agrippa and Pinus (?), deacons (1.381[b]; 1.398.2)

Romanus, presbyter, and Victor, exorcist, of Apta Julia (Apt) (1.404)

Mercurius and Leontinus, presbyters of Ostia (1.414.44)

* Arpi is probably modern-day Arpinova, 6 km north of Foggia. While the manuscript tradition is fairly consistent for locating this city in Apulia and regarding the names of the clergy (Pardus or Pandus), the spelling of the city varies from manuscript to manuscript (i.e., Alpiensium, Salpientiu, Salpuensium, Alpientium), leaving uncertainty about its precise location (Di Gioia 1984, 283–84; Otranto 1991, 164; Mullen 2004, 204).

racina, Secundus of Praeneste (Palestrina), Felix of Tres Tabernae, Maximus of Ostia, Evandrus of Ursinum [presumably Urvinum] (Urbino), and Donatianus of Forum Clodii (Forum of Claudius).[26]

THE COUNCIL OF ARLES (314)

When Constantine was asked to review the acquittal of Caecilian, another council was convened. It met in Arles in 314, composed of Italian and Gallic bishops, again under the leadership Miltiades of Rome. Letters were sent to bishops in all the Western provinces, and the names of those who attended the council are listed in its *acta* (Augustine, *Don.* 1.18.27; PL 43.124) (see sidebar 9.3).[27]

There is some overlap of bishops who attended the councils of 313 and 314 (i.e., those from Milan, Capua, and Ostia). If we consider the geographical regions from which the attendees of both councils came, we notice that most of the churches with known bishops are aggregated in two areas: (1) around Rome and to the south along the coast (within Regio I), and (2) between Ariminum

26. The Forum Clodii was another "halting station," northeast of Rome, on the Via Clodii, at the present site of the ruins of the ninth-century Church of SS. Marcus, Marianus, and Liberatus.

27. See Wataghin 2000, 210.

on the Adriatic across the neck of the peninsula to Pisa on the coast of the Ligurian Sea. Only Milan and Aquileia can be accounted for in northern Italy. Three bishops came from unlikely towns in the Apulian region in the southeast along with representatives from Cagliari and Syracuse, whose attendance became commonplace in future councils. While the importance of these findings must not be overstated, this examination of the spread of Christianity in Italy before Constantine qualifies the commonly accepted theory that Christian growth was initially and primarily an urban phenomenon. Among the Italian episcopates identified, no less than half were from small towns, some quite a distance from the coast. Modern studies about the Christianization in northern Italy show a similar balance between urban and rural (Lizzi 1990, 157).

EMPERORS AND COUNCILS

Of course, the spread of Christianity in Italy, as elsewhere throughout the empire, was greatly facilitated by patronage from Constantine and, later, Constantius II (r. 337–361). Continuing largely without interruption for centuries, imperial support, monies, and privileges flowed into the Christian community and its institutions in Italy. Milan and Aquileia were already home to imperial residences. Throughout Italy bishops came to take on increasingly prominent social and political roles over the course of the fourth and fifth centuries (Salzman 2007, 210–12).

Since the Council of Nicaea was primarily an Eastern affair, the list of bishops extant in several manuscripts sheds almost no light on the ecclesiastical organization of Italy around 325. In addition to the two presbyters representing Rome, Marcus of Calabria was the only Italian bishop in attendance (*EOMIA* 1.84–85, 250).[28]

THE SYNOD OF SERDICA (343) AND THE COUNCIL OF ROME (350)

It is confusing and misleading to refer to the episcopal support for Athanasius of Alexandria (bp. 328–373) and Marcellus of Ancyra (bp. pre-314–374) as "Western." Conciliar documents that survive from the Synod of Serdica (Sofia), held in 343, show how churches in Italy, particularly those in Campania, were divided over the proper ecclesial direction to take concerning theological and conciliar matters. By no means did all Italian bishops side with Julius I of Rome (bp. 337–352) and the small council held in Rome (350) exonerating Athanasius and Marcellus of the charges laid against them by several Eastern councils. Among the recipients of the conciliar letter issued

28. Before the division of the empire under Diocletian, Calabria was the farthest southeastern region in Italy.

by the opponents of Athanasius and Marcellus were Desiderius of Campania, Fortunatus of Neapolis (Naples) in Campania, Euthicius of Campania, and, somewhat curiously, "the clergy of Ariminum."[29] This is not to say that these bishops were necessarily complicit with the aims of the senders, but since these were the only addressees in Italy and their names do not appear with the Italians present at Serdica, it is enough to presume that there was some dissension among regions.

The next known episcopal list is found in a copy of Serdica's decisions sent to Julius of Rome in which ten Italian bishops (out of sixty-one) subscribed to the exoneration of Marcellus, Athanasius, and Asclepius of Gaza (*CAP* B.4.2, 5).[30] Athanasius also inserts several synodical letters from Serdica in his *Defense against the Arians*. The last letter is a general encyclical containing the names (no sees) of those bishops from each diocese who subscribed either at the council or added their names afterward, which puts the total at over three hundred (Athanasius, *Apol. sec.* 50).[31]

Judging from the locales of attending bishops, Christianity had developed more widely in the north since the beginning of the fourth century. Severus of Ravenna, Ursacius of Brixia (Brescia), Protasius of Milan, Fortunatianus of Aquileia, and Lucius of Verona represented previously unreported sees. From central and southern Italy came Maximus of Luca (Lucca) in Tuscia, Vincentius of Capua in Campania, Januarius of Beneventum in Campania, Calepodis of Neapolis in Campania, and Stercorius of Canusium (Canosa di Puglia) in Apulia.

Council of Arles (353) and Milan (355)

At Arles, in 353, Vincentius of Capua was present as a representative of Liberius of Rome (bp. 352–366). Much to Liberius's chagrin, Vincentius caved in to the pressures laid on bishops present to sign an unknown document condemning Athanasius and Marcellus (*CAP* B.7.6).[32] This action was a surprise because Vincentius was at Serdica and was on record against the condemnations. Apparently, everyone subscribed except Paulinus of Trier (bp. ca. 346–358), who was immediately exiled.[33] Liberius wrote to Constantius asking for a second council. The bishops reconvened in Milan in 355, the see of Dionysius

29. Undoubtedly, Westerners are cited earlier in this conciliar letter, since it was addressed to the North African churches.

30. CSEL 65.132–39.

31. Athanasius claims that sixty-three bishops actually subscribed at the council. If we add the names of the two presbyter legates from Rome (Archidamus and Philoxenus), who were representing the bishop of Rome, then the number matches that of Hilary's account.

32. CSEL 65.167.

33. Probably to Pepouza in Phrygia. See Tabbernee forthcoming c.

(bp. 351–355), formerly of Alba Pompeia. This time more Italian bishops attended, among them Fortunatianus of Aquileia, Lucifer of Cagliari,[34] Eusebius of Vercelli,[35] Marcellus of Campania, and, again, Vincentius of Capua. Caecilianus of Spoletium (Spoleto) was not present but received a report from Liberius before the latter's exile (CAP B.7.6).[36] Presumably, the rest of the bishops at Milan agreed to the condemnation of Athanasius and to signing a confessional document.[37] Liberius himself capitulated. In a letter, written while in exile, Liberius avows that he has now separated from Athanasius and can be in communion with Epictetus of Centumcellae and Auxentius of Milan (CAP B.7.10),[38] the most vocal critics of the pro-Athanasian movement. In the letter Liberius asks Vincentius (his one-time ally) to inform "all the bishops of Campania" of his new peaceful intentions (CAP B.7.10 [2]).[39] Apparently, Marcellus was not the only bishop in Campania who had opposed Liberius.

THE COUNCIL OF ARIMINUM (359)

The largest council ever to convene in the West met in the Adriatic port city of Ariminum in 359. Approximately four hundred bishops attended, with the likelihood that Italian clergy constituted a majority. Proceedings probably commenced in the late third or fourth week of May.[40] Since the mid-350s, the momentum for which Constantius II had hoped had been building: a consolidation of Eastern and Western bishops behind a single profession of faith. To that end, Constantius sought to convoke a single great council along the same design as Nicaea, but it was apparent that more bishops could participate if separate (but related) councils were held in the East (Seleucia)[41] and the West (Ariminum).[42]

Select documents of the council's correspondence are preserved in Hilary of Poitiers's Against Valens and Ursacius and in Athanasius's On the Councils. Apart from these, we have only post hoc reports in the Chronicle of Sulpicius

34. Lucifer may have prompted Liberius's insistence for holding another council after Arles (CCSL 9.121).

35. Ancient Vercellae, a city of Liguria.

36. CSEL 65.167.

37. The document may have been a variant of the Sirmium Creed, though this is by no means certain.

38. CSEL 65.172.

39. CSEL 65.173.

40. The Fragmenta of Hilary of Poitiers (bp. ca. 350–367) contain a letter of Constantius to the council at Ariminum giving final instructions on matters of procedure (CAP A.8 [CSEL 65.93–94]). The letter is dated May 28 (datum V. Kal. Iunias Eusebio et Ypatio conss.), the second imperial communication to this council.

41. That is, Seleucia ad Calycadnum (Silifke).

42. For details about the council at Ariminum, see D. Williams 1995, 11–37.

Severus (ca. 363–ca. 420) and in *Against the Luciferians*, penned by Jerome (ca. 347–419), which contains a lively summary of the council's decisions. Regrettably, no subscription list of the council survives. A new Homoian creed was embraced that announced that the Son was like the Father and forbade the use of *homoousios* (same substance) or any theological term that uses substance:

> The Son of God was not a creature as were other creatures; and the deceit of this profession bypassed the notice of those hearing. Even though he [Valens of Mursa] denied in these words that the Son was like other creatures, the Son was, nevertheless, pronounced to be a creature, only superior to other creatures. (Sulpicius Severus, *Chron.* 2.44.7 [CSEL 1.97–98])

Ariminum did indeed have a galvanizing effect on bishops throughout the West, but not as the emperor had planned. In the years that followed, pro-Nicene fervor took hold of most churches. A gathering of bishops in Paris, in 360, condemned the Ariminum Creed as the "deceit of the devil" and declared that Western bishops who subscribed to the acts of the council had done so out of ignorance. This protest is echoed in Liberius's general letter to the Italian bishops (362/3) when he describes the bishops at Ariminum as deceived and *ignorantes*.[43] About this same time, an unnamed gathering of Italian bishops professed that they had renounced the decrees of Ariminum, and that, in order for their episcopal colleagues in Illyricum to establish communion with them, the latter must not only subscribe to the Nicene faith but also unambiguously disavow Ariminum.[44]

Still, little could be done about those Homoian bishops who tenaciously clung to their sees. The only way for a see to be opened for the election of a candidate favorable to Nicaea was through the death of its Homoian incumbent (D. Williams 1995, 70–73). There had been several attempts to remove Auxentius of Milan (an outspoken "Arian" Homoian), none of which was successful. An otherwise unattested Italian synod, held in Rome around 368, sent the results of its decisions to pro-Nicene bishops in Illyricum publicly condemning Auxentius and all supporters of Ariminum (Sozomen, *Hist. eccl.* 6.23.7–15 [GCS 1.266–68]; Theodoret, *Hist. eccl.* 2.22 [GCS 44.147–50]). Nevertheless, Auxentius remained bishop of Milan until his death in 374. Similarly, Urbanus of Parma (bp. ca. 359–378) is said to have retained his see despite conciliar attempts to have him ejected as an "Arian."[45] As the first and

---

43. This synodical letter (*CAP* B.4.1 [CSEL 65.156–57]) seems to be the only remnant of this council.

44. "Exemplum Epistulae Episcoporum Italiae," *CAP* B.4.2 (CSEL 65.158–59).

45. Collatio Avellana 13.6–7: "Gratianus et Valentinianus Augg. Aquilino vicerio" (CSEL 35.55–56).

only known bishop of Parma in Antiquity, Urbanus's condemnation was the subject of protest by Homoian sympathizers at the Council of Aquileia (381).[46]

Theological discord such as that described above was not limited to the North. In the early 360s Florentius of Puteoli (bp. 355–ca. 373 and post-388) had been condemned by his peers for theological reasons that almost certainly are linked to the anti-Ariminum fervor that swept across Italy after 359. An isolated record of another unidentified Italian council complained to the emperor Gratian (r. 375–383) in 378 that Florentius was still active in the city and "by his persuasive speech, corrupted a multitude of lost souls" (CSEL 35.56.7–8). Earlier and more influential than Florentius was Epictetus of Centumcellae, bishop of an important city north of the Tiber. On more than one occasion Athanasius expressed frustration that Epictetus had the support of the emperor (Constantius II), which allowed this bishop to oppose all attempts to resurrect the Creed of Nicaea as a standard of faith (*Ep. Aeg. Lib.* 7 [PG 25.553B]; *H. Ar.* 75 [PG 25.784C]). After Constantius's death in 361, we hear no more about Epictetus, though he likely remained in his see till death.

COUNCIL OF AQUILEIA (381)

By the time of the Council of Aquileia, Italy's bishops were almost solidly pro-Nicene, a situation created by the theological unity of the most influential sees—Milan, Aquileia, and Rome.[47] The identities of the bishops known to be at the council also reveal how the weight of episcopal authority had shifted to northern Italy, largely due to the influence of Ambrose over the region. At the council, an event that Ambrose orchestrated to remove the last pockets of Homoian Christianity in Italy and Illyricum, twelve North Italian bishops presented themselves as theological supporters of Neo-Nicenism and of Ambrose's cause to eradicate Homoian bishops.

Valerianus of Aquileia (bp. 369–388) presided over the synodical proceedings as the host bishop, although the *acta* record that Ambrose led the questioning of the accused. But perhaps Ambrose's most influential activity was following the council in the consecration of new bishops in the cities of Comum (Como): Felix; Laus Pompeia (Lodi): Bassianus; Ticinum: Profuturus; and Aquileia: Chromatius (Paoli 1998, 129). Besides these, there is from Ambrose's extensive correspondence positive reference to other North Italian bishops such as Gaudentius of Vercelli (ca. 379) and Felix of Bologna (d. 429), all of which provide

46. *Scholia* 344ᵛ.125–26 (Gryson 1980, 308).

47. Ironically, the church at Milan would continue to experience discord between Nicenes and Homoians, exacerbated by the arrival of Valentinian II (r. 375–392) in the imperial residence. For the young emperor's pro-Ariminum policies, see D. Williams 1995, 259–71.

us with a broader picture of
the sphere of episcopal influence at the end of the fourth
century.

North Italy

Northern Italy was largely
peripheral during the late
Republic and early Principate,
not coming under Roman authority until the reign of Augustus. The south slopes and
valleys of the Alps, as well as
the territories to the northeast, were inhabited by various
tribal federations, such as the

9.4 Anti-Homoian Bishops at Council of Aquileia

Valerianus of Aquileia (Aquileia)
Ambrose of Mediolanum (Milan)
Eusebius of Bononia (Bologna)
Abundatius of Tridentum (Trent)
Bassianus of Laus Pompeia (Lodi Vecchio)
Diogenes of Genua (Genoa)
Eventius of Ticinum (Pavia)
Exsuperantius of Dertona (Tortona)
Filastrius of Brixia (Brescia)
Heliodorus of Altinum (near modern
    Quarto di Altino)
Limenius of Vercellae (Vercelli)
Sabinus of Placentia (Piacenza)
[and other bishops from Gaul and Pannonia]

Raeti. To protect the peace of Italy, it was necessary for the Romans to establish military and administrative hegemony. The strategic importance of upper
Italy meant positioning troops in the Po Valley and in the Alpine passes. As a
result, three small military districts separated Italy from southern (Cisalpine)
Gaul: the Cottian Alps (Alpes Cottiae), the Graian Alps (Alpes Graiae), and
the Maritime Alps (Alpes Maritimae) (see Mommsen 1968, 15–18).

By the time of Constantine, Roman emperors rarely traveled to Rome.[48]
Cities in the north—Milan and Aquileia—grew in importance by hosting
imperial residences. Having acquired an increasingly cosmopolitan population, northern Italy was no longer a territorial outpost. By the fourth century
it had become the hub of political and social activity equal to and sometimes
superseding that of central and southern Italy. North Italy, however, remained
on the periphery of Christian activity until the early fourth century. No writings were produced by North Italian Christians to compare with those of
Hippolytus, Novatian, or Cyprian. Not until the councils held in Rome (313)
and Arles (314) is the silence broken and, as noted, do indications of bishoprics in North Italy appear. The two most important North Italian bishoprics

---

48. After 313 Constantine returned to Rome only twice, in the summers of 315 and 326 (Seeck
1919, 163–64, 177). During his entire *imperium* Constantius II appeared in the city only once,
for a two-month stay in 357 (Seeck 1919, 204); there is no evidence that Valens (r. 364–378),
Valentinian I (r. 364–375), Gratian, or Theodosius I ever made an appearance there.

in the fourth and fifth centuries were Milan and Aquileia. Ravenna became significant in the late fifth and early sixth centuries.

Mediolanum

From the time of Augustus, Mediolanum (Milan) was already an important transportation hub, though the city rose in status under the tetrarchy of Diocletian by becoming the site of an important mint and the site of an imperial residence because of its advantageous strategic location. It was there that Constantine and Licinius (r. 308–324) met in 313 and agreed to tolerate Christianity and other religions (Lactantius, *Mort.* 48.2). The presence of the emperor and his court opened up new possibilities for Milan's provincials as the city grew in prominence and size. The best estimates indicate that the city increased from a pre-fourth-century population of 30,000–50,000 to 130,000–150,000. By the end of the fourth century, Milan had earned a reputation as a wealthy and important city (Salzman 2007, 225).

How much and how quickly Milan's Christian community grew is hard to say with certainty, since the origin and the extent of the Christian community prior to Constantine are unknown. Supposedly, the first bishop was Anatelon, a disciple of Barnabas, though there are no concrete data to make a secure determination. The episcopal *fasti* for Milan record Maternus as bishop sometime before the fourth century. The first bishop known to us from other evidence is Merocles (listed at Arles in 314), after whom came Protasius, a member of the so-called Western delegation at Serdica (*CAP* B.1.4 [CSEL 65.134]). Eustorgius (exact dates unknown) was next, then Dionysius. The latter was deposed in 355 for his refusal to condemn Athanasius.[49] Dionysius was immediately replaced with Auxentius, an Easterner, who remained until his death in 374 (despite multiple attempts to unseat him as an Arian).

The dramatic story of Ambrose as bishop of Milan in 374 is found in the hagiographic *Vita Ambrosii* (*Life of Ambrose*). His successful influence over three emperors (Gratian, Valentinian II, and Theodosius I) concerning pro-Nicene and antipagan issues augmented the importance of the city in civil and church politics. Indeed, Ambrose used intracity conflict to further the conversion of Milan's elite to Nicene Christianity, which, by the 370s, was the dominant version of Christianity in the West.[50]

---

49. "Oratio synodi Sardicensis ad Constantium imperatorem" [= Hilary of Poitiers, *Ad Const. 1*] in *CAP* II.B.2, "Appendix ad *Collectanea antiariana parisina*" (CSEL 65.187).

50. In the last decade of the fourth century under Theodosius I the senatorial elite of Rome had converted in large numbers (Salzman 2007, 217).

The imperial court continued to make Milan its seat of power; emperors returned there after military campaigns and intermittently resided there to administer the Western empire from the time of Constans I (r. 337–350) and Constantius II, continuing down to Theodosius II (r. 408–450).

Before the episcopacy of Ambrose, Milan could claim one cathedral complex, later known as the *Basilica Vetus* (Old Basilica), although its original form is uncertain. An extensive building program after 380 evidently served to showcase the city's transformation from a pagan imperial capital to a Christian ecclesial metropolis (Krautheimer 1983, 69–92; McLynn 1994, 226–37; Lizzi 1990, 164–66), as well as solidify Ambrose's place as the defender of pro-Nicene orthodoxy.

Aquileia

Aquileia, in the northeastern region of Italy, was one of the great Italian cities during the Roman Empire. Ausonius (ca. 310–ca. 394) praised the grandeur of its walls and harbors, ranking the city fourth in Italy and ninth in the empire when, in about 388, he wrote his *Catalogue of Famous Cities*. As a commonly used transit point in trade between the transalpine regions and the Mediterranean, goods produced in the northern regions passed through Aquileia on to the Eastern empire and/or to Rome, Africa, or Illyria.

Although a Christian community must have been present by the third century, no surviving public places of worship or titular churches are attested until the time of Constantine. The earliest monumental evidence comes from the so-called Theodorian Complex, whose first level of mosaic flooring dates to the years of Aquileia's first known bishop, Theodorus (bp. ca. 308–319), who was present at Arles in 314.

The uniformity and organization of the mosaic flooring have led scholars to see a centralized control of the design, under the supervision of the clergy and bishop, whose identification and designation as *felix* provide a terminus ante quem for the mosaic, since Theodorus died in 319 (Caillet 1993, 127–30). From this same period the foundations of a church building have been uncovered that reveal not a basilica format but two parallel rectangular halls. This design was largely predetermined by reuse of the foundations of earlier buildings.

A second period of construction took place in the 340s under Fortunatianus (bp. pre-343–pre-369). This activity marked a substantial increase to the dimensions of the Theodoran northern hall, almost doubling the earlier dimensions (Humphries 1999, 194). Despite his successes in Aquileia, Fortunatianus seems to have had a rather jaded career. He is listed as among the "Westerners," supporting Rome's exoneration of Athanasius and others at the Council of

Serdica (*CAP* B.2.4 [CSEL 65.137]). However, he capitulated to the emperor's demands that Athanasius be condemned at the Council of Milan in 355, and presumably he signed the Creed of Ariminum in 359. It is not known whether he "repented" of this action, as did so many Italian bishops, though it is likely that he did so once Constantius II was gone.

Valerianus (bp. 369–388) was pro-Nicene and a stalwart colleague of Ambrose, as already demonstrated by his hosting and presiding at the Aquileian council (381). The sole purpose of this council was to drive out the remaining elements of Homoian Arianism in Italy and Illyricum, a feat that was accomplished by the condemnation of three bishops: Palladius of Ratiaria (bp. 346–381), Secundianus of Singidunum (bp. ca. 375–381), and Julian Valens, the Homoian bishop of Milan (bp. ca. 378), on doctrinal grounds.[51] Chromatius (bp. 392/3–407) continued Valerianus's ecclesial policies in the churches of Aquileia, solidifying this episcopal pattern for the next century.

Ravenna

Although today quite far inland, the ancient city of Ravenna lay on the Padus River (Po), just at the point that it flowed into the Hadriaticum Mare (Adriatic Sea) and in a marshy area that was surrounded by swampy lagoons on its western and southern sides. Although Ravenna was under Roman dominance since the late third century BCE, it was Augustus who first recognized these natural defenses as well as the city's strategic importance. Situated on the northeastern part of the Italian Peninsula and protected on both sea and land sides by waterways, the city provided an ideal harbor for the imperial fleet. The city of Classis (Classe), 4 km to the north, grew up around this naval base and, surrounded by a common city wall, became a sister city to Ravenna.

Ravenna's early Christian history can be divided into three main eras, each characterized by a distinct ecclesial and cultural identity. The earliest evidence for Christianity in the region dates to the second or third century, although, according to legend, the city's first bishop, Apollinaris, was a follower of St. Peter. During the latter part of this first era, the Western Roman emperor Honorius (r. 395–423) made Ravenna his seat of government in 402. The second era commenced in the late fifth century, when the Ostrogothic king Theodoric the Great (r. 471–526) made Ravenna his capital in 493 (Moorhead 1992). This short-lived Gothic era ended with the city's reconquest in 534 by the Greek general Belisarius (ca. 505–565) on behalf of Justinian I (r. 527–565), which

---

51. The conditions that Theodosius I (*Cod. theod.* 16.5.6 [January 10, 381]) laid down against heretics in the East appear to have been applied by Gratian also in the West.

ushered in the next period, one of Eastern Roman dominance and the city's position as exarchate of the Byzantine emperor (Deliyannis 2010). Each of these eras has distinct political, ecclesial, and art historical significance.

In addition to documentary evidence, the archaeological record provides essential data regarding early Christian Ravenna. The written record primarily consists of sermons by Ravenna's early fifth-century bishop, Peter Chrysologus (bp. 433–450), and the *Liber pontificalis ecclesiae Ravennatis* (*The Book of Pontiffs of the Church of Ravenna*), compiled by the ninth-century ecclesiastical chronicler Andreas Agnellus (ca. 805–post-846). Agnellus relied on legends and oral traditions, especially regarding the earliest years of Ravenna's ecclesiastical history. In general, the story of early Christianity in Ravenna highlights central characters from both lay and clerical worlds: St. Apollinaris, Empress Galla Placidia, Bishop Peter Chrysologus, King Theodoric, the philosopher Boethius, and Bishop Maximian. These individuals' stories are essential threads in the fabric of Ravenna's theological, architectural, and political tapestry.

Pre-Gothic Era

According to both Peter Chrysologus and Agnellus, Ravenna's first bishop was the martyr Apollinaris. Peter says very little about the saint's life other than that he shed his blood on more than one occasion for the sake of the church, but that by the dint of its prayers, his life was prolonged. In a sermon (*Serm.* 128), preached about the saint's shrine on his feast day (July 23), Peter describes Apollinaris as a shepherd in the midst of his flock, an allusion illustrated a

Fig. 9.5. Apse Mosaic, Sant'Apollinare in Classe

century later in the apse mosaic of the sixth-century church constructed in about 549 in Classe to honor Apollinaris's memory.

Following later sources, especially the *Passio Sancti Apollinaris episcopi Ravennatensis* (*The Martyrdom of St. Apollinaris*),[52] Agnellus claims that Apollinaris was ordained by St. Peter and sent to Ravenna as a missionary bishop (*Pont. Rav.* 1–2). Doubtless, this story met a need to establish a kind of apostolic foundation for the city, and scholars tend to judge Agnellus's historical reliability as somewhat dubious.[53] Agnellus's twelfth bishop, Severus, was listed as among those who attended the Council of Serdica in 343 (*Pont. Rav.* 13). Even allowing for extra-long reigns, these numbers suggest that Apollinaris's episcopacy probably began in the early third century rather than in the first. Also according to Agnellus, the seventh bishop, Probus (d. ca. 175), constructed the cathedral of Classe, where the first bishops of Ravenna were buried (indicating that Classe, not Ravenna, was the original episcopal see).

The shift from Classe to Ravenna as the Christian center probably began around the year 402, when, as already noted, Honorius transferred his capital to Ravenna from Milan. Honorius made this move in the face of the threat posed to Italy by Alaric I, king of the Visigoths (r. 395–410), Ravenna being a more strategically placed and defensible stronghold. In addition to gaining metropolitan status, the benefits to Ravenna of being an imperial capital included the building of grand architectural monuments, church buildings, and imperial palaces (M. Johnson 1988).

Just before sacking Rome in 410, Alaric captured Honorius's stepsister, Galla Placidia (ca. 388/90–450), daughter of Emperor Theodosius I (r. 379–395), and brought her as hostage to Gaul. Eventually she was married to his successor, Ataulf, king of the Visigoths (r. 410–415), who entered into an alliance with Honorius. After Ataulf's murder, his successor, Wallia (r. 415–419), surrendered to Honorius, and Galla Placidia was married to Constantius III (r. 421), who briefly ruled the West as Honorius's co-emperor. By this second marriage, Galla Placidia gave birth to Valentinian III (r. 425–455) in 419. When he was just five years old, Valentinian ascended the Western throne. Galla Placidia served as regent until he came of age (Oost 1968).

Galla Placidia's reign as Augusta (425–437) coincided with Peter Chrysologus's tenure as bishop. Peter's gift for oratory earned him his title, Golden-Word. A fervent Chalcedonian Christian (like his patroness, despite her associations with Arian Goths), Peter's sermons railed against Jews, Arians,

---

52. On the *Passio Sancti Apollinaris episcopi Ravennatensis*, see the bibliography provided in Deliyannis 2006, 39n70.

53. On Agnellus's sources and reliability, see Deliyannis 2006, 20–52, esp. 39–43.

Robin Jensen

Fig. 9.6. Baptism of Jesus, Neonian Baptistery, Ravenna

and "Monophysites," attending carefully to orthodox Christian doctrine and offering typological interpretations of biblical stories and parables.[54]

Peter's immediate predecessor, Ursus (bp. 399–426), had constructed Ravenna's first actual cathedral. Ursus also built the adjoining (and still existing) baptistery on the site, although its opulent decoration was the work of Peter's successor, Neon (bp. ca. 449–473). Like Ursus and Neon, Galla Placidia made a permanent physical imprint on Ravenna by constructing churches in the city. These included the Basilica of the Holy Cross, the Church of the Apostles (now the Basilica of St. Francis), and the Basilica of St. John the Evangelist, dedicated by Galla Placidia in gratitude for surviving a shipwreck.[55] A chapel, probably dedicated to the Roman martyr St. Lawrence (d. 258), is now known as Galla Placidia's mausoleum, although it is quite unlikely that this was her actual burial place (she died in Rome in 450).

Gothic Era

When the German chieftain Odoacer (r. 435–493) deposed the last Western emperor, Romulus Augustus (r. 475–476), the Byzantine emperor Zeno

54. For the English translation of Peter Chrysologus's sermons, see Ganss and Palardy 1953; 2004; 2005. Each volume contains a helpful introduction.

55. The inscription giving thanks for this rescue (*ILS* 1.818.1) is still in situ in St. John's in Ravenna.

Fig. 9.7. Baptism of Jesus, Arian Baptistery, Ravenna

(r. 474–491) agreed to Odoacer functioning as king of Italy. Ultimately, however, Odoacer's power threatened the Eastern ruler, and Zeno formed an alliance with the Ostrogothic leader Theodoric the Great, promising him the Italian Peninsula if he could overcome his rival. Theodoric went to war against Odoacer and was fairly successful until a fruitless three-year-long siege of Ravenna ended, in 493, in a pact that specified that the two should share the rule of Italy. This pact was rendered void when Theodoric murdered Odoacer at the very banquet arranged to celebrate the pact.

Theodoric had been taken hostage as a child to Constantinople, where he was raised and educated. Accepted as ruler by Emperor Anastasius (r. 491–518), he established Ravenna as the capital of an Ostrogothic kingdom. Although an Arian Christian, Theodoric initially showed tolerance toward his Nicene-Christian subjects, allowing them to continue to assemble in Ursus's cathedral. Meanwhile, he built his own palace and installed an Arian bishop, Drogdone (fl. ca. 520), the *episcopus Gothicorum* (Bishop of the Goths),[56] in a newly built Arian cathedral called the Hagia Anastasis (Holy Resurrection), now the Basilica of the Holy Spirit. Another Arian basilica, now called Sant'Apollinare Nuovo, was originally dedicated to Christ the Savior. Some time later (possibly after Theodoric's death in 526) a separate, freestanding

56. On this title, see Urbano 2005, 74n6.

baptistery near the Arian basilica was constructed to serve the Arians, its mosaic decoration modeled closely on the decor of the Neonian (orthodox) Baptistery.

Toward the end of the fifth century, the relatively friendly relations between the Arian and Nicene communities began to disintegrate, worsened by Theodoric's vehement objection to decrees against Arians promulgated by Emperor Justin I (r. 518–527). Theodoric demanded that Rome's Pope John I (bp. 523–526) travel to Constantinople to seek retractions, threatening reprisals against the city's orthodox Christians. John's failure to achieve compromise caused Theodoric to charge him with conspiring with the enemy. John died in a Ravenna prison.

Anicius Manlius Severinus Boethius (ca. 480–525) was also among those who suffered from Theodoric's anger. A member of the ancient Roman nobility and a profoundly learned philosopher and statesman, he had become Theodoric's chief officer in about 520. Three years later, however, he fell out of favor. Theodoric suspected him, like John, of duplicitous associations with the court at Constantinople, charged him with treason, and had him executed. While in prison, Boethius wrote his most famous work, the *Consolatio philosophiae* (*Consolation of Philosophy*), a reflection on the unreliability of human friendship and the instability of political power. Orthodox sources consider Theodoric's own death in 526 as an instance of divine justice, and many regard both John and Boethius (St. Severinus) as martyrs. Nevertheless, Theodoric's two-story mausoleum is still a well-known Ravenna landmark.

After Theodoric's death, his daughter Amalasuntha (ca. 495–534/5) acted as regent Augusta for her son Althalaric (r. 526–534). Althalaric's death in 534 made her queen in her own right, but she made the fateful mistake of asking her elderly cousin Theodahad (r. 534–536) to rule with her. Theodahad's weakness and the Goths' dissatisfaction led to Amalasuntha's assassination and a power vacuum that left the Gothic kingdom of Ravenna vulnerable to invasion by armies of the Eastern emperor, Justinian.

Byzantine Era

Justinian's ascent to the Byzantine throne in 527 marked the process of gradual retaking of lost territory in the West. In 533 his leading general, Belisarius, landed near Carthage and began to reclaim North Africa. Two years later Belisarius turned northward, and by 540 he had captured Ravenna, making it the western capital (exarchate) of the Byzantine Empire.

Once in power, the Byzantine authorities began to erase evidence of the Gothic occupation. Toward the end of his reign, Justinian gave Agnellus (bp. 557–570)[57] rights to all Arian (Gothic) churches, so that they could be reconsecrated to the Nicene faith (Agnellus, *Pont. Rav.* 85–86). The Arian cathedral and its adjacent baptistery were among the reconsecrated properties. The other Arian basilica, eventually named for St. Apollinaris,[58] actually was not fully reconciled until 561, when it was rededicated to St. Martin of Tours (bp. 371/2–397), the legendary foe of heretics. This transformation required the obliteration of many mosaics that apparently depicted the Gothic court (remnants of some figures are still visible). In their place, two processions of orthodox saints, depictions of the enthroned Madonna and Christ, and the adoration of the Magi were installed.

The most significant orthodox building projects, however, took place during the prior episcopate of Maximian (bp. 546–556). Maximian, whose ivory *cathedra* may still be seen in a museum annexed to the Archiepiscopal Chapel, was not a native of Ravenna. Rather, he was a deacon of the church of Pola (Pula, Croatia), well connected inside the Byzantine court, and specifically patronized by Justinian himself. Maximian's outsider status made him unpopular at first, but he showed exceptional ability to unite dissenting groups, and soon he became recognized as de facto primate of Italy during the controversy over the Three Chapters. Pope Vigilius of Rome (bp. 537–555) tended to side with Western opponents and suffered condemnation for his position.

Under the leadership of Maximian, Ravenna achieved an architectural golden age. Although Ecclesius (bp. 522–532) began construction of a basilica dedicated to St. Vitalis,[59] during the late Gothic period, Maximian directed its completion and ensured that the stunningly beautiful basilica, consecrated in 548, would be one of the most significant Byzantine-styled buildings in the West. The project was funded by an exceptionally wealthy local banker, Julius Argentarius (the silversmith), who also subsidized the building of the new basilica of Sant'Apollinare in Classe.

All of San Vitale's patrons are depicted in its mosaic program. The apse shows Bishop Ecclesius presenting a model of the church to the enthroned Christ, in the company of two archangels and St. Vitalis himself. The walls of the raised, apsed sanctuary portray Justinian and his consort, Theodora

---

57. Not to be confused with Andreas Agnellus, the ecclesiastical chronicler of the bishops of Ravenna.

58. The renaming of this church for St. Apollinaris did not take place until the mid-ninth century, when the relics were moved from Classe to Ravenna.

59. St. Vitalis, although from Milan, allegedly was martyred at Ravenna in the reign of Marcus Aurelius (r. 161–180). The church is built on the presumed site of his martyrdom (he was, according to tradition, buried alive).

Fig. 9.8. Justinian Carrying Eucharistic Paten, San Vitale, Ravenna

(r. 527–548), presenting the elements of the Eucharist. Justinian, carrying the paten, is joined by Maximian (named in the mosaic). Others in the group include Belisarius (leading a group of Byzantine soldiers) and Julius Argentarius. Directly across the chancel is a representation of Theodora carrying a large chalice and accompanied by an entourage of noble ladies. Although the images are fictional (Justinian and Theodora never visited Ravenna), this gathering of royalty, saints, soldiers, and bishops graphically illustrates the complex intersections of imperial and religious politics and parallels between liturgy and court ceremony in the Byzantine Empire.

Fig. 9.9. Theodora Carrying Eucharistic Chalice, San Vitale, Ravenna

South Italy and the Islands

Fewer early Christian communities existed in southern Italy than in central or northern Italy. Of special interest are Pompeii, because of its possible archaeological evidence of Christianity prior to 79 CE, and Neapolis.

Pompeii

Volcanic activity features prominently in Italy's history. With the exception of the Po Valley, which stretches west-east in the form of a crescent across Aemilia, Italy is essentially a mountainous region with small plains. Its major range, the Mons Apenninus, runs from the most southerly tip all the way to the Alps. Consequently, the land has been subject to frequent earthquakes, volcanic eruptions, and changes in coastlines. Mount Vesuvius is Italy's most famous volcano because of its eruption on August 24, 79 CE, which completely engulfed the towns of Pompeii, Herculaneum, Stabiae, and Oplontis, thus preserving the layout of their buildings and various artifacts.

On a priori grounds, it is not unlikely that a Christian community existed in Pompeii. A community of Jews, which often was the catalyst for Christian missionaries, inhabited the city. The nearby town of Puteoli was home to a Christian community since the time of St. Paul,[60] and Neapolis, on the other side of Mount Vesuvius, is known to have had a bishop before Constantine.

Finding specific signs of a thriving Christian community in Pompeii, however, has been notoriously difficult, such that certain scholars have declared that Christianity was not present at the time of the eruption. Admittedly, the famous Rotas-Sator Square[61] and an inscription found on a city wall (*CIL* 4.3.10000)[62] provide inconclusive evidence. A distinct *chi-rho* symbol on the side of a garden vase (*CIL* 4.3.10477) may be no more than an attestation of local trade. There is, however, a more noteworthy figure in the shape of a cross with the letters "VV" at the top (*CIL* 4.3.10062). The double "V" is similar to part of an inscription on a Christian gravestone located in the ancient town of Abellinum (Atripalda near Avellino) in Campania (*CIL* 10.1.1192).[63]

Neapolis

Neapolis (Naples) is on the Campanian coast, just north of Mount Vesuvius. From the various *monumenta*, Neapolis shows the continuation of Greek culture, being called *Graeca urbs* by Tacitus (*Ann.* 15.33.2). Other than Milan, no Italian Christian community has preserved such comprehensive episcopal *fasti* from the first half of the fourth to the seventh centuries as has

60. Not until the mid-fourth century, however, is there evidence for a bishop. Florentius of Puteoli was deposed from his see in about 373 for unknown reasons, though he is later associated with Homoian theology.
61. Two such inscriptions have been found thus far in this city; see Atkinson 1951, 1–18; Last 1954, 112–15; Fishwick 1964, 39–53.
62. "ROMANUS ARMI[S] VITI." Cf. Romans 6:13; Augustine, *Civ.* 13.4.
63. "Hic requiescat in pace dei serus Ioannic vv praesbyt."

Neapolis/Naples (Mullen 2004, 194–95). Calepodius (bp. ca. 343) subscribed at the Council of Serdica (*CAP* B.2.4 [CSEL 65.138]; B.2.4 [CSEL 65.134]) in support of Athanasius and Marcellus's innocence.

Both Bishop Maximus (otherwise unknown) and Zosimus (bp. ca. 351– ca. 361) sided with the Homoianism of Valens of Mursa (d. ca. 375) and Ursacius of Singidunum (d. ca. 371). Soon after Constantius's death in 361, however, Zosimus is known to have favored a pro-Nicene position (CSEL 35.23). Subsequent Neapolitan bishops continued this theological legacy.

Sicilia

Because of Sicily's strategic value, especially in agriculture, Julius Caesar granted all freeborn Sicilians full Roman rights (*ius Latii*)[64] to ensure that they remained loyal. Even so, most Sicilians did not think of themselves as Italians or Romans. Nevertheless, the resources of the island, known as the breadbasket of Rome, were depleted by the Romans, who also founded large estates (*latifundia*) that subsequently hampered the economic development of Sicilia as an independent province. Because Rome's interest in Sicily was entirely marginal, the island was regarded as land to be exploited, especially agriculturally, to supply Rome with grain. The only two cities deemed noteworthy, politically speaking, were Syracusae (Syracuse) and Agrigentum (Agrigento).

Greek language continued to be predominant in the early stages of Sicily's incorporation into the Roman "sphere of influence," and the Sicilian Greek calendar remained in use (R. Wilson 1996, 441). Buildings were still erected in traditional Greek fashion, with mud-brick walls on stone foundations. Six military veteran colonies were founded at Syracusae and elsewhere on the island in 21 BCE (Cassius Dio, *Hist. rom.* 54.7.1), intended as a spur for the Romanization of Sicily.

Sicily underwent certain changes when Latin finally became the principal spoken language in the imperial era. Official inscriptions were increasingly written in that language; it was used on coins, and people wanted to be buried in tombs with Latin epitaphs. The island continued to sell grain to Rome and also exported wool, timber, and wine. The money was reinvested in new, Roman-style buildings, especially in the cities along the coast. At the same time, the small towns of the interior of Sicily were converted into large villas, occupied by the senatorial class, whose presence had become superfluous in Rome.

Because the most ancient catacomb iconography in Syracuse is dated to about 250, a Christian community probably existed on the east coast of Sicily

---

64. This is not the same thing as Roman citizenship, which few Sicilians enjoyed.

no later than the beginning of the third century (Greco 1999, 55–56). Other data confirm a Christian presence in Syracuse by the end of third and very early fourth centuries. As already noted, Bishop Chrestus (or Crescens) (*EOMIA* 1.379) and a deacon named Florus (*EOMIA* 1.398) attended the Council of Arles (314). Intriguingly, the governor of Sicily, Domitius Latronianus, furnished transport for these clergy to the Italian mainland. It is unknown whether the governor was required to perform this service or did so at his own initiative.

An important mosaic comes from the south aisle of an early Christian church excavated in 1962 at Pirrera, near an as-yet-unidentified ancient site, Santa Croce Camarina, in the southeast corner of Sicily. Although the dating of the building's construction is not exact, the mosaics probably were laid in the later fifth century or at the latest before the Byzantine conquest of Sicily in 535 (R. Wilson 1982, 422, plate 54, fig. 21).[65]

Syracusae

Despite its late arrival in comparison to the Italian coasts, Christianity in Syracuse continued to expand during the fourth century. A council of Italian bishops (size unknown) met there in 365 to ratify pro-Nicene decisions that had been made in Paris, Sirmium, and Rome (Barnes 1993, 162). This insinuates that the metropolitan city of Sicily had joined with most of Italy in affirming the Nicene faith as the sole standard of orthodoxy.

Syracusan catacombs lie just north of the city center and consist of three separate passageways: Cassia, Santa Maria di Gesù, and San Giovanni. These have yielded hundreds of inscriptions. In the recess of an *arcosolium* tomb in Cassia is a mosaic of Christ that dates to the late third century, as does a fresco of the Good Shepherd with an *orans* (Spender 1900, 126–27). In the same catacomb is a mid-fourth-century *arcosolium* with a striking fresco of a young woman kneeling in prayer with arms outstretched toward figures of Christ (on one side) and Peter and Paul (on the other side). Near her head is a Greek inscription: "Marcia, aged twenty-five years, eight months, fifteen days" (Spender 1900, 127).

Catacombs in Syracuse show approximately two phases of construction: moderate growth between the Valerianic and Diocletianic persecutions and strong growth after the Constantinian reform, when the conversion of the upper

---

65. A similar distinctive design is found in a group of church mosaics around Aquileia and Ravenna that belong to the second half of the fifth century. The curved acanthus leaves occur on a border strip in the baptistery of the Santa Eufemia Church (ca. 470) in Grado (ancient Ad Aquas Gradatas), the port of Aquileia in Roman times, and in the mosaics of Santa Maria delle Grazie, also in Grado. See Brusin and Zovatto 1957, 427–30.

social strata is also reflected in more impressive *cubicula* (Zimmermann 1999, 322–33). Inscriptions in Greek and Latin can be found in all the catacombs.

Sardinia

Despite their proximity, Sardinia and Corsica were culturally distinct from Sicily. Greek influence in both islands was negligible, whereas a considerable legacy of Carthaginian culture has been identified in Sardinia (R. Wilson 1996, 442). In 509 BCE, with Phoenician expansion inland becoming ever more menacing and penetrating, the native Sardinians attacked the coastal cities of the Phoenicians. To defend themselves, the Phoenicians called on Carthage for help. The Carthaginians, after a number of military campaigns, overcame the Sardinians and conquered the most mountainous region, later referred to as Barbaria or Barbagia (Gennargentu).

When the Carthaginians were defeated by the Romans in the First Punic War (238 BCE), Sardinia became a province of Rome. The Romans enlarged and embellished the coastal cities, and Sardinia adopted Latin language and civilization in the process. Although the Romans dominated Sardinia for the next seven hundred years, they often were opposed by the local Sardinians. Nevertheless, Sardinia developed into a major source of grain and salt for the empire. It also exported wines and olives and was home to several mining operations.

CHRISTIANITY

The first time we hear of an association of Christians in Sardinia, they and others deemed criminals were sent to the mines. The *Refutatio omnium haeresium*, attributed to Hippolytus (ca. 170–235), mentions how the future pope Callistus endured the mines for a previous theft that he had committed, and how there he met Marcia, a Christian and former concubine of the emperor Commodus (*Ref.* 9.4). About forty years later another Roman bishop, Pontian (bp. 230–235), and the presbyter Hippolytus were exiled to work in these mines during the age of Maximinus Thrax (r. 235–238), implying that Sardinia was still considered a place of exile populated by pagans (Mastino 1999, 268).

Well over four hundred Christian inscriptions have been found in Sardinia, most located in the Catacomb of San Giovanni, just outside the city limits of Cagliari. About thirty of the oldest inscriptions are from the fourth century (Corda 1999).

CARALIS

In Athanasius's second letter to Lucifer, bishop of Cagliari (ancient Caralis), he speaks of Lucifer's predecessors as martyrs. It is certain, however, that

Juvenal, during the reign of Diocletian, escaped death by flight. Quintasius, who attended Arles (314), is possibly identical with the bishop of Cagliari present at Serdica (343). Very little is known about the development of Christianity in Caralis before the fourth century. In 354 Lucifer, the champion of orthodoxy against Arianism and a friend of Athanasius, became bishop. One of his contemporaries praises his unworldliness, his constancy in the faith, and his knowledge of sacred literature. Toward the end of his life, however, Lucifer became the author of a schism that rejected the decision by the Council of Alexandria (362) to offer communion to penitent bishops who had signed the Ariminum Creed (359). The fruits of this schism could still be found among the bishops of Sardinia after Lucifer's death (ca. 370). There is preserved in a funeral address delivered by Ambrose, *De excessu fratris sui Satyri* (*On the Death of His Brother Satyrus*), the story of how Satyrus's ship, sailing to Rome from North Africa, sank near where Lucifer had his schismatic supporters (1.47: *et forte ad id locorum in schismate regionis illius erat Ecclesia*).[66] Satyrus, grateful for having escaped the sinking of the vessel, nevertheless refused to be baptized by a bishop who continued to propagate the rending of the church.

At the end of the seventh century the mortal remains of Augustine of Hippo were kept secure in Cagliari for fear of the Arab invasions. Eventually, Augustine's body was interred in the basilica of Pavia.

Environs

During the time Christianity was spreading throughout central Europe, the lands north of Italy and east of Germania Superior were composed of Roman provinces named Raetia and Noricum. Both provinces extended as far north as the Danuvius (Danube), although at various times the borders, especially that of Raetia, were pushed well beyond the river. To the east of Noricum was Pannonia, created in 10 CE when Illyricum was divided into two provinces, the other being Dalmatia. In 294 Diocletian created the diocese known as Pannoniae, which encompassed the (smaller) administrative units of Pannonia Prima, Pannonia Secunda, Noricum Ripense, Noricum Mediterraneum, as well as the new provinces of (Pannonia) Savia, and (Pannonia) Valeria. It also included Dalmatia, but Raetia (divided into Prima and Secunda) was added to the Diocese of Italia. The name Illyricum was reinstated in 337 to refer to the new prefecture of Illyricum, Italia, and Africa. Later in the century Illyricum became a separate praetorian prefecture, encompassing most of the Balkan Peninsula (apart from Thrace) (see chap. 8).

66. PL 16.1306A–B: "Lucifer enim se a nostra tunc temporis communione diviserat. . . ."

Fig. 9.10. Map of Raetia, Noricum, Pannonia, and Dalmatia

Italy's environs, therefore (however divided politically at any given time), included not only the Gallic, Alpine, and Germanic provinces but also the area consisting of much of modern-day eastern Switzerland, Lichtenstein, eastern Germany, Austria, the Czech Republic, western Hungary, western Slovakia, Slovenia, Croatia, Serbia, and Bosnia-Herzegovina. These territories were inhabited, at the time, by local Illyricans as well as immigrant Celtic tribes. Mountainous Raetia produced timber, cattle, and, in the valleys, corn and wine. Noricum was famous for its gold, iron, and steel, especially its finely crafted swords. Pannonia produced timber, iron, and silver and grew oats and barley. Dalmatia, on the Adriatic, prospered as a result of its maritime activities. As elsewhere in the Roman Empire, despite a certain amount of Romanization, the inhabitants of these lands continued to maintain their own cultures, customs, and religions.

The Celtic sea-god Bedaius, from the lake district around Bedaium (Seebruck) in Noricum, was popular also in Raetia and often appears in inscriptions alongside the Celtic-Roman Jupiter Arubianus (e.g., *CIL* 3.5575), who hailed from Arubium (Măcin) in Moesia. In Western Raetia another Jupiter (Jupiter Poeninus) was the Roman version of the Gallic Kenninos (or Penninos): god of the summit and protector of the Great St. Bernard Pass.

The chief goddess of the Norici was Noreia, the name also of Noricum's first capital city (now Neumarkt-Einöd). Another Gallic goddess, Vibes, is attested only epigraphically in Noricum, as is Latobius (Mars Latobius), the tutelary god of the Latobici, a Celtic-Illyrican tribe centered in what is now Slovenia. The worship of Teutanus (Jupiter Optimus Maximus Teutanus) was ubiquitous in Pannonia, and the cult of the Illyrian mother goddess Genusus was popular in Dalmatia.

Christianity in parts of the region may date back to the apostolic era. St. Paul claims to have preached the gospel "as far as around Illyricum" (Rom. 15:19), stressing that he made it his practice to go only to those regions where no Christian missionary preceded him (Rom. 15:20). According to 2 Timothy 4:10, Titus also spent time in Dalmatia. Extensive Christianization of Italy's environs, however, does not appear to have occurred until much later. There is literary evidence of mixed value regarding some pre-Constantinian martyrs, and some archaeological remnants attest fourth-century churches in the area. Numerous cities in the region, such as Sabiona (Tre Chiesa), however, may not have had bishops until the sixth century (Mullen 2004, 220).

Raetia

A fourth-century inscription from Castra Regina (Regensburg) recording the death of a woman named Sarmannina concludes with the formula *quiescenti in pace mart(i)r(i)bus sociatae* (she rests in peace in the company of the martyrs), presumably indicating that she was buried near the graves of earlier martyrs (Gamber 1982). There certainly was an earlier martyr, Afra, at Augusta Vindelicum (Augsburg), who died on August 5, 304 (Mullen 2004, 222).

In the mid-fifth century, during the aftermath of the "barbarian invasion" of the region, a monk named Severinus (d. 482) (re)evangelized Raetia and Noricum, establishing numerous churches and monasteries.

Noricum

According to the *Martyrologium hieronymianum* (4 non. Maii), a Florianus was martyred at Lauriacum (Lorch) in 304 during the Diocletianic persecution. Apparently, Florianus had earlier lived in Cetium (St. Pölten) (*Pass. Flor.* 2), which suggests the existence of third-century Christian communities in both cities. The remains of an early church building, with an apse perhaps constructed around 300–310, have been discovered at Lavant, 2 km east of Dölsach, the site of ancient Aguntum, where there are remnants of a late fourth-century church and a fifth-century double-apsed funerary chapel.

A beautifully carved fourth-century tombstone, commissioned by a soldier named Flavius Januarius for his deceased thirty-nine-year-old wife, Ursa, describes her as *crestiana* [*sic*] *fidelis* (a faithful Christian) (*CIL* 3.13529). The stone was found in a field just east of Wels (ancient Ovilava) and is on display in the Wels City Museum. *Corpus Inscriptionum latinarum* 3.4921, from ancient Virunum (Zollfeld), commemorates a fourth-century woman named Herodiana. The Good Shepherd motif decorating her tombstone makes it almost certain that she was a Christian.

A number of bishops from Noricum and surrounding provinces attended Serdica in 343 (Athanasius, *Apol. Sec.* 37.1; *H. Ar.* 28.2), but both they and their sees are unnamed. In addition to the Christian communities mentioned above, however, it is clear from archaeological and literary evidence that Teurnia (St. Peter-in-Holz) and Celeia (Celje) were bishoprics by the sixth century.

Pannonia

The earliest evidence for Christianity in Pannonia comes from various "acts of the martyrs" (*acta martyrum*). Diocletianic martyrs include Quirinius of Siscia (Sisak), who was put to death at Savaria (Szombathely) on June 4 of an uncertain year, and Victorinus of Pettau (ancient Poetovio), who died most likely in 304. Victorinus wrote a number of commentaries, including one on the book of Revelation (Jerome, *Vir. ill.* 74). He may also have been the person responsible for producing the earliest Latin translations of the originally Greek *Muratorian Canon* and Pseudo-Tertullian's *Against All Heresies* (Tabbernee 2007, 79–80, 106–7; Armstrong 2008). As well as Irenaeus, bishop of Sirmium (Sremska Mitrovica), who was martyred in 303/4, a number of slightly later Christians were buried near the shrine of Synerotas (*CIL* 3.10232, 10233), who was beheaded at Sirmium in 307. Literary evidence attests the existence of pre-Constantinian Christians at Scarbantia (Sopron) (Mullen 2004, 108).

A ring containing the word *Eusebi* may indicate the presence of Christians at Mursa (Osijek) as early as the third century. Mursa, as noted above, was the see of the Homoian bishop Valens, who died in about 375. Valens had been among bishops at Philippopolis (Plovdiv) in Thrace who opposed the decisions made at Serdica (Socrates, *Hist. eccl.* 2.20.9; 2.22.1; Sozomen, *Hist. eccl.* 3.11.4). Other, probably fourth-century, inscriptions suggest Christian communities at Alisca (Ocsény), Aquae Balissae (Daruvar), and Ulcisia Castra (Szentendre). Remains of fourth-century Christian cemeteries and/or basilicas exist at the sites of ancient Alisca, Aquae Balissae, Aquincum (Budapest), Carnuntum (near Petronell), Cibalae (Vincovci), Cirtisa (Strbinci), Donnerskirchen (between Petronell and Sopron), Intercisa (Dunaújváros), Kékkút, Savaria, Sirmium, Sopianae (Pécs), Tricciana (Ságvár), and Vindobona (Vienna) (Mullen 2004, 179–83).

Dalmatia

Salona (Solin), the capital of Roman Dalmatia, must have had a significant Christian community by the end of the third century. Its early fourth-century bishop, Domnio, was put to death in 304 (*Mart. hier.* 3 id. Apr.), as were a number of others—for example, Anastasius (*Mart. hier.* 7, 8 kal. Sept.) and Severus (*Mart. hier.* 14 kal. Maii). A martyrium was built soon after to commemorate Domnio (*CIL* 3.9575, 12870b), whose nephew, Primus (*CIL* 3.14897), was the bishop about the time of the Council of Nicaea in 325.

In the mid-fourth century the then-bishop of Salona, probably Maximus (d. 346), may have sided with the bishops who met at the Synod of Philippopolis (Zeiller 1967, 100), suggesting that Dalmatia, as well as Noricum and Pannonia, was "pro-Arian." A late fourth-century memorial to Maximus has been discovered at Majsan (Chevelier 1996, 312–15).

Diocletian, who was born at Doclea (Podgorica) in Dalmatia, abdicated in 305. He retired to his newly constructed palace at the port city of Spalatum (Split), 5 km southwest of Salona. An early fourth-century sarcophagus from Spalatum may provide evidence of a preexistent Christian community there (Mullen 2004, 172). There must also have been a pre-Nicene Christian community at Stridon, where Jerome was born around 347, but the exact location of that city has not yet been identified.

10

The Western Provinces and Beyond

GRAYDON F. SNYDER AND WILLIAM TABBERNEE

Introduction

In describing the martyrdom of the apostle Paul, *1 Clement* claims that Paul had preached throughout the whole world as far as the "limit of the West" (5.5–7). The anonymous author, perhaps Clement of Rome (fl. ca. 95 CE), may simply have had in mind the city of Rome itself, since immediately after mentioning the "limit of the West" he refers to Paul's execution (5.7). Pious legend (e.g., *Acts Pet. Paul* 1) and scholarly speculation, however, have taken the reference as proof that St. Paul traveled at least to Spain and possibly even to Britain.

That Paul wanted to go to Spain is clear from Romans 15:22–29. Indeed, one of the purposes, if not the main purpose, behind Paul's writing of the letter to the Romans was to lay the groundwork for soliciting the Roman Christians' support for his proposed mission to Spain (Lampe 2003a, 80). Despite the author of the *Muratorian Fragment*'s assumption that all this eventuated (38–39), there is no proof other than the ambiguous statement in *1 Clement* that Paul ever went farther west than Rome. His hopes for evangelizing the western provinces of the Roman Empire (and beyond?) were to be realized by Christians other than himself.

This chapter was written by **Graydon F. Snyder** (The Western Provinces, Beyond the Borders) and **William Tabbernee** (Introduction).

Rome's Westward Expansion

SPAIN

That St. Paul should wish to conduct a missionary journey to Spain is perfectly understandable. Most of the region had been under Roman control ever since the Carthaginians, who had colonized most of the southern and eastern part of Spain, lost the Second Punic War in 206 BCE. In 197 BCE two Roman provinces had been created: Hispania Citerior (Nearer Spain) and Hispania Ulterior (Farther Spain). In 19 CE, under Augustus (r. 31 BCE–14 CE), these were renamed Hispania Tarraconensis and Hispania Baetica respectively. Augustus also added a third province: Hispania Lusitania (western Spain and Portugal). Following standard practice, a number of settlements, including Tarraco, Corduba, and Emerita Augusta, the capitals of the three Hispanic provinces, were refounded as Roman colonies. These, like the Roman colonies that Paul evangelized in the East, were potential centers for proclaiming the gospel concerning Jesus Christ.

New roads, such as the Via Augusta from Gades (Cadiz) in the southeast through Corduba, Carthago Nova, Tarraco, and Barcino to the northwest, facilitated the transport of local commodities and safe passage for travelers. Small farmlets rather than large estates continued to dominate the landscape in the first two centuries CE, producing wheat, grapes, olives, and horses. Toward the end of the fourth century, however, land was accumulated by an increasingly powerful Romano-Spanish elite living in huge Roman-style villas. Gold mines were abundant in the northwest, as were silver and copper mines in the southwest. Fishing industries thrived on both the Atlantic and Mediterranean coasts, and Hispania was famous for its garum, a highly sought-after fish sauce, which it exported throughout the empire.

By the time of Paul's proposed mission to Hispania, its population consisted not only of the descendants of the Iberians who had settled there during the second millennium BCE, probably from elsewhere in southern Europe (rather than from North Africa, as was once thought), and of various Celtic tribes that had arrived sometime between 900 and 800 BCE, but also of the descendants of Greek, Phoenician, Carthaginian, and, more recently, Roman settlers. Each of these peoples and subgroups had brought to the Iberian Peninsula its own gods and goddesses, many of them eventually being assimilated to the gods of the Roman pantheon. Candimo, the sky-god, for example, became identified with Jupiter, and Nabia, the protectoress of health, wealth, and fertility, was linked to aspects of the goddesses Diana, Juno, Tutela, and Victoria. Especially popular, as in the other Western provinces, were the pan-Celtic Matres, Lug, and Epona. Epona was invariably depicted riding a horse, often sidesaddle.

The Matres or Ma-
tronae were mother
goddesses, akin to
the Phrygian Cybele,
but always depicted
as three women. Sim-
ilarly, Lug, the Celtic
protector of artisans,
travelers, and com-
merce, is frequently
portrayed as a plural
deity, sometimes with
three heads.

Fig. 10.1. Map of the Western Provinces

GAUL

A sanctuary dedi-
cated to Lug at what
is now Lyons in France
became the city of
Lugdunum. The Ro-
mans had first annexed
part of Gallia Transal-
pina (Gaul across the
Alps)[1] in 121 BCE by creating the province of Gallia Narbonensis. Between
56 and 51 BCE Julius Caesar (ca. 100–44 BCE) conquered the rest of what
is now France, Switzerland, Belgium, and Germany south and southwest of
the Rhenus (Rhine). This area, first known as Gallia Comata (Long-Haired
Gaul), was divided by Augustus into three provinces: Gallia Belgica, Gallia
Lugdunensis, and Gallia Aquitania. The combined Tres Galliae (Three Gauls)
encompassed a huge territory from the Rhine in the north to the Pyrenees
in the south and the Swiss Alps in the southwest. More than sixty *civitates*
(tribal groups) were represented at the Festival of the Three Gauls conducted
annually at Lugdunum at the great altar of the cult of Roma and Augustus.

Most of Gallia Transalpina was inhabited in pre-Roman times by a variety
of Celtic tribes whose ancestors had crossed the Alps no later than around
1200 BCE. Numerous beautifully crafted artifacts, discovered near Hallstatt
in Austria and La Tène (The Hollows) at the northern end of Lake Neuchâtel

---

1. So called in contrast to Gallia Cisalpina (Gaul on this Side of the Alps)—that is, North
Italy, on which, see chap. 9.

in Switzerland, confirm a unique culture in the widespread region that can be defined as Celtic. The Roman invasion of the area pushed many Celts toward the Atlantic coast and, at the same time, made room for a Romano-Gallic culture—the demographic basis for the later Francia. The Belgae in the north probably were a mixed Celtic/Germanic race, and the Aquitani in the southeast were predominantly of Iberian origin. Descendants of Greek and Phoenician traders were also to be found on the Mediterranean coast of Gaul, and during the Roman period immigrants from Asia Minor settled in cities such as Lugdunum and Vienna (Vienne),[2] a little farther south than Lugdunum and, like it, accessible from Massilia (Marseilles) via the River Rhodanus (Rhône).

Lugdunum, situated strategically at the confluence of the Rhodanus and the Arar (Saône) Rivers and at the crossroads of major highways, became a significant trading and shipping center. The immediate region produced wheat, wine, olive oil, and lumber, some of which also came from elsewhere in Gaul, as did lead, silver, and marble.

In addition to Lug and the other Celtic gods and goddesses already mentioned in connection with Hispania, epigraphic evidence exists for the popularity, among many others, of the following deities in Gaul: Adsmerius, god of providence (= Mercury); Belenos, god of sun, light, fire (= Apollo); Ogmios, god of eloquence, poetry, and learning (= Hercules); and Taranis, god of thunder (= Jupiter).

GERMANY

At first merely military districts under the control of the governor of Gallia Belgica, Germania Superior (Upper Germania) and Germania Inferior (Lower Germania) became separate Roman provinces in 90 CE. Germania Superior encompassed most of what is now Switzerland, and Germania Inferior covered the territory of the "Low Lands" along the south bank of the Rhine to the Germanicum Mare (North Sea). The capital of Germania Inferior was Colonia Agrippinensis (Cologne); the capital of Germania Superior was Moguntiacum (Mainz), named after the Celtic god Moguns. Helvetii and Sequani were major Celtic tribes in Germania Superior, whereas Ubii, Treveri, and Belgae predominated in Germania Inferior.

Abundant grasslands in Germania meant that many inhabitants herded cattle and produced milk, cheese, and leather. Various cereal grains were also grown in the area. Ancient forests yielded lumber and beautiful amber, the latter highly prized in Roman society.

Shrines and inscriptions have identified almost one hundred gods and goddesses in the two Germaniae, including the Aufaniae, local versions of the

2. Not to be confused with the Vienna (ancient Vindobona) in Austria.

Matres, and similar fertility goddesses such as Nehallenia (popular in Germania Inferior) and Herecura (popular in Germania Superior), both of whom, surprisingly, were also goddesses of death. Male deities included Granus, Celtic god of corn and of the healing warmth of hot springs, whose cult center was in Germania. In Roman times Granus became associated with Apollo. Another healing god, Lenus, popular among the Treveri, became linked to Mars. Cissonius, probably, like Lug, a Celtic god of trade and protection of travelers, was equated with Mercury. The non-Celtic Germanic gods Tiu (god of war), Wodan (god of the dead), and Donar (or Thor, god of thunder), whose names (along with that of Wodan's wife, Frija) came to designate "Tuesday" through "Friday," were equated with Mars, Mercury, and Jupiter (Hercules) by the Romans.

BRITAIN

Julius Caesar, in 55 and 54 BCE, was the first to lead Roman armies across the Britannicum Mare (English Channel) onto British soil. The lands now comprising England, Wales, and southern Scotland, however, were not annexed by the Romans until almost a century later. In 43 CE Claudius (r. 41–54) invaded Britain and captured Camulodunum (Colchester), the headquarters of the Catuvellauni, a Celtic tribe probably originally from Belgica. During the next four decades the Romans gradually conquered most of the other tribes of the Scottish Highlands before withdrawing to the isthmus between Solway Firth and the North Sea, where Hadrian (r. 117–138) eventually constructed his famous stone wall, 120 km in length.

Aulus Plautius, the first governor of the Roman province of Britannia, made Camulodunum his capital. After the defeat of Boudicca (Boadicea) of the Iceni (r. 60–61), however, the capital was moved to Londinium (London). Britannia was a rich prize for the Romans, supplying grain, cattle, leather, iron, tin, silver, and even gold to the rest of the empire. It was also a source of slaves and even of hunting dogs.

Camulodunum was named after the Celtic god Camulos, a Belgic god of war, assimilated into the Roman pantheon as Mars Camulus. Other popular Celtic gods of war worshiped in Britannia were Belatucadros Veteris and, as in Germania, Moguns. Celtic female deities in Britannia, as elsewhere, were frequently personifications of wells or springs. Examples are Senua, Coventina, and, especially, Sulis, whose name was incorporated into the Roman name for the city of Bath: Aquae Sulis. Sulis and some of the other "water goddesses" were identified with Minerva by the Romans.

When the Romans arrived, they, like modern visitors, were impressed by still-existing megaliths such as those at Stonehenge and Avebury—reminders of a high-level Neolithic culture dating back perhaps as far as the fourth millennium BCE, visible not only in Britain but also in Ireland (e.g., at Newgrange and the Knowth Valley) and Britanny (e.g., near Carnac). The precise ways in which this Neolithic society interacted with and shaped the development of Celtic religion and culture and exactly how, in turn, Celtic religion and culture interacted with the Romanization of Britain and other Western provinces remain debatable. It is clear, however, that a great deal of religious and cultural diversity remained and was tolerated by the Romans, as long as the diverse groups showed publicly their loyalty to the empire when called on to do so. Christianity's inability to demonstrate such loyalty in ways acceptable to the empire made it much less able to be accommodated within the empire than other religions and societies.

Changing Borders

In 294 Diocletian (r. 284–305) reorganized the provinces of the Roman Empire into twelve "dioceses," each containing a number of provinces that were smaller than their predecessors. The original single province of Britannia had already been divided by Septimius Severus (r. 193–211) into Britannia Superior (capital: Londinium) and Britannia Inferior (capital: Eboracum [York]). These two provinces, reduced in size, were renamed Britannia Prima and Britannia Secunda by Diocletian, to which were added Maxima Caesariensis and Flavia Caesariensis. A fifth Britannic province, Constantia Valentia, was created by Constans I (r. 337–350). The exact boundaries of these latter provinces are still unclear.

In about 400, after the permanent division of the Roman Empire into East and West, even larger administrative units, called prefectures, were established. Britanniae was incorporated into the prefecture Gallia, which also included the Diocletianic dioceses Hispaniae, Viennensis (southern Gaul), and Galliae (northern Gaul, including Germania Superior and Germania Inferior, renamed Germania Prima and Germania Secunda respectively).

During the late fourth and early fifth centuries, for various political reasons and reasons related to the personal ambitions of military commanders, Roman troops were taken from Britanniae to Galliae and elsewhere. This left Britanniae vulnerable to invasions by Saxons, Jutes, and Angles—Germanic tribes that, by the 440s, had virtually taken control of Roman Britanniae.

SCOTLAND AND IRELAND

Apart from a brief period of five years (79–84), when C. Julius Agricola, the governor of Britannia, gained some temporary victories there, the Romans were content to leave Caledonia (Scotland)[3] to the Caledonii and the other Celts residing north of Hadrian's Wall. Nor did the Romans bother to occupy Hibernia (Ireland), even though Agricola had the opportunity to do so. No great threat was perceived from Hibernia, and Hadrian's Wall provided all the protection needed from potentially hostile tribes in the north.

NORTH OF THE RHINE

Similarly, after some initial forays into the lands of the Batavii, the Frisii, and other tribes north of the Rhine, the Romans built a timber palisade, 550 km in length, to secure its border between the Rhenus and the Danuvius (Danube). They also used these rivers as natural boundaries between the empire and nonoccupied lands belonging to various Germanic tribes. Although Romans scorned the lifestyle of these tribes (fur-and-skin clothing, long hair, strange food, nomadic living conditions), the two sides had reasons to establish a fairly peaceful relationship. The Romans needed food and able warriors. The so-called barbarians needed Roman products, political connections, and a more elite way of life. So the border became a bargaining line. Members of some Germanic tribes living on or near the border crossed over into the empire, where they lived as *laeti* (serfs), cultivating their own land in small villages. As the immigrants grew in power and prestige, the distinction between barbarian Romans and Roman barbarians disappeared in the borderlands.

WESTERN EUROPE AND BRITAIN IN LATE ANTIQUITY

Eventually, demographic pressures in the lands north of the border and the general weakness of the Western empire following the division of the empire into East and West in 395 led to a series of Germanic invasions, treatises, and, ultimately, conquests within the Western provinces. In December 406 the Rhine froze over, allowing vast groups of Vandals, Alani, and Suebi to cross into Roman Gaul. After plundering Galliae, they invaded Hispaniae in 409. The new, but somewhat powerless, Western emperor, Honorius I (r. 395–423), enlisted the aid of another Germanic tribe, the Visigoths (Western Goths), to defeat the invaders in Hispaniae. As a reward, in 418 Honorius granted the Visigoths lands in Gallia Aquitania. Later in that century, under their ruler Euric (r. ca. 466–488), the Visigoths established an independent kingdom based at Tolosa (Toulouse), which, in about 500, stretched from Aquitania to Spain. The northern part of this kingdom was lost to Clovis I (r. 481–511), king of the Franks, in 407/8. The Franks, yet another Germanic tribe, consolidated their

---

3. The modern name Scotland comes from the Scotti, immigrants from Ireland during the fourth century CE who settled in great numbers on the west coast of Caledonia and as far south as Wales.

power in what had been Roman Galliae and created the Merovingian kingdom of Francia. Francia eventually developed into the Carolingian Empire under Charlemagne (r. 800–814). The Visigoths continued to rule the former Roman Hispaniae until the Arab invasion of Spain in 711 under the Islamic general Tariq ibn Ziyad (689–720). Newly created Anglo-Saxon kingdoms thrived in Britain, despite Viking raids and the conquest of parts of Britain especially by the Danes, from the fifth century until the Norman Conquest in 1066.

The Western Provinces

Hispania

Although St. Paul probably never personally made it to Spain, as he had hoped he would, other Christians obviously did. Irenaeus of Lyons (bp. ca. 177–200) knew of churches in Spain founded well before 180 (*Haer.* 1.10.2; cf. Tertullian, *Adv. Jud.* 7.4; Arnobius the Elder, *Nat.* 1.16). An inscription found at Tarragona dated around 200 (Alföldi 1975, no. 236) may possibly be Christian, as are others from the third and early fourth centuries (Alföldi 1975, nos. 93, 95–97). Judging from the thirty-nine churches represented at the Council

Fig. 10.2. Map of Hispania

of Elvira (see below), Christianity was well established in the Spanish provinces by the beginning of the fourth century.[4]

According to Cyprian of Carthage (bp. ca. 248/9–258), a man named Sabinus was ordained during the Decian persecution as bishop of Emerita Augusta, as customary, by all the other bishops of the province (*Ep.* 67.5). By this, Cyprian may

---

4. For all known or likely Christian communities in Spain prior to 325, see Mullen 2004, 250–59.

have meant the bishops of Lusitania only or of all of Hispania. In either case, Cyprian's letter attests the existence of a number of (mainly unspecified) bishoprics in Spain in about 250. Cyprian (*Ep.* 67.1.6) does, however, refer specifically to a Christian community at Caesaraugusta (Zaragoza) and to what appears to have been a joint see consisting of Legio (León) and Asturica Augusta (Astorga). A beautiful sarcophagus depicting biblical scenes including the miracle of the loaves and fishes, the raising of Lazarus, and the arrest of Peter, datable to about 305–312, has been found at Asturica Augusta (Sotomayor y Muro 1975, 11, 47–54). It is one of more than thirty extant Spanish Christian *sarcophagi* from the Constantinian or immediate pre-Constantinian period (Sotomayor y Muro 1979, 136–42).

TARRACO

In 259 Fructuosus, bishop of Tarraco (Tarragona), capital of Hispania Tarraconensis, was brought before Aemilianus the governor and ordered to worship the gods and adore the images of the emperors in compliance with the second edict issued by Valerian (r. 253–260). Fructuosus refused to do so, and, according to the account of his martyrdom, Aemilianus then asked him, "Are you a bishop?" "I am," said Fructuosus. "You *were*," replied Aemilianus and sentenced him to be burned alive (*Pass. Fruct.* 2.8–9). Martyred along with Fructuosus were two deacons: Augurius and Eulogius (1.1; 2.9; 5.2). Mentioned also in the account are Augustalis, a *lector* (reader) (3.4); Felix, a "fellow soldier" and *frater nostri* (a [Christian] brother of ours) (3.5); numerous other, but unnamed, "brethren" (e.g., 1.4; 3.1–3; 4.1–2; 6.1; 6.3); as well as Babylas and Mygdonius, described as "[Christian] brethren of ours in the household of Governor Aemilianus" (5.1). The *Passio Sanctorum Martyrum Fructuosi Episcopi, Auguri et Eulogi Diaconorum* (*The Martyrdom of Bishop Fructuosus and His Deacons Augurius and Eulogius*) probably was composed early in the fourth century (Musurillo 1972, xxxii). There is no need to doubt the general accuracy of the picture that it presents of a sizable Romano-Hispanic Christian congregation at Tarraco by the middle of the third century. A spectacular early Christian cemetery at Tarraco, comparable only to that beneath the Vatican in Rome, dates from that period. How much earlier this Christian community had been founded and who its earlier bishops were, however, are unknown. The same is true of Corduba, the capital of Baetica, and of Emerita Augusta, the capital of Lusitania.

CORDUBA

Very few traces of early Christianity at Corduba (Cordova) remain (Knapp 1983, 69). The first bishops of Corduba mentioned in tradition are Severus (fl. ca. 269 or 279), followed by Gratus and Berosus later in the third century. A precise date occurs with Hosius (ca. 256–ca. 358), who became bishop of Corduba in 294. He is mentioned as one of nineteen bishops attending the provincial Council of Elvira in about 309. Apart from the later stunning Mosque of Mesquita, built in 784 on the site of the former Temple of Janus, Cordova's current fame rests almost entirely with Bishop Hosius, who from 313 onward became one of the most trusted agents of Constantine I (r. 306–337) in dealing with Christian bishops and communities (Eusebius, *Hist. eccl.* 10.6.2).

When the Arian controversy started, Constantine asked Hosius to deliver a letter seeking reconciliation between Arius (ca. 256/60–ca. 336) and Alexander of Alexandria (bp. 313–328) (Eusebius, *Vit. Const.* 2.63–72). Reliable detailed information regarding the Council of Nicaea (325) is scarce, but it is at least possible that Hosius presided.

The powerful Arians frequently succeeded in securing the exile of some of their theological opponents. After returning from one such exile in 340, Athanasius of Alexandria (bp. 328–373) conferred with Hosius in Gaul. They appeared together at the Council of Serdica (343) in Illyrium, called by Emperors Constans I (r. 337–350) and Constantius II (r. 337–361). Hosius presided and proposed canons that would resolve the Arian-Nicene conflict. Although the council spoke of Hosius as "one who on account of his age, his confession, and the many labors he had undergone, is worthy of all reverence" (Athanasius, *Apol. sec.* 44), the canons regarding the Arians failed to receive support. The Council of Serdica did, however, accept canons that limited the authority of the bishops to their own dioceses.

Arians continued the theological and political dispute after Serdica. Still Hosius continued to resist strongly any attempt to condemn Athanasius. Arian pressure caused Constantius II to write Hosius a letter asking whether he alone was going to remain obstinate in the struggle. Hosius responded with a letter, preserved by Athanasius (*H. Ar.* 42–45 [text in Leclercq 1906, 113–16]), protesting imperial interference in church affairs (353). This led to Hosius's exile, in 355, to Sirmium, Pannonia (modern Serbia).

Regrettably, because Hosius spent so much time away from his own bishopric, it is difficult to gain a full appreciation of the issues facing him in Spain. Two of these issues, however, may have been land-owning bishops and the promotion of bishops by an increasingly powerful lay elite (Bowes 2005, 237–38). The Council of Elvira (Albaicin, a suburb of Granada), held in Hosius's own province (although not presided over by him), also reveals a number of issues confronting Spanish bishops such as Hosius in the pre-Constantinian period. Many of these issues, including those related to Jewish-Christian relations (*Can.* 16, 36, 49, 50, 78), undoubtedly remained issues after the official "toleration" of Christianity.

Some of the canons of Elvira do deal specifically with the pre-Constantinian situation. Clerics are forbidden to enter temples or offer sacrifices (*Can.* 1–4). Canon 36 forbids art (pagan temple art) in the church building. Most of the canons, however, deal with the behavior of clerics, especially *flamines* and *duumviri*—Greco-Roman officials who had converted and also begun to serve as Christian officials. Sexuality is a major concern. Besides inappropriate sexual behavior such as adultery, the canons even forbid sexual intercourse between the clerics and their wives (*Can.* 33). Celibacy does not seem to be the issue, so much as asceticism. Abstinence identifies the clerics over against the pagan rulers. The members of the Council of Elvira drew up stern measures against themselves and their fellow male clerics, often with no opportunity for repentance. Their strong ascetic stance granted them the authority to express power over others. For example, they wrote harsh requirements for women (about 40 percent of the canons). These included such minutiae as dealing with hairdressers (*Can.* 67), writing letters without their husband's permission (*Can.* 81), and lending fine clothes to others for public use (*Can.* 57). It is unknown whether the canons were written to correct existing problems or to establish the authoritative position of the clerics (Laeuchli 1972, 101–2). Nor is it clear what impact the Elvira canons had on later councils. The canons do, however, show how minority, sectarian Christians were moving into authority and power (Laeuchli 1972, 68).

Emerita Augusta

There was a Christian community at Emerita Augusta (Mérida) by the time of the Decian persecution in about 250. During that persecution the then-bishop, whose name most likely was Martialis, obtained a certificate (*libellus*) stating that he had sacrificed and was subsequently replaced by Sabinus (Cyprian, *Ep.* 67.1, 5–6, 9), the bishop mentioned above.

It is possible that Eulalia, one of Spain's most revered martyrs, died at Emerita during the Decian persecution, but it is more likely that she was a victim of the Diocletianic persecution (ca. 304), perhaps at Barcino (Barcelona) rather than Emerita. Whatever the precise historic details, in the latter part of the fourth century a small martyrial shrine was built to venerate her at Emerita (Mateos Cruz 1999). Not until a century later was a basilica built on the site, encompassing the shrine and adjacent mausoleums (Bowes 2005, 195).

Indeed, it appears that not just in Emerita, but also in Spain generally, the only late fourth- and early fifth-century, purpose-built Christian structures were mausoleums and martyria. Further examples of the latter are a martyrium at Tarraco, dedicated to Fructuosus and his deacons, and another one at Castrum Octavianum (San Cugat), traditionally believed to be that of the Decian martyr Cucuphas (Bowes 2005, 195).

Episcopal churches (cathedrals), especially those within the walls of the major cities, first appear in Hispania somewhat later than elsewhere in the empire. This may be attributed to a unique feature of fourth- and fifth-century Christianity in Hispania. From about 380 a large number of members of the Romano-Hispanic aristocratic elite converted to Christianity and used their vast resources to expand their enormous villas by adding not only mausoleums to bury the (now-Christian) members of their families but also chapels and shrines to contain the relics of martyrs and saints, thus blurring the distinction between public and private liturgical functions. Instead of supporting financially the building of cathedrals, the lay-based rural cultural elite directed their funds to their own properties and/or to empirewide Christian projects, including pilgrimages to the Holy Land. This group of Christian elites perhaps included Maternus Cynegius (d. 388), praetorian prefect under Theodosius I (r. 379–395) (see Bowes 2005, 218–26). It certainly included the family of Melanie the Elder (ca. 341/2–ca. 410), her husband, and her granddaughter Melanie the Younger (ca. 383–439). The latter funded her patronage of Jerome (ca. 347–419) in Bethlehem by selling some of her estates in Spain. Although little is known about Egeria, the Spanish pilgrim who visited most of the holy sites in biblical lands circa 381–384, her resources were obviously sufficient for her extensive journey. The famous Latin poet Prudentius (ca. 348–ca. 413) was also one of the new Spanish Christian elites of the late fourth and early fifth centuries.

Gallia

Irenaeus (*Haer*. 1.10.2), Tertullian (ca. 160/70–ca. 220) (*Adv. Jud.* 7.4), and Arnobius the Elder (d. ca. 330) (*Nat*. 1.16) mention Gaul as well as Spain in their lists of Roman provinces that included Christian communities. Some of these communities owned identifiable church buildings by the time of the Great Persecution (303–313). Constantius I (r. 305–306), the father of Constantine, appears on the whole to have avoided destroying the churches in Gaul (Eusebius, *Hist. eccl.* 8.13.13; but cf. Lactantius, *Mort.* 15). The earliest known Christians in Gaul are those who suffered during a local pogrom in Lugdunum in about 177.

Lugdunum

Before the Roman period, a settlement named Condate (Confluence) was inhabited by river-fishing people on the left bank of the Arar (Saône) at the spot where that river meets the Rhodanus (Rhône). Another settlement existed above the right bank of the Arar on the hill now known as the Fourvière, near the sanctuary of the god Lug. The population of both settlements consisted primarily of members of an extensive Celtic tribe, the Allobroges, known to the Romans as a barbarian people—undisciplined, individualistic, who loved war in order to prove their courage (Chevallier 1958, 42). Pre-Roman coins and pottery have been discovered in the bed of the Arar/Rhodanus confluence, but no Celtic examples have been positively identified (Desbat and Walker 1981). However, the archaeological remains around

Fig. 10.3. Map of Gaul

Lugdunum show similarities to the La Tène Celtic culture (S. Walker 1981). In 43 BCE Lucius Munatius Plancus (ca. 87–15 BCE), a former lieutenant of Julius Caesar, established a military colony there, Colonia Copia Felix Munatia. Julius Caesar subsequently made it the capital of Gallia Transalpina, and he named his son-in-law, Marcus Vipsanius Agrippa (63–12 BCE), governor of the province. Agrippa created a network of roads that converged in the city. Among the visible Roman sites is a still-usable theater. Augustus made Lugdunum the capital of Gallia Lugdunensis when he divided Gallia Transalpina into three provinces.

For three hundred years after its foundation, Lugdunum remained the most important city in northwestern Europe. Two emperors, Claudius (r. 41–44) and Caracalla (r. 211–217), were born there. Claudius renamed the city "Colonia Copia Claudia Augusta Lugdunum." The Christian community at Lugdunum appears to have been founded by merchants, immigrants, and missionaries from the East. The late second-century epitaph of one such missionary, Euteknios, from Laodicea in Syria, was found in 1974 (*EG* 4, 494–98, no. 2). Eusebius of Caesarea (ca. 264/5–ca. 339/40) wrote of a "blessed Pothinus" as the first bishop of Lyons, consecrated perhaps as early as 150. During a persecution in the time of Marcus Aurelius (r. 161–180), in about 177, the ninety-year-old Pothinus was dragged before the authorities and died two days later (Eusebius, *Hist. eccl.* 5.1.29–31).

Among the approximately forty-eight martyrs of the persecution were Blandina and Attalus. The Christians of Lugdunum and neighboring Vienna sent a letter to the churches in Asia and Phrygia describing the martyrdoms (Eusebius, *Hist. eccl.* 5.1). The story of the renowned slave Blandina has inspired many. After refusing to recant her faith, she was bound to a stake in the amphitheater, and wild beasts were set on her. They did not, however, touch her. Finally, as the last of the martyrs, she was scourged, placed on a red-hot grate, enclosed in a net, and thrown to a wild steer, which tossed her into the air with its horns. Finally, she was killed with a dagger. Attalus was paraded in the arena with a placard identifying him as a Christian. Following the directions of Marcus Aurelius, the governor had him and the other Roman citizens among the prisoners beheaded (Eusebius, *Hist. eccl.* 5.1.43–47).

The best-known Christian leader of Lugdunum/Lyons was Irenaeus. Irenaeus was born in Smyrna, where, apparently, he knew Bishop Polycarp (d. ca. 155/6), who may have passed on to Irenaeus the Johannine tradition

William Tabbernee

Fig. 10.4. Amphitheater, Lugdunum

(Mutschler 2004, 9, 21–23; Grant 1997, 36–37); then he studied and taught in Rome before shifting to Lugdunum. Irenaeus wrote a number of books, but the most important survival is the five-volume *On the Detection and Overthrow of the So-Called Gnosis*, normally referred to by the Latin title *Adversus haereses* (*Against Heresies*). Book 1 talks about the Valentinian Gnostics and their predecessors, who, according to Irenaeus (*Haer.* 1, preface 1), go as far back as the magician Simon Magus (Acts 8:9; *Acts of Peter*). Gnostics talk like Christians but mean something else. Book 2 provides rational proof that

> ## 10.1 Irenaeus on the Gospels
>
> But it is not possible that the Gospels can be either more or fewer in number than they are. For since there are four zones of the world in which we live, and four principal winds, while the church has been scattered throughout the world, and since the "pillar and ground" of the church is the Gospel and the spirit of life, it is fitting that she should have four pillars, breathing incorruption on every side, and vivifying humanity afresh. (*Haer.* 3.11.8 [*ANF* 1:428–29, altered])

Valentinianism contains no merit in terms of its doctrines. Book 3 shows that Gnostic doctrines falsify evidence from the Gospels. Book 4 consists of Jesus's sayings and stresses the unity of the Old Testament with the gospel. Book 5, the final volume, focuses on more sayings of Jesus plus the letters of Paul the apostle (Grant 1997, 6). In his attempt to subvert the Gnostics, Irenaeus insisted on the necessity for and validity of four Gospels. He was the first to propose a four-Gospel canon (see sidebar 10.1).

Successors to Irenaeus include Faustinus (bp. ca. 254 [Cyprian, *Ep.* 63.1]) and Eucherius (bp. ca. 433/4–349/50). The latter wrote the widely used *De laude eremi* (*In Praise of Hermits*) (see below).

Vienna

Vienna developed on the left bank of the Rhodanus approximately 27 km south of Lugdunum. Vienna (modern Vienne) was originally the capital of the Allobroges. Excavations have uncovered not only remains of early Celtic life but also some first-century walls of a temple dedicated to Cybele (Pelletier 1980, 6–8). These are the only traces of the Cybele cult in France. Remnants of a theater indicate that Vienna was used as a commercial town by the Greeks as well as the Romans. The Romans were present in Vienna from 122 BCE to 275 CE, but Vienna first became a Roman colony under Julius Caesar.

There are perhaps more visible Roman ruins in modern-day Vienne than any other city in France. The Temple of Augustus and Livia was built by Claudius. A truncated quadrangular pyramid is generally believed to have been part of the *spina* (central dividing barrier) of a large circus (racetrack), the outlines of which have been traced. The remains of a large Roman theater on the slopes of Mont Pipet, one of five hills surrounding the city, are still used for performances today. Vienna was named "Colonia Julia Augusta Florentia Vienna" under Augustus and made the capital of Gallia Narbonensis. From 259 to 269 it was the capital of the new Provincia Viennensis (Pelletier 1980, 10).

Although the arrival of Christians in Vienna cannot be precisely determined with historical accuracy, we know there was a faith community present by 177, as it is mentioned in the letter to churches in Asia Minor, which recounted the persecution in Lugdunum. The letter identifies the martyr Sanctus as a deacon of the Vienna church (Eusebius, *Hist. eccl.* 5.1.17). Like Lugdunum, Vienna appears to have been among the earliest Christian communities in Gaul.

According to tradition, the first bishop of Vienna was Crescens, who converted the city to Christianity well before 177. This Crescens has traditionally been identified with the Crescens of 2 Timothy 4:10. That text says Titus went to Dalmatia, and Crescens to Galatia. However, the Codex Sinaiticus and others read "Gaul" rather than "Galatia." Even Eusebius (*Hist. eccl.* 3.3.8) assumes that Crescens was sent by Paul to Gaul. Apart from this interesting tradition, the first bishop known for certain is Verus, who was present at the Council of Arles in 314.

Avitus (bp. ca. 490–ca. 523) was highly influential in the church life of Burgundy. Avitus came from a prominent Gallo-Roman family, an example of the several Gallo-Roman aristocrats who became prominent leaders of the church in Gaul (Shanzer and Wood 2002, 3–6). His father, Isychius (bp. ca. 475–ca. 490), had preceded him in the see. It was Avitus, however, who brought the Arian king Sigismund (r. 516–523) into the Catholic faith and in that way contributed greatly to the formation of a Catholic Gaul (Shanzer and Wood 2002, 8–9). Avitus's literary works include many surviving letters and a long poem, *De spiritualis historiae gestis* (Shea 1997). The interpretative method employed by Avitus, discerning the faith meaning of historical narratives, set the stage for medieval hermeneutics. His letters reflect the relationship between Catholics and Merovingians between 499 and 518. They include letters to the Arian king Gunobad (r. 473–516) and his son Sigismund. The most significant letter is *Epistle* 46, a letter written to Clovis at the latter's baptism (Shanzer and Wood 2002, 362–73). Clovis became king of the Franks after the death of his father, King Childeric (r. 457–481). Though a pagan, Clovis was careful in his treatment of Christians. The Law of the Salian Franks (the *Lex Salica*),[5] produced around 508–511, reflects Clovis's thoughtfulness. He married an Arian Burgundian, Chlothild, in about 490. Consequently, there were efforts to convert Clovis to Arian Christianity, but he (along with his army) was finally baptized in 496 by Remigius of Rheims (bp. ca. 459/60–ca. 530). At that point, the Franks essentially became Catholic Christians (P. Brown 2003, 133–38).

5. This subgroup of Franks settled in what is now the northern part of the Netherlands.

10.2 Pectorius's Epitaph

Divine race of the heavenly Fish, with a noble heart draw, receiving, amongst mortals, the immortal spring of oracular water. Friend, warm your soul in the eternal waters of bounteous wisdom; Receive the food, sweet as honey, of the Saviour of the saints; Eat with zest, holding the Fish in your hands. That I may be filled with the Fish, I ardently desire, Master and Saviour. That my mother may be in blessed calm, I beseech, Light of the dead. Ascandios, my father, so dear to my heart, with my sweet mother and brothers, in the peace of the Fish, remember your Pectorius. (Behr 2013, 71; cf. Behr 2006, 378–79)

AUGUSTODUNUM

A large Celtic tribe, the Aeduli, settled in the Burgundy area, with the *op-pidium* (fortified town) Bibracte as its center (Chardron-Picault and Pernot 1999, 11). The settlement reflected the La Tène lifestyle (Audouze and Büchsen-schütz 1992, 25, 27). After Augustus assimilated the area, he founded ex nihilo within the province of Gallia Lugdunensis a new town 15 km northeast of Bribracte, appropriately named *Augustodunum* (Autun). Several elements of Roman architecture such as city walls, gates (La porte d'Arroux; La porte Saint-André), a Roman theater, and an amphitheater are still visible (Rebourg 2002, 48–57, 72–76). The metrical epitaph of a man named Pectorius indicates a Christian presence in the third century (see sidebar 10.2).

The inscription consists of two sections: the first addresses the Christian readers, while in the second Pectorius prays for his mother and asks his father and brothers to pray for him. The initial letters of the first five lines form a Greek acrostic spelling *ichthys* (fish). The inscription centers on the fish as "Jesus Christ, Son of God, Savior," a symbolic reference seen in early Christian art as well as, possibly, in Tertullian (*Bapt.* 1.3). In the middle section of the inscription, the readers are instructed to hold the fish in their hands, an obvious reference to the feeding of the five thousand as well as to the presence of fish in eucharistic meals (also seen in early Christian art).[6]

According to tradition, the first bishop of Augustodunum was St. Ama-tor (fl. ca. 250), but historically the first-known was Reticius, bishop at the time of Constantine. At the request of Constantine, Reticius, with two other Gallic bishops and fifteen Italian ones, attended a council in Rome in 313 to discuss the Donatist conflict. Because the Roman synod did not prove fruit-ful, Constantine sent a second invitation, including one to Reticius, for the

---

6. Compare the reference to a fish in the epitaph of Avircius of Hieropolis (see sidebar I.1 in the general introduction).

First Council of Arles (314), where Donatism was eventually rejected. The letters inviting Reticius to Rome and Arles are preserved by Eusebius (*Hist. eccl.* 10.5.18–24). A prolific writer, Reticius was one of the first to compose a commentary in Latin on a book of the Bible: *Commentarii in Canticum canticorum* (*Commentary on the Song of Songs*).

In the fifth century a cathedral was begun in Autun and dedicated to St. Nazarius. Since the cathedral also contained the alleged relics of Lazarus (see John 11:1–44), it made Autun a popular pilgrimage center.

Arelate

Although evidence exists for prehistoric caves in the area, Arles in southeastern France was first established by the Greeks, who wanted access to southern Gaul port cities for commercial reasons. Later it was taken over by the Celts, coming from northern Gaul, in 535 BCE. They named it Arelate (Town in the Marsh). Absorbed by the Romans in 123 BCE, Arelate was reestablished by Nero (r. 54–68) as a military *colonia* in Gallia Narbonensis (I. Wood 1999). Romanization of the Celtic city included the construction of a theater and a stadium (Rouquette and Sintès 1989, 17).

Little is known about the early presence of Christianity in Arelate/Arles. Tradition makes St. Trophimus the first bishop, sent there by Pope Fabian (bp. 236–250) in about 250 (Gregory of Tours, *Hist.* 1.30). Local legend anachronistically associates this Trophimus with Paul's companion mentioned in Acts 21:29. The Catholic Church honors Trophimus with a feast day on December 29, and a fine cathedral bearing his name was built in Arles in the Middle Ages. Another tradition places the martyrdom of St. Genesius around 303 in the town, though the Arles Genesius may have been confused with the actor and martyr-saint of the same name who died in Rome. Regardless, two sanctuaries outside the walls of ancient Arelate exist for Genesius: the alleged site of his martyrdom at what is now the suburb of Trinquetaille, and that of his burial at the Alyscamps necropolis (Klingshirn 1994, 59).

The first historically reliable information about Christianity in Arles comes from Cyprian, who in 254 referred to it as an episcopal city. Cyprian suspected its bishop Marcianus of Novatianism. In 313 Bishop Marinus attended the Synod of Rome (Eusebius, *Hist. eccl.* 10.5.19). The next year, Marinus hosted a council of Western bishops at Arles. The council dealt with celibacy, consecration of bishops, and rebaptism (Rosenberg 1997). Donatists strictly opposed clergy who had been ordained without the participation of validly ordained bishops. In Carthage, however, Caecilian (bp. pre-311–ca. 345) had been consecrated under questionable circumstances (see chap. 6). The Donatists brought their case against Caecilian to the new emperor, Constantine, who in turn passed the case over to Miltiades of Rome (bp. 310–314). Miltiades convened the council in Arles, though he died before it met in 314. The council vindicated Caecilian, and in 317 Constantine ordered the forceful suppression of the Donatists.

Cyprian had denied the validity of baptism performed by anyone outside the church (*Ep*. 69–75), while Stephen I of Rome (bp. 254–257) argued that the water and the confession made baptism valid regardless of who administered it. Consequently, Stephen opposed rebaptism. While supporting the validity of the original baptism, the Donatists also insisted on the moral character of the administrator as well as doctrinal correctness. So for them, rebaptism was sometimes necessary. The Donatist position, however, was denied at Arles.

At a later date monasticism was of considerable interest in Arles. Honoratus (bp. ca. 426/7–ca. 429/30) had founded the monastic community at Lerina (Lérins) before coming to Arles as bishop. He was followed by another Lérins leader, Hilary (bp. ca. 429/30–449). Honoratus supported monasticism but also defended Nicene Christianity—an issue at the Second Council of Arles in 353. Hilary, however, defended Semi-Pelagianism as a theological basis for monasticism. He also struggled with Leo I of Rome (bp. 440–461) over jurisdictional powers. These struggles cost Arles its important status for a time.

Caesarius (bp. ca. 502/3–542), born into a Gallo-Roman aristocratic family in 469, was able to restore Arles to its preeminent position. Caesarius himself was caught in a conflict with the Arian Visigoths, particularly Alaric II (r. ca. 484/5–507), and from time to time he was exiled from Arles, though eventually he was restored. Caesarius's rule for nuns (the *Regula virginum*),

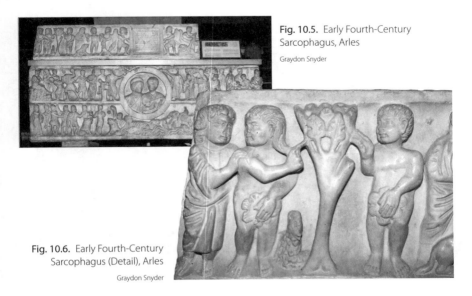

Fig. 10.5. Early Fourth-Century Sarcophagus, Arles

Graydon Snyder

Fig. 10.6. Early Fourth-Century Sarcophagus (Detail), Arles

Graydon Snyder

a kind and thoughtful reflection on the common life of women, has remained a standard. His sister Caesaria (d. 529) became the abbess of a convent that he founded in 512 near the Alyscamps (Benoît 1927, 90–93). Caesarius was a devotee of Augustine of Hippo (bp. ca. 395/6–430). He used Augustine's sermons as his own when preaching in Arles. Caesarius altered the form of mission work in western Europe. He did not attempt to destroy paganism but rather sought to make it subordinate to Christianity (Klingshirn 1994, 226).

In addition to the convent, Arles is best known to many for the marvelous assembly of about fifty Christian *sarcophagi* dating from the early fourth century (e.g., Koch 2000, nos. 24, 88, 110–13, 184–86, 236, 252). The rich collection reflects a fairly wealthy and prominent Christian community at the time of Caesarius (Benoît 1954, 30).

Augusta Treverorum

According to a legend preserved in the *Gesta Treverorum* (*Deeds of the Treveri*), St. Peter sent Eucherius, allegedly one of the Seventy (cf. Luke 10:1–12), as bishop to Gaul, where he became the first bishop of Augusta Treverorum (Trier). In reality, given the late evidence for Christianity in the city, it is unlikely that a Christian community was established in Augusta Treverorum before the second half of the second century (Harnack 1908, 2:407).

Founded in 16 BCE on the banks of the Mosella (Moselle) River within the territory of the Treveri, Augusta Treverorum, the capital of Gallia Belgica, was made a Roman colony in the time of Claudius. Eventually it became one of the more significant Roman cities in northern Europe. During the reorganization of

Fig. 10.7. Pre-Constantinian Sarcophagus (Detail: Noah in Ark), Trier

the empty by Diocletian, Caesar Constantius I established his headquarters there in 293.

Constantine, Constantius's son, later also resided periodically in Augusta Treverorum (e.g., in 310 and in 328). Portraits of his wife, Fausta, and of his mother, Helena, survive on the ceilings of the imperial palace. Two large basilicas were constructed in the city during Constantine's reign; the earlier was started in about 321, perhaps at the site of an earlier house-church. Bishop Agricius attended the Council of Arles in 314, and Bishop Maximinus was at the Council of Serdica in 343 and of Cologne in 346.

> ### 10.3 Christian Graffiti at Trier
>
> *Verna vivas* ☧ (Verna, live [in Christ]!)
> *Viva in Domino* ☧ (Live in the Lord [Christ]!)
> (Snyder 2003, 265–66, fragments 5–6, altered)

In the Rheinisches Landesmuseum at Trier are two pre-Constantinian *sarcophagi*. Numerous *sarcophagi* and early Christian graves are visible in the extensive necropolis under the Church of St. Maximinus. Fifteen graffiti inscriptions found under the choir of the Liebfrauenkirche indicate a strong presence of Christianity between 350 and 380, reflecting a simple form of faith (see sidebar 10.3).

BURDIGALA

Burdigala (Bordeaux), the capital of Gallia Aquitania, was also its main port. Situated on the left bank of the Garumna (Garonne) River, Burdigala was originally the main center of a Celtic tribe, the Bituriges Vivisci. In 56 BCE the settlement was captured by Publius Licinius Crassus (ca. 115–53 BCE), one of Julius Caesar's generals. In Roman times the region was already famous for its vineyards. Bishop Orientalis attended Arles in 314, but Christianity may have been long established at Burdigala by then. An inscription from 258 (*CIL* 13.633) may be Christian.

LERINA

The Isles of Lérins consist of four small islands off what is now the coast of Provence, France. For reasons no longer clear, the Greek god Lero and goddess Lerina became associated with the islands (Cooper-Marsdin 1913, 3–4). Two of the islands are barren. At one time the other islands had served as commercial and military ports for the Phoenicians and the Greeks.

The main island was originally called Lerina but is now named Saint-Honorat, after the Honoratus already mentioned in connection with Arelate/Arles. Honoratus, born in about 350 of socially significant parents in northern Gaul, settled on the deserted island in about 400–410 and created there a monastic community (*congregatio* or *coenobium*) and also provided opportunities for religious hermits (*cellulae*) (see Pricoco 1978, 43). The Lérins community, one of the oldest and most influential monastic institutions in western Europe (Cooper-Marsdin 1913, 3, 36), nurtured many for leadership in the churches of Gaul (Cavadini 1997). As noted above, Honoratus became bishop of Arles around 426/7 and was followed in that position by Hilary, another Lérins compatriot, around 429/30.

Eucherius joined the Lérins community in about 410. Inspired by a letter from John Cassian (ca. 360–post-432) on hermit life in Egypt, Eucherius described Lérins in his *De laude eremi*, which he wrote for Hilary (ca. 428) (Pricoco 1978, 44–47). In this well-known epistle he describes, among other things, affirmations of desert existence in the Hebrew Scriptures (Pricoco 1978, 154–64), the heavenly life of Jesus in the wilderness (Pricoco 1978, 66–69), and the magnificence of Lérins (Pricoco 1978, 59–73). In another essay, the *Liber formularum spiritalis intelligentiae* (*Formulas of Spiritual Intelligence*), following Origen (ca. 185–ca. 253), he defended the reading of Scripture in an allegorical sense. This work presaged medieval biblical hermeneutics. Eucherius was elected to the see of Lyons around 433/4. Eucherius's sons, who had been with him at Lérins, also became bishops: Salonius of Geneva (bp. ca. 440) and Varanius of Lyons (bp. ca. 449/50).

Many others from the Lérins community also impacted the life and theology of Gaul and beyond. Salvian (presbyter) of Marseilles (d. ca. 480), for example, was a monk at Lérins from about 424 and became renowned as a preacher and teacher of rhetoric. Of his several works, two treatises and nine letters are extant. The *De gubernatione Dei* (*On the Governance of God*) consists of eight books, of which the first five are by Salvian (Quasten 1950–1986, 4:531–33). Incomplete though it is, it is a moving indictment of contemporary Roman and Gallic society and calls for true Christian living. The other work, usually called *Contra avaritiam* (*Against Avarice*), is a plea for generosity to the church.

About the same time, a monk named Vincent (d. pre-450) also lived at Lérins. He shared in the general monastic Semi-Pelagianism (a life requiring discipline and a general dissatisfaction with Augustinian teaching on grace). In 434 Vincent wrote the *Commonitorium* (*An Aid to Memory*), a work intended to distinguish Catholic truth from heresy. He makes the Bible the authority for determining truth—the truth being the way Scripture has been interpreted universally, even from Antiquity. Consequently, he is best known for his famous adage, in *Commonitorium* 2, about truth: *Quod ubique, quod semper, quod ab omnibus* (What is believed everywhere, always, and by all people). This axiom has served as a powerful defense for tradition against theological novelty (Cooper-Marsdin 1913, 62).

In about 426 Faustus of Riez (ca. 410–ca. 495), apparently originally from Britain, joined the community of Lérins, where he became the abbot in 433. In about 459 he was consecrated bishop of Colonia Julia Augusta Apollinaris Reiorum (Riez). As did others from the Lérins monastery, Faustus struggled with Merovingian Arianism. At the same time, he championed a Semi-Pelagian free will combined with the necessity to cooperate with the divine will (Quasten 1950–1986, 4:483–84).

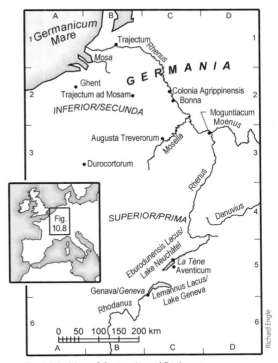

Fig. 10.8. Map of Germania and Environs

Another Lérins expatriot was Lupus (393–479), brother of Vincent, born in Tullum (Toul), Gaul. He married Pimeniola, the sister of Hilary of Arles, but after six years they mutually decided on the monastic life. Lupus entered the Lérins monastery under Honoratus. In about 426 he became bishop of Augustobona Tricassium (Troyes). Legend recounts that when Attila the Hun (r. 433–453) invaded Gaul in 451, Lupus met him and, by offering himself as a hostage, managed to persuade Attila to spare the city (Pricoco 1978, 51).

As noted, Caesarius, bishop of Arles, had also dwelled in Lérins around 490 and shared the monastic vision of Honoratus. The Lérins community was a powerful proponent for monasticism, the educational base of many Gallic bishops, and a strong theological opponent of Augustinianism.

Germania

In his representative list of Christian communities throughout the world, Irenaeus (*Haer.* 1.10.2) mentions churches in Germania. Similarly, Tertullian (*Adv. Jud.* 7.4) and Arnobius the Elder (*Nat.* 1.16) refer to the spread of Christianity among the German people. Consequently, as with Spain and Gaul, there

Fig. 10.9. Martyrium, Bonn

is literary evidence for pre-Constantinian Christianity in Germania Inferior and Germania Superior dating back at least to the end of the second century.

Exactly where in Roman-controlled Germania the first Christian communities were located is difficult to determine. A glass beaker with the phrase *Vivas in Deo* (Live in God) and decorated with a palm branch (Drack and Fellmann 1988, 308, 337–48) provides evidence of Christianity in Colonia Aventicum (Avenches, Switzerland) in Germania Superior by the early fourth century. Excavations underneath the Cathédrale St.-Pierre in Geneva (ancient Genava) have revealed two fourth-century churches. However, since the first attested bishop is Isaac (d. ca. 400), it is unclear when the Christian community in Geneva was first established.

In Bonn (ancient Bonna in Germania Inferior) an early Christian martyrium has been discovered next to the minster. It indicates the presence of pre-Constantinian Christians who were persecuted by the border-dwelling Gauls.

We may presume that the capitals of the two Roman German provinces were among the earliest cities to have Christian communities in the region.[7]

Colonia Agrippinensis

Sometime after the battles of Julius Caesar against the Ubii in 55 BCE, a settlement was founded on the west bank of the Rhine by Marcus Vipsanius Agrippa. This occurred most likely in 38 BCE (but perhaps as late as 19 BCE), when the Ubii asked to be moved from the other side of the river (Dietmar and Jung 2002, 15–17). The settlement that they built there was simply known as Oppidum Ubiorum—that is, the "fortified town of the Ubii" (La Baume

7. For all possible places in Germany where pre-Constantinian Christianity may have existed, see Mullen 2004, 223–26.

1964, 10). Oppidum Ubiorum was refounded as a Roman colony in 50 CE by Claudius. The colony was named Colonia Claudia Ara Agrippinensis in honor of Claudius's second wife, Agrippina the Younger (15–59 CE), as well as referring to the Altar (Ara) of Roma and Augustus, for which the city had become famous. Colonia Agrippinensis (Cologne) became the capital of Germania Inferior in 69 CE.

Some elements of a Roman wall with remains of nineteen towers that surrounded the old city still exist (Dietmar and Jung 2002, 18; Signon 1970, 76–87), as does a Roman aqueduct. Most notable is the Dionysus mosaic from the third century found in the dining room of a Roman villa (Signon 1970, 15, 22, plate 1). In 1956 a Roman-Frankish cemetery was uncovered under the Church of St. Severin, one of twelve Romanesque churches (Dietmar and Jung 2002, 30; Signon 1970, 50).

Colonia Agrippinensis's first-known Christian bishop was Maternus. He visited Rome in 313 and attended the Council of Arles in 314. Maternus was also responsible for the construction of the first cathedral, a square building erected early in the fourth century (Dietmar and Jung 2002, 29). The later great dome cathedral was constructed over this earlier church (Signon 1970, 50). Very little evidence for early Christianity in Colonia Agrippinensis exists apart from this. Colonia Agrippinensis had a number of workshops producing glassware. Some early fourth-century gold glasswork depicting biblical scenes, Christian symbols, and a few possibly early Christian inscriptions have been found in the area (Mullen 2004, 224). A church council was held at Colonia Agrippinensis/Cologne in 346.

MOGUNTIACUM

In about 15–12 BCE the Romans, under their general Nero Claudius Drusus (38–39 BCE), constructed a fort a short distance from the left bank of the Rhine near its junction with the River Main (ancient Moenus). The territory, on which the fort and the city that grew up between it and the Rhine were built, belonged to the Vangiones, a Germanic/Celtic tribe. The city, now known as Mainz, 130 km upstream from Colonia Agrippinensis, became, as already noted, the capital of Germania Superior in 69 CE. Remnants of an aqueduct and a Roman gate, as well as Drusus's cenotaph, still exist from this early period.

A third-century inscription (*CIL* 13.11834) with the words *innocenti spirito* (those innocent in the spirit) may be Christian. The earliest known bishop, however, is Martin, who definitely attended the Council of Cologne in 346 and perhaps the Council of Serdica in 343 (Mullen 2004, 226). The story that, when in December 406 the Germanic tribes crossed the frozen Rhine, Moguntiacum

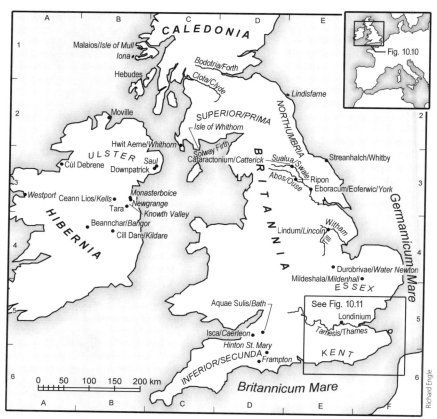

Fig. 10.10. Map of Britannia and Environs

was the first city to be taken and that the then bishop, Aureus, and some others who had sought refuge in the cathedral were killed by Alamanni invaders, is problematic; Aureus may have been a later bishop.

Britannia

Studies from the late twentieth century (Painter 1989; Hassall and Tomlin 1982; 1993; Watts 1991) have shown that early Christianity in Britain was more widespread, more syncretistic, and more continuous than previously thought. It was originally introduced by Britain's Roman conquerors and viewed as a "Roman religion" by Britain's Celtic inhabitants, who, when they converted, retained many of their Celtic traditions, practices, and symbols. Especially in the fourth and early fifth centuries Christianity attracted the new Romano-British elites, who, as did their contemporaries in Spain, lived in splendid rural *villae*,

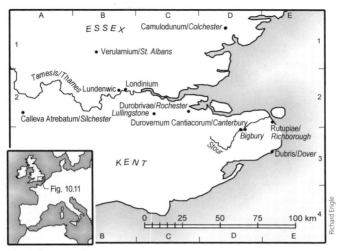

Fig. 10.11. Map of Southwestern Britannia (Detail)

some of which became richly decorated with mosaics displaying Christian symbolism, as at Frampton, Hinton St. Mary, and Lullingstone (Painter 1972; 1989, 2056–58; Bowes 2005, 232–33; Hartley et al. 2006, 72–73, 91–92).[8] A hoard of silver plates, chalices, and other objects decorated with Christian symbols from Water Newton (ancient Durobrivae) appears to have come from a local Christian community. Buried in about 350, this Christian silver is arguably the oldest known as some of the pieces may date to the third century (Painter 1975; Hartley et al. 2006, 92; but see also Mawer 1995, 18, 87–89). Another hoard, found at Mildenhall (ancient Mildeshala) in Suffolk, contains silver spoons with Christian inscriptions and *chi-rho* monograms (Frend 1996, 350–51).

Both Tertullian (*Adv. Jud.* 7.4) and Origen (*Fragmenta ex commentariis in Ezechielem* 4) indicate that they took it for granted that Christianity had been established in the British Isles before their own time (cf. Eusebius, *Dem. ev.* 3.5; Sozomen, *Hist. eccl.* 2.6.1). Exactly when the first Christians arrived in Britannia is, however, unknown. Legends about the apostles preaching in Britain (Eusebius, *Dem. ev.* 3.5) and the conversion of a British king named Lucius through correspondence with Eleutherius (i.e., Eleutherus) of Rome (bp. ca. 174/5–ca. 189) (*Lib. pont.* 14; cf. Bede, *Hist. eccl. Angl.* 1.4) are surely spurious.

St. Alban may have been martyred around 250 at Verulamium (St. Albans) during the Decian persecution (Thomas 1981, 48–50), but it is also possible that he died during the Diocletianic persecution in the early years of the fourth century.

8. The ancient names of these villages are unknown.

The same holds for two other martyrs, Aaron and Julius, who were put to death at Isca (Caerleon) (Gildas, *Exc. Brit.* 9.1; 10.2; Bede, *Hist. eccl. Angl.* 1.7, 18).

At least three bishops from Britain attended the Council of Arles in 314. However, no Christian inscriptions or other extant archaeological materials can be dated securely before the fourth century.[9] The earliest-known church buildings located in Britain also date to the (late) fourth century—for example, at Calleva Atrebatum (Silchester), Durovernum Cantiacorum (Canterbury), Lindum (Lincoln), and Rutupiae (Richborough) (see Thomas 1981, 168–74, 216–17; Watts 1991, 111–12, 119–22).

When the Romans withdrew from Britannia in about 410, their troops being needed in Gaul and Spain to deal with the Germanic invasions from across the Rhine, the popularity of Christianity waned, but, contrary to earlier scholarly views, it did not virtually die out. The absence of the Romans and especially of the elites who had adopted Christianity, however, enabled the Celtic elements within early British Christianity to predominate. This is not to say that the term "Celtic Church" should be applied to Christianity in the British Isles at that time, but rather that in Britain the Christian church continued to exist in Celtic-speaking regions as well as elsewhere (W. Davies 1992).

There is a rather cynical account of the Saxon conquest of Britain that occurred in the middle of the fifth century CE. This work, the *De excidio et conquestu Britanniae* (*On the Ruin and Conquest of Britain*), was written by a monk named Gildas, perhaps as early as the late fifth century. Judging by a series of freestanding Christian memorial stones with inscriptions in a style similar to those common in western Gaul, it appears that contact between Gaul and western Britain led to a revitalization of Christianity, especially in Wales (Knight 1992, 45–50). Roman-influenced Christianity was reintroduced to Britain in 597 with the arrival of Augustine of Canterbury (d. pre-610). The Saxon king of Kent at that time, Ethelbert (r. 560–616), had married a Christian woman, Bertha, daughter of Charibert I (r. 561–567), king of the Franks. Bertha may have convinced Gregory I of Rome (bp. 598–604) to (re)evangelize Britain. In any case, it was Gregory who commissioned Augustine to carry the gospel to England. Ethelbert granted him Canterbury as the primary location for his work (see below).

Londinium

The origins of London remain a conundrum, partially because of inconclusive archaeological and historical data, and partially because of deep

9. For all known and possible locations of pre-Constantinian Christianity in Britannia, see Mullen 2004, 243–48.

preconceptions. Some Londoners prefer a pre-Roman beginning. A favored legend comes from Geoffrey of Monmouth (1100–1154). In his *Historia regum Britanniae* (*History of the Kings of Britain*), written in about 1136, he claims that Brutus, a leader of the Trojans and great-grandson of Aeneas, traveled to Britain, and "coming to the River Tamesis [Thames], he walked along the shore and at last pitched upon a place very fit for his purpose" where he "built a city, which he called New Troy" (1.16) (see Giles 1968, 108; Merrifield 1983, 1). Legend notwithstanding, little evidence exists for any settlement prior to the Roman creation of London. Some prehistoric artifacts have been uncovered in the London area (Merrifield 1983, 2–9).[10] Then, perhaps one hundred years before the Roman invasion, there were Belgic (or Gallo-Belgic) incursions south and west of present-day London (Morris 1982, 30). About the same time, native tribes such as the Catuvellauni, Trinovantes, and Cantiaci entered the region. Because of their similarity and relationship, they are referred to collectively as the "Aylseford-Swarling culture" (Watts 2005, 1). The Atrebates, Dobunni, Durotriges, and Dumnonii tribes, also closely related, were more Belgic in origin.

Following his initial failure to invade Britain in 55 BCE, Julius Caesar made a more successful attempt in 54. His army reached the Thames, and near "London" it encountered stiff opposition from British tribes led by Cassivellaunus, a powerful and skilled leader. Although these tribes eventually were defeated, Caesar did not stay and, contrary to his intentions, did not return. The history of London really began when the Romans invaded England in 43 CE. To move farther inland, they built a bridge over the Thames at a place approximately the site of the present-day London Bridge. The Romans soon realized the usefulness of this site as a way to cross to western Britain, so they rather quickly developed a town at the northern end of the bridge. The Romans called it "Londinium," possibly a Latinized Celtic term. Historians generally assume the founding of London served the military purposes of the Romans. However, very few military artifacts have been discovered from that earliest period, nor was London ever a *colonia* (Tacitus, *Ann.* 15.33). When Claudius arrived in 43, he made Camulodunum (Colchester), not London, a *colonia* and the capital of Britannia. London may actually have originated more as a commercial site than as a military outpost (Haverfield 1912, 26–28, 169–70; Merrifield 1983, 41; P. Marsden 1980, 26–27).

The first Londinium was short-lived. It was sacked around 60 CE by Boudicca (Watts 2005, 8) in retaliation for the Roman violent seizure of the kingdom that she had inherited and the rape of her daughters (Tacitus, *Ann.* 14–16;

10. Note the remarkable Battersea Shield (see Merrifield 1969, 16–18).

Cassius Dio, *Hist. rom.* 61.1–12). It was rebuilt in about ten years. When London reached its apex in the second century, it replaced Camulodonum as the capital of Roman Britain. Structurally it was a Roman city containing a civic basilica five hundred feet in length, a large garrison-fort (Cripplegate), and even a fine mithraeum. Only at the end of the second century was the London Wall built. Remains of each of these are to some extent still visible. The city slowly declined until 410, when the Romans left Britannia, abandoning London. By 600 the Anglo-Saxons had created a new settlement, Lundenwic (London Trading-Post), upstream and 1.6 km west of the old Roman city.

Early Christian evidence in London is very slight. Restitutus of London attended the Council of Arles in 314. The current St. Paul's Cathedral may have been built over a pre-604 church. In 604 Augustine of Canterbury consecrated Mellitus (d. 624), a person sent by Pope Gregory to support Augustine's work, as bishop for the province of the East Saxons with its headquarters in London. Mellitus baptized King Saebert of Essex (r. ca. 604–616), King Ethelbert's nephew. Despite the conversion, Saebert's non-Christian sons drove Mellitus from London to Gaul in 616. Laurence, the second archbishop of Canterbury (bp. pre-601–619), brought Mellitus back to Britain. In 619 Mellitus succeeded Laurence as the third archbishop of Canterbury. Trying to assure the Christianization of Britain, Pope Gregory, according to Bede (ca. 673–735), addressed a letter to Mellitus regarding pre-Christian festivals. He urged Mellitus not to scorn pagan holy days but rather to coalesce them with the celebration of a Christian saint (Bede, *Hist. eccl. Angl.* 1.29–30; 2.3–7).

Another important bishop of London was Cedd (bp. ca. 658–664). He had been trained at Iona under Aidan (d. 651) and founded three monasteries (Bede, *Hist. eccl. Angl.* 4.23). Because of the connection with Iona, Cedd held to the Irish approach to Christianity (e.g., concerning the tonsure and the date of Easter). He participated in the Synod of Whitby (664), then shifted his allegiance to Rome after the council rejected the Irish tradition.

St. Dunstan (bp. 958–960) established a Benedictine monastery. In the next century, Edward the Confessor (r. 1042–1066), the next-to-last Anglo-Saxon king, built the abbey's chapel. This church became known as the "west minster" to distinguish it from St. Paul's Cathedral (the "east minster").

EBORACUM/EOFERWIC/YORK

In Northern Britain, on territory belonging to the Brigantes tribe, the Romans founded a new city, Eboracum, in 71 CE (Wenham 1970, 5–6, 12–13; Ottaway 1993, 19–26). Strategically located, Eboracum was destined to become the capital of Britannia Inferior and, later, of Britannia Secunda. Two Roman emperors resided in Eboracum during British military actions and died there of natural causes: Septimius Severus (between 208 and 211) and Constantius I (in 295 and 305–306). On the latter's death, his son Constantine was proclaimed emperor there by the troops (Hartley et al. 2006, 31–35). The city's imperial palaces have not survived, although large parts of the Roman fortress have. The invading Angles named the city Eoferwic and made it the capital of Northumbria. Eventually, in about 1000 CE, it became known by its present name, York.

In 601 Gregory I sent Paulinus, a monk at St. Andrew's Monastery in Rome, to join Mellitus in the second group of missionaries sent to Britannia. Bede describes Paulinus as "a tall man having a slight stoop, with black hair, an ascetic face, a thin hooked nose, and a venerable and majestic presence" (*Hist. eccl. Angl.* 2.16). Paulinus stayed in Kent until 625, when he was consecrated as a bishop by Justus of Canterbury (bp. 624–627).

To establish Christianity in the region, Paulinus accompanied Ethelburga, the sister of King Eadbald of Kent (r. 616–640), in 627 to Northumbria, where she was to marry King Edwin (r. 616–632/3). Ethelburga was the daughter of Bertha, the wife of Ethelbert, the woman who had first encouraged the mission to England (Bede, *Hist. eccl Angl.* 2.9). According to tradition, Eadbald would not let his sister Ethelburga marry Edwin unless he allowed freedom of worship. Eventually Edwin was convinced by Paulinus and Ethelburga to convert. Paulinus baptized him in a church at Eoferwic especially constructed for that purpose. That small wooden church ultimately gave rise to the great York Minster. Edwin's kingdom encompassed an area from the Abos River (Humber) to the Clota (Clyde) and the Bodotria (Forth). There are traces of Paulinus and his mission in many parts of this vast district. According to Bede (*Hist. eccl. Angl.* 2.14), Paulinus used to baptize in the River Sualua (Swale), near "Cataractum"—that is, Cataractonium, the modern Catterick. After Edwin was killed in a battle, Paulinus took Ethelburga and her children to Kent. There, Paulinus was made bishop of Rochester (Roman Durobrivae) in 633, and he died in 644.

The first native Saxon to become bishop of Eoferwic was Wilfrid (634–709), who held office from 664 until 666 and again from 669 until 678 (Bede, *Hist. eccl. Angl.* 5.19) (Duckett 1947, 146). He was born in Northumbria and, as a young man, spent time on the holy island of Lindisfarne at the monastery founded there in about 635 (see below). After some time in Rome and Lyons he returned to Britain around 657/8, and around 660/1 he became abbot of a recently established monastery at Ripon. Wilfrid managed to polarize the Northumbrian churches by insisting on the Roman, rather than Celtic, way of life for the churches of the English (Bede, *Hist. eccl. Angl.* 4.2). In 664 he was influential at the Synod of Whitby, where the Northumbrian date of Easter was made to conform to that of Rome (Duckett 1947, 135–36). Wilfrid's success at Streaneshalch (the Anglo-Saxon name for Whitby), where the synod was held at the Monastery of St. Hilda, resulted in his appointment as bishop of Eoferwic.

LINDUM/LINCOLN

Early remains of Lincoln can be found in a group of first-century BCE wooden dwellings. Only a few artifacts from that period are available, most notably the Witham Shield (M. Jones 1993, 2). The earliest settlement on the territory of the Coritani existed close to what is known as the Brayford Pool, where the River Witham meets the River Till (M. Jones 1993, 1). The name Lincoln probably came from the settlement's Brythonic language as *Lindu*, *Lindo*, or *Lindum* (or possibly *Lindon* or *Lindunon*). The name may have referenced either the Brayford Pool itself (dark pool [cf. *llyn* in Welsh]), or possibly the location of the early settlement (fort on a hill by a pool [*Lindun*]). Whatever the origin of this early name, it was subsequently Latinized in the Roman period to "Lindum" (or *Colonia Lindum* from around 90 CE), which in Anglo-Saxon became *Lincoln* (J. Hill 1948, 3).

When the Romans conquered the area in 48 CE, they built a fortress for the Ninth Legion on the hill overlooking Brayford Pool at the northern end of the Fosse Way—the main Roman road from southwestern Britain to the northeast. The legion moved from Lindum to Eboracum in 71 CE. Under Diocletian, Britannia Inferior was divided into four parts. Lindum was made the capital of Flavia Caesariensis (M. Jones 1993, 9). As with other locations in Britannia, there is little literary or archaeological indication of a Christian presence before the time of Augustine of Canterbury. We know, however, that there was a Christian community by the beginning of the fourth century because, as with York and London, a bishop of Lincoln (Adelphius) attended the Council of Arles in 314.

Following the evacuation of the Roman troops in 410, Lincoln became less populous. There are, nevertheless, significant visible remains of the Roman period. The most notable of these include the Mint Wall from the Roman forum and the well-preserved Newport Arch (M. Jones 2002, 59). It appears that two timber churches might have been built in the courtyard of the forum. The northern center of the Roman town was called "Bailgate," so the later St. Paul-in-the-Bail might have been constructed over one of these early churches (Painter 1989, 2043–44; M. Jones 1993, 11–12). In the southern section of Roman Lincoln (modern Wigford), two other churches might have been started during the Roman period. The present day St. Mary-le-Wigford Church is a medieval building with a Norman nave. But intriguingly, it contains a Roman grave slab inscribed by both Romans and Saxons. St. Peter-at-Gowts, however, appears to be somewhat later than the Roman period (Steane 2001, 1–3).

Paulinus, while Bishop of Eoferwic, visited Lincoln and reestablished a Christian presence in about 629. Bede writes:

> His first convert was Blecca, Reeve [*Praefectus civitatis*] of the city of Lincoln, with all his family. Here he built a beautiful stone church, which today, either through neglect or enemy damage, has lost its roof, although the walls are still standing. And each year miracles of healing occur in this place among those who seek it in faith. (*Hist. eccl. Angl.* 2.16 [trans. Sherley-Price 1955])

DOROVERNUM CANTIACORUM/CANTWAREBYRIG/CANTERBURY

Canterbury lies in eastern Kent, the southeast region of England. The original settlement straddled the River Stour at what was probably the lowest crossing point (Tatton-Brown 1994, 1). This means that it existed on the easiest route from the continent via Dubris (Dover) to London (Lyle 1994, 15). Excavations around the settlement have uncovered pre-Roman pots, hand axes, and other implements from as far back as 3000 BCE (Lyle 1994, 16; J. Boyle 1974, 20–22). In 54 BCE Julius Caesar, attempting to invade Britain, stormed a hilltop near the Stour ford. He described the people as a farming people with long-haired warriors and military chariots (*Bell. Gal.* 5.14) (Lyle 1994, 17). This hilltop settlement mentioned by Caesar was likely Bigbury (Crouch 1970, 20–21), the predecessor of nearby Durovernum (British *duro* [fort], *verno* [swamp]). The present name Canterbury derives from the Old English, or Anglo-Saxon, *Cantwarebyrig*, meaning "fortress of the people of Kent." The Romans called it Durovernum Cantiacorum because the pre-Roman, Belgic people were called the Cantiaci (Tatton-Brown 1994, 1). Durovernum Cantiacorum continued as a key town in Kent during the Roman occupation (48–410 CE). It was abandoned at the end of the Roman period and then resettled by the Saxons. Although the Saxons were quite pagan, some evidence of earlier and continuing Christianity exists.

Canterbury Cathedral and the Church of St. Pancras appear to have been built on the sites of late fourth-century Christian structures (Thomas 1981, 168, 170–74). Similarly, a late Roman church, St. Martin's, still existed when Augustine arrived in 597. According to Bede, "[Augustine] proceeded with the king's approval to repair a church which he was informed had been built long ago by Roman Christians . . . and established a dwelling for himself and his successors nearby" (*Hist. eccl. Angl.* 1.33 [trans. Sherley-Price 1955]). St. Martin's is the oldest church in England that is still functioning (Tatton-Brown 1994, 12).

Augustine also built a monastery outside the city: St. Augustine's Abbey. It was first dedicated to St. Peter, but later it was dedicated to Augustine after his death. Although Gregory had planned the division of England into two archbishoprics, one at London (under Bishop Mellitus) and one at Eoferwic,

Augustine's success explains why the southern archiepiscopal see came to be fixed at Canterbury instead of London.

Beyond the Borders

Caledonia

Tertullian may have had Caledonia (Scotland) in mind when he referred to regions of the Britons "inaccessible to the Romans but accessible to Christ" (*Adv. Jud.* 7.4). Alternatively, he may not have known very much about the Romans in Britain (Dunn 2008, 167). Apart from some long-cist (stone-coffin) cemeteries and a few memorial stones (Proudfoot 1995), little but legend exists about the earliest Christians in Caledonia. Even the historicity of the story of Ninian, traditionally considered to be the first bishop to have evangelized Scotland, is problematic.

Hwit Aerne/Whithorn

According to Bede (*Hist. eccl. Angl.* 3.4), Ninian built a church made of white stone, the *Candida Casa* (White House or Shining House), and established an episcopal see named after Martin of Tours (bp. ca. 371/2–397). If historically accurate, this may have occurred in the year of, or soon after, Martin's death. It is also possible that "Ninian" has been confused with "Finian" (Clancy 2001). Finian of Moville (ca. 495–589), spent time at *Candida Casa* in the early sixth century and (as with a tradition concerning Ninian) was a mentor of St. Columba (on whom, see below).

Regardless of who actually built the first church in Scotland, the modern town of Whithorn and the nearby Isle of Whithorn, on the tip of the southwest coast of Scotland, take their names from the white church via the name given to it by the local Picts: *Hwit Aerne*. Excavations on the grounds of the medieval St. Ninian's Priory have discovered remnants of a white-plastered wall (which may belong to the original *Candida Casa*), as well as an ancient cemetery, remains of two mid-sixth-century shrines, a seventh-century church, an eighth-century church, and a number of Celtic crosses and commemorative stones. Among the latter is a rectangular stone pillar decorated with a *chi-rho* in a style popular from about 450. The inscribed text, arguably the oldest extant Christian inscription from Scotland, reads:

> We praise you, O Lord.
> Latinus a descendant of Barrovados, aged 35, and his daughter, aged 4, made (this) sign.[11]

11. Translation by the author.

The stone pillar presumably signified and commemorated the completion of a pilgrimage to the site.

IONA

Since early medieval times a small island in the Scottish Hebrides (ancient Hebudes), 1.6 km west of the Isle of Mull (ancient Malaios), has been called Iona. The name comes from the Latin *Ioua Insula*, a translation of an original Old Irish designation probably meaning "Yew-Tree Island." According to the *Life of Columba* by Adomnán (ca. 627/8–704), Columba[12] (ca. 521–597) sailed with twelve companions to the Scottish western seaboard, the Dál Riata, in 563 (iii.3–4) and landed at Iona, since then also known as Columba's Island.

Why the great Irish saint traveled to the small Scottish island cannot be determined for certain. Irish monks were famous for their peregrinations, often without any specific goal. Columba may have simply continued that tradition. Some say that he sought God's favor for his family and thereby alienated his political contemporaries. Since Columba belonged to a royal family (Uí Níall, or "O'Neill"), he may well have been involved in bloody clan battles between the northern Uí Níalls and the southern Uí Níalls, such as the battle at Cúl Drebene in 561. Others say that he fell into disfavor with St. Finian of Moville because of plagiarism and had to leave Ireland. In any case, Columba developed one of the most famous monastic communities outside his homeland (Walsh and Bradley 2003, 98–99; P. Brown 2003, 327).

Ireland had been barely touched by the Roman occupation of Britannia. Irish monasteries, consequently, developed as centers of high-level learning independent of Romanized Christianity. The monks of Iona, continuing the Irish tradition, not only formed an academic center but also developed their own unique, high-level artistic skills, known to us especially through the creation of the famous *Book of Kells*, or *Book of Columba*, a copy of the four Gospels produced in what is known as insular art. We know of Columba primarily through Adomnán, who, while serving as the abbot of Iona from 679 to 704, ninth after Columba, wrote Columba's *vita*. The *vita* (*Life of Columba*), according to Adomnán (Anderson and Anderson 1991, lvii), consisted of three parts: revelations (i.1), miracles of power (ii.11), and angelic visions (iii.1). In addition, Adomnán was an ecclesiastical politician as well as a writer. In 700 he wrote *Cain Adomnáin* (*Adomnán's Law*). This document, also known as the *Law of Innocents*, served to protect persons such as women and clerics from clan violence (Anderson and Anderson 1991, xli; P. Brown 2003, 329).

12. The Latinized form of Colum Cille (The Church's Dove).

According to tradition, Columba set out from Iona to convert Scotland (*Life of Columba* i.1; ii.10, 26 [Anderson and Anderson 1991]). However, there were Christian communities among the Picts well before the time of Columba (MacArthur 1995, 9), including the earliest Scottish church at Whithorn. The archaeological discoveries at Whithorn indicate the presence of a vital fifth-century Christian community in Scotland. The vigor of Pictish Christianity can also be seen in later monuments such as the marvelous eighth-century Aberlemno Cross, as well as monuments in the Miegle Sculptured Stone Museum collection in eastern Scotland.

Fig. 10.12. Aberlemno Cross, Aberlemno

The influence of Iona community members was widespread. The Monastery of Lindisfarne, referred to above, founded by Irish-born St. Aidan (d. 651), became a key center for evangelizing Northumbria and Scotland. Aidan had moved from Iona at the request of King Oswald (r. 634–642) in about 635 (Bede, *Hist. eccl. Angl.* 111.3). Monks from the community of Iona populated Lindisfarne, also well known for such artistic masterpieces as the Lindisfarne Gospels.

Some clear conflicts existed between the Irish/Scottish "Ionian position" and the English "Roman position." The date of Easter, however, was the primary issue that divided Christianity in the Celtic world from the rest of the West. As noted already, a synod to discuss the issue took place in Streaneshalch (Whitby) in 664. Along with King Oswiu (r. 642–670), the communities of Iona and Linisfarne defended the Celtic calendar, whereas Wilfrid, while still abbot of Ripon, championed the Roman practice. The conflict was settled in favor of the Roman calendar (Walsh and Bradley 2003, 156–65).

Iona has been a center for pilgrimages for centuries. It may have been a sacred place well before Christianity came to the region, but it was a barren island when Columba and the Irish monks arrived. They lived in simple huts, built of wood, and they constructed an abbey of wood. The present Iona Abbey, built around 1200, is one of the best-preserved monastic buildings from the Middle Ages. In front of the abbey stands the ninth-century St. Martin's High Cross, one of the finest Celtic crosses outside Ireland. An ancient burial ground, called the Reilig Odhráin, contains the graves of many early kings of Scotland (Thomas 1971, 105–11). St. Oran's Chapel, constructed before the present-day abbey, shows the style of architecture utilized on the island.

Hibernia

As in the case of Caledonia, although Christianity may have been established in Hibernia (Ireland) before the fifth century, any reliable knowledge has been long lost to posterity. Presumably, contact between the Romans who occupied Britannia and the Celtic inhabitants of Hibernia, especially on the southeast coast, may, as elsewhere, have led to some, albeit limited, early Christianization. A reference by Prosper of Aquitaine (ca. 390–post-455) that a Roman deacon named Palladius was sent by Pope Celestine I (bp. 422–432) "to the Irish who believe in Christ" (*Chron.* anno 431) indicates that a Christian community existed in Ireland by 431. The wording suggests that, as in the case of a similar mission to Britannia at the time, Celestine was concerned about the influence of the teachings of Pelagius (d. ca. 431) on the Christians in the region (Ó Corráin 1989, 8).

At about the same time, Patrick, the more famous missionary, came to Hibernia from Britannia, perhaps settling at or near what is now Armagh. While Irish Christianity was known particularly through St. Patrick (ca. 390–ca. 460), St. Bridget of Kildare (451–525), and St. Columba, other great Irish saints, similar to the Ionians, represented the Celtic gospel to the Roman world (Herbert 1988, 146–47). The best-known missionary was Columban (d. 615),[13] a monk of the Monastery of Beannchar (Bangor) in northern Ireland, who founded monastic centers in France, Switzerland, and Italy. They became centers of evangelization and learning for much of Europe—for example, in Bobium (Bobbio), northern Italy, in about 612 (Munro 1993, 6; Walsh and Bradley 2003, 118–38).

EMAIN MACHA/ARMAGH

The name Emain Macha derives from the appellation of a mythological war-goddess Macha. Her name is contained in the name Armagh, which derived from "Ard Macha" (Height of Macha). Emain Macha may have been the ancient capital of Ulster, the location of ancient kings, the spiritual center of the area (McCreary 2001, 15). There were several such "royal centers" in Hibernia, one of which was Emain Macha (Navan Fort in English). Prehistoric artifacts have been discovered dating as far back as five thousand years, while remains of the royal center itself go back to the Iron Age (Aitchison 1994,

---

13. Not to be confused with St. Columba.

19–20). Navan Fort was a large wooden structure with a gigantic central totem pole (McCreary 2001, 17), quite like the Irish ring-forts of a later time (Walsh and Bradley 2003, 43–44).

Muirchu's seventh-century *Life of Patrick* relates that Patrick founded a church near Emain Macha, the local chieftain Daire having granted Patrick a small tract of land down the hill from Navan Fort. That, according to Irish tradition, was the origin of Armagh, the primary ecclesiastical city of Ireland (Bury 1905, 155–56). There is, however, no mention of any connection with Armagh in the writings of Patrick himself, nor are there any historical or archaeological data to substantiate the ecclesiastical and political claims of Armagh as the place of origin for Patrick (see Thomas 1971, 84; Hanson 1983, 34–35).

We know Patrick best through his *Confession*. He writes that his father was "Calpornius, a deacon, a son of Potitus, a presbyter, who was at the village of Bannavern Taberniae" (*Conf.* 1). Such a location is unknown, but still it has been assumed he probably spent his childhood in a Celtic Christian environment (west Britain). During an Irish raid Patrick was seized and taken to northern Ireland as a slave. After six years of captivity, responding to a vision, he escaped Ireland on a merchant ship headed for Gaul (*Conf.* 17). Eventually he returned to his family in Britain, but, again responding to a vision, in 431 he felt called to return to Ireland as a missionary (*Conf.* 23).

It is nearly impossible to distinguish between Patrick and Palladius. If the two missionaries were sent to Ireland to convert the Irish to a Roman form of Christianity, they did not succeed (De Paor and De Paor 1958, 30). First, some elements of Christianity already existed, probably brought from Spain by traders and merchants. Second, instead of forming Catholic dioceses and bishoprics, the Irish established monasteries directed by abbots. Irish Christians tended to be ascetic, spiritualistic, even Pelagian, and they followed a pre-Nicene calendar. Indeed, Patrick's account of the Ireland to which he returned sounds very much like the Celtic world from which he had come. He mentions kings and subkings (*Conf.* 52). Officials who administered early Irish law were titled brehons (*Conf.* 53). Patrick was a gentle, humble Christian. He often gave thanks to God for pardoning his weaknesses. At least once, however, he lost his temper (*Conf.* 46). The British king Coroticus (r. ca. 450) captured, enslaved, and murdered a group of Irish Christians recently baptized by Patrick. Patrick wrote a scathing letter to Coroticus and formally excommunicated him.

Patrick is best remembered for his famous poem, the *Lorica Sancti Patricii*, commonly called "St. Patrick's Breastplate." No one knows whether Patrick actually wrote the poem, though in it an early Irish Christian faith has been preserved in the Old Irish language. The poem has been translated into many languages and

appears in many hymn-
books. It reflects a standard faith yet expresses
the unique, beautiful
world of Celtic Chris-
tianity (see sidebar 10.4).

Patrick was buried
not in Armagh but in
Downpatrick, County
Down. According to
legend, he died in Saul,
a small village just out-
side Downpatrick. Saul
is named after the barn

> ### 10.4 St. Patrick's Breastplate
>
> Christ with me, Christ before me,
> Christ behind me, Christ within me,
> Christ beneath me, Christ above me,
> Christ at my right, Christ at my left,
> Christ in my lying, my sitting, my rising;
> Christ in the heart of everyone who knows of me,
> Christ in the mouth of everyone who speaks to me,
> Christ in every eye that sees me,
> Christ in every ear that hears me.
> (Stanzas 8–9 [adapted from translation by
>   Cecil Frances Alexander])

(Irish: *Sabhall*) where Patrick allegedly preached his first sermon after landing
in Ireland (Hanson 1983, 35). The cult of St. Patrick is also celebrated on a
mountain in the west of Ireland located 8 km from Westport, County Mayo.
The mountain originally served as a place to celebrate the summer solstice and
to share in the feast of the Celtic god Lug. It was also deemed to be the dwelling place of another Celtic deity named Crum Cru. Patrick allegedly fasted
there before banishing all snakes from Ireland. Now on "Reek Sunday," the
last Sunday in July, over twenty-five thousand pilgrims climb the mountain,
known as Croagh Patrick, to commemorate the life of Ireland's primary saint
(Walsh and Bradley 2003, 49).

Ceann Lios/Kells

According to legendary tradition, Kells became a fortified royal residence
in about 1204 BCE under the name *Dun Chuile Sibhrinne* (Aitchison 1994).
In the third century CE, though ruling from Tara, Cormac mac Airt, the most
famous king of Ireland, may have used Kells as a residence (Stokes 1877). It
was subsequently named Ceannannas or Ceann Lios. The name Kells is an
Anglicization of that Irish-language name. Located in County Meath, north of
Dublin, the Abbey of Kells was first founded by Columba probably in 554 on
land granted by Diarmuid mac Fergusso Cerrbheoil. Diarmuid and Columba,
though probably related, often disagreed violently. The abbey land was given
as an act of recompense (Roe 1966, 1).

Little else is known about Kells until it was "refounded" around 804 by
monks who escaped successive Viking invasions of St. Columba's monastery
on Iona (in 795, 802, and 806) (Kenney 1929, 445). In 814 Cellach, then abbot
of Iona, also moved to Kells (*Annals of Ulster* 807.4; 814.9) (Bannermann

1999, 74). After further Viking raids the Iona shrine of St. Columba also was transferred to the Abbey of Kells (Herbert 1988, 69). The international fame of Kells rests primarily on the famous illustrated Gospels, the *Book of Kells*, also known as the Great Gospel of Colum Cille (Columba). According to legend, the book was produced by Columba himself and was preserved in Kells down to Archbishop James Usher's time (bp. 1625–1656). Historians now believe that the *Book of Kells* may have been either started in Iona and finished in Kells or written entirely in Kells by successive generations of monks (Kenney 1929, 640–41; Walsh and Bradley 2003, 176). It has often been regarded as the "chief relic of the western world" (*Annals of Ulster* 1007.11).

The *Book of Kells* is the finest example from a group of manuscripts, in what is known as the insular style, produced in monasteries of Ireland, Scotland, and England from the late sixth through the early ninth centuries. These manuscripts include the *Cathach of St. Columba* and the *Book of Durrow* (from the second half of the seventh century) (O'Neill 1997, 69). The *Book of Durrow* contains the four Gospels in the Vulgate. Artistic symbolism marks the beginning of each Gospel (Walsh and Bradley 2003, 174–75). The *Cathach of St. Columba* is an early seventh-century Irish Psalter, traditionally associated with Columba himself. It may be the copy made by him of a book loaned to him by St. Finian. The so-called resultant plagiarism led to the Battle of Cúl Drebene in 561, a fight that, as noted, may have caused Columba to flee Ireland and found Iona (Walsh and Bradley 2003, 98–100). It could be the oldest known Irish manuscript and contains the earliest examples of a written Goidelic language (Q-Celtic, spoken by the Irish and Scots) other than Ogham inscriptions (pre-Christian stones with Latin-type marks).

Kells still contains several ancient monuments that tradition attaches to Columba's residence there. "Columba's House" is a tall, high-pitched building, of which the ground floor formed an oratory while the croft between the oratory and the roof served as the sleeping compartment for the saint. There are some fine crosses dating probably from the ninth century. One stands in the marketplace, the other in the churchyard. The latter is a fairly well-sculpted cross, though others elsewhere, such as one at Monasterboice, have clearer and more extensive art. Irish crosses primarily portray biblical scenes (Snyder 2002, 176–83, plates 7, 9, 11, 14, 15, 16). The Kells South Cross has been called the "Cross of Patrick and Columba" because the plinth (base) was inscribed *Patricii et Columbae Crux*, implying that it was intended to commemorate both Patrick and Columba, the founder of the monastery (Roe 1966, 10). Art on this cross depicts the fall of Adam, the death of Abel, the three young men in the fiery furnace, Daniel in the lions' den, and the multiplication of the loaves and fishes. On the Market-Place Cross we see four horsemen on the base (common in Celtic art); the resurrection of Jesus, showing two tomb guards armed with spears; Christ as the King of Glory, dressed in military costume and surrounded by three pairs of armed men; the fall of Adam; the death of Abel; Daniel in the lions' den; and the sacrifice of Isaac. Early Irish crosses, which first appeared in the eighth and ninth centuries, are a signal mark of Irish Christianity. Three types exist: those with pierced rings, those with solid rings, and those with no rings. Early examples, like the Reask Cross, normally have no rings but only an interior symbol, such as a cross. Later crosses, as those in Kells, normally with pierced rings, are marked with beautiful illustrative sculptures. There is also a fine round tower in Kells, about 27 m in height, built during the Danish Wars to protect the church and monastery. Citizens would climb to the top of the tower to avoid the invaders.

Germania North of the Border

The Germanic tribes north of the Rhine and the Danube had, at first, little contact with and certainly no interest in Christianity. The earliest Christians among the Goths, for example, appear to have been persons captured from within the Roman Empire and taken north across the border by raiding parties. Among these were the grandparents (or great-grandparents) of Ulfila and the clergy of their village (Philostorgius, *Hist. eccl.* 2.5).

Ulfila (Wulfila: Little Wolf) was born circa 306/11 in the Gothic territory ruled by Tervingian kings, north of the Danube, which by then must have had a sizable Christian community. Theophilus, "bishop of the Goths," attended Nicaea (325), and Ulfila is said to have been one of his disciples (Socrates, *Hist. eccl.* 2.41.23). Ulfila's own disciple and foster son, Auxentius of Durostorum (d. ca. 400), in his epistolary eulogy, written soon after Ulfila's death in 383, states that Ulfila had been a lector before his ordination as bishop at the age of thirty (*Ep. de fide Ulfilae* 56). This ordination was presided over by Eusebius of Nicomedia (d. 341/2). Just before his ordination, Ulfila, as a Christian, had been chosen to be part of a Gothic delegation to the Christian emperor (Philostorgius, *Hist. eccl.* 2.5). According to Philostorgius (ca. 368–ca. 439), the visit was to Constantine. If so, it may have occurred as part of Constantine's tricentennial in 336, and Ulfila then may have been ordained during the time of the synod held in Constantinople during the same year (Barnes 1990, 541–45). It is more likely, however, that both the visit and the ordination occurred sometime early in the reign of Constantius II (r. 337–361), as the accession of a new ruler would be the logical occasion for a delegation to have been sent (Sivan 1996).[14]

14. In that case, the reference to Constantine in Philostorgius, *Hist. eccl.* 2.5, is, of course, a mistake.

Perhaps, since Eusebius of Nicomedia became bishop of Constantinople in 338/9, Ulfila's ordination as "Bishop of the Goths" occurred between 338/9 and 341/2. Eusebius of Nicomedia, although he had attended Nicaea and subscribed to its creed, was and remained a supporter of Arius (d. 336) and championed a "Semi-Arian" theology, adopted also by Constantius II. Whether Ulfila, who similarly had great difficulties with the Catholic formulation of the Trinity, had always ascribed to a kind of "Arianism" or, as argued by later Catholic historians, was virtually forced into "Arianism" out of political and ecclesiastical necessity (Socrates, *Hist. eccl.* 2.41.23; 4.33.6–7; Sozomen, *Hist. eccl.* 6.37.6–12; Theodoret, *Hist. eccl.* 4.37.3–5) remains debatable. Ulfila certainly assented to the creed put forward by the so-called Homoian Arians,[15] which was adopted at Constantinople in 360, and not only eliminated the terms "substance" and "subsistence" in connection with the godhead in that particular creed but also prohibited their use altogether (Socrates, *Hist. eccl.* 2.41.43; Sozomen, *Hist. eccl.* 4.21.4).

Regardless of when or why Ulfila adopted a particular brand of "Arian" or "Arian-like" Christianity, his espousal of this kind of Christianity inevitably caused the members of his Gothic flock, especially new converts, to also become "Arian" in theology. Auxentius, who around 384 appears to have become the "Arian" bishop of Milan, states that Ulfila, after having completed only seven years of his episcopate, brought a large number of Gothic Christians with him across the border in the time of Constantius II and settled within the empire (*Ep. de fide Ulfilae* 59). Socrates (*Hist. eccl.* 4.33), Sozomen (*Hist. eccl.* 6.37), and Theodoret (*Hist. eccl.* 4.37) describe a similar migration involving Ulfila and some of the Goths, but they place it in the latter part of the reign of Valens (r. 364–378). Presumably, Ulfila, the "Bishop of the Goths," carried out his pastoral and evangelistic mission on both sides of the border, at times living within and at times outside that border.

By the late 370s, "Arian Christianity" had become almost the predominant form of religion among the Tervingian Goths, not only because of Ulfila but also because of the decision by King Fritigern (r. ca. 376–ca. 380) to adopt (along with his subjects) the ("Arian") Christianity of Valens in gratitude for the latter's support against his rival Athanaric (r. 369–381) (Sozomen, *Hist. eccl.* 6.37).

Athanaric's resultant retributive persecution of Gothic Christians led not only to some of these crossing the Lower Danube but probably also to the western migration of some Christian Goths. Aided by the translation produced by Ulfila of almost the whole Bible into the Gothic language (Sozomen, *Hist. eccl.* 6.37), Christianity spread throughout the Western Goths and to similar

---

15. A group of "Semi-Arians," led by Acacius of Caesarea (d. 366).

Germanic tribes such as the Vandals. When, after the collapse of the Western Roman Empire, the Visigoths, the Vandals, and other "barbarians" invaded Europe and North Africa in the fifth century, they brought their "Arian" Christianity with them and, like Fritigern in the previous century, all but imposed it on their subjects.

Not until the seventh and eighth centuries did Christian missionaries have any permanent success in the Low Countries (Netherlands), north of the Rhine. A monk named Amandus (d. ca. 675), originally from Nantes in Aquitaine, established a missionary center in Ghent in about 625 and from there, with the support of the Merovingian kings Clotaire II (r. 613–629) and Dagobert I (r. 629–639), evangelized among the Northern Franks and the Frisians. He established a monastery at Trajectum ad Mosam (Maastricht) around 647 and he may also have been bishop of that city between 649 and 652.

In 678 Wilfrid, bishop of York, visited Frisia and apparently baptized a large number of Frisians. In 690 Willibrord (658–739), one of the monks of the Ripon Monastery, of which Wilfrid had been abbot (ca. 660/1–664), led a group of twelve British missionaries to Frisia. Five years later he was made "Archbishop of the Frisians" by Pope Sergius (bp. 687–701). Pepin II (r. 687–695), the early Carolingian ruler who consolidated the control of the Franks over the Frisians and the Alamanni, supported Willibrord's mission and gave him property near Trajectum (Utrecht) to build a cathedral.

From 716 onward, Willibrord's work in Frisia was continued by another British-born missionary originally named Winfrith but better known by his subsequent name, Boniface (680–754). Boniface gained the official support of Pope Gregory II (bp. 715–731) in 722 and extended his mission geographically to the east of Frisia to Hesse and eventually as far as Thuringia. Boniface was by no means the first to bring Christianity to this area north of the Rhine but was very successful at converting the still-pagan Saxons and members of other Teutonic tribes. He also consolidated and provided an organizational structure for the Christian communities already established in the region, bringing them more closely into the fold of the Roman Church.

British-born clergy also participated in the eventual Christianization of the Scandinavian countries even farther north. The history of the beginnings of the official establishment of Christianity in Denmark, Norway, and Sweden, during the tenth century, however, falls outside of the chronological scope of this book.

References

Abbott, Nabia. 1937. *The Monasteries of the Fayyūm*. SAOC 16. Chicago: University of Chicago Press.

Abuladze, Ilia, ed. 1971. *Dzveli kʿartʿuli agiograpʿiuli literaturis dzeglebi*. MAGHL 3. Tbilisi: Mecʾniereba.

Adams, William Y. 1977. *Nubia: Corridor to Africa*. Princeton, NJ: Princeton University Press.

———. 2005. *Sites of Meroitic and Ballaña Age*. Vol. 2 of *The West Bank Survey from Faras to Gemai*. BARIS 1335. Oxford: Archaeopress.

Agathangelos. 1976. *History of the Armenians*. Translated by R. W. Thomson. Albany: State University of New York Press.

Aitchison, Nicholas Boyter. 1994. *Armagh and the Royal Centres in Early Medieval Ireland: Monuments, Cosmology, and the Past*. Glasgow: Cruithne.

Aland, Barbara. 1980. "Bibelübersetzungen I. Neues Testament." *TRE* 6:189–96.

Alcock, Susan E. 1993. *Graecia Capta: The Landscapes of Roman Greece*. Cambridge: Cambridge University Press.

Alemany, Augustí. 2000. *Sources on the Alans: A Critical Compilation*. HO 5/8. Leiden: Brill.

Alexidze, Zaza. 2002. "Four Recensions of the 'Conversion of Georgia.'" In *Die Christianisierung des Kaukasus*, edited by W. Seibt, 9–16. VKB 9. Vienna: Österreichische Akademie der Wissenschaften.

Alföldi, Géza. 1975. *Die Römischen Inschriften von Tarraco*. 2 vols. MF 10. Berlin: de Gruyter.

Amat, Jacqueline, ed. 1996. *Passion de Perpétue et de Félicité suivi des Actes*. SC 417. Paris: Cerf.

Anderson, John G. C., Franz V. M. Cumont, and Henri Grégoire, eds. 1910. *Recueil des inscriptions grecques et latines du Pont et de L'Arménie*. SPon 3/1. Brussels: Lamertin. [Abbr.: *IPont*]

Anderson, Marjorie O., and Alan O. Anderson, eds. and trans. 1991. *Adomnán's Life of Columba*. OMT. Oxford: Clarendon.

Andreas, F. C., and K. Barr. 1933. "Bruchstücke einer Pehlevi-Übersetzung der Psalmen." SPAW 2:91–152.

Angelov, Anastas. 2002. *Martsianopol: Istoriia i arkheologiia* [*Marcianopolis: History and Archaeology*] (in Bulgarian). Varna: [s.n.].

Angus, Samuel. 2011. *The Mystery-Religions*. New York: Dover.

Appelbaum, Shimon, and Arthur Segal. 1993. "Gerasa." *NEAEHL* 2:470–79.

Armstrong, Jonathan J. 2008. "Victorinus of Pettau as the Author of the Canon Muratori." *VC* 62:1–34.

Arnal, William. 2001. *Jesus and the Village Scribes: Galilean Conflicts and the Setting of Q.* Minneapolis: Fortress.

Arnaud, Pascal. 2005. *Les routes de la navigation antique: Itinéraires en Méditerranée.* Paris: Errance.

Ascough, Richard S. 2000. "Christianity in Caesarea Maritima." In *Religious Rivalries and the Struggle for Success in Caesarea Maritima,* edited by Terence L. Donaldson, 153–80. SCJ 8. Waterloo, ON: Wilfrid Laurier University Press.

Ashbrook Harvey, Susan. 2000. "Antioch and Christianity." In *Antioch: The Lost Ancient City,* edited by Christine Kondoleon, 39–50. Princeton, NJ: Princeton University Press.

Ashbrook Harvey, Susan, and Heinzgerd Brakmann. 1998. "Johannes von Ephesus." *RAC* 18:553–64.

Asmussen, Jes P. 1983. "Christians in Iran." In *The Seleucid, Parthian and Sasanian Periods,* edited by Ehsan Yarshater, 924–48. Vol. 3.2 of *The Cambridge History of Iran,* edited by William B. Fischer et al. Cambridge: Cambridge University Press.

Atiya, Aziz S. 1952. "The Monastery of St. Catherine and the Mount Sinai Expedition." *PAPhS* 96:578–86.

Atkinson, Donald. 1951. "The Origin and Date of the 'Sator' Word Square." *JEH* 2:1–18.

Audouze, François, and Olivier Büchsenschütz. 1992. *Towns, Villages and Countryside of Celtic Europe.* Translated by Henry Cleere. London: Batsford.

Aviam, Mordechai. 1990. "Horvath Hesheq—A Unique Church in Upper Galilee: Preliminary Report." In *Christian Archaeology in the Holy Land: New Discoveries; Essays in Honour of Virgilio C. Corbo, OFM,* edited by G. C. Bottini, L. Di Segni, and E. Alliata, 351–77. Jerusalem: Franciscan Printing Press.

Aviam, Mordechai, and Peter Richardson. 2001. "Josephus' Galilee in Archaeological Perspective." In *Life of Josephus, Translation and Commentary,* 177–209. Vol. 9 of *Flavius Josephus: Translation and Commentary,* edited by Steve Mason. Leiden: Brill.

Avi-Yonah, Michael. 1984. *The Jews under Roman and Byzantine Rule: A Political History of Palestine from the Bar Kokhba War to the Arab Conquest.* New York: Schocken.

Ayres, Lewis. 2004. *Nicaea and Its Legacy: An Approach to Fourth-Century Trinitarian Theology.* Oxford: Oxford University Press.

Babalikashvili, N. 1970. "O pamjatnikah evreiskoj epigrafiki iz Mckheta." *Macne* 6:271–88.

Bagnall, Roger S. 1988. "Combat ou vide: Christianisme et paganisme dans l'Égypte romaine tardive." *Ktema* 13:285–96.

———. 1993. *Egypt in Late Antiquity.* Princeton, NJ: Princeton University Press.

———. 2001. "Monks and Property: Rhetoric, Law, and Patronage in the Apophthegmata Patrum and the Papyri." *GRBS* 42:7–124.

———. 2002. "Public Administration and the Documentation of Roman Panopolis." In *Perspectives on Panopolis: An Egyptian Town from Alexander the Great to the Arab Conquest,* edited by Arno Egberts, Brian P. Muhs, and Jacques van der Vliet, 1–12. PLB 31. Leiden: Brill.

———. 2003a. "Conversion and Onomastics: A Reply." In *Later Roman Egypt: Society, Religion, Economy and Administration,* edited by Roger S. Bagnall, article IX. VCSS 758. Aldershot: Ashgate Variorum.

————. 2003b. "Religious Conversion and Onomastic Change in Early Byzantine Egypt." In *Later Roman Egypt: Society, Religion, Economy and Administration*, edited by Roger S. Bagnall, article VIII. VCSS 758. Aldershot: Ashgate Variorum.

————. 2008. "Models and Evidence in the Study of Religion in Late Roman Egypt." In *From Temple to Church: Destruction and Renewal of Local Cultic Topography in Late Antiquity*, edited by Johannes Hahn, Stephen Emmel, and Ulrich Gotter, 23–41. RGRW 163. Leiden: Brill.

————. 2009. *Early Christian Books in Egypt*. Princeton, NJ: Princeton University Press.

Bagnall, Roger S., and Dominic W. Rathbone, eds. 2004. *Egypt from Alexander to the Copts: An Archaeological and Historical Guide*. London: British Museum.

Bakirtzis, Charalambos. 1988. *The Basilica of St. Demetrios*. Thessaloniki: Institute of Balkan Studies.

Bakirtzis, Charalambos, Eftychia Kourkoutidou-Nikolaidou, and Chrysanthi Mavropoulou-Tsioumi. 2012. *Mosaics of Thessaloniki: 4th–14th Century*. Athens: Kapon Editions.

Balicka-Witakowski, Ewa, Sebastian P. Brock, David G. K. Taylor, and Witold Witakowski, eds. 2001. *The Heirs of the Ancient Aramaic Heritage*. Vol. 2 of *The Hidden Pearl: The Syrian Orthodox Church and Its Ancient Aramaic Heritage*, edited by Sebastian P. Brock and David G. K. Taylor. Rome: Trans-World Film Italia.

Ball, Warwick. 2003. *Rome in the East: The Transformation of an Empire*. London: Routledge.

Ballance, Michael H. 1957. "The Site of Derbe: A New Inscription." *AnSt* 7:147–51.

Balty, Janine. 1977. *Mosaïques antiques de Syrie*. Brussels: Centre Belge de recherches archéologiques à Apamée de Syrie.

Bandy, Anastasius C. 1970. *The Greek Christian Inscriptions of Crete*. Athens: Christian Archaeological Society.

Bannermann, John. 1999. "The Scottish Takeover of Pictland and the Relics of Columba." In *Spes Scotorum = Hope of Scots: Saint Columba, Iona and Scotland*, edited by Dauvit Brown and Thomas Owen Clancy, 71–91. Edinburgh: T&T Clark.

Baratte, François. 2005. "La sculpture en Numidie à la fin de l'antiquité." In *Saint Augustin: La Numidie et la société de son temps; Actes du colloque SEMPAN-AUSONIUS, Bordeaux, 10–11 octobre 2003*, edited by Serge Lancel, Stéphanie Guédon, and Paul Maurin, 153–71. Paris: de Boccard.

Baratte, François, and Bernard Boyaval. 1979. "Catalogue des étiquettes de momies du Musée du Louvre (C.E.M.L.): Textes grecs. 4ème partie." *CRIPEL* 5:237–339.

Barbet, Alix, and Florence Monier. 2001. "La crypte funéraire de la basilique sous le lycée M. Eminescu à Constantza (Roumanie)." In *La peinture funéraire antique IVe siècle av. J.-C.-IVe siècle ap. J.-C*, 221–28. Actes du VIIe colloque de l'AIPMA, 221–28. Paris: [s.n.].

Barbet, Alix, et al. 1996. "L'hypogée paléochrétien des orants à Constanza (Roumanie), l'ancienne Tomis." *MEFRA* 108, 105–58.

Barbieri, Guido. 1952. *L'albo senatorio da Settimio Severo a Carino (193–285)*. SIISA 6. Rome: Signorelli.

Bardill, Jonathan. 1997. "The Palace of Lausus and the Nearby Monuments in Constantinople." *AJA* 101:69–83.

————. 1999. "The Great Palace of the Byzantine Emperors and the Walker Trust Excavations." *JRA* 12:216–30.

Barnard, Leslie W. 1983. *The Council of Serdica, 343 A.D.* Sofia: Synodal Publishing House.

Barnea, Ion. 1980. "L'épigraphie chrétienne de l'Illyricum oriental." In *Rapports présentés au Xe congrès international d'archéologie chrétienne, Thessalonique, 28 septembre–4 octobre 1980*, 447–95. Thessalonikē: Société d'études macédoniennes.

Barnes, Timothy D. 1968. "Pre-Decian Acta Martyrum." *JTS*, NS 19:509–31.

———. 1971. *Tertullian: A Historical and Literary Study*. Oxford: Clarendon.

———. 1982. *The New Empire of Diocletian and Constantine*. Cambridge, MA: Harvard University Press.

———. 1985. "Constantine and the Christians of Persia." *JRS* 75:126–36.

———. 1990. "The Consecration of Ulfila." *JTS*, NS 41:541–45.

———. 1993. *Athanasius and Constantius: Theology and Politics in the Constantinian Empire*. Cambridge, MA: Harvard University Press.

Barsanti, Claudia. 1992. "Costantinopoli: Testimonianze archeologiche di età costantiniana." In *Costantino il grande dall'antichità all'umanesimo: Colloquio sul cristianesimo del mondo antico, Macerata 18–20 dicembre 1990*, edited by Giorgio Bonamente, 115–50. Macerata: Università di Macerata, Facoltà di lettere e filosofia.

Bartol'd, Vasilii V. 1977. *Turkestan Down to the Mongol Invasion*. 4th ed. London: Gibb Memorial Trust.

Basset, Sarah. 2004. *The Urban Image of Late Antique Constantinople*. Cambridge: Cambridge University Press.

Bauckham, Richard. 1992. "Jude." *ABD* 3:1098–1103.

Bauer, Walter. 1934. *Rechtgläubigkeit und Ketzerei im ältesten Christentum*. BHT 10. Tübingen: Mohr.

———. 1964. *Rechtgläubigkeit und Ketzerei im ältesten Christentum*. 2nd ed. BHT 10. Tübingen: Mohr Siebeck.

———. 1971. *Orthodoxy and Heresy in Earliest Christianity*. Edited and translated by Robert A. Kraft and Gerhard Krodel. Philadelphia: Fortress. [English edition of Bauer 1964.]

Baum, Wilhelm, and Dietmar W. Winkler. 2003. *The Church of the East: A Concise History*. London: RoutledgeCurzon.

Baumer, Christoph. 2006. *The Church of the East: An Illustrated History of Assyrian Christianity*. London: Tauris.

Baumgarten, Albert I. 1992. "Literary Evidence for Jewish Christianity in the Galilee." In *The Galilee in Late Antiquity*, edited by Lee I. Levine, 39–50. New York: Jewish Theological Seminary.

Baumstark, Anton. 1922. *Geschichte der syrischen Literatur mit Ausschluß der christlich-palästinensischen Texte*. Bonn: Marcus & Weber.

Bavant, Bernard. 2004. "L'Illyricum." In *L'Empire romain d'Orient, 330–641*, 303–28. Vol. 1 of *Le monde byzantin*, edited by Cécile Morrisson and Bernard Bavant. Nouvelle Clio. Paris: Presses universitaires de France.

Bavant, Bernard, Vladimir Kondić, and Jean-Michael Spieser, eds. 1990. *Le quartier sud-ouest de la ville haute*. Vol. 2 of *Caričin Grad*, edited by Noël Duval et al. CEFR 75/2. Rome: École française de Rome.

Bavant, Bernard, Vujadin Ivanišević, and Veroljub Trajković. 2006. *Justiniana Prima – Caričin grad*. Belgrade: National Museum.

Bayet, Charles Marie C. 1878a. *De titulis atticae christianis antiquissimis: Commentatio historica et epigraphica; Thesim proponebat Facultati litterarum parisiensi*. Paris: Thorin.

———. 1878b. "La nécropole chrétienne de Milo." *BCH* 2:347–59.

Beck, Edmund, ed. and trans. 1957. *Des heiligen Ephraem des Syrers: Hymnen contra Haereses.* 2 vols. CSCO 169, 170. Louvain: Durbecq.

———, ed. and trans. 1961–1963. *Des heiligen Ephraem des Syrers: Carmina Nisibena.* 2 vols. in 4 parts. CSCO 218, 219, 240, 241. Louvain: Secrétariat du Corpus scriptorum christianorum orientalium.

Beck, Roger. 2006. "The Religious Market of the Roman Empire." In *Religious Rivalries in the Early Roman Empire and the Rise of Christianity,* edited by Leif Vaage, 233–52. SCJ 18. Waterloo, ON: Wilfrid Laurier University Press.

Becker, Adam H. 2006. *Fear of God and the Beginning of Wisdom: The School of Nisibis and Christian Scholastic Culture in Late Antique Mesopotamia.* Divinations. Philadelphia: University of Pennsylvania Press.

———. 2008. *Sources for the History of the School of Nisibis.* TTH 50. Liverpool: Liverpool University Press.

Becker-Bertau, Friedrich. 1986. *Die Inschriften von Klaudiu Polis.* Bonn: Habelt. [Abbr.: IKlaudiop]

Bedjan, Paul. 1895. *Histoire de Mar-Jabalaha: De trois autres patriarches, d'un prêtre et de deux laïques, Nestoriens.* 2nd ed. Paris: Harrassowitz.

———. 1968. *Acta martyrum et sanctorum Syriace.* 7 vols. Leipzig: Harrassowitz, 1890–1897. Reprint, Hildesheim: Olms.

Behr, John. 2006. "Gaul." In *Origins to Constantine,* edited by Margaret M. Mitchell, Frances M. Young, and K. Scott Bowie, 366–79. Vol. 1 of *The Cambridge History of Christianity,* edited by Margaret M. Mitchell et al. Cambridge: Cambridge University Press.

———. 2013. *Irenaeus of Lyons: Identifying Christianity.* Oxford: Oxford University Press.

Bell, Gertrude L. 1907. *The Desert and the Sown.* New York: Dutton.

Bell, H. Idris. 1924. *Jews and Christians in Egypt: The Jewish Troubles in Alexandria and the Athanasian Controversy, Illustrated by Texts from Greek Papyri in the British Museum; With Three Coptic Texts Edited by W. E. Crum.* London: British Museum.

———. 1946. "Alexandria ad Aegyptum." *JRS* 36:130–32.

Bell, H. Idris, and T. C. Skeat. 1935. *Fragments of an Unknown Gospel and Other Early Christian Papyri.* London: British Museum. [Abbr.: P.Egerton]

Bell, H. Idris, and Herbert Thompson. 1925. "A Greek-Coptic Glossary to Hosea and Amos." *JEA* 11:241–46.

Ben Khader, Aïcha Ben Abed, and David Soren, eds. 1987. *Carthage: A Mosaic of Ancient Tunisia.* New York: American Museum of Natural History, with W. W. Norton.

Benoît, Fernand. 1927. *Arles: Ses monuments, son histoire.* Lyon: Rey.

———. 1954. *Sarcophages paléochrétiens d'Arles et de Marseille.* Supplément à "Gallia" 5. Paris: Centre national de la recherche scientifique.

———. 1959. *Mars et Mercure: Nouvelles recherches sur l'interprétation gauloise des divinités romaines.* Aix-en-Provence: Ophrys.

———. 1999. "Maximus of Madauros." In *Augustine through the Ages: An Encyclopedia,* edited by Allen Fitzgerald, 550. Grand Rapids: Eerdmans.

Berger, Albrecht 1988. *Untersuchungen zu den Patria Konstantinupoleos.* PB 8. Bonn: Habelt.

———. 1997. "Regionen und Straßen im frühen Konstantinopel." *IstMitt* 47:349–414.

———. 2000. "Streets and Public Spaces in Constantinople." *DOP* 54:161–72.

Bernoulli, Carl A. 1968. *Hieronymus und Gennadius: De viris illustribus.* Freiburg im Breisgau: Mohr, 1895. SAKDQ 11. Reprint, Frankfurt: Minerva.

Beševliev, Veselin. 1964. *Spätgriechische und spätlateinische Inschriften aus Bulgarien.* BBA 30. Berlin: Akademie-Verlag.

Betz, Hans Dieter, ed. 1986. *The Greek Magical Papyri in Translation: Including the Demotic Spells.* Chicago: University of Chicago Press.

Betz, Hans Dieter, et al., eds. 1998–2007. *Religion in Geschichte und Gegenwart: Handwörterbuch für Theologie und Religionswissenschaft.* 4th rev. ed. 8 vols. Tübingen: Mohr. [Abbr.: *RGG*]

Bickerman, E. 1983. "Time-Reckoning." In *The Seleucid, Parthian and Sasanian Periods*, edited by Ehsan Yarshater, 778–91. Vol. 3.1 of *The Cambridge History of Iran*, edited by William B. Fisher et al. Cambridge: Cambridge University Press.

Bienert, Wolfgang A. 1978. *Dionysius von Alexandrien: Zur Frage des Origenismus im dritten Jahrhundert.* PTS 21. Berlin: de Gruyter.

Biernacki, A. B. 1990. "Remarks on the Basilica and Episcopal Residence at Novae." *TAB* 5:187–208.

Bikai, Patricia. 2002. "ACOR Report: The Churches of Byzantine Petra." *NEA* 65:271–76.

Bintliff, John L. 2004. "Town and Chora of Thespiae in the Imperial Age." In *Roman Rule and Civic Life: Local and Regional Perspectives*, edited by L. de Ligt, E. A. Hemelrijk, and H. W. Singor, 199–229. IE 4. Amsterdam: Gieben.

———. 2005. "The Leiden University Ancient Cities of Boeotia Project: 2005 Season at Tanagra." *Pharos* 13:29–38.

Bintliff, John L., Phil Howard, and Anthony Snodgrass, eds. 2007. *Testing the Hinterland: The Work of the Boeotia Survey (1989–1991) in the Southern Approaches to the City of Thespiae.* Cambridge: MacDonald Institute for Archaeological Research.

Bintliff, John L., et al. 2004–2005. "The Tanagra Project: Investigations at an Ancient Boeotian City and Its Countryside (2000–2002)." *BCH* 128:541–606.

Biran, Michal. 2005. *The Empire of the Qara Khitai in Eurasian History: Between China and the Islamic World.* CSIC. Cambridge: Cambridge University Press.

Bitrakova-Grozdanova, Vera. 2006. "Lychnidos in the Early Christian Period and Its Urban Nucleus." In *Jubileen Zbornik–25 Godini Mitropolit Timotei*, 257–68. Ohrid, Macedonia: Makedonska Pravoslavna Tsurkva, Debarsko-Kichevska Eparchiya.

Bitton-Ashkelony, Brouria, and Aryeh Kofsky. 2000. "Gazan Monasticism in the Fourth–Sixth Centuries." *POC* 50:14–62.

Blanchetière, François. 1981. *Le christianisme asiate aux IIe et IIIe siècles.* Lille: Service de reproduction des thesès, Université de Lille.

Blockley, R. C. 1987. "The Division of Armenia between the Romans and the Persians at the End of the Fourth Century." *Historia* 36:222–34.

Blumell, Lincoln. 2010. "Is P.Oxy. XLII 3057 the Earliest Christian Letter?" In *Early Christian Manuscripts: Examples of Applied Method and Approach*, edited by T. J. Kraus and T. Nicklas, 97–113. Leiden: Brill.

Blumell, Lincoln, and Jenn Cianca. 2008. "The Oratory of St. George in Rihab: The Oldest Extant Christian Building or Just Another Byzantine Church?" *BAR* Online Archives. http://www.bib-arch.org/online-exclusives/oldest-church.pdf.

Bolman, Elizabeth S., Stephen J. Davis, and Gillian Pike. 2010. "Shenoute and a Recently Discovered Tomb Chapel at the White Monastery." *JECS* 18:453–62.

Bolotov, Vassilii V. 1994. *Lektsii po istorii drevnei tserkvi* [*Lectures on the History of the Ancient Church*] (in Russian). 4 vols. St. Petersburg: Merkusheva, 1907–1918. Reprint, Moscow: Spasso-Preobrazhenskiy Balaam Monastery.

Bonanno-Aravantinou, M. 1988. "Oi Sarkofagoi Romaikis Periodou tis Boiotias: Synoptiki Theorisi." In *1 Diethnes Synedrio Boiotikon Meleton, Theba, 10–14 Septembriou 1986*, edited by P. Bekiaris, 307–24. Athens: Epeteris tes Hetaireias Boiotikon Meleton.

Borkowski, Zbigniew. 1975. *Une description topographique des immeubles à Panopolis*. Translated by Zsolt Kiss. Warsaw: PWN-Éditions scientifiques de Pologne.

Bosch, Emin, ed. 1967. *Quellen zur Geschichte der Stadt Ankara im Altertum*. Türk Tarih Kurumu, 76.46. Ankara: Türk Tarih Kurumu Basımevi. [Abbr.: *IAnkyraBosch*]

Bospačieva, Mina. 2001. "An Early Christian Martyrium from Philippopolis." *ABulg* 5:59–69.

———. 2002. "A Small Early Christian Basilica with Mosaics at Philippopolis (Plovdiv)" (in Bulgarian). *ABulg* 6:55–76.

———. 2005. "Spätantike (frühchristliche) Denkmäler in Philippopolis (Plovdiv, Bulgarien)." *MCA* 11:24–55.

Bospačieva, Mina, and Vera Kolarova. 2014. *Plovdiv, grad varhu gradovete: Filipopol – Pulpudeva – Paldin*. [*Plovdiv, City on Top of Cities: Philippopolis – Pulpudeva – Paldin*]. Sofia: Tola.

Bounni, Adnan. 1997. "Syria in the Persian through Roman Periods." *OEANE* 5:134–39.

Bowen, Gillian. 2002. "The Fourth-Century Churches at Ismant el-Kharab." In *Dakhleh Oasis Project: Preliminary Reports on the 1994–1995 to 1998–1999 Field Seasons*, edited by Colin A. Hope and Gillian E. Bowen, 65–85. Oxford: Oxbow.

———. 2003. "The Small East Church at Ismant el-Kharab." In *The Oasis Papers III: Proceedings of the Third Conference of the Dakhleh Oasis Project*, edited by Gillian E. Bowen and Colin A. Hope, 153–66. Oxford: Oxbow.

Bowersock, Glen W. 1990. *Hellenism in Late Antiquity*. Cambridge: Cambridge University Press.

Bowersock, Glen W., Peter Brown, and Oleg Grabar, eds. 1990. *Late Antiquity: A Guide to the Postclassical World*. HUPRL. Cambridge, MA: Belknap Press of Harvard University Press. [Abbr.: *LAGPW*]

Bowes, Kim. 2005. "'Une coterie espagnole pieuse': Archaeology and Christian Communities in Fourth- and Fifth-Century Hispania." In *Hispania in Late Antiquity: Current Perspectives*, edited and translated by Kim Bowes and Michael Kulikowski, 189–258. MEMIW 24. Leiden: Brill.

Bowman, Alan K. 2005. "Egypt from Septimius Severus to the Death of Constantine." *CAH* 12:311–26.

Bowman, Alan K., et al., eds. 2007. *Oxyrhynchus: A City and Its Texts*. GRM 93. London: Egypt Exploration Society.

Boyadjiev, Stefan. 1969. "Rannohristiyanska tsarkva krai s. Golyamo Belovo, Pazardjishki okrag" ["An Early Christian Church near Golyamo Belovo, Pazardjik District"] (in Bulgarian). *Arheologiya* (Sofia) 9:10–20.

———. 1976. "L'église rouge de Perustitca et le problème des édifice à toiture en terrase." In vol. 3 of *Actes du XIVe congrès des études byzantines: Bucarest, 6–12 septembre*

1971, edited by Mihai Berza and Eugen Stanescu, 289–93. Bucharest: Editura Acacemiei Republicii România.

———. 1994. "Hristiyanska grobnichna arhitektura v Serdica prez II–VI vek" ["Christian Tomb Architecture in Serdica, II–VI C"] (in Bulgarian). Bulgarsko arhitekturno nasledstvo [*Bulgarian Architectural Heritage*] 1:3–27.

———. 1998. "Arhitektura, parvonachalno prednaznachenie i preustroistva na Chervenata tsarkva krai Perushtitsa" ["Architecture, Original Design, and Reconstruction of the Red Church near Perushtitsa"] (in Bulgarian). Arheologiya (Sofia) 39:24–38.

———. 2001. "L'aspect architectural du martyrium dans la nécropole orientale de Philippopolis." *ABulg* 5:71–75.

———. 2002. "Serdica." In vol. 1 of *Rimski i rannovizantiiski gradove v Bulgariia* [*Roman and Early Byzantine Cities in Bulgaria*] (in Bulgarian), edited by Rumen T. Ivanov, 125–80. Sofia: Ivray.

———. 2009. *Rannochristijanski hram "Sveta Sofija," Premadrost Bozhiya* [*The Early Christian Church of "St. Sophia," The Wisdom of God*] (in Bulgarian). 2nd rev. ed. Sofia: "St. Kliment Ohridski" Sofia University Press.

Boyce, Mary. 1983. "Parthian Writings and Literature." In *The Seleucid, Parthian and Sasanian Periods*, edited by Ehsan Yarshater, 1151–65. Vol. 3.1 of *The Cambridge History of Iran*, edited by William B. Fisher et al. Cambridge: Cambridge University Press.

Boyle, John. 1974. *Portrait of Canterbury*. London: Hale.

Boyle, John A., ed. and trans. 1958. *The History of the World-Conqueror by 'Ala-ad-Din 'Ata-Malik Juvaini*. 2 vols. Manchester, UK: Manchester University Press.

———, trans. 1971. *The Successors of Genghis Khan: Translated from the Persian*. PHS 10. New York: Columbia University Press.

Brakke, David. 1994. "The Authenticity of the Ascetic Athanasiana." *Or*, NS 63:17–56.

———. 1995. *Athanasius and the Politics of Asceticism*. Oxford: Oxford University Press.

Brashear, William, and Helmut Satzinger. 1990. "Ein akrostichischer griechischer Hymnus mit koptischer Übersetzung (Wagner-Museum K 1003)." *JCoptS* 1:37–58.

Bratož, Rajko. 2004a. "Die Diokletianische Christenverfolgung in den Donau- und Balkanprovinzen." In *Diokletian und die Tetrarchie: Aspekte einer Zeitenwende*, edited by Alexander Demandt, Andreas Goltz, and Heinrich Schlange-Schöningen, 115–40. M-S 1. Berlin: de Gruyter.

———. 2004b. "Verzeichnis der Opfer der Christenverfolgung in den Donau- und Balkanprovinzen." In *Diokletian und die Tetrarchie: Aspekte einer Zeitenwende*, edited by Alexander Demandt, Andreas Goltz, and Heinrich Schlange-Schöningen, 209–51. M-S 1. Berlin: de Gruyter.

Braun, Oskar. 1915. *Ausgewählte Akten persischer Märtyrer, mit einem Anhang: Ostsyrisches Mönchsleben*. BK 22. Kempten: Kösel.

Braund, David. 1994. *Georgia in Antiquity*. Oxford: Oxford University Press.

Brent, Allen. 2007. *Ignatius of Antioch: A Martyr Bishop and the Origin of Monarchical Episcopacy*. London: Continuum.

Brett, Michael, and Elizabeth Fentress. 1996. *The Berbers*. Oxford: Blackwell.

Breydy, Mich[a]el. 1983. *Études sur Saʿīd ibn Baṭrīq et ses sources*. CSCO 450. Louvain: Peeters.

———. 1985. *Das Annalenwerk des Eutychios von Alexandrien: Ausgewählte Geschichten und Legenden kompiliert von Saʿīd ibn Baṭrīq um 935 A.D.* CSCO 471. Louvain: Peeters.

Briquel-Chatonnet, Françoise, and Alain Desreumaux. 2004. "Les inscriptions syriaques de Turquie et de Syrie." In *Les inscriptions syriaques*, edited by Françoise Briquel-Chatonnet, Muriel Debié, and Alain Desreumaux, 15–27. ES 1. Paris: Geuthner.

Briquel-Chatonnet, Françoise, Muriel Debié, and Alain Desreumaux, eds. 2004. *Les inscriptions syriaques*. ES 1. Paris: Geuthner.

Brock, Sebastian P. 1968. Review of *Zur Märtyrerüberlieferung aus der Christenverfolgung Schapurs II*, by Gernot Wiessner. *JTS*, NS 19:300–309.

———. 1978. "A Martyr at the Sasanid Court under Vahran II: Candida." AnBoll 96:167–81.

———. 1981–1982. "A Syriac Life of John of Dailam." *ParOr* 10:123–90.

———. 1982. "Christians in the Sasanian Empire: A Case of Divided Royalties." In *Religion and National Identity: Papers Read at the Nineteenth Summer Meeting and the Twentieth Winter Meeting of the Ecclesiastical History Society*, ed. Stewart Mews, 1–19. SCH 18. Oxford: Blackwell.

———. 1990. *Saint Ephrem the Syrian: Hymns on Paradise*. Crestwood, NY: St. Vladimir's Seminary Press.

———. 1992. "Eusebius and Syriac Christianity." In *Eusebius, Christianity, and Judaism*, edited by Harold W. Attridge and Gohei Hata, 212–34. Detroit: Wayne State University Press.

———. 1995. "Bar Shabba/Mar Shabbay: First Bishop of Merv." In *Syrisches Christentum weltweit: Studien zur syrischen Kirchengeschichte; Festschrift Prof. Hage*, edited by Martin Tamcke, Wolfgang Schwaigert, and Egbert Schlarb, 190–201. SOK 1. Münster: LIT.

———. 1996a. "The 'Nestorian Church': A Lamentable Misnomer." In *The Church of the East: Life and Thought*, edited by J. F. Coakley and Ken Parry, special issue, *BJRL* 78 (3): 23–35. Manchester, UK: John Rylands University Library of Manchester.

———. 1996b. *Syriac Studies: A Classified Bibliography, 1960–1990*. Kaslik, Lebanon: Université Saint-Esprit de Kaslik.

Brock, Sebastian P., and Susan Ashbrook Harvey, trans. 1987. *Holy Women of the Syrian Orient*. TCH 13. Berkeley: University of California Press.

Brook, Kevin A. 2006. *The Jews of Khazaria*. 2nd ed. Lanham, MD: Rowman & Littlefield.

Brooten, Bernadette. 2000. "The Jews of Ancient Antioch." In *Antioch: The Lost Ancient City*, edited by Christine Kondoleon, 29–37. Princeton, NJ: Princeton University Press.

Brouquier-Reddé, Véronique. 1992. *Temples et cultes de Tripolitaine*. EAA. Paris: Éditions du Centre National de la Recherche Scientifique.

Brown, L. W. 1956. *The Indian Christians of St. Thomas*. Cambridge: Cambridge University Press.

Brown, Peter. 1998. "Christianization and Religious Conflict." CAH 13:632–64.

———. 2003. *The Rise of Western Christendom: Triumph and Diversity, A.D. 200–1000*. Malden, MA: Blackwell.

Brown, Raymond E., and John P. Meier. 1983. *Antioch and Rome: New Testament Cradles of Catholic Christianity*. New York: Paulist Press.

Browning, Ian. 1982. *Jerash and the Decapolis*. London: Chatto & Windus.

Bruneau, Philippe. 1963. "La Synagogue Juive de Délos." *BCH* 87:873–75.

———. 1982. "Les Israélites de Délos et la Juiverie Délienne." *BCH* 106:465–504.

Bruns, Peter. 1991. *Unterweisungen: Aphrahat*. 2 vols. FC 5/1–2. Freiburg im Breisgau: Herder.

———. 2000. "Ephraem the Syrian." *DECL* 195–99.

486   References

Brusin, Giovanni, and Paulo L. Zovatto. 1957. *Monumenti paleocristiani di Aquileia e di Grado*. Udine: Deputazione di storia patria per il Fruili.

Budge, E. A. Wallis, ed. and trans. 1893. *The Book of Governors: The Historia Monastica of Thomas, Bishop of Marga, A.D. 840*. 2 vols. London: Paul, Trench, Trübner.

———, trans. 1928. *The Monks of Kublai Khan, Emperor of China*. London: Religious Tract Society.

———, trans. 1976. *The Chronography of Gregory Abu'l-Faraj*. 2 vols. London: Oxford University Press, 1932. Reprint, Amsterdam: Philo.

Bundy, David. 1989–1990. "*The Life of Abercius*: Its Significance for Early Syriac Christianity." *SecCent* 7:163–76.

Burckhardt, Jacob. 1990. *Die Zeit Constantins des Grossen*. Kettwig: Athenaion.

Burns, J. Patout. 2002. *Cyprian the Bishop*. London: Routledge.

Burns, J. Patout, and Robin M. Jensen, in collaboration with Graeme W. Clarke, Susan T. Stevens, William Tabbernee, and Maureen A. Tilley. 2014. *Christianity in Roman Africa: The Development of its Practices and Beliefs*. Grand Rapids: Eerdmans.

Burns, Ross. 1994. *The Monuments of Syria: A Guide*. London: Tauris.

Burrell, Barbara. 2004. *Neokoroi: Greek Cities and Roman Emperors*. Cincinnati Classical Studies. Leiden: Brill.

Burton, Anne. 1972. *Diodorus Siculus, Book I: A Commentary*. EPROER 29. Leiden: Brill.

Bury, John B. 1905. *The Life of St. Patrick and His Place in History*. London: Macmillan.

Butler, Howard C. 1969. *Early Churches in Syria: Fourth to Seventh Centuries*. Edited and completed by E. Baldwin Smith. Princeton, NJ: Department of Art and Archaeology of Princeton University, 1929. PMAA 1. Reprint, Amsterdam: Hakkert.

Cabrol, Fernand, and Henri Leclerq, eds. 1907–1953. *Dictionnaire d'archéologie chrétiennes et de liturgie*. 15 vols. Paris: Letouzey et Ané. [Abbr.: *DACL*]

Caillet, Jean-Pierre. 1993. *L'évergétisme monumental chrétien en Italie et à ses marges: D'après l'épigraphie des pavements de mosaïque (IVᵉ–VIIᵉ s)*. CEFR 175. Rome: École française de Rome.

———. 2005. "La réalité de l'implantation monumentale chrétienne au temps d'Augustin: L'example de quelques cités de Numidie." In *Saint Augustin: La Numidie et la société de son temps; Actes du colloque SEMPAN-AUSONIUS, Bordeaux, 10–11 octobre 2003*, edited by Serge Lancel, Stéphanie Guédon, and Louis Maurin, 55–66. Paris: de Boccard.

———. 2008. "Vie (et survie) des sanctuaries chrétiens du Maghreb: Le cas de la Maurétanie Césarienne." In *Lieux de cultes: Aires votives, temples, églises, mosquées; IXᵉ Colloque international sur l'histoire et l'archéologie de l'Afrique du Nord antique et médiéval, Tripoli, 19–25 février 2005*, 239–46. EAA. Paris: CNRS.

Caillet, Jean-Pierre, and Miroslav Jĕremić, eds. 2010. *L'acropole et ses monuments (cathédrales, baptistère et bâtiments annexes)*. Vol. 3 of *Caričin Grad*, edited by Noël Duval et al. CEFR 75/3. Rome: École française de Rome.

Calder, William M. 1922–1923. "Philadelphia and Montanism." *BJRL* 7:309–53.

———. 1923. "The Epigraphy of the Anatolian Heresies." In *Anatolian Studies Presented to Sir W. M. Ramsay*, edited by William M. Calder and Josef Keil, 59–91. Manchester, UK: Manchester University Press.

———. 1955. "Early Christian Epitaphs from Phrygia." *AnSt* 5:25–38.

Calder, William M., et al., eds. 1928–1993. *Monumenta Asiae Minoris*. Vols. 1–8. Manchester, UK: Manchester University Press. Vols. 9–10. London: Society for the Promotion of Roman Studies. [Abbr.: *MAMA*]

Calderini, Aristide, and Sergio Daris, eds. 1935–. *Dizionario dei nomi geografici e topografici dell'Egitto greco-romano*. 5 vols. with supplements. Cairo: Società reale di geografia d'Egitto.

Cameron, Averil. 1981. "The Sceptic and the Shroud: An Inaugural Lecture in the Departments of Classics and History Delivered at King's College London on 29th April 1980." In *Continuity and Change in Sixth Century Byzantium*, article V. VCSS 143. London: Variorum Reprints.

———. 1993. *The Late Roman Empire (284–430)*. Cambridge, MA: Harvard University Press.

Cameron, Averil, and Judith Herrin. 1984. *Constantinople in the Early Eighth Century: The Parastaseis syntomoi chronikai*. Series Columbia Studies in the Classical Tradition, 10. Leiden: Brill.

Caner, Daniel. 2002. *Wandering, Begging Monks: Spiritual Authority and the Promotion of Monasticism in Late Antiquity*. Berkeley: University of California Press.

Capponi, Livia. 2005. *Augustan Egypt*. London: Routledge.

Casson, Lionel. 1989. *The Periplus Maris Erythraei: Text with Introduction, Translation, and Commentary*. Princeton, NJ: Princeton University Press.

Casson, Lionel, and Ernest L. Hettisch, eds. and trans. 1950. *Excavations at Nessana: Literary Papyri*. Vol. 2. Princeton, NJ: Princeton University Press. [Abbr.: P.Ness. 2]

Cavadini, John C. 1997. "Lérins." *EEC*² 2:677–78.

Cecchelli, Carlo, Giuseppe Furlani, and Mario Salmi, eds. 1959. *The Rabbula Gospels: Facsimile Edition of the Miniatures of the Syriac Manuscript Plut. 1,56 in the Medicaean-Laurentian Library*. MO 1. Olton: Urs Graf.

Cereti, Carlo G., et al. 2002. "The Problem of the Saint Thomas Crosses and Related Questions: Epigraphical Survey and Preliminary Research." *EW* 52:285–310.

Charachidzé, Georges. 1968. *Le système religieux de la Géorgie païenne: Analyse structurale d'une civilization*. Paris: Maspero.

Chardron-Picault, Pascale, and Michel Pernot. 1999. *Un quartier antique d'artisanat métallurgique à Autun (Saône-et-Loire): Le site du Lycée militaire*. Paris: Maison des sciences de l'homme.

Charlesworth, James H. 1985a. "Odes of Solomon." *OTP* 2:725–71.

———, ed. 1985b. *The Old Testament Pseudepigrapha*. 2 vols. Garden City, NY: Doubleday. [Abbr.: *OTP*]

———, ed. 2006. *Jesus and Archaeology*. Grand Rapids: Eerdmans.

Chaumont, Marie-Louise. 1988. *La christianisation de l'Empire iranien: Des origines aux grandes persécutions du IVᵉ siècle*. CSCO 499. Louvain: Peeters.

Cherry, John F., Jack L. Davis, and Helene Mantzourane, eds. 1991. *Landscape Archaeology as Long-Term History: Northern Keos in the Cycladic Islands from Earliest Settlement until Modern Times*. Los Angeles: University of California at Los Angeles Institute of Archaeology.

Chevallier, Gabriel. 1958. *Lyon 2000*. Le quadrige d'Apollon. Paris: Presses universitaires de France.

Chevelier, Pascale. 1996. *Salona II,1–2: Ecclesiae Dalmatiae*. CEFR 194/1. Rome: École française de Rome.

Chin, Catherine M. 2006. "Rhetorical Practice in the Chreia Elaboration of Mara bar Serapion." *Hugoye* 9 (2): 145–71.

Chitty, D. J. 1966. *The Desert a City: An Introduction to the Study of Egyptian and Palestinian Monasticism under the Christian Empire*. Oxford: Blackwell.

Choat, Malcolm. 2002. "The Development and Use of Terms for 'Monk' in Late Antique Egypt." JAC 45:5–23.

———. 2006. *Belief and Cult in Fourth-Century Papyri*. SAAus 1. Turnhout: Brepols; Sydney: Ancient History Document Research Centre.

———. 2007. "Fourth-Century Monasticism in the Papyri." In *Akten des 23. Internationalen Papyrologenkongresses, Wien, 22.–28. Juli 2001*, edited by Bernhard Palme, 95–101. PV 1. Vienna: Verlag der Österreichischen Akademie der Wissenschaften.

———. 2012. "Christianity." In *The Oxford Handbook of Roman Egypt*, edited by Christina Riggs, 474–89. Oxford: Oxford University Press.

Christern, Jürgen. 1976. *Das frühchristliche Pilgerheiligtum von Tebessa: Architektur und Ornamentik einer spätantiken Bauhütte in Nordafrika*. Wiesbaden: Steiner.

Clancy, Thomas O. 2001. "The Real St. Ninian." *InnisR* 52:1–28.

Clarke, Graeme W. 1984–1989. *The Letters of St. Cyprian of Carthage*. 4 vols. ACW 43, 44, 46, 47. New York: Newman.

———. 1998. "Two Mid-Third Century Bishops: Cyprian of Carthage and Dionysius of Alexandria; Congruences and Divergences." In *Early Christianity, Late Antiquity, and Beyond*, edited by Thomas W. Hillard, 317–28. Vol. 2 of *Ancient History in a Modern University: Proceedings of a Conference Held at Macquarie University, 8–13 July 1993, to Mark Twenty-Five Years of the Teaching of Ancient History at Macquarie University and the Retirement from the Chair of Professor Edwin Judge*, edited by Thomas W. Hillard et al. Grand Rapids: Eerdmans.

———. 2005. "Third-Century Christianity." CAH 12:589–671.

Colless, B. 1986. "The Nestorian Province of Samarqand." *Abr-Nahrain* 24:51–57.

Collins, Adele Yarbro. 1998. "Pergamon in Early Christian Literature." In *Pergamon: Citadel of the Gods; Archaeological Record, Literary Description and Religious Development*, edited by Helmut Koester, 163–84. HTS 46. Harrisburg, PA: Trinity Press International.

———. 2006. "Satan's Throne: Revelations from Revelation." *BAR* 12:26–39.

Cooper-Marsdin, Arthur. 1913. *The History of the Islands of the Lérins: The Monastery, Saints and Theologians of St. Honorat*. Cambridge: Cambridge University Press.

Corda, Antonio M. 1999. "Iconografia e simbolismo nelle iscrizioni paleocristiane della Sardegna." In *La Sardegna paleocristiana tra Eusebio e Gregorio Magno: Atti del convegno nazionale di studi, Cagliari, 10–12 ottobre 1996*, edited by Attilo Mastino, Giovanna Sotgiu, and Natalino Spaccapelo, 49–64. SRCR, NS 1. Cagliari: Pontificia facoltà teologica della Sardegna.

Cormack, Robin, and Maria Vassilaki, eds. 2008. *Byzantium 330–1453*. London: Royal Academy of Arts.

Cornell, Tim, and John Matthews. 1982. *Atlas of the Roman World*. Oxford: Phaidon.

Cragg, Kenneth. 1991. *The Arab Christian: A History in the Middle East*. Louisville: Westminster John Knox.

Crouch, Marcus. 1970. *Canterbury*. London: Longman Young.

Crowe, S. Peter. 2011. "Armenian Hagiography." In *Periods and Places*, edited by Stephanos Efthymiadis, 299–322. Vol. 1 of *The Ashgate Research Companion to Byzantine Hagiography*. Farnham, UK: Ashgate.

Crum, Walter E. 1934. "Un psaume en dialecte d'Akhmim." In *Orient grec, romain, et byzantin*, 73–76. Vol. 2 of *Mélanges Maspero*. Cairo: Institut français d'archéologie orientale.

Cugusi, Paolo. 1992. *Corpus epistolarum latinarum: Papyris tabulis ostracis servatarum (CEL)*. 2 vols. PF 23/1–2. Florence: Gonnelli.

Ćurčić, Slobodan. 2010. *Architecture in the Balkans from Diocletian to Suleyman the Magnificent*. New Haven: Yale University Press.

Cureton, William. 1965. *Spicilegium Syriacum: Containing Remains of Bardesan, Meliton, Ambrose, and Mara Bar Serapion*. London: Rivington, 1855. Reprint, Lexington, KY: American Theological Library Association.

Dagron, Gilbert. 1974. *Naissance d'une capitale: Constantinople et ses institutions de 330 à 451*. BBE 7. Paris: Presses universitaires de France.

———. 1984a. *Constantinople imaginaire: Études sur le recueil des Patria*. BBE 8. Paris: Presses universitaires de France.

———. 1984b. "Les villes dans l'Illyricum protobyzantin." In *Villes et peuplement dans l'Illyricum protobyzantin: Actes du colloque organisé par l'École française de Rome (Rome, 12–14 mai 1982)*, 1–20. CEFR 77. Rome: École française de Rome.

———. 1996. *Empereur et prêtre: Étude sur le "césaropapisme" byzantin*. Paris: Éditions Gallimard.

Dahari, Uri. 2000. *Monastic Settlements in South Sinai in the Byzantine Period: The Archaeological Remains*. Jerusalem: Israel Antiquities Authority.

Dann, Rachael J. 2009. *The Archaeology of Late Antique Sudan: Aesthetics and Identity in the Royal X-Group Tombs at Qustul and Ballana*. Amherst, NY: Cambria.

Danov, Christo. 1979. "Philippopolis, Serdica, Odessos: Zur Geschichte und Kultur der bedeutendsten Städte Thrakiens von Alexander d.Gr. bis Justinians." *ANRW* II.7.1:241–300.

Dar, Shimon. 1993. *Settlements and Cult Sites on Mount Hermon, Israel: Ituraean Culture in the Hellenistic and Roman Periods*. Translated by M. Erez. BARIS 589. Oxford: Tempus Reparatum.

Darmon, Jean-Pierre. 1994. "Les mosaïques de la synagogue de Hammam Lif: Un reexamen du dossier." In *Acts of the Fifth International Colloquium on Ancient Mosaics Held at Bath, England, on September 5–12, 1987*, edited by Roger Ling, 7–30. JRASup 9. Ann Arbor, MI: Journal of Roman Archaeology.

Dauvillier, Jean 1948. "Les provinces chaldéennes 'de l'extérieur' au Moyen Age." In *Mélanges offerts au R. P. Ferdinand Cavallera, doyen de la faculté de théologie de Toulouse à l'occasion de la quarantième année de son professorat à l'Institut catholique*, 260–316. Toulouse: Bibliothèque de l'Institut Catholique.

Davies, John G. 1968. *The Secular Use of Church Buildings*. New York: Seabury.

Davies, Wendy. 1992. "The Myth of the Celtic Church." In *The Early Church in Wales and the West: Recent Work in Early Christian Archaeology, History and Place-Names*, edited by Nancy Edwards and Alan Lane, 12–21. OM 16. Oxford: Oxbow.

Davis, Stephen J. 1999. "Namesakes of Saint Thekla in Late Antique Egypt." *BASP* 36:71–81.

———. 2004. *The Early Coptic Papacy: The Egyptian Church and Its Leadership in Late Antiquity*. Cairo: American University in Cairo Press.

———. 2005. "Biblical Interpretation and Alexandria: Episcopal Authority in the Early Christian Fayum." In *Christianity and Monasticism in the Fayoum Oasis*, edited by G. Gabra, 45–61. Cairo: American University in Cairo Press.

Dawes, Elizabeth A. S., and Norman H. Baynes, trans. 1977. *Three Byzantine Saints: Contemporary Biographies*. Oxford: Clarendon, 1948. Reprint, Crestwood, NY: St. Vladimir's Seminary Press.

Debié, Muriel, et al., eds. 2005. *Les apocryphes syriaques*. ES 2. Paris: Geuthner.

de Blois, François. 2002. "*Nasrani* (Nazwraios) and *Hanif* (Ethnikos): Studies on the Religious Vocabulary of Christianity and Islam." *BSOAS* 65:1–30.

Decret, F. 1979. "Les conséquences sur le christianisme en Perse de l'affrontement des empires romain et sassanide: De Shapur Iᵉʳ à Yazdgard Iᵉʳ." *RAug* 14:91–152.

Deeg, M. 2006. "Towards a New Translation of the Chinese Nestorian Documents from the Tang Dynasty." In *Jingjiao: The Church of the East in China and Central Asia*, edited by Roman Malek and Peter Hofrichter, 115–31. CS. Sankt Augustin: Institut Monumenta Serica.

Delattre, Alfred-Louis. 1907a. "Inscriptions chrétiennes de Carthage." *RT* 14:405–19.

———. 1907b. "Lettre du R. P. Delattre à M. Héron de Ville fosse sur l'inscription des martyrs de Carthage, Sainte Perpétue, Sainte Félicité et leur companions." CRAI, 5th series, 8:193–95.

———. 1908. "La basilica majorum." CRAI, 5th series, 9:59–69.

Delehaye, Hippolyte, ed. 1902. *Synaxarium ecclesiae Constantinopolitanae e codice Sirmondiano nunc Berolinensi*. Brussels: Société des Bollandistes.

Deliyannis, Deborah M., ed. 2006. *Agnelli Ravennatis: Liber pontificalis ecclesiae Ravennatis*. CCCM 199. Turnhout: Brepols.

———. 2010. *Ravenna in Late Antiquity*. Cambridge: Cambridge University Press.

Demandt, Alexander. 1989. *Die Spätantike: Römische Geschichte von Diocletian bis Justinian 284–565 n. Chr.* Munich: Beck.

Demougeot, E. 1947. "Les partages de l'Illyricum à la fin du IVe siècle." *RH* 197:16–31.

———. 1950. "A propos des partages de l'Illyricum en 386–387." In vol. 1 of *Actes du VIe congrès international des Études byzantines, Paris, 27 juillet–2 aout 1948*, 87–92. Paris: École des hautes études, à la Sorbonne.

———. 1981. "Le partage des provinces de l'Illyricum entre la pars orientalis et la pars occidentalis de la Tétrarchie au règne de Théodoric." In *La géographie administrative et politique d'Alexandre à Mahomed: Actes du colloque de Strasbourg, 14–16 juin 1979*, 229–53. TCRPOGA 6. Leiden: Brill.

De Paor, Márie, and Liam De Paor. 1958. *Early Christian Ireland*. APP 8. London: Thames & Hudson.

Depuydt, Leo. 1993. *Catalogue of Coptic Manuscripts in the Pierpont Morgan Library*. 2 vols. CIMOS 1, 2. Louvain: Peeters.

de Rachewiltz, Igor, trans. 2006. *The Secret History of the Mongols: A Mongolian Epic Chronicle of the Thirteenth Century*. 2 vols. BIAL 7. Leiden: Brill.

Desbat, Armand, and Stephen Walker. 1981. "Le probleme des origins de Lyon." In *Récentes recherches en archéologie gallo-romaine et paléochrétienne sur Lyon et sa région*, edited by Stephen Walker, 29–54. BARIS 108. Oxford: Archaeopress.

Desanges, Jehan, Noël Duval, Claude Lepelley, and Sophie Saint-Amans, eds. 2010. *Carte des routes et des cités de l'est de l' 'Africa' à la fin de l'Antiquité: Nouvelle édition des 'Voies romaines de l'Afrique du Nord' conçue en 1949, d'après les tracés de Pierre Salama*. BAT 17. Turnhout: Brepols.

Desreumaux, Alain, Andrew Palmer, and Robert Beylot. 1993. *Histoire du roi Abgar et de Jésus*. Apocryphes 3. Paris: Brepols.

de Vos, Mariette. 2003. "Documentation archéologique à Hippone (Hippo Regius)." In *Augustinus Afer: Saint Augustin, africanité et universalité; Actes du colloque international, Alger-Annaba, 1–7 avril 2001*, edited by Pierre-Yves Fux, Jean-Michel Roessli, and Otto Wermelinger, 401–11. 2 vols in 1. Paradosis 45. Fribourg: Éditions Universitaires Fribourg.

di Berardino, Angelo, ed. 1992. *Encyclopedia of the Early Church*. Translated by Adrian Walford. New York: Oxford University Press. [Abbr.: EECh]

di Cesnola, Luigi P. 1877. *Cyprus: Its Cities, Tombs and Temples; A Narrative of Researches and Excavations during Ten Years' Residence as American Consul on That Island*. London: Murray.

Dick, Ignace. 1994. *Les Melkites: Grecs-Orthodox et Grecs-Catholiques des patriarcats d'Antioche, d'Alexandrie et de Jérusalem*. Turnhout: Brepols.

Dickens, M. 2010. "Patriarch Timothy I and the Metropolitan of the Turks." *Journal of the Royal Asiatic Society* 20:117–39.

Diebner, Bernd, and Rodolphe Kasser, eds. 1989. *Hamburger Papyrus bil. 1: Die alttestamentlichen Texte des Papyrus bilinguis 1 der Staats- und Universitätsbibliothek Hamburg*. Geneva: Cramer.

Dieleman, Jacco. 2005. *Priests, Tongues, and Rites: The London-Leiden Magical Manuscripts and Translation in Egyptian Ritual (100–300 CE)*. RGRW 153. Leiden: Brill.

Dietmar, Carl, and Werner Jung. 2002. *Kleine illustrierte Geschichte der Stadt Köln*. Cologne: Bachem.

Di Gioia, Michele. 1984. "La diocesi di Arpi e il vescovo Pardo." *ArSP* 37:283–89.

Dihle, A. 1998. "Early Christianity in India." In *Early Christianity, Late Antiquity, and Beyond*, edited by Thomas W. Hillard, 305–16. Vol. 2 of *Ancient History in a Modern University: Proceedings of a Conference Held at Macquarie University, 8–13 July 1993, to Mark Twenty-Five Years of the Teaching of Ancient History at Macquarie University and the Retirement from the Chair of Professor Edwin Judge*, edited by Thomas W. Hillard et al. Grand Rapids: Eerdmans.

Dijkstra, Jitse H. F. 2008. *Philae and the End of Ancient Egyptian Religion: A Regional Study of Religious Transformation (298–642 CE)*. OLA 173. Louvain: Peeters.

———. 2011. "The Fate of the Temples in Late Antique Egypt." In *The Archaeology of Late Antique "Paganism,"* edited by Luke Lavan and Michael Mulryan, 389–436. LAA 7. Leiden: Brill.

———. 2012. "Blemmyes, Noubades, and the Eastern Desert in Late Antiquity: Reassessing the Written Sources." In *The History of the Peoples of the Eastern Desert*, edited by Hans Barnard and Kim Duistermaat, 238–47. Los Angeles: Cotsen Institute of Archaeology.

Dillemann, Louis. 1962. *Haute Mésopotamie et pays adjacents: Contribution à la géographie historique de la région*. Paris: Geuthner.

Dintchev, Ventzislav. 2009. "The Antique Towns' Square Complexes and Their Fate in Late Antiquity." In *LAURA: In honorem Margaritae Vaklinova*, 63–80. Sofia: The National Archaeological Institute.

Di Segni, Leah. 1990. "Horvath Hesheq: The Inscriptions." In *Christian Archaeology in the Holy Land: New Discoveries; Essays in Honour of Virgilio C. Corbo, OFM*, edited by G. C. Bottini, L. Di Segni, and E. Alliata, 351–90. Jerusalem: Franciscan Printing Press.

Divjak, Johannes. 1987. *Lettres 1*–29**. Vol. 46B of *Œuvres de Saint Augustin*. BAug. Paris: Études augustiniennes. [Abbr.: Augustine of Hippo, *Ep.**]

Dodge, Bayard, ed. and trans. 1970. *The Fihrist of al-Nadīm: A Tenth-Century Survey of Muslim Culture*. 2 vols. RCSS 83. New York: Columbia University Press.

Dodgeon, Michael H., and Samuel N. C. Lieu. 1994. *The Roman Eastern Frontier and the Persian Wars (AD 226–363): A Documentary History*. London: Routledge.

Dolbeau, François. 1996. *Vingt-six sermons au peuple d'Afrique*. CEASA 147. Paris: Institut d'Études augustiniennes.

Donaldson, Terence L., ed. 2000. *Religious Rivalries and the Struggle for Success in Caesarea Maritima*. SCJ 8. Waterloo, ON: Wilfrid Laurier University Press.

Döpp, Siegmar, and Wilhelm Geerlings, eds. 2000. *Dictionary of Early Christian Literature*. New York: Crossroad. [Abbr.: *DECL*]

Doran, Robert. 2006. *Stewards of the Poor: The Man of God, Rabbula, and Hiba in Fifth-Century Edessa*. CSS 208. Kalamazoo, MI: Cistercian Publications.

Dorival, Gilles. 1999. "Les débuts du christianisme à Alexandrie." In *Alexandrie: Une mégapole cosmopolite; Actes du 9ème colloque de la Villa Kérylos à Beaulieu-sur-Mer, les 2 & 3 octobre 1998*, edited by Jean Leclant, 157–74. Paris: Académie des Inscriptions et Belles-Lettres.

Dosseva, Iva. 2000. "Early Byzantine Chancel Screens in Thrace and Dacia" (in Bulgarian). *Problemi na izkustvoto/Art Studies Quarterly* (Sofia) 3:9–18.

———. 2011. "Early Byzantine Ambos on the Territory of Contemporary Bulgaria: Samples and Adaptions" (in Bulgarian). In *Studies in Honor of Stefan Boyadzhiev*, edited by Stanislav Stanev, Valeri Grigorov, and Vladimir Dimitrov, 139–60. Sofia: The National Archaeological Institute.

Downey, Glanville. 1957. "Description of the Church of the Holy Apostles at Constantinople." *TAPA*, NS 47:857–924.

Drack, Walter, and Rudolf Fellmann. 1988. *Die Römer in der Schweiz*. Stuttgart: Theiss.

Drew-Bear, Thomas. 1981. "Les voyages d'Aurélius Gaius, soldat de Dioclétien." In *La géographie administrative et politique d'Alexandre à Mahomet: Actes du colloque de Strasbourg, 14–16 juin 1979*, edited by Toufic Fahd, 93–141. TCRPOGA 6. Leiden: Brill.

Drijvers, H. J. W. 1965. *The Book of the Laws of Countries: Dialogue on Fate of Bardaisan of Edessa*. STT 3. Assen: Van Gorcum.

Drijvers, Jan W. 1992. *Helena Augusta: The Mother of Constantine the Great and the Legend of Her Finding of the True Cross*. BSIH 27. Leiden: Brill.

———. 1997. "The Protonike Legend, the Doctrina Addai, and Bishop Rabbula of Edessa." *VC* 51:298–315.

Drijvers, Jan W., and John F. Healey. 1999. *The Old Syriac Inscriptions of Edessa and Oshroene: Texts, Translations, and Commentary*. HO 1/42. Leiden: Brill.

Driver, Godfrey R., and Leonard Hodgson, trans. 2002. *The Bazaar of Heracleides*. Oxford: Clarendon, 1925. Reprint, Eugene, OR: Wipf & Stock.

Duchesne, Louis. 1879. "Inscription chrétienne de Tanagre." *BCH* 3:144–46.

Duckett, Eleanor S. 1947. *Anglo-Saxon Saints and Scholars*. New York: Macmillan.

Dunbabin, Katherine. 1978. *The Mosaics of Roman North Africa: Studies in Iconography and Patronage*. Oxford: Clarendon.

Dunderberg, Ismo. 2005. "The School of Valentinus." In *A Companion to Second-Century Christian "Heretics,"* edited by Antti Marjanan and Petri Luomanen, 64–99. VCSup 76. Leiden: Brill.

Dunn, Geoffrey D. 2002. "The Carthaginian Synod of 251: Cyprian's Model of Pastoral Ministry." In *I concili della cristianità occidentale secoli III–V: XXX Incontro di studiosi dell'antichità cristiana, Roma, 3–5 maggio 2001*, 235–57. SEAug 78. Rome: Institutum Patristicum Augustinianum.

———. 2004. *Tertullian*. The Early Church Fathers. London: Routledge.

———. 2007. *Cyprian and the Bishops of Rome: Questions of Primal Papacy in the Early Church*. ECS 11. Strathfield, NSW: St. Pauls.

———. 2008. *Tertullian's Aduersus Iudaeos: A Rhetorical Analysis*. PMS 19. Washington, DC: Catholic University of America Press.

Durkin-Meisterernst, Desmond. 2006. "The Pahlavi Psalter Fragment in Relation to Its Source." *SIAL* 21:1–19.

Duval, Noël. 1972. "Études d'architecture chrétienne nord-africaine." *MEFRA* 84:1072–125.

———. 1990. "Chronique d'antiquité tardive et de christianisme ancien et medieval." *REA* 92:347–87.

———. 1993. "Vingt ans de recherches archéologiques sur l'antiquité tardive en Afrique du Nord, 1975–1993." *REA* 95:583–640.

———. 1997. "L'État actuel des recherches archéologiques sur Carthage chrétienne." *AT* 5:309–50.

Duval, Noël, and Vladislav Popović. 1980. "Urbanisme et topographie chrétienne dans les provinces septentrionales de l'Illyricum." In *Rapports présentés au Xe Congrès international d'archéologie chrétienne, Thessalonique, 28 septembre–4 octobre 1980*, 369–402. Thessalonikē: Société d'études macédoniennes.

———. 1984. *Les basiliques B et J de Caričin Grad*. Vol. 1 of *Caričin Grad*, edited by Noël Duval et al. CEFR 75. Rome: École française de Rome.

Duval, Yvette. 1982. *Loca sanctorum Africae: Le culte des martyrs en Afrique du IVe au VIIe siècle*. 2 vols. CEFR 58. Rome: École française de Rome.

———. 1984. "Densité et repartition des évêchés dans les provinces africaines au temps de Cyprien." *MEFRA* 96:493–521.

———. 1988. *Auprès des saints, corps et âme: L'inhumation "ad sanctos" dans la chrétienté d'Orient et d'Occident du IIIe au VIIe siècle*. Paris: Études augustiniennes.

———. 1995a. "L'Afrique: Aurelius et Augustin." In *Naissance d'une chrétienté (250–430)*, edited by Charles and Luce Pietri, 799–812. Vol. 2 of *Histoire du christianisme*. Paris: Desclée.

———. 1995b. "L'Église d'Afrique au IIIe siècle." In *Naissance d'une chrétienté (250–430)*, edited by Charles and Luce Pietri, 127–33. Vol. 2 of *Histoire du christianisme* Paris: Desclée.

————. 2000. *Chrétiens d'Afrique à l'aube de la paix constantinienne: Les premiers échos de la grande persecution*. CEASA 164. Paris: Institut d'Études augustiniennes.

————. 2003. "Sur les conciles africains antérieurs à Cyprien." *REAug* 49:239–51.

————. 2005. *Les chrétientés d'Occident et leur évêque au IIIe siècle: "Plebs in ecclesia constituta"(Cyprien, Ep. 63)*. CEASA 176. Paris: Institut d'Études augustiniennes.

Dyck, Jonathan. 2002. "Philo, Alexandria and Empire: The Politics of Allegorical Interpretation." In *Jews in the Hellenistic and Roman Cities*, edited by J. R. Bartlett, 149–74. London: Routledge.

Ebersolt, Jean, and Adolphe Thiers. 1913. *Les églises de Constantinople*. MAB 3. Paris: Leroux.

Edgington, Sue B. 1985. *The Life and Miracles of St. Ivo*. St. Ives: Friends of the Norris Museum.

Edwards, David N. 2001. "The Christianisation of Nubia: Some Archaeological Pointers." *Sudan & Nubia* 5:89–96.

————. 2004. *The Nubian Past: An Archaeology of the Sudan*. London: Routledge.

Edwards, Mark J., ed. and trans. 1997. *Optatus: Against the Donatists*. TTH 27. Liverpool: Liverpool University Press.

Edwell, Peter. 2008. *Between Rome and Persia: The Middle Euphrates, Mesopotamia, and Palmyra under Roman Control*. RMCS. London: Routledge.

Eide, Tormod, T. Hägg, R. H. Pierce, and László Török, eds. 1998. *From the First to the Sixth Century AD*. Vol. 3 of *Fontes Historiae Nubiorum: Textual Sources for the History of the Middle Nile Region between the Eighth Century BC and the Sixth Century AD*. Bergen: University of Bergen.

Eisen, Ute E. 2000. *Women Officeholders in Early Christianity: Epigraphical and Literary Studies*. Translated by Linda M. Maloney. Collegeville, MN: Liturgical Press.

Elishē'. 1982. *History of Vardan and the Armenian War*. Translation and Commentary by R. W. Thomson. HATS. Cambridge, MA: Harvard University Press.

Elliott, John H. 2000. *1 Peter: A New Translation with Introduction and Commentary*. AB 37B. New York: Doubleday.

Elm, Susanna. 1994. *Virgins of God: The Making of Asceticism in Late Antiquity*. Oxford: Oxford University Press.

Emerson, W. 1946. "The Basilica of Belovo." *BBI* 1:43–59.

Emmel, Stephen. 2004. *Shenoute's Literary Corpus*. 2 vols. CSCO 599, 600. Louvain: Peeters.

————. 2005. "The Library of the Monastery of the Archangel Michael at Phantoou (al-Hamuli)." In *Christianity and Monasticism in the Fayoum Oasis: Essays from the 2004 International Symposium of the Saint Mark Foundation and the Saint Shenouda the Archimandrite Coptic Society in Honor of Martin Krause*, edited by Gawdat Gabra, 63–70. Cairo: American University in Cairo Press.

Ennabli, Liliane. 1972. *Les inscriptions funéraires chrétiennes de Carthage. I: De la basilique dite de Sainte Monique à Carthage*. CEFR 25. Rome: École française de Rome.

————. 1997. *Carthage: Une métropole chrétienne du IV siècle à la fin du VIIe siècle*. EAA. Paris: Éditions du Centre National de la Recherche Scientifique.

Epstein, A. 1982. "The Rebuilding and Redecoration of the Holy Apostles in Constantinople: Reconsideration." *GRBS* 23:79–92.

Eshel, Hanan. 2006. "The Bar Kochba Revolt, 132–135." *CHJ* 4:105–27.

Eshel, Hanan, Peter Richardson, and Yitshak Jamitowsky. Forthcoming. "Josephus' Judea, Samaria, and Perea in Archeological Perspective." In *Judean War 1*, appendix A. Vol. 1A of *Flavius Josephus: Translation and Commentary*, edited by Steve Mason. Leiden: Brill.

Evelyn-White, Hugh G. 1932. *The History of the Monasteries of Nitria and of Scetis*. Part 2 of *The Monasteries of Wâdi 'n Natrûn*, edited by Hugh G. Evelyn-White and Walter Hauser. PMMAEE 7. New York: Metropolitan Museum of Art.

———. 1933. *The Architecture and Archaeology*. Part 3 of *The Monasteries of Wâdi 'n Natrûn*, edited by Hugh G. Evelyn-White and Walter Hauser. PMMAEE 8. New York: Metropolitan Museum of Art.

Evetts, B., ed. and trans. 1904. *Sawirus ibn al-Muqaffa: History of the Patriarchs of the Coptic Church of Alexandria (S. Mark to Benjamin I)*. PO 1. Paris: Firmin-Didot.

Fairley, William. 1900. *Notitia Dignitatum or Register of Dignitaries*. Translations and Reprints from Original Sources of European History 6/4. Philadelphia: Department of History of the University of Pennsylvania.

Falivene, Maria R. 1998. *The Herakleopolite Nome: A Catalogue of the Toponyms, with Introduction and Commentary*. ASP 37. Atlanta: Scholars Press.

Féghali, Paul, and Claude Navarre, trans. 1989. *Saint Ephrem: Les chants de Nisibe*. AC 3. Paris: Cariscript.

Feissel, Denis. 1983. *Recueil des inscriptions chrétiennes de Macédoine du IIIe au VIe siècle*. BCH Supplément 8. École française d'Athènes.

Feltoe, Charles L. 1918. *St. Dionysius of Alexandria: Letters and Treatises*. London: Society for Promoting Christian Knowledge.

Ferguson, Everett, Michael P. McHugh, and Frederick W. Norris, eds. 1990. *Encyclopedia of Early Christianity*. 2nd ed. 2 vols. Garland Reference Library of the Humanities 1839. New York: Garland. [Abbr.: *EEC²*]

Février, Paul-Albert. 1986. "Aux origènes du christianisme en Maurétanie Césarienne." *MEFRA* 98:767–804.

Fiema, Zbigniew T. 2003. "The Byzantine Church at Petra." In *Petra Rediscovered: Lost City of the Nabataeans*, edited by Glenn Markoe, 239–49. New York: Harry N. Abrams, with the Cincinnati Art Museum.

Fiensy, David A., and David R. Darnell. 1985. "Hellenistic Synagogal Prayers." *OTP* 2:671–97.

Fiey, Jean-Maurice. 1964. "Vers la réhabilitation de l'*Histoire de Karka d'Bét Slōḥ*." AnBoll 82:189–222.

———. 1965–1968. *Assyrie chrétienne: Contribution à l'étude de l'histoire et de la géographie ecclésiastiques et monastiques du nord de l'Iraq*. 3 vols. Recherches publiées sous la direction de l'Institute de lettres orientales de Beyrouth 22, 23, 42. Beirut: Imprimerie Catholique.

———. 1970. *Jalons pour une histoire de l'Église en Iraq*. CSCO 310. Louvain: Secrétariat du Corpus scriptorum christianorum orientalium.

———. 1975. "Iconographie syriaque: Hulagu, Doquz Khatun et six ambons?" *Le muséon* 88:59–68.

———. 1977. *Nisibe, métropole syriaque orientale et ses suffragants des origines à nos jours*. CSCO 388. Louvain: Secrétariat du Corpus scriptorum christianorum orientalium.

Figueras, P. 1995. "Monks and Monasteries in the Negev Desert." *LASBF* 45:401–50.

Filov, Bogdan. 1913. *Sofiiskata tsurkva Sv. Sofii* [*The St. Sophia Church in Sofia*] (in Bulgarian). MIS 4. Sofia: Sofia Archaeological Society.

————. 1933. *Sofiiskata tsurkva Sv. Georgi* [*The St. George Church in Sofia*] (in Bulgarian). MIS 7. Sofia: Bulgarian Archaeological Institute.

Finegan, Jack. 1992. *The Archeology of the New Testament: The Life of Jesus and the Beginning of the Early Church.* Rev. ed. Princeton, NJ: Princeton University Press.

Fingarova, Galina. 2011. *Die Baugeschichte der Sophienkirche in Sofia.* Spätantike – Frühes Christentum – Byzanz 33. Wiesbaden: Reichert Verlag.

Finley, Moses I. 1973. *The Ancient Economy.* Berkeley: University of California Press.

Fishwick, Duncan. 1964. "On the Origin of the ROTAS-SATOR Square." *HTR* 57:39–53.

Foss, Clive. 1987. "St. Autonomous and His Church in Bithynia." *DOP* 41:187–98.

————. 2000. "Late Antique Antioch." In *Antioch: The Lost Ancient City*, edited by Christine Kondoleon, 23–28. Princeton, NJ: Princeton University Press.

Fowden, Elizabeth K. 1999. *The Barbarian Plain: Saint Sergius between Rome and Iran.* TCH 28. Berkeley: University of California Press.

Fowden, Garth. 1998. "Polytheist Religion and Philosophy." CAH 13:538–60.

Franceschini, Aetio, and Robert Weber, eds. 1965. *Itineraria et alia geographica.* CCSL 175. Turnhout: Brepols.

Frankel, Rafael, et al. 2001. *Settlement Dynamics and Regional Diversity in Ancient Upper Galilee: Archaeological Survey of Upper Galilee.* IAAR 14. Jerusalem: Israel Antiquities Authority.

Frankfurter, David. 1993. *Elijah in Upper Egypt: The Apocalypse of Elijah and Early Egyptian Christianity.* Minneapolis: Fortress.

————. 1998. *Religion in Roman Egypt: Assimilation and Resistance.* Princeton, NJ: Princeton University Press.

————. 2005. "Beyond Magic and Superstition." In *Late Ancient Christianity*, edited by Virginia Burrus, 255–84. PHC 2. Minneapolis: Fortress.

Frantz, Alison. 1965. "From Paganism to Christianity in the Temples of Athens." *DOP* 19:185–205.

Frantz, Alison, Homer A. Thompson, and Ioannes N. Travlos. 1988. *Late Antiquity, A.D. 267–700.* AA 24. Princeton, NJ: American School of Classical Studies at Athens.

Frazier, Nancy. 1999. *The Penguin Concise Dictionary of Art History.* New York: Penguin.

Freeman-Grenville, G. S. P., Rupert L. Chapman, and Joan E. Taylor. 2003. *Palestine in the Fourth Century A.D.: The Onomasticon by Eusebius of Caesarea.* Jerusalem: Carta.

Frend, W. H. C. 1971. *The Donatist Church: A Movement of Protest in Roman North Africa.* Oxford: Clarendon.

————. 1972. *The Rise of the Monophysite Movement: Chapters in the History of the Church in the Fifth and Sixth Centuries.* Cambridge: Cambridge University Press.

————. 1975. "The Christian Period in Mediterranean Africa, c. AD 200 to 700." In *From the Earliest Times to 500 B.C.*, edited by J. Desmond Clark, 410–89. Vol. 1 of *The Cambridge History of Africa*, edited by J. D. Fage and R. A. Anthony. Cambridge: Cambridge University Press.

————. 1977. "The Early Christian Church in Carthage." In vol. 3 of *Excavations at Carthage 1976, Conducted by the University of Michigan*, edited by John H. Humphrey, 21–35. Ann Arbor: Kelsey Museum of the University of Michigan.

————. 1981. *Martyrdom and Persecution in the Early Church: A Study of a Conflict from the Maccabees to Donatus.* Oxford: Blackwell, 1965. Reprint, Grand Rapids: Baker.

———. 1982. "The North African Cult of Martyrs: From Apocalyptic to Hero-Worship." In *Jenseitsvorstellungen in Antike und Christentum: Gedenkschrift für Alfred Stuiber*, edited by Theodor Klauser, Ernst Dassmann, and Klaus Thraede, 154–67. JACE 9. Münster: Aschendorffsche Verlagsbuchhandlung.

———. 1984. *The Rise of Christianity*. Philadelphia: Fortress.

———. 1988. "Montanism: A Movement of Prophecy and Regional Identity in the Early Church." *BJRL* 70:25–34.

———. 1996. *The Archaeology of Early Christianity: A History*. Minneapolis: Fortress.

———. 1997. "'*Donatus paene totam Africam decepit.*' How?" *JEH* 48: 611–27.

———. 2004. "From Donatist Opposition to Byzantine Loyalism: The Cult of Martyrs in North Africa, 350–650." In *Vandals, Romans, and Berbers: New Perspectives on Late Antique North Africa*, edited by A. H. Merrills, 259–69. Aldershot, UK: Ashgate.

———. 2006. "Persecutions: Genesis and Legacy." In *Origins to Constantine*, edited by Margaret M. Mitchell, Frances M. Young, and K. Scott Bowie, 503–23. Vol. 1 of *The Cambridge History of Christianity*, edited by Margaret M. Mitchell et al. Cambridge: Cambridge University Press.

Friesen, Stephen J. 1993. *Twice Neokoros: Ephesos, Asia and the Cult of the Flavian Imperial Family*. RGRW 116. Leiden: Brill.

———. 2001. *Imperial Cults and the Apocalypse of John: Reading Revelation in the Ruins*. Oxford: Oxford University Press.

———. 2005. "Prospects for a Demography of the Pauline Mission." In *Urban Religion in Roman Corinth: Interdisciplinary Approaches*, edited by Daniel Schowalter and Steven J. Friesen, 351–70. Cambridge, MA: Harvard University Press.

Gaddis, Michael. 1999a. "Chalcedon, Council of." *LAGPW* 369–70.

———. 1999b. "Cyril of Alexandria." *LAGPW* 403–4.

———. 1999c. "Ephesus, Councils of." *LAGPW* 426–27.

———. 1999d. "Nicaea, Council of." *LAGPW* 604–5.

Galey, John. 1980. *Sinai and the Monastery of St. Catherine*. New York: Doubleday.

Galvão-Sobrinho, Carlos R. 1995. "Funerary Epigraphy and the Spread of Christianity in the West." *Athenaeum* 83:431–66.

Gamber, Klaus. 1982. *Sarmannina*. SPL 11. Regensburg: Pustet.

Ganss, George E., and William B. Palardy, trans. 1953, 2004, 2005. *St. Peter Chrysologus: Selected Sermons*. 3 vols. FCh 17, 109, 110. Washington, DC: Catholic University of America Press.

Gardner, Iain. 2000. "He Has Gone to the Monastery." In *Studia Manichaica: IV. Internationaler Kongress zum Manichäismus, Berlin, 14.–18. Juli 1997*, edited by Ronald E. Emmerick, Werner Sundermann, and Peter Zieme, 247–57. Berlin: Akademie-Verlag.

Gardner, Iain, Anthony Alcock, and Wolf-Peter Funk, eds. 1999. *Coptic Documentary Texts from Kellis*. Oxford: Oxbow.

Gardner, Iain, and Samuel N. C. Lieu, eds. 2004. *Manichaean Texts from the Roman Empire*. Cambridge: Cambridge University Press.

Garsoïan, Nina G. 1997. "The Aršakuni Dynasty." In *The Armenian People from Ancient to Modern Times*, edited by Richard G. Hovannisian, 63–94. New York: St. Martin's Press.

———. 2004. "Janus: The Formation of the Armenian Church from the IVth to the VIIth Century." In *The Formation of a Millennial Tradition: 1700 Years of Armenian*

Christian Witness (301–2001), edited by Robert F. Taft, 79–95. OrChrAn 271. Rome: Pontificio Istituto Orientale.

———. 2005–2007. "Introduction to the Problem of Early Armenian Monasticism." *REArm* 30:177–236.

Gascou, Jean. 1998. "Les églises d'Alexandrie: Questions de méthode." In *Alexandrie médiévale 1*, edited by Christian Décobert and Jean-Yves Empereur, 23–44. EA 3. Cairo: Institut français d'archéologie orientale.

Gauckler, Paul. 1903. "Le quartier des thermes d'Antonin et le couvent de Saint-Étienne à Carthage." *BCTHS* 20:410–20.

Gero, Stephen. 1981. *Barsauma of Nisibis and Persian Christianity in the Fifth Century.* CSCO 426. Louvain: Peeters.

Gibbon, Edward. 1908. *The History of the Decline and Fall of the Roman Empire.* Edited by John B. Bury. 3rd ed. 7 vols. London: Methuen.

Giles, John A. 1968. *Six Old English Chronicles.* Bohn's Antiquarian Library. London: Henry G. Bohn, 1848. Reprint, New York: AMS.

Gilles, Pierre. 1988. *The Antiquities of Constantinople.* 2nd ed. New introduction and bibliography by Ronald G. Musto. New York: Italica.

Gillman, Ian, and Hans-Joachim Klimkeit. 1999. *Christians in Asia before 1500.* Ann Arbor: University of Michigan Press.

Gingras, George E., trans. 1970. *Egeria: Diary of a Pilgrimage.* ACW 38. New York: Newman.

Giorgetti, Dario. 1983. "Ratiaria and Its Territory." In vol. 2 of *Ancient Bulgaria: Papers Presented to the International Symposium on the Ancient History and Archaeology of Bulgaria, University of Nottingham, 1981*, edited by A. G. Poulter, 19–39. Nottingham, UK: University of Nottingham, Department of Classical and Archaeological Studies, Archaeology Section.

———. 1987. "Res ad topographiam veteris urbis Ratiariae pertinente: Prolegomeni all'urbanistica della città romana." *Ratiariensia* 3/4:33–84, and tables V–XXII.

Glucker, Carol A. M. 1987. *The City of Gaza in the Roman and Byzantine Periods.* BARIS 325. Oxford: Archaeopress.

Glueck, Nelson. 1939. "Excavations in Eastern Palestine, III." *AASOR* 1939:18–19.

Goehring, James E. 1990. *The Crosby-Schøyen Codex MS 193 in the Schøyen Collection.* CSCO 521. Louvain: Peeters.

———. 1999a. "Hieracas of Leontopolis: The Making of a Desert Ascetic." In *Ascetics, Society, and the Desert: Studies in Early Egyptian Monasticism*, 110–33. Harrisburg, PA: Trinity Press International.

———. 1999b. "Melitian Monastic Organization: A Challenge to Pachomian Originality." In *Ascetics, Society, and the Desert: Studies in Early Egyptian Monasticism*, 187–95. Harrisburg, PA: Trinity Press International.

———. 1999c. "The Origins of Monasticism." In *Ascetics, Society, and the Desert: Studies in Early Egyptian Monasticism*, 13–35. Harrisburg, PA: Trinity Press International.

———. 1999d. "Withdrawing from the Desert: Pachomius and the Development of Village Monasticism in Upper Egypt." In *Ascetics, Society, and the Desert: Studies in Early Egyptian Monasticism*, 89–109. Harrisburg, PA: Trinity Press International.

————. 1999e. "The World Engaged: The Social and Economic World of Early Egyptian Monasticism." In *Ascetics, Society, and the Desert: Studies in Early Egyptian Monasticism*, 39–52. Harrisburg, PA: Trinity Press International.

Goehring, James E., and Janet Timbie, eds. 2007. *The World of Early Egyptian Christianity: Language, Literature, and Social Context; Essays in Honor of David W. Johnson*. CUASEC. Washington, DC: Catholic University of America Press.

Grabar, André. 1928. *La peinture religieuse en Bulgarie*. Paris: Geuthner.

————. 1972. *Martyrium: Recherches sur le culte des reliques et l'art chrétien antique*. 2 vols. London: Variorum Reprints.

Graf, David F., Benjamin Isaac, and Israel Roll. 1992. "Roads and Highways: Roman Roads." *ABD* 5:782–87.

Grant, Robert. 1997. *Irenaeus of Lyons*. London: Routledge.

Greatrex, Geoffrey. Forthcoming. "The Romano-Persian Frontier and the Context of the Book of Steps." In *Breaking the Mind: New Studies in the Syriac Book of Steps*, edited by Kristian S. Heal and Robert Kitchen. Washington, DC: Catholic University of America Press.

Greatrex, Geoffrey, and Samuel N. C. Lieu. 1994. *The Roman Eastern Frontier and the Persian Wars: Part II, AD 363–630; A Narrative Sourcebook*. London: Routledge.

Greco, Rosario. 1999. *Pagani e cristiani a Siracusa tra il III e il IV secolo d.C.* Supplementi a "Kókalos" 16. Rome: Bretschneider.

Green, Tamara M. 1992. *The City of the Moon God: Religious Traditions of Harran*. RGRW 114. Leiden: Brill.

Gregg, Robert C., and Dan Urman. 1996. *Jews, Pagans, and Christians in the Golan Heights: Greek and Other Inscriptions of the Roman Byzantine Eras*. SFSHJ 140. Atlanta: Scholars Press.

Grégoire, Henri. 1909. "Rapport sur un voyage d'exploration dans le Pont et en Cappadoce." *BCH* 33:3–169.

————. 1922. *Recueil des inscriptions grecques chrétiennes d'Asie Mineure*. Fascicle 1. Paris: Leroux. [Abbr.: *IAsMinChr*]

Gregory, Timothy E. 1983. "The Oracle at Delos in Late Antiquity." *CW* 76:290–91.

————. 1986. "The Survival of Paganism in Christian Greece: A Critical Essay." *AJP* 107:229–42.

————. 1993. *The Hexamilion and the Fortress*. Isthmia 5. Princeton, NJ: American School of Classical Studies at Athens.

Grenfell, Bernard P., Arthur S. Hunt, et al., eds. 1898–. *The Oxyrhynchus Papyri*. 72 vols. London: Egypt Exploration Fund. [Abbr.: P.Oxy.]

Grenier, Jean-Claude. 1983. "La stèle funéraire du dernier taureau Bouchis (Caire JE 31901 = Stèle Bucheum 20), Ermant–4 novembre 340." *BIFAO* 83:197–208.

————. 2002. "La stèle de la mère d'un Bouchis datée de Licinius et de Constantin." *BIFAO* 102:247–58.

————. 2003. "Remarques sur les datations et titulatures de trois stèles romaines du Bucheum." *BIFAO* 103:267–79.

Grierson, Roderick, and Stuart C. Munro-Hay. 2002. *Red Sea, Blue Nile: The Civilisation of Ancient and Medieval Ethiopia*. London: Weidenfeld & Nicolson.

Griffith, Francis Llewellyn. 1935–1937. *Catalogue of the Demotic Graffiti of the Dodecaschoenus*. 2 vols. Oxford: Oxford University Press.

Griffith, Sidney H. 2003. "The *Doctrina Addai* as a Paradigm of Christian Thought in Edessa in the Fifth Century." *Hugoye* 6 (2): 269–92.

———. 2006. "The Church of Jerusalem and the 'Melkites': The Making of an 'Arab Orthodox' Christian Identity in the World of Islam (750–1050 C.E.)." In *Christians and Christianity in the Holy Land: From the Origins to the Latin Kingdoms*, edited by Ora Limor and Guy G. Stroumsa, 175–204. CELAMA 5. Turnhout: Brepols.

Grig, Lucy. 2004. *Making Martyrs in Late Antiquity*. London: Duckworth.

Griggs, C. Wilfred. 2000. *Early Egyptian Christianity: From Its Origins to 451 C.E.* BSL. Leiden: Brill.

Grillmeier, Alois. 1990. *Die Kirche von Alexandrien mit Nubien und Äthiopien nach 451.* Vol. 2.4 of *Jesus der Christus im Glauben der Kirche*. Freiburg: Herder.

Gros, Pierre. 2008. "De Cyrène à *Lepcis Magna*: L'investissement des centres urbains par le pouvoir." In *Lieux de Cultes: Aires votives, temples, églises, mosquées; IXe colloque international sur l'histoire et l'archéologie de l'Afrique du Nord, Tripoli, 19–25 février 2005*, 47–59. EAA. Paris: Éditions du Centre National de la Recherche Scientifique.

Grossman, Peter. 1996. "Report on the Season in Fayran (March 1990)." *ByzZ* 89:11–36.

———. 2002. *Christliche Architektur in Ägypten*. HO 62. Leiden: Brill.

Gryson, Roger. 1980. *Scolies ariennes sur le concile d'Aquilée*. Paris: Cerf.

Guadelli, J.-L., et al. 2005. "Une séquence du Paléolithique inférieur au Paléolithique récent dans les Balkans: La grotte Kozarnika à Oréchets (Nord-Ouest de la Bulgarie)." In *Les premiers peuplements en Europe: Colloque international "Données récentes sur les modalités de peuplement et sur le cadre chronostratigraphique, géologique et paléogéographique des industries du Paléolithique inférieur et moyen en Europe," Rennes, 22–25 septembre 2003*, edited by Nathalie Molines, M.-H. Moncel, and J.-L. Monnier, 87–103. BARIS 1364. Oxford: Archaeopress.

Gui, Isabelle, Jean-Pierre Caillet, and Noël Duval. 1992. *Inventaire de l'Algérie*. Vol. 1.1 of *Basiliques chrétiennes d'Afrique du Nord (Inventaire et Typologie)*. 1 vol. in 2 parts. CEASA 129, 130. Paris: Institut d'Études augustiniennes.

Guidi, Ignazio, ed. and trans. 1955. *Chronica minora*. Vol. 1. CSCO 1. Paris: E Typographeo Reipublicae, 1903. Reprint, Louvain: Durbecq.

Guillaumont, Antoine, et al. 1991. "Kellia." In vol. 5 of *The Coptic Encyclopedia*, edited by Aziz S. Atiya, 1396–410. New York: Macmillan.

Haas, Christopher. 1997. *Alexandria in Late Antiquity: Topography and Social Conflict*. Baltimore: Johns Hopkins University Press.

———. 2008. "Mountain Constantines: The Christianization of Aksum and Iberia." *JLA* 1:101–26.

Haider, Peter W. 1996. "Eine christliche Hauskirche in Dura Europos." In *Religionsgeschichte Syriens: Von der Frühzeit bis zur Gegenwart*, edited by Peter W. Haider, Manfred Hutter, and Siegfried Kreuzer, 284–88. Stuttgart: Kohlhammer.

Halbertsma, Tjalling H. F. 2008. *Early Christian Remains of Inner Mongolia: Discovery, Reconstruction and Appropriation*. SL 88. Leiden: Brill.

Hanson, R. P. C. 1983. *The Life and Writings of the Historical Saint Patrick*. New York: Seabury.

———. 1988. *The Search for the Christian Doctrine of God: The Arian Controversy, 318–381*. Edinburgh: T&T Clark.

Harmless, William. 2004. *Desert Christians: An Introduction to the Literature of Early Monasticism*. New York: Oxford University Press.

Harnack, Adolf. 1908. *The Mission and Expansion of Christianity in the First Three Centuries*. Translated and edited by James Moffatt. 2nd enlarged and rev. ed. 2 vols. TTL 20. New York: Putnam.

Harrak, Amir, ed. and trans. 2005. *The Acts of Mār Māri the Apostle*. SBLWGRW 11. Atlanta: Society of Biblical Literature.

Harrison, R. M., and Nezih Firatlı. 1967. "Excavations at the Sarçhane in Istanbul: Fourth Preliminary Report." *DOP* 21:272–78.

Hartley, Elizabeth, et al., eds. 2006. *Constantine the Great: York's Roman Emperor*. York: York Museum and Gallery Trust.

Haspels, Caroline H. E. 1971. *The Highlands of Phrygia: Sites and Monuments*. 2 vols. Princeton, NJ: Princeton University Press.

Hassall, [Mark] W. C., and Roger S. O. Tomlin. 1982. "Roman Britain in 1981. II. Inscriptions." *Britannia* 13:396–422.

———. 1993. "Roman Britain in 1992. II. Inscriptions." *Britannia* 24:310–22.

Hatch, William H. P. 1937. "The Subscription in the Chester Beatty Manuscript of the Harclean Gospels." *HTR* 30:141–55.

Hatlie, Peter. 2007. *The Monks and Monasteries of Constantinople, ca. 350–850*. Cambridge: Cambridge University Press.

Hauben, Hans. 1998. "The Melitian 'Church of the Martyrs': Christian Dissenters in Ancient Egypt." In *Early Christianity, Late Antiquity, and Beyond*, edited by Thomas W. Hillard, 329–49. Vol. 2 of *Ancient History in a Modern University: Proceedings of a Conference Held at Macquarie University, 8–13 July 1993, to Mark Twenty-Five Years of the Teaching of Ancient History at Macquarie University and the Retirement from the Chair of Professor Edwin Judge*, edited by Thomas W. Hillard et al. Grand Rapids: Eerdmans.

Haverfield, Francis. 1912. *The Romanization of Roman Britain*. Oxford: Clarendon.

Heine, Ronald E. 1989. *The Montanist Oracles and Testimonia*. PMS 14. Macon, GA: Mercer University Press; Washington, DC: Catholic University of America Press.

———. 1998. Review of *Montanist Inscriptions and Testimonia: Epigraphic Sources Illustrating the History of Montanism*, by William Tabbernee. *JTS*, NS 49:824–27.

Hemer, Colin J. 1986. *The Letters to the Seven Churches of Asia in Their Local Setting*. JSNTSup 11. Sheffield: JSOT Press.

———. 1990. *The Book of Acts in the Setting of Hellenistic History*. Edited by Conrad H. Gempf. Winona Lake, IN: Eisenbrauns.

Hengel, Martin. 1979. *Acts and the History of Earliest Christianity*. Translated by John Bowden. Philadelphia: Fortress.

Hennessy, Cecily. 2008. "Topography of Constantinople." In *The Oxford Handbook of Byzantine Studies*, edited by Elizabeth Jeffreys, John F. Haldon, and Robin Cormack, 202–16. Oxford: Oxford University Press.

Henning, Walter B. 1948. "The Date of the Sogdian Ancient Letters." *BSOAS* 12:601–15.

Herbert, Máire. 1988. *Iona, Kells, and Derry: The History and Hagiography of the Monastic Familia of Columba*. Oxford: Clarendon.

Herrmann, John J., and Annewies van den Hoek. 2002. *Light from the Age of Augustine: Late Antique Ceramics from North Africa (Tunisia)*. Cambridge, MA: Harvard Divinity School.

Herzfeld, Ernst. 1935. *Archaeological History of Iran*. London: Oxford University Press.

Hess, Hamilton. 1958. *The Canons of the Council of Sardica, AD 343: A Landmark in the Early Development of Canon Law*. OTM. Oxford: Clarendon.

Hewsen, Robert H. 2000. *Armenia: A Historical Atlas*. Chicago: University of Chicago Press.

Hickley, Dennis. 1966. "The Ambo in Early Liturgical Planning: A Study with Special Reference to the Syrian Bema." *HeyJ* 7:407–27.

Hill, Charles E. 2006. *From the Lost Teaching of Polycarp: Identifying Irenaeus' Apostolic Presbyter and the Author of* Ad Diognetum. WUNT 186. Tübingen: Mohr Siebeck.

Hill, George F. 1922. *Catalogue of the Greek Coins of Arabia, Mesopotamia, and Persia*. London: British Museum.

Hill, James W. M. 1948. *Medieval Lincoln*. Cambridge: Cambridge University Press.

Hiller von Gaertringen, Friedrich, et al. 1924–. *Inscriptiones graecae*. Editio minor. Berlin: de Gruyter. [Abbr.: *IG*]

Hirschfeld, Yizhar. 1990. "List of the Byzantine Monasteries in the Judean Desert." In *Christian Archaeology in the Holy Land: New Discoveries; Essays in Honour of Virgilio C. Corbo, OFM*, edited by G. C. Bottini, L. Di Segni, and E. Alliata, 1–90. Jerusalem: Franciscan Printing Press.

———. 2002. "Deir Qal'a and the Monasteries of Western Samaria." In *Late-Antique Petra, Nile Festival Building at Sepphoris, Deir Qal'a Monastery, Khirbet Qana Village and Pilgrim Site, 'Ain-'Arrub Hiding Complex and Other Studies*, edited by John H. Humphrey, 155–89. Vol. 3 of *The Roman and Byzantine Near East*. JRASup 49. Portsmouth, RI: Journal of Roman Archaeology.

———. 2004. "The Monasteries of Gaza: An Archaeological Review." In *Christian Gaza in Late Antiquity*, edited by Brouria Bitton-Ashkelony and Aryeh Kofsky, 61–88. JSRC 3. Brill: Leiden.

Hirschmann, Vera-Elisabeth. 2005. *Horrenda Secta: Untersuchungen zum frühchristlichen Montanismus und seinen Verbindungen zur paganen Religion Phrygiens*. HE 179. Stuttgart: Steiner.

Hirth, Friedrich, and William W. Rockhill, trans. 1911. *Chau Ju-Kua: His Work on the Chinese and Arab Trade in the Twelfth and Thirteenth Centuries, Entitled Chu-fan-chī*. St. Petersburg: Imperial Academy of Sciences.

Hoddinott, Ralph F. 1981. *The Thracians*. London: Thames & Hudson.

Hoffmann, Georg. 1966. *Auszüge aus syrischen Akten persischer Märtyrer*. AKM 7/3. Leipzig: Brockhaus, 1880. Reprint, Nendeln, Liechtenstein: Kraus Reprint.

Höffner, Richard. 2000. "Archaeus." *DECL* 46.

Hollerich, Michael J. 1999. *Eusebius of Caesarea's Commentary on Isaiah: Christian Exegesis in the Age of Constantine*. Oxford: Clarendon.

Hollerweger, Hans, Andrew Palmer, and Sebastian P. Brock. 1999. *Lebendiges Kulturerbe: Turabdin: Wo die Sprache Jesu gesprochen wird*. Linz: Freunde des Tur Abdin.

Holm, Frits. 1924. *My Nestorian Adventure in China: A Popular Account of the Holm-Nestorian Expedition to Sian-Fu and Its Results*. London: Hutchinson.

Holum, Kenneth G. 1982. *Theodosian Empresses: Women and Imperial Dominion in Late Antiquity*. TCH 3. Berkeley: University of California Press.

Honigmann, E. 1939. *Le synekdèmos d'Hiéroklès et l'opuscule géographique de Georges de Chypre: Texte, introduction, commentaire et cartes.* Brussels: Éditions de l'Institut de philologie et d'histoire orientales et slaves.

Hopkins, Keith. 1998. "Christian Number and Its Implications." *JECS* 6:185–226.

Horbury, William. 2006. "Beginnings of Christianity in the Holy Land." In *Christians and Christianity in the Holy Land: From the Origins to the Latin Kingdoms*, edited by Ora Limor and Guy G. Stroumsa, 7–89. CELAMA 5. Turnhout: Brepols.

Horn, Cornelia B. 2006. *Asceticism and Christological Controversy in Fifth-Century Palestine: The Career of Peter the Iberian.* Oxford: Oxford University Press.

———. 2010. "Apocryphal Gospels in Arabic, or Some Complications on the Road to Traditions about Jesus." In *Jesus in apokryphen Evangelienüberlieferungen: Beiträge zu außerkanonischen Jesusüberlieferungen aus verschiedenen Sprach- und Kulturtraditionen*, edited by Jörg Frey and Jens Schröter, with Jakob Spaeth, 583–609. WUNT 254. Tübingen: Mohr Siebeck.

———. 2013. "Jesus' Healing Miracles as Proof of Divine Agency and Identity: The Trajectory of Early Syriac Literature." In *The Bible, the Qur'ān, and Their Interpretation: Syriac Perspectives*, edited by Cornelia Horn, 69–97. Eastern Mediterranean Texts and Contexts 1. Warwick, RI: Abelian Academic.

Horn, Cornelia B., and Robert R. Phenix. 2005. "Eastern Catholic Churches of the Syriac Tradition in the Near East: Their Origins, History and Place in Ecumenical Dialogue." *BRIIFS* 7:159–82.

———. 2010. "Apocryphal Gospels in Syriac and Related Texts Offering Traditions about Jesus." In *Jesus in apokryphen Evangelienüberlieferungen: Beiträge zu außerkanonischen Jesusüberlieferungen aus verschiedenen Sprach- und Kulturtraditionen*, edited by Jörg Frey and Jens Schröter, with Jakob Spaeth, 527–55. WUNT 254. Tübingen: Mohr Siebeck.

Horsley, G. H. R., and S. R. Llewelyn, eds. 1981–. *New Documents Illustrating Early Christianity: A Review of Greek Inscriptions and Papyri.* North Ryde, NSW: Macquarie University Ancient History Documentary Research Centre; Grand Rapids: Eerdmans. [Abbr.: *NewDocs*]

Horsley, Richard A. 2005. "Paul's Assembly in Corinth: An Alternative Society." In *Urban Religion in Roman Corinth: Interdisciplinary Approaches*, edited by Daniel Schowalter and Steven J. Friesen, 371–95. Cambridge, MA: Harvard University Press.

Horton, Charles. 2004. "The Chester Beatty Biblical Papyri: A Find of the Greatest Importance." In *The Earliest Gospels: The Origins and Transmission of the Earliest Christian Gospels—The Contribution of the Chester Beatty Gospel Codex P45*, edited by Charles Horton, 149–60. JSNTSup 258. London: T&T Clark.

Horton, Mark. 1991. "Africa in Egypt: New Evidence from Qasr Ibrim." In *Egypt and Africa: Nubia from Prehistory to Islam*, edited by W. V. Davies, 264–76. London: Egypt Exploration Society.

Howard, George, ed. and trans. 1981. *The Teaching of Addai.* SBLTT 16. Chico, CA: Scholars Press.

Hoyland, Robert G. 2001. *Arabia and the Arabs from the Bronze Age to the Coming of Islam.* London: Routledge.

Humbert, J.-B. 1990. "Khirbet es-Samra du Diocèse de Bosra." In *Christian Archaeology in the Holy Land: New Discoveries; Essays in Honour of Virgilio C. Corbo, OFM*, edited by G. C. Bottini, L. Di Segni, and E. Alliata, 467–74. Jerusalem: Franciscan Printing Press.

Humphries, Mark. 1999. *Communities of the Blessed: Social Environment and Religious Change in Northern Italy*, AD 200–400. Oxford: Oxford University Press.

Hunger, Herbert, et al., eds. 1976–. Tabula Imperii Byzantini. Vienna: Verlag der Österreichischen Akademie der Wissenschaften. [Abbr.: TIB]

Hunter, Erica C. D. 1996. "The Church of the East in Central Asia." In *The Church of the East: Life and Thought*, edited by J. F. Coakley and Ken Parry, special issue, *BJRL* 78 (3): 29–42. Manchester, UK: John Rylands University Library of Manchester.

Hunter, Erica C. D., and Judah B. Segal. 2000. *Catalogue of the Aramaic and Mandaic Incantation Bowls in the British Museum*. London: British Museum.

Hurtado, Larry W. 2006. *The Earliest Christian Artifacts: Manuscripts and Christian Origins*. Grand Rapids: Eerdmans.

Hutter, Manfred. 2003. "Mār Abā and the Impact of Zoroastrianism on Christianity in the 6th Century." In *Religious Themes and Texts of Pre-Islamic Iran and Central Asia: Studies in Honour of Professor Gherardo Gnoli on the Occasion of His 65th Birthday on 6th December 2002*, edited by Carlo G. Cereti, Mauro Maggi, and Elio Provasi, 167–73. BI 24. Wiesbaden: Reichert.

Huttner, Ulrich, 2014. *Early Christianity in the Lycus Valley*. AJEC 85. Leiden: Brill.

Illert, Martin, ed. 2007. *Doctrina Addai: De imagine Edessina* [= *Die Abgarlegende: Das Christusbild von Edessa*]. FC 45. Turnhout: Brepols.

Innemee, Karel. 2000. "Deir al-Baramus: Excavations at the So-Called Site of Moses the Black 1994–1999." *BSAC* 39:123–35.

———. 2005. "Excavations at Deir al-Baramus 2002–2005." *BSAC* 44:55–68.

Ireland, Robert H., ed. 1997. *Notitia dignitatum*. Stuttgart: Teubner.

Irshai, Oded. 2006. "From Oblivion to Fame: The History of the Palestinian Church (135–303 C.E.)." In *Christians and Christianity in the Holy Land: From the Origins to the Latin Kingdoms*, edited by Ora Limor and Guy G. Stroumsa, 91–139. CELAMA 5. Turnhout: Brepols.

Ivanov, Rumen T., ed. 2002. *Rimski i rannovizantiiski gradove v Bulgariia* [*Roman and Early Byzantine Cities in Bulgaria*] (in Bulgarian). Sofia: Ivray.

Ivashchenko, M. 1980. "Samtavroijskie pogrebenija pervyh trex vekov nashej ery." *Mtskheta* 1:189–215.

Jackson, Peter, trans. 1990. *The Mission of Friar William of Rubruck: His Journey to the Court of the Great Khan Möngke, 1253–1255*. London: Hakluyt Society.

Jacoby, Felix, ed. 1993–. *Die Fragmenta der griechischen Historiker: (F GR HIST)*. 15 vols. Leiden: Brill. [Abbr.: FGH (cited by entry number)].

Jadir, Adil H. al-. 1983. *A Comparative Study of the Script, Language, and Proper Names of the Old Syriac Inscriptions*. Self-published.

Jakab, Attila. 2001. *Ecclesia alexandrina: Evolution sociale et institutionnelle du christianisme alexandrin (IIe et IIIe siècles)*. CA 1. Bern: Lang.

Jakobielski, Stefan, and Piotr O. Scholz, eds. 2001. *Dongola-Studien: 35 Jahre polnischer Forschungen im Zentrum des makuritischen Reiches*. Warsaw: Zaś Pan.

Jameson, Michael H., Curtis N. Runnels, and Tjeerd H. van Andel, eds. 1994. *A Greek Countryside: The Southern Argolid from Prehistory to the Present Day*. Stanford, CA: Stanford University Press.

Janin, Raymond. 1964. *Constantinople byzantine: Développement urbain et répertoire topographique*. 2nd ed. AOC 4A. Paris: Institut français d'études byzantines.

———. 1969. *Les églises et les monastères*. Part 1, vol. 3 of *La géographie ecclésiastique de l'empire byzantin*. 2nd ed. PIFEB. Paris: Institut français d'études byzantines.

Jarry, Jacques. 1972. "Inscriptions syriaques et arabes du Tur Abdin." *AI* 10:207–50.

Jensen, Robin M. 2005. "Baptismal Rites and Architecture." In *Late Ancient Christianity*, edited by Virginia Burrus, 117–44. Vol. 2 of *The People's History of Christianity*, edited by Denis R. Janz. Minneapolis: Fortress.

———. 2012. *Baptismal Theological Imagery in Early Christianity: Ritual, Visual, and Dimensions*. Grand Rapids: Baker Academic.

Jěremić, Miroslav. 2005. "Adolf Hytrek et les premières fouilles archéologiques à Sirmium." *Starinar* 55:115–32.

Jewell, Harry H., and F. W. Hasluck. 1920. *The Church of Our Lady of the Hundred Gates (Panagia Hekatontapyliani) in Paros*. London: Macmillan, for the Byzantine Research Fund.

Johnson, Gary J. 1995. *Early-Christian Epitaphs from Anatolia*. SBLTT 35. Atlanta: Scholars Press.

Johnson, Mark. 1988. "Towards a History of Theodoric's Building Program." *DOP* 42:73–96.

Jones, Arnold H. M. 1964. *The Later Roman Empire, 284–602: A Social, Economic, and Administrative Survey*. 3 vols. Oxford: Blackwell.

Jones, Michael J. 1993. *Lincoln: History and Guide*. Dover, NH: Sutton.

———. 2002. *Roman Lincoln: Conquest, Colony and Capital*. Charleston, SC: Tempus.

Jordan, D. R., and R. D. Kotansky. 1996. "Two Phylacteries from Xanthos." *RAr* 21:161–74.

Judge, Edwin A. 1977. "The Earliest Use of Monachos for 'Monk' (P. Coll. Youtie 77) and the Origins of Monasticism." *JAC* 20:72–89.

Judge, Edwin A., and Stuart R. Pickering. 1977. "Papyrus Documentation of Church and Community in Egypt to the Mid-Fourth Century." *JAC* 20:47–71.

Jullien, Christelle, and Florence Jullien. 2001. "La *Chronique d'Arbèles*: Propositions pour la fin d'une controverse." *OrChr* 85:41–83.

———. 2003. *Aux origines de l'église de Perse: Les Actes de Mar Mari*. CSCO 604. Louvain: Peeters.

Kakhidze, Emzar. 2008. "Apsaros: A Roman Fort in Southwestern Georgia." In *Meetings of Cultures in the Black Sea Region: Between Conflict and Coexistence*, edited by Pia Guldager Bilde and Jane Hjarl Petersen, 303–32. BSS 8. Aarhus: Aarhus Universitetsforlag.

Kákosy, László. 1995. "Probleme der Religion im römerzeitlichen Ägypten." *ANRW* II.18.5:2894–3049.

Kalopisi-Verti, Sophia. 1991. "Kos tardoantica e bizantina nelle scoperte archaeologiche dal IV secolo al 1314." In *XXXVIII corso di cultura sull'arte ravennate e bizantina: Seminario internazionale di studi sul tema; "La Grecia insulare tra tardoantico e medioevo,"* *Ravenna, 15–20 marzo 1991*, 233–51. Ravenna: Edizioni del Girasole.

Kantor, Marvin. 1983. *Medieval Slavic Lives of Saints and Princes*. MST 5. Ann Arbor: University of Michigan Press.

Karivieri, Arja. 1994. "The So-Called Library of Hadrian and the Tetraconch Church in Athens." In *Post-Herulian Athens: Aspects of Life and Culture in Athens, A.D. 267–529*, edited by Paavo Castrén, 89–113. PMFIA 1. Helsinki: Suomen Ateenan-instituutin säätiö.

———. 1995. "The Christianization of an Ancient Pilgrimage Site: A Case Study of the Athenian Asklepieion." In vol. 2 of *Akten des XII Internationalen Kongresses für christliche Archäologie, Bonn, 22–28 September 1991*, 898–905. JACE 20. Münster: Aschendorff.

Karwiese, Stefan. 1995. "The Church of Mary and the Temple of Hadrian Olympios." In *Ephesos: Metropolis of Asia; An Interdisciplinary Approach to Its Archaeology, Religions, and Culture*, edited by Helmut Koester, 311–19. HTS 41. Valley Forge, PA: Trinity Press International.

Kasher, Aryeh. 1988. *Jews, Idumaeans, and Ancient Arabs: Relations of the Jews in Eretz-Israel with the Nations of the Frontier and the Desert during the Hellenistic and Roman Era (332 BCE–70 CE)*. TSAJ 18. Tübingen: Mohr Siebeck.

Kasser, Rodolphe. 1960. *Papyrus Bodmer VI: Livre des Proverbes*. 2 vols. in 1. CSCO 194, 195. Louvain: Secrétariat du Corpus scriptorum christianorum orientalium.

Katsarova, Vesselka. 2005. *Pautaliia i neinata territoriia prez I–VI vek [Pautalia and Its Territory: I–VI Centuries]* (in Bulgarian, with German summary, "Pautalia und ihr Territorium im 1.–6. Jh."). Veliko Tarnovo, Bulgaria: Faber.

Kautzsch, Rudolf. 1936. *Kapitellstudien: Beiträge zu einer Geschichte des spätantiken Kapitells im Osten vom vierten bis ins siebente Jahrhundert*. SSK 9. Berlin: de Gruyter.

Kawerau, Peter, ed. and trans. 1985. *Die Chronik von Arbela*. 2 vols. CSCO 467, 468. Louvain: Peeters.

Keenan, James. 2000. "Egypt." CAH 14:612–37.

Kennedy, Hugh. 1998. "Egypt as a Province in the Islamic Caliphate, 641–868." In *Islamic Egypt, 640–1517*, edited by Carl F. Petry, 62–85. Vol. 1 of *The Cambridge History of Egypt*, edited by Carl F. Petry and M. W. Daly. Cambridge: Cambridge University Press.

Kenney, James F. 1929. *The Sources for the Early History of Ireland: An Introduction and Guide*. New York: Columbia University Press.

Kenrick, Phillip. 2009. *Tripolitania: Libya Archaeological Guides*. London: Silphium Books.

Kenyon, Frederick G. 1937. *Isaiah, Jeremiah, Ecclesiasticus*. Vol. 6 of *The Chester Beatty Biblical Papyri: Descriptions and Texts of Twelve Manuscripts on Papyrus of the Greek Bible*. London: Walker.

Keramopoullos, Antonios. 1917. "Thivaika." *AD* 3:1–503.

———. 1926. "Palaiai Christianikai kai Byzantinai Tafai en Thivais." *AD* 10:124–36.

Kerkslager, Allen. 1998. "Jewish Pilgrimage and Jewish Identity in Hellenistic and Roman Egypt." In *Pilgrimage and Holy Space in Late Antique Egypt*, edited by David Frankfurter, 99–225. RGRW 134. Leiden: Brill.

Kesyakova, Elena. 1989a. "Ancient Synagogue of Philippopolis" (in Bulgarian with French summary). *Arheologiya* (Sofia) 1:20–33.

———. 1989b. "Une nouvelle basilique à Philippopolis." In *Actes du XIe CIAC*, 2539–59. Paris.

Kettenhofen, Erich. 1994. "Deportations ii. In the Parthian and Sasanian Periods." *EncIran* 7:297–308.

Khazanov, Anatolii M. 1994. "The Spread of World Religions in Medieval Nomadic Societies of the Eurasian Steppes." In *Nomadic Diplomacy, Destruction and Religion from the Pacific to the Adriatic: Papers Prepared for the Central and Inner Asian Seminar, University of Toronto, 1992–93*, edited by Michael Gervers and Wayne Schlepp, 11–23. TSCIA. Toronto: Joint Centre for Asia Pacific Studies.

Khimshiashvili, Kaha. 1999. "The Architecture of Uphlistsikhe, Georgia." *TAMS* 43:77–100.

Khosroyev, Alexandr. 1995. *Die Bibliothek von Nag Hammadi: Einige Probleme des Christentums in Ägypten während der ersten Jahrhunderte.* Altenberge: Oros.

Khouri, Maysoun al-. 2003. *Il limes arabicus.* MSBC. Rome: CISU.

King, Karen L. 2003. *What Is Gnosticism?* Cambridge, MA: Belknap.

Kiourtzian, Georges. 2000. *Recueil des inscriptions grecques chrétiennes des Cyclades: De la fin du IIIe au VIIe siècle après J.-C.* Paris: de Boccard.

Kirin, Asen. 2000. "The Rotunda of St. George and Late Antique Serdica: From Imperial Palace to Episcopal Complex." PhD diss., Princeton University.

Kirk, Geoffrey Stephen. 1985. *The Iliad: A Commentary.* Vol. 1: books 1–4. Cambridge: Cambridge University Press.

Kirschbaum, Engelbert. 1959. *The Tombs of St. Peter and St. Paul.* Translated by John Murray. London: Secker & Warburg.

Kirwan, Laurence. 1982. "Some Thoughts on the Conversion of Nubia to Christianity." In *Nubian Studies: Proceedings of the Symposium for Nubian Studies, Selwyn College, Cambridge, 1978,* edited by J. Martin Plumley, 142–45. Warminster: Aris & Phillips.

———. 1984. "The Birth of Christian Nubia: Some Archaeological Problems." *RSO* 58:119–34.

Kitzinger, Ernst. 1978. "The Cleveland Marbles." In vol. 1 of *Atti de IX congresso internazionale di archaeologia cristiana, Roma, 21–27 settembre 1975,* 653–75. Vatican City: Pontificio istituto di archeologia cristiana.

Klauser, Theodor, et al., eds. 1950–. *Reallexikon für Antike und Christentum: Sachwörterbuch zur Auseinandersetzung des Christentums mit der Antiken Welt.* Stuttgart: Hiersemann. [Abbr.: *RAC*]

Klein, Wolfgang W. 1999. "Das Orthodoxe Katholikat von Romagyris in Zentralasien." *ParOr* 24:235–65.

———. 2000. *Das Nestorianische Christentum an den Handelswegen durch Kyrgyzstan bis zum 14. Jh.* SRS 3. Turnhout: Brepols.

Kleinbauer, W. Eugene. 1973. "The Origin and Functions of the Aisled Tetraconch Churches in Syria and Northern Mesopotamia." *DOP* 27:89–114.

———. 2000. "The Church Building at Seleucia Pieria." In *Antioch: The Lost Ancient City,* edited by Christine Kondoleon, 217–18. Princeton, NJ: Princeton University Press.

Klingshirn, William, 1994. *Caesarius of Arles: The Making of a Christian Community in Late Antique Gaul.* CSMLT 4/22. Cambridge: Cambridge University Press.

Kloppenborg, John S. 2000. *Excavating Q: The History and Setting of the Sayings Gospel.* Minneapolis: Fortress.

Knapp, Robert C. 1983. *Roman Córdoba.* Berkeley: University of California Press.

Knight, Jeremy. 1992. "The Early Christian Latin Inscriptions of Britain and Gaul: Chronology and Context." In *The Early Church in Wales and the West: Recent Work in Early Christian Archaeology, History and Place-Names,* edited by Nancy Edwards and Alan Lane, 45–50. OM 16. Oxford: Oxbow.

Knox, John. 1942. *Marcion and the New Testament: An Essay in the Early History of the Canon.* Chicago: University of Chicago Press.

Kobischchanov, Yuri M. 1979. *Axum.* Translated by Joseph W. Michaelo. Rev. ed. University Park: Pennsylvania State University Press.

Koch, Guntram. 1982. "Probleme des nordmesopotamischen Kirchenbaus: Die Längston-nenkirchen im Ṭūr 'Abdīn." In *Studien zur spätantiken und frühchristlichen Kunst und Kultur des Orients*, edited by Guntram Koch, 117–35. GO 2/6. Wiesbaden: Harrassowitz.

————. 2000. *Frühchristliche Sarkophage*. HA. Munich: Beck.

Koder, Johannes, and Friedrich Hild. 1976. *Hellas und Thessalia*. TIB 1. Vienna: Öster-reichische Akademie der Wissenschaften.

Koenen, Ludwig. 1983. "Manichäische Mission und Klöster in Ägypten." In *Das römisch-byzantinische Ägypten*, edited by G. Grimm, H. Heinen, and E. Winter, 93–108. Mainz: P. von Zabern.

Koester, Helmut. 1982. *Introduction to the New Testament*. 2 vols. Berlin: de Gruyter.

————. 1995. "Ephesos in Early Christian Literature." In *Ephesos: Metropolis of Asia; An Interdisciplinary Approach to Its Archaeology, Religions, and Culture*, edited by Helmut Koester, 119–40. HTS 41. Valley Forge, PA: Trinity Press International.

Kofsky, Aryeh. 1997. "Peter the Iberian: Pilgrimage, Monasticism and Ecclesiastical Politics in Byzantine Palestine." *LASBF* 47:209–22.

Koilakou, Charikleia. 2006. "I Boiotia kata tin Palaiochristianiki Periodo (4os–7os ai.): Mia Proti Proseggisi." In *Thessalia*, 1105–18. Vol. 1 of *Archaiologiko Ergo Thessalias kai Stereas Elladas: Praktika Epistimonikis Synantisis, Volos 27.2–2.3.2003*, edited by Alexander M. Ainian. Volos: Ergastirio Archaiologias Panepistimiou Thessalias.

Kollaparampil, J. R. K. 1992. *The Babylonian Origin of the Southists among the St. Thomas Christians*. OrChrAn 241. Rome: Pontificum Institutum Orientalium Studiorum.

Kollias, Elias. 2000. "I Palaiochristianiki kai Byzantini Rodos: I Antistasi mias Ellinistikis Polis." In vol. 2 of *Rodos 2400 Chronia: I Poli tis Rodou apo tin Idrysi tis mechri tin Karalipsi apo tous Tourkous (1523); Diethnes Epistimoniko Synedrio, Rodos, 24–29 Ok-tobriou 1993*, 299–308. HP 22. Athens: Ephoreia Proïstorikōn kai Klassikon Archaiotētō.

Kondoleon, Christine, ed. 2000. *Antioch: The Lost Ancient City*. Princeton, NJ: Princeton University Press.

Konrad, Michaela, Hans R. Baldus, and Thilo Ulbert. 2001. *Der spätrömische Limes in Syrien: Archäologische Untersuchungen an den Grenzkastellen von Sura, Tetrapyrgium, Cholle und in Resafa*. Resafa 5. Mainz: P. von Zabern.

Konstantinidis, Emmanuel I. 1998. "*Ecclesiastiki* Organosis tis Parou." In *Ekatontapyliani kai Christianiki Paros: Praktika Epistemonikou Symposiou, Paros 15–19 Septembriou 1996*, 205–10. Paros: Iera Mitropolis Paronaxias.

Konstas, D. D. 1890. "Anaskafai Tanagras." *PAE* 1890:33–35.

Korać, Miomir. 2007. *The Paintings of Viminacium*. Belgrade: Viminacium Center for New Technology.

Koriwn. 1941. *Vark' Maštoc'i*. Edited by M. Abelean. Reprint, with English translation by B. Norehad, Delmar, NY: Caravan, 1985.

Kovács, Péter. 2003. "Christianity and the Greek Language in Pannonia." *AAASH* 43:113–24.

Kraeling, Carl H., ed. 1935. *A Greek Fragment of Tatian's Diatessaron from Dura*. Lon-don: Christophers.

Kraemer, Ross S. 1991. "Jewish Tuna and Christian Fish: Identifying Religious Affiliation in Epigraphic Sources." *HTR* 84:141–62.

Kraus, Johann. 1930. *Die Anfänge des Christentums in Nubien*. Mödling: St. Gabriel.

Krause, Gerhard, and Gerhard Müller, eds. 1977–. *Theologische Realenzyklopädie*. Berlin: de Gruyter. [Abbr: *TRE*]

Krautheimer, Richard. 1981. *Early Christian and Byzantine Architecture*. 3rd ed. PHA. Harmondsworth: Penguin.

———. 1983. *Three Christian Capitals: Topography and Politics*. Una's Lectures 4. Berkeley: University of California Press.

Krawiec, Rebecca. 2002. *Shenoute and the Women of the White Monastery: Egyptian Monasticism in Late Antiquity*. New York: Oxford University Press.

Kropp, Angelicus, ed. and trans. 1930–1931. *Ausgewählte koptische Zaubertexte*. 3 vols. Brussels: Fondation égyptologique reine Élisabeth.

Kuzmanov, Georgi, and Julia Valeva. 2001. "Mosaïque d'une salle d'audience de Ratiaria (Dacia Ripensis)." In vol. 2 of *La mosaïque gréco-romaine VIII: Actes du VIIIème colloque international pour l'étude de la mosaïque antique et médiévale; Lausanne (Suisse), 6–11 octobre 1997*, edited by Daniel Paunier and Christophe Schmidt, 255–368. CAR 85. Lausanne: Cahiers d'archéologie romande.

La Baume, Peter. 1964. *Colonia Agrippinensis: Kurzer Rundgang durch das römische Köln*. 3rd ed. Cologne: Greven.

Labourt, Jérôme. 1904. *Le christianisme dans l'empire perse sous la dynastie sassanide (224–632)*. 2nd ed. Paris: Lecoffre.

Laeuchli, Samuel. 1972. *Power and Sexuality: The Emergence of Canon Law at the Synod of Elvira*. Philadelphia: Temple University Press.

Lalonde, Gerald V. 2005. "Pagan Cult to Christian Ritual: The Case of Agia Marina Theseiou." *GRBS* 45:91–125.

Lambrinoudakis, B., G. Gruben, and M. Korres. 1976. "Anaskafi Naxou." *PAE* 1976:299–307.

Lampe, Peter. 1989. *Die stadtrömischen Christen in den ersten beiden Jahrhunderten: Untersuchungen zur Sozialgeschichte*. 2nd ed. WUNT 2/18. Tübingen: Mohr Siebeck.

———. 1991. "The Roman Christians of Romans 16." In *The Romans Debate*, edited by Karl P. Donfried, 216–30. Rev. ed. Peabody, MA: Hendrickson.

———. 1998a. "Anacletus (Cletus) von Rom." *RGG* 1:446.

———. 1998b. "Anicetus von Rom." *RGG* 1:503.

———. 1998c. "Aquila/Prisca (Priszilla)." *RGG* 1:666.

———. 2003a. *From Paul to Valentinus: Christians at Rome in the First Two Centuries*. Translated by Michael Steinhauser. Edited by Marshall D. Johnson. Minneapolis: Fortress. [English edition of Lampe 1989]

———. 2003b. "Petrus: I. Neues Testament." *RGG* 6:1160–65.

———. 2003c. "Pius I." *RGG* 6:1363.

———. 2004a. "Early Christians in the City of Rome: Topographical and Social Historical Aspects of the First Three Centuries." In *Christians as a Religious Minority in a Multicultural City: Modes of Interaction and Identity Formation in Early Imperial Rome*, edited by Michael Labahn and Jürgen Zangenberg, 20–32. London: Continuum.

———. 2004b. "Paths of Early Christian Mission into Rome: Judaeo-Christians in the Households of Pagan Masters." In *Celebrating Romans: Template for Pauline Theology; Essays in Honor of Robert Jewett*, edited by Sheila E. McGinn, 143–48. Grand Rapids: Eerdmans.

————. 2004c. "Soter." *RGG* 7:1458.

————. 2005a. "Rom—Hauptstadt und größte Metropole des römischen Reiches." In *Familie, Gesellschaft, Wirtschaft*, edited by Kurt Erlemann and Klaus Scherberich. Vol. 2 of *Neues Testament und antike Kultur*, edited by Kurt Erlemann et al., 165–71. Neukirchen-Vluyn: Neukirchener Verlag.

————. 2005b. "Victor [röm. Bischof]." *RGG* 8:1103–4.

Lancel, Serge. 1995. *Carthage: A History.* Translated by Antonia Nevill. Oxford: Blackwell.

————. 2002. *St. Augustine.* Translated by Antonia Nevill. London: SCM.

Lancel, Serge, Stéphanie Guédon, and Louis Maurin, eds. 2005. *Saint Augustin: La Numidie et la société de son temps; Actes du colloque SEMPAN-AUSONIUS, Bordeaux, 10–11 octobre 2003.* Paris: de Boccard.

Lancel, Serge, and Paul Mattei. 2003. *Pax et Concordia: Chrétiens des premiers siècles en Algérie (IIIe–VIIe siècles).* Paris: Marsa.

Lane Fox, Robin. 1989. *Pagans and Christians.* New York: Knopf.

Lange, Christian. 2008. *Ephraem der Syrer: Kommentar zum Diatessaron.* 2 vols. FC 15/1–2. Turnhout: Brepols.

Langer, Gerhard. 1996. "Das Judentum in Syrien von den Hasmonäern bis um 700 n. Chr." In *Religionsgeschichte Syriens: Von der Frühzeit bis zur Gegenwart*, edited by Peter W. Haider, Manfred Hutter, and Siegfried Kreuzer, 242–60. Stuttgart: Kohlhammer.

Laronde, André, and Gérard Degeorge. 2005. *Leptis Magna: La splendeur et l'oubli.* Paris: Hermann.

Lassus, Jean. 1958. Preface to *Monuments chrétiens d'Hippone: Ville épiscopale de Saint Augustin*, by Erwan Marec, 5–14. Paris: Arts et Métiers Graphiques.

Last, Hugh. 1954. Review of *Études d'histoire chrétienne: Le christianisme secret du carré magique; Les fouilles de Saint-Pierre et la tradition*, by Jérôme Carcopino. *JRS* 44:112–16.

Lauffray, Jean. 1983–1991. *Halabiyya-Zenobia: Place forte du limes oriental et la Haute-Mésopotamie au VIe siècle.* 2 vols. BAH 119, 138. Paris: Geuthner.

Laurent, J. 1899. "Delphes Chrétien." *BCH* 23:206–79.

Layton, Bentley. 2007. "Rules, Patterns, and the Exercise of Power in Shenoute's Monastery: The Problem of World Replacement and Identity Maintenance." *JECS* 15:45–73.

Le Bas, Philippe, and William H. Waddington. 1870. *Inscriptiones grecques et latines recueillies en Asie Mineure.* 2 vols. Voyage archéologique en Grèce et en Asie Mineure 3/5, Subsidia epigraphica 1–2. Paris: Didot. [Abbr.: LBW]

Leclercq, Henri. 1906. *L'Espagne chrétienne.* Paris: Lecoffre.

————. 1933. "Mésopotamie." *DACL* 11 (1): 508–13.

————. 1937. "Osrhoène." *DACL* 13 (1): 21–22.

Le Coq, Albert von. 1913. *Chotscho: Facsimile-wiedergaben der wichtigen Funden der ersten königlich preussischen Expedition nach Turfan in Ost-Turkistan, im Auftrage der Generalverwaltung der königlichen Museen aus Mitteln des Baessler-Institutes.* Ergebnisse der königliche preussischen Turfan-Expedition 1. Berlin: Reimer.

Lefort, Louis-Théophile. 1955. *Athanase: Lettres festales et pastorales en copte.* 2 vols. CSCO 150, 151. Louvain: Durbecq.

Leglay, Marcel. 1961–1966. *Saturne africaine.* 3 vols. Paris: Arts et Métiers Graphiques.

Legutko, Paul. 2003. "The Letters of Dionysius: Alexandrian and Christian Identity in the Mid-Third Century A.D." *AW* 34:27–42.

Lehto, Adam Isaac. 2003. "Divine Law, Asceticism, and Gender in Aphrahat's Demonstrations: With a Complete Annotated Translation of the Text and Comprehensive Syriac Glossary." PhD diss., University of Toronto.

Leipoldt, Johannes. 1903. *Shenute von Atripe und die Entstehung des national ägyptischen Christentums*. Leipzig: Hinrichs.

Lemerle, Paul. 1945. *Philippe et la Macédoine orientale à l'époque chrétienne et byzantine: Recherches d'histoire et d'archéologie*. BEFAR 1/58. Paris: de Boccard.

Lepelley, Claude. 1981. *Notices d'histoire municipal*. Vol. 2 of *Les cites de l'Afrique romaine au Bas-Empire*. Paris: Études augustiniennes.

Lerner, Constantine B. 2003. *The Wellspring of Georgian Historiography: The Early Medieval Historical Chronicle, the Conversion of Kartli, and the Life of St. Nino*. London: Bennett & Bloom.

Lerner, Judith A. 1977. *Christian Seals of the Sasanian Period*. Istanbul: Nederlands Historisch-Archaeologisch Instituut.

Licheli, Vakhtang. 1998. "St. Andrew in Samtskhe—Archaeological Proof?" In *Ancient Christianity in the Caucasus*, edited by Tamila Mgaloblishvili, 25–37. Richmond: Curzon.

Lieu, Samuel N. C. 1986. "Captives, Refugees and Exiles: A Study of Cross-Frontier Civilian Movements and Contacts between Rome and Persia from Valerian to Jovian." In vol. 2 of *The Defence of the Roman and Byzantine East: Proceedings of a Colloquium Held at the University of Sheffield in April 1986*, edited by Philip Freeman and David Kennedy, 475–505. BARIS 297. Oxford: British Archaeological Reports.

———. 1992. *Manichaeism in the Later Roman Empire and Medieval China*. 2nd ed. WUNT 63. Tübingen: Mohr Siebeck.

———. 1994. *Manichaeism in Mesopotamia and the Roman East*. RGRW 118. Leiden: Brill.

———. 1998. *Manichaeism in Central Asia and China*. NHMS 45. Leiden: Brill.

———. 2009. "Epigraphica Nestoriana Serica." In *Exegisti monumenta: Festschrift in Honour of Professor Nicholas Sims-Williams*, edited by W. Sundermann, A. Hintze, and F. de Blois, 227–46. Wiesbaden: Harrasowitz.

Lieu, Samuel N. C., Lance Eccles, Majella Franzmann, Iain Gardner, and Ken Parry. 2012. *Medieval Christian and Manichaean Remains from Quanzhou (Zayton)*. CFM 2. Turnhout: Brepols.

Lieu, Samuel N. C., and Dominic Montserrat, eds. 1998. *Constantine: History, Historiography, and Legend*. London: Routledge.

Lightfoot, Chris S. 1990. "Trajan's Parthian War and the Fourth-Century Perspective." *JRS* 80:115–26.

Lin Wushu, and Rong Xinjiang. 1996. "Doubts concerning the Authenticity of Two Nestorian Christian Documents Unearthed at Dunhuang from the Li Collection." *CAAD* 1:9–13.

Liščák, Vladimír. 2006. "The Early Christianity in Tang China and Its Scriptures in Chinese." In *Trade, Journeys, Inter- and Intracultural Communication in East and West (Up to 1250): Papers Presented at the International Workshop (Humboldt-Kolleg), Dolná Krupá, Slovak Republic, June 2–6, 2004*, edited by Marián Gálik and Tatiana Štefanovičowá, 160–81. Bratislava: Institute of Oriental Studies, Slovak Academy of Sciences.

Li Tang. 2002. *A Study of the History of Nestorian Christianity in China and Its Literature in Chinese: Together with a New English Translation of the Dunhuang Nestorian Documents*. EUS 87. Frankfurt: Lang.

————. 2011. *East Syriac Christianity in Mongol-Yuan China*. OBC 18. Wiesbaden: Harrasowitz.

Lizzi, Rita. 1990. "Ambrose's Contemporaries and the Christianization of Northern Italy." *JRS* 80:156–73.

Llewelyn, Stephen R., and Alanna M. Nobbs. 1997. "P. Grenf. II 73: A Reconsideration." In vol. 2 of *Akten des 21. Internationalen Papyrologenkongresses, Berlin 13.–19.8.1995*, edited by Bärbel Kramer, Wolfgang Luppe, and Herwig Maehler, 613–30. APVG 3. Stuttgart: Teubner.

Locher, Josef. 1999. *Topographie und Geschichte der Region am ersten Nilkatarakt in griechisch-römischer Zeit*. APVG 5. Stuttgart: Teubner.

————. 2002. "Die Anfänge der römischen Herrschaft in Nubien und der Konflikt zwischen Rom und Meroe." *ASoc* 32:73–133.

Lochman, Tomas. 1991. "Deux reliefs anatoliens au Musée des beaux-arts de Budapest." *BMHB* 74:11–24.

Löhr, Winrich. 2007. "Western Christianities." In *Constantine to c. 600*, edited by Augustine Casiday and Frederick W. Norris, 9–51. Vol. 2 of *The Cambridge History of Christianity*, edited by Margaret M. Mitchell et al. Cambridge: Cambridge University Press.

Loosley, Emma. 2001. "The Early Christian Bema Churches of Syria Revisited." *Antiquity* 75:509–10.

Lordkipanidze, Otar. 2000. *Phasis: The River and City in Colchis*. Stuttgart: Steiner.

Lourié, Basil. 2010. "Peter the Iberian and Dionysius the Areopagite: Honigmann–Van Esbroeck's Thesis Revisited." *Scrinium* 6:143–213.

Lüdemann, Gerd. 1980. "The Successors of Pre-70 Jerusalem Christianity: A Critical Evaluation of the Pella Tradition." In *The Shaping of Christianity in the Second and Third Centuries*, edited by E. P. Sanders, 161–73. Vol. 1 of *Jewish and Christian Self-Definition*, edited by E. P. Sanders, A. I. Baumgarten, and Alan Mendelson. Philadelphia: Fortress.

————. 2005. *The Acts of the Apostles: What Really Happened in the Earliest Days of the Church*. Amherst, NY: Prometheus.

Luibhéid, Colm. 1982. *The Council of Nicaea*. Galway, Ireland: Officina Typographica.

Luijendijk, AnneMarie. 2008. *Greetings in the Lord: Early Christians and the Oxyrhynchus Papyri*. HTS 60. Cambridge, MA: Harvard Divinity School and Harvard University Press.

Łukaszewicz, Adam. 1998. "Une momie en exil." *JJP* 28:85–94.

Lyle, Marjorie. 1994. *Canterbury: 2000 Years of History*. Stroud: Tempus.

MacArthur, E. Mairi. 1995. *Columba's Island: Iona from Past to Present*. Edinburgh: Edinburgh University Press.

Machitadze, Zakaria. 2006. *Lives of the Georgian Saints*. Platina, CA: St. Herman of Alaska Brotherhood.

MacKendrick, Paul. 1980. *The North African Stones Speak*. Chapel Hill: University of North Carolina Press.

MacKenzie, David N. 1970. "The Kartir Inscriptions." In *W. B. Henning Memorial Volume*, edited by Mary Boyce and Ilya Gershevitch, 109–20. London: Lund Humphries.

MacKenzie, Duncan. 1897. "Excavations of the British School at Melos: The Site of the 'Three Churches.'" *JHS* 17:122–33.

Mackerras, Colin. 1972. *The Uighur Empire according to the T'ang Dynastic Histories: A Study in Sino-Vighur Relations 744–840*. Canberra: Australian National University Press.

MacMullen, Ramsay. 1982. "The Epigraphic Habit in the Roman Empire." *AJP* 103:233–46.

———. 2009. *The Second Church: Popular Christianity A.D. 200–400*. SBLWAW 1. Leiden: Brill.

Madigan, Kevin, and Carolyn Osiek, ed. and trans. 2005. *Ordained Women in the Early Church: A Documentary History*. Baltimore: Johns Hopkins University Press.

Magen, Yitzhak. 1990. "A Roman Fortress and a Byzantine Monastery at Khirbet el-Kîliya." In *Christian Archaeology in the Holy Land: New Discoveries; Essays in Honour of Virgilio C. Corbo, OFM*, edited by G. C. Bottini, L. Di Segni, and E. Alliata, 275–86. Jerusalem: Franciscan Printing Press.

Mai, Angelo. 1839–1844. *Specilium romanum*. 10 vols. Rome: Typis Collegii Urbani.

———. 1930. "Ex sermonibus ab Angelo editis." In *Sancti Augustini sermones post Maurinos reperti*, edited by Germain Morin, 285–386. MA 1. Vatican City: Typis Polyglottis Vaticani. [Abbr.: Augustine of Hippo, *Serm*. Mai]

Maier, Jean-Louis. 1973. *L'Épiscopat de l'Afrique romaine, vandale, et byzantine*. Rome: Institut Suisse de Rome.

Mango, Cyril. 1978. "The Date of the Studios Basilica at Istanbul." *Byzantine and Modern Greek Studies* 4:115–22.

———. 1990a. *Le développement urbain de Constantinople (IVe–VIIe siècles)*. 2nd ed. TMCRHCB 2. Paris: de Boccard.

———. 1990b. "Constantine's Mausoleum and the Translation of Relics." *ByzZ* 83:51–61.

———. 1995. "The Conversion of the Parthenon into a Church: The Tübingen Theosophy." *DCAE* 18:201–3.

Mango, Cyril, and Ihor Ševčenko. 1961. "Remains of the Church of St. Polyeuktos at Constantinople." *DOP* 15:243–47.

Manns, F. 1990. "Joseph de Tibériade, un Judéo-chrétien du quatrième siècle." In *Christian Archaeology in the Holy Land: New Discoveries; Essays in Honour of Virgilio C. Corbo, OFM*, edited by G. C. Bottini, L. Di Segni, and E. Alliata, 353–59. Jerusalem: Franciscan Printing Press.

Mansi, Giovanni D. 1960. *Sacrorum conciliorum nova et amplissima collectio*. 57 vols. Florence: Expensis Antonii Zatta, 1761–1762. Reprint, Ganz: Verlaganstalt.

Marec, Erwan. 1958. *Monuments chrétiens d'Hippone: Ville épiscopale de Saint Augustin*. Paris: Arts et Métiers Graphiques.

Maresch, Klaus, and Isabella Andorlini, eds. 2006. *Das Archiv des Aurelius Ammon (P. Ammon) 2,A Text: Papyri aus den Sammlungen des Istituto Papirologico "G. Vitelli" (Università di Firenze), der Duke University, Durham N.C., und der Universität zu Köln*. PC 26/2A. Paderborn: Schöningh.

Marguerat, Daniel. 2002. *The First Church Historian: Writing the "Acts of the Apostles."* Translated by Ken McKinney, George J. Laughery, and Richard Bauckham. Cambridge: Cambridge University Press.

Markham, Clements R., trans. 1859. *Narrative of the Embassy of Ruy Gonzalez de Clavijo to the Court of Timour, at Samarcand A.D. 1403–6*. London: Hakluyt Society.

Markoe, Glenn, ed. 2003. *Petra Rediscovered: Lost City of the Nabataeans*. New York: Harry N. Abrams, with the Cincinnati Art Museum.

Markschies, Christoph. 1992. *Valentinus Gnosticus? Untersuchungen zur valentinianischen Gnosis mit einem Kommentar zu den Fragmenten Valentins*. WUNT 65. Tübingen: Mohr Siebeck.

Markus, Robert A. 1979. "Carthage–Prima Justiniana–Ravenna: An Aspect of Justinian's Kirchenpolitik." *Byzantion* 49:277–302.

Marrou, Henri-Irénée. 1960. "La basilique chrétienne d'Hippone d'après les résultats des dernières fouilles." *REAug* 6:105–54.

Marsden, Peter. 1980. *Roman London*. London: Thames & Hudson.

Marsden, W., trans. 1997. *The Travels of Marco Polo*. London: Cox & Baylis, 1818. Reprint, Ware: Wordsworth.

Martin, Annick. 1996. *Athanase d'Alexandrie et l'église d'Égypte au IVᵉ siècle (328–373)*. CEFR 216. Rome: École française de Rome.

Maspero, Jean. 1909. "Théodore de Philae." *RHR* 59:299–317.

Mastino, Attilo. 1999. "La Sardegna Cristiana in età tardo-antica." In *La Sardegna paleocristiana tra Eusebio e Gregorio Magno: Atti del convegno nazionale di studi, Cagliari, 10–12 ottobre 1996*. Edited by Attilo Mastino, Giovanna Sotgiu, and Natalino Spaccapelo, 263–307. SRCR, NS 1. Cagliari: Pontificia facoltà teologica della Sardegna.

Mateos Cruz, Pedro. 1999. *La Basilica de Santa Eulalia de Mérida: Arquelogía y urbanismo*. AAEA 19. Madrid: Consejo superior de investigaciones cientificas.

Mathews, Thomas F. 1971. *The Early Churches of Constantinople: Architecture and Liturgy*. University Park: Pennsylvania State University Press.

Matthews, John. 2006. *The Journey of Theophanes: Travel, Business and Daily Life in the Roman East*. New Haven: Yale University Press.

Mattingly, David. 1995. *Tripolitania*. London: Batsford.

Mavromataki, Maria. 2003. *Paul: The Apostle of the Gentiles*. Athens: Haitalis.

Mawer, C. Frances. 1995. *Evidence for Christianity in Roman Britain: The Small Finds*. BARBS 243. Oxford: Tempus Reparatum.

McCreary, Alf. 2001. *Saint Patrick's City: The Story of Armagh*. Belfast: Blackstaff.

McGuckin, John A., ed. 2004. *The Westminster Handbook to Origen*. Louisville: Westminster John Knox.

McKenzie, Judith. 2007. *The Architecture of Alexandria and Egypt 300 B.C.–A.D. 700*. New Haven: Yale University Press.

McLean, Bradley H. 2000. "Epigraphical Evidence in Caesarea Maritima." In *Religious Rivalries and the Struggle for Success in Caesarea Maritima*, edited by Terence L. Donaldson, 57–64. SCJ 8. Waterloo, ON: Wilfrid Laurier University Press.

McLynn, Neil B. 1994. *Ambrose of Milan: Church and Court in a Christian Capital*. TCH 22. Berkeley: University of California Press.

McVey, Kathleen. 1990. "A Fresh Look at the Letter of Mara bar Serapion to His Son." In *V Symposium Syriacum, 1988: Katholieke Universiteit, Leuven, 29–31 août 1988*, edited by René Lavenant, 257–72. OrChrAn 236. Rome: Pontificum Institutum Orientalium Studiorum.

Medlycott, A. E. 2005. *India and the Apostle Thomas: An Inquiry with a Critical Analysis of the Acta Thomae*. London: Nutt, 1905. Reprint, Piscataway, NJ: Gorgias.

Menze, Volker-Lorenz. 2008. *Justinian and the Making of the Syrian Orthodox Church*. OECS. Oxford: Oxford University Press.

Merdinger, Jane E. 1997. *Rome and the African Church in the Time of Augustine*. New Haven: Yale University Press.

———. Forthcoming. "North African Councils and Canons." In *The History of Western Canon Law to 1000*, edited by Kenneth Pennington and Wilfried Hartmann. Washington, DC: Catholic University of America Press.

Merell, Jean. 1938. "Nouveaux fragments du papyrus 4." *RB* 47:5–22.

Merrifield, Ralph. 1969. *Roman London*. London: Cassell.

———. 1983. *London: City of the Romans*. Berkeley: University of California Press.

Meyer, Marvin, ed. 2007. *The Nag Hammadi Scriptures*. New York: HarperCollins.

Meyer, Marvin, and Richard Smith, eds. 1994. *Ancient Christian Magic: Coptic Texts of Ritual Power*. San Francisco: HarperSanFrancisco.

Meyers, Eric M. 1997. *The Oxford Encyclopedia of Archaeology in the Near East*. 5 vols. New York: Oxford University Press. [Abbr.: OEANE]

Mgaloblishvili, Tamila, and Yulon Gagoshidze. 1998. "The Jewish Diaspora and Early Christianity in Georgia." In *Ancient Christianity in the Caucasus*, edited by Tamila Mgaloblishvili, 39–58. Iberica Caucasica 1. Richmond: Curzon.

Michałowski, Kazimierz. 1967. *Faras: Die Kathedrale aus dem Wüstensand*. Einsiedeln: Benziger.

Micheau, Françoise. 2006. "Eastern Christianities (Eleventh to Fourteenth Century): Copts, Melkites, Nestorians and Jacobites." In *Eastern Christianity*, edited by Michael Angold, 373–403. Vol. 5 of *The Cambridge History of Christianity*, edited by Margaret M. Mitchell et al. Cambridge: Cambridge University Press.

Michel, Anne. 2005. "Aspects du culte dans les églises de Numidie au temps d'Augustin: Un état de la question." In *Saint Augustin: La Numidie et la société de son temps; Actes du colloque SEMPAN-AUSONIUS, Bordeaux, 10–11 octobre 2003*, edited by Serge Lancel, Stéphanie Guédon, and Louis Maurin, 67–108. Paris: de Boccard.

Migne, Jacques-Paul., ed. 1844–1864. Patrologiae cursus completus: Series latina. 217 vols. Paris: Migne. [Abbr.: PL]

———, ed. 1857–1866. Patrologiae cursus completus: Series graeca. 162 vols. Paris: Migne. [Abbr.: PG]

Mikulčić, Ivan. 2004. *Stobi: An Ancient City*. Skopje: Magor.

Milik, Józef T. 1962. "Á propos d'un atelier monétaire d'Adiabène: Natounia." *RevNum* 6 (4): 51–58.

Millar, Fergus. 1993. *The Roman Near East, 31 B.C.–A.D. 337*. Cambridge, MA: Harvard University Press.

Milne, H. J. M., and T. C. Skeat. 1963. *The Codex Sinaiticus and Codex Alexandrinus*. London: Trustees of the British Museum.

Milošević, Gordana. 2004. "The Martyry and the Cemetery Basilica in Jagodin Mala in Niš." In *Niš and Byzantium: Second Symposium, Niš, 3–5 June 2003; Collection of Scientific Works, II*, edited by Miša Rakocija, 121–40. Niš: University of Niš.

Milošević, Petar. 2001. *Arheologija i istorija Sirmijuma* [Archaeology and History of Sirmium] (in Serbian). Novi Sad: Matica srpska.

Minchev, Alexander. 2003. *Early Christian Reliquaries from Bulgaria (4th–6th Century AD)*. Varna Regional Museum of History. Varna: Stalker.

Mingana, Alfonse, ed. and trans. 1907. *Sources syriaques*. Leipzig: Harrassowitz.

———. 1925. "The Early Spread of Christianity in Central Asia and the Far East: A New Document." *BJRL* 9:297–367.

————. 1926. "The Early Spread of Christianity in India." *BJRL* 10:435–514.

Mitchell, Stephen. 1982. "The Life of Saint Theodotus of Ancyra." *AnSt* 32:93–113.

————. 1988. "Maximinus and the Christians in A.D. 312: A New Latin Inscription." *JRS* 78:105–24.

————. 1993. *Anatolia: Land, Men, and Gods in Asia Minor*. 2 vols. Oxford: Clarendon.

————. 2005. "An Apostle to Ankara from the New Jerusalem: Montanists and Jews in Late Roman Asia." *SCI* 25:207–23.

Mitchell, Stephen, and Marc Waelkens, with contributions by Jean Burdy et al. 1998. *Pisidian Antioch: The Site and Its Monuments*. London: Duckworth.

Mitchell, Stephen, and Peter Van Nuffelen, eds. 2010. *One God: Pagan Monotheism in the Roman Empire*. Cambridge: Cambridge University Press.

Mitford, Terrence B. 1971. *The Inscriptions of Kourion*. MAPS 83. Philadelphia: American Philosophical Society. [Abbr.: *IKourion*]

————. 1990. "The Cults of Roman Cyprus." *ANRW* II.18.3:2175–211.

Mitteis, Ludwig, and Ulrich Wilcken, eds. 1912. *Chrestomatie*. Vol. 1.2 of *Grundzüge und Chrestomathie der Papyruskunde*. 2 vols. in 4 parts. Leipzig: Teubner. [Abbr.: W.Chr.]

Mitthof, Fritz. 2002. *Ein spätantikes Wirtschaftsbuch aus Diospolis Parva: Der Erlanger Papyruskodex und die Texte aus seinem Umfeld*. Munich: Saur.

Modrzejewski, Joseph. 1997. *The Jews of Egypt: From Rameses II to Emperor Hadrian*. Princeton, NJ: Princeton University Press.

Momigliano, Arnaldo, ed. 1963. *The Conflict between Paganism and Christianity in the Fourth Century: Essays*. OWS. Oxford: Clarendon.

Mommsen, Theodor. 1968. *The Provinces of the Roman Empire: The European Provinces*. Chicago: University of Chicago Press.

Monneret de Villard, Ugo. 1938. *Storia della Nubia cristiana*. OCA 118. Rome: Pontificium Institutum Orientalium Studiorum.

Montevecchi, Orsolina. 2000. "'ΤΗΝ ΕΠΙΣΤΟΛΗΝ ΚΕΧΙΑΣΜΕΝΗΝ': P.Oxy. XLII 3057." *Aegyptus* 80:189–94.

Moorhead, John. 1992. *Theodoric in Italy*. Oxford: Clarendon.

Morin, Germain. 1930. *Sancti Augustini sermones post Maurinos reperti*. MA 1. Vatican City: Typis Polyglottis Vaticani. [Abbr.: Augustine of Hippo, *Serm.* Morin]

Morony, Michael G. 2003. "Magic and Society in Late Sasanian Iraq." In *Prayer, Magic, and the Stars in the Ancient and Late Antique World*, edited by Scott Noegel, Joel Walker, and Brannon Wheeler, 83–107. University Park: Pennsylvania State University Press.

————. 2007. "Religion and the Aramaic Incantation Bowls." *RelC* 1 (4): 414–29.

Morris, John. 1982. *Londinium: London in the Roman Empire*. Revised by Sarah Macready. New York: St. Martin's Press.

Mosig-Walburg, Karin. 2009. *Römer und Perser: Vom 3. Jahrhundert bis zum Jahr 363 n. Chr.* Gutenberg: Computus.

Moule, Arthur C. 1930. *Christians in China before the Year 1550*. London: Society for Promoting Christian Knowledge.

Movses Khorenats'i. 1978. *History of the Armenians*. Translated by R. W. Thomson. Cambridge, MA: Harvard University Press.

Mullen, Roderic L. 2004. *The Expansion of Christianity: A Gazetteer of Its First Three Centuries.* VCSup 69. Leiden: Brill.

Müller, Friedrich W. K. 1907. "Neutestamentliche Bruchstücke in soghdischer Sprache." SPAW 13:260–70.

Müller, Friedrich W. K., and Wolfgang Lentz. 1934. "Soghdische Texte: II. Aus dem Nachlass." SPAW 21:520–22.

Müller-Wiener, Wolfgand. 1977. *Bildlexikon zur Topographie Istanbuls: Byzantion – Konstantinupolis – Istanbul bis zum Beginn des 17. Jahrhunderts.* Tübingen: Wasmuth.

Munro, Dana C., ed. 1993. *Life of St. Columban.* Translations and Reprints from the Original Resources of European History 2/7. Philadelphia: Department of History of the University of Pennsylvania, 1895. Reprint, Felinfach, Wales: Llanerch.

Munro-Hay, Stuart C. 1991. *Aksum: An African Civilization of Late Antiquity.* Edinburgh: Edinburgh University Press.

Murre-Van Den Berg, Helene H. L. 1999. "The Patriarchs of the Church of the East from the Fifteenth to Eighteenth Centuries." *Hugoye* 2 (2): 235–64.

Musurillo, Herbert. 1972. *The Acts of the Christian Martyrs: Introduction, Text, and Translations.* Oxford: Clarendon.

Mutschler, Bernhard. 2004. *Irenäus als johanneischer Theologe: Studien zur Schriftauslegung bei Irenäus von Lyon.* STAC 21. Tübingen: Mohr Siebeck.

Myers, Elaine A. 2010. *The Ituraeans and the Roman Near East: Reassessing the Sources.* SNTSMS 147. Cambridge: Cambridge University Press.

Myers, Susan E. 2006. "Revisiting Preliminary Issues in the Acts of Thomas." *Apocrypha* 17:95–112.

Naldini, Mario. 1998. *Il cristianesimo in Egitto: Lettere private nei papiri dei secoli ii–iv.* New ed. Florence: Nardini.

National Museum of Korea. 2003. *Arts of Central Asia: Collections in the National Museum of Korea: Special Exhibition, 16.12.2003–1.2.2004.* Seoul: Tongchun.

Naumkin, Vitaly V. 1993. *Island of the Phoenix: An Ethnographic Study of the People of Socotra.* Translated by Valerie A. Epstein. MECS 16. Concord, MA: Paul.

Naveh, Joseph, and Sha'ul Shaked. 1985. *Amulets and Magic Bowls: Aramaic Incantations of Late Antiquity.* Jerusalem: Magnes.

———. 1993. *Magic Spells and Formulae: Aramaic Incantations of Late Antiquity.* Jerusalem: Magnes.

Negev, Avraham. 1977. *The Inscriptions of Wadi Haggag, Sinai.* Jerusalem: Hebrew University of Jerusalem.

Neill, Stephen. 1984. *A History of Christianity in India: The Beginnings to AD 1707.* Cambridge: Cambridge University Press.

Neusner, Jacob 1971. *Aphrahat and Judaism: The Christian-Jewish Argument in Fourth-Century Iran.* StPB 19. Leiden: Brill.

Nigdelis, Pantelis M. 2010. "Voluntary Associations in Roman Thessalonikē: In Search of Identity and Support in a Cosmopolitan Society." In *From Roman to Early Christian Thessalonikē: Studies in Religion and Archaeology,* edited by Laura Nasrallah, Charalambos Bakirtzis, and Steven Friesen, 13–47. Cambridge, MA: Harvard University Press.

Nikolov, Vasil. 2006. *Kultura i izkustvo na praistoricheska Trakiya* [*Culture and Art of Prehistoric Thrace*] (in Bulgarian). Sofia: Letera.

Nissen, Theodor. 1912. *S. Abercii vita*. BSGRT. Leipzig: Teubner.

Nongbri, Brent. Forthcoming. "The Limits of Paleographical Dating of Literary Papyri: Some Observations on the Date and Provenance of P.Bodmer II (P66)." *Museum Helveticum*.

Nordenfalk, Carl A. J. 1938. *Die spätantiken Kanontafeln: Kunstgeschichtliche Studien über die eusebianische Evangelien-konkordanz in den vier ersten Jahrhunderten ihrer Geschichte*. Göteborg: Isacsons Boktryckeri.

Oates, David. 1968. *Studies in the Ancient History of Northern Iraq*. London: Oxford University Press.

Ochała, Grzegorz. 2011. "The Date of the Dendur Foundation Inscription Reconsidered." *BASP* 48:217–24.

Ó Corráin, Donnchadh. 1989. "Prehistoric and Early Christian Ireland." In *The Oxford Illustrated History of Ireland*, edited by R. F. Foster, 1–52. Oxford: Oxford University Press.

Okada, Yasuyoshi. 1991. "Early Christian Architecture in the Iraqi South-Western Desert." *Al-Rafidan* 12:71–83.

O'Neill, Timothy. 1997. "Columba the Scribe." In *Studies in the Cult of Saint Columba*, edited by Cormac Bourke, 69–79. Dublin: Four Courts Press.

Oost, Stewart Irvin. 1968. *Galla Placidia Augusta: A Biographical Essay*. Chicago: University of Chicago Press.

Oppermann, Manfred. 2010. *Die frühe Christentum an der Westküste des Schwarzen Meeres und im anschiessenden Binnenland: Historische und archäologische Zeugnisse*. Langenweissbach: Beier & Beran.

Orlandi, Tito. 2002. "The Library of the Monastery of Saint Shenute at Atripe." In *Perspectives on Panopolis: An Egyptian Town from Alexander the Great to the Arab Conquest*, edited by Arno Egberts, Brian P. Muhs, and Jacques van der Vliet, 211–31. PLB 31. Leiden: Brill.

Orlandos, Anastasios. 1926. "Neoterai Ereunai en Agio Tito Gortynas." *EEBS* 3:297–328.

———. 1936. "Delos Chrétienne." *BCH* 60:68–100.

Otranto, Giorgio. 1991. *Italia meridionale e Puglia paleocristiane: Saggi storici*. SR 5. Bari: Edipuglia.

Ottaway, Patrick. 1993. *Book of Roman York*. London: Batsford/English Heritage.

Painter, Kenneth S. 1972. "Villas and Christianity in Roman Britain: Recent Finds 1962–69." In vol. 1 of *Actas del VIII Congreso internacional de arqueología cristiana, Barcelona, 5–11 oct. 1969*, 149–66. StACr 30. Barcelona: Consejo superior de investigaciones cientificas.

———. 1975. "A Fourth-Century Christian Silver Treasure Found at Water Newton, England, in 1975." *RivAC* 51:333–45.

———. 1989. "Recent Discoveries in Britain." in *Actes du XIe Congrès international d'archéologie chrétienne: Lyon, Vienne, Grenoble, Genève et Aoste (21–28 septembre 1986)*, 2031–72. CEFR 123. Rome: École française de Rome.

Pallas, Dimitrios I. 1977. *Les monuments paléochrétiens de Grèce découverts 1959 à 1973*. Rome: Pontificio istituto di archeologia cristiana.

———. 1979–1980. "Monuments et texts: Rémarques sur la liturgie dans quelques basiliques paléochrétiens." *EEBS* 44:37–116.

———. 1980. "L'édifice cultuel chrétien et la liturgie dans l'Illyricum oriental." In *Rapports présentés au Xe Congrès international d'archéologie chrétienne, Thessalonique, 28 septembre–4 octobre 1980*, 497–570. Thessalonikē: Société d'études macédoniennes.

———. 1986. "I Palaiochristianiki Notioanatoliki Attiki." In *Praktika B' Epistemonikis Synantisis Notioanatolikis Attikis, Kalyvia 1985*, 43–80. Kalyvia: Epimorphotikos Syllogos Kalyvion.

———. 1990. "Korinth." In *Reallexikon zur Byzantinischen Kunst*, edited by Klaus Wessel and Marcell Restle, 476–811. Stuttgart: Hiersemann.

Palmer, Andrew. 1990. *Monk and Mason on the Tigris Frontier: The Early History of Tur 'Abdin*. UCOP 39. Cambridge: Cambridge University Press.

———. 2001. "Procopius and Edessa." *Antiquité tardive* 8:127–36.

———. 2002. "Les Actes de Thaddée." *Apocrypha* 13:63–84.

———, trans. 2005. "Actes de Thaddée." In vol. 2 of *Écrits apocryphes chrétiens*, edited by Pierre Geoltrain and Jean-Daniel Kaestli, 645–60. BP 516. Paris: Gallimard.

Panossian, Razmik, 2006. *The Armenians*. New York: Columbia University Press.

Paoli, Elizabeth. 1998. "Remarques sur l'apport des Œuvres d'Ambroise de Milan à la prosopographie chrétienne de l'Italie." In *Atti del congresso internazionale di studi ambrosiani nel XVI centenario della morte di sant'Ambrogio: Milano, 4–11 aprile 1997*, edited by Luigi F. Pizzolato and Marco Rizzi, 119–40. SPM 21. Milan: Vita e Pensiero.

Papanikola-Bakirtzi, Dimitra, ed. 2002. *Kathimerini Zoi sto Byzantio*. Athens: Kapon.

Papazoglu, Fanula. 1976–. *Inscriptions de la Mésie superieure*. Belgrade: Centre d'Études epigraphiques et numismatiques de la faculté de philosophie de l'Université de Beograd. [Abbr.: *IMS*]

———. 1988. *Les villes de macédoine a l'époque romaine*. Paris: de Boccard.

Parker, Samuel T. 1979. "The Historical Development of the Limes Arabicus." PhD diss., University of California Los Angeles.

———. 2006. *The Roman Frontier in Central Jordan*. Washington, DC: Dumbarton Oaks.

Parry, Ken. 2005. "The Stone Crosses of Kerala." *TAASA Review* 14 (2): 10–12.

———. 2006. "The Art of the Church of the East in China." In *Jingjiao: The Church of the East in China and Central Asia*, edited by Roman Malek and Peter Hofrichter, 321–39. CS. Sankt Augustin: Institut Monumenta Serica.

———. 2012. "Byzantine-Rite Christians (Melkites) in Central Asia in Late Antiquity and the Middle Ages." In *Thinking Diversely: Hellenism and the Challenge of Globalization*, edited by E. Kefallinos, 91–108. *Modern Greek Studies (Australia and New Zealand)* 16 [Special issue]. Sydney, Australia: Modern Greek Studies Association of Australia and New Zealand.

———. 2013. "'Rejoice for Me, O Desert': Fresh Light on the Remains of Nestorius in Egypt." StPatr 68:41–49.

———. Forthcoming. "An Early 'Christian' Painting from Toyuk in the Turfan Oasis." JIAAA.

Parsons, Peter J. 1970. "A School-Book from the Sayce Collection." *ZPE* 6:133–49.

———. 1980. "The Earliest Christian Letter." In *Miscellanea papyrologia*, edited by Rosario Pintaudi, 289. Florence: Gonnelli.

———. 2007. *City of the Sharp-Nosed Fish: Greek Lives in Roman Egypt*. London: Weidenfeld & Nicolson.

Patrich, J. 2000. "A Chapel of St. Paul at Caesarea Maritima?" *LASBF* 50:363–82.

Pauli, Judith, and Christiane Schmidt. 2000. "Methodius of Olympus." DECL 421–23.

P'awstos Buzand, *Buzandaran Patmut'iwnk'*. 1883. Edited by K. Patkanean. St. Petersburg. English translation: *The Epic Histories (Buzandaran Patmut'iwnk')*. 1989. Translated by Nina G. Garsoïan. Cambridge, MA: Harvard University Press. [Abbr.: P'awstos Buzand]

Pearson, Birger A. 1990. "Pre-Valentinian Gnosticism in Alexandria." In *The Future of Early Christianity: Essays in Honor of Helmut Koester*, edited by Birger A. Pearson, 455–66. Minneapolis: Fortress.

———. 2003. "Cracking a Conundrum: Christian Origins in Egypt." *ST* 57:61–75.

———. 2004. *Gnosticism and Christianity in Roman and Coptic Egypt*. SAC. London: T&T Clark International.

———. 2005. "Basilides the Gnostic." In *A Companion to Second-Century Christian "Heretics,"* edited by Antti Marjanan and Petri Luomanen, 1–31. VCSup 76. Leiden: Brill.

———. 2006. "Egypt." In *Origins to Constantine*, edited by Margaret M. Mitchell, Frances M. Young, and K. Scott Bowie, 331–50. Vol. 1 of *The Cambridge History of Christianity*, edited by Margaret M. Mitchell et al. Cambridge: Cambridge University Press.

Peeters, Paul. 1924. "S. Demetrianus évêque d'Antioch?" AnBoll 42:288–314.

Pelletier, André. 1980. *Histoire de Vienne et de sa région: Saint-Colombe, Saint-Romain-en-Gal*. CHVF. Roanne: Horvath.

Pelliot, Paul. 1973. *Recherches sur les chrétiens d'Asie centrale et d'Extrême-Orient*. Paris: Imprimerie nationale.

———. 1996. *L'Inscription nestorienne de Si-ngan-fou*. Edited with supplements by Antonio Forte. Italian School of East Asian Studies, Epigraphical Series 2/College de France Œuvres posthumes de Paul Pelliot. Kyoto: Scuola di studi sull'Asia orientale.

Perler, Othmar. 1955. "L'Église principale et les autres sanctuaires chrétiens d'Hippone-la-Royale d'après les textes de saint Augustin." *REAug* 1:299–343.

———. 1956. "La *memoria* des vingt martyrs d'Hippone-la-Royale." *REAug* 2:435–46.

Perler, Othmar, and Jean-Louis Maier. 1969. *Les voyages de saint Augustin*. Paris: Études augustiniennes.

Perrin, Michel-Yves. 1995. "Le nouveau style missionaire: La conquête de l'espace et du temps." In *Naissance d'une chrétienté (250–430)*, edited by Charles and Luce Pietri, 585–621. Vol. 2 of *Histoire du christianisme*. Paris: Desclée.

Pervo, Richard I. 1987. *Profit with Delight: The Literary Genre of the Acts of the Apostles*. Philadelphia: Fortress.

———. 2006. *Dating Acts: Between the Evangelists and the Apologists*. Santa Rosa, CA: Polebridge.

Peschlow, Urs. 1977. *Die Irenenkirche in Istanbul: Untersuchungen zur Architektur*. Istanbuler Mitteilungen. Beiheft [Supplement] 18. Tübingen: Wasmuth.

———. 1982. "Die Johanneskirche des Studios in Istanbul: Bericht über die jüngsten Untersuchungsergebnisses." *JÖB* 32/4:429–34.

Peterson, Erik, and Christoph Markschies. 2012. *Heis Theos: Epigraphische, formgeschichtliche und religionsgeschichtliche Untersuchungen zur antiken "Ein-Gott"=Akklamation*. Ausgewählte Schriften 8. Wurtzburg: Echter.

Peterson, John B. 1907. "Bacchylus." In vol. 2 of *The Catholic Encyclopedia*, edited by Charles G. Herbermann and Edward A. Pace, 189–90. New York: Appleton.

Phenix, Robert R., Jr., and Cornelia B. Horn. 2005. "Syriac-Speaking Churches: Their Origins and History to the Eighteenth Century." *BRIIFS* 7:9–35.

———. Forthcoming. *The Rabbula Corpus: Comprising the Life of Rabbula, His Correspondence, a Homily Delivered in Constantinople, Canons, and Hymns; With Texts in Syriac and Latin, English Translations, Notes and Introduction.* SBLWGRW 17. Atlanta: Society of Biblical Literature.

Pierre, Marie-Joseph, ed. 1988–1989. *Les exposés: Aphraate le Sage Persan.* 2 vols. SC 349, 359. Paris: Cerf.

Piovanelli, Pierluigi. 2009. "Thomas in Edessa? Another Look at the Original Setting of the *Gospel of Thomas.*" In *Myths, Martyrs, and Modernity: Studies in the History of Religions in Honour of Jan N. Bremmer*, edited by Jitse Dijkstra, Justin Kroesen, and Yme Kuiper, 443–61. SHR 127. Leiden: Brill, 2009.

Pizzuto-Pomaco, Julia. 2001. "Unity in the Midst of Diversity: The Early Church at Rome as Reflected in Romans 16." In *Who Killed Goliath? Reading the Bible with Heart and Mind*, edited by Robert Shedinger and Deborah J. Spink, 88–103. Valley Forge, PA: Judson.

Plassart, André. 1926. "Fouilles de Thespies et de l'hiéron des muses de l'Hélicon: Inscriptions: Dédicaces de caractère religieux ou honorifique, bornes de domaines sacrés." *BCH* 50:383–462.

Platon, Nikolaos. 1937. "Christianiki Epigrafi ek Tanagras." *AE* 2:655–67.

Poidebard, Antoine. 1934. *La trace de Rome dans le desert de Syrie: Le "limes" de Trajan à la conquête arabe, recherches aérienes (1925–1932).* 2 vols. BAH 18. Paris: Geuthner.

Polidori, Robert, et al. 1999. *Libya: The Lost Cities of the Roman Empire.* Cologne: Könemann.

Popović, Svetlana. 1998. "Prolegomena to Early Monasticism in the Balkans as Documented in Architecture." *Starinar* 49:131–44.

Popović, Vladislav. 2003. *Sirmium, Grad careva i mućenika: (Sabrani radovi o arheologiji i istoriji Sirmiuma)* [*Sirmium, City of Kings and Martyrs: (Collected Papers on the Archaeology and History of Sirmium)*] (in Serbian). Stremska Mitrovica: Projekat Blago Sirmijuma.

Preger, Theodor. 1901–1907. *Scriptores originum Constantinopolitanarum.* 2 vols. Leipzig: Teubner.

Preisendanz, Karl. 1973–1974. *Papyri Graecae Magicae: Die griechischen Zauberpapyri.* 2 vols. Stuttgart: Teubner.

Preisigke, F., et al., eds. 1915–. *Sammelbuch griechischer Urkunden aus Ägypten.* Strassburg: Trübner. [Abbr.: *SB*]

Preusser, Conrad. 1911. *Nordmesopotamische Baudenkmäler altchristlicher und islamischer Zeit.* Leipzig: Hinrichs.

Price, Simon R. F. 1998. *Rituals and Power: The Roman Imperial Cult in Asia Minor.* 8th ed. Cambridge: Cambridge University Press.

Pricoco, Salvator. 1978. *L'Isola dei santi: Il cenobio de Lerino e le origini del monachesimo gallico.* FilCr 23. Rome: Edizioni dell'Ateneo & Bizzarri.

Prior, J. W. 2002. "Awaiting the Trumpet of God." *NewDocs* 9:102–5.

Proudfoot, Edwina. 1995. "Archaeology and Early Christianity in Scotland." In *A Pictish Panorama: The Story of the Picts and a Pictish Bibliography*, edited by Eric H. Nicoll, 26–30. Balgavies, Scotland: Pinkfoot.

Pullan, Wendy. 2000. "'Ascent and Descent' in the Constantinian Church of the Holy Nativity in Bethlehem." In *Text and Artifact in the Religions of Mediterranean Antiquity: Essays in Honour of Peter Richardson*, edited by Stephen G. Wilson and Michel Desjardins, 308–21. SCJ 9. Waterloo, ON: Wilfrid Laurier University Press.

Quasten, Johannes. 1950–1986. *Patrology.* 4 vols. Westminster, MD: Newman.

Quecke, Hans. 1975. *Die Briefe Pachoms: Griechischer Text der Handschrift W.145 der Chester Beatty Library; Anhang: Die koptischen Fragmente und Zitate der Pachombriefe.* TPL 11. Regensburg: Pustet.

Rakocija, Miša. 2008. "New Insight into the Early Christian Past of Niš." In *Niš and Byzantium: Sixth Symposium, Niš, 3–5 June 2005; Collection of Scientific Works, VI,* edited by Miša Rakocija, 45–57. Niš: University of Niš.

Rakocija, Miša, and Milica Todorović, eds. 2013. *Niš and Christian Heritage: Niš and Byzantium.* Niš: Niški Kulturini Centar [Cultural Center of Niš].

Ramelli, Ilaria. 2000. "Una delle più antiche lettere cristiane extracanoniche?" *Aegyptus* 80:169–88.

———. 2006. "Possible Historical Traces in the *Doctrina Addai.*" *Hugoye* 9 (1): 51–127.

Ramsay, William M. 1882a. "The Tale of St. Abercius." *JHS* 3:339–53.

———. 1882b. "Trois villes phrygiennes: Brouzo, Hierápolis, et Otrous." *BCH* 6:503–20.

———. 1883. "The Cities and Bishoprics of Phrygia." *JHS* 4:370–436.

———. 1889. "Early Christian Monuments in Phrygia: A Study in the Early History of the Church, V." *Expositor* 9:392–400.

———. 1895–1897. *The Cities and Bishoprics of Phrygia: Being an Essay of the Local History of Phrygia from the Earliest Times to the Turkish Conquest.* 1 vol. in 2 parts [cited as 1 and 1.2]. Oxford: Clarendon. [Abbr.: *CB* (only when cited by inscription number)]

———. 1904. *The Letters to the Seven Churches of Asia.* London: Hodder & Stoughton.

———. 1908. *Luke the Physician and Other Studies in the History of Religion.* London: Hodder & Stoughton.

———. 1915. *The Bearing of a Recent Discovery on the Trustworthiness of the New Testament.* London: Hodder & Stoughton.

Rapp, Stephen H. 1998. *K'art'lis c'xovreba: The Georgian Royal Annals and Their Medieval Armenian Adaptation.* 2 vols. Delmar, NY: Caravan.

———. 2003. *Studies in Medieval Georgian Historiography: Early Texts and Eurasian Contexts.* CSCO 601. Louvain: Peeters.

Rapports présentés au Xe Congrès international d'archéologie chrétienne, Thessalonique, 28 septembre–4 octobre 1980. 1980. (*Ellinika* 26). Thessalonikē: Société d'études macédoniennes.

Raschke, M. 1975. "Papyrological Evidence for Ptolemaic and Roman Trade with India." In *Proceedings of the XIV International Congress of Papyrologists, Oxford, 24–31 July, 1974,* 241–46. GRM 61. London: Egypt Exploration Society.

Raven, Susan. 2002. *Rome in Africa.* 3rd ed. New York: Routledge.

Reade, Julian. 2001. "More about Adiabene." *Iraq* 63:187–99.

Rebillard, Éric. 1993. "KOIMHTHRION et COEMETERIUM: Tombe, Tombe sainte, Nécropole." *MEFRA* 105:975–1001.

———. 1996. "Les *areae* carthaginoises (Tertullien, *Ad Scapulam* 3,1): Cimetières communautaires ou enclos funéraires de chrétiens?" *MEFRA* 108:175–89.

———. 2008. "The West (2): North Africa." In *The Oxford Handbook of Early Christian Studies,* edited by Susan Ashbrook Harvey and David G. Hunter, 303–22. Oxford: Oxford University Press.

————. 2009. *The Care of the Dead in Late Antiquity.* Translated by Elizabeth Trapnell Rawlings and Jeanine Routier-Pucci. CSCP 59. Ithaca, NY: Cornell University Press.

————. 2012. *Christians and Their Many Identities in Late Antiquity: North Africa, 200–450 CE.* Ithaca: Cornell University Press.

Rebourg, Alain. 2002. *Autun antique.* GEF 39. Paris: Monum.

Reich, Ronnie. 1996. "'God Knows Their Names': Mass Graves Revealed in Jerusalem." *BAR* 11:26–33, 60.

Reitz, F. 2001. "Is the Origin of the Granite Crosses of Kerala Indigenous or Foreign?" In *Tohfa-e-Dil: Festschrift Helmut Nespital,* edited by Dirk W. Loenne, 799–819. Reinbek: Verlag für Orientalistische Fachpublikationen.

Renaudot, E. trans. 1995. *Ancient Accounts of India and China by Two Mohammedan Travellers Who Went to Those Parts in the 9th Century.* London: Harding, 1733. Reprint, New Delhi: Asian Educational Services.

Renfrew, Colin, and Malcolm Wagstaff. 1982. *An Island Polity: The Archaeology of Exploitation in Melos.* Cambridge: Cambridge University Press.

Rensberger, David. 2010. "Reconsidering the Letter of Mara bar Serapion." In *Aramaic in Postbiblical Judaism and early Christianity: Papers from the 2004 National Endowment for the Humanities Summer Seminar at Duke University,* edited by Eric M. Meyers and Paul V. M. Flesher, 3–21. DJS 3. Winona Lake, IN: Eisenbrauns.

Reynolds, J. M., ed. 1976. *Libyan Studies: Select Papers of the Late R. G. Goodchild.* London: Elek.

Rheidt, Klaus. 1998. "In the Shadow of Antiquity: Pergamon and the Byzantine Millennium." In *Pergamon: Citadel of the Gods: Archaeological Record, Literary Description and Religious Development,* edited by Helmut Koester, 395–423. HTS 46. Harrisburg, PA: Trinity Press International.

Richardson, Peter. 1996. *Herod: King of the Jews and Friend of the Romans.* SPNT. Columbia: University of South Carolina Press.

————. 2000. "Archaeological Evidence for Religion and Urbanism in Caesarea Maritima." In *Religious Rivalries and the Struggle for Success in Caesarea Maritima.* Edited by Terence L. Donaldson, 11–34. SCJ 8. Waterloo, ON: Wilfrid Laurier University Press.

————. 2002. *City and Sanctuary: Religion and Architecture in the Roman Near East.* London: SCM.

————. 2004. *Building Jewish in the Roman East.* Waco: Baylor University Press.

————. 2006. "The Beginnings of Christian Anti-Judaism." *CHJ* 4:244–58.

Richardson, Peter, and M. B. Shukster. 1983. "Barnabas, Nerva and the Yavnean Rabbis." *JTS,* NS 34:31–55.

Richter, Siegfried G. 2002. *Studien zur Christianisierung Nubiens.* SKCO 11. Wiesbaden: Reichert.

Riggs, David. Forthcoming. "Berber Cults, Punic Cults, and Graeco-Roman Cults at Carthage until 400 C.E." In *Religious Life at Carthage in Late Antiquity,* edited by Jane E. Merdinger. Leiden: Brill.

Ritner, Robert K. 1998. "Egypt under Roman Rule: The Legacy of Ancient Egypt." In *Islamic Egypt, 640–1517,* edited by Carl F. Petry, 1–33. Vol. 1 of *The Cambridge*

History of Egypt, edited by Carl F. Petry and M. W. Daly. Cambridge: Cambridge University Press.

Rives, James. 1995. *Religion and Authority in Roman Carthage from Augustus to Constantine.* Oxford: Clarendon.

Roberts, Colin H. 1979. *Manuscript, Society, and Belief in Early Christian Egypt.* London: The British Academy.

Robinson, Edward. 1970. *Biblical Researches in Palestine and the Adjacent Regions: A Journal of Travels in the Years 1838 and 1852 Drawn Up from the Original Diaries, with Historical Illustrations.* 3rd ed. Jerusalem: Universitas Booksellers.

Robinson, James M. 1990. *The Pachomian Monastic Library at the Chester Beatty Library and the Bibliothèque Bodmer.* Claremont: Institute for Antiquity and Christianity.

Roe, Helen M. 1966. *The High Crosses of Kells.* Rev. ed. Meath, Ireland: Meath Archaeological and Historical Society.

Rogers, Francis M. 1962. *The Quest for Eastern Christians: Travels and Rumor in the Age of Discovery.* Minneapolis: University of Minnesota Press.

Roller, Lynn E. 1999. *In Search of God the Mother: The Cult of Anatolian Cybele.* Berkeley: University of California Press.

Rose, Pamela J. 2007. *The Meroitic Temple Complex at Qasr Ibrim.* London: Egypt Exploration Society.

Rosenberg, Harry. 1997. "Arles." *EEC*[2] 1:115–16.

Ross, Steven K. 2001. *Roman Edessa: Politics and Culture on the Eastern Fringes of the Roman Empire, 114–242 CE.* London: Routledge.

Rothaus, Richard M. 2000. *Corinth: The First City of Greece: An Urban History of Late Antique Cult and Religion.* RGRW 139. Leiden: Brill.

Rouquette, Jean-Maurice, and Claude Sintès. 1989. *Arles antique: Monuments et sites.* GAF 17. Paris: Imprimerie nationale.

Rousseau, Philip. 1999. *Pachomius: The Making of a Community in Fourth-Century Egypt.* 2nd ed. Berkeley: University of California Press.

Rubenson, Samuel. 1995. *The Letters of St. Antony: Monasticism and the Making of a Saint.* Minneapolis: Fortress.

———. 2007. "Asceticism and Monasticism, I: Eastern." In *Constantine to c. 600*, edited by Augustine Casiday and Frederick W. Norris, 637–68. Vol. 2 of *The Cambridge History of Christianity*, edited by Margaret M. Mitchell et al. Cambridge: Cambridge University Press.

Runesson, Anders, Donald D. Binder, and Birger Olsson. 2008. *The Ancient Synagogue from Its Origins to 200 C.E.: A Source Book.* AJEC 72. Leiden: Brill.

Russell, James R. 1987. *Zoroastrianism in Armenia.* Cambridge, MA: Harvard University Press.

———. 1991. "Christianity i. in Pre-Islamic Persia: Literary Sources." *EncIran* 5:523–28.

Russell, Paul S. 2005. "Nisibis as the Background to the Life of St. Ephraem the Syrian." *Hugoye* 8 (2): 179–235.

Rutgers, Leonard V., et al. 2005. "Radiocarbon Dating: Jewish Inspiration of Christian Catacombs." *Nature* 436:339.

———. 2009. "Stable Isotope Data from the Early Christian Catacombs of Ancient Rome: New Insights into the Dietary Habits of Rome's Early Christians." *JAS* 36:1127–34.

Sabw Kanyang, Jean-Anatole. 2000. *Episcopus et plebs: L'évêque et la communauté ecclésiale dans les conciles africains (345-525)*. EUS 701. Bern: Peter Lang.

Sachau, C. Edward, ed. and trans. 1879. *The Chronology of Ancient Nations: An English Version of the Arabic Text of the Athâr-ul-Bâkiya of Albîrûnî, or "Vestiges of the Past."* London: Allen.

Saeki, P. Yoshiro. 1935. *Keikyō no kenkyu [Researches on Jingjiao]* (in Japanese). Tokyo: Tōhō bunkwa gakuin Tokyō Kenkyūjo [Academy of Oriental Culture, Tokyo Institute].

———. 1937. *The Nestorian Monuments and Relics in China*. Tokyo: Academy of Oriental Culture, Tokyo Institute.

———. 1951. *The Nestorian Monuments and Relics in China*. 2nd ed. Tokyo: Maruzen.

Saldarini, Anthony J. 1992. "The Gospel of Matthew and Jewish-Christian Conflict in the Galilee." In *The Galilee in Late Antiquity*, edited by Lee I. Levine, 23–38. New York: Jewish Theological Seminary.

Salzman, Michelle. 2007. "Christianity and Paganism, III: Italy." In *Constantine to c. 600*, edited by Augustine Casiday and Frederick W. Norris, 210–30. Vol. 2 of *The Cambridge History of Christianity*, edited by Margaret M. Mitchell et al. Cambridge: Cambridge University Press.

Sanders, Guy D. R. 2005. "Archaeological Evidence for Early Christianity and the End of Hellenic Religion in Corinth." In *Urban Religion in Roman Corinth: Interdisciplinary Approaches*, edited by Daniel Schowalter and Steven J. Friesen, 419–42. Cambridge, MA: Harvard University Press.

Sanders, Ian F. 1982. *Roman Crete: An Archaeological Survey and Gazetteer of Late Hellenistic, Roman and Early Byzantine Crete*. Warminster: Aris & Phillips.

Sanikidze, Tamaz. 2004. "On the Genesis and Typological Peculiarities of One Pagan Temple Complex." In *Emǧvneba akademikos Vaxtang Beriżis 90 clist'aks [= In Honour of Professor Vakhtang Beridze]*, 65–77. Studies on Georgian Art 3. Tblisi: G. Chubinashvili Institute of History of Georgian Art.

———. 2009. "General Aspects of the History and Architecture of Uplistsikhe." In *Georgian Art in the Context of European and Asian Cultures: Proceedings of the 1st International Symposium of Georgian Culture, June 21–29, 2008, Georgia*, edited by Peter Skinner, Dimitri Tumanishvili, and Anna Shanshiashvili, 51–57. Tbilisi: Georgian Arts and Culture Center.

Saradi, Hélène G. 2006. *The Byzantine City in the Sixth Century: Literary Images and Historical Reality*. MSMAS. Athens: Perpinia.

Saradi-Mendelovici, Helen. 1990. "Christian Attitudes toward Pagan Monuments in Late Antiquity and Their Legacy in Later Byzantine Centuries." *DOP* 44:47–61.

Sas-Zaloziecky, Wladimir R. 1936. *Die Sophienkirche in Konstantinopel und ihre stellung in der geschichte der abendländischen architektur*. StACr 12. Vatican City: Pontificio istituto di archeologia cristiana.

Satzinger, Helmut. 1991. "Old Coptic." In vol. 8 of *The Coptic Encyclopedia*, edited by Aziz S. Atiya, 169–75. New York: Macmillan.

Saxer, Victor. 1980. *Morts, martyrs, reliques en Afrique chrétienne aux premiers siècles: Les témoignages de Tertullien, Cyprien et Augustin à la lumière de l'archéologie africaine.* TH 55. Paris: Beauchesne.

———. 1984. *Vie liturgique et quotidienne à Carthage vers le milieu du IIIe siècle: Les témoignages de saint Cyprien et de ses contemporains d'Afrique.* 2nd ed. Vatican City: Pontificio istituto di archeologia cristiana.

———. 1992a. "Archaeus." *EECh* 71.

———. 1992b. "Caesarea in Mauretania." *EECh* 138.

———. 1992c. "Mauretania." *EECh* 543–44.

———. 1995. "La mission: L'Organisation de l'église au IIIe siècle." In *Naissance d'une chrétienté (250–430)*, edited by Charles and Luce Pietri, 41–75. Vol. 2 of *Histoire du Christianisme*. Paris: Desclée.

———. 2000. "L'Afrique chrétienne (180–260)." In *Le nouveau peuple (des origines à 250)*, edited by Charles and Luce Pietri, 579–623, 784–815. Vol. 1 of *Histoire du christianisme*. Paris: Desclée.

Scheil, Vincent. 1893. *Deux traités de Philos.* Mémoires publiés par les membres de la mission archéologique française au Caire 9/2. Paris: Leroux.

Scherrer, Peter. 1995. "The City of Ephesos from the Roman Period to Late Antiquity." In *Ephesos: Metropolis of Asia; An Interdisciplinary Approach to Its Archaeology, Religions, and Culture*, edited by Helmut Koester, 1–25. HTS 41. Valley Forge, PA: Trinity Press International.

Schmitz, Philip C. 1992. "Phoenician Religion." *ABD* 5:357–63.

Schnabel, Eckhard J. 2004. *Early Christian Mission.* 2 vols. Downers Grove, IL: InterVarsity.

Schneemelcher, Wilhelm, ed. 1991–1992. *New Testament Apocrypha.* Translated by Robert McL. Wilson. Rev. ed. 2 vols. Louisville: Westminster John Knox.

Scholl, Reinhold. 2002. "Libellus aus der Christenverfolgung des Kaisers Decius." In *Griechische Urkunden der Papyrussammlung zu Leipzig (P.LIPS.II)*, edited by Ruth Duttenhöfer, 218–41. APVG 10. Munich: Saur.

Schöllgen, Georg. 1984. *Ecclesia sordida? Zur Frage der socialen Schichtung frühchristlicher Gemeinden am Beispiel Karthagos zur Zeit Tertullians.* JACE 12. Münster: Aschendorff.

Scholten, Clemens. 1995. "Die alexandrinische Katechetenschule." *JAC* 38:16–37.

Schowalter, Daniel, and Steven J. Friesen, eds. 2005. *Urban Religion in Roman Corinth: Interdisciplinary Approaches.* HTS 53. Cambridge, MA: Harvard University Press.

Schroeder, Caroline T. 2007. *Monastic Bodies: Discipline and Salvation in Shenoute of Atripe.* Philadelphia: University of Pennsylvania Press.

Scranton, Robert L., Joseph W. Shaw, and Leila Ibrahim. 1978. *Topography and Architecture.* Vol. 1 of *Kenchreai: Eastern Port of Corinth; Results of Investigations by the University of Chicago and Indiana University for the American School of Classical Studies at Athens.* Leiden: Brill.

Sears, Gareth. 2007. *Late Roman African Urbanism: Continuity and Transformation in the City.* BARIS 1693. Oxford: Archeopress.

Sebeos. 1999. *The Armenian History Attributed to Sebeos.* Translated and edited by R. W. Thomson and James Howard-Johnston. 2 vols. TTH 31. Liverpool: Liverpool University Press.

Seeck, Otto. 1876. *Notitia dignitatum accedunt Notitia urbis Constantinopolitanae et laterculi provinciarum.* Berlin: Weidmann.

———. 1919. *Regesten der Kaiser und Päpste für die Jahre 311 bis 476 n. Chr.: Vorarbeit zu einer Prosopographie der christlichen Keizerzeit.* Stuttgart: Metzler.

Segal, Judah B. 2001. *Edessa: "The Blessed City."* Oxford: Clarendon, 1970. Reprint, Piscataway, NJ: Gorgias.

Seipel, Wilfried, ed. 2002. *Faras: Die Kathedrale aus dem Wüstensand.* Vienna: Kunsthistorisches Museum.

Ševčenko, Ihor. 1966. "The Early Period of the Sinai Monastery in Light of Its Inscriptions." *DOP* 20:255–64.

Seyrig, Henri. 1955. "Trésor monétaire de Nisibe." *RevNum* 5 (17): 85–128.

Shalganov, Konstantin. 2002. "New evidence about the early architectural history of Saint-Sophia basilica in Sofia" (in Bulgarian). In Πιτύη: *Studies in Honor of Prof. I. Marazov*, 581–92. Sofia: Anubis.

———. 2005. "Archaeological Excavations beneath the Basilica of Santa Sophia in Sofia from 1991 to 2002" (in Bulgarian, with English abstract). In *Heros Hephaistos: Studia in honorem Liubae Ognenova-Marinova*, edited by Totko Stoyanov, 52, 469–79. Veliko Tarnovo, Bulgaria: Faber.

Shanks, Hershel. 1998. "Gaza Update: Excavation Yields Huge Church." *BAR* 24.4:12.

Shanks, Hershel, and Ben Witherington III. 2003. *The Brother of Jesus: The Dramatic Story and Meaning of the First Archaeological Link to Jesus and His Family*. London: Continuum.

Shanzer, Danuta, and Ian N. Wood. 2002. *Avitus of Vienne: Letters and Selected Prose*. TTH 38. Liverpool: Liverpool University Press.

Shaw, Brent. 1995. "Climate, Environment and History: The Case of Roman North Africa." In *Environment and Society in Roman North Africa: Studies in History and Archaeology*, article III. VCSS 479. Aldershot, UK: Ashgate Variorum.

———. 2004. "The Passion of Perpetua." In *Studies in Ancient Greek and Roman Society*, edited by Robin Osborne, 286–325. PPP. Cambridge: Cambridge University Press.

Shea, George. W. 1997. *The Poems of Alcimus Ecdicius Avitus*. MRTS 172. Tempe, AZ: Medieval and Renaissance Texts and Studies.

Sheppard, A. R. R. 1979. "Jews, Christians and Heretics in Acmonia and Eumeneia." *AnSt* 29:169–80.

Sherley-Price, Leo, trans. 1955. *Saint Bede the Venerable: A History of the English Church and People*. Harmondsworth, UK: Penguin.

Sherwin-White, Adrian N. 1966. *The Letters of Pliny: A Historical and Social Commentary*. Oxford: Clarendon.

Signon, Helmut. 1970. *Die Römer in Köln: Altertümer zwischen Eifel und Rhein*. Frankfurt: Societäts-Verlag.

Sijpesteijn, Pieter J. 1980. "List of Nominations to Liturgies." In *Miscellanea papyrologica*, edited by Rosario Pintaudi, 341–47. PF 7. Florence: Gonnelli.

Silberman, Neil A. 1991. "Desolation and Restoration: The Impact of a Biblical Concept on Near Eastern Archaeology." *BA* 54:76–87.

Sima, Alexander. 2002. "Religion." In *Queen of Sheba: Treasures from Ancient Yemen*, edited by St John Simpson, 161–79. London: British Museum Press.

Simonsen, J. Baek. 1988. *Studies in the Genesis and Early Development of the Caliphal Taxation System with Special Reference to the Circumstances in the Arab Peninsular, Egypt and Palestine*. Copenhagen: Akademisk Forlag.

Sims-Williams, Nicholas, ed. and trans. 1985. *The Christian Sogdian Manuscript C2.* SGKAO 12. Berlin: Akademie-Verlag.

———. 1990a. "Bible v. Sogdian Translations of the Bible." *EncIran* 4:207.

———. 1990b. "Bulayïq." *EncIran* 4:545.

———. 1992. "Sogdian and Turkish Christians in the Turfan and Tun-Huang Manuscripts." In *Turfan and Tun-Huang: The Texts; Encounters of Civilizations on the Silk Route,* edited by Alfredo Cadonna, 43–61. OV 4. Florence: Olschki.

———. 1993. "The Sogdian Inscriptions of Ladakh." In vol. 2 of *Antiquities of Northern Pakistan: Reports and Studies,* edited by Karl Jettmar, 151–63. Mainz: P. von Zabern.

Sironen, Erkki. 1997. *The Late Roman and Early Byzantine Inscriptions of Athens and Attica: An Edition with Appendices on Scripts, Sepulchral Formulae and Occupations.* Helsinki: University of Helsinki.

Sivan, Hagith. 1996. "Ulfila's Own Conversion." *HTR* 89:373–86.

Skeat, Theodore C. 2004. "The Oldest Manuscript of the Four Gospels?" In *The Collected Biblical Writings of T. C. Skeat,* introduced and edited by James K. Elliott, 158–92. NovTSup 113. Leiden: Brill.

Slokoska, L., L. Staykova-Aleksandrova, and R. Spassov. 2002. "Pautalia." In vol. 1 of *Rimski i rannovizantiiski gradove v Bulgariia [Roman and Early Byzantine Cities in Bulgaria]* (in Bulgarian), edited by Rumen Ivanov, 251–66. Sofia: Ivray.

Smith, Dennis E. 2009. "The Idealization of Christian Origins in Acts of the Apostles." In *A Passion for Christian Unity: Essays in Honor of William Tabbernee,* edited by John M. Imbler, 47–57. St. Louis: Chalice.

Smith, Mark. 1998. "Coptic Literature, 311–425." CAH 13:720–35.

———. 2002. "Aspects of the Preservation and Transmission of Indigenous Religious Traditions in Akhmim and Its Environs during the Graeco-Roman Period." In *Perspectives on Panopolis: An Egyptian Town from Alexander the Great to the Arab Conquest; Acts from an International Symposium Held in Leiden on 16, 17, and 18 December 1998,* edited by Arno Egberts, Brian P. Muhs, and Jacques van der Vliet, 233–47. PLB 31. Leiden: Brill.

Snegarov, Ivan. 1944. *Kratka istoriia na suvremennitie praroslavni tsurkvi (Ierusalimska, Antiokhiiska, Aleksandriiska, Tsarigradska, Kip'rska, Sinaiska, i Gruzinska) [Concise History of the Orthodox Churches of Today (in Jerusalem, Antioch, Alexandria, Constantinople, Cyprus, Sinai and Georgia)]* (in Bulgarian). Sofia: Sofia University Press.

Snively, Carolyn S. 1984. "Cemetery Churches of the Early Byzantine Period in Eastern Illyricum: Location and Martyrs." *GOTR* 29:117–24.

———. 2005. "Dacia Mediterranea and Macedonia Secunda in the Sixth Century: A Question of Influence on Church Architecture." In *Niš and Byzantium: Sixth Symposium, Niš, 3–5 June 2004; Collection of Scientific Works, III,* edited by Miša Rakocija, 213–24. Niš: University of Niš.

Snyder, Graydon F. 2002. *Irish Jesus, Roman Jesus: The Formation of Early Irish Christianity.* Harrisburg, PA: Trinity Press International.

———. 2003. *Ante Pacem: Archaeological Evidence of Church Life before Constantine.* Rev. ed. Macon, GA: Mercer University Press.

Solzbacher, Rudolf. 1989. *Mönche, Pilger und Sarazenen: Studien zum Frühchristentum auf der südlichen Sinaihalbinsel; Von den Anfängen bis zum Beginn islamischer Herrschaft.* MTA 3. Altenberge: Telos.

Sommer, Michael. 2005. *Roms orientalische Steppengrenze: Palmyra-Edessa-Dura Europos-Hatra; Eine Kulturgeschichte von Pompeius bis Diocletian*. OrOc 9. Stuttgart: Steiner.

Song, Lian, et al. 1976. *Yuan shi*. Nanjing: Nei fu, 1370. Reprint, Beijing: Zhonghua shuju. [Abbr.: Lian Song]

Sotiriou, Georgios A. 1928. "I Christianiki Katakomvi tis Nisou Milou." *PAA* 3:33–46.

———. 1929. "Ai Christianikai Thivai tis Thessalias kai ai Palaiochristianikai Basilikai tis Ellados." *AE* 1929:198–201.

Sotomayor y Muro, Manuel. 1975. *Sarcofagos romano-cristianos de España: Estudio iconográfico*. BTG 16. Granada: Facultad de Teología.

———. 1979. *La iglesia en la España romana y visigoda (siglos I–VIII)*. Vol. 1 of *Historia de la iglesia en España*, edited by Ricardo Garcia Villoslade and Manuel Sotomayor y Muro. BAC 16. Madrid: Edica.

Spassov, Roumen, Vesselka Kazarova [Katsarova], Rositta Mladenova, and Svetoslava Filipova. 1999. "The Early Christian Basilica No. 7 at Pautalia." *MCA* 5:18–44.

Speck, P. 1973. "Der Mauerbau in 60 Tagen: Zum Datum der Errichtung der Landmauer von Konstantinopel mit einem Anhang über die Datierung der *Notitia urbis Constantinopolitanae*." In *Studien zur Frühgeschichte Konstantinopels*, edited by Hans-George Beck, 135–78. MBM 14. Munich: Institut für Byzantinistik und Neugriechische Philologie der Universität München.

Spender, Arthur F. 1900. "The Catacombs of Syracuse." *DubRev* 127:123–44.

Spieser, Jean-Michel. 1984. *Thessalonique et ses monuments du IVe au VIe siècle. Contribution à l'étude d'une ville paléochrétienne*. BEFAR 254. Paris: de Boccard.

Spyridakis, Stylianos V. 1988. "Notes on the Jews of Gortyna and Crete." *ZPE* 73:171–75.

Stanev, Stanislav. 1999. "The Basilica of Belovo." *Μνημείο & περιβάλλον/Monument and Environment* 5:35–52.

Stanev, Stanislav, and Zarko Zhdrakov. 2009. "The Old Metropolitan Church in Nessebar/Mesembria after New Epigraphical 7th Century Evidence." *ABulg* 13:87–101.

Stark, Rodney. 1996. *The Rise of Christianity: A Sociologist Reconsiders History*. Princeton, NJ: Princeton University Press.

Steane, Kate. 2001. *The Archaeology of Wigford and the Brayford Pool*. LAS 2. Oxford: Oxbow.

Stein, Aurel. 1921. *The Thousand Buddhas: Ancient Buddhist Paintings from the Cave-Temples of Tun-Huang on the Western Frontier of China*. London: Quaritch.

Stern, Ephraim, ed. 1993. *The New Encyclopedia of Archaeological Excavations in the Holy Land*. 4 vols. New York: Simon & Schuster. [Abbr.: NEAEHL]

———. 1994. *Dor: Ruler of the Seas*. Jerusalem: Israel Exploration Society.

Stern, Karen B. 2008. *Inscribing Devotion and Death: Archaeological Evidence for Jewish Populations of North Africa*. RGRW 161. Leiden: Brill.

Stevenson, James, ed. 2012. *Creeds, Councils and Controversies: Documents Illustrating the History of the Church AD 337–461*. Revised with additional documents by W. H. C. Frend. Grand Rapids: Baker Academic.

———. 2013. *A New Eusebius: Documents Illustrating the History of the Church to AD 337*. Revised with additional documents by W. H. C. Frend. Grand Rapids: Baker Academic.

Stewart, Alistair C. 2014. *The Original Bishops: Office and Order in the First Christian Communities*. Grand Rapids: Baker Academic.

Stokes, Whitley, ed. and trans. 1877. *Three Middle-Irish Homilies on the Lives of Saints Patrick, Brigit, and Columba*. Calcutta: Privately printed.

Stone, Michael, ed. 1982. *The Armenian Inscriptions from the Sinai*. Cambridge, MA: Harvard University Press.

———, ed. 1992–1994. *Rock Inscriptions and Graffiti Project: Catalogue of Inscriptions*. 3 vols. SBLRBS 28, 29, 31. Atlanta: Scholars Press.

Strzygowski, Josef. 1973. *Origin of Christian Church Art: New Facts and Principles of Research*. Translated by O. M. Dalton and H. J. Braunholtz. New York: Hacker Art Books.

Sundermann, Werner. 1981. "Nachlese zu F. W. K. Müller, 'Soghdischen Texten I.'" AoF 8:171–95.

Sutherland, Carol H. W., and Robert A. G. Carson. 1967. *From Diocletian's Reform (A.D. 294) to the Death of Maximinus (A.D. 313)*. Vol. 6 of *The Roman Imperial Coinage*. London: Spink.

Tabbernee, William. 1983. "Christian Inscriptions from Phrygia." *NewDocs* 1:128–39.

———. 1989. "Remnants of the New Prophecy." StPatr 21:193–201.

———. 1993. "Montanist Regional Bishops: New Evidence from Ancient Inscriptions." *JECS* 1:249–80.

———. 1997. *Montanist Inscriptions and Testimonia: Epigraphic Sources Illustrating the History of Montanism*. PMS 16. Macon, GA: Mercer University Press. [Abbr.: *IMont* (only when cited by inscription number)]

———. 2001. "To Pardon or Not to Pardon? North African Montanism and the Forgiveness of Sins." StPatr 36:375–86.

———. 2002. "'Keeping the Faith': Montanism and Military Service." In *Actes du Ier Congrès international sur Antioche de Pisidie*, edited by Thomas Drew-Bear, Mehmet Taşlıalan, and Christine M. Thomas, 123–36. CAHA 5. Paris: de Boccard.

———. 2003. "Portals of the New Jerusalem: The Discovery of Pepouza and Tymion." *JECS* 11:87–94.

———. 2005. "Perpetua, Montanism, and Christian Ministry in Carthage *c*. 203 C.E." *PRSt* 32:421–41.

———. 2006. "Recognizing the Spirit: Second-Generation Montanist Oracles." StPatr 40:521–26.

———. 2007. *Fake Prophecy and Polluted Sacraments: Ecclesiastical and Imperial Reactions to Montanism*. VCSup 84. Leiden: Brill.

———. 2008a. "Epigraphy." In *The Oxford Handbook of Early Christian Studies*, edited by Susan Ashbrook Harvey and David G. Hunter, 121–39. Oxford: Oxford University Press.

———. 2008b. "Scillitan Martyrs." In *The Early, Medieval, and Reformation Eras*, edited by Robert Benedetto, 598. Vol. 1 of *The New Westminster Dictionary of Church History*, edited by Robert Benedetto et al. Louisville: Westminster John Knox.

———. 2009. *Prophets and Gravestones: An Imaginative History of Montanists and Other Early Christians*. Peabody, MA: Hendrickson.

———. 2011. "Initiation/Baptism in the Montanist Movement." In *Ablution, Initiation and Baptism: Late Antiquity, Early Judaism, and Early Christianity*, edited by David Hellholm et al., 917–45. BZNW 176. Berlin: de Gruyter.

———. 2012. "The Appearance of the New Jerusalem in the Montanist Interpretation of the Revelation of John." In *Die Johannesapokalypse: Kontexte–Konzepte–Rezeption*, edited by Jörg Frey, James A. Kelhoffer, and Franz Tóth, 651–82. WUNT 1/287. Tübingen: Mohr Siebeck.

———. 2013a. "Material Evidence for Early Christian Groups during the First Two Centuries C.E." *ASA* 30/2:287–301 and I–XII (plates).

———. 2013b. "The World to Come: Tertullian's Christian Eschatology." In *Tertullian and Paul*, edited by Todd D. Still and David E. Wilhite, 259–77. Vol. 1 of *Pauline and Patristic Scholars in Debate*, edited by Todd D. Still and David E. Wilhite. New York: Bloomsbury.

———. Forthcoming a. "Early Christianity in Carthage." In *Religious Life at Carthage in Late Antiquity*, edited by Jane E. Merdinger. Leiden: Brill.

———. Forthcoming b. "Epigraphy: Clandestine and Crypto-Christian." In *The Encyclopedia of Early Christian Art and Architecture*, edited by Paul C. Finney. Grand Rapids: Eerdmans.

———. Forthcoming c. "Exiled to Pepouza: Consorting Unwillingly with Heretical Montanists." StPatr.

Tabbernee, William, and Peter Lampe. 2008. *Pepouza and Tymion: The Discovery and Archaeological Exploration of a Lost Ancient City and an Imperial Estate*. Berlin: de Gruyter.

Tabor, James D., and Simcha Jacobovici. 2012. *The Jesus Discovery: The New Archaeological Find That Reveals the Birth of Christianity*. New York: Simon & Schuster.

Tacheva-Khitova, Margarita. 1982. *Istoriia na iztochnite kultove v Dolna Miziia i Trakiia V v. pr. n.e.–IV v. ot n.e.* [*History of the Oriental Cults in Moesia Inferior and Thracia (5th Century BC–4th Century AD)*] (in Bulgarian). Sofia: Nauka i izkustvo.

———. 1983. *Eastern Cults in Moesia Inferior and Thracia (5th Century BC–4th Century AD)*. EPROER 95. Leiden: Brill.

Taft, Robert. 1998. "Women at Church in Byzantium." *DOP* 52:27–88.

———. 2004. *A History of the Liturgy of St. John Chrysostom*. Vol. 2: *The Great Entrance: A History of the Transfer of Gifts and Other Pre-anaphoral Rites*. 4th ed. Rome: Pontificium Institutum Studiorum Orientalium.

Tatton-Brown, Tim. 1994. *Canterbury: History and Guide*. Dover, NH: Sutton.

Taylor, Joan E. 1993. *Christians and Holy Places: The Myth of Jewish-Christian Origins*. Oxford: Clarendon.

Taylor, Nicholas. 1992. *Paul, Antioch and Jerusalem: A Study in Relationships and Authority in Early Christianity*. JSNTSup 66. Sheffield: Sheffield Academic Press.

Tchalenko, Georges. 1980. *Églises de village de la Syrie du nord*. Paris: Geuthner.

Teeter, Timothy M. 1997. "Letters of Recommendation or Letters of Peace?" In vol. 2 of *Akten des 21. Internationalen Papyrologenkongresses, Berlin 13.–19. 8. 1995*, edited by Bärbel Kramer, Wolfgang Luppe, and Herwig Maehler, 954–60. APVG 3. Stuttgart: Teubner.

Telfer, W. 1961. "The Origins of Christianity in Africa." StPatr 4:512–17.

Temporini, Hildegard, and Wolfgang Haase, eds. 1972–. *Aufstieg und Niedergang der römischen Welt: Geschichte und Kultur Roms im Spiegel der neueren Forschung*. Berlin: de Gruyter. [Abbr.: ANRW]

Tepper, Yotam, and Leah Di Segni. 2006. *A Christian Prayer Hall of the Third Century CE at Kefar 'Othnay (Legio): Excavations at the Megiddo Prison 2005*. Jerusalem: Israel Antiquities Authority.

Theissen, Gerd. 1982. *The Social Setting of Pauline Christianity: Essays on Corinth*. Translated and edited by John H. Schütz. Philadelphia: Fortress.

Thelamon, Françoise. 1981. *Païens et chrétiens au IVe siècle: L'apport de l'"Histoire ecclésiastique" de Rufin d'Aquilée*. Paris: Études augustiennes.

Thomas, Charles. 1971. *Britain and Ireland in Early Christian Times, AD 400–800*. London: Thames & Hudson.

———. 1981. *Christianity in Roman Britain to AD 500*. London: Batsford.

Thomson, Robert W., trans. 1991. *The History of Lazar P'arpec'i*. Atlanta: Scholars Press. [Abbr.: *Lazar P'arpec'i*]

———. 1994. *Studies in Armenian Literature and Christianity*. Aldershot, UK: Ashgate.

———, trans. 1996. *Rewriting Caucasian History: The Medieval Armenian Adaptation of the Georgian Chronicles*. Oxford: Oxford University Press.

———. 2000. "Armenia in the Fifth and Sixth Century." CAH 14:662–77.

———. 2008. "Eastern Neighbours: Armenia (400–600)." In *The Cambridge History of the Byzantine Empire c. 500–1492*, edited by Jonathan Shepard, 156–72. Cambridge: Cambridge University Press.

Tilley, Maureen, trans. 1996. *Donatist Martyr Stories: The Church in Roman North Africa*. TTH 24. Liverpool: Liverpool University Press.

———. 1997. *The Bible in Christian North Africa: The Donatist World*. Minneapolis: Fortress.

Timm, Stefan. 1984. *Das christlich-koptische Ägypten in arabischer Zeit: Eine Sammlung christlicher Stätten in Ägypten in arabischer Zeit, unter Ausschluß von Alexandria, Kairo, des Apa-Mena-Klosters (Dēr Abū Mina), der Skētis (Wādi n-Natrūn) und der Sinai-Region*. Vol. 2. TAVO B41/2. Wiesbaden: Reichert.

Tkaczow, Barbara. 1990. "Archaeological Sources for the Earliest Churches in Alexandria." In *Coptic Studies: Acts of the Third International Congress of Coptic Studies, Warsaw, 20–25 August 1984*, edited by Wlodzmierz Godlewski, 431–35. Warsaw: PWN-Éditions scientifiques de Pologne.

Todorova, Maria. 1997. *Imagining the Balkans*. Oxford: Oxford University Press.

Tomašević, Gordana, and Milorad Medić. 1967. *Heraclea III: Mosaic Pavement in the Narthex of the Large Basilica*. Bitola: Board of Heraclea.

Tomber, Roberta. 2008. *Indo-Roman Trade: From Pots to Pepper*. Duckworth Debates in Archaeology. London: Duckworth.

Topalilov, Ivo. 2012. *Das römische Philippopolis. B. 1. Topografie, Städtebau und Architektur* (in Bulgarian with German summary). Bulgaria: Faber.

Török, László. 1988a. "Geschichte Meroes: Ein Beitrag über die Quellenlage und den Forschungsstand." *ANRW* II.10.1:107–341.

———. 1988b. *Late Antique Nubia: History and Archaeology of the Southern Neighbour of Egypt in the 4th–6th c. A.D.* Budapest: Archaeological Institute of the Hungarian Academy of Sciences.

———. 1997. *The Kingdom of Kush: Handbook of the Napatan-Meroitic Civilization*. HO 1/31. Leiden: Brill.

———. 1999. "The End of Meroe." In *Recent Research in Kushite History and Archaeology: Proceedings of the 8th International Conference for Meroitic Studies*, edited by Derek A. Welsby, 133–56. London: British Museum Press.

Torp, Hjalmar. 1963, *Mosaikkene i St. Georg-Rotunden I Thessaloniki.* Oslo: Gyldendal.

Toumanoff, Cyril. 1963. *Studies in Christian Caucasian History.* Washington, DC: George-town University Press.

Travlos, John. 1988. *Bildlexikon zur Topographie des Antiken Attika.* Tübingen: Wasmuth.

Trebilco, R. 1991. *Jewish Communities in Asia Minor.* Cambridge: Cambridge University Press.

Trevett, Christine. 1996. *Montanism: Gender, Authority and the New Prophecy.* Cambridge: Cambridge University Press.

Trimingham, J. Spencer. 1979. *Christianity among the Arabs in the Pre-Islamic Times.* London: Longman.

Trombley, Frank R. 1989. "Boeotia in Late Antiquity: Epigraphic Evidence on Society, Economy, and Christianization." In *Boiotika: Vorträge vom 5. Internationalen Böotien-Kolloquium zu Ehren von Professor Dr. Seigfried Laufer: Institut für Alte Geschichte, Ludwig-Maximilians-Universität München 13.–17. Juni 1986,* 215–28. Munich: Maris.

———. 1993–1994. *Hellenic Religion and Christianity, c. 370–529.* 2 vols. RGRW 115. Leiden: Brill.

Trombley, Frank R., and Josef Rist. 1999. "Christentum." In vol. 13 of *Der Neue Pauly: Enzyklopädie der Antike,* edited by Hubert Cancik, Helmuth Schneider, and Manfred Landfester, cols. 1154–62. Leiden: Brill.

Tsafrir, Yoram, and Yizhar Hirschfeld. 1993. "The Byzantine Church at Horvat Berachot." In *Ancient Churches Revealed,* edited by Yoram Tsafrir, 207–18. Jerusalem: Israel Exploration Society.

Tsetskhladze, Gocha R. 1994. "The Silver Phiale Mesomphalos from the Kuban (Northern Caucasus)." *OJA* 13:199–215.

———. 1998. *Die Griechen in der Kolchis.* Amsterdam: Hakkert.

Tyson, Joseph B. 2006. *Marcion and Luke-Acts: A Defining Struggle.* Columbia: University of South Carolina Press.

Tzaferis, Vasilios. 1993. "Early Christian Churches at Magen." In *Ancient Churches Revealed,* edited by Yoram Tsafrir, 283–85. Jerusalem: Israel Exploration Society.

Uray, G. 1983. "Tibet's Connections with Nestorianism and Manichaeism in the Eighth–Tenth Centuries." In *Contributions to Tibetan Language and Culture,* edited by Ernst Steinkellner, 399–429. Vol. 1 of *Proceedings of the Csoma de Körös Symposium, Held at Velm-Vienna, Austria, 13–19 September 1981,* edited by Ernst Steinkellner and Helmut Tauscher. Vienna: Arbeitskreis für Tibetische und Buddhistische Studien, University of Vienna.

Urbano, Arthur. 2005. "Donation, Dedication, and *Damnatio Memoriae*: The Catholic Reconciliation of Ravenna and the Church of Sant'Apollinare Nuovo." *JECS* 13:71–110.

Usener, Hermann. 1907. *Der Heilige Tychon.* Berlin: Teubner.

Vaage, Leif, ed. 2006. *Religious Rivalries in the Early Roman Empire and the Rise of Christianity.* SCJ 18. Waterloo, ON: Wilfrid Laurier University Press.

Vailhé, S. 1912. "Adiabène." In vol. 1 of *Dictionnaire d'histoire et de géographie ecclésiastiques,* edited by Alfred Baudrillart et al., 561–63. Paris: Letouzey et Ané.

Valeva, Julia. 1986. "La tombe aux archanges de Sofia: Signification eschatologique et cosmogonique du décor." *CahArch* 34:5–28.

———. 1998. "Les tombes ornées de croix et de chrismes peints." In *Acta XIII congressus internationalis archaeologiae christianae, Split–Poreč, 25.9.–1.10.1994,* edited by

Nenad Cambi and Emilio Marin, 761–86. StACr 54. Vatican City: Pontificio istituto di archeologia cristiana.

———. 2001a. "La peinture funéraire dans les provinces orientales de l'Empire romain dans l'Antiquité Tardive." *HAM* 7:167–208.

———. 2001b. "Mosaïque à croix de Marcianopolis (diocèse de Thrace)." In vol. 2 of *La mosaïque gréco-romaine VIII: Actes du VIIIème colloque international pour l'étude de la mosaïque antique et médiévale; Lausanne (Suisse), 6–11 octobre 1997*, edited by Daniel Paunier and Christophe Schmidt, 369–77. CAR 86. Lausanne: Cahiers d'archéologie romande.

———. 2011a. "Galerius, Constantine and the Imperial Palace in Serdica (Status quaestionis)." In *Variae Thracica: Studia in honorem Mariae Čičikova*, edited by Zlatozara Gocheva, Kamen Dimitrov, and Michaela Alexieva, 132–39. Sofia: Prof. Marin Drinov Academic Publishing House.

———. 2011b. "Elite House Architecture and Decoration in the Diocese of Thrace (4th–7th centuries)" (in Bulgarian). In *Studies in honour of Stefan Boyadzhiev*, edited by Stanislav Stanev, Valeri Grigorov, Vladimir Dimitrov, 17–56. Sofia: The National Archaeological Institute.

van Berchem, Max. 1910. *Amida: Matériaux pour l'épigraphie et l'histoire musulmanes du Diyar-bekr; Beiträge zur Kunstgeschichte des Mittelalters von Nordmesopotamien, Hellas und dem Abendlande, mit einem Beitrag "The Churches and Monasteries of the Tur Abdin" von Gertrude L. Bell*. Heidelberg: Winter.

Van Dam, Raymond, trans. 1988. *Gregory of Tours: Glory of the Martyrs*. TTH 3. Liverpool: Liverpool University Press.

van den Broek, Roelof. 1996. "Juden und Christen in Alexandrien im 1. und 3. Jahrhundert." In *Studies in Gnosticism and Alexandrian Christianity*, edited by Roelof van den Broek, 181–96. NHMS 39. Leiden: Brill.

van den Hoek, Annewies. 1997. "The 'Catechetical' School of Early Christian Alexandria and Its Philonic Heritage." *HTR* 90:59–87.

van der Vliet, Jacques. 2005. Review of *Studien zur Christianisierung Nubiens*, by Siegfried G. Richter. *VC* 59:219–23.

Van de Sandt, Huub, and David Flusser. 2002. *The Didache: Its Jewish Sources and Its Place in Early Judaism and Christianity*. CRINT 3. Assen: Van Gorcum.

Van Esbroeck, Michel. 1990. "La religion géorgienne pré-chrétienne." *ANRW* II.18.4:2694–725.

van Ginkel, Jan J. 1995. "John of Ephesus: A Monophysite Historian in Sixth-Century Byzantium." PhD diss., University of Groningen.

van Haelst, Joseph. 1970. "Les sources papyrologiques concernant l'église en Égypte à l'époque de Constantin." In *Proceedings of the Twelfth International Congress of Papyrology, Ann Arbor, 13–17 August 1968*, edited by Deborah H. Samuel, 497–503. *ASP* 7. Toronto: Hakkert.

Van Millingen, Alexander. 1912. *Byzantine Churches in Constantinople: Their History and Architecture*. London: Macmillan.

van Minnen, Peter. 1994. "The Roots of Egyptian Christianity." *APF* 40:71–85.

van Peursen, W. Th., and R. B. ter Haar Romeny, eds. 2006. *Text, Translation, and Tradition: Studies on the Peshitta and Its Use in the Syriac Tradition Presented to Konrad D. Jenner on the Occasion of His Sixty-Fifth Birthday*. MPIL 14. Leiden: Brill.

van Tongerloo, Alois. 1992. "Ecce Magi ab Oriente venerunt." In *Philosophie = Philosophy: Tolérance*, edited by A. Théodoridès, P. Naster, and J. Ries, 57–74. AOB 7. Brussels: Société belge d'études orientalis.

Vásáry, István. 1988. "Orthodox Christian Qumans and Tatars of the Crimea in the 13th– 14th Centuries." *CAJ* 32:260–71.

Veilleux, Armand. 1981. *Pachomian Chronicles and Rules*. Vol. 2 of *Pachomian Koinonia: The Lives, Rules, and Other Writings of Saint Pachomius and His Disciples*. Kalamazoo, MI: Cistercian Publications.

Velkov, Velizar. 1966. "Ratiaria (eine römische Stadt in Bulgarien)." *Eirene* 5:155–75.

———. 1977. *Cities in Thrace and Dacia in Late Antiquity (Studies and Materials)*. 2nd ed. Amsterdam: Hakkert.

Venedikov, Ivan, and T. Petrov. 1964. "The St. George Church in Sofia" (in Bulgarian). *Serdica* 1:77–108.

Venit, Marjorie. 2004. "The Remarkable Western Cemetery of Alexandria." *JRA* 17:551–55.

Villes et peuplement dans l'Illyricum protobyzantin: Actes du colloque organisé par l'École française de Rome (Rome, 12–14 mai 1982). 1984. CEFR 77. Rome: École française de Rome.

Volanakis, Ioannis. 1998. "Edifici paleocristiani dell' isola di Rodi (IV–VI sec.)." In *XLIV Corso di cultura sull'arte ravennate e bizantina: Seminario internazionale di studi sul tema; "Le grandi isole del Mediterraneo orientale tra terda antichità e medioevo," Ravenna, 19–21 Settembre 1991*, 311–30. Ravenna: Edizioni del Girasole.

Volbach, Wolfgang F. 1976. *Elfenbeinarbeiten der Spätantike und des frühen Mittelalters*. 3rd ed. Mainz: P. von Zabern.

von Tischendorf, Constantine. 1862. *Travels in the East*. Translated by W. E. Schuckard. London: Longman, Brown, Green & Longmans.

Vööbus, Arthur, ed. and trans. 1961. *The Statutes of the School of Nisibis*. PETSE 12. Stockholm: Estonian Theological Society in Exile.

———. 1965. *History of the School of Nisibis*. CSCO 266. Louvain: Secrétariat du Corpus scriptorum christianorum orientalium.

Vorster, Willem S. 1992. "James, Protevangelium of." *ABD* 3:629–32.

Waelkens, Marc. 1986. *Die kleinasiatischen Türsteine: Typologische und epigraphische Untersuchungen der kleinasiatischen Grabreliefs mit Scheintür*. Mainz: P. von Zabern.

Wagner, Guy. 1987. *Les oasis d'Égypte à l'époque grecque, romaine et byzantine d'après les documents grecs: Recherches de papyrologie et d'épigraphie grecques*. BE 100. Cairo: Institut français d'archéologie orientale.

Waley, Arthur, trans. 1931. *The Travels of an Alchemist: The Journey of the Taoist Ch'ang-ch'un from China to the Hindukush at the Summons of Chingiz Khan*. London: Routledge.

Walker, Joel T. 2006. *The Legend of Mar Qardagh: Narrative and Christian Heroism in Late Antique Iraq*. TCH 40. Berkeley: University of California Press.

Walker, Stephen. 1981. "La campagne lyonnaise du 1ᵉ siècle av. J.C. jusqu'au 5ᵉ siècle ap. J.C." In *Récentes recherches en archéologie gallo-romaine et paléochrétienne sur Lyon et sa région*, edited by Stephen Walker, 279–325. BARIS 108. Oxford: Archaeopress.

Walsh, John R., and Thomas Bradley. 2003. *A History of the Irish Church, 400–700*. 2nd ed. Blackrock, Ireland: Columba Press.

Ward-Perkins, J. Bryan, and Richard G. Goodchild. 1953. "The Christian Antiquities of Tripolitania." *Archaeologia* 95:1–83.

Wataghin, Gisella Cantino. 2000. *Christianisation et organisation ecclésiastique des campagnes: L'Italie du Nord aux IVᵉ–VIIᵉ siecles.* In *Towns and Their Territories between Late Antiquity and the Early Middle Ages,* edited by G. P. Brogiolo, N. Gauthier, and N. Christie, 209–34. TRW 90. Leiden: Brill.

Watts, Dorothy. 1991. *Christians and Pagans in Roman Britain.* London: Routledge.

———. 2005. *Boudicca's Heirs: Women in Early Britain.* London: Routledge.

Weerakkody, D. P. M. 1997. *Taprobanê: Ancient Sri Lanka as Known to the Greeks and Romans.* Indicopleustoi: Archaeologies of the Indian Ocean. Turnhout: Brepols.

Weitzman, Michael P. 1998. *The Syriac Version of the Old Testament: An Introduction.* UCOP 56. Cambridge: Cambridge University Press.

Weitzmann, Kurt, ed. 1979. *Age of Spirituality: Late Antique and Early Christian Art, Third to Seventh Century; Catalogue of the Exhibition at the Metropolitan Museum of Art, November 19, 1977, through February 12, 1978.* New York: Metropolitan Museum of Art.

Welles, C. Bradford, et al., eds. 1959. *The Parchments and Papyri.* The Excavations at Dura-Europos; Final Report 5.1. New Haven: Yale University Press. [Abbr.: P.Dura]

Welsby, Derek A. 1996. *The Kingdom of Kush: The Napatan and Meroitic Empires.* London: British Museum Press.

———. 1998. *Soba II: Renewed Excavations within the Metropolis of the Kingdom of Alwa in Central Sudan.* London: British Museum Press.

———. 2002. *The Medieval Kingdoms of Nubia: Pagans, Christians and Muslims along the Middle Nile.* London: British Museum Press.

Wenham, Leslie P. 1970. *Eboracum.* London: Ginn.

Wessel, Susan. 2004. *Cyril of Alexandria and the Nestorian Controversy: The Making of a Saint and the Making of a Heretic.* OECS. Oxford: Oxford University Press.

Westphalen, Stephen. 2006. "'Niedergang oder Wandel?': Die spätantiken Städte in Syrien und Palästina aus archäologischer Sicht." In *Die Stadt in der Spätantike: Niedergang oder Wandel?: Akten des Internationalen Kolloquiums in München am 30. und 31. Mai 2003,* edited by Jens-Uwe Krause and Christian Witschel, 181–97. HE 190. Stuttgart: Steiner.

White, L. Michael. 1990. *Building God's House in the Roman World: Architectural Adaptation among Pagans, Jews, and Christians.* LBNEA. Baltimore: Johns Hopkins University Press.

———. 1997. *Texts and Monuments for the Christian Domus Ecclesiae in Its Environment.* Vol. 2 of *The Social Origins of Christian Architecture.* Valley Forge, PA: Trinity Press International.

Whitehorne, John E. G. 1977. "P.Oxy. XLII 3119: A Document of Valerian's Persecution?" *ZPE* 24:187–96.

Wiessner, Gernot. 1967. *Zur Märtyrerüberlieferung aus der Christenverfolgung Schapurs II.* USL 1. Göttingen: Vandenhoeck & Ruprecht.

Wilfong, Terry G. 1998. "The Non-Muslim Communities: Christian Communities." In *Islamic Egypt, 640–1517,* edited by Carl F. Petry, 175–97. Vol. 1 of *The Cambridge History of Egypt,* edited by Carl F. Petry and M. W. Daly. Cambridge: Cambridge University Press.

Wilkinson, John. 1977. *Jerusalem Pilgrims before the Crusades.* Warminster: Aris & Philips.

———. 1999. *Egeria's Travels.* 3rd ed. Warminster: Aris & Phillips.

————. 2002. *Jerusalem Pilgrims before the Crusades*. Rev. ed. Warminster: Aris & Philips.

Williams, D. H. 1995. *Ambrose of Milan and the End of the Nicene-Arian Conflicts*. Oxford: Clarendon.

Williams, Michael A. 1996. *Rethinking "Gnosticism": An Argument for Dismantling a Dubious Category*. Princeton, NJ: Princeton University Press.

Willis, William H., and Klaus Maresch, eds. 1998. *The Archive of Ammon Scholasticus of Panopolis (P.Ammon) 1: The Legacy of Harpocration: Texts from the Collection of Duke University and the Universität zu Köln*. PC 26/1. Opladen: Westdeutscher Verlag.

Wilmshurst, David. 2000. *The Ecclesiastical Organisation of the Church of the East, 1318–1913*. CSCO 582. Louvain: Peeters.

Wilson, E. Jan. 2003. *The Old Syriac Gospels: Studies and Comparative Translations*. Rev. ed. EastCS 1, 2. Louaize, Lebanon: Notre Dame University; Piscataway, NJ: Gorgias.

Wilson, Roger J. A. 1982. "Roman Mosaics in Sicily: The African Connection." *AJA* 86:413–28.

————. 1996. "The West: Sicily, Sardinia and Corsica." CAH 10:434–48.

Wilson, Stephen G. 1995. *Related Strangers: Jews and Christians 70–170 C.E.* Minneapolis: Fortress.

Winkler, Dietmar W. 1997. "Miaphysitism: A New Term for Use in the History of Dogma and in Ecumenical Theology." *The Harp* 10 (3): 33–40.

————. 1999. "Monophysites." *LAGPW* 586–88.

Wipszycka, Ewa. 1986. "La valeur de l'onomastique pour l'histoire de la christianisation de l'Égypte: À propos d'une étude de R. S. Bagnall." *ZPE* 62:173–81.

————. 1996. "Le monachisme égyptien et les villes." In *Études sur le christianisme dans l'Égypte de l'antiquité tardive*, edited by Ewa Wipszycka, 281–336. SEAug 52. Rome: Institutum Patristicum Augustinianum.

————. 2001. "P.Coll.Youtie II 77 = P.Col. VII 171 Revisited." In *Essays and Texts in Honor of J. David Thomas*, edited by Trianos Gagos and Roger S. Bagnall, 45–50. Oakville, CT: American Society of Papyrologists.

————. 2006. "The Origins of the Monarchic Episcopate in Egypt." *Adamantius* 12:71–89.

Wischmeyer, Wolfgang K. 1980. "Die Aberkiosinschrift als Grabepigramm." JAC 23:22–47.

Wood, Ian N. 1999. "Arles." *LAGPW* 315.

Wood, Philip. 2010. *"We Have No King but Christ": Christian Political Thought in Greater Syria on the Eve of the Arab Conquest (c. 400–585)*. Oxford: Oxford University Press.

Worp, Klaas A. 1994. "A Checklist of Bishops in Byzantine Egypt (A.D. 325–c. 750)." *ZPE* 100:283–318.

————. 1998. "A Note on the Provenances of Some Greek Literary Papyri." *JJP* 28:203–18.

Wright, William. 1968. *Apocryphal Acts of the Apostles*. 2 vols. London: Williams & Norgate, 1871. Reprint, 2 vols. in 1, Amsterdam: Philo.

Xi'an beilin bowuguan. 1993. *Xi'an beilin bowuguan [Xi'an Forest of Stone Tablets Museum Exhibition Catalogue]* (in Chinese). Xi'an: Xi'an beilin bowuguan.

Xu Longfei. 2004. *Die nestorianische Stele in Xi'an: Begegnung von Christentum und chinesischer Kultur*. Bonn: Borengässer.

Xydis, Stephen G. 1947. "The Chancel Barrier, Solea and Ambo of Hagia Sophia." *ArtBul* 29:1–24.

Yarshater, Ehsan, ed. 1985–. *Encyclopaedia Iranica*. London: Routledge & Kegan Paul. [Abbr.: *EncIran*]

Yates, Jonathan. Forthcoming. "Christianity and Sacred Texts in Carthage ca. 180 C.E. to 258 C.E." In *Religious Life at Carthage in Late Antiquity*, edited by Jane E. Merdinger. Leiden: Brill.

Young, Frances. 2002. "Ministerial Forms and Functions in the Church Communities of the Greek Fathers." In *Community Formation in the Early Church and in the Church Today*, edited by Richard N. Longenecker, 157–76. Peabody, MA: Hendrickson.

Zayadine, F. 1994. "Ayla-ʿAqaba in the Light of Recent Excavations." *ADAJ* 38:484–505.

Zeiller, Jacques. 1918. *Les origines chrétiennes dans les provinces danubiennes de l'Empire Romain*. BEFAR 112/1. Paris: de Boccard.

———. 1967. *Les origines chrétiennes dans la province romaine de Dalmatie*. SH 47. Paris: Bibliothèque de l'École des hautes études, 1906. Reprint, Rome: Bretschneider.

Zelinger, Y., and Leah Di Segni. 2006. "A Fourth-Century Church Near Lod (Diospolis)." *LASBF* 56:459–68.

Zertal, Adam, Shemon Dar, and Itzak Magen. 1993. "Samaria." *NEAEHL* 4:1311–18.

Zetterholm, Magnus. 2003. *The Formation of Christianity in Antioch: A Social-Scientific Approach to the Separation between Judaism and Christianity*. London: Routledge.

Zhang Naizhu. 2007. "Ba Henan Luoyang xin chutu de yijian Tangdai Jingjiao shike" ["On a Recently Excavated Jing-jiao Inscription of the Tang Period from Luoyang, Henan"] (in Chinese). *Xiyu yanjiu* [*Western Regions Studies*] 17:65–73.

Zimmermann, Norbert. 1999. "Katakombenmalerei." In vol. 6 of *Der Neue Pauly: Enzyklopädie der Antike*, edited by Hubert Cancik, Helmuth Schneider, and Manfred Landfester, cols. 322–24. Leiden: Brill.

Contributors

Lincoln Blumell (PhD, University of Toronto) is assistant professor in the department of ancient scripture at Brigham Young University. (**Chapter 1: Sinai and the Negev, Arabia Felix**)

Malcolm Choat (PhD, Macquarie University) is senior lecturer in the department of ancient history at Macquarie University. (**Chapter 5: Egypt**)

Jenn Cianca (PhD, University of Toronto) is assistant professor of classics and liberal arts at Bishop's University. (**Chapter 1: Antioch, the Tetrapolis, and Syria Coele**)

Jitse Dijkstra (PhD, University of Groningen) is associate professor of classics at the University of Ottawa. (**Chapter 5: Nubia**)

Christopher Haas (PhD, University of Michigan) is associate professor of history and classical studies at Villanova University. (**Chapter 3: The Caucasus; Chapter 5: Alexandria**)

Cornelia Horn (PhD, The Catholic University of America; DrHabil, Eberhard Karls Universität, Tübingen) is currently affiliated with the Institut für Byzantinistik, Freie Universität Berlin; Philosophische Fakultät, Universität Tübingen, Germany; and is a research fellow at the Institute for Christian Oriental Research, CUA, Washington, DC. (**Chapter 2: Introduction, Northern Mesopotamia**)

Robin M. Jensen (PhD, Columbia University and Union Theological Seminary) is the Luce Chancellor's Professor of History of Christian Art and Worship at Vanderbilt University. (**Chapter 9: Ravenna**)

Peter Lampe (DrTheol, DrHabil, University of Bern) is professor of New Testament theology and the history of early Christianity at the University of Heidelberg, Germany, and honorary professor at the University of the Free State, Bloemfontein, South Africa. (**Chapter 9: Rome**)

Samuel N. C. Lieu (DPhil, Oxford, FAHA) is inaugural distinguished professor in ancient history at Macquarie University. (**Chapter 2: Persia; Chapter 4: Introduction, China**)

Jane Merdinger (PhD, Yale) is a member of the Augustinian Institute, Villanova University and formerly assistant professor of church history and theology at The Catholic University of America. (**Chapter 6: Roman North Africa**)

Ken Parry (PhD, University of Manchester) is senior research fellow in the department of ancient history at Macquarie University. (**Chapter 4: Introduction, Central Asia, India**)

Robert R. Phenix Jr. (Chapter 2: Introduction, Northern Mesopotamia)

Peter Richardson (PhD, Cambridge University, FRSC) is professor emeritus of the Centre for the Study of Religion at the University of Toronto. (**Chapter 1: Introduction, Judaea, Samaria, Galilee, Syria Phoenice, Phoenicia/Phoenica Libanensis, The Decapolis, Northern Arabia, Central Arabia, Southern Arabia, Complexity of Christianity in the Roman Near East**)

Graydon F. Snyder (PhD, Princeton University), now retired, was dean and professor of New Testament at Chicago Theological Seminary. (**Chapter 10: The Western Provinces, Beyond the Borders**)

William Tabbernee (PhD, LittD, University of Melbourne) is executive director of the Oklahoma Conference of Churches. He formerly served as president and Stephen J. England Distinguished Professor of the History of Christianity at Phillips Theological Seminary. (**General Introduction; Chapter 1: Jerusalem; Chapter 5: Introduction, Axum; Chapter 7: Asia Minor and Cyprus; Chapter 9: Environs; Chapter 10: Introduction**)

Julia Valeva (PhD, DrHabil, Institute of Art Studies, Bulgarian Academy of Sciences) is a professor at the Institute of Art Studies at the Bulgarian Academy of Sciences. (**Chapter 8: Introduction, Thracia, Eastern Illyricum, Constantinople**)

Athanasios K. Vionis (PhD, Leiden University) is an assistant professor in the department of history and archaeology at the University of Cyprus. (**Chapter 8: Achaea, The Greek Islands**)

D. H. Williams (PhD, University of Toronto) is professor of patristics and historical theology in the department of religion at Baylor University. (**Chapter 9: Introduction, Central Italy, North Italy, South Italy and the Islands**)

Subject Index

Ancient Writings Index

Other Premodern Authors and Works

English translations of the titles of premodern works are not necessarily literal translations of the original, but they are the titles most commonly used in English for those works.

89 158
134 159

Libanius

Orationes [Orations] (Or.)
14.41 333

Liber graduum [Book of Steps]

in toto 65

Liber pontificalis [Book of Pontiffs] (Lib. pont.)

in toto 82
14 459
30.2 405n21

Life of Nino

in toto 127

Life of St. John the Almsgiver

in toto 175

Life of St. Shio of Mghvime

in toto 131

Lucian

De morte Peregrini [On the Death of Peregrinus] (Peregr.)
11–16 305

Lugdunenses martyres [The Martyrs of Lyons] (Mart. Lugd.)

17 282
37 282
44 282

Mani

Kephalaia [Teachings]
in toto 167

Marco Polo

Travels of Marco Polo (Travels)
in toto 174, 176

Martyrdom and Passion of St. Eustace of Mtskheta (Pass. Eust.)

in toto 122
7.43 127
7.89 127
9.73 127

Martyrium Carpi, Papyri, et Agathonicae [Martyrdom of Carpus, Papylus, and Agathonicê] (Mart. Carp.)

(A) (Recensio A) [Recension A]
27 282

(B) (Recensio B) [Recension B]
in toto 282
1 282

Martyrium Polycarpi [Martyrdom of Polycarp] (Mart. Pol.)

preface 281
13–18 280
19.1 286

Martyrium Simeonis bar Sabba'e [Martyrdom of Simeon bar Shaba] (Mart. Simeon.)

7 102

Martial

Epigrammata libri xii [Epigrams] (Epigr.)
1.41 392
4.59 187

Minucius Felix

Octavius (Oct.)
in toto 382
31.7 395
36.3 393

Mokcevay Kartlisay

in toto 127

Movses Khorenats'i

History of the Armenians (Hist. Arm.)
2.34 137
2.74 137

Muratorian Canon

in toto 430

Narratio de Simeone bar Sabba'e [The Story of Simeon bar Shaba] (Narr. Simeon.)

4 102
58 103

Nestorius

Liber Heraclidis [The Bazaar of Heracleides]
in toto 148

Nicephorus Callistus

Historia ecclesiastica [Ecclesiastical History] (Hist. eccl.)
17.10 371
2.40 124–25

Nicetas of Paphlagonia

Orationes laudatoriae aliaeque nonnullae festivae [Prayers of Praise and Some Other Festive Prayers] (Or.)
in toto 275

Notabilia of the Tang Dynasty

in toto 164

Notitia dignitatum [Register of Offices]

in toto 324

Notitia urbis Constantinopolitanae [Register of the City of Constantinople]

in toto 324

Olympiodorus

Fragmenta [Fragments] (Fr.)
35.2 217

Optatus of Milevis

Adversus Donatistas [Against the Donatists] (Donat.)
in toto 405
1–23 405
1.18 244
2.18 256
Appendix 1 246
Appendix 4 254
Appendix 5 254
Appendix 10 247

Oration of Meliton the Philosopher

in toto 64

Origen

Contra Celsum [Against Celsus] (Cels.)
3.30 333, 335
3.55 396